A Breed So Rare

A Breed So Rare

The Life of J. R. Parten,
Liberal Texas Oil Man,
1896–1992

DON E. CARLETON

*Published by the Texas State Historical Association in cooperation with
the Center for American History, University of Texas at Austin*

Copyright ©1998 by the Texas State Historical Association, Austin, Texas. All rights reserved.
Printed in the United States of America.

Library of Congress Cataloging-in-Publication Data:
Carleton, Don E., 1947–
 A breed so rare : the life of J. R. Parten, liberal Texas oil man, 1896–1992 / Don E.
Carleton.
  p. cm.
  Includes bibliographical references and index.
  ISBN 0–87611–166–5 (alk. paper)
  1. Parten, J. R. (Jubal Richard), 1896–1992. 2. Texas—Politics and government—
1951– 3. Texas—Politics and government—1865–1950. 4. Democratic Party (Tex.)—Biography.
5. Businessmen—Texas—Biography. 6. Petroleum industry and trade—Texas—History—20th
century. 7. Madison County (Tex.)—Biography.
  I. Title.
  F391.4.P265C37   1998
  338.7'6223382'092—dc21
  [B]   98–14630
                                                               CIP

        5 4 3 2 1   98 99 00 01 02

Published by the Texas State Historical Association in cooperation with the Center for American
History at the University of Texas at Austin.

Book design by David Timmons. Dustjacket design by David Timmons.

∞The paper used in this book meets the minimum requirements of the American National
Standard for Permanence of Paper for Printed Library Materials, z39.48—1984.

Dedicated to my parents,
Edward and Jo Carleton,
and to the memory of
John Henry Faulk.

Contents

Introduction

The Alamo. The Cowboy. The Longhorn. Texas has produced several potent images that are internationally recognized. No archetype is more indelibly stamped on the public perception than the Texas oil man—a shrewd, flamboyant figure captured most recently in the character of J. R. Ewing in the long-running television series "Dallas." During the 1980s when this program was playing worldwide, reinforcing the stereotype of the oil man as a rapacious, conservative, unprincipled rogue, another Texas oil man named J. R.—in this case, J. R. Parten—was quietly concluding a remarkable career that spanned much of the twentieth century. Although J. R. Parten shared some characteristics with the fictional J. R. Ewing—he was a highly successful entrepreneur capable of playing hardball with the sharpest of the Texas oil men— he was a quiet gentleman, loyal to his friends, and a man of honor and principle. Little known during his lifetime, he remains a relatively anonymous figure despite the fact that he played a number of historically significant roles in Texas and the nation, and counted numerous bigger-than-life characters as colleagues, associates, and friends: Huey Long, Sam Rayburn, Lyndon B. Johnson, Harry Truman.

J. R. Parten did not occupy that highest rank of public figures that includes presidents and other major celebrated players. Instead, he is an archetype of the echelon of powerful men and women just below the highest levels of fame, who nevertheless make a major difference in the lives of their fellow citizens. And J. R. Parten did make a difference. After studying government and law at the University of Texas from 1913 to 1917, followed by service in the army during World War I as the youngest major in the field artillery, Parten entered the oil business as a young man in 1919. A pioneer in the American oil industry, he made the discovery well at the fabled El Dorado field in southern Arkansas in 1922. Starting with the Woodley Petroleum Company in the 1920s, Parten founded several highly successful businesses, including Pan American Sulphur, which operated one of North America's most prolific and profitable sulphur mines. His businesses earned millions of dollars and employed thousands of people.

While serving on the University of Texas Board of Regents from 1935 to 1941 Parten used his knowledge of the oil business to greatly increase the university's income from its oil holdings, and fought tenaciously for academic excellence and the right to freedom of speech on behalf of students and faculty. When the very existence of democracy was threatened during World War II, Parten was a dominant figure in the development of the "Big Inch" and "Little Inch" pipelines, which stretched from East Texas to New York and Pennsylvania and provided a secure system of transportation for American oil and fuel, critical to the victorious Allied war effort. In 1945 Parten served as chief of staff for the U.S. delegation to the Allied War Reparations Commission in Moscow and later participated in the Potsdam Conference in Berlin. During the Korean War, Parten organized the Petroleum Administration for Defense, which ensured that the military efforts in Korea were supported by adequate supplies of oil. Parten also served as an oil policy advisor during the Kennedy administration.

A lifelong Democrat of moderately liberal cast, Parten was extremely active behind the scenes in promoting candidates and ideas. His work in Texas campaigns found him frequently on the losing side, as he was associated with the loyalist faction of the Texas Democratic Party, which supported the national party's platform and ticket in presidential elections from the 1940s to the 1970s. In 1954, he joined other wealthy loyalists in establishing the *Texas Observer*. His support for the *Observer*, his support for sometimes unpopular politicians and ideas, and his work with the Fund for the Republic and the Center for the Study of Democratic Institutions, a think tank for the study of public policy, brought important liberal ideas to the forefront on a statewide and national level.

Throughout his life, Parten was fully engaged in the events and ideas of his times. As a philanthropist, Parten supported a wide range of nonprofit programs and institutions, including the University of Texas, and as an activist he worked until the end of his life in support of world peace and in opposition to nuclear weapons. He continued to belie the conservative stereotype of the Texas oil man in many ways, most notably by his strong opposition to the Vietnam war.

Parten was proud of his heritage and of his accomplishments, and he had reason to be. He was especially pleased when the University of Texas named him one of its distinguished alumni on October 2, 1987. Faculty, administrators, and prominent former students had gathered at the university's Bass Auditorium to honor Parten, Speaker of the House of Representatives Jim Wright, and two others. To Parten's surprise, the house lights suddenly dimmed and a video was projected at the center of the stage. Images of people and events from Parten's past filled the screen as television commentator and author Bill Moyers narrated highlights of Parten's life.

At the end of the video, the audience gave Parten a standing ovation. Frail and unsteady at the age of ninety-one, Parten summoned all his energy and, carefully supported by his son Randy, slowly walked to the podium at center stage. Tears welled in his eyes as he tried to express his feelings, but the emotions were too strong. Parten had worked tirelessly as a regent to improve the university's status, and, in spite of the political strife that had kept him from playing an active role in the university for many years, he retained throughout his life a deep love for the university. The distinguished alumni award was in a way a form of reconciliation as well as recognition for his service. Parten finally pulled himself together enough to tell an anecdote about his days as a university student and then he left the stage.

The next morning, Parten attended an outdoor brunch at Bauer House, the official residence of the Chancellor of the University of Texas System. Among the guests were members of Parten's family as well as many of his old friends, including Lady Bird Johnson, Ralph W. Yarborough, John Henry Faulk, and John B. Connally. As the brunch drew to a close, Parten chatted with Ambassador Edward Clark, one of his oldest acquaintances—though they had opposing political views—about their loyalty and affection for the University of Texas and their love for their East Texas homeland. An out-of-state observer asked from where in East Texas did Clark and Parten come? Clark quickly replied that he was proud to be from San Augustine, while Parten replied that he was "from the county named for the greatest of all Americans." The observer assumed that the old Texan must be referring to a county named for one of the heroes of the Texas Revolution and asked if he meant Crockett, Houston, or Austin? "No," Parten answered firmly, "I'm from James Madison's county."

James Madison's Constitution and the small town in Texas named after him each had significant influences on J. R. Parten. His lifelong support for the Jeffersonian-Jacksonian view of democracy made him a man of principles and integrity. His small-town upbringing made him value loyalty and friendship. J. R. Parten was a quiet doer in a culture that is more likely to recognize the flamboyant gesture. A man who stood firmly behind his beliefs, but who was willing to change when he thought he had learned a better way, J. R. Parten was a man who made a difference. He was an uncommon man whose life spanned a remarkable century.

Part One

1896–1935

Jube Parten of
Madison County

ounded in 1854 and named for the fourth president of the United States,
Madisonville, Texas, is a town of thirty-five hundred people located one
hundred miles northwest of Houston. Madisonville is the county seat of
Madison County. Cotton was king in Madison County for the first seventy-five years of its existence, but cattle ranches and farms growing food for cattle now dominate the land. A few oil wells are scattered among the ranches. It was
in Madisonville, in a house on a ten-acre lot on Commerce Street, that Jubal
Richard "J. R." Parten was born on February 16, 1896.[1]

Jubal, whose nickname soon became "Jube," was the sixth child and the first
son born to Ella May Brooks Parten and Wayne Lafayette Parten. Five more children, two boys and three girls, eventually followed. Jube's parents were among the
leading citizens of Madisonville. His mother was an active member of several of
Madisonville's community organizations when she was not busy taking care of her
family. His father was a prosperous merchant with substantial land holdings. He
and his brother Oscar owned the Parten Brothers general store, located on the
courthouse square. Originally from Nanafalia, a small village in Marengo County,
Alabama, Wayne, Oscar, and their older brother Reuben were brought to Texas
after the Civil War by an uncle, Dr. James Law Jr. They were the orphaned children of Nancy Agnes and Asa J. Parten. Their mother had been the victim of
pneumonia, while their father, a soldier in the Confederate Army, had died in a
Union prisoner-of-war camp.[2]

Wayne Parten and Ella May Brooks met in 1875 when Wayne took a job as a
laborer-in-residence at the Brooks family farm near the Madison County village of
Midway. He was sixteen and she was only ten. Ella May's mother, Emily Montague
Brooks, was a widow in her mid-forties with two young children. Wayne brought

some needed cheer to the Brooks homestead. Blessed with an outgoing personality, he was "happy and cheerful, really the life of the . . . Parten brothers," a family member recalled. He grew especially close to Emily, a strong-willed matriarch who had for five years held the family together and almost singlehandedly kept the farm going. Physically able and devoted to hard work, Emily possessed a shrewd mind for business and a deep passion for books and learning. She was an insatiable reader; her children would recall years later how she often sat in the evenings on the front porch, churning butter while she read a book. Emily passed on to her children her love for reading and education. Although she died the year before Jube's birth, this remarkable woman left her strong imprint on his character by way of her daughter, who was the dominant force in shaping Jube's life.[3]

Eventually, Emily's daughter, Ella May, attracted Wayne Parten's romantic attention. They married in Midway on December 18, 1882, following Ella's graduation from Sam Houston Normal Institute. They lived on the Brooks farm for almost eleven years. When an economic depression swept the country in 1893, causing a drastic plunge in agricultural prices, Wayne decided that there was no future in farming one's own land. He rented the Brooks farm to tenant farmers and moved his growing family and his mother-in-law to a house on Commerce Street in Madisonville, where he joined his brother Oscar to open the "Parten Brothers" general merchandising store. Jube was born in Madisonville three years later.[4]

The Parten family enjoyed a comfortable and stable life by the time of Jube's birth. His father had acquired several small tenant farms and the Parten Brothers store was well established. Jube's childhood experiences were typical for a white, middle-class youth living in a rural East Texas town at the turn of the century. Growing up in a home dominated by women (he later recalled that his five older sisters were "good at giving me directions"), Jube sought out male playmates and joined with them in the usual boyish adventures and escapades. When he was not in school or working in his father's cotton fields or store, Jube was with his friends swimming and diving at spring-fed "Price's tank," hunting and trapping rabbits and opossums, playing baseball in a cleared pasture, or horseback riding. Jube learned how to ride a horse by his fifth birthday. Wayne sometimes received horses in payment for debts and Jube would throw his little red saddle on every new horse and "try him out." Jube became an expert horseman, but as a child he often came home bruised and bleeding from his misadventures on horseback. He later joked that his sisters, who became registered nurses, did so as a result of the experience they gained from tending his wounds.[5]

Jube Parten's childhood was shaped by the influences of a small town in the South at the end of the Victorian era. Madisonville had a population of only a few hundred people throughout the late 1890s and early 1900s. Family, church, school, and the public square dominated social life. Although the rapid changes flowing from the onset of the petroleum revolution and the outbreak of world war soon brought profound changes to small-town life, Madisonville was still a typically American rural "island" community: self contained, nearly uniform in terms of

North Madison Street, Madisonville, Texas, in 1909. *CN 09626. Courtesy Parten Photograph Collection, Center for American History, University of Texas at Austin (cited hereafter as CAH).*

ethnicity and religion (overwhelmingly Anglo-Saxon and Protestant), and little influenced by the outside world.

The primary influence in Jube Parten's life was his family and in that realm his mother dominated. A family friend recalled that Ella Parten "was a very strong, capable pioneer-type woman. J. R. had his mother's personality." Jube's first teacher was his mother, who preferred to teach her children at home the basic lessons normally taught in the first grade. When he finally entered the local school, he was sent to the second grade. Even after her children entered Madisonville's public school, Ella brought them together in the evenings and conducted what her children called "the roundtable." They did homework and discussed the day's lessons with her, often until late in the evening. One of his mother's traits that Jube Parten always remembered was her ability to focus on a task and see it through to the end. She taught her son from a very early age that it was important that he set goals and work hard to achieve those goals in order to become a success in life. As an elderly man, Jube Parten would say that his mother's hard work and "stick-to-it" philosophy had driven him throughout his business career. His father's own single-minded dedication to hard work reinforced that philosophy by example.[6]

Ella also inculcated in her son a devotion to reading. His mother, Jube noted, "read everything that she could get her hands on." Another influence from his

Wayne L. and Ella May Parten. *CN 09639. Courtesy Parten Photograph Collection, CAH.*

mother that Jube would retain throughout his life was a deep dedication to learning. "She felt that the only way that a democratic government could be held
together," Parten recalled, "is by more and more education." Ella's husband
respected his wife's own educational experience, which was superior to his own. In
many ways she served as his teacher and he shared her fervor for education. Wayne
urged his daughters to go to college, offering to support their education financially. Six of the girls accepted his invitation, a remarkable family achievement during
an era when a college-educated woman was a rarity.[7]

One of the outstanding characteristics of J. R. Parten's life was his love of
learning and his ability to grow and change. Throughout his life as a businessman,
public servant, and political activist, Parten demonstrated an ability to learn from
his experiences and from others. Parten often referred to some phase of his life—
his experience as a regent at the University of Texas at Austin, for example, or his
work with Robert Hutchins on the board of the Fund for the Republic—as a new,
higher level of education. An intelligent, well-read, and well-educated man, Parten
was never satisfied that life had no more to teach him. Living well into his nineties,
he grew and changed constantly over the years, always following his mother's
example and admonition that education would constantly renew one's ability to
think and learn. This was a standard that served Parten well. His core sense of values gave him the ability throughout his long and varied life to draw new lessons
from whatever experience came his way.

Although Ella Parten was the most important influence on J. R. during his formative years, his father contributed to his son's development in the realm of politics and business. Wayne Parten had a deep interest in current events and political affairs. Like most Texans in the decades after the Civil War, he was a "yellow dog" Democrat imbued with a strong streak of Jacksonian economic liberalism mixed with the republicanism of Thomas Jefferson and James Madison. In the Parten family, Jefferson and Madison symbolized everything good in the American system of government. At the dinner table, Wayne lectured his family on Jefferson's faith in reason and education, his preference for rural over city life, his opposition to the economic aristocracy, and his firm belief in states' rights, the separation of powers in the federal government, and the protection of civil liberties as embodied in the federal Bill of Rights. Wayne Parten acquired a set of Jefferson's published writings and speeches, which Jube read during his high school years. A version of Jeffersonian and Madisonian values, as Jube interpreted them, served as the lifelong basis for much of his political philosophy, especially with respect to civil liberties issues.[8]

Wayne Parten was also a Jacksonian Democrat who impressed on his son the evils of business monopoly and the dangers of federal intervention in the economic affairs of the people. As a small-town merchant and producer of agricultural commodities, Wayne Parten was squeezed by the rate tyranny of the railroads and threatened by the encroachment of corporate monopolies into his business market. Small-town entrepreneurs such as Wayne Parten perceived the railroads, with their discriminatory rate structures, restraint of trade, and involvement in political corruption, to be the embodiment of the evils of business monopolies. Nevertheless, as a prosperous merchant and landowner, Wayne was never a Populist. Indeed, as a farm landlord and creditor, he was a member of the economic group targeted by the Populists for reform and government regulation.

Jubal Richard Parten, age thirteen months. *CN 09614. Courtesy Parten Photograph Collection, CAH.*

11

Accordingly, Wayne Parten was an active supporter of Texas Democrat and moderate reformer James S. Hogg, who served as the state's chief executive from 1891 to 1895 and who provided small businessmen like Wayne Parten an alternative to the Populists and to reactionary Democrats. In 1891 Hogg played a key role in establishing the Texas Railroad Commission as the state agency responsible for supervising railroad operations. The philosophy behind the Railroad Commission embodied much of Wayne Parten's own political and economic beliefs. The Commission would intervene in the state's economy by regulating the railroads, but it would be a popularly elected body operating at the state rather than at the federal level. State rather than federal power would be used to fight the hated monopolies and to ensure equality of business opportunity.[9]

As Jube Parten grew to adulthood, his political and economic philosophy was shaped profoundly by his father's discussions and dinner-table talks. Although Wayne's opinions over the years were as contradictory and inconsistent as those of other Americans in regard to specific political issues—for example, he later strongly favored Woodrow Wilson while also supporting the virulently anti-Wilson Joseph Bailey—his allegiance to the national Democratic Party, his hostility toward industrial monopolies, and his opposition to federal rather than state regulation of business remained steadfast. Jube also acquired his father's reverence for Jeffersonian democracy and his belief in the sanctity of individual liberty. This latter component of his intellectual and emotional framework nurtured a strong sense of social justice in Jube. Most significant, a Jeffersonian passion for education, reinforced by his mother's almost religious fervor for learning, provided Jube with an open mind and a hunger for knowledge that allowed him to grow and to develop intellectually throughout his life. J. R. Parten accumulated a fortune as a successful businessman, but he never allowed his material success to convert him to an economic reactionary. He remained a Jacksonian conservative in economic matters, equally suspicious of big government and big business. But Jeffersonian democratic principles, with their emphasis on personal liberty, toleration, and the critical need for an educated citizenry, dominated his political and social world view.[10]

Like his father, J. R. Parten was an eminently practical man of some complexity who embodied contradictions, especially when his strongly held principles stood in the way of a practical result. As an independent oil man, albeit a wealthy and powerful one, who saw himself as quite different from a major oil power such as Humble or Mobil, Parten objected on principle to government regulation of the oil business. Throughout his life, as a matter of principle, he strenuously opposed such governmental interference. It is clear that this stand had a practical side: Parten firmly believed that government interference would hurt the business of independent oil men. Yet he supported government controls when it benefited him and his fellow independents, and he admitted that at times such control was for the good of the industry and the country. He was, in many ways, the embodiment of the American "can do" pragmatist. But this is not to say that he was an unprincipled opportunist. His thoughts may rarely have been far from his pocket-

Jube Parten (right) working in his father's store in 1912. To his right is his father's partner, Tom Byers. *CN 09596. Courtesy Parten Photograph Collection, CAH.*

book, but his mind was always engaged; he was adaptable, a man who studied and learned from life.

"High Pockets" Parten and the Five-Dollar Prize

As important as political issues were to the Parten family and to the intellectual development of young Jube, the routine of daily life in a small town ruled their lives as much as it ruled the lives of others similarly situated. Although not wealthy, his family prospered economically, enjoying the comforts of a middle-class affluence. Nevertheless, Wayne and Ella frowned on idleness, and were not inclined to spoil their children. When Jube and his siblings were not in school, they were expected to work at a job, so most of Jube's out-of-school time was spent either in the general store or picking cotton. He had to work not only in his father's fields, but also in those of the Parten extended family, which were scattered throughout the county. Although Jube was eager to get away from the hot and backbreaking work of picking cotton, the experience played an important role in his development. He became accustomed to hard work, a habit reinforced by the exhortations of his parents. Work, not play or leisure, became the most important thing in his life. Jube learned something in those cotton fields that served him well in his later business career. He discovered that one of the most effective ways to get productive labor out of co-workers and employees was by example—the supervisor must always attempt to out-work the supervised.

13

Jube had learned that lesson well by the time he was a teenager. Late in the summer when Jube was fifteen, Wayne told him to make certain that the cotton crop was gathered from the Parten fields before the beginning of the school term in mid-September. Jube's father provided him with several field hands to get the job done. Instead of just supervising, however, Jube devised a method to increase productivity that required him to pick cotton with his workers. At the beginning of the job, young Parten announced his "five-dollar bill award" system. Holding the money high above his head, Jube promised a five-dollar bonus to anyone who picked more cotton than he, an attractive lure to people whose pay was based on the number of pounds of cotton they picked each day and who could hope to earn at the very best no more than three or four dollars for the day. By this time, Jube had developed into a tall, thin, and strong young man. As he later remembered the episode, "I picked four hundred pounds of cotton in one day and I never spent that five-dollar bill. And we got those fields cleared in plenty of time before school began." The episode taught Jube a lesson about managing people that he never forgot.[11]

But life was not all work for Jube. In his high school years Jube enjoyed organized sports and other extracurricular activities, especially baseball. Jube played third base for the Madisonville High School squad. The tallest member of the team, Jube with his long legs soon earned a new nickname: "High Pockets" Parten. Jube was also in the debating club in high school. In his senior year, he made the school's varsity debating team and competed in the statewide high school contest held in Houston. Like his father, Jube admired those who could speak effectively in public. He later credited his debate experience in high school and college with giving him the self-confidence later in life to serve in leadership positions that required public speaking.[12]

Jube dated several girls in Madisonville before graduating from high school, but one of his favorites was Vivian Dean, the daughter of Frank Dean, a local merchant and a close friend of Jube's father. Jube's and Vivian's relationship never developed into anything serious, but Jube's romance with Vivian was important to him for other reasons. He and Vivian often visited her uncle, W. Luther Dean, a prominent attorney and politician in Huntsville. A native of Madison County, W. L. Dean was also a longtime friend of Wayne Parten. After serving as Madison County's representative in the state legislature in the early 1890s, Dean moved his law practice to Huntsville in 1900. Dean, whom his associates referred to as "Judge," was an important role model for Jube Parten. He enjoyed talking about law and politics with "Judge" Dean, who had become an important Texas Democratic Party leader after his move to Huntsville, eventually winning a seat in the Texas Senate in 1916. Dean was a member of the prohibitionist faction of the party, which was identified with the Southern progressive reform movement. After Texas ratified the Prohibition (Eighteenth) Amendment to the United States Constitution in 1919, Dean authored the stringent enforcement statute, which became known as "the Dean Law." Although Jube's father was never an enthusiast for prohibition, he and Dean agreed on most other political issues, taking basically

Jube Parten during his senior year at Madisonville High School. *CN 09601. Courtesy Parten Photograph Collection, CAH.*

the same positions advocated by Woodrow Wilson. With such powerful influences working on him, Jube also became a staunch Wilsonian Democrat. More important, it was his discussions with W. L. Dean that convinced Jube Parten to study law in college.[13]

"one hell of a bang"

Jube made top marks in all of his classes at Madisonville High, excelling in history, government, English, Latin, and mathematics. By his senior year, school was so easy for Jube that he became bored, and his boredom eventually got him into trouble. A few days before the Christmas holiday, Jube and a friend decided to break the monotony, so Jube exploded a firecracker against a wall on the school grounds during lunch. The result, he recalled later, was "one hell of a bang." No attempt was made to discover the offender until the end of the day, when all of the boys were told to stay after school to meet with the superintendent of schools, M. L. "Mack" Bennett. When Jube admitted that he was the culprit, Bennett suspended him from school until after the Christmas holidays.

When Jube returned to school in early January, Bennett told him that he was certain to be the class valedictorian, which meant he would receive a scholarship from Baylor University, the college with which Madisonville High School was affiliated. Knowing Jube wanted to be a lawyer, Bennett advised him to waive the scholarship and go to the University of Texas in Austin, where he could attend law school. That course, however, meant that Jube would have to take the university's entrance exam and pay for his tuition and books. Bennett assured Jube that he could probably pass the exam, but that he would improve his chances by doing some extra work. He offered to tutor Jube in subjects like trigonometry and advanced United States history and government, which were not taught in the Madisonville school. This extra work would also take care of Jube's boredom. Jube accepted Bennett's offer. For the remainder of the school year, he and the superintendent spent their afternoons preparing for the entrance exam. Jube never forgot Bennett's generous help. In gratitude, he later financed Bennett's son's education at the University of Texas.[14]

Jube completed his senior year in May 1913, ranked first in his graduating class of twenty-two. His decision to give up his scholarship presented him with an immediate problem. He had a summer job in his father's general store, but the pay was too meager to cover his college expenses. Although his father had willingly paid for his daughters' college educations, his son refused to ask him for help. Jube had turned down a scholarship to one of the best schools in Texas and he felt uncomfortable about asking his business-minded father to pay for something he could have had for free. Jube, who had also become fiercely independent, decided to raise the money himself, without his father's help or knowledge.[15]

One afternoon in the summer of 1913, Jube rode horseback to the tiny village of Connor to ask his aunt Nannie Parten for a loan to pay for his college education. Nannie was the well-to-do widow of his father's older brother "Doc" Parten, who had died three years earlier. Sitting on the front porch of Nannie's house, Jube made his first business deal. Jube proposed to borrow five hundred dollars for each of his four years at the university. Five hundred dollars would pay for his tuition, books, room and board, and all other expenses for the entire school year. Nannie Parten made a hard bargain. Jube did not have to repay the loan until after his graduation, but Nannie insisted that he pay 10 percent interest, a very high rate for the time. Family relations were one thing, but this was business. Jube agreed and the loan was made. He returned to Madisonville with five hundred dollars and a practical lesson in capitalism.[16]

While Jube was still a student at the university, his father found out about Nannie's loan and paid it off without telling his son. After Jube had made some money in the drilling business and was living in Louisiana, he tried to repay his debt to Nannie, only to learn that his father had taken care of it. When Jube tried to reimburse his father, Wayne refused it. He told Jube that he was proud of his effort in self-help, but he was unhappy that his son had borrowed money at such a high rate of interest. After his father's lecture, Jube was even more determined to maintain his independence in the matter. Seeing that it was futile to force his father to take the money, Jube paid cash for a new Buick automobile, put it in his father's name, parked it in front of his parents' house, and left for Louisiana without another word.[17]

"Pushing to the Front"

With his Aunt Nannie's five hundred dollars in his pocket, Jube Parten departed from Madisonville on September 20, 1913, on the train for Austin. Jube's excitement about becoming "a university man" was tempered by deep anxieties. Not only was he leaving home for the first time, but he had never been to Austin and he had no idea what it or the university even looked like. His worries were alleviated somewhat by the fact that his cousins Ben and Reuben Parten were students at the university. Jube had additional concerns, however. Despite Superintendent Bennett's assurances, he was nervous about the exams he had to pass before he would be permitted to enroll.

Arriving at Austin's Congress Avenue train depot early the next morning, Jube looked around, trying to get his bearings. Too shy to ask directions, he gazed to the north and saw the great dome of the Texas State Capitol. He turned and saw another impressive building on a hill across the Colorado River to the south and concluded that he had found the university. Jube lugged his trunk and bag aboard a south-bound streetcar and headed across the Congress Avenue bridge, only to discover when he got there that he was at the wrong university. The large building on the hill was Saint Edward's, a Catholic college on the opposite side of town from the University of Texas. Embarrassed but not defeated, Jube took a streetcar going north and finally found his new school.[18]

After seeing the beautiful and impressive Saint Edward's College, Jube was disappointed by what he found at the University of Texas. He was shocked to see a large but decaying "main building" surrounded by eight plain, brick buildings and several wooden shacks to which the students referred derisively as "shack-o'tec-ture." There was one impressive and beautiful new structure to the southwest of the main building which housed the library, but most of the campus was in scandalous shape, the legacy of three decades of legislative neglect. The main building, not yet thirty years old but flawed structurally, was literally falling apart. Its auditorium, which was the university's only large indoor meeting place, was a fire trap. Actually, most of the campus was one large fire hazard because of the poorly constructed wooden shacks, which included the University Commons or "Caf" that served as the dining room, and the men's and women's gymnasiums. A severe shortage of dormitories forced many of the school's seven thousand students to live in boarding houses near campus.[19]

Jube's cousin Benjamin Lafitte Parten lived on Nueces Street a few blocks

Jube Parten in his room at Mrs. Berry's boarding house, Austin, 1913. *CN 09610. Courtesy Parten Photograph Collection, CAH.*

west of the campus. With Ben's help, Jube found a room to rent in Mrs. Berry's boarding house, across the street from Ben's place. The next day Jube took the entrance exam. He did well in all sections except Latin, which caused him to be short one high school credit for admission. Fortunately, at Mack Bennett's suggestion, Jube had brought with him to Austin some examples of his best work in high school, including a batch of his mechanical drawings. He took those to T. U. Taylor, the dean of the School of Engineering, who granted him the one credit he needed to enroll.[20]

Jube wasted little time in getting into the swing of things on campus. Freshmen were not allowed to join a fraternity or sorority, but the first-year class did organize and elect officers. His classmates elected Jube sergeant-at-arms. As a freshman officer, Jube had an opportunity to meet many of the incoming class of 1917. Among them was a combative and outspoken boy from San Antonio named Maury Maverick. "Maury was always a little advanced for me," Jube later recalled of the future New Deal congressman and San Antonio mayor. "I was willing to make a little trouble, but he always wanted to make a lot, even then." Although he was a freshman officer and participated in campus social events, Jube's main concern that first year was in the classroom. Enrolled in a scholastically rigorous program that would let him graduate in five years with two degrees (a bachelor's degree in government and a law degree), Jube worked hard and passed all of the required first-year courses. Surviving his initial year at the university, Jube returned home triumphantly in the summer of 1914.[21]

After his return to Austin in September 1914, Jube landed a part-time job, which freed him from a need for Aunt Nannie's money for at least a year. As a sophomore, Jube was eligible to join a fraternity. He chose Delta Chi, the law fraternity to which his cousins Ben and Reuben belonged. Jube's heavy academic load, his part-time job, and the fraternity and campus social scene (he was elected vice president of the Speakers' Club in the spring semester) left him little extra

18

time during his sophomore year. Whenever he could, however, Jube walked the short distance from the campus to the Capitol to observe the state legislature at work. Because the Texas legislature is in session only once every two years, it was not until the last semester of his second year in college that Jube had an opportunity to observe its members in collective action. Pondering a possible future in politics, Jube sat in the spectators' gallery and took notes on the proceedings. He also frequently visited two state representatives he knew personally, Walter "Uncle" Elmer Pope and Myron G. Blalock. The latter was one of Jube's law school classmates who was serving his second term as state representative from Harrison County. Pope, the state representative from Corpus Christi, was a former resident of Madison County and an old friend of Jube's father.[22]

Jube's access to the legislature improved significantly in 1917 when W. L. Dean became a member of the Texas Senate. Jube enrolled in Prof. Charles G. Haines's course on state government and administration, and the legislature became his unofficial off-campus laboratory. After Jube's daily visits to the Capitol during his senior year, he met with Haines to report the latest developments. This was during the height of Gov. James Ferguson's attempt to purge the university's faculty and administration, so there was usually something of great interest to Haines for Jube to report. The lessons Jube learned from Haines, Pope, and Dean, as well as from his own firsthand observations, were invaluable later when developments in his career required frequent dealings with the state legislature and the United States Congress.[23]

At the end of his sophomore year in June 1915, Jube decided to spend the summer working in Houston. His older sister "Miss Malcolm" had moved to Houston in 1910 to work as a registered nurse at Houston Heights Hospital and she had invited him to stay with her. Jube had recently read and enjoyed Orison Swett Marsden's *Pushing to the Front*, a popular "self-motivation" book typical of the period. A forerunner of the Norman Vincent Peale approach, Marsden's book was crammed with trite "positive thinking for success" exhortations such as "the world makes way for the determined man." The book featured chapters with titles such as "The Man With an Idea," "The Will and the Way," and "One Unwavering Way." It reinforced Jube's already strong belief in will power, determination, and persistence as the essential keys to success in life, a belief he never really abandoned. Jube decided to order a supply of *Pushing to the Front* and try his hand at peddling them door-to-door in Houston. Because of the recent opening of the Houston Ship Channel and Gulf Coast oil discoveries, the city was enjoying an immense economic boom. Jube thought that Marsden's book would have great appeal in a city in which the self-made-man myth had become a civic religion. His guess was correct. *Pushing to the Front* sold well, earning Jube enough money to make Nannie Parten's money unnecessary for yet another year.[24]

George Butte and the *Lusitania*

While Jube sold books in Houston during the summer of 1915, the daily newspapers were filled with stories about the incident in which the British luxury ship

Above: George Charles Butte, Parten's international law professor. *CN 09616. Courtesy Prints and Photographs Collection, CAH.*

Parten and his debate partner, Sam Baggett, 1917. *CN 09611. From the 1917* Cactus, *CAH.*

Lusitania had been sunk by a German U-boat, with the loss of twelve hundred lives, of which one hundred and twenty-four were U. S. citizens. The *Lusitania* incident initiated a heated national debate about the rights of citizens from neutral nations during a war. Jube followed the unfolding events with fascination throughout the summer. When he returned to school in September, Jube was so enthralled with the national discussion about neutral's rights and other issues of international law raised by the European war that he enrolled in Prof. George Charles Butte's elective course on the subject. Jube's decision to take Butte's senior-level course resulted in his most rewarding intellectual experience at the university. Butte was a thirty-eight-year-old law graduate of the University of Texas who had made a small fortune in the Oklahoma oil boom. He had studied international law at the University of Berlin and at Heidelberg University, where he had earned a doctorate in jurisprudence. Butte joined the law faculty in 1914 and soon earned a reputation as a brilliant teacher, intellectually rigorous but personally accessible and popular with his students.[25]

Jube fell under George Butte's spell the first day of class. Declaring that he was "an enthusiast on the subject of international law," Butte told the class that they had chosen a timely subject because of the "great conflict now going on in Europe." Because the war was raising "many interesting current questions of international law," Butte noted, the students would have the exciting opportunity to "observe a science in the . . . making." International law, Butte argued, was "living law," determined by the way nations actually behave, so students had to approach the subject in the manner of naturalists studying flowers and animals— by observation of behavior. "Hence," he announced to Parten's delight, "contemporary events will engage much of our time."[26]

International relations dominated Jube Parten's junior year, as Butte's class exposed him to a new and fascinating world filled with arguments about such topics as freedom of the seas, the rights of neutral nations in wartime, and U.S. military interventions in Mexico and Central America. The daily newspaper served as a class textbook. Because of his experience in Germany and the fact that the United States was not yet in the war, Butte was able to teach the course in an even-handed manner. It was from Butte that Jube learned to appreciate the complexities and contradictions inherent in diplomatic disputes, and the dangers involved in viewing international conflict in simplistic black-and-white terms.[27]

In the late fall of 1915, one of Jube's debating assignments as a member of the university's Speakers' Club reinforced these lessons. The semester debate question asked: "Were the Germans justified in the sinking of the *Lusitania* ?" With Butte's lectures on the subject fresh on his mind, Jube volunteered to argue in favor. During his preparations for the debate, Jube learned that the *Lusitania*'s passengers had been warned in writing that the ship was carrying munitions into a war zone and that it might be sunk before it got to London. With that information, Jube argued that if a ship carried munitions of war to a combatant nation and its civilian passengers were given prior warning, then it could be sunk with justification under the "evolving" rules of naval warfare. The Germans were arguing that submarines, because of their vulnerability after surfacing, could not stop and search ships as required by the established rules of war. Therefore, the "living law" of international relations had to accommodate technical developments making earlier rules obsolete. In the debate, which was judged by three members of the Texas Court of Civil Appeals, Jube concluded his argument with the bold statement that "therefore the German submarine commander was thoroughly justified in the sinking of the *Lusitania.*" To the surprise of his friends who thought the affirmative position was a lost cause, Jube won the debate.[28]

As a result of Butte's influence, Jube seriously considered the Foreign Service for a career, but he eventually decided against it. Jube was determined to be his own boss and he concluded that the State Department bureaucracy was no place for the independent minded. Nevertheless, Butte's class made a lifelong impression on Jube, greatly encouraging his interest in world affairs and issues of war and peace.[29]

The Little Woodley Girl and the Single Tax

There was one other reason why the Foreign Service lost its appeal before Jube left the university. He was distracted by romance. The source of which was Opal Woodley, an attractive and vivacious freshman from the little town of Shamrock, in the Texas Panhandle near the Oklahoma border. Jube met Opal at a campus football rally in the fall of 1915. After that chance encounter, Jube's and Opal's relationship flowered. By the spring of 1916 they were a steady pair. "Jube Parten rushes the little Woodley girl," declared the student yearbook, the *Cactus*, in a listing of campus social "developments" during the 1915–1916 school year. The couple seemed to confirm the old saying that in romance opposites often attract. Opal was outgoing and informal. She loved parties and the opportunity to mix with strangers in social situations and to meet new people. Her fellow students selected her as one of the seven campus "Bluebonnet" beauty queens for 1916. Despite Jube's participation in the debate club, he remained somewhat shy and reserved, uncomfortable with strangers and not interested in the social scene. Despite these personality differences, Jube fell in love with Opal. They talked marriage, but decided to wait until after Jube's graduation.[30]

Jube began his senior year at the university with much anticipation. He was eager to escort Opal, now a Chi Omega pledge, to campus social events—carrying the dark-brown walking cane used by male seniors as a badge of upperclass status. Jube was also determined to make the varsity intercollegiate debate team, which was a big step up from the campus Speakers' Club, of which he had served as president the previous year. The Chautauqua and lyceum movements, religious revivals, and traditional political "stump" speaking had made public oratory a communications art form much coveted by anyone interested in public leadership. In the era before radio and motion picture "talkies," public lectures and debates were also a major form of mass entertainment. Accordingly, intercollegiate debating was among the most popular activities on campuses throughout the United States. Making the varsity debate team conferred the status that in later years would be given to those making the football or basketball team, so competition was strong. Jube's success in the *Lusitania* debate gave him the confidence he needed to make the attempt.[31]

To be eligible for the team, Jube enrolled in the debate class instructed by Charles I. Francis, a graduate student in law who also served as the coach. After several weeks of preparation and class debates, Jube won a place on the varsity's two-man squad representing the university in the season's first debate. Their opposition was a team visiting from the University of Colorado. The national subject for all intercollegiate debates in the 1916–1917 school year was Henry George's "single tax," which had been introduced by the social reformer in his 1879 book *Progress and Poverty*. George argued for a tax on the unearned surplus value of appreciated land to redistribute wealth, alleviate poverty, and eliminate the need for other kinds of taxes. George's proposal had been widely discussed for almost four decades, but it had lost most of its popular appeal by 1916.[32]

Jube agreed with those who criticized the single tax as utopian and fatally flawed. He and his debate partner, Sam Baggett, therefore hoped that they would be assigned the negative side of the debate. The *Daily Texan* promoted the debate with several front-page stories, and broadsides announcing the event were plastered on walls all over campus. On the night of the debate, as the University String Band played "Hawaiian" music, Jube and Sam sat on the stage of the YMCA auditorium, awaiting the arrival of the large crowd that typically attended the varsity debates. They were disappointed but not surprised when few spectators appeared. Momentous events in Washington had distracted everyone, including the debaters. That afternoon, April 6, 1917, Congress had declared war on Germany and intercollegiate debate now seemed trivial in the extreme. Jube and Sam drew the affirmative side of the single-tax question and lost the debate. "To debate the single tax on the affirmative side on the evening after World War I was declared was the worst damn job I ever had in my life," Jube later said.[33]

The University Goes to War

"University Prepares for War" screamed the *Daily Texan*'s headlines the next day. War fever and patriotic posturing swept the campus. The university administration dismissed classes at noon and requested that every student and faculty member attend a mass meeting in front of the Law Building to pledge support for the U.S. war effort. Jube dutifully reported to a shady spot beneath the trees in front of the building to listen to Dean T. U. Taylor's speech on patriotism and the need for every able-bodied young male student to join the army. At the end of his speech, Taylor pulled a small American flag out of his vest pocket and waved it above his head as the crowd cheered. Two days later, Jube joined his fellow students and the faculty in a "Loyalty Day Parade" down Guadalupe Street. Within two weeks, the university administration required that every male student register for a course titled Military Science 101 or be expelled. The entire male student body was organized into fourteen military companies, drilling daily under the supervision of a regular U.S. Army officer.[34]

News about war preparations on campus filled the *Daily Texan*. The army announced the May 8 opening of an officers training camp for college men from Texas and Oklahoma at Camp Leon Springs near San Antonio. In an editorial, the *Daily Texan* called upon every able-bodied male student to go to the training camp and prepare to lead soldiers to France. Coeds circulated petitions declaring that they would "socially ostracize" any healthy boys who stayed at school rather than go to officers camp. University officials declared that anyone with passing grades could leave school early for officers camp and receive full credit for their courses. The pressure to conform was tremendous; dissent was not tolerated.[35]

Jube had opposed U.S. entrance into the European war. His work in George Butte's class had reinforced his view and now that war was a reality he had no enthusiasm for it. "But like most everyone else," Parten recalled, "I figured once we were in it, I had . . . to prepare to go in the Army." After the army announced the first officers training camp, students, including many of his fraternity brothers, rushed to sign up. Jube, however, lacked one year of course work for graduation. He feared that once he entered the army, he might never return to school. Jube considered skipping the first officers training camp so that he could attend summer school and take two law courses critical to his preparation for the bar exam in August. Once he passed the exam, he would not have to return to school. Opal urged him to take that option. As Jube wrestled with his problem, pressured by the intolerant war environment and the call to enlist immediately, the army announced on May 2 that the officers camp was full. A second camp would be available in September, after the current crop of men had competed their three months of training. Jube's future course was set, he applied for admission to the second officers training camp and made ready for summer school.[36]

The last weeks of the spring semester of 1917 at the University of Texas were memorable for reasons other than the war. In late May, a power struggle broke out between Gov. James E. "Pa" Ferguson and the university's board of regents, administration, and faculty. Ferguson, whose demands for a purge of his political opponents from the university payroll had been ignored by the administration, called a meeting of the board of regents for May 28 with the implied purpose of firing Pres. Robert E. Vinson and other university administrators. News of the impending action roused students and powerful alumni leaders to action. Large and noisy protest rallies were held on campus and thousands of students marched on the Capitol on the day Governor Ferguson met with the regents. Although the governor vetoed the university's state appropriation a few weeks later, the action initiated a series of events that eventually lead to his impeachment and removal from office.[37]

Jube's friends in law school opposed Ferguson, and some of them led the student protests. His father, however, was an ardent supporter of Pa Ferguson, also called "Farmer Jim," because of his strong identification with rural Texas. Although independent in most matters, Jube at this age generally accepted his father's choice in political leaders, so he supported Ferguson. As a result, he not only refused to take part in the campus protest, he told his friends that they were wrong and that "their demonstrations did a great injustice to an able government." Jube changed his mind, however, when he attended the impeachment hearings during the summer and read the evidence. The hearings convinced him that Ferguson was "guilty of misuse of state funds," a conclusion his father rejected. The Ferguson fight impressed Jube with the need to keep the university out of partisan politics. Years later, when he served as a University of Texas regent, he had frequent opportunities to remember that lesson.[38]

After finishing his course work for the summer session, Jube passed the bar exam in the middle of August. When he applied for army officers training, he and Opal agreed to delay marriage until he had completed his army service. She wanted to finish her degree in English at the University of Texas and Jube assumed that he would be sent overseas as soon as he received his commission. With law license in hand, he packed his trunk and left Opal and the university for three months of officers school. He hoped to return after the war and finish his degree, but he did not. His student days had ended but his relationship with the University of Texas was far from over.[39]

"delighted to have the privilege of firing a French '75'"

Jube entered the army on August 24, 1917, when he arrived at the Leon Springs Military Reservation located twenty-six miles northwest of San Antonio. Upon his arrival, Jube was given the option of service in the infantry or the horse artillery. Jube choose the artillery, a choice which proved to be a good one. His mathematical skills, organizational talents, and fondness for work made him an ideal artillery-officer candidate, especially after the army adopted the so-called French method of artillery fire soon after his training began. The French method aims the artillery piece directly at the target, so that it fires its shell like a rifle rather than lobbing it like a howitzer. Proper aiming required rapid and accurate mathematical calculations. Use of the new method was necessitated by the U.S. Army's acquisition of the French "75" cannon after entering the war. Jube soon became a specialist in the firing of the French gun. Because many of the old army officers resisted learning the French method, younger artillery officers like Jube had an opportunity to advance rapidly in rank as they became skilled in its use.[40]

Jube found the discipline and order of army life appealing. Characteristically, he was determined to rise as high as possible in the officer corps, so he took advantage of every opportunity for extra training, even to the extent of forgoing weekend leave. Because of the extra practice, Jube regularly outperformed most of the other men in maneuvers and he received top evaluations from his instructors. When he completed his training on November 24, he was one of only four of the class to be commissioned as a captain.[41]

Jube was ordered to report for duty on December 18, 1917, to the 343rd Field Artillery of the Ninetieth Division based at Camp Travis, Fort Sam Houston, in San Antonio. When he left Leon Springs on November 27, however, he headed straight to Memphis, Tennesse, to marry Opal. It was his first trip out of Texas. Opal's father, Edward L. Woodley, who was practicing law in Memphis, had met

Parten in his army officer's uniform, 1918. *CN 09607. Courtesy Parten Photograph Collection, CAH.*

Jube during a visit to Austin to see his daughter and the two had gotten along very well. Jube and Opal had a private wedding ceremony in the Woodley home on December 15, 1917. The next morning, Jube rushed back to San Antonio to report to his new post.[42]

A few days before Christmas, Opal joined Jube in San Antonio, where he waited for his new orders. The Partens enjoyed the social scene at huge Fort Sam Houston, one of the army's most desirable posts. Despite the war, the Christmas season at "Fort Sam" was a swirl of parties and activities. Aware of the danger awaiting them overseas, the post's young officers enjoyed themselves while they could. It was not a bad place to be for a newly married couple. The Parten's made several new friends, including a twenty-seven-year-old law professor from Indiana, Capt. Paul Vories McNutt, and his fiancee Kathleen Timolat of San Antonio, with whom they went out nightly to dances and other events. McNutt, a future Democratic governor of Indiana and presidential aspirant, remained a friend of Jube's for many years to come.[43]

The week after New Year's Day, 1918, Jube's orders arrived from the War Department. It was not the assignment he had anticipated, however. He had done so well with the new French gun that the army decided he should instruct the next group of officer candidates in the third training camp at Leon Springs (now renamed Camp Stanley). Jube had to live on base, but he found an apartment for Opal in the nearby town of Boerne, where he joined her every Saturday night. He remained at Camp Stanley for the remainder of the winter, hoping for a "real" war assignment in Europe.[44]

Jube thought his opportunity had arrived when the army ordered him in late March to Camp Jackson, near Columbia, South Carolina. Camp Jackson's mission was to train artillery-officer replacements for the front. When he and Opal arrived in South Carolina on April 5, 1918, the army gave Jube the same job he had had at Camp Stanley and he spent the remainder of the war instructing artillery officers who were on their way to France. Jube was disappointed about being kept in the states, but he enjoyed his work in South Carolina. Like Fort Sam Houston, Camp Jackson offered a vibrant social life for the officers and their wives. Paul McNutt and his new wife were stationed there, as well as some of the former artillery instructors who had helped Jube at Leon Springs. When they were not teaching the French method of artillery fire, Jube, McNutt, and their buddies went horseback riding, hunting, and hiking in the thick pine forest nearby. After the war, Jube admitted to one of his former colleagues at Camp Jackson that he looked back with "pleasure" on his army experience and that he often felt that he would once again be "delighted to have the privilege of firing a '75' from the hillside in South Carolina where we used to burn so much ammunition for Uncle Sam."[45]

The Youngest Major

The army brass noted Jube's outstanding performance at Camp Jackson. On September 20, 1918, he was appointed to the rank of major in command of the Fifty-ninth Battalion of the Field Artillery and reassigned to the Twentieth

Division of the regular army at Camp Jackson. Soon after the promotion, Jube's commanding officer informed him that at age twenty-two he was now the youngest major in the artillery section of the army.[46]

When news of the armistice reached Camp Jackson in November, Jube and his fellow officers were disappointed because they had missed the action. He envied his older sister, Lucy, who was serving overseas as an army nurse. Jube had worked hard to make himself a good artillery officer and he felt that he had not made much of a contribution to the war effort. With the war over, he and Opal had to decide their future course. In early December 1918, the army offered Jube an assignment as an artillery instructor in the officers training program at Harvard University. It was an appealing offer because Jube would have the opportunty to continue his law studies at Harvard. After he left the army, he would be well fixed with an advanced degree from the nation's most prestigious law school. Opal urged Jube to accept the job because it gave her an opportunity to finish her undergraduate course work in Boston and then to go on to graduate school. However, Jube decided to postpone his decision until after he and Opal had spent the Christmas holidays in Shreveport, Louisiana, where Opal's parents had recently moved. Almost certain that they would soon be on their way to Boston, Jube and Opal boarded a train for Shreveport.[47]

CHAPTER 2

The Major Becomes an Oil Man

Arkansas and Louisiana, 1919–1930

Jube's Christmas visit to Shreveport was his first real opportunity to become acquainted with his father-in-law, Edward (E. L.) Woodley, a forty-six-year-old businessman and sometime attorney. Woodley and his wife had decided to move from Memphis to Shreveport in June 1917 to get in on the oil boom in northwest Louisiana. E. L. joined with his brother Tom ("T. J.") and two other men to organize Farmers Oil Company, which bought and sold oil and gas leases. By the time the Partens arrived in Shreveport for the holidays, E. L. and his brother had also started an oil-well drilling business.[1]

When Jube told his father-in-law about his opportunity to go to Harvard, E. L. urged him not to do it. Instead, E. L. argued, Jube should move to Shreveport and join him in the drilling business. Oil had been discovered near Shreveport at Caddo Lake in 1905 and within five years Caddo wells were pumping more than five million barrels of crude a year. E. L. claimed that landowners throughout northern Louisiana wanted their property drilled for oil, so there was plenty of business waiting for their new drilling company. He offered to help Jube get a loan to buy his own drilling rig. Jube could manage their drilling projects in the field, while E. L. managed the company office in Shreveport and drummed up clients. Eventually, they could drill their own wells. To help convince Jube that this was a great business opportunity, E. L. drove him out to Pine Island, fifteen miles northwest of Shreveport and at that time one of the most active fields in the Caddo oil pool. Jube was impressed by what he saw at Pine Island, and later recalled that he had gotten his "first taste of oil" there. Oil operators were drilling shallow wells and producing thousands of barrels of low-gravity crude oil a day with relatively small investments. It was apparent to Jube that this was a real entrepreneurial opportunity for a young man with little capital.[2]

Woodley also took Jube to downtown Shreveport to get a look at a boomtown. In coffee shops and hotel lobbies, on street corners and courthouse steps, oil entrepreneurs gathered in small groups trading information, buying and selling, making deals and feverishly searching for the big play that might result in a new Rockefeller. Like Tulsa had been earlier, and Houston would be later, Shreveport was the place to be for anyone wanting to get a piece of the action in the sudden-wealth world of oil. It was an exciting scene to a young man eager to make his mark. When Jube discussed E. L.'s offer with Opal, however, she pleaded with him to reject it. Opal warned Jube that her father had lost most of the family's savings in get-rich-quick schemes. Her father had spent most of his adult years restlessly in search of the quick dollar, speculating in real estate and oil leases in the Texas Panhandle, trading in cotton futures, and hustling a South American soft drink, called *El Mate*, which he had hoped would be the next Coca Cola. As far as Opal was concerned, the oil business was just another one of her father's harebrained ideas, it was just too risky. Opal yearned for a more stable and contemplative life and she wanted to go back to school.[3]

Jube realized that he was at an important crossroads in his career. One of the reasons he had considered remaining in the army was because he had doubts about making the law his profession. "My classmates who . . . got their law licenses . . . went to work in Houston for seventy five dollars a month," he said later. "I figured I could beat that. I was making three hundred and sixty dollars a month in the Army plus some allowance." As Jube saw it, his future was either in the army or in the oil business. Pulled in both directions, he decided to get the advice of his commanding officer, Col. Phillip Woodfin Booker. Leaving Opal with her parents in Shreveport, Jube returned to South Carolina. When he told Colonel Booker about his father-in-law's proposal, Booker advised his young officer to accept it. He told Jube that the peacetime army had few opportunities for career advancement. "I'll never forget Booker," Parten later said. "I resigned the next day and was on a train back to Shreveport."[4]

Woodley Drilling Company

Delighted by Jube's decision, E. L. backed a loan from a local bank for him to purchase a rig. Jube then joined with E. L. and T. J. Woodley to create Woodley Drilling Company. Opal did not share her father's enthusiasm about this change in her life. Jube tried to persuade his deeply skeptical wife that he had made the right choice. He also made her a promise. As soon as the business made money, she could return to school and get her degree. Filled with misgivings, Opal found an apartment at 1534 Highland Avenue, not far from her parents' home on Line Avenue in central Shreveport, and she and Jube moved in.[5]

Opal's fears about the extremely risky nature of the oil business were legitimate. Her husband and her father had entered an industry that was unpredictable in the best of times, and, despite E. L.'s unrestrained enthusiasm, 1919 was not a good time. The industry was in a state of confusion made worse by a national economy suffering through a critical period of postwar adjustment. The economic problems were especially evident in Shreveport. The end of the war had terminated a major and ready market, especially for Pine Island's low-gravity oil, which at the time was suitable only for fueling naval vessels. Demand for northern Louisiana oil had fallen after the signing of the armistice in November 1918, resulting in a plunge in price from $1.55 to about fifty cents a barrel by the spring of 1919. Widespread predictions of an impending oil shortage, however, soon restored prices to an acceptable level, until the discovery of new fields lowered prices again. This pattern continued for decades. The enormous rise in the number of automobiles, the widespread shift of homeowners to fuel-oil, and the expansion of the chemical and synthetic industries created unprecedented demand, though huge new oil discoveries in the midcontinent region, in the Gulf area, and in California often exceeded the growth rates of these new markets. The result was increasingly frequent maladjustments between supply and demand and a highly fluctuating price structure.[6]

Parten was well aware of these problems when he entered the business in January 1919. The very conditions that repelled Opal, however, attracted her husband. When he first saw Pine Island, he quickly realized that the risky business of discovering and producing oil was one enterprise still open to the aspiring entrepreneur. The inability to know with certainty where oil was located underground had kept the major companies from monopolizing the finding and producing of crude oil. Although the major oil companies were producing some of their own crude oil by 1919, a large amount was still being found and produced by individual entrepreneurs who were independent of those companies. Parten's goal was to join the ranks of those "independents." Parten's Jeffersonian-Jacksonian view of the world also fueled his desire to be his own man, and an independent oil company provided him the economic freedom that for Parten and his ideological idols was a hallmark of the American dream. The risks were real enough, but Parten intended to proceed with relative caution. He knew nothing about oil-well drilling. "In those early days, you didn't learn how to drill an oil well by going to a university," Parten explained. So he and E. L. hired experienced drillers to work their rigs until they learned the operational side of the business. Parten planned to learn the business carefully without taking the kind of financial risk inherent in a wildcat oil-well venture. He and E. L. would earn their drilling fees whether a well was successful or not. Once their rigs were paid off and the time was ripe, they could assume the risk of drilling their own wells. Drilling for others also provided them valuable information that could be used to buy potential leases.

Parten was also optimistic about future oil supply. He believed that there was much more oil yet to be discovered and that the demand would always be sufficient to guarantee a profit. Although 1918 proved to be the production high-point for the Caddo Lake oil fields, the decline was slow and plenty of new sources in northern Louisiana and southern Arkansas were soon discovered. Indeed, four months after he and E. L. opened for business, a large oil field was discovered near the town of Homer, about forty miles northeast of Shreveport. Other discoveries quickly followed, making Louisiana the third-largest oil-producing state, behind Texas and Oklahoma.[7]

Shreveport, Parten's new home, was a prime location in which to start a new oil enterprise. With five large oil fields producing fifty thousand barrels of oil a day within a fifty-mile radius of its central business district, Shreveport was the oil center of the state, "the hub about which the spokes of fortune revolved." Located at the head of navigation on the Red River and at the center of a major railroad network, Shreveport served as a great inland cotton market with one of the largest cotton-compress operations in the world. The city's location near extensive forests of yellow pine made it a major lumber center. The gas produced nearby from some of the largest natural gas fields in the world gave Shreveport an abundant source of cheap fuel. The second-largest city in Louisiana with a population of about fifty thousand in 1919, Shreveport nearly doubled in size during the prosperous decade of the 1920s. Shreveport was also a pleasant place in which to live and work for young couples such as the Partens and others of the growing professional and business class who flocked to the city after the First World War. Because the city had close cultural and economic ties to East Texas, Shreveport felt very much like home to J. R. Parten.[8]

In mid-January 1919, E. L. leased office space in the City National Bank building in downtown Shreveport and spread word around town that the Woodley Drilling Company was ready to drill oil wells. Barely twenty-three years old, Jube now decided to replace the nickname of his youth with one that was more business-like. Following the example of his partners, he decided to use his initials. Henceforth, Jube would be "J. R." He also acquired a title that remained with him for the rest of his life. During his holiday visit, he had been in uniform and had been introduced to the Woodley family friends as "Major" Parten. Although now out of the army, his new friends still called him "Major," a title Parten did not discourage. As "Major" Parten, the young entrepreneur enjoyed a social status among Shreveport's elite that a person of his tender years normally would not be granted.[9]

In the early months of 1919, E. L. and J. R. busily made contacts, talking deals and pushing the new Woodley Drilling Company. Because the most important place in Shreveport to make contacts was in the lobby and the restaurant of the city's largest hotel, the Youree, they spent much time there in the beginning. As Woodley Drilling Company's business grew, however, J. R. and E. L. abandoned the Youree for an office on the tenth floor of the City Bank Building. "We developed a pretty good name quickly, and people found us rather than us having to go find them," Parten later said. The Pine Island boom got Woodley Drilling off to a fast start and its twenty-three-year-old field supervisor soon had all the work he could handle.[10]

Woodley drilling rigs were active in Pine Island and the new fields in Red River Parish and Sabine Parish to the south of Shreveport. In the latter parish, they drilled in the so-called "Bull Bayou" field near Bayou Toro, where they eventually

Parten (right) observes crude oil gushing from his new well at Pine Island near Shreveport, Louisiana, about 1922. *CN 09606. Courtesy Parten Photograph Collection, CAH.*

conducted some oil production of their own. With the rapid growth of their business, Parten was soon spending all of his time in the field supervising operations, while E. L. ran the office. It became clear to E. L. that his son-in-law partner was responsible for much of the company's hard-driving energy and that his brother Tom had very little interest in the business and contributed nothing to it. So E. L. renamed the business Woodley *and Parten* to reflect more accurately the true nature of the partnership.[11]

Parten spent his first seven years in the oil business out in the field working as a "tool pusher," which was the term used in the oil fields for the person responsible for obtaining all the necessary supplies for the operation and seeing that the drilling site was prepared properly. He also supervised the work crew on a daily basis. Woodley and Parten usually signed turn-key contracts for a flat fee that required drilling to a specified depth, typically three thousand feet. After the contract was signed, Parten travelled to a site and hired a building crew of six or seven men to construct a wooden drilling derrick. Once the derrick was completed, Parten brought in his own drilling crew and a rig with a rotary bit. He used two crews of five men each, consisting of a driller, a derrick man, and three helpers called "roughnecks" who worked in twelve-hour shifts, drilling around the clock seven days a week. Typically, the crew members were white men from rural areas who were attracted by wages much higher than anything they could earn as farm laborers. As one veteran driller from the Caddo fields later recalled, they were "pretty well all nesters . . . like myself . . . from up there in the country and looking for a job. And they were anxious to . . . get out of that pea patch." Parten frequently stayed overnight on the work site, usually sleeping on the ground with his men and putting in eighteen-hour days. Parten followed this work routine until he took over the company's office management in the late 1920s.[12]

El Dorado

Most of Parten's jobs as a drilling contractor in these early years were routine, with modest results. One job, however, led to a significant discovery that opened up a large new oil field in Arkansas and pushed Woodley and Parten into the production side of the oil business. In December 1919, J. J. Victor, a geologist with Constantin Refining Company of Oklahoma, told Parten that his company had been hired to drill a test well on a block of leases west of El Dorado, in Union County, Arkansas. They had a rig on the site, but no driller. The lease owner, Bruce Hunt, was desperate because his lease would expire on December 31 unless he had started a well. Victor wanted to borrow one of Parten's men to drill the well to about three thousand feet. It was well known that Woodley and Parten had the services of some of the best drillers in North Louisiana, but they were already committed to other jobs. "Drillers were just as scarce as hen's teeth," Parten said. "I just thought there was nothing I could do for him." Then Parten remembered that he had a young driller named Lee Sharp working at Bull Bayou. Parten told Victor that Sharp had a "sweet little wife" living in a tent with him down by the bayou in knee-deep mud. "I thought it would be a nice thing to let Sharp and his wife go up to those hills of Arkansas and drill a wildcat well in the spring," Parten said.[13]

Sharp went to El Dorado and began to drill the well, which was called Hill number 1, on December 30, 1919. It turned out to be a difficult job, taking longer to drill than he had anticipated. Finally, late in the evening of April 22, 1920, when Sharp's drill reached 2,243 feet, it hit an enormous pocket of gas that exploded a stream of saltwater over the derrick. The roar could be heard in the town of El Dorado, nearly three miles away. The gas spewed from the wellhead at a rate equivalent to forty million cubic feet a day. Sharp ran to a telephone near the drilling site and called Parten at his home in Shreveport. Over the telephone, Parten could hear the roar of the gas as it spewed from Hill number 1. Parten rushed to the site the next morning. J. J. Victor had one of the few land-ownership maps in Union County, Arkansas. As a favor for having loaned him a driller, Victor let Parten use the map to identify the open acreage in the block. Parten bought leases on six tracts of land before midnight, three turned out to be good oil producers.[14]

It was soon obvious that the land around Hill number 1 had a large pool of oil and gas near the surface. Within a short time after Lee Sharp's drill hit the gas pocket, hundreds of small craters pockmarked a ten-acre area surrounding the well. Water wells and creeks within four miles boiled and gurgled as gas seeped to the surface. Leases quickly rose in value after the news spread about Hunt's gas well. J. R. and E. L. had not yet made the move into drilling their own wells, but they had purchased some promising leases at Pine Island and Bull Bayou with that in mind. Now they had leases in Arkansas with the potential to make them rich. As Parten later recalled, the leases near El Dorado promised to be "real barn-burners." He and E. L. decided it was time to do more than drill other people's wells. As soon as they completed their contracted drilling jobs, they moved their rigs to El Dorado. Parten spent the next four years in Arkansas.[15]

By the summer of 1921, the El Dorado field was undergoing rapid development. More than one hundred wells had been drilled and another 340 wooden derricks were under construction. The field eventually proved to be ten miles long and two miles wide, covering nearly eight thousand acres. Among the new wells dotting the Union County landscape were five belonging to Woodley and Parten, all located in the southern part of the field. These wells proved to be excellent producers of "sweet oil," meaning the crude was relatively free of sulphur. The sulphur content of oil must be reduced by refining before the oil can be sold as a lubricant or before gasoline or kerosene can be made. The lower the sulphur content, the cheaper it is to refine, giving sweet oil a high market value. The fact that El Dorado oil was located close to the surface meant that it was also cheaply produced. With five highly profitable wells in El Dorado located on the leases he had acquired soon after the discovery well, J. R. Parten, only twenty-five years old, had now joined the ranks of the affluent.[16]

Also hoping to join those ranks were thousands of fortune hunters who streamed into Union County, attracted by the lure of easy money. As these restless men streamed from the trains arriving almost by the hour, one of the first things they saw was the message of a large billboard on the street in front of the station: "As Brigham Young Said of Utah Valley—'This Is the Place.'" Most new arrivals headed straight to El Dorado's main hostelry, the four-story Garrett Hotel. Another oil man later remembered that "a person literally had to shoulder his way through the [Garrett] lobby from early in the morning until late at night. It was a seething mass of humanity. More wells were drilled in its lobby than in the field." Unable to accommodate the huge number of men pouring through its front door, the Garrett filled its halls with cots and rented the chairs in the lobby to sleepers. An enterprising barber rented his chairs for two dollars a night. Parten, however, was among the lucky who were able to get a room. He set up an office in his room at the hotel, and for several years it was the headquarters for his and E. L.'s Arkansas oil leases.[17]

Future Texas oil-billionaire H. L. Hunt was among those expectant entrepreneurs who arrived in El Dorado eager to cash in on the bounty. Not yet an oil man, Hunt's income came from another source. He opened a gambling house across the street from Hamburger Row, a hastily assembled row of shacks built by the city to serve new businesses ranging from shoe stores to fortune tellers. "I met Hunt in El Dorado," Parten recalled, "but as a gambler, not as an oil man." El Dorado was also notorious for Pistol Hill, the location of the town's bawdy houses and saloons called "barrel houses" which sported names such as Dago Red's, Blue Moon, and

Smackover Sal's. "Barrel house" referred to the imaginative method used by the management of these establishments to remove drunken customers. They stuffed the customers who were too drunk to walk into barrels and rolled them out the front door of the saloon. Parten went through Pistol Hill often because it was in the middle of the oil field. "But I didn't stop," Parten claimed. "I was too busy drilling wells." Although still a young man, Parten was already showing his life-long, single-minded focus on the business at hand. He had little time for distractions while there was work to be done.[18]

Paying close attention to his business was an especially good idea in an oil boomtown. Not only were gamblers, hookers, and bartenders eager to take the money men made in the oil patch, there were plenty of "businessmen" just as anxious to take it all. El Dorado was full of con artists and hustlers engaged in frauds of all types. Especially popular was the selling of fraudulent oil leases. Parten's legal education proved to be a valuable asset in this regard, giving him the knowledge and skills to navigate through a treacherous landscape filled with swindlers who took advantage of many of the uneducated and overeager. Although a certain amount of good luck had played a role in Parten's getting into El Dorado early, when leases were still available at cheap prices, his background in the law and his growing knowledge of the oil business made it possible for him to move quickly to take advantage of the ever changing situation and to avoid traps.

The situation in El Dorado changed rapidly. In the month of August 1921, 1.7 million barrels of crude flowed from the El Dorado pool. Oil came out of the ground so fast that most of it had to be channeled to open-air earthen pits, which allowed the oil to leak into the subsoil, where it spread into the fields of surrounding farms and ruined crops. Occasionally, a storage pit's earthen walls collapsed, spilling huge amounts of crude oil directly into streams and creeks. The producers at El Dorado, hastily taking the "black gold" out of the ground without much regard for safety or conservation, soon lowered the field's gas pressure, resulting in a rapid decline in production after 1922. Nevertheless, Parten and Woodley were now active oil producers, joining the ranks of Shreveport's up-and-coming businessmen.[19]

The Frenchman and the Kingfish

One reason Parten could take advantage of the situation in El Dorado so quickly was that he had a ready source of capital with which to acquire leases. This was the result of a strong personal relationship he had forged with Andrew Querbes, the president of the First National Bank of Shreveport. Like most of the independents in the oil business, Parten needed a readily available source of financing. Without it, he could not buy leases or pay drilling expenses when unexpected opportunities such as the discovery at El Dorado arose. Andrew Querbes, the man who financed Parten's first drilling rig, provided this critical support. Parten's business relationship with Querbes played a crucial role in his success during the first decade of his career as an oil man. Parten relied heavily on the banker's counsel, spending much time in his office discussing business strategy and getting his advice on a wide variety of political, as well as financial matters. As a former mayor of Shreveport, Querbes also served as an important political connection for Parten. "[Querbes] was very influential in politics and he was very influential in other matters affecting Shreveport," recalled one Louisiana political leader.[20]

Another person who played an important role in Parten's early business development was a rough-edged young lawyer and politician from rural northern Louisiana by the name of Huey Long. After his election in November 1918 to the Louisiana Public Service Commission, the state agency empowered to regulate railroads, Long moved from his hometown of Winnfield to Shreveport. One of his first clients in Shreveport was E. L. Woodley, who hired Long to recover a five-hundred-dollar check given as earnest money on a house. Woodley and Huey Long became friends. After Woodley and Parten formed their drilling company, they hired Long whenever they needed legal services. By hiring Long, Woodley and Parten went against the grain in Shreveport's conservative community. Long was extremely unpopular with the town establishment, who disliked his brash manner, his championship of workers' rights, and his attacks on corporate greed. Long became an early and loud critic of "Big Oil," especially Standard of Louisiana. Long also specialized in workers' compensation cases, which did nothing to endear him to the business leaders of Shreveport. "He took a great delight in being a plaintiff's advocate," Parten recalled, "the smaller the plaintiff and the bigger the claim was, he liked it the better." Parten claimed that "there were just two kinds of folks in Shreveport—those for Long and those against Long. Rich people didn't have much to do with Huey because he was a little more than an ordinary tantalizer of the wealthy class." According to one Shreveport attorney who also knew Woodley and Parten, Long's reputation when he was doing work for the drilling company in the early 1920s was that he was "an unethical lawyer, a very crude individual. . . ."[21]

None of this bothered Parten. Indeed, many of the things that alienated Long from the Shreveport power elite were the very things that Parten liked about him, especially his denunciations of the big oil companies and his championing of small independents. Although they never became close friends, Parten and Long met frequently in each other's offices and Long occasionally visited the Parten home. J. R. liked Huey's breezy style and seemingly inexhaustible capacity for work. "He had the energy of a mad man," recalled Cecil Morgan, one of Long's political opponents, "he never entered a room, he stormed in, waving his arms and talking loud. . . ." Ignoring Long's many critics in Shreveport, Woodley and Parten hired him to handle a number of cases, most of them minor lease disputes, but all of them potentially troublesome for a small company struggling to succeed. Obviously, Long's services were not as expensive as the more established lawyers in Shreveport, which was another reason Woodley and Parten forged a business relationship with him. "I didn't mind giving Long some business," Parten recalled, "because he was a hungry lawyer and he had a hard time making a living."[22]

Another struggling young lawyer to whom Woodley and Parten gave work whenever Long was unavailable was Cecil Morgan, who eventually became one of Long's bitterest enemies. After Long became governor in the late 1920s, Morgan,

by then a state representative, led the unsuccessful fight in the Louisiana legislature to remove Long from office. Morgan later recalled that Parten "wasn't giving
me the best of his business [that went to Long] but he was giving me what he
could to help me out a little bit in this area." Although the opposite of Huey Long
in world view and personal and political style, Morgan also became a good business and political contact for Parten. After serving in the Louisiana legislature
from 1928 until the mid-1930s, Morgan became chief counsel for the Standard Oil
Company of Louisiana. Thus Parten's friendship with Long and Morgan in the
early days of their careers, gave him access to the two dominant opposing factions
in Louisiana politics.[23]

Woodley Petroleum Company

By the end of 1921, Woodley's and Parten's personal oil production at El
Dorado and at Pine Island and Bull Bayou was earning them significantly more
money than their drilling business. As their business dealings became more complex legally, they decided to incorporate as a new company. They agreed to
exchange their personal oil leases and other holdings for stock in the new company, which they named the Woodley Petroleum Company. When Parten asked
Huey Long if he knew how to incorporate a company, Long assured him that he
knew a great deal about the procedure and that he was an "old hand at creating
corporations." Long got the job. He promptly ordered a kit through the mail
which explained in simple language how to carry out what Long claimed he was
"an old hand" at doing. Following the instructions carefully, Long accomplished
the incorporation entirely through the mail. On March 27, 1922, the Woodley
Petroleum Company was officially incorporated. E. L. Woodley took the title of
president and Parten assumed the official position of secretary-treasurer, although
he also served unofficially as the general manager.[24]

With a solid base of assets worth a little more than a million dollars and a
total debt of less than a hundred thousand dollars, Parten decided in June 1922 to
raise additional funds for Woodley to explore its undeveloped properties and to
acquire new leases.[25] With E. L.'s agreement, J. R. asked Huey Long to find a
national company to handle Woodley's new stock offer. Long sent letters to several firms around the country, declaring "the management of this Company is as
good as can be found in southern Arkansas and northern Louisiana. They wish to
store their oil when it is bringing the low price and to sell it when it is bringing the
most." Having suffered from the loss in value of his own oil investments a few
years before, Long could add with confidence that "nothing is surer in the oil business than a fluctuation of prices up and down." Woodley eventually issued one
hundred thousand new shares of stock through C. T. Morgan of New York City.[26]

Smackover

As a company strategy, Parten and Woodley concentrated on buying small
acreage adjacent to wildcat oil wells to gain access to potential fields at a low price,
before any oil was found and letting the wildcatters take most of the risk. This

Left: Woodley's Richardson number 1 site, Smackover, Arkansas, 1922. *CN 09593. Courtesy Parten Photograph Collection, CAH.*

Below: Woodley's work crew at Smackover, Arkansas, 1922. Parten is third from left at the rear. *CN 09592. Courtesy Parten Photograph Collection, CAH.*

WooDLEY No.
Boiler House and Pump Station
Richardson Farm.

Woodley was among those oil companies at Smackover that stored their crude in open earthen pits, 1922. *CN 09595. Courtesy Parten Photograph Collection, CAH.*

strategy paid off handsomely in Arkansas. In July 1922, Parten bought a spread of acreage near Smackover, a tiny village of sixty people, fourteen miles northwest of El Dorado. Although oil had never been discovered in that area, Parten purchased the lease when he learned that Shreveport's V. K. F. oil company planned to drill a wildcat well there. V. K. F. was owned by members of the Friedman family, who also operated a jewelry business in Shreveport and were among the Woodley Company's new investors. Parten leased the land surrounding V. K. F.'s "Richardson number 1" site, just in case the Friedmans got lucky. Lucky they were. Oil gushed out of V. K. F.'s well on July 1, 1922. Parten, who happened to be in nearby El Dorado, rushed to the site as soon as the news reached him. "We went into production right there," he later recalled, "offsetting that discovery."[27]

The new Smackover field eventually became a greater find than El Dorado, resulting in a boom that expanded the little town's population to over twenty thousand in a period of only six months. Drilling in the area was exceedingly difficult, however, so the oil field was developed at a slightly slower pace than El Dorado. Woodley's lease was located in the clay hills along Smackover Creek just north of the Union County line with Ouachita County. "Drilling was really rough," Parten said. "That Smackover creek bottom was wide and muddy, and it had a lot of quicksand in it. It was awful." Because there were no roads, Parten and his crew were forced to move around the field on horseback. The mud and slime made the drilling sites almost inaccessible. "I had to quit my horses as many as three or four times a day because they would just bog down in the mud," Parten recalled. In order to move heavy drilling equipment to the oil field, J. R. had to clear pathways through the surrounding forests. His crews would split the felled trees into log rails and lay them over the muddy path. The result was what oil men usually called a corduroy road, but in Smackover it was known as an "Arkansas gravel" road. Even these labor intensive tactics sometimes failed. Oxen and mules, which were used to move heavy equipment often bogged down and suffocated in the deep mudholes before they could be pulled out.[28]

Parten soon struck oil in four small wells on his Smackover leases. Although none of his new wells were major producers, Parten quickly accumulated more oil than he could sell, a problem that plagued the entire Smackover field. A number of factors hindered the marketing of Smackover crude. One was the price of oil, which had plunged to a new low. Another was the field's location. There were no pipelines nearby and the area was suffering from a lengthy railroad strike, which created a serious transportation problem. In addition, the oil from the portion of the field in which Parten was operating was so-called heavy oil (eighteen to twenty-three degrees in gravity) with a high sulphur content, making it expensive to refine.[29]

Parten built a small pipeline to the nearest rail terminal at the tiny village of Louann, seven or eight miles away from his lease, but he was unable to find a buyer for the oil. Faced with the problem of too much oil and no place to put it, Parten ceased his drilling operations. A few days later, the Humble Oil Company drilled a well two hundred feet from the boundary line of one of his leases that produced about seventy-five barrels a day. Sid Umbstead, the landowner of Parten's lease, demanded that Woodley immediately drill a well to offset the new Humble well. Producing wells are usually offset by wells on adjoining tracts to prevent the migratory loss of oil from tract to tract. The last thing Parten wanted to do was drill another well, but the lease contract required it. "I resisted as long as I could," Parten recalled, "not only did I have more oil than I could do anything with, I had to drill the offset well in the middle of a damn pond."[30]

Bound by his lease contract, Parten reluctantly built an earthen mound and drilled a well down to the oil sand. "It was such an awful place that I decided to erect a five hundred barrel tank on the platform right beside the derrick and flow this well into that tank," Parten said. "We planned to transfer the oil from that tank to an open-air pit." After his crew began drilling, Parten went down the creek to inspect another lease. When he returned an hour later, he was shocked to learn that oil was already flowing from the well. His five-hundred-barrel tank was full and oil was gushing out the flume at its top. Parten had the well shut in immediately. Working all night, his crew built a four-inch pipeline across the swamp to take the oil to storage. Woodley's Umbstead "A" Lease turned out to be a very rich strike, producing twenty-five to thirty thousand barrels a day for over a month, offsetting Humble's little seventy-five-barrel pumper. "I got on the map with the

Humble Oil Company with that discovery," Parten noted. "Humble's geologists came to the tract and they just shook their heads."[31]

With the addition of the Umbstead well, Woodley Petroleum was producing two thousand barrels of oil a day at Smackover by the middle of 1923, with an additional four hundred thousand barrels in storage. Parten and his fellow producers were swimming in oil, but drilling and pumping nevertheless continued at a frenzied pace. The prevailing attitude was to get the oil out of the ground as quickly as possible, before your neighbor drained your lease. "Smackover was a giant field and it was cut all to pieces in development because there was no market for the oil," Parten noted, "and people were just drilling wells here and there and yonder, and storing the oil in earthen pits." Smackover operators resorted to open-pit storage so frequently that, during the first twelve years, much of the field's total crude-oil production was lost through leakage and evaporation. Parten stored most of his oil in steel tanks, but continuing market problems forced him to put large amounts of oil in the open air on the ground. "I learned then and there never to store crude oil on the ground," Parten admitted. "The rain water would stratify in it and it was very expensive to treat that water out. Open storage was also dangerous in the respect that a levee might break, and a lot of oil would go down a creek or a valley."[32]

At Smackover, such accidents happened with disturbing frequency, turning the area into an environmental nightmare. One of the worst incidents occurred in November 1922, when a large wooden storage tank and several earthen storage ponds broke, pouring more than a hundred thousand barrels of crude oil into Smackover Creek. The oil caught fire, turning the little stream into a roaring inferno. On other occasions terrible fires erupted in the Smackover field when lightning struck the open pits. Because of the enormous gas pressure in the Smackover field and the careless haste with which many of the drillers operated, wells often blew out of control when the drill struck the oil pool. When this occurred, the oil and gas surged out of the well, creating conditions ripe for explosions and fires. Once these wells went wild, they were difficult to cap. Although well blowouts were common at Smackover, Parten's careful management and his close supervision of his wells helped his company to avoid such costly accidents. Indeed, Woodley earned a reputation at Smackover as one of the safest independent companies in the field, a reputation the company retained throughout its history.[33]

By the end of its first year, the Woodley Company had produced nearly seven hundred thousand barrels of oil from five different fields in Louisiana and Arkansas, with the vast majority coming from Smackover and El Dorado. The total amount of oil produced from these new fields glutted the market, however, causing prices to plunge and increasing the rivalry between various segments of the industry. As the price situation worsened in July 1923, Woodley found itself without a market for its oil and no place to store it. Running out of cash to pay for new drilling expenses, Parten suspended Woodley's drilling operations not only in Smackover but everywhere else. Woodley had assets four times its liabilities, but most of those assets were sitting in storage with no buyer in sight. For most of the fall of 1923, Andrew Querbes made loans to Woodley to alleviate the cash problem, but continued borrowing was obviously a short-term solution. The company issued more stock, but it sold slowly. After several months of stagnation Woodley Oil was facing the real possibility of going under, when a saviour suddenly appeared in the form of the Louisiana Oil Refining Company, which needed oil for its refinery. "I was just happy to accommodate them," Parten said. "We sold that stored oil at Smackover plus some new production for about a 1.5 million dollars and that saved us." With the infusion of cash it received from the sale to Louisiana Standard in 1924, Woodley continued to develop its properties at Smackover, expanding into a portion of the field near Louann, where a higher quality crude had been found.[34]

Woodley prospered throughout much of 1925. As the company grew, E. L. deferred more and more to his energetic son-in-law who now managed most of the growing company's operations, not only in the field but in the Shreveport office. With money in the bank and oil flowing from Woodley's wells in Arkansas and North Louisiana, J. R. and Opal were living the good life. These were the best years of their marriage. J. R. was spending more time in his Shreveport office than he was in the field, making it possible for the Partens to enjoy the first extended period of togetherness they had ever had. They purchased a new house on Jordan Street in the city's fashionable Highland area, the first house they could call their own. J. R. and Opal joined the Shreveport Country Club and spent much of their leisure time there, golfing, swimming, and horseback riding. Andrew Querbes pulled J. R. into charitable activities of the city's businessmen's organizations, while Opal, who had been in the drama club at the University of Texas, became involved in Shreveport's new amateur theater. J. R. also took an interest in the athletic program at Shreveport's Centenary College, a small liberal arts school affiliated with the Methodist Church. Parten helped Centenary's coach, Homer Norton, scout and recruit promising high school athletes and gave some of the recruits summer employment at Woodley.[35]

By the end of 1925, E. L. decided that Woodley was doing so well and the company's stock value was so high that it would be a good time for him to sell out. E. L. wanted to buy a long-dreamed-of West Texas cotton farm, and though Parten had often heard his father-in-law talk about this, he was shocked when E. L. finally announced he was going to do it. To give J. R. an opportunity to retain control of the company, E. L. gave him the first option on his seventy-six thousand shares of stock, which had a value of $380,000. J. R., however, could not afford to buy E. L.'s entire share. He appealed to Opal to talk her father out of selling his stock. "There's nothing you can do with Daddy," she told him, "if he's made up his mind he wants to go back to farming, he's going to go back to farming." Parten turned to Andrew Querbes, who counseled him to let E. L. go. Querbes advised Parten to form a syndicate of investors to buy the stock and to draw up an agreement that gave him first right of purchase whenever any of them decided to sell.[36]

Parten persuaded his friend Gene Palmer, the fifty-five-year-old former president of Standard Oil of Louisiana, now a successful independent, to help him form a group to acquire E. L.'s stock. They attracted four other investors who agreed to share the expense equally. In February 1926 Parten, who was now Woodley's largest stockholder, assumed his father-in-law's former title of general manager. This latter change was largely symbolic; Parten had performed the duties of general manager in fact if not in title for years. Gene Palmer became Woodley Petroleum's new chairman of the board. Parten was delighted that a person of Palmer's financial strength and reputation had joined the company. "Palmer was an active chairman," Parten noted, "he paid close attention to the business, and he was a big help to me through his counsel and advice." Palmer remained chairman until his death in the early 1930s.[37]

Expansion into Texas

Woodley continued its steady, if unspectacular, growth in 1926, but the company was depleting its oil reserves more rapidly than it was discovering new sources. "We weren't finding oil too freely in north Louisiana," Parten later recalled, "and south Louisiana hadn't shown great prospects at that time." As a result, Parten went to Houston in the summer of 1926 to see if Eugene Holman, a friend who was a geologist with Humble Oil, could give him some leads on promising locations in Texas for oil exploration.

Holman had become one of Parten's closest friends when Holman lived in Shreveport in 1923 and 1924 as the supervisor of Humble's operations in North Louisiana and Arkansas. Gene's wife Edith had worked with Opal Parten in plays at the Shreveport Little Theater, while J. R. and Gene occasionally traveled together to Austin, Dallas, and College Station to attend University of Texas football games. His friendship with Holman became an important busi-

Opal Woodley Parten, Shreveport, Louisiana, sometime in the early 1930s. *CN 09615. Courtesy Dayson Photograph Collection, CAH.*

ness connection for Parten. By the mid-1920s, Humble, which had been organized in the first decade of the century by a small group of Texas investors, was one of the largest subsidiaries of Standard Oil of New Jersey. One of Parten's best friends in law school, Hines Baker, was now one of Humble's fast-rising corporate lawyers. Through Gene Holman, Parten met other key members of the company's management. Parten consulted often with Holman about developments in the oil patch, sometimes swapping information with him about oil leases and other business matters while they played golf at the country club. Holman became a small stockholder in Woodley and he joined with Parten in a real estate venture near Abilene, Texas. Humble promoted Holman to chief geologist in 1925 and transferred him to Houston, but he and Parten remained in contact.[38]

Holman urged Parten to move Woodley into Texas. He felt that the west central area of Texas to the east of Abilene was a promising area, especially Brown and Callahan Counties. Holman recommended that Parten also take a look at far West Texas, specifically the region of the Permian Basin between Fort Stockton and Midland. A major discovery had been made in March 1926 in Crane County, just to the north of Fort Stockton, and wildcatters were drilling wells throughout the region. He advised Parten to acquire some offsetting leases. In November 1926, Parten toured the areas in Texas Holman had recommended. He returned to Shreveport enthusiastic about the oil potential of the region and determined to get Woodley involved. The company soon opened field offices in Ft. Stockton and Brownwood and purchased a spread of leases in several counties in the Permian Basin and in the area between Abilene and Brownwood. Full of optimism, Parten told a friend in Beaumont that the "oil prospects of West Texas look mighty good to me. Needless to say that it is always a fine feeling to get back to Texas."[39]

Moutray Oil

In the early fall of 1928, Gene Holman told Parten that 51 percent of the stock of the Moutray Oil Company, a small firm in west central Texas, was available for purchase at a very fair price. Parten knew that Moutray owned a large block of potentially valuable acreage near Baird, in Callahan County, just west of Cisco. The company was already producing oil from shallow wells only a few hundred feet deep, but it was having serious financial difficulties. Moutray Oil had no access to pipeline transportation for its crude, so it was forced to ship its oil to a refinery in Fort Worth by railroad, greatly increasing costs. Holman revealed that Humble was going to build a pipeline through the area and that it would be available to carry Moutray's crude to the refinery. Moutray's value was certain to increase significantly once Humble's plans became public, so Parten had to move quickly. He returned to Texas and contacted Beauford Jester, a young lawyer in Corsicana who was one of Moutray's major stockholders. Parten had known Jester when they were both students at the University of Texas. Jester told his former schoolmate that he could acquire a majority of Moutray's stock for four hundred thousand dollars. Because of Holman's tip, Parten believed the price was too good to pass up, despite current oil prices.[40]

In fact, low oil prices created a significant problem for Parten. The discovery of huge oil fields such as Yates in West Texas and the Greater Seminole in Oklahoma had hurled the oil-price roller coaster into one of its downward plunges, forcing Woodley to suspend all drilling operations in Arkansas and Louisiana during the entire year of 1928 in an attempt to contain expenses. Woodley had recently become involved in a new oil field in Cotton Valley, approximately forty miles northeast of Shreveport. Although Cotton Valley eventually produced a large amount of oil, the initial production was natural gas, which proved to be a fortunate development for Woodley. The price of crude oil was so low that the sale of gas from Cotton Valley helped to offset some of the loss in Woodley's oil income, but the company's earnings were much reduced nevertheless. Woodley was fortunate to have one hundred thousand dollars in cash from its Arkansas profits in the bank, but still needed an additional three hundred thousand to acquire Moutray. Since entering the oil business nine years earlier, Parten had been very conservative about borrowing money, but he believed the Moutray property was far more valuable than the purchase price. Unfortunately, money was tight, interest rates were high, and very few banks were making large loans for oil production.

For help, Parten went to his old banker friend, Andrew Querbes, who quickly put together a loan package that gave Parten his three hundred thousand dollars. He made one loan in the amount of $115,000 directly to Woodley Petroleum, secured by a mortgage on Woodley's crude oil in storage. Another loan for the remaining $185,000 was made to a special consortium composed of Parten, Gene Palmer, and, as trustees, two other Woodley stockholders, R. J. O'Brien and Rutledge Deas. The Moutray stock served as collateral for that loan. When Parten asked Querbes how much the loan was going to cost, he replied, "Well, that's a surprise. It's going to cost you six per cent, because whether you know it or not, that is all you are able to pay." Parten had expected to pay a minimum of 9 percent—some banks in New York were charging even more for similar loans. Woodley purchased controlling interest in Moutray Oil, and Humble subsequently made its pipeline available to carry crude from Moutray's field. Texas soon dominated Parten's and Woodley's interests.[41]

Educating Huey

Not long before Parten was arranging the Moutray loan with Querbes, his sometime attorney Huey Long ran for governor in a heated and controversial election campaign. The campaign put Parten in an uncomfortable position because Andrew Querbes was a vocal supporter of one of Long's opponents, Riley Joe Wilson. As a result, Querbes frequently found himself on the receiving end of some of Long's devastating demagoguery. "Andrew Querbes was one of a group of men here in Shreveport," remembered one close observer of the campaign, "who were 100 per cent against Huey and putting up money to fight him and all that. [Long] called Andrew every kind of SOB in the world. . . ." With Huey Long on one side and Cecil Morgan and Andrew Querbes on the other, Parten was caught between the two strongest competing political factions in the state. Despite Querbes's urging, Parten chose not to get involved in the governor's race in 1928. He begged off from both camps with two excuses: his heavy workload and the fact that he still considered himself to be a Texan and, thus, an outsider to Louisiana's politics.[42]

After Long's election in January 1928, however, Parten found that his friendship with the new governor, plus his own self-interest, forced him to become involved in his adopted state's political affairs. A few months after his inauguration, Huey Long succeeded in passing a severance tax on natural resources that based levies on the quantity produced rather than on the monetary value of the product. In other words, tax was charged per barrel of oil, per ton of sulphur, and per foot of lumber. This "quantity" tax fell most heavily on the oil and gas industries, especially those in North Louisiana. Long's critics assumed that he had aimed the tax at his old political enemy, the Standard Oil Company of Louisiana, but Long never publicly admitted it. Actually, the tax increase was modest and Long needed the revenue to pay for his bridge, road, and free-school-textbooks programs. The law provided for a sliding scale based on the gravity of the oil, from four cents a barrel on oil of low gravity to eleven cents on oil of high gravity. Because North Louisiana oil was usually much higher in gravity than that in South Louisiana, operators in the north, especially the independents, charged that the tax was discriminatory.[43]

J. R. Parten was among those independents outraged by the tax. Most of his production was high gravity so he was forced to pay the top rate of eleven cents a barrel. The tax made no sense to Parten from the standpoint of potential revenue. High-gravity oil was selling at a much lower price than the low-gravity crude, yet the highest tax rate was applied to the commodity with the lowest value. To help in the effort to repeal the tax, Parten became active in the Louisiana chapter of the Mid-Continent Oil and Gas Association. He attended the association's annual meeting in Shreveport and at one point took the floor and denounced the severance tax. The association formed a six-man committee to lobby the legislature to repeal the tax. Impressed by his speech and the fact that he knew Long, they elected Parten chairman of the protest committee. Parten told his committee colleagues, most of whom were attorneys for oil companies, that the first thing he was going to do when they got to Baton Rouge was to go see the governor. He was optimistic. "I thought I could explain to Huey that this tax was impossible, unfair, and discriminatory."[44]

When they arrived in Baton Rouge, Parten told his colleagues that he preferred to see Long alone. Parten walked over to the governor's apartment in the Heidelberg Hotel, where he spent most of his nights in a suite on the seventh floor. Armed guards escorted Parten to a small sitting room where the governor was reading a morning newspaper, still dressed in his pajamas; dirty dishes and the remains of breakfast scattered around the table. Parten explained his mission and complained that the tax was discriminatory. With a big smile on his face, Long declared, "Well, that's about right. That's fair. Why? Because those Cajuns in the south supported me, but you highlanders didn't." Parten replied that he realized that Long's real target was Standard of Louisiana. "You err when you think you're hurting them with this bill," Parten explained, "because the Standard Oil Company has only one hundred and fifty barrels of oil production daily in Louisiana. The independents have most of the oil production, and they're the ones you're hurting." Standard of Lousiana purchased rather than produced most of the oil it refined and marketed. With an expression of surprise on his face, Long wheeled around in his chair. Gazing out on the Mississippi River, he suddenly saw a barge carrying oil. He looked back at Parten and said: "I know what I can do to the Standard Oil Company. I can put a five-cent-a-barrel tax on that foreign oil they're refining in Baton Rouge." Parten admitted that he had no objection to that; he shared the general view held by many independents that foreign-oil imports were resulting in low crude-oil prices. Long promised Parten that he would propose a compromise that would include a refinery tax on foreign oil and a more equitable system for determining severance tax rates.[45]

Parten felt Long's offer was an acceptable option, but his committee of oil company lawyers rejected it. They preferred to challenge the tax in court. Parten returned to Shreveport and the legislature subsequently passed the original version of Long's bill. The Ohio Oil Company challenged the tax in court, demanding protection under the Fourteenth Amendment, but lost the suit in the lower federal courts. In 1929, Ohio Oil won a stay from the U.S. Supreme Court on collecting the tax. Long immediately called a special legislative session to consider the same five-cents-a-barrel tax on refined oil that he had proposed to Parten. This was obviously an attack on Standard Oil of Louisiana, the most powerful corporation in the state. The negative reaction was fierce, setting off a chain of events that led to Governor Long's impeachment in April 1929.[46]

Parten opposed Long's impeachment, but he played no role in the affair. The issues were complex and deeply rooted in a tangle of political rivalries, and he had good friends on both sides. His banker, Andrew Querbes, advocated Long's ouster and Cecil Morgan, now a legislator, was a leader of the impeachment forces. But Parten liked Huey Long and admired the populist streak in his politics. "Long built more bridges and more hospitals and schools and roads than any other Governor in the state of Louisiana," Parten later explained. He also admired the role Long played in transforming Louisiana State University into a modern institution of higher learning. The effort to remove Long from office eventually failed. The U.S. Supreme Court finally upheld the severance tax in April 1930 and it remained in force for several years. As for Parten, his experience in the severance tax matter served as his initial foray into the world of oil politics. Many more were to come.[47]

Learning to Fly

By the summer of 1929, Parten had completed the Moutray Oil Company purchase and Woodley was deeply involved in West Texas. With Woodley's operations scattered over a three-state area, Parten decided to take flying lessons. The primitive condition of the road system made car travel between Shreveport and

Parten (with aviator goggles) poses with his buddies in front of his Stearman airplane. His flying instructor, Currie Sanders, is on the extreme right, 1929. *CN 09599. Courtesy Parten Photograph Collection, CAH.*

Woodley's drilling sites in Arkansas and West Texas difficult and time consuming. With an airplane, Parten could supervise Woodley's scattered operations with relative ease and efficiency. Shreveport in the 1920s was a good place to be interested in aviation. The city had more than its share of flight pioneers engaged in barnstorming and experimental aviation; among them was W. Currie Sanders, whom Parten hired as his flight instructor. Sanders taught Parten how to fly in a Stearman, a sturdy open-cockpit biplane used to train army pilots. By late September, Parten had his license. A month later he purchased a Stearman C-3-B with a 225-horsepower Wright engine. From the fall of 1929 until the late 1930s, Parten flew his Stearman all over Texas, Louisiana, and New Mexico looking after his oil operations and tending to a host of other activities.[48]

J. R. Parten had worked hard during the 1920s to build a business and to achieve financial security. Except for his attempted intervention with Huey Long in the severance tax episode, he had avoided politics. The future, however, would be much different.

CHAPTER 3

East Texas and the Oil Crisis

1930–1931

Parten was enjoying a rare Sunday morning at home in Shreveport on December 28, 1930, when he received a telephone call from P. J. Slimer, Woodley's oil scout who was monitoring the progress of a competitor's wildcat well near the small East Texas town of Kilgore. A few days earlier the driller, Ed Bateman, had produced a core sample stained with oil. When this development was reported, Parten asked Slimer to stay close to the well to monitor its progress. Slimer was now reporting on the telephone that Bateman had "struck a gusher." He had seen Malcolm Crim, the owner of the land, run from the well site, his clothes dripping with crude oil. Upon hearing this news, Parten went immediately to the airport and flew his Stearman to Longview, a few miles to the northeast of Kilgore. Eager to get ahead of his competition, he hurried out to buy whatever leases he could find in the region between Longview and Kilgore.[1]

Parten had been among those oil men who had accepted the conventional wisdom that there was almost no prospect of finding oil in East Texas. However, when Gene Holman told Parten that Humble planned to drill test wells in Rusk County, Parten acquired a few leases adjoining Humble's drilling sites. On October 3, Parten learned that a small-time promoter by the name of Columbus Marion "Dad" Joiner had struck oil just to the west of his new leases. Many in the industry, including Parten, believed that Joiner had discovered a marginal well. "I had one eye on the Joiner well," Parten later recalled, "but after it came in, I felt that it was probably just a residual oil deposit." Just in case, he also leased some acreage close to Joiner's well.

The Bateman discovery indicated that Joiner's well was anything but marginal. Flowing high-quality oil at an estimated rate of ten thousand barrels a day, the Bateman well provided compelling evidence that a big oil field lurked beneath the sandy soil of East Texas. No one really understood how big until a few months later when another gusher (Lathrop's number 1 well) was struck in Gregg County to the northwest of Longview. Other discoveries soon revealed that the new field was a vast lake of oil, forty-three miles long and three to ten miles wide. Covering most of five counties, "the Black Giant" was the largest oil field the industry had ever seen. "I flew across the East Texas field one hundred and fifty times without discovering it," Parten lamented.[2]

News of the enormity of the East Texas field soon sparked a frenzied oil rush. With most of East Texas unleased, "lease hounds" soon swarmed over every square mile of the region. Leases similar to those that Parten and other independents had purchased a few weeks earlier at ten dollars to one hundred dollars an acre were now going for several thousand dollars an acre. Parten was as eager as anyone to take a deep plunge into this vast new oil pool, but he and his company were desperately short of cash. Two weeks before the Bateman discovery, Humble sold the pipeline near the Moutray field that had carried Woodley's oil to market and the new owner had cut off Woodley's access. Because Parten was unable to reach an agreement with Sinclair, the company with the only other pipeline in the area, he had no way to get his oil to market. The result for Woodley was a loss in income of thirty-five thousand dollars per month. Parten was now in the frustrating situation of suffering a serious cash shortage despite the fact that he was producing about fifteen hundred barrels of good-quality oil a day from the fifty shallow wells in the Moutray field.[3]

To raise money quickly in order to buy more leases in East Texas, Parten sold Woodley's six drilling rigs for one hundred thousand dollars with the idea that for future wells he would contract with drilling companies. There was an unusually large amount of land available for leasing in the East Texas oil field because of the field's sheer size and the fact that the major companies had not locked everything up. Leases were eventually grabbed up by more than four thousand individuals and companies. The fact that oil was less than four thousand feet below the surface meant that just about anyone with a modest amount of credit or cash could join the boom, provided that they had been lucky enough to get a cheap lease. For that reason, East Texas was a major incubator for the independent oil man, creating vast fortunes for men such as H. L. Hunt and Clint Murchison and smaller fortunes for hundreds of others. The process of leasing in East Texas was more complicated than in most of the other areas where oil had been discovered. The land was divided into a maze of thousands of tiny farms. Because of the Depression, many of these farms had been abandoned, sold for taxes, or occupied by people who failed to register the change of ownership. When oil was found on one of these farms, the claimants were often many and the resulting litigation costly and complicated. Eager to get into the oil play, some operators bought oil and gas leases on faith and oral promises from the landowner. As Parten later recalled, the

J. R. and his siblings during a rare family reunion in Madisonville about 1930. In front, from left to right are Alice, Grace, Bessie, and Lizzie. In back are Bobby, Sam, Lucy, Agnes, Malcolm, and J. R. *CN 09608. Courtesy Parten Photograph Collection, CAH.*

thought was "get the lease now, you can always check the title later." As a result of this confusion and overeager leasing, the East Texas courts were soon clogged with land-dispute cases.[4]

Because of his legal training, Parten had handled most of Woodley's legal affairs except for the courtroom work the company gave to Huey Long and Cecil Morgan. But the legal traps in the East Texas field were so numerous and complex that Parten realized he could not manage the company and also do its legal work. For help, he turned to one of his friends from law school, Myron Blalock, who had opened a law firm in Marshall, a Texas town located between Shreveport and the East Texas field. Blalock's expertise was land law, a specialty which was particulary valuable in East Texas. In the spring of 1931, Myron Blalock and his younger brother Jack agreed to represent Woodley. The skillful Blalocks succeeded in keeping to a minimum Woodley's lease and royalty problems in East Texas. Within a year, Myron Blalock joined Woodley's board of directors and became vice president.[5]

Parten's new alliance with the two Blalock brothers initiated a close and valuable business and political relationship that endured for more than three decades. Myron had served in the Texas legislature from 1913 until 1917, when he resigned to join the army. After the war, he returned to his hometown to practice law with T. Whitfield Davidson, a former state senator and lieutenant governor and a future federal judge. Myron, who eventually became a member of the National Democratic Party Committee, was a confidant of powerful Texas congressmen John Nance Garner and Sam Rayburn. As a result, he and his brother Jack gained reputations as highly influential "political lawyers." Eventually, the Blalocks became more important to Parten as political allies than as business associates.[6]

The Flamboyant Frenchman: Sylvester Dayson

Early in 1931, Parten was facing the prospect of having to sell his Callahan County property for a huge loss unless he found a market for his Moutray oil. While Parten wrestled with this problem, a refiner by the name of Sylvester Dayson paid him a timely visit. Parten had first met the flamboyant Dayson in El Dorado in 1925. Born in France in 1892, Dayson had learned the refinery business while working in the Rumanian oil fields as a teenager before the outbreak of World War I. After the war, Dayson supervised the building of oil refineries for the Royal Dutch Shell Company in Borneo and Mexico. In 1921, he moved to the United States and constructed refineries in Massachusetts, Wyoming, and Texas

before eventually making his way to Arkansas. By the time he arrived in El Dorado in 1922 to work for the Lion Oil Company, Dayson had gained a reputation not only as a highly competent refining engineer but also as an innovator in devising new techniques to "crack" low-quality crude oil. Lion Oil had constructed a large refinery in El Dorado, but the equipment it had installed could not properly refine the Smackover crude oil because of its high sulphur content—a problem Dayson managed to solve. He married and settled down in El Dorado, eventually becoming a director and vice president of Lion Oil.[7]

Dayson suffered extensive losses in the stock market crash of 1929 and went

J. R. (left) and Sylvester Dayson stroll down a street in downtown Shreveport, early 1930s. *CN 09600. Courtesy Parten Photograph Collection, CAH.*

deeply into debt. He resigned from the Lion Oil Company in October 1930 with the hope of finding someone to back him in a new refining venture. It was his search for an investor that brought Dayson to Parten. Dayson told Parten that he had heard about his difficulties in Callahan County and he thought that he might have a solution for both their problems. He recommended that he and Parten form a business partnership to build and operate a small refinery at Baird, near Woodley's Moutray field, to produce gasoline for the local market. This refinery would free Woodley from its dependency on pipeline companies and the refinery in Fort Worth. It would also provide an outlet for Woodley's oil and boost the company's revenue. Dayson estimated that it would cost about three hundred thousand dollars to build the refinery. When Parten asked Dayson how much money he had to invest in the partnership, Dayson replied that he only had "$4000 in musty $100 bills" stored in his safe-deposit box. Parten told Dayson to hold on to his cash, because he believed he could get most of the project financed. Dayson could pay back his share interest free after they earned money from the refinery.[8]

To finance the Baird refinery, Parten turned once again to Andrew Querbes. Parten's banker had his own problems, however. The nation was now in the grips of the Depression and Querbes's bank had been hit hard by a large number of bad cotton loans. Given the desperate economic conditions, the bank's officers were extremely reluctant to commit large sums of money to such a risky business. Aided by the fact that the value of Woodley's assets was seven times larger than its liabilities, Querbes eventually persuaded his loan committee that despite the bad economic conditions, Woodley would "stand the storm" because of its oil reserves in Callahan County and elsewhere. Although prices were still falling, Querbes shared Parten's feeling that the oil Woodley had in the ground would soon be much more valuable when production stabilized and prices went back up. Accordingly, Querbes convinced his bank colleagues that the loan could be secured with a mortgage on the oil that Woodley already had in reserve. When prices rose, as Querbes reasoned that they surely must, Parten could sell his stored oil and pay off his loan with relative ease. The trick was to generate enough cash from the Callahan refinery to pay the bills and buy new leases until prices returned to a high level. Querbes had given similar advice to Parten the previous December, urging him to keep his oil in storage as long as possible to wait out the low prices. "In other words," the banker argued, "prosperity for your company is simply delayed and not destroyed."[9]

With Woodley's oil reserves serving as security, Querbes arranged a loan similar to the one Parten had received two years earlier to purchase the Moutray field. Half of the three-hundred-thousand-dollar loan went directly to Woodley Petroleum, while the other half went to Parten and Eugene Palmer. Querbes's faith in Parten proved to be well placed, but his belief that oil prices would soon rise was wrong. The price of oil continued to sink, reaching depths unimaginable to anyone in the industry at the time.[10]

In early June 1931, Woodley struck a major oil well on its two-hundred-acre

Laura Walker lease in East Texas. The well was a big enough producer to attract the immediate attention of the Magnolia Petroleum Company, a subsidiary of Standard of New York (Mobil). Magnolia's subsequent purchase of the lease greatly alleviated Woodley's cash-flow problem. It also provided Parten with enough money for him and Dayson to purchase two-thirds of their new refining company, which they called Centex Refining. After Woodley Petroleum bought the other third of Centex in the fall of 1931, Dayson moved to Baird to supervise the construction of the refinery. When the refinery was completed in June 1932, Parten gave E. L. Woodley, now in his late fifties, a job as refinery manager at Baird with additional authority for marketing. The plunge in cotton prices that had threatened Querbes's bank had bankrupted E. L. during the previous summer. He and his wife had lost nearly everything and were living in a house in Dallas that J. R. had bought for them. The Woodleys were thankful not only for E. L.'s job, but for the opportunity to return to their native West Texas.[11]

Thus was Parten launched on a close association with Sylvester Dayson that would last twenty-five years. Their friendship puzzled many of Parten's associates. Dayson was in many ways Parten's opposite in style and outlook, but they shared a progressive political world view. "Sylvester was very liberal," one friend has noted, "he was as liberal as the Major, but he just didn't get so involved." Dayson, only five feet seven inches in height, was a profane-speaking, cigar-smoking gambler and woman chaser who wore flashy cowboy hats and black boots. As one friend later observed, "People never knew what to make of him. He made a lot of huge mistakes by overdoing in a lot of ways. But that was his way." Fred Mayer, the person responsible for much of the financing behind Parten's and Dayson's joint ventures, remembered that whenever they had made the last payment on their latest loan, Dayson liked to come into his office, put his feet up on Mayer's desk, light a cigarette, and announce with his heavy French accent, "Freddy, you leetuhl-son-of-a-beech, treat me like a gentleman for once, I'm paid up." Dayson also became good friends with Myron and Jack Blalock, especially Jack with whom he shared a love of the good life. For the next several years, Dayson and the Blalock brothers were key members of Parten's small inner circle of business and political allies.[12]

Oil at Ten Cents a Barrel: Prorationing and Unitization

While Parten was busy trying to solve his problem in Callahan County by forming a new refining company, his industry had become immersed in the most serious crisis it had ever faced—a crisis in which Parten was soon deeply involved. Despite the largesse that it created for many, the East Texas field was not good news for the oil industry in general and the major oil companies in particular. The oil gushing from its many wells flooded a market already stagnating from the worldwide economic depression. The price of oil had dropped steadily since the mid-1920s, from $1.88 per barrel in 1926 to $1.10 per barrel in October of 1930; a drop greater than the decline in the general wholesale commodities price level. The discovery of the East Texas oil field quickly turned this price decline into a dizzy free-fall. While industrial growth had stopped and even declined, the supply of oil suddenly and dramatically increased. As a result, by the end of 1931 the price of East Texas crude fell to an incredible ten cents per barrel.[13]

The price crisis created by the East Texas field led to a bitter struggle within the oil industry between those calling for government control of production (generally the majors and larger independents) at the state or federal level and those opposed to such controls (mainly small and medium-sized independents). As prices plunged, some of the major oil companies pressed the state governments of Oklahoma and Texas to impose strict production limits to restore stability to the industry nationally. Most of the majors and many of the larger independents urged that a method known as prorationing be used to control production. Under prorationing, each operator in a field produces only a stipulated proportion (called the "allowable") of the oil his wells are capable of producing. The allowable is set by order of a regulatory agency, which applies the allowable to individual wells or to total acreage. If the controls are based on acreage, the field is said to be "unitized," meaning that an entire oil field is operated as one production unit. The unitized field is assigned a total allowable and the individual producers (usually operating as a committee) determine how the allowable is to be divided among wells. Any oil produced in excess of the amount allowable, whether under well prorationing or under field unitization, is called "hot oil."[14]

Those in favor of prorationing stressed that it prevented waste and ensured the equitable withdrawal of oil in all fields, especially in East Texas. An oil field could be permanently damaged and much of the recoverable oil lost if drilling was conducted without regard for geological factors such as bottom-hole gas pressure. It was gas pressure that "drove" East Texas crude out of the ground. Careless production practices could exhaust the field's gas prematurely, resulting in the loss of millions of barrels of oil with no way to recover it. In addition, because oil is usually found in a pool extending beneath the property of several different individuals, the uncontrolled, flush-pumping of the pool by one individual could literally drain the oil from beneath everyone else's land. Naturally, the major companies that were creating oil reserves opposed anyone who wanted to produce oil from leases adjacent to their reserve fields. Such production could drain their field or exhaust its generating gas. By the mid-summer of 1931 the nineteen largest oil companies in East Texas produced only 36 percent of its total output, while the six hundred smallest operators produced nearly 50 percent. As one student of the field has charged, "the independents . . . pumping away, draining oil from other leases and winning the race to drain the field." Proration supporters therefore argued for unitization or acreage prorationing in East Texas. They declared that each landowner was entitled to recover only that portion of the oil in the pool that underlay his land. Acreage prorationing, it was argued, would establish an equitable allocation and eliminate the independents' production advantage.[15]

While opponents of prorationing often ignored or downplayed the conservation argument, they confronted head-on the argument that one's flush production might drain the oil from a neighbor's lease. They argued that it was impossible to determine with any precision how much of the oil in a pool actually lay beneath one piece of land. They also denounced as a threat to personal liberty any plan that prevented a landowner from exploiting his land to the fullest. Antiprorationists claimed that the ancient English common law concept known as the "rule of capture" entitled a property owner to produce as much oil as he could from beneath his property whenever he wanted. The argument was that oil was like fugitive wildlife, if a deer or game bird from one property moved over to another, the owner of the latter had the right under this concept to hunt and kill the animal as long as it was on his property. If a neighbor wanted to preserve the oil that was beneath his own land, then he needed to pump it out. To deny one the "right" to do whatever one wanted to do with oil under the surface of one's own land was, independent geologist A. D. Lloyd declared, "naked confiscation of private property."[16]

The independents opposed to controls argued that major oil companies, bolstered by other sources of revenue, could afford to keep much of their oil in the ground. The majors also needed to maintain reserves to keep all units of their huge systems (pipelines, refineries, and filling stations) operating on a predictable and consistent production schedule. The small independents, however, often faced bankruptcy if they were not allowed to produce and sell their oil as quickly as possible.

The most effective charge the antiprorationists used was that prorationing was just another name for legal price-fixing. Limiting production obviously restricted supply and raised prices. Most proration advocates (especially the majors) tended to downplay that side of the argument because of the antitrust and price-fixing implications. Nevertheless, as it became clear that allowables based only on conservation factors could not cut production to levels low enough to restore higher prices, advocates for controls argued for market-demand prorationing, which limited production to whatever level met the current demand for oil.[17]

The argument over government control of production did not begin with the discovery of oil in East Texas, but dated back to the discovery at Spindletop and earlier. In 1919, the Texas legislature granted the Texas Railroad Commission the authority to prevent the waste of natural resources. But the only proration orders issued by the Railroad Commission during the 1920s (for the Yates field in West Texas) had been voluntary. The Railroad Commission did not issue its first mandatory and statewide production-control order until August 27, 1930, two months before the Joiner discovery. That order was in response to accusations made by the major companies that independents were engaging in massively wasteful practices that were destroying productive oil fields. The August order limited statewide production to 750,000 barrels daily. The order also required producers to follow certain conservation practices. Monthly quotas were determined through information secured at hearings and by reliance on the production forecasts of the U.S. Bureau of Mines. This first mandatory order created a serious dispute within the industry over prorationing even before the discovery of the East Texas field. Several independents rejected the Railroad Commission's authority and obtained court injunctions allowing them to continue production without restriction. As a result of these legal attacks, many oil producers at the time the East Texas field was discovered were ignoring the Railroad Commission's proration order.[18]

When the dispute over the Railroad Commission's first mandatory order broke out, J. R. Parten voiced his opposition to production controls. In the Woodley Company's 1930 annual report, written before the Bateman discovery, Parten claimed that "proration umpires" were issuing "greatly exaggerated" reports of an oversupply of oil to scare the industry into supporting prorationing. Arguing that the law of supply and demand could not "tolerate manipulation," Parten declared that "the oil man . . . should entertain himself with the hope that the government will permit him to conduct his own business so long as he does not stoop to the crime of actual waste."[19]

Parten sided with those who claimed that the demand for government controls was essentially an attempt by the major companies to run independents such as himself out of the industry. His views were tempered somewhat as Woodley enjoyed financial success, partially because of government intervention. In the early 1930s, however, Parten believed that the major oil companies were using the conservation argument, for example, as an excuse for government support of price-fixing and monopolistic activity. Parten supported conservation of natural resources, but only as it related to the reduction of physical waste, not to "guarantee profits to an industry." He thought the idea that government regulation of production could be based on market demand was especially bogus. "Oil production," Parten argued, "has been naturally . . . limited to market demand from the beginning of time. Producers can only produce what they can sell or store. . . ." Parten was equally opposed to government-imposed unitization, although he had no objection to the idea of producers voluntarily agreeing to operate an oil field as one production unit. Woodley Petroleum participated in a unit operation of fifteen thousand acres in the Cotton Valley field in 1935. Parten believed that production controls would drive the small operators out of business, force landowners to sell, and result in consolidation of the industry into a few large companies which would set consumer prices at a high level for greater profits. The industry's return to good health could come about only through the preservation of competition, more efficient and economical oil production, and increased consumption. Indeed, Parten argued, rather than produce less oil the industry needed to increase consumption by developing more uses for petroleum products.[20]

Martial Law in East Texas

As oil production in East Texas climbed to a record high and as prices fell to new lows during the early months of 1931, major companies such as Humble Oil, as well as some of the larger independents, called on the Texas Railroad Commission to control production. They demanded that production allowables be based on market demand in order to drive prices to higher levels. As these calls for a stricter system of production control grew louder and more insistent, Parten worried about the possibilities of either the individual oil-producing states or the federal government taking control of oil production. His concern deepened on April 3, 1931, when the Railroad Commission issued its first proration order for the East Texas field, limiting each well in the field to about one thousand barrels a day.[21]

At the same time the Railroad Commission was issuing these new orders, rumors circulated that some of the major companies planned to ask the federal government to impose production controls. Parten believed that the major oil companies, especially Jersey Standard, Standard of New York, and Standard of Indiana, hoped federal control would lead to the creation of a national oil utility. Because of their political clout, such a utility would inevitably be dominated by Standard and the other major companies. As far as Parten was concerned, the government had shown that it was incapable of regulating such huge and complicated enterprises as railroads, with the usual result being that the "regulated become the regulators." Disturbed by the specter of an alliance between the major oil companies and the federal government, Parten wrote Huey Long, now a United States senator-elect, to express his concern. Complaining to Long that "the whole procedure seems to be . . . price fixing," he expressed his concern that any controlled price would be "a very low price" that favored the major companies because of their huge volume of production. During a private visit a few weeks later, Long encouraged Parten to call on his help if the issue of federal control arose in Congress. That battle, however, was two years away.[22]

The Railroad Commission's production orders for the East Texas field were almost completely ignored. The Commission set the field's allowable at seventy thousand barrels a day, but the field's oil operators produced twice that amount. When the allowable was raised to ninety thousand barrels a day, production jumped to three hundred thousand barrels daily and the price of crude oil dropped to twenty cents a barrel. As the Railroad Commission's orders continued to be ignored, the major oil companies pressured Gov. Ross Sterling to call a special legislative session to pass a prorationing law with legal penalties for those who refused to observe it. Rejecting these demands, the governor requested that the operators in East Texas join together voluntarily to control the problem of overproduction. In response to Sterling's suggestion, on June 15 Parten met in Tyler with other small East Texas independents and royalty owners to create such a voluntary program in an attempt to avoid government regulation. They accepted fellow independent Tom Cranfill's plan to limit the production of individual wells to a maximum of three hundred barrels per day with the hope that it would cut daily production by a total of about one hundred thousand barrels.[23]

To monitor their plan, the Tyler group created the East Texas Oil Arbitration Committee, which consisted of three independents, two royalty owners or landowners, and two representatives of major oil companies. Parten agreed to serve as one of the independents' representatives on the committee and also as the committee's secretary. Although he remained strongly opposed to prorationing in theory, he realized that the industry crisis caused by the unusual situation in East Texas had panicked so many independents that some type of action was necessary to avoid the much greater danger of compulsory control. Accepting the inevitable, he focused his efforts on implementing a proration program that would not be linked to market demand and that could be dismantled easily once the crisis was over. Sending a copy of the Cranfill plan to a friend in Houston, Parten wrote, "you will notice that there is no reference to price. Nature must take care of that." The Tyler group announced that the East Texas Oil Arbitration Committee gave the people of East Texas the opportunity to regulate themselves without outside help or legislation.

Governor Sterling endorsed the Cranfill plan and urged "speedy" compliance. The major purchasing companies, including Texaco and Humble, declared their support for the plan, but only if the Railroad Commission adopted it as an official order. After a meeting with an advisory committee of East Texas producers in Longview on June 18, the East Texas Oil Arbitration Committee sent a copy of their plan to the Texas Railroad Commission, urging its adoption by the commission.[24] The Cranfill plan went into effect on June 20. Parten told East Texas newspaper publisher Carl Estes that voluntary production controls were "nothing less than a 'home rule' plan for East Texas." He warned, however, that "much diligent labor will be required to make any plan effective."[25]

On June 22, Parten and his colleagues on the Arbitration Committee travelled to Austin and met with Governor Sterling, who voiced his continuing support for the plan, but expressed skepticism that a voluntary program could succeed. The Arbitration Committee also gave testimony at public hearings of the Railroad Commission in support of the plan. When Commissioner Pat Neff (a former Texas governor) asked the East Texans why they believed most of their fellow producers would voluntarily comply with their plan, Parten replied that the people of the region supported the plan so strongly that "violators will bring down a wrath [from their neighbors] that can not be long endured." Parten's statement proved to be wishful thinking. Thumbing their noses at any attempt to control their private property, many independents produced oil far in excess of the limits called for by the voluntary plan. In a newspaper interview, Parten pleaded in vain with East Texas producers to cooperate. "The committee has no status in law," Parten explained, "and can hope to accomplish nothing without the whole hearted support of . . . nearly all of the interested parties."[26]

As it became obvious that the Cranfill plan was not working, Parten's last hope was for the Railroad Commission to adopt the plan as an official order, allowing the major oil companies to participate without fear of violating antitrust laws. Parten's hopes were dashed on July 2 when the Railroad Commission decided to adopt a greatly modified version of the Cranfill plan that prorationed the field on an acreage basis and raised the total allowable to 250,000 barrels a day. This decision was as unsatisfactory to the major companies as it was to Parten and his fellow antiproration independents. The former demanded much lower allowables to raise prices, while the latter strongly opposed acreage prorationing. The fight soon shifted to the legislature when Governor Sterling, declaring a "grave crisis," gave in to demands for a special session to strengthen the Railroad

Commission's power to regulate oil production. The governor asked the legislature to stop the "orgy of disorderly production" by devising regulations to control East Texas. From July 14 through August 12, the lawmakers debated whether to base prorationing on market demand or on a formula to prevent physical waste.[27]

While the legislators grappled with the proration problem, the Federal District Court in East Texas complicated the situation by ruling in the MacMillan case that the Railroad Commission's original East Texas order in April was invalid because the legislature had not given the commission the authority to use market price as a guide for oil production quotas. The court also ruled that the order violated contracts, deprived plaintiffs of property without due process, and interfered with interstate commerce. Sterling interpreted the decision as an antimonopoly warning from the courts and told the legislature that he would veto any bill linking prorationing with market demand and prices. After much legislative maneuvering, the so-called Anti-Market Demand Prorationing Act was passed on August 12, 1931. The new law strengthened the Railroad Commission's ability to control physical waste but it also specifically prohibited market-demand allowables, compulsory unitization, and consideration of economic waste. Although the law did uphold the Railroad Commission's power to issue statewide proration orders, it could do so only for conservation purposes. Parten, who had spent much time in Austin lobbying in favor of the legislation, was delighted by its passage.[28]

Interpreting the law as voiding all previous proration orders, producers throughout East Texas turned their wellhead valves wide open. In mid-August, production soared to one million barrels per day, the world record for an individual field. Flush production had thrown fifty-six million barrels of East Texas oil onto the market in less than nine months. This flood of oil suddenly plunged crude prices in Texas from slightly more than one dollar to as low as two cents a barrel in some markets, sending a shock wave felt throughout the world market. A condition of near anarchy prevailed in the East Texas field as producers pumped as much oil as quickly as they could from their wells.[29]

As the situation worsened, Gov. "Alfalfa Bill" Murray of Oklahoma shut down Oklahoma's oil production and imposed martial law in the state's fields. He called on Texas to do likewise. Accordingly, on August 17, only five days after the new conservation bill had been enacted, Governor Sterling declared that the East Texas field was in a "state of insurrection" and imposed martial law on the East Texas counties of Upshur, Gregg, Rusk, and Smith. He ordered the closing of all wells and called out the National Guard, placing it under the command of Gen. Jacob F. Wolters, who in civilian life served as chief counsel to the Texas Company. National Guardsmen patrolled the field on horseback to enforce the Railroad Commission's proration orders.[30]

Parten opposed martial law and he criticized Sterling for declaring it. He and other independents were especially upset that a major oil company attorney was now administering the field. When General Wolters explained to the press that martial law had been necessitated by an imminent threat of violence in the oil field, Parten's reaction was documented in a letter to his hometown newspaper, the Madisonville *Meteor.* "To my certain knowledge, there has never been any act of violence or any threat of violence which should justify such a statement. . . ." Parten complained that Wolter's "exaggerated statements . . . are designed particularly to encourage more governmental control in private industry, which would . . . eradicate free competition."[31]

Nevertheless, Sterling's drastic action stabilized the situation in East Texas. On September 2, the Railroad Commission issued a new order for a production allowable of four hundred thousand barrels per day on a well basis of approximately 225 barrels per well, without regard to individual well potential. The order was to be enforced by the National Guard in East Texas and voluntarily in other Texas fields. When Governor Sterling reopened the East Texas oil field on September 5, prices climbed quickly to sixty-eight cents a barrel. On October 13, antiproration independents persuaded a federal judge to issue an order restraining the Railroad Commission, the Texas attorney general, and General Wolters from enforcing proration until a suit challenging martial law could be decided. Accordingly, Governor Sterling stepped in and issued his own proration order for the field, which simply copied the one previously issued by the Railroad Commission. The National Guard continued to enforce the order with the result that crude-oil prices were lifted "at the point of the bayonet" to eighty-three cents a barrel by the end of 1931.[32]

Despite the rise in prices and the restoration of order to the field, the basic dispute remained unresolved. The major companies worked for compulsory market-demand prorationing while Parten and other independents worked just as hard to prevent it. Parten was deeply distressed by Sterling's imposition of martial law. To him, it symbolized the ultimate danger to the oil industry: nationalization. It also hurt his pocketbook. Although Woodley Petroleum had thirteen wells in East Texas with an estimated potential of 150,000 barrels per day, the Railroad Commission's proration order restricted Woodley's production to only 1,300 barrels per day. Parten believed that the price increases were artificial, that they had been raised by the major companies to show how government control could help the industry. He wrote Querbes that he was obviously happy to be paid more for the oil that he was allowed to sell, but he doubted it would last: "The increased price is the wage . . . that is being paid the Governors of Texas and Oklahoma for certain regulatory acts."[33]

In early November, Governor Sterling, who was temporarily the only official permitted to order proration allowables, announced that he was considering changing the proration basis from individual wells to acreage, which more effectively limited the number of wells drilled and benefited those who owned larger leases. This acreage plan was being pushed by the Texas Oil and Gas Conservation Association, which was pressuring Sterling to implement it while martial law was still in effect. J. Edgar Pew of the Sun Oil Company urged Charles F. Roeser of Fort Worth, an independent oil man who supported strong production controls, to do everything he could to persuade Sterling to act quickly because ". . . we can put this over under martial law when it might be very difficult otherwise." Outraged by this effort, a group of East Texas independents organized a delegation to go to Austin and meet with the governor to argue against the acreage plan. Parten was an eager member of this delegation and his attorney, Myron Blalock, was elected spokesman.

When the delegation of East Texas independents met with Sterling on November 4, he asked the group if unitization was a possible solution to the problems in East Texas. Parten spoke up, telling the governor that the theory of unitization was impractical because of too many unknown factors in the underground structures of a pool. He argued that the industry should be left alone, subject only to the "natural law" of supply and demand. Sterling questioned Parten at length and in detail about his view of the situation in East Texas. Parten repeated that he preferred that the governor turn the field "loose" and let the natural order work everything out, but in deference to his colleagues who refused to go that far he could support some form of regulation if it was not at the expense of the small independent and if it did not encourage the creation of an oil monopoly. After this meeting, Sterling announced that he no longer supported acreage prorationing.[34]

Parten's work with the East Texas Oil Arbitration Committee and the prominent role he played in the meeting with Governor Sterling in November, thrust him into a leadership position in the fight against government controls. His university education and legal training, his experience as an intercollegiate debater and as an officer and instructor in the army, as well as his strong and long-standing interest in public affairs, gave him the tools and motivation to assume leadership. Men with his background and experience were rare among independent oil men. Beginning with his work with the East Texas Oil Arbitration Committee, it became common for Parten to receive letters from other independent oil men seeking his advice on a variety of public policy issues related to their industry. He usually responded with detailed critiques of such issues as market-demand prorationing and unitization, with several pages of charts and graphs enclosed.[35]

The Independent Petroleum Association of Texas

Parten's new visibility among the state's oil men led to his election in June 1931 as vice president of the Independent Petroleum Association of Texas (IPAT). A group of small independent oil men, led by Tom Cranfill of Dallas and E. B. Germany of Tyler, had organized the IPAT at a meeting in Fort Worth in February 1930 to represent the interests of Texas independents in legislative and other governmental matters. A meeting of oil men in Colorado Springs the previous summer had resulted in the creation of the Independent Petroleum Association of America (IPAA) and its existence had inspired the subsequent creation of the IPAT. The Texans' initial effort was in support of the national organization's campaign to win passage of a federal tariff on oil imports. Many independents blamed cheap foreign oil as one of the reasons for the depression in oil prices. The IPAT soon broadened its program, however, to focus on state legislation. It lobbied the Texas legislature for a law declaring the state's natural gas pipelines to be common carriers and eventually helped to secure the passage of the Common Purchaser

Parten's official portrait as IPAT president, 1931. *Courtesy Parten Photograph Collection, CAH.*

Law; it worked for passage of the state Conservation Act of 1931; and it sponsored the Texas "marginal well" act, exempting the small stripper wells in old fields from proration. By late 1931, the IPAT concentrated on the fight against the proration and unitization movement, which ultimately put the organization in opposition to the national association. A number of the IPAT's founding members, including Clint Murchison of Tyler and Joe Danciger of Fort Worth, strongly opposed any type of government regulation of production, including prorationing in any form.

At its annual meeting in Chicago in November 1931, the American Petroleum Institute (API), which was controlled by the major oil companies, endorsed the oil tariff. As domestic oil prices plunged, major companies such as Standard of New Jersey who were also oil importers were willing to support a tariff as part of their larger strategy to get domestic production controls. The idea was to demonstrate that imports were actually having little effect on the price structure. Accordingly, the API also passed a formal resolution demanding compulsory unitization and market-demand prorationing, giving notice that the integrated companies and large independents were launching a vigorous campaign for domestic production controls.[36]

As a result of the API's actions, the IPAT's annual meeting in Dallas on December 15 became a rally against government controls. Serving as the meeting's keynote speaker, Parten told IPAT members that unitization was unworkable and inherently unfair to the small producer because of the lack of knowledge about underground pools. He claimed that compulsory unitization would encourage monopoly, depress the price of oil in the long run, and destroy small refineries. Unitization would raise oil prices to a certain level and keep them there, Parten claimed, insuring stable prices for the majors, who would buy cheap crude from independents and sell products at high prices set by the monopoly. Parten declared that the "business of today needs. . . . less centralized control by government or private interests " and more "free and untrammeled . . . competition." The members responded enthusiastically to the speech, which was subsequently published as a pamphlet and distributed nationwide, attracting much attention in the oil industry. Parten's speech also convinced the members that he should be their new president. Elected as the IPAT president, Parten now turned his full attention to the politics of oil.[37]

CHAPTER 4

Oil and Politics

*"Red" Thompson, and the Fight to Preserve
the Railroad Commission, 1932–1933*

Near the end of 1931, the Independent Petroleum Association of Texas (IPAT), seemed to be an organization without a future. The IPAT was on the verge of bankruptcy and hampered by a membership composed of a quarrelsome group of small independents who preferred not to pay their dues. J. R. Parten's election to the presidency, however, brought new life to a dying organization. Convinced that market-demand prorationing and other government controls posed an unprecedented threat to the survival of the oil industry's small independents, he was determined to reshape and transform the IPAT into an effective political pressure group to fight such controls. To Parten and his fellow IPAT members, that basically meant opposing market-demand prorationing and compulsory unitization of oil fields (or prorationing based on acreage). Actually, Parten made one strategic compromise on the issue of prorationing. Although he hated prorationing, he was beginning to see that an allowable allocated to individual wells was much preferable to acreage allowables. He also believed that well-based prorationing, which was opposed by many of the major oil companies, would not work in the long run and would thus demonstrate the foolishness of production controls. Parten confided to one ally in the fight against government controls that "this [well-based] plan, rigidly applied, will make proration unpopular with the very people who started the practice."[1]

Parten's IPAT agenda was ambitious. He wanted to expand the association's membership, raise its public profile, disseminate its message, and attract badly needed funds to replenish its depleted treasury. The IPAT's financial situation was so desperate that the organization owed its only full-time employee, executive vice president Claude Wild, several thousand dollars in back pay. The forty-year-old Wild, who managed the association from his office in Fort Worth, was slated to play a critical role in Parten's effort to fight production controls. An attorney by profession, Wild was also an astute and skilled political strategist and lobbyist whose talents had been wasted by previous IPAT presidents. Parten, however, appreciated Wild's skills and resolved to make good use of them.[2]

With Wild at his side, Parten launched an aggressive campaign for the IPAT in the early weeks of 1932, hosting public programs and luncheons throughout the tri-state region. Flying his Stearman, he was able to cover a wide area on a tight schedule. His itinerary during the first week in January was typical, as he attended meetings in Shreveport, Oklahoma City, Dallas, and Tyler within a four-day period. These public meetings, which attracted much attention from the local press, served as forums for Parten to preach the antiproration gospel. "Potential production, not actual, is being used as a bugaboo in East Texas," he complained to his audiences. "They are holding the oil we carry underground as an axe against us to beat down the price." Parten also initiated a "Directors Bulletin" to serve as the IPAT's newsletter, but its "news" was largely Parten's editorial views on current political developments related to the oil industry.[3]

Parten's goal to replenish the IPAT treasury proved to be more elusive than his other goals. A visit to Houston to raise money brought Parten into contact for the first time with such politically active independents as James Abercrombie, Elwood Fouts, Dan Harrison, Hugh Roy Cullen, and Jim West. Parten formed important relationships with each of these men, but only Cullen and West provided any financial help for the IPAT. Eventually, Parten managed to squeeze nearly twelve thousand dollars out of the IPAT's 175 members. Nevertheless, he was forced to personally provide more than one-fourth of the association's operational funds for the entire year of 1932. Acknowledging Parten's success at keeping the IPAT alive, Hines Baker of Humble Oil admitted that before Parten had become president, most of the oil industry had expected the IPAT to die "a natural death." Parten's "intelligent leadership," however, had almost single-handedly made the association an influential voice in the industry.[4]

"Swattin' Hokum"

While Parten worked to strengthen the IPAT internally, external developments at the state and national levels required his attention as the association's president. On February 18, 1932, a federal district court declared Governor Sterling's martial law order unconstitutional on the grounds that martial law could only be invoked when there was an actual insurrection or "the menacing threat of one." The court, however, ordered restrictions on production to remain in place until the Railroad Commission could issue a proration order based on physical conservation. One week later the commission set allowables in East Texas at about seventy-five barrels per well. Fearing that many independents would ignore the new allowables and once again flood the market, Parten urged IPAT members to cooperate in the effort to enforce "orderly production in the East Texas field." Parten worried that if the independents ignored the new production order, such action would play into the hands of those who favored compulsory controls.[5]

Although Parten grudgingly voiced his support for a temporary program of prorationing, he believed that the "excessive" importation of foreign oil by the major companies was the primary reason for low oil prices. Parten believed that the reduction of imports would raise the price for domestically produced oil and make market-demand prorationing unnecessary. Accordingly, Parten enlisted the IPAT in the national effort in the spring of 1932 to persuade Congress to pass an oil import tariff. Here was an area in which Parten and his IPAT colleagues not only welcomed government regulation, they demanded it. Describing the tariff matter as "probably the most important oil issue of the day," Parten and the IPAT linked up with a national organization, the Independent Petroleum Association of America (IPAA), to campaign for a high tariff on imported oil. Parten coordinated a letter-writing campaign in Louisiana and Arkansas as well as in Texas to "exert all the influence possible" on Congress to support the tariff. Parten told IPAT members to spread the word that the "future of the American oil industry" depended on a high oil tariff.[6]

Parten also traveled throughout Texas speaking to local organizations and urging them to write their congressional representatives. A prominent article in the Dallas Morning News on Parten's activities on behalf of the oil tariff gave his views even wider distribution. His work in Texas and the efforts of his allies in other states helped the oil tariff receive a favorable hearing in Washington. Congress had rejected the tariff in previous sessions, but the revenue the tariff would produce for the federal budget in a time of worsening economic conditions now made it more attractive. Huey Long's active support gave momentum to the oil tariff in the Senate, which passed it as an amendment to the general revenue bill on May 20. The following month, President Hoover signed the oil tariff into law.[7]

Most of the major oil companies and some of the large independents, however, did not view the oil tariff as the answer to their problems. In May, Congress considered legislation to create a Federal Interstate Oil Board to recommend production quotas for each state, approve private unitization agreements, and promote uniform state conservation laws. The sharp controversy caused by these proposals, which were known as the Thomas-McKeown bills, eventually caused their withdrawal. Nevertheless, the American Petroleum Institute (API), which had helped write the proposals, served notice that they would push similar bills in the new congress in 1933. Parten reacted to the Thomas-McKeown bills with intense hostility, which was reflected by Claude Wild's public declaration that the "sinister" and "evil" bills were part of a plot "by certain integrated oil concerns . . . to gain complete control of the oil industry." Echoing Parten, Wild declared that the major oil companies could control the federal government "much more easily than they can the States."[8]

Parten had anticipated a move toward federal control ever since November 1931, when the API had issued a call for compulsory unitization to be enforced by "the police power of the State," market-demand prorationing, and a change in the concept of oil ownership to eliminate the rule of capture. Parten knew that most of the major oil companies had concluded that the independents in California and Texas were strong enough to ward off production limits imposed by their states, so the power of the federal government would have to be invoked to compel controls. He feared this would ultimately result in making the oil industry a utility subject to rigid price controls and regulation by government bureaucracy. He believed that such a development would destroy the independent segment of the industry, end competition, and leave the oil business entirely in the hands of a few major companies. By the summer of 1932, the battle lines were being drawn, and it looked bad for Parten and his fellow opponents of government control. Not only would they have to fight the federal government, but also a powerful array of forces within the industry itself, including the influential API and a well-organized and financed pressure group called the Texas Oil and Gas Conservation Association.[9]

Five small organizations of independents who supported market-demand prorationing had merged in October 1931 to form the Texas Oil and Gas Conservation Association. Before the merger, the most visible lobbyists for prorationing had been the major oil companies, particularly Humble. The major companies had such a poor public image in Texas, however, that it was necessary for them to help organize a group of independents to take the public lead in the fight for market-demand prorationing. The Oil and Gas Conservation Association served this purpose, advocating cooperation with the majors to rationalize and stabilize the industry through the use of unitization, an interstate oil compact, and market-demand prorationing. Its leaders included Fort Worth independent Charles Roeser, who became president; H. L. Hunt, now rich with East Texas oil; and J. Edgar Pew of the Sun Oil Company. Headquartered in Fort Worth because of Roeser, the association worked to counter Parten's and the IPAT's activities. This included publication of a propaganda magazine, the *Conservationist.*

Parten's group was at a distinct disadvantage in this battle between independent associations. While the IPAT struggled to pay its monthly bills, the Texas Oil and Gas Conservation Association enjoyed bountiful financial support from the major oil companies. Because their membership rules were less exclusive than the IPAT's, the Texas Oil and Gas Conservation Association also had a much larger membership than their rival. Claiming to be the true representative of Texas independents, the IPAT strictly limited its membership to companies and individuals not affiliated with any major oil company.[10]

As part of his effort to counter the Texas Oil and Gas Conservation Association, the API, and their allies, Parten created a monthly magazine called the *Texas Independent.* The publication was targeted at legislators, judges, and Railroad Commission members and staff, each of whom received complimentary copies. Parten's first editorial in the journal made clear that he and the IPAT were framing their arguments in the concepts of traditional American values. Explaining that the *Texas Independent* was waging a battle for "free and fair competition in the oil industry," he declared that it would have a special appeal to those "who believe in the principles of individual and independent opportunity as the foundation of American progress."[11]

Beginning with the first issue in June 1932, the *Texas Independent* regularly featured detailed articles, many written by Parten, which analyzed specific economic and legal issues related to market-demand prorationing and compulsory unitization. To attract readers who might not be inclined to read such technical articles, Wild added cartoons, jokes, and a "news" column called "Swattin' Hokum" which stressed in more simplistic terms that the fight against government controls was really a "populist" fight against Big Business. Wild argued that the typical independent "has a family to support, and his children to educate. He is not extensively interested in other fields. His life work may be wrapped up in [one] lease." Cartoons consistently depicted the "average" independent as a poorly clothed and ill-housed farmer with one well on his tiny lease, fighting off a huge man who symbolized the major oil companies and who looked very much like the Daddy Warbucks character from the "Orphan Annie" comic strip. Standard of New Jersey and Humble Oil, its Texas subsidiary, were frequent targets of Wild's editorial barbs. In one column, Wild characterized Humble president W. S. Farish as the "John D. Rockefeller of Texas" and charged that his company "is seeking to own the entire oil fields of Texas."[12]

Although based on the accurate understanding that Humble was the driving force behind the movement to unitize the East Texas field, Wild's attacks nevertheless caused Parten some discomfort. In response to a complaint from his friend Hines Baker, Parten ordered Wild to stop the personal attacks. Parten's friendship with Baker, Farish, Gene Holman, and other Humble executives blinded him to the fact that they not only supported Standard's policies, they had helped formulate them. Despite all evidence to the contrary, he preferred to believe that Standard's New York executives, especially its president Walter Teagle, had forced Humble's executives to push for unitization in East Texas.[13]

Jimmy Allred

The state and federal elections to be held in 1932 were far more crucial to the ultimate outcome of Parten's fight than his articles in the *Texas Independent* or his other IPAT activities. Accordingly, Parten's heavy involvement in the politics of his industry now led to his direct involvement in partisan electoral politics. Although his political choices in future years were determined by his views on a variety of issues and his politics would become more ideology-oriented toward the end of his life, his political motivation in 1932 sprang from a single issue rooted in business self-interest. To J. R. Parten the political campaigns of 1932 were strictly battles against government control of his business. The Depression was also an issue, but to Parten, ending the economic crisis and preserving his business were so intimately connected that they were one and the same. As a result, he searched for candidates who would come closest to his position on this single issue of the relationship between oil and the government. His search brought him to two men with whom he would be closely linked in politics for several decades to come: James V. Allred and Ernest O. Thompson.

In May of 1932, Parten was listening to Shreveport radio station KWKH when James V. "Jimmy" Allred, running for reelection as attorney general of Texas, came on the air to make a campaign speech. Allred had purchased time on KWKH because the station transmitted a powerful signal that could be heard clearly throughout Texas (as well as much of the United States).[14] Allred's oratorical talents made a strong impression on Parten. "He had a very smooth speaking voice," Parten noted, "and he could thread a needle with his arguments." More important, however, were Allred's antitrust views. During his first term as attorney general, Allred had filed a suit against seventeen major oil companies, alleging a conspiracy to monopolize the oil business in Texas. Allred specifically charged that Jersey Standard's control of Humble Oil violated the Texas antitrust law. The suit wound its way through the court system until 1938. The companies were eventually acquitted, except for the Texas Petroleum Marketers Association, which was fined. Parten supported the antitrust suit and he admired the young attorney general for filing it. After hearing Allred speak on KWKH, Parten was eager to meet him. The next time Allred was in Shreveport, Parten went to KWKH and introduced himself to him. Parten took Allred to dinner and they spent the evening discussing politics. Parten learned that Allred had become district attorney in Wichita Falls at the age of twenty-five and that he had waged an effective war on the Ku Klux Klan while in that post. Close in age and sharing the same views about the evils of corporate monopolies and the need to protect the "independent" businessman, Parten and Allred forged a close political bond that night in Shreveport that lasted until Allred's death a quarter of a century later.[15]

As his campaign continued during that summer, Allred made frequent use of KWKH's facilities, and he and Parten dined together whenever Parten was in Shreveport. Likewise, whenever Parten made one of his frequent trips to Austin, he paid a visit to the attorney general's office, where he also forged an important friendship with Allred's assistant attorney general, Ralph W. Yarborough. Allred had appointed the twenty-nine-year-old Yarborough to the position of assistant attorney general in April 1931, even though he had supported Allred's opponent, Robert Lee Bobbitt. Allred made the young East Texan responsible for legal matters related to the state's Permanent School Fund and for the University of Texas's Permanent Fund, both largely supported by oil royalties from Texas public lands. The latter fund was of particular interest to Parten because of its importance to the economic well-being of his beloved alma mater. Yarborough won a critical lawsuit against the Magnolia Oil Company (Standard of New York) involving the state's right to royalties from oil land that ultimately earned hundreds of millions of dollars for the University of Texas and the public schools. Nearly six decades later, Yarborough's memory of his first meetings with Parten remained fresh. "[Parten] was one of the most impressive persons I had ever seen," Yarborough recalled. "He wasn't an effusive backslapper; he had incredible control and his strength of personality was seen rather than expressed. It wasn't long before he became one of Allred's top advisors." Later, when Yarborough sought political office on his own, Parten served as one of his most important advisors and financial backers.[16]

Parten was actively involved in the 1932 Texas Democratic primary campaign. Texas was a one-party state, so winning the Democratic primary was tantamount to election. Because Allred's reelection was almost a sure thing, Parten's efforts on his behalf were largely to demonstrate to the attorney general that he had more than Parten's rhetorical support. Although the IPAT did not officially endorse any candidate, Parten directed Claude Wild to send a letter to the its directors urging them to work for Jimmy Allred's reelection and warning them that Allred's defeat would be a "calamity" because it would mean that "three or four oil concerns with headquarters in New York City are going to run the State of Texas. . . ." Parten sent Wild to several towns in East Texas to give speeches for Allred on the IPAT's time. Besides making a large cash donation to Allred's general campaign fund, Parten helped finance Allred's radio campaign speeches.[17]

"Red" Thompson

In the Texas governor's race, Ross Sterling was seeking reelection to a second term. His principal opponent was former governor Miriam "Ma" Ferguson. Parten supported Sterling, largely because Myron Blalock was one of the governor's campaign managers. Parten also had second thoughts about his opposition to Sterling's imposition of martial law. "I am frank to admit," Parten confided to his sister Lizzie, "[that Sterling's] course was that of wisdom. I happen to know that it did not help the Standard Oil Company as much as it is reputed to have helped it." Nevertheless, Parten's support for Sterling was without enthusiasm, especially after Sterling refused to denounce market-demand prorationing in his campaign. Believing that Ma Ferguson was a tool of the major oil companies, Parten finally decided that Sterling was simply the lesser of two evils.[18]

Parten concentrated his energy during the 1932 Texas Democratic primary campaign on the Railroad Commission, where two of the three positions on the commission were up for election. A strong Railroad Commission, supportive of well-based prorationing and willing to enforce its orders, was a key factor in Parten's strategy to keep the federal government out of the oil fields. For one position, he supported the reelection of Commissioner Charles V. Terrell, who had held the post for eight years. Terrell had been sympathetic to the independents' cause and he had been personally helpful to Parten, who was a frequent visitor to his office at the Railroad Commission. Parten did what he could for Terrell's campaign. He contributed money and made a few speeches for him, including one that was broadcast over a statewide radio hook-up. Terrell's reelection, however, was never really in doubt.[19]

The other Railroad Commission race was hotly contested. Ernest O. Thompson, the recently appointed incumbent, was facing several opponents, the strongest being former Texas state treasurer Gregory Hatcher. When Commissioner Pat Neff resigned to become president of Baylor University, Governor Sterling appointed Thompson to the Railroad Commission just one month before the July primary election. Parten supported Thompson's election, but he had not always looked with favor on the red-headed war hero from Amarillo. He had, in fact, actively opposed Thompson's appointment. Parten had known "Red" Thompson favorably during their law-school student days at the University of Texas and also during the war, but Thompson had recently served as

James V. Allred (center) and Ernest O. Thompson (right), early 1930s. *CN 09627. Courtesy E. O. Thompson Photograph Collection, CAH.*

a vice president of the IPAT's bitter foe, the Texas Oil and Gas Conservation Association. Parten had been impressed, however, by Thompson's progressive record as mayor of Amarillo, where he had battled with the city's utility companies to lower consumer rates. Parten was even less enchanted with Thompson's opponents, especially Hatcher, who he felt was a political opportunist likely to sell out to the major oil companies.[20]

Soon after Sterling appointed Thompson to the Railroad Commission, Parten met with him in Austin to see if he could support his election. Thompson admitted to Parten that he had much to learn about the oil business, but he assured him that he had no special agenda other than to stabilize the Texas oil industry in such a way as to protect everyone's basic interests. He convinced Parten that he was neither a representative of the major oil companies nor of the Texas Oil and Gas Conservation Association. He understood the vital stake the independents had in whatever course the Railroad Commission took in regulating oil production. Thompson did much to reassure Parten when he insisted that he was "bitterly opposed to any sort of Federal Control. . . ." Parten subsequently contributed money to Thompson's brief campaign, but his IPAT responsibilities and the need to pay close attention to Woodley's affairs during the early part of the summer restricted his activity during the first primary.[21]

On July 23, Ross Sterling lost to Miriam Ferguson in an extremely close election marred by allegations of voter fraud. As expected, Allred and Terrell won decisive victories but Thompson was forced into a runoff with Hatcher. Concerned that Hatcher might win, Parten went to work full time on Thompson's behalf in the runoff campaign. Operating out of a room in Austin's Stephen F. Austin Hotel, Parten worked closely with Thompson's campaign manager, Carl Calloway, to raise money and to provide Thompson with material for speeches. He spent much of his time on the telephone, calling on his associates in the oil industry to work for Thompson's victory and asking them to persuade their employees to vote for him. To make certain that Thompson knew what he had done on his behalf, Parten sent him a full report about his work on the day before the election. Emphasizing his hope that his efforts "will bear fruit," he told Thompson that he personally expected nothing in return. His self-interest would be served, he insisted, by Thompson's "common honesty and ability in office."[22]

The 1932 runoff campaign and Thompson's victory over Hatcher initiated a political relationship between Parten and Thompson that became increasingly close as they worked together to fight against federal control of the oil industry. They sometimes disagreed about Railroad Commission policy, especially in the early days of Thompson's appointment, but Parten never regretted his decision to support Thompson. Parten's active support of Allred, Thompson, and Terrell gave him valuable access to some of the key players in the oil regulation fight in Texas.[23]

"Mr. Hoover must be beaten"

Although Parten played no role in national presidential politics in 1932, his opinions about the campaign and the candidates reveal much about his world view during this period in his life. At this point, the thirty-six-year-old Parten was, within the context of his industry, a successful but small businessman, who had retained the Jacksonian economic and political principles he had imbibed as a youth. Because of the instability plaguing the oil business, as well as business in general during the bleakest days of the Depression, Parten worried that what he had achieved and built could be easily taken away from him by one or both of the twin evils: Big Business and Big Government. He feared both equally. Accordingly, he was a strict constructionist in his interpretation of the federal Constitution and a firm believer in states' rights. He advocated rigid economy in government spending and an absolute minimum of business regulation. He interpreted almost every demand by the major oil companies for federal regulation of production as a push for unitization or cartelization, and he viewed the API as the agent for such a development. He was opposed to any expansion of the federal bureaucracy, fearing that unless the growth of the federal government was checked "all of the legislative, judicial, and executive powers of our original government will have been usurped and destroyed by a bureaucracy far more vicious and dangerous than the monarchies of old." He voiced few other public-issue concerns. There is no evidence, for example, that such social problems as the plight of the unemployed, the sick and disabled, and the poverty-stricken elderly, or the injustice of racial discrimination were of any special concern to him in this period. Parten may have had sympathy for the needy, but there is no reference in his private correspondence, his writings, or his public statements in these years to indicate that issues of social and economic justice were of any interest to him. In the early 1930s, J. R. Parten's involvement in public affairs essentially sprang from motives of economic self-defense. Accordingly his choice for the presidential nomination reflected this dominant attitude.[24]

As Parten expressed it in a letter to Huey Long, "the paramount problem before this country today is that Mr. Hoover must be beaten for reelection to the Presidency . . . for otherwise the country will suffer for many decades to come." Parten not only opposed Herbert Hoover because of his loyalty to the Democratic Party, he also opposed him because he believed his administration had sought to create an American oil cartel that would destroy the independent sector of the industry. He was eager to see the Republicans removed from the White House and he was sympathetic to anyone with the same goal.[25]

An example of Parten's eagerness to seize almost any issue to use against Hoover in his campaign efforts among his friends was his brief attraction to the "radio priest" Father Charles E. Coughlin, a pseudo-populist Catholic demagogue whose radio show was broadcast from his church in Royal Oak, Michigan, over an extensive network of independent stations. Coughlin, who was near the peak of his popularity in 1932, was conducting a public campaign against Herbert Hoover's reelection. In April, Parten learned from a friend in Shreveport about Coughlin's radio diatribes against the Republicans and Hoover. He was enticed by the news that Coughlin had charged in a radio address, titled "The Secret is Out," that Hoover was actually a British citizen who had used the presidency to further British interests. Parten wrote Coughlin asking for a copy of the address and any other literature he might have on Hoover, adding that he was "undoubtedly rendering a great service to the United States in the discussion of its current problems." Coughlin's staff sent Parten multiple copies of some anti-Hoover pamphlets and a membership card in the priest's organization, the League of the Little Flower. Parten subsequently distributed the pamphlets among friends, with the explanation that he thought it might "warm your heart to the Democratic candidate." Later, when Coughlin's radio populism moved toward fascism and he turned against Franklin Roosevelt, Parten rapidly lost whatever enthusiasm he had for the demagogic priest.[26]

As the 1932 presidential election campaign drew closer, Parten's first choice for the Democratic nomination was Melvin Alvah Traylor, a moderately conservative business leader and president of the First National Bank of Chicago. Part of Traylor's appeal was the fact that he had entered the banking business in Texas where he had earned a reputation among some of Parten's acquaintances for fairness and sound judgement. Parten was impressed with the banker's calls for a stringent fiscal conservatism in government, his criticism of federal taxation poli-cy, and his attacks on "unnecessary" bureaucracy. Accordingly, Parten promoted Traylor among his friends and business associates. "In my opinion," he declared to Myron Blalock, "Traylor is one of the outstanding Americans today."[27]

Traylor was among a large group of minor candidates and favorite sons who scrambled for the nomination against Franklin D. Roosevelt and the unsuccessful 1928 candidate, Al Smith. Traylor, who claimed Texas as one of his three home-states, had a small but aggressive organization promoting his name in the state. Traylor's candidacy never really gained any momentum in Texas, however, because the Speaker of the House of Representatives, John Nance Garner, held firm control of the state's convention delegation. When Roosevelt won the Democratic nomination and then added Garner to the ticket as the nominee for vice president, Parten was disappointed but not dispirited. "I am convinced that the Democrats were wise in selecting Roosevelt and Garner for I believe that they will make the strongest race," he admitted to a friend, "they are both good men." He still hoped that if elected, Roosevelt would appoint Traylor secretary of the treasury. Although Roosevelt ignored Traylor after he won the election, Parten was still delighted to be rid of the Herbert Hoover administration. Ironically, however, Roosevelt's administration posed a far greater threat to Parten's ideas about feder-al regulation than Hoover's ever had.[28]

A New Market Demand Act

A few days before the general election of 1932, in the People's Petroleum Producers suit, the district court in East Texas ruled that the Railroad Commission's latest proration order violated the state law against market-demand prorationing. The court also killed the well-based formula much favored by Parten, ruling that the Railroad Commission's per-well allowable had discriminat-ed against wells with greater potential. The court upheld the commission's right to prorate oil production, but the overall decision once again undermined the power of the state to control the East Texas field. "The so-called hot oil boys ran oil with-out any respect to the Commission orders," Parten said, "on the assumption that their lawyers were going to have the courts strike them down anyway." Although no supporter of prorationing (he still hoped prorationing would be done away with as soon as the economy improved), Parten nevertheless feared that the deci-sion in the People's case would cause a further breakdown in the East Texas oil field and the resulting panic would lead to a market-demand prorationing law at the state level, or something even worse—federal controls. Upset by the decision, he warned his allies to prepare for yet another "heavy siege of fighting" over mar-ket-demand prorationing and unitization.[29]

The decision in the People's case left East Texas without any effective regula-tion, which frightened some of the people who had previously opposed market-demand prorationing. Prior to the People's decision, oil prices had not only stabi-lized but had increased. Now there was general fear of another price collapse. There was also a growing acceptance of the scientific arguments about the proper development of oil pools and the dangers of a too rapid depletion. Many people were now convinced that uncontrolled production was destroying the field. In addition, the recently imposed federal tariff on imported crude made it difficult to blame low prices on imports. Public opinion and the attitude among operators and royalty owners in East Texas was shifting rapidly in favor of tighter production controls. The most surprising example of this shift was journalist Carl Estes, heretofore one of Parten's staunchest allies. Fearing chaos in the East Texas field, Estes issued a public call for more controls. His change of mind caught Parten completely off guard and badly damaged the IPAT's cause.[30]

As expected, Governor Sterling called a special session of the legislature to convene on November 3, 1932, to address the problem of the Railroad Commission's inability to issue a legal allowable order based on economic waste. Bills were immediately filed to allow market-demand prorationing and acreage-based allocations. The latter was widely acknowledged to be a step toward allowing the Railroad Commission to order compulsory unitization. Parten, backed by Attorney General Allred, immediately announced his opposition to the bill. Ernest Thompson, however, supported the legislation and he did his best to persuade Parten to do the same. Assuring Parten that he did not favor any law allowing compulsory unitization, he argued that market-demand prorationing would make it unnecessary. He also believed a market-demand law was the only way to preserve the Railroad Commission's authority over oil and gas matters. He warned Parten that a failure to act could easily lead to federal intervention, which Thompson believed would create "the greatest monopoly ever conceived by the mind of man."[31]

Rejecting Thompson's argument, Parten joined Wild in Austin to fight the proposed market-demand law. It was soon apparent, however, that their efforts would fail. The major oil companies had their lobbyists all over the legislature, twisting arms for the market-demand law and for unitization. Among them was Houston attorney James A. Elkins, legal counsel for the Pure Oil Company of Chicago. Elkins, who was on his way to becoming one of the most effective business lobbyists in the state capitol and a powerful behind-the-scenes force in Texas politics, worked as a direct counterweight to Parten and the IPAT, severely criticizing Parten personally and alleging that his company was producing hot oil. Elkins's personal attacks got back to Parten, who soon developed a lifelong dislike for the powerful Houston attorney. Their paths would cross frequently in the future. Also effective was the lobbying work performed by the Texas Oil and Gas Conservation Association, which allowed the unpopular Humble Oil to remain out of sight during the battle.[32]

The legislature passed a market-demand bill on November 12, 1932, but by a surprisingly close vote. The new law gave the Railroad Commission the authority to set allowables based not only on physical-waste factors but also on oil in excess of "reasonable demand." Although this was a major shift in legislative policy, it was not a reversal of antitrust policy and it did not alter the rule of capture by allowing forced unitization. Although Parten was disappointed by the passage of the new law, he and his colleagues were able to defeat the much loathed compulsory unitization. Their arguments convinced the legislature that market-demand prorationing left control of the oil fields to an elected state agency, while unitization would place the oil fields in the hands of the majors, who, of necessity, would be the unit operators. This argument scared many of the legislators who feared that unitization might allow the major companies to starve out the independents with restrictive allowables. The defeat of unitization was a major victory for Parten and his independent allies. To this day, compulsory unitization is illegal in Texas, although voluntary unitization is widespread.[33]

One reason for the legislature's reversal in favor of market-demand prorationing was the changed view of many of its members toward the Railroad Commission. Ernest Thompson's strong and skilled leadership had transformed the commission's image almost overnight from one of ineptness to one of competency, giving the legislators confidence in its ability to enforce prorationing with fairness to majors and independents alike. One oil man later recalled that Thompson took charge of the Railroad Commission as soon as he was appointed, totally dominating his colleagues. "And it was a good thing he did," the oil man noted, "because the Lord knows, the other two wouldn't have been capable of doing it." Thompson's views were also having an effect on Parten, who grudgingly admitted to Thompson that market-demand prorationing enforced by a strong, popularly elected state commission might eventually be the only way to avoid federal control.[34]

The day after the passage of the new state law, Parten attended the annual meeting of the Independent Petroleum Association of America in Tulsa. As a new member of the association's policy committee, Parten was forced to fight yet another battle at his first committee meeting. Some of his fellow committee members demanded passage of a resolution calling for federal regulation of oil production, possibly through an oil states' compact board that would replace regulation by state commissions. After a heated and protracted debate, Parten was able to defeat the resolution in the committee. He knew, however, that those in favor of federal control would not give up that easily. He left Tulsa fearful that the IPAA's executives would carry the fight to Washington and press their views on the new administration.[35]

After his battle in Tulsa, Parten rushed back to Austin to join Claude Wild and Jack Blalock in the effort to produce a new proration plan for the Railroad Commission that would do the least harm to the small independents in East Texas. Now that the courts had disallowed per-well allocations and the new state law permitted allowables based on market demand, the commission had to devise alternative methods for determining allowables and distributing allocations. On November 26, the Railroad Commission began public hearings to receive the testimony of representatives from the oil industry. A parade of witnesses appeared before the commission, Parten among them, offering various versions of the old well-based proration plan. Parten argued that a system should be used that determined the allowable production for each well by measuring its bottom hole pressure; the higher the pressure, the higher the allowable. This would deal with the court's ruling that the old system allocated production arbitrarily. The Railroad Commission's staff engineer, E. O. Buck, submitted an alternative plan which retained Parten's bottom-hole-pressure method but added acreage as a factor. The Texas Oil and Gas Conservation Association supported Buck's plan. "There was a very bitter fight," Parten later reported to Claude Wild. "I am quite fearful that the . . . acreage basis will be adopted. In this event I anticipate . . . a possible break-down of the order."[36]

In early December 1932, the Railroad Commission issued a new proration order allowing a total daily production of less than four hundred thousand barrels in East Texas. In an attempt to placate the two opposing sides in the issue, the commission adopted a complex, hybrid method of allocation, based on both of the plans offered during the hearings. It maintained the per-well allocation advocated by Parten and the IPAT for two-thirds of the field. The remaining third of the field was prorated on a twenty-acre basis with bottom hole pressure to serve as a factor in determining allowables. Disappointed by the acreage provision, Parten complained to Thompson that he could not see the justification for its inclusion in the order. He believed that allocating production by acreage rather than by well was a violation of the concept of the rule of capture. Thompson responded by reminding Parten that a federal court had ordered the Railroad Commission to use some other method of allocation than by the well. And, Thompson emphasized, the Railroad Commission did retain the old per-well basis on two-thirds of the field, and limited the field size for the allocation on the remaining third to less than twenty acres, which, he argued, was not a large tract. "It was not an easy matter to please everybody," Thompson complained, but the commission had tried to "be as really fair to everyone as possible" and still issue an order that could be upheld in court.[37]

The Railroad Commission's new order cut daily production to about thirty-seven barrels of oil for each well. Because many of these wells were capable of ten thousand barrels per day, some of the independents so affected rushed back to court in search of relief. Many independents simply thumbed their noses at the order and continued to produce oil far in excess of the allowable. Hot oil in the amount of one hundred thousand barrels a day was now flowing out of East Texas. In a punitive reaction, the major oil companies dropped prices in December from about one dollar to sixty-five cents. Some crude was sold "off the market" for prices as low as fifty cents per barrel.[38]

Faced with a rapidly deteriorating situation, Thompson thought seriously about shutting down the field to give the Railroad Commission time to formulate yet another plan. When he heard that Thompson was considering a shutdown, Parten sent him a telegraph arguing that a shutdown would force producers to lay off their field workers, resulting in large-scale unemployment. Parten feared that the resulting economic dislocations in the local economies would increase criticism of the Railroad Commission and give support to those arguing for federal control. Thompson rejected Parten's advice and voted with his colleagues to order an immediate closure of the East Texas field until January 1, 1933. Parten's displeasure ended a few days later, however, when the Railroad Commission completely abandoned its compromise approach and issued new orders restoring allowables to Parten's favored per-well basis. The commission also issued a complicated formula limiting most wells to a production limit of from twenty-six to thirty-three barrels per day. The major oil companies reacted negatively to the commission's action. In January, in an apparent move to pressure the Texas Railroad Commission, Standard Oil of Indiana (Stanolind) cut its official East Texas price to fifty cents a barrel. Parten declared that Stanolind's action demonstrated "where proration has finally led us. As I see it East Texas will be compelled to demand a higher allowable oil production. . . ."[39]

The Railroad Commission's drastic curtailment of production in East Texas, coupled with the plunge in oil prices, was a severe blow to Parten's business interests. The Centex refinery had finally begun operations on June 13, 1932, more than two months later than planned. Refining twelve hundred barrels a day of the crude oil produced by the 160 stripper wells in the Moutray field, the refinery was pulling Parten out of an extremely tight financial jam. By mid-June, Parten informed Andrew Querbes that he could pay off his $150,000 loan within a few months. This prediction proved hopelessly optimistic, however. The Railroad Commission's proration order cut Woodley's production in East Texas by two-thirds, drastically reducing the company's income. As a result, Woodley's executive committee pleaded with Parten to open up the company's wells in East Texas to produce hot oil. Parten refused and told his board colleagues that regardless of what others were doing, Woodley would live within the proration allowable whether they liked the law or not. The year 1932, which started out so promising, ended badly for Woodley as the company actually earned less than it had the previous year.[40]

"A policy of vigilant combat"

In early December, as the latest oil-price crisis continued, the IPAT held its annual meeting in Fort Worth. In his keynote address, Parten denounced unitization, declaring that it threatened the sacred rule of capture, "our fundamental law of oil ownership." Parten called on the oil industry to work harder to increase consumption as a solution to low prices rather than forcing producers to keep their oil in the ground. Rallying his troops for the battle ahead, he argued that the IPAT could not afford a strategy of passive resistance. Instead, he urged the membership to embrace "a policy of vigilant combat." The IPAT's membership responded to Parten's call by passing resolutions denouncing market-demand prorationing, unitization, and the concept of an interstate oil compact to replace the state regulatory commissions. Pleased with their aggressive leadership, IPAT members reelected Parten as their president and Claude Wild as their executive vice president. They ended the meeting with a resolution instructing them to continue the fight against government intrusions into their business. Aware of an intense effort already being made by some major oil company executives to persuade President-elect Roosevelt to intervene in the oil crisis after his inauguration in March 1933, Parten now prepared for "vigilant combat" in the halls of Congress.[41]

Parten had thought about giving up the IPAT presidency at the annual meeting, but his fear of federal control eventually won out over his desire to give up the office. He was determined to fight any move by the federal government to control his business and the IPAT provided him a platform from which he could launch his attacks. The IPAT presidency gave Parten status as the official representative of a business organization, which in turn gave him better access to the press, legitimized his claims to be a representative of independent oil men, and granted him more authority when dealing with elected and appointed government officials.

Threatening Parten's plans for the IPAT, however, was the membership's refusal to provide their organization adequate financial support. Parten had been forced to provide nearly twenty-five thousand dollars of his own money to sustain the IPAT's daily operations and to publish the *Texas Independent* during the last four months of the year. In early January 1933, the IPAT was once again in financial difficulty. Adding to the organization's woes, Wild was forced to sue the IPAT for his unpaid back salary; its directors removed him as vice president, replacing him with Bailey W. Hardy, a former state legislator from Breckenridge. Hardy opened a new IPAT office in Austin.[42]

Despite this episode, Claude Wild maintained a close professional relationship with Parten. Wild knew Parten had done everything he could to solve the IPAT's financial problems and he did not hold the oil man responsible for what had happened. Parten, on the other hand, valued Wild's skills and judgement. He hired Wild to serve as his personal lobbyist in Austin. For the next several years, Wild lobbied the legislature and drafted bills for Parten and his associates to give to allied legislators, and he frequently represented Parten at Railroad Commission hearings.[43]

"Everybody got excited"

Despite the Texas Railroad Commission's new authority to restrict production to market demand, by the spring of 1933 the East Texas oil field was again out of control. A small group of East Texas independents continued their efforts in the courts to weaken the state's ability to restrict production. They filed suit asking the federal district court in Houston to overturn the commission's December 1932 proration order. In late January 1933, Parten and the Blalock brothers testified at the court hearings in support of the commission's order. Nevertheless, on March 17, 1933, the court ruled the commission's orders invalid, nullifying its December order. Although the court upheld market-demand prorationing because of the new Texas law, it ruled that the commission's arbitrary production allocation was confiscatory and overly restrictive because it failed to consider individual factors for each well. It ordered the commission to issue a new order. This was the final blow to Parten's fight for arbitrary allocations on a per-well basis. Attorney General Allred advised the Railroad Commission that the court decision meant that any total allowable under four hundred thousand barrels would be invalid. When the commission failed to issue a new order quickly enough, the court cited it for contempt for not having written an allowable order.

While the Railroad Commission deliberated, the situation in East Texas again became desperate. Oil flowed from wells pumping at flush production, sending prices to the bottom, as low in some cases as two-and-a-half cents a barrel (one lease owner posted a sign declaring "Three barrels of the best crude in the world for a bottle of beer.") Unable to produce oil as cheaply as the hundreds of small independents scattered throughout the field, some of the larger independents faced financial ruin. Several pipelines operated by persons suspected of running hot oil were mysteriously dynamited. The Texas Company slashed its official posted price from seventy-five cents to ten cents a barrel, an action which the Railroad Commission denounced as "the boldest and most sinister, coercive and high-handed action the major oil companies have yet taken in their efforts to control Texas."[44]

Fearful that state governments were unwilling to control the situation, many oil men who had previously opposed strict production controls now demanded relief. And it was apparent to many that only the federal government was capable of exercising effective control. Ray Dudley, an editorial writer for the *Oil Weekly*, charged that the Railroad Commission's allowable figures were "a ghastly joke. The Texas Railroad Commission has had its chance," Dudley wrote, ". . . results speak for themselves and the results indicate to us that the Commission is a failure." Parten later claimed that many oil men "panicked" and were "quite irrational" as a result of the crisis. "I think it's fair to say that the Texas Railroad Commission didn't have control of the situation," Parten admitted. "When the price of crude oil went down to ten cents a barrel, everybody got excited. They decided that they had to have federal control of oil production."[45]

CHAPTER 5

Oil and Politics

The New Deal and the Texas Legislature,
1933–1934

Franklin Delano Roosevelt took the oath of office as President of the United States on Saturday, March 4, 1933. In his stirring inaugural speech, the new president declared to the solemn crowd attending the ceremony that the American people were demanding that the federal government take "action, and action now" to restore prosperity in "these dark days" of the country's general economic emergency. A call for the president to back up his words with action soon emanated from such expected places as labor halls and soup lines, but an urgent demand also came from an unlikely source: the Standard Oil Company of New Jersey and other major oil companies.[1]

Almost immediately after Roosevelt moved into the White House, the American Petroleum Institute urged the new administration to impose production controls to stabilize the oil industry. Parten was not particularly alarmed by the API's demand for federal intervention. He was confident that Roosevelt was committed to the Democratic Party's campaign platform, which called for a balanced federal budget, the preservation of states' rights, and the strict enforcement of antitrust laws. Unknown to Parten, however, the API's executive committee sent James A. Moffett, a vice president of Standard of New Jersey, to lobby FDR three days after the inauguration to support a plan for the federal government to impose a reduction of about half a million barrels in daily national oil production. During the campaign, Moffett had been one of Roosevelt's strongest supporters within the business community and had served as a major fund-raiser for the Democratic Party. Moffett told the president that the oil industry was in chaos because a small minority of oil men were refusing to cooperate in the effort to curb production. Hot oil was driving the price of oil to such low levels, Moffett argued, that one of the country's basic industries was on the verge of collapse. The Standard Oil executive argued that the states were not enforcing their conservation laws, thus relief had to come from the federal government.[2]

Moffett's arguments persuaded the new president to act. On March 14, Roosevelt instructed his secretary of the interior, Harold L. Ickes, to invite representatives of the governors of Oklahoma, Texas, Kansas, and California to meet with federal officials and oil industry leaders on March 27 in Washington to propose ways to stabilize the oil industry and to determine to what extent the federal government should be involved in such an effort. The president asked Ickes, as the head of the federal department responsible for oil matters, to chair the conference and steer its deliberations.[3]

With his decision to turn the oil conference over to Ickes, Roosevelt was initiating a thirteen-year love-hate relationship between the oil industry and a man who was as strong-willed, persistent, and self-righteous as any person in government or business. Sharp of tongue, hypersensitive to criticism, protective of his bureaucratic fiefdom, and a formidable foe in the in-house administrative power struggles that afflicted the New Deal, Ickes quickly assumed a position as one of the new administration's most visible and controversial members. As an antitrust progressive who believed that the excesses of Big Business could be curbed only by the power of Big Government, Ickes's solution to most of the nation's economic ills and social injustices was for the federal government to play an active and, if necessary, a controlling role in whatever sector of the nation's business and public life intervention was warranted.[4]

When Ickes and his Interior Department staff examined the oil industry, they found, as one staffer described it, "a discouraged and disorderly mob." Ickes concluded that here was an industry to which only the federal government could bring order. As he learned more about the oil business, Ickes eventually came to view it as a public utility—with its activities, prices, and profits in need of strict federal controls. The secretary believed that the importance of oil to the economy and to national defense made federal control an absolute necessity. Holding strong views about the need to conserve nonrenewable natural resources, Ickes was also shocked by what he considered to be the terrible waste of a resource critical to the nation's economic health. Believing he was one of the few men capable of exercising vast powers over an industry like oil without being corrupted, Ickes wanted to be the oil industry's benevolent despot. Accordingly, he tried to broaden federal power over the industry, especially with respect to prices and production.[5]

As his staff prepared for the oil conference, Ickes anticipated a trouble-free and harmonious meeting. He asked Moffett to select the oil executives to serve as the industry spokesmen at the meeting. Moffett's choices came from the membership of the API. When Ickes invited the governors to attend or send their representatives to the conference, however, he ran into trouble. J. Edward Jones, a New York lawyer and oil investor close to the independent side of the industry and hostile to federal controls, found out about the conference. Jones quickly concluded that it was the opening move toward federal control. On March 16 he sent a telegram to the governors of the twenty-one oil-producing states informing them about the meeting and the fact that seventeen of the states were not invited. Jones warned that critical national problems related to the production of oil should not be resolved by only four governors, the secretary of the interior, and the API. He sent copies of the telegram to Parten and other leaders among the independents. Jones's telegram shocked Parten. Although he was expecting such a move toward federal control, he had thought that it would originate in Congress. The day after he received Jones's telegram, Parten sent Ickes a message expressing his concern that only the views of the major oil companies would be presented at the conference. He urged Ickes to invite J. Edward Jones to represent the independent view.[6]

Parten's telegram was among many others Ickes received protesting the absence of "true" independent representation at the oil conference. The protest was large enough to force Ickes to expand the conference to include nearly every faction in the oil industry: the API and the majors, the moderate independents represented by the IPAA, and dissident independents rigidly opposed to any regulation by the federal government. After Ickes broadened his invitation list, the IPAA's Wirt Franklin called a meeting of representatives of the independent component of the industry to meet in a pre-conference on March 26 at the Mayflower Hotel in Washington. Franklin wanted to formulate a program to submit to the official conference the next day. Parten was invited to attend as president of the IPAT. Eagerly accepting the invitation, he was convinced that "the forces of monopoly" had persuaded Roosevelt and Ickes to call the conference to further their scheme to control the oil industry and that most of the representatives were "hand picked by the API."[7]

Fight at the Mayflower

Accompanied by Myron and Jack Blalock, Parten traveled to Washington to attend the oil conference. When he arrived at the pre-conference gathering at the Mayflower Hotel on Sunday morning, March 26, he was not pleased with what he found. "The room was full of people hoping to make Harold Ickes the federal oil czar," Parten recalled. J. Edward Jones, who entered the meeting room with Parten and the Blalocks, later wrote that when he and his companions saw all of the API staff members and employees of the major oil companies, their suspicions about the conference were deepened. "It appeared to be the same old story," Jones wrote, "a meeting of independents packed by representatives of the majors!" The opening speeches confirmed their suspicions. Wirt Franklin informed the conferees that they were there to approve a statement that could be presented to the oil conference the next day as the official position of the country's independent oil men. Insisting on "harmony," Franklin declared that any person unwilling to cooperate with the will of the majority should leave the room. After Charles Roeser of the Texas Oil and Gas Conservation Association and other speakers declared that the federal government should take immediate action to end "the evil of overproduction," William Boyd, API vice president, read the draft of a resolution urging federal control of oil production at the wellhead. When one of Ickes's assistants declared that the resolution had the secretary's endorsement, Boyd made a motion that it be approved by voice vote.[8]

Outraged at an obvious attempt to cram the resolution down their throats,

Parten and Jack Blalock persuaded J. Edward Jones to go to the podium to denounce it. When Jones charged that the majors had taken over the meeting and were dictating a position to the independents, shouts and catcalls from the audience drowned him out. Wirt Franklin interrupted Jones to claim that the Independent Petroleum Association of America had joined with the API to endorse federal control of production. Franklin's statement outraged Parten. He had defeated the resolution to endorse federal controls at the last IPAA meeting the previous November. While statements were still being made from the floor, Parten quickly made his way up to the rear of the podium to confront Franklin. He reminded him that production controls had been voted down at the previous IPAA meeting. Franklin conceded that Parten was correct, but he believed that because new conditions now prevailed, the IPAA's membership would want him to support the API resolution. Angered by Franklin's unilateral and unauthorized decision, Parten shook his finger in Franklin's face and told him that he would do whatever he could to defeat his plan. Without waiting for a reply, Parten turned his back on Franklin and returned to his chair.[9]

When it came time to vote on Boyd's resolution, Parten made a statement from the floor challenging Wirt Franklin's right to make an official endorsement on behalf of the IPAA membership. Jumping to his feet and waving a clenched fist, Charles Roeser interrupted Parten by shouting that anybody opposed to the motion should "get the hell out of this room." Parten turned toward his critic and yelled, "Well, Mr. Roeser, I'm not going out of the room, and I don't think there's anybody in here who can put me out." As men in the audience moved between Parten and Roeser to prevent a physical confrontation, Franklin declared from the podium that Parten had a right to state his view and that no one needed to leave the room. "I want to say that Mr. Parten is exactly right," Franklin announced, "our Association did refuse to take such a stand in the month of November." He pointed out, however, that Parten was ignoring a resolution passed that same day endorsing the general idea of some type of restriction on domestic production. "I feel that if all of my membership were present today," Franklin said, "ninety percent of them would instruct me to vote for this resolution." The audience cheered.[10]

Feeling very much like the odd man out, Parten soon had another ally: John B. Elliott of California, an associate of William "Kill 'Em" Keck's Superior Oil Company, one of the nation's largest independent producers. "He was a very impressive figure," Parten recalled, "a big Democrat, and a great friend of Roosevelt." Elliott stood up, and with Bill Keck sitting quietly in the chair next to his, identified himself as representing the Independent Petroleum Association of California. He announced that his association joined Parten and Jones in opposition to the resolution. Suddenly confronted with an open rebellion, Franklin made a motion to have an eleven-man committee meet and discuss the issue immediately and prepare a formal plan for the independents to consider when they reconvened late that afternoon. Elliott, Keck, and their associates from California, however, denounced the entire proceeding as a frame-up by the majors and walked out of the meeting, taking Jones with them. Parten and the Blalocks remained, however, and Parten agreed to serve as a member of the committee.[11]

At the committee meeting, Parten discovered that a proposal to support federal control had already been drafted. Without discussion, the committee voted to accept the proposal and submit it to the general meeting. Parten wrote a minority report arguing that the delegates to the Washington Oil Conference were not "duly constituted to act as representative of the whole industry." He condemned the majority report's definition of waste as being economic rather than physical and criticized its call for the federal government to control production in order to manipulate prices, a practice, he declared, that was "both economically and socially wrong." Parten demanded the continuation of the oil import tariff; rigid enforcement of the antitrust laws; and a reduction in the size of the federal bureaucracy. When the general meeting reconvened, Parten read his report from the floor and announced that he would not waste his time trying to get it adopted because it was obvious that the meeting "had been stacked and steam rolled by the majors." He declared instead that his dissenting report would be hand-delivered to Ickes. Not surprisingly, the committee's majority report was adopted overwhelmingly.[12]

The Independent Petroleum Association Opposed to Monopoly

At two o'clock on the afternoon of March 27, the oil conference officially opened in the auditorium of the Interior Department building. Over two hundred industry leaders had rushed to Washington to attend. As Parten entered the auditorium with Jones, the Blalocks, and Elliott, they were stopped by a doorman who handed a telegram to Jones. It was an official communication from Gov. Ruby Laffoon of Kentucky, removing Jones as his state's representative at the conference. Laffoon had received a number of telephone calls the night before demanding that he remove Jones because of his alleged "anti-Roosevelt" stance. The governor did not want to offend the new presidential administration at a time when his state was hoping for federal relief from the Depression. As a result of the loss of his credentials, Jones was refused entrance into the auditorium. Outraged, Parten and Jones gathered their allies in another room in the Interior building, where they created an informal committee to work against Wirt Franklin, Charles Roeser, and their API associates.[13]

Meanwhile, Ickes opened the official conference without the dissident independents. At Ickes's request, Gov. Alf Landon of Kansas agreed to serve as chairman. Landon strongly supported the idea of appointing a federal dictator to allocate oil production quotas, declaring that "even the iron hand of a national dictator is preferable to a paralytic stroke." Ickes also requested the majors, independents, and other elected officials present to appoint three committees of five members each to hammer out an oil plan in consultation with Interior Department staff members. Walter Teagle of Standard of New Jersey and R. C. Holmes of Texaco represented the majors, while Wirt Franklin and Charles Roeser were among those chosen for the independents.[14]

After the morning session, Parten and his fellow dissidents met with California senators Hiram Johnson and William Gibbs McAdoo at a luncheon arranged by John Elliott, who was one of McAdoo's chief fund-raisers in California. Hiram Johnson was a close friend of Ickes. Pledging their support for the dissident's cause, both senators encouraged them to form a committee to meet privately with Ickes, who the senators believed could be won over to their side against the major companies. Accordingly, the dissidents organized themselves into a committee consisting of John Elliot (chairman), Parten, Jack Blalock, Will Reid of California, J. Edward Jones, and E. B. Howard and H. H. Champlin of Champlin Oil of Oklahoma.

When the dissident committee met with Ickes the next morning, he was overtly cold and aloof and clearly angered by their opposition. Ickes later noted in his diary that the oil men were "certainly all hot and bothered. They did a lot of haranguing and speech making. They really had a chip on their shoulders. In the end, I managed to find out they don't want . . . to curtail oil production, but they do want action to break up the big oil companies." While Elliott explained his committee's views, Ickes interrupted him, complaining loudly that they had caused all of the trouble by walking out of the meeting at the Mayflower Hotel the night before in an attempt to disrupt the conference before it even started. Ickes also attacked Jones for sending the telegram alerting all of the governors about the conference. Jones argued back, telling Ickes that he had been duped by the major oil companies. The problem with the oil industry, he argued, was not domestic overproduction, it was foreign imports. This tense discussion lasted nearly an hour. When it was over, however, Ickes surprised the oil men by asking them to return for more discussion the next morning. The committee's cause was not helped when Elliot met privately with Ickes after the others had left. Elliot warned Ickes that he needed to back the dissidents in the oil fight because he had considerable political clout in the White House as a result of having managed the Roosevelt campaign in California. Ickes wrote in his diary that Elliott had "threatened me rather crudely."[15]

During dinner that evening at the Shoreham Hotel, Parten and the other dissidents decided to create a more formal organization, naming it the Independent Petroleum Association Opposed to Monopoly. "In the New Deal era, you had to have a national organization to be heard," Parten later explained. The dissidents issued a press release the next morning claiming that they represented independent oil men who controlled 5 to 10 percent of the nation's total production. "The title was too long," Parten admitted, "but its purpose was expressed in its title." Some members of Parten's group, such as Fort Worth refiner Joe Danciger, represented the interests of small refiners in the Southwest and Southern California who lacked access to interstate pipelines and who depended on a supply of cheap crude oil to compete with the major refineries. The group also reflected the position of some independents whose oil properties were located in the high-production fields of East Texas, Southern California, and Oklahoma, and who felt that state production control unduly restricted their wells for the benefit of others.

Thinking in terms of their economic survival, these producers were more interested in antitrust reform than in federal intervention into their affairs. For example, when Jack Blalock was asked at a congressional committee hearing what role Congress could play to help solve the problems in the oil industry, he replied that it was simple, Congress could "revitalize the antitrust laws [and] dismember . . . these gigantic holding companies. . . ." The members of the Association Opposed to Monopoly also denied that oil was being overproduced, arguing instead that the excess oil coming into the domestic market was from foreign production. They agreed with the IPAA and Wirt Franklin that imports of petroleum should be restricted; but, unlike Franklin, who tried to bargain and work with the majors, they wanted a total embargo on oil imports.[16]

When Parten, Elliott, Jones, and their associates met with Ickes at ten o'clock the next morning, they handed the secretary the minority report Parten had written earlier. The only addition they made to the report was a demand to take pipelines away from the integrated companies. Small refiners and independent producers had demanded such action for years, arguing that through ownership of the primary means of transporting crude oil, the major corporations had restrained competition and controlled prices. Although the Hepburn Act of 1906 had declared interstate pipelines to be common carriers, small refiners and oil producers had not obtained open access to their use. In this second discussion with Ickes, the dissidents claimed that the oil industry was healthier than American industry in general. What problems it did have, they told Ickes, were caused by the monopolistic practices of the majors, burdensome taxation, and excessive government regulation. Charging that the Department of the Interior was full of spies and stooges for the majors who had deliberately misled him about the true state of the oil industry, the dissidents also warned Ickes to seek information from more trustworthy sources, such as themselves. Ickes, who was friendlier than he had been the previous day, promised the men that their proposals would be given a fair hearing. Nonetheless, Ickes was not persuaded by their arguments. He complained in private that the only thing the dissidents really wanted was to be free to pump "as much oil as possible, without restraint." He continued to work with the conference's formal committee of fifteen, which represented the vast majority of the capital invested in oil, if not the views of every oil producer. Although Elliott, Keck, and most of the other members of the group left Ickes's office with a firm dislike for the "old curmudgeon," Parten later admitted that Ickes was only taking a position advocated by "a vast majority of the oil and gas people of the nation. They wanted a Czar. He only showed a willingness to make the sacrifice and be that Czar."[17]

The next day, on March 30, the Association Opposed to Monopoly went to the White House and made their appeal to the president. Elliott, who had persuaded Senator McAdoo to arrange the appointment, served with Jack Blalock as a co-spokesman for the group. Roosevelt, who spent more than an hour with the men, captivated the group with his charm and ability to make them feel as though he were solidly on their side, although he was actually undecided. As the dissidents took their seats in a semicircle around his huge desk, the president smiled and declared that ordinarily there was only one teacher and many students, but today he was the one pupil and they were the teachers. "What can you teach me," Roosevelt asked, "what can the pupil do for the teachers?" Parten later recalled that they were received "most graciously and courteously by our great President. He showed immediate grasp of the tremendous problem." Roosevelt assured the men that he supported the principle of free competition and was opposed to monopolies. He agreed, for example, that pipelines should be divorced from the integrated companies. "With a rather grandiose, flourishing toss of his head," J. Edward Jones later recalled, "[the president] said . . . 'I think you are right. I am going to recommend it.'" Parten left the White House "greatly heartened." He and his companions were completely disarmed, confident that the president was on their side.[18]

Parten and his dissident colleagues bolstered Roosevelt's reluctance to add control over oil production to his executive powers. On April 4, the president sent word to Governor Landon that he could not accept the conference's recommendation that the federal government impose production controls, explaining that such action was a power reserved exclusively to the states. He did recommend, however, the passage of legislation prohibiting the interstate transportation of hot oil, as well as a law divorcing pipelines from the integrated companies. The first recommendation had been submitted by the official conference, while the second was the dissident group's suggestion. Roosevelt was giving something to both groups. Otherwise, he merely recommended that the governors continue to consult and work on the problem and that other actions could be taken at a future date after additional study.[19]

The dissidents' protest had affected Roosevelt's thinking, causing him to retreat, at least temporarily. Realizing the oil issue was far more complex and divisive than he and Ickes had originally assumed, the president sidestepped the issue and decided to do nothing until his administration could work out a general plan to address the overall problem of industrial recovery and reform. Parten, Elliott, and their allies had also made an impression on Ickes by appealing to his deeply ingrained antitrust sympathies, though those sympathies were restrained by his conviction that the dissidents were a bunch of greedy hot-oilers. Privately, Ickes also thought the time was not quite right for strong action. A week after the conference, he told a friend that the federal government should not make any "drastic" moves until they knew more about the oil industry "than we now know. . . ." Although Parten felt that the president's decision was an important victory for the dissidents, Roosevelt had endorsed only one of their recommendations—pipeline divorcement. Parten later admitted that as far as he was concerned the pipeline divorcement demand "was just a side issue that we knew would be very discomforting to the major oil companies, who were the principal support." Even this turned out to be an empty gesture. When the major oil companies protested, the administration dropped the idea.[20]

The Washington Oil Conference shattered the solidarity of the Independent

Petroleum Association, whose fragile unity had been maintained only because the organization had focused on one issue, oil imports. Wirt Franklin's stand in favor of federal controls led to the departure of several independents from the organization, including Parten and his Texas allies. When Franklin learned that Parten was leaving the IPA, he urged him to reconsider, arguing that they should continue working together in favor of policies on which they could agree, such as tighter restrictions on oil imports. Their differences over the federal control issue, Franklin said, should not "in any way affect our friendship. . . ." Parten, however, was not in a generous mood. Now convinced that Franklin was deceptive and untrustworthy, Parten broke off relations with him.[21]

"the law of the tooth and claw"

As soon as it appeared that the Washington Oil Conference was going to end inconclusively, the oil-war battle lines shifted to Austin, where Humble, Texaco, and the Texas Oil and Gas Conservation Association teamed with Gov. Miriam Ferguson in an attempt to transfer regulatory authority over the state's oil and gas production from the Railroad Commission to a proposed new Oil and Gas Commission whose members would be appointed by the governor. The major companies and their allies believed that an appointed commission would be easier to control than the popularly elected Railroad Commission. This effort gained momentum when it became apparent in late March 1933, that the Railroad Commission (over the strenuous objection of the Texas Oil and Gas Conservation Association) planned to issue a new proration order allowing high production quotas.[22]

A bill to create the new regulatory commission was submitted on April 3 and placed as the number-one item on the calendar of the Texas House of Representatives. When Parten heard this news, he rushed back to Austin, leaving Jack Blalock to monitor developments in Washington. As soon as he arrived in Austin, he hurriedly organized a small group to fight the bill. "We had to stop the bill in the House," he said, "we figured if it got to the Senate, it was going to be hard to beat, because many of the Senators were doing work for the major oil companies." Parten's strategy against the proposed commission included the submission of two other bills that could be used as bargaining chips in the event of a legislative stalemate. One bill divorced the state's pipelines from ownership by integrated companies, while the other taxed oil on a graduated basis, the higher the production, the higher the tax, forcing the majors to bear the brunt. Parten's legislative tactics effectively stalled the Oil and Gas Commission bill in committee. In an attempt to break the stalemate, the commission's advocates added a tax provision to their legislation with the idea that the Senate would delete it. This ploy failed and the bill was held up in the House for three additional weeks.[23]

While the maneuvering in the House continued, the Railroad Commission, under threat of another contempt citation from the federal court, finally issued a new proration order on April 22 which set the total East Texas allowable at the extremely high level of 750,000 barrels per day. Although the allowable level was double the amount that engineers claimed could be safely pumped out without damaging the field, the Railroad Commission had finally issued an order that was acceptable to the courts. The timing could not have been worse as far as Parten's efforts in the legislature were concerned. The new order was seen by some law-makers as final proof that the Railroad Commission was incapable of managing the problem of overproduction. Ernest Thompson, Parten later noted, "just took the bull by the horns" and raised the allowable high enough for the commission to get a legal proration order in place. When the commission issued its order, Parten claimed, "Roeser and his crowd went to Austin and cried, 'You've wrecked the oil business, you've wrecked everything.'"[24]

The major oil companies, invoking what Humble's Will Farish described as "the law of the tooth and claw," immediately announced drastic cuts in the price of East Texas crude. Texaco took the lead by dropping its price from fifty cents to ten cents a barrel. The other major companies quickly followed. Although this price-cut was partially the result of the Railroad Commission's new allowable, there is much evidence to suggest that it was more drastic than was necessary and that it was done to pressure the Texas House into passing the Oil and Gas Commission bill. Parten reacted bitterly to the price-cut. Invoking vivid Populist rhetorical images, he complained in an interview published in the Fort Worth *Star-Telegram* that "no more merciless rawhide was ever used on the backs of slaves than this political whip which is being wielded on the backs of our present Railroad Commission in order to have them obey those monopolistic interests who would be their masters. If the great octopus slashes the price of oil . . . from fifty cents . . . to ten cents per barrel over night and then blames it on the Railroad Commission . . . how much longer will the people of Texas stand for this outra-geous abuse by the forces of monopoly?" [25]

Crude oil at ten cents a barrel was all the advocates of the Oil and Gas Commission needed. The House passed the bill by a six-vote margin on April 24. "They got it out about 5:30 in the afternoon," Parten noted, "and it looked like the jig was up." Parten and his allies believed there was no possibility of defeating the bill in the Senate. The same evening the House passed the bill, Parten was in his room in the Stephen F. Austin Hotel visiting with Claude Wild and Jim Abercrombie, a prominent Houston independent oil man, when a loud rapping on the door interrupted their conversation. Parten opened the door and in stepped Charles Roeser and three drilling contractors. Full of alcohol and arro-gance, Roeser sprawled on Parten's bed and declared in a loud voice, "well now, Major, we've beaten you in the House, and we're gonna pass this bill in the Senate. Won't you be a good fellow and join us to make it unanimous, so we can all be happy with the new Oil and Gas Commission?" Roeser laughed and then asked if there was any liquor in the room. Parten poured them all a drink. "Charlie was a very likable fellow until he had a few drinks," Parten later claimed, "but when he had a few drinks, it seemed to change his whole personality." Parten and Abercrombie chatted with the men for a few minutes and then left them with Claude Wild, telling Wild to "give them all they want to drink and take care of them." Parten went to dinner. After consuming more of Parten's liquor, Roeser and his colleagues went to the lobby of the hotel, where they spied Cong. Gordon Burns of Huntsville, one of the leading opponents of the Oil and Gas Commission bill. Roeser staggered over to Burns and began yelling and cursing at him, accusing the legislator of accepting bribes to vote against the Oil and Gas Commission. Burns, who was in his early thirties and younger than Roeser, yelled back and the two threw punches at each other. Some of Roeser's burly friends pulled Burns off Roeser, threw him to the floor, and kicked him savagely. Badly bruised and bleeding, Burns was rushed to the hospital.[26]

The next morning, after visiting Burns in the hospital, Parten went straight to the Capitol to see what was happening in the House and Senate. Members were on the floor taking turns condemning the "oil lobbyists" who had assaulted their colleague. "And that didn't displease me," Parten admitted. As he was leaving the Capitol, Parten ran into an old law-school friend who was working for the Roeser group. "The Legislature this morning is wholly irrational," he complained to Parten, "can't you agree with me that we ought not to let any consideration of that new Oil and Gas Commission bill be considered until this irrationality can quiet down?" Parten replied, "I want to be utterly frank with you. If there's any way in the world I can help get that bill up in the Senate before nightfall, I'm gonna do it." Although the vote on the bill did not come that soon, Parten, Wild, and their associates worked to keep emotions high and saw to it that everyone kept the incident in their minds. Nevertheless, the Senate State Affairs Committee passed the bill on Friday, April 28. On May 1, Humble turned the screws tighter, declaring that it would no longer post prices for oil in East Texas. The pressure intensified.[27]

The Senate convened as a committee of the whole on May 2 to hear testimony on the Oil and Gas Commission bill. Attorney General Allred, Commissioner Thompson, and Parten were chosen to make the opposition case. In his testimony, Parten made a strongly legalistic argument, reading extensively from court decisions. He told the Senate that the majors were seeking the establishment of the new commission as part of their effort to drive the small independents out of business. He charged that the proposed Oil and Gas Commission would help bring about federal control. Because the members of the new commission would be appointed, he declared, it would soon fall under the control of the major companies. The major companies would have the commission issue a proration order that would lower allowables to such an extent that the federal courts would overturn it. Parten argued that this would remove all controls from the field, resulting in a panic that would force the federal government to take over the industry. He stressed that if the Railroad Commission's recent prorationing order was valid, "it can and will be enforced and the need for a Federal Dictator of Oil production will be totally eliminated." Parten admitted to the senators that he had opposed market-demand prorationing until recently. He was now willing to accept it, but only if managed by the Railroad Commission. He believed that agency, as presently structured, would protect the interests of the independents.[28]

Because of the friendly questions he was asked afterward, Parten was encouraged by the Senate's reaction to his testimony. Allred and Thompson also made presentations that seemed to be well received by the Senate. But Parten's forces still had one more card to play. During the debate that followed, Congressman Burns was brought into the Senate chamber in a wheelchair. He did not speak, but everyone had an opportunity to see how badly injured he was. After the hearing, the Senate voted against the new commission bill by a vote of twenty to ten. The next day, the major oil companies raised oil prices from ten cents to twenty-five cents a barrel, providing further evidence that the majors had cut the price in an attempt to force the legislature to pass the Oil and Gas Commission bill. The vote was a significant victory for Parten, Allred, Thompson, and their allies in the IPAT. "The situation in Texas is apparently safe," Parten told John Elliot, "we have beaten them badly in this fight, and they were hard losers . . . ." Parten's leadership in this affair earned him Ernest Thompson's respect as well as his gratitude. "Ernest has a very high regard for your opinion," one of the commissioner's friends told Parten after the defeat of the Oil and Gas Commission bill. "In recent months I have grown to feel that he welcomes frank advice from you. . . ."[29]

After the Railroad Commission's authority over oil had been preserved in the legislature, the federal courts gave the commission some significant help. In decisions issued in May and June, the courts upheld the commission's proration order as well as the state's Market Demand Proration Law. Most important, the court deferred to the judgement of the commission on technical questions related to the determination of appropriate prorationing levels. This shifted the burden of proof to the plaintiffs and bolstered the commission's authority. For the first time, the Texas Railroad Commission could enforce its proration orders with the confidence that the federal courts would uphold them. Armed with a valid proration order, the commission focused its attention on enforcement.[30]

Before the end of the 1933 session, the legislature passed a law making violations of the Railroad Commission's proration orders a felony. Nevertheless, hot oil continued to be a severe problem. Hot-oilers were too numerous and some too clever for the Railroad Commission's understaffed and underpaid enforcement agents to handle. Bill Murray, a Railroad Commission field investigator in the 1930s and later a commissioner, has recalled that there was a "Robin Hood philosophy that the oil belongs to everybody . . . I wouldn't steal from my neighbor, but if I steal from the field as a whole, that's all right. So it became sort of a community philosophy that running hot oil wasn't really bad." Hot-oilers devised a number of imaginative methods to get oil out of the field, such as installing valves that opened the wrong way so that when an agent believed it was being closed it was actually being opened. Perhaps the most popular trick was one known as the "bypass," which involved a series of piping arranged in such a complicated pattern that investigators never knew from what wells the oil was actually flowing. An operator in Gladewater used one of the more outrageous ploys. He built a concrete blockhouse over his oil well and attached the structure to a house he subsequently claimed was his home. Local people referred to the building as the "fortress of

Gladewater." The operator claimed that his home was his castle, and therefore, no representative of the Texas Railroad Commission could legally enter and check the well. Some operators simply hired guards who kept agents out at gunpoint. Rural residents in East Texas became accustomed to oil-tank trucks full of hot oil driving recklessly fast down gravel back roads in the forest at all times of the night with their headlights off.[31]

Parten and many of his allies in the fight against federal control recognized that hot oil was now their most serious problem. Accordingly, they supported the Railroad Commission's intensified efforts to stop the hot-oil trade during the summer of 1933. Parten believed that the current allowable would support reasonable prices, but that hot oil would continue to disrupt that plan. As IPAT president, Parten pleaded with his colleagues to support the Railroad Commission's proration order. "Regardless of our personal likes or dislikes for proration," Parten told the membership, "unless the East Texas situation is so handled to eliminate . . . all of the proration violations, we will have federal control from which we will never recover. It is in view of this that we are requesting all individual oil men to cooperate in support of the present order. . . ." Parten advised John Elliot that the elimination of hot oil in Texas was "the only thing, in my opinion, that will avoid Federal interference."[32]

Despite Parten's pleas and the Railroad Commission's stepped-up efforts to enforce its proration order, hot oil flowed out of East Texas in the spring and summer of 1933. Demands for federal intervention continued, soon leading to the formal introduction in Congress of the type of federal legislation J. R. Parten feared the most. The oil-war battlefront now returned to Washington.

CHAPTER 6

Oil and Politics

"A Small, Pugnacious and Selfish Minority," 1933

W hen the major oil companies dropped the price of oil to ten cents a barrel during the battle to pass the Oil and Gas Commission bill in the Texas legislature in mid-spring 1933, Harold Ickes decided that federal intervention could no longer be delayed. Frustrated by the industry's inability to get its own house in order, Ickes instructed the Interior Department's solicitor, Nathan Margold, to draft a bill to bring the oil industry under federal control. In April, Cong. Ernest W. Marland of Oklahoma submitted Margold's draft to the House of Representatives, while Arthur Capper of Kansas submitted it to the Senate. The Marland-Capper bill proposed to grant sweeping powers to Secretary Ickes to control oil production, oil imports, and storage. Among these powers was the authority to set maximum and minimum prices and to assign legally binding production quotas to each state. The law banned from interstate commerce oil from any state that failed to enforce its quota.[1]

Ickes sent a copy of the bill to Roosevelt on May 1, explaining that it provided for the secretary of the interior to "in effect be an oil dictator. . . ." Ickes told Roosevelt that "whatever may be the cause for the low price for oil, the fact is it is . . . now selling in the east Texas field at the ruinous rate of ten cents a barrel." When Sen. Hiram Johnson urged Ickes to withdraw the Interior Department's support for Marland-Capper, Ickes refused, claiming that "only a very small group in the oil industry are opposing Federal control." Referring to the Elliott-Parten dissidents, Ickes told Johnson that they had promised that the oil-price crisis "will right itself if left alone." Ickes argued that because he and Roosevelt had taken "this small minority at its word . . . prices have become demoralized and the utter collapse of this important industry is threatened." Ickes was now convinced that the Elliott-Parten dissidents were acting as a front for the hot-oilers and that hot oil was "one of the major difficulties of this whole situation." He felt that if the independents were so frightened by the majors, they should welcome federal control because "there is only one power in the US stronger than the major oil companies, and that is the Federal Government. The states have shown themselves to be helpless."[2]

Believing he was responding to the wishes of the vast majority of the oil industry, Ickes had made certain that the Marland-Capper bill gave him all the authority he needed to restore order in the oil patch. The bill, however, alarmed many in the industry who had earlier supported the call for federal regulation of production. The head of Stanolind declared that federal regulation was necessary but a federal oil dictator was not. However, R. C. Holmes, president of Texaco, strongly supported the bill, as did Wirt Franklin. Governor Ferguson of Texas also announced support for the bill, explaining that it was necessary because she believed the Railroad Commission was in collusion with the hot-oil runners. The Texas legislature, on the other hand, passed a resolution against Marland-Capper. Reflecting the split that was developing among those who had advocated federal controls, the API's board of directors decided not to take a public position on the Marland-Capper bill.[3]

In late May, when Parten was certain that the Oil and Gas Commission was dead, he and Jack and Myron Blalock rushed to Washington to work against Marland-Capper. Jack Blalock served as the Parten-Keck coalition's main lobbyist against the bill, meeting with individual congressmen and testifying at hearings. Although he was officially working on behalf of the IPAT, Parten paid all of his own expenses as well as most of the expenses of the Blalocks. As one of the Blalock brothers noted, Parten was spending "much more money on this fight than any-one else" among the independents. However, unlike the situation with the IPAT, in which Parten had been forced to pay most of the association's expenses out of his own pocket, the increased threat of federal control now opened the wallets of some of the independents in Houston, including Jim Abercrombie, Hugh Roy Cullen, Mike Hogg, and Jim West Sr.[4]

One source of support Parten studiously avoided was the hot-oil crowd. Not only was Parten seeking to stop hot oil, he also knew that Ickes suspected him of being a hot-oiler. Ickes's suspicions were understandable but misdirected. Parten steadfastly refused to produce hot oil, even when Woodley's directors had pleaded with him to do so in 1932. "These hot oilers were very pleased to see the resistance we were giving to federal control," Parten recalled, "but, hell, they weren't financ-ing us, and we weren't a part of them. That puzzled a lot of people." Among Parten's erstwhile supporters was Clint Murchison, who openly admitted to trad-ing in hot oil. When Murchison showed up in Washington and asked what he could do to help, Parten told him "you can get out of town and stay out." Murchison accepted the advice and returned to Texas.[5]

The National Industrial Recovery Act

The opponents of the Marland-Capper bill were able to stall it in committee. By then, however, President Roosevelt had become interested in New York senator Robert Wagner's bill to establish a federally monitored national system of indus-trial self-regulation and cooperation to allow businesses to coordinate activity without fear of antitrust laws. On May 20, 1933, the president suggested to Congress that it might incorporate regulation of the oil industry in Wagner's general industrial recovery program, which was officially called the National Industrial Recovery Act (NIRA).[6]

The Marland-Capper bill was redrafted as an amendment to Wagner's NIRA bill. Parten was appalled when he discovered that the amendment retained most of the original Marland-Capper provisions, including the one authorizing the federal government to set production quotas. Parten and Blalock lobbied Texas's influential congressman Sam Rayburn, Texas senator Tom Connally, and Vice Pres. John Nance Garner, urging them to modify the NIRA oil-industry amendment to preserve the Railroad Commission's authority to set its own production quotas. In response, Senator Connally drafted another version of the amendment that eventually became section nine of the NIRA bill. It included a key subsection nine (c) which gave the president power to ban hot oil from interstate commerce, but left it to the state regulatory agencies to determine their own allowables. While subsection nine (c) was being written in committee, Blalock monitored every word, notifying Parten, Thompson, and Allred by telegram every time the committee considered a change in the amendment and asking for their immediate reaction. Blalock passed their suggestions on to Connally and Rayburn.[7]

Blalock's hard work paid off. The Connally amendment represented the most in power over oil that Parten, Thompson, and their allies were willing to see transferred from Austin to Washington. When Ickes had another amendment submitted to Congress in an effort to kill Connally's, Senator Connally and Senator McAdoo of California threatened to kill the entire NIRA bill. Roosevelt quickly forced Ickes to retreat. The president hoped to make the National Industrial Recovery Act the cornerstone of his program to pull the country out of the Depression. On June 8, a happy Jack Blalock wired IPAT vice president Bailey Hardy that "the Ickes Amendment [to the Wagner bill] was killed tonight on floor of Senate. . . . I regard this as a signal victory. . . ."[8]

President Roosevelt signed the National Industrial Recovery Act into law on June 16, 1933, calling it the "most important and far-reaching legislation ever enacted by . . . Congress." The law gave Roosevelt unprecedented peacetime authority to regulate the nation's business sector. As one student of the act has concluded, the NIRA was popular because in the vagueness of its prescriptions it meant very different things to different people. To many of the nation's largest corporations, it meant the beginning of a type of legalized monopoly. Unions saw it as a fair-labor law. To others it offered an opening move toward the creation of a centrally planned, collectivist democracy. To J. R. Parten and his allies opposed to federal regulation, it was a decidedly mixed blessing. They deplored the fact that the NIRA guaranteed a larger role for the federal government in their industry. Nevertheless, they had thwarted Ickes's attempt to impose federal control over every important phase of their business. Parten understood that one reason Marland-Capper had been killed was because of the alternative represented by the NIRA bill. In addition, subsection nine (c) strengthened the Texas Railroad

Commission by empowering the federal government to serve as the commission's hot-oil policeman. Overall, Parten had reason to be relieved if not happy.[9]

The NIRA was an experiment in industrial self-government that required each industry to devise a code to govern its activities. The National Recovery Administration, headed by Gen. Hugh Johnson, was created to work with every major industry to produce the codes and to supervise their implementation. The continuing tensions within the oil industry, however, threatened to undermine the attempt to produce an oil code. On June 17, 1933, the API and representatives of some of their allied associations met in Chicago to draft the version of the oil code they expected to be adopted at the NRA conference in Washington in July. Although Parten grudgingly accepted some kind of oil code as inevitable (he admitted to the IPAT membership that the code would be written "regardless of our personal likes or dislikes"), he and his IPAT colleagues boycotted the code meeting in Chicago. He expected the API leadership to force the Chicago conference to accept the type of code the API wanted. Writing off the Chicago meeting as a lost cause, he decided to save his efforts for the Washington conference, where he could use his political influence to better advantage.[10]

The API's attempt to present the Chicago meeting with a fait accompli met with unexpected contention. There were disputes among the majors over the issues of federal authority to set a minimum price for oil and whether the industry should establish a minimum wage and a forty-hour work week. The labor wage-and-hours provision was especially unpopular and was deleted from the final plan, only to be reinserted after the NRA's General Johnson told them it was required. These disputes and others were carried over to the Washington hearings. John Elliott, who attended the Chicago meeting as a member of the NRA administrative board, sent Parten a copy of the final draft. Parten was displeased when he saw that the draft code took away each state's right to set its own production allowable. Concluding that the draft code would be "derogatory to the interests of Texas . . . producers," Parten prepared for yet another battle in Washington.[11]

Before the Washington NRA conference began, Ernest Thompson made a decision that ultimately did much to help Parten and his allies in their effort to get a final oil code that was more acceptable to the Texas Railroad Commission and the IPAT. On July 8, Thompson asked President Roosevelt to invoke NIRA's subsection nine (c) for Texas. The president agreed. He issued an executive order four days later designating Secretary Ickes as his enforcement agent. Ickes and his staff reacted almost immediately, issuing a set of enforcement regulations requiring well owners to file monthly production and sales reports to the Interior Department's investigation division and to sign an oath that they had not run hot oil. Oil transporters and refiners also had to file reports. Ickes sent federal agents into the East Texas field to examine refinery records, test oil gauges, and inspect storage tanks. Agents even dug up pipelines to verify the accuracy of reports. Hot-oil producers filed dozens of lawsuits demanding injunctions to stop the inspections. Nonetheless, Roosevelt's quick response to Thompson's request had an immediate and significant effect on hot-oil movements out of East Texas.[12]

The NRA Code Conference

The results of this new enforcement activity were not yet apparent, however, when the NRA code conference opened in Washington on July 24. More than a thousand oil men from every oil-producing region in the United States gathered in the heat and humidity of late summer in the nation's capital. Among them were Parten, Jack Blalock, and San Antonio oil man Harry Pennington, who were attending the conference as IPAT representatives. Parten brought with him a proposal for an oil code that an IPAT committee had drafted under Bailey Hardy's supervision and that Parten planned to offer as an alternative to the API's code.[13]

Harold Ickes was determined to play an influential role in the oil-code conference. After the fiasco of the oil conference the previous March, Ickes realized that he needed his own sources of expert advice on the legal issues relating to the oil industry. To meet that need, he hired two young legal scholars, J. Howard Marshall and Norman Meyers, to serve as his personal aides. Marshall, a Quaker with a chemistry degree from Havorford College, was a brash, highly opinionated, twenty-eight-year-old assistant to the dean of the Yale Law School. Meyers, an economist at the Brookings Institute, had been a friend of Marshall's while working on his doctorate at Yale. Both were strong advocates of federal regulation of oil production. To bring stability to the industry, they advised Ickes that the federal government would have to impose oil production quotas for each state. If a state failed to enforce its quota, its oil would be prohibited from interstate commerce. They also urged mandatory unitization of oil-field pools. Marshall and Meyers reported to Ickes that the Parten-Keck dissident group was a "small pugnacious and selfish minority" within the industry that had grown wealthy running hot oil. They warned that even though the dissidents were small in number they were persistent, aggressive, and enjoyed significant political influence through Vice President Garner and other key Texas and California congressmen. Among the dissidents, Marshall and Meyers considered J. R. Parten to be the most articulate and effective foe of federal control.[14]

Taking the offensive against Parten and "his pals," Ickes asked Marshall and Meyers to gather evidence to prove Parten was dealing in hot oil. Ickes hoped to use such evidence to embarrass Parten at the appropriate time during the oil-code conference. While Marshall and Meyers travelled throughout East Texas as part of another assignment to gather information to be used in drafting regulations for subsection nine (c), they also quietly searched for the evidence needed to expose Parten. "We searched and searched," Marshall reported back to Ickes, "and discovered that Parten is clean as a whistle. Even his worst enemies say he is no hotoiler; he obeys the rules even if he dislikes them. Parten's concerns are pretty clearly based on principles." Marshall came away from the assignment with a newly found respect for the Texas oil man. During the Washington code conference, Marshall walked up to Parten and Blalock and announced that he and Meyers had just returned from Texas on their special mission to discover if Parten was running hot oil. He told Parten that they failed to find one speck of dirt on his record and had duly reported that to Ickes. Although Marshall thought Parten's fight against the government was wrongheaded, he wanted him to know that he respected his integrity. Parten and Marshall soon became good friends, despite their differences over oil policy.[15]

At the code conference, the Parten dissidents pushed the same agenda they had favored at the first oil conference in March: pipeline divorcement, strict enforcement of antitrust laws, a ban on oil imports, a continuation of the executive order prohibiting the transport of hot oil in interstate commerce, administration of the code by the Department of Commerce rather than the NRA itself, and opposition to unitization. Although most of them disliked it, the Parten group agreed to accept a minimum-wage and maximum-work-week provision. This was partly a strategic move, because Blalock was convinced that it would not hurt the industry and that it would please Roosevelt. Blalock told Parten that the president was "concerned . . . almost exclusively . . . with this feature in order to put men to work and increase purchasing power of labor. . . ." They also did not object to federal recommendations on future market demand, but insisted that production quotas had to consider a state's potential production.[16]

Early in the conference, Parten persuaded Jimmy Allred to come to Washington and testify. Allred told the conference that the code should require uniform prices for crude of the same gravity and quality in all fields. He pointed out that purchasers were posting West Texas oil at prices far below the average market price. Howard Marshall and Norman Meyers encouraged Allred to talk with Ickes about the problem because the same discrimination was being made against oil on western federal lands and the federal government was losing money on royalties. At the meeting, Ickes stubbornly refused to consider the Texan's proposal. Ickes grumbled that he would not be interested in trying to do anything for a state whose senators opposed a bill (Marland-Capper) that would have given him the power to deal with just such a problem. Allred left Ickes's office angry and determined to fight harder against the secretary's schemes.[17]

A disagreement between key executives within Standard of New Jersey over the price-control issue soon surfaced at the conference. Jersey Standard vice president J. A. Moffett agreed with Ickes in strongly favoring federal price-regulation. He was bitterly opposed by his fellow Jersey executives Will Farish and Walter Teagle, who eventually forced Moffett to resign over the issue. Parten decided to accept some type of price-regulation feature, but not price-fixing. Harry Sinclair convinced Parten that regulating the supply but not the price of oil would give the majors an unfair advantage. It would force small refiners, such as Parten, to buy crude at a high price determined by market-demand proration allowables and sell gasoline in a highly competitive market at an unregulated low price. Bailey Hardy polled the IPAT directors on the issue. They agreed to the change as long as it was "fair to all of the affected branches of the industry."[18]

The Parten group, now joined by Edwin A. Pauley, a forceful independent from California, submitted the only oil-code alternative to the API plan. Their version was not accepted, but the group did influence overall deliberations and the final code. After a few days of contentious debate, NRA administrator Hugh Johnson realized that the oil industry was too deeply divided to produce a code on its own. The oil codes were especially critical for the prestige and ultimate success of the NRA because oil was such a basic industry. Johnson decided to hammer out his own version, which provided for federal quotas but not for price controls. Johnson's plan failed to satisfy the quarreling oil men, so the hearings adjourned on August 2 without producing a code. Defeated, General Johnson announced that it would now be up to the president to have an oil code written.[19]

Parten and his associates were now determined to play a role in the effort to produce a final version in the White House. Joining forces with Thompson and Allred, they launched an all-out lobbying campaign in Congress and with the president's staff against any provision in the final code giving the federal government control over production. General Johnson's version provided that if a state exceeded its federal quota, all of its oil would be banned from interstate commerce. Parten argued that this provision would transfer power from Austin to Washington. Under subsection nine (c), the president was given the power to enforce state quotas, but nothing was said about compulsory federal quotas. This battle had been waged over the Marland-Capper bill and the NIRA legislation. Now the Interior Department, some of the major companies, and the IPAA were trying to get it in from another direction, through the NRA code.

When General Johnson submitted his draft to the president, Ickes immediately countered with an alternative proposal calling for rigid price and production controls. By this time, however, the federal agents Ickes had sent to East Texas had stemmed the flow of hot oil. On August 17, Ernest Thompson appealed directly to President Roosevelt in a letter, declaring that Johnson's revised code "violated the sovereignty of Texas." He told the president that because nine (c) was proving to be an effective weapon against hot oil, compulsory federal quotas were unnecessary. He urged that the code simply be revised to allow the federal government to recommend quotas. Thompson's appeal was effective. On August 19, Roosevelt ordered Ickes and Johnson to accept the Railroad Commissioner's recommendation. This was done and the president approved the code that same day.

The final code gave the president the power to ban interstate and foreign shipment of hot oil by executive order, as well as the authority to set minimum and maximum prices for periods not to exceed ninety days. The code also preserved limitations on foreign imports. Roosevelt, who was losing confidence in Johnson, designated the interior secretary to be the oil code administrator on August 30, 1933. The president gave Ickes the authority to recommend monthly production quotas to each state based on oil-demand forecasts from the Bureau of Mines and on advice from a committee of fifteen industry representatives. Theoretically representative of the industry, in reality this Production and Coordination Committee was stacked heavily in favor of those supporting federal price-fixing authority. Ickes made certain that the Parten group was ignored when Roosevelt made the appointments. When he heard who had been appointed to the committee, John Elliott complained to Jack Blalock that he felt he had been "left naked before mine enemies." Parten and his associates refused to sign the code because of their lack of representation on the committee of fifteen and because of the code's failure to demand antitrust reform.[20]

Some of the dissidents felt that the oil code represented a total defeat for their cause. Parten disagreed. Despite his refusal to sign the code, Parten believed that their effort had not been entirely without results. Parten told John Elliott that he was certain "that the Code as finally written was a distinct improvement over the Chicago Code." He believed that they had also educated Roosevelt, Ickes, and Congress about the pitfalls of federal controls, which would "serve our purpose well in time to come." Parten admitted to his fellow IPAT members that the code had "several imperfections," but he urged them to abide by it, warning that the code's failure could lead to harsher regulations. Nevertheless, Parten retained a skeptical attitude toward the NRA oil code, believing it might prove destructive to free enterprise in the long run. "I realize fully that my viewpoint is that of a distinct minority among oil men," Parten admitted to a colleague. "I am sincerely hoping that this whole program will have good results, even though I can't help thinking silently that one day the oil business will be very glad to retrace some of the steps we are now taking."[21]

Despite his negative opinion, Parten was earning much more money as a result of the NRA. The ban on hot oil in interstate commerce raised the price of oil to one dollar a barrel, where it remained as long as the NRA code was in effect. In May, when the price of oil had fallen to twenty-five cents a barrel, Parten had made the wise decision to place about three hundred thousand barrels of Woodley's crude in storage. Soon after the completion of the NRA oil code, he told Andrew Querbes that the jump in price would almost double the value of Woodley's stored oil. In addition, Parten's net monthly income from production more than doubled. Parten admitted in Woodley's 1933 annual report that "the restricted flow of wells will greatly lengthen the . . . life of production . . . of oil in [East Texas]." Woodley reported a "sharp gain" of 66 percent in per-share earnings for 1933 over the previous year.[22]

"It is admitted that this is a profitable price"

While Parten was working in Washington as IPAT president, the organization itself was barely breathing. Its members continued to act as though the IPAT could exist without money. Compounding the problem was Claude Wild's lawsuit seeking payment of past-due salary. Before leaving Texas to attend the oil-code conference, Parten made an effort to get the delinquent oil men to pay their debt to Wild so that the suit could be dismissed. Parten tried to keep the suit as quiet as possible because of his fear that it might hurt the IPAT's reputation and destroy his credibility in Washington. Wild warned Parten that he was "fully aware . . . that such action would destroy the influence of the association, but if no one is interested in it then evidently there won't be much to destroy." Despite this threat, Parten was able to keep the IPAT together until the code conference adjourned. When he returned to Texas, Parten raised enough money to settle the suit out of court, sparing the IPAT much embarrassment.[23]

Believing the fight against federal control and market-demand prorationing to be over for the immediate future, tired of the never-ending need to raise money for the IPAT, and frustrated by the difficulties of trying to organize people who distrusted organizations, Parten refused to accept another term as IPAT president. He told a friend that he planned to "sit back and ride in the boat for a while and let others navigate." In his farewell speech at the annual meeting in December 1933, Parten observed that "at this time most operators appear to be very well satisfied because they have one dollar oil. It is admitted that this is a profitable price." He hoped that it would continue, but he still believed that "much work remains to be done in Texas if the interest of the independent oil man is to be protected."[24]

As the months passed, a growing number of independents came to share Parten's negative view of the NRA. The industry committee working with Ickes to administer the code raised suspicions by holding closed meetings to discuss policy. Because the major companies controlled the committee, some independents complained that they were being regulated and judged by their giant competitors who were getting vital competitive information from the Interior Department, fixing production and refining quotas, and generally implementing trade practices that limited competition. Big Oil had moved into the federal government in a significant way.[25]

CHAPTER 7

Oil and Politics

The Ickes Bill, 1934

Expansion into Texas had been a positive development for Woodley Petroleum, but it had an ultimately negative impact on the Parten marriage. It encouraged J. R.'s workaholic lifestyle, taking him away from home for weeks at a time. Even at home, his mind tended to remain in the office or in the oil field. Making matters worse was his inability to share his emotions with others. Reserved and somewhat self-absorbed, J. R.'s inner life remained very much his own. Too often he left Opal wondering how he really felt about their relationship. Not surprisingly, their marriage suffered. Unable to have a child, bored with the daily routine of life in Shreveport, emotionally deprived by a frequently absent husband, and eager to see more of the world, Opal made a separate life for herself. In January 1928, she moved to New York City to begin work on her master's degree in English at Columbia University. She rented an apartment in Greenwich Village and spent most of the next three years there. Aware of Opal's boredom as well as her need for an intellectual challenge, J. R. encouraged and supported the move. Neither of them saw it as a "separation" in terms of their marriage, but in reality that was what it was.[1]

J. R. Parten's responsibilities as IPAT president in 1932 and 1933 and his direct involvement in the struggle over governmental regulation of the oil industry dominated nearly all of his time during this period of his life. One diversion he did allow himself in these years was an interest in intercollegiate football and baseball. With Jack Blalock and Sylvester Dayson, Parten travelled to Dallas, Fort Worth, and Austin to see the University of Texas play their Southwest Conference rivals. More than just a spectator, Parten recruited athletes for the university, frequently sending detailed scouting reports on high school players in northern Louisiana and East Texas to football coach Clyde Littlefield and baseball coach "Uncle" Jimmy Disch. Parten helped pay the expenses of some of those who wound up at the University of Texas and he hired a few of the boys for summer jobs.[2] A grateful Coach Littlefield undoubtedly spoke for Disch as well as himself when he wrote

Parten at the end of the 1932 season that he did "not believe that I could find another man in the country that takes as much sincere interest in our work as you have been taking the past several years."[3]

In his effort to find prized athletes for the university, Parten attended some of the inter-service football games between Shreveport's Barksdale Army Airfield and other army bases. Many of the army's athletes had entered the service right out of high school, so they were eligible for collegiate sports at the end of their enlistment. Barksdale played a football game with Galveston's Fort Crockett "Flyers" in Shreveport in late October 1933. It was J. R.'s interest in this game that brought him into contact with a dashing and handsome young army pilot who soon became intimately entangled in the lives of both J. R. and Opal Parten.

A pilot for one of the transport planes carrying the Fort Crockett "Flyers" to Shreveport, Dallas Sherman was a member of the Army Air Corps' Third Attack Group. The Partens had first met him eight months earlier at the dedication ceremony for Barksdale. J. R. had been one of a group of Shreveport's civic leaders who had helped persuade the army to build the airfield on a section of land northeast of the city. The city held a gala opening on February 2, 1933, that attracted a crowd of more than forty thousand people, including J. R and Opal, who were among the special guests invited by the dedication committee. The highlight of the celebration was an aerial demonstration involving nearly 150 airplanes, including eighty-eight Curtis Falcon "A-3's" from the army's training schools at Kelly, Randolph, and Brooks airfields in San Antonio. After the air show, the dedication committee held a reception for the flyers in one of the new airplane hangars. As the Partens mingled with the crowd at the reception, word spread among the army pilots that J. R. was a former army major who had struck it rich as an oil man. That Major Parten also flew his own plane impressed the pilots even more.[4]

Among the pilots most curious about J. R. Parten was Dallas Sherman. Sherman later recalled that he and some of his fellow pilots soon realized that "the famous and alert young Major Parten was eyeballing us with deeper penetration than we were him." The reason for Parten's curiosity soon became clear: he was looking for soldier athletes who might consider switching their army hitches for student status at the University of Texas and the greater glory of the Longhorn football team. Parten quickly spotted the tall and muscular Dallas Sherman. After he and Opal introduced themselves, the three hit it off immediately. The Partens learned that the personable airman was the son of a professor at Clemson, in South Carolina, where Dallas had graduated in 1929 with a degree in architecture. With few job opportunities available to novice architects in the worst days of the Depression, he had enlisted in the army, which sent him to the new flight school at Randolph Field in San Antonio.[5]

The Partens and Dallas Sherman had gone their separate ways after the Barksdale dedication ceremony. The following October, the Partens learned that Dallas had been transferred from San Antonio to Fort Crockett in Galveston and that he was among the group coming to Shreveport for the football game with Barksdale. They invited the young pilot to join them for dinner at their new home at 586 Oneota Street in the Shreveport suburb of South Highland Addition. During dinner, Parten began quizzing Dallas about the playing talents of individual players on the Fort Crockett team. Dallas realized that J. R. was scouting for soldier athletes he could get out of the army and send to play football at the University of Texas. "In those days, you could buy out of the army," Dallas recalled, "and J. R. was willing to pay soldier athletes to do that." Dallas knew nothing about the athletic ability of his army colleagues. Disappointed, Parten's interest in the conversation waned rapidly, but Opal saved Dallas. She had just returned from a trip to Europe, so after the meal, she brought out her postcard pictures of sites she had visited. Because of his professional training, Dallas was able to explain the architectural styles of the various buildings and monuments. As Opal and Dallas looked at the pictures and discussed architecture, J. R. told them to entertain themselves. He went to his study, leaving them alone for the rest of the evening. Dallas and Opal talked and laughed for hours. When Dallas walked out of the Parten house late that night, he left feeling that he and Opal had developed more than a friendship, but he believed they could never be more than just friends. He liked and respected J. R. and he believed that Opal was still very much in love with her husband.[6]

After Sherman returned to Galveston, he invited the Partens to one of the city's biggest social events, the annual Christmas benefit dance for the Red Cross. J. R. welcomed an opportunity to visit his sister, Malcolm, and her husband, Dr. Earl Cone, who were still residing in Galveston, and Opal was eager to see Dallas again, so they accepted the invitation. At the conclusion of the IPAT annual meeting in Dallas, J. R.'s last as the association's president, the Partens flew to Galveston in their open-cockpit Stearman. Sherman and the Partens attended parties at Fort Crockett's officers' club and at several private homes around Galveston. Galveston enjoyed an unusually warm holiday period, so Sherman, the Partens, and Earl Cone played several rounds of golf. Winter returned with a vengeance on the day the Partens were scheduled to return to Shreveport. Dallas was not surprised when J. R. determined that the weather was too turbulent for flying and that the return to Shreveport would have to be by train. Dallas was stunned, however, when J. R. said, "Dallas, take care of my wife and my airplane for me, and I'll come back when the weather's good." Recalling the incident nearly six decades later, Dallas Sherman smiled and said, "so he left the airplane and the wife and I took very good care of both of them."[7]

Although Opal and J. R. continued to live together as man and wife, Opal and Dallas became lovers, beginning an open relationship that lasted for more than forty years. "J. R. never had any outright objections," Sherman claimed, "there never was any enmity. As a matter of fact, Opal and I had more togetherness than she and he did and that went on for a long, long time." Not only were there no visible bad feelings, Dallas and J. R. became good friends.[8]

Whatever sexual tensions were at work in this unusual arrangement remain unknown. Dallas Sherman, however, simply attributed J. R.'s behavior to his obsession with building his oil business and his political activities. "J. R. was married to his work," Dallas claimed. "He loved Opal and I know for certain that Opal loved him, but he was bored and unhappy unless he was studying an oil map, walking around an oil lease or discussing politics over drinks with friends." Opal needed an outlet and Dallas provided it. He loved parties and going out to dinner and was a great raconteur. He made a perfect escort and companion for Opal during J. R.'s extended absences from home. Dallas and Opal had much in common, but perhaps the most important interest they shared was a love of touring and sightseeing, activities of no interest whatsoever to J. R. Parten. So the two travelled extensively together without J. R. On the other hand, J. R.'s favorite leisure activity was to attend University of Texas football games, which Opal and Dallas both disliked. Opal especially hated football. On the few occasions when J. R. was able to persuade her to accompany him to a football game, Opal would bring a thick book and read for the entire game. Eventually, J. R. welcomed the fact that Opal had optional entertainment when he travelled to Texas for a football weekend. "J. R. was rather loyal to his football games," Dallas claimed, "so Opal and I got some nice weekends together."⁹

"vicious legislation . . . so destructive of freedom"

Parten had left the presidency of the IPAT with the hope that he would be free from the politics of oil for awhile. During the last few months of 1933, it seemed that the Texas Railroad Commission, with the help of federal marshalls empowered by subsection nine (c) of the NIRA, had finally taken control of East Texas. Uncomfortable with the NRA, but resigned to accommodate themselves to the reality of its existence, Parten and his allies looked forward to a period of peace within the industry. Those hopes were soon dashed, however.

Many of the small oil-producers in East Texas soon devised new ways to get hot oil past the federal marshalls and the Railroad Commission agents who had the difficult task of policing nearly fifteen thousand wells and an estimated one hundred small refineries. In the early months of 1934, Texas produced more than 110,000 barrels of oil a day in excess of the allowable. This new flow of hot oil from East Texas created much frustration within the industry. It was apparent to everyone that the Railroad Commission was incapable of effectively policing the field, even with federal help. This situation played into the hands of Harold Ickes and some of the oil men who had never given up on the idea of making the industry a public utility. Ickes continued to lobby within the Roosevelt administration for legislation to increase and expand his power over oil production and distribution. Hearing of Ickes's renewed efforts to get a federal oil-control bill passed, E. O. Thompson worked to head him off. He wrote Sen. Tom Connally in early March to urge him to oppose Ickes's new efforts. "Please don't give them any more authority," Thompson pleaded, "they have all the power they ought to have now." Thompson also sent a telegram to his proration enforcement officer in Kilgore, Capt. E. N. Stanley, declaring that he had a job to do "and that is to stop hot oil [so] let nothing stop you from enforcing it."¹⁰

Thompson's concerns proved to be well founded. On April 2, a delegation of major oil company executives, led by Walter Teagle, the powerful head of Standard of New Jersey, told Ickes they were willing to support legislation giving him "the fullest possible power to regulate the production of crude oil." Ickes claimed that Teagle came to his office the following day and urged him to get the federal government to confiscate the East Texas field and declare it a federal reserve. Even Ickes admitted that this "seemed rather a startling proposition to come from the president of the Standard Oil Company of New Jersey." This request encouraged Ickes to move ahead with a new federal oil-control plan, the draft of which had been written several weeks before by Parten's old debate coach, Charles I. Francis, who was now a senior partner of the Vinson, Elkins law firm in Houston. Francis was serving as a special assistant to the U.S. attorney general. Jess Walker, who was teaching oil and gas law at the University of Texas School of Law, helped Francis prepare the draft. According to J. Howard Marshall, Francis's original draft was "about as long as a telephone book," so Marshall and Meyers condensed and simplified it. Ickes sent this new draft to Sen. Elmer Thomas of Oklahoma, who agreed to submit it to Congress. Although this activity was kept quiet, word leaked out a few days before Thomas submitted it to the Senate. On April 30, IPAT executive director Bailey Hardy issued a circular to his directors warning that Ickes had written a new bill to "provide for an oil dictatorship . . ." Bailey urged the directors to contact the Texas congressional delegation to demand the defeat of this "vicious legislation . . . so destructive of freedom . . ."[11]

On April 30, the day Hardy issued his warning, Senator Thomas submitted a bill to Congress to strip state commissions of all authority to regulate oil production and to grant Ickes broad and sweeping powers to restrict imports and to set quotas for each state, even down to individual wells if necessary. Although the president of the API quickly announced his endorsement of what was unofficially referred to as the "Ickes bill," it proposed far more power for the secretary of the interior than what many of the major oil companies had envisioned. It soon became apparent that there would be no more of a consensus within the industry on the Ickes bill than there had been on earlier bills. Another divisive controversy over public policy now tore the industry apart. Back in Texas, Carl Estes and the East Texas Chamber sponsored a public rally in Tyler to support the Ickes bill. At the rally, attorney W. F. Weeks declared that everyone should realize that God was now intervening on behalf of the oil industry because it was obvious that President Roosevelt was "divinely inspired." Bewildered by this and similar rhetoric at the rally, Parten complained to Sylvester Dayson that everyone in East Texas had "simply lost their heads."[12]

Alarmed by these developments, IPAT directors passed a resolution denouncing the Ickes bill and designating Parten, Jack Blalock, and Bailey Hardy as a committee empowered to represent the association in Washington. After the meeting, Parten issued a press release attacking the Ickes plan, claiming that it would give the interior secretary "virtual dictatorial powers" over the oil industry. Blalock soon left for Washington, while Parten and Hardy stayed behind to rally opposition to the bill in Texas and Louisiana. Parten organized a group of Houston independents, including Jim Abercrombie, Mike Hogg, and Dan Harrison, to go with him to Washington to lobby the Texas delegation.[13]

As opposition to the so-called Ickes bill increased, Cong. W. M. Disney of Oklahoma filed a modified version of the bill in the House of Representatives. Disney's revision made it easier for oil producers to appeal their federally imposed quota and provided for a two-year time limit on the federal government's authority to impose quotas, but it was no more satisfactory to Parten and his IPAT allies than the original version. A key person in their strategy to stop the Disney bill in the House was Sam Rayburn, the representative from Texas's Fourth Congressional District and chairman of the powerful Interstate and Foreign Commerce Committee, the committee to which the Disney bill would be routinely assigned. Although Rayburn had not announced a position on the bill, Blalock and Parten were hopeful that he could be persuaded to oppose it. Rayburn had been a protégé of Vice Pres. John Nance Garner. An old friend of Myron Blalock, Garner also opposed the federal control bills. Ickes later complained that Garner was "tied hand and foot with the Blalock group." Myron Blalock told Parten that with Garner's help they might be able to bring Rayburn into their camp, which would give them a fighting chance to defeat the bill. On May 16, however, Jack Blalock sent a telegraph to Parten warning that supporters of the Disney bill were trying to bypass Rayburn by assigning the bill to the House Committee on Mines and Mining (which had no Texan members). He urged Parten to get to Washington as soon as possible because the "fight is on. . . ."[14]

After reporting these developments to Parten, Jack Blalock immediately went to Sam Rayburn and told him about the scheme to bypass his committee. Ickes had earlier tried to get Rayburn, whose district had no oil, to sponsor the bill, but he had refused. Angered by the attempt to deny him the opportunity to play a role in legislation of such importance to his home state, Rayburn called House Speaker William Bankhead and persuaded him to assign the Disney bill to his committee. On May 17, Blalock informed Parten that they had won the "first skirmish" because Rayburn's committee had retained jurisdiction. Delighted by this encouraging development, Parten wired Blalock that he was leaving immediately for Washington, but that Ernest Thompson had decided to stay in Austin to "bolster up East Texas enforcement." Thompson also sent a telegram to Blalock asking him to make it clear to Rayburn and others that the Railroad Commission was determined to stop excessive production. "The job will be done. That can be depended upon."[15]

Parten, Jack and Myron Blalock, and their allies (Roosevelt called them the "Blalock Crowd") set up headquarters in Washington's Shoreham Hotel and went to work, meeting with a series of key congressional leaders to argue against the Thomas and Disney bills. They were discouraged by the response they received, especially from the members of the Texas delegation who were being pressured to support the legislation by such powerful Texans as Amon Carter, the influential publisher of the Fort Worth *Star-Telegram*. Claiming that only those who ran hot oil opposed the bills, Carter warned President Roosevelt that unless federal control was established, "there will be no escape from the chaotic conditions. . . ." Texas governor Miriam Ferguson also urged the president to support federal controls.[16]

Generally discouraged by the attitudes of most of the members of the Texas delegation, the "Blalock Crowd" decided to concentrate on Sam Rayburn, whose decision to support or oppose the bill would prove crucial. Parten and the Blalock brothers arranged to meet privately with Rayburn on a Sunday afternoon at his tiny apartment on Massachusetts Avenue where they could talk without distractions or interruptions. Parten had never met Rayburn, but he had long admired his reputation for integrity and legislative skill. When Parten was a student at the University of Texas, he learned from his government professors about Rayburn's impressive record as a young state representative. Rayburn attended the University of Texas School of Law while serving in the legislature. In 1911, at the age of twenty-nine, he was elected Speaker of the Texas House of Representatives, at that time the youngest person in Texas history to serve in that position. As Parten discussed the oil-regulation fight with Rayburn, he was deeply impressed by the congressman's ability to absorb the technical information about unitization and prorationing and to apply it to the larger issue of federal regulation. Rayburn was particularly responsive to Parten's arguments about the dangers to business competition posed by the big oil companies. The congressman had learned about the power of business monopolies as a member of the Texas legislature when he had attacked the railroad monopolies. After Parten's presentation, Rayburn declared that he could not make a public announcement against the oil regulation bill because of its apparent support in the White House, but he promised to give the bill a full and "very lengthy" hearing. Parten and the Blalocks left Rayburn's apartment confident that they had an ally.[17]

Although he never spoke out against the Disney bill, Rayburn's management of the bill soon made it evident that he would kill it by stalling it in his committee. Parten later claimed that in regard to the Ickes oil-control plan, Rayburn was "the only Texas congressman who didn't look out the window on us. He just decided it would put all the oil business on the Potomac." Rayburn's decisive support initiated a friendship with Parten, one that grew increasingly close and lasted until Rayburn's death more than a quarter of a century later. Rayburn, a man of modest material needs, basically distrusted men of wealth. Through Parten, however, he became friends with several of the richest people in Texas, including independent oil men Sid Richardson of Fort Worth and Jim Abercrombie of Houston. Although they were partisan Republicans, such men appreciated Rayburn's consistent and often crucial support of the oil depletion tax allowance and other federal laws helpful to the oil industry and the independents in particular. They also respected his integrity and his deeply held ethical standards, traits J. R. Parten also strongly appreciated. "Rayburn knew how to pull people together and he was a man of deep conviction," Parten later stated, "once he had a conviction, nothing could shake him. I regarded Mr. Rayburn as one of the [most] outstanding statesmen I have ever known. . . ." In turn, Rayburn respected Parten and he learned to trust his judgement. Parten became Rayburn's unofficial advisor on the oil industry and, in the last decade of Rayburn's life, he would serve as an important link between Rayburn and the liberal wing of the Democratic Party in Texas.[18]

"I'll filibuster that God-damn thing till frost"

Through J. R. Parten, the opponents of the Ickes oil-control plan also had an important contact in the Senate—Huey P. Long. Because of his public criticisms of the president and the Democratic leaders in the Senate, the "Kingfish" was not popular in the White House or among the Senate leadership. His support therefore had to be managed carefully or it could harm more than help Parten's cause. Parten met with Long in his senate office and explained his opposition to the Ickes plan. When he heard Parten's argument, Long exclaimed "My God, that's not good for Louisiana or Texas! What are Texas' senators doing about it?" Parten admitted that they had not been helpful. "Well," Long said, "you just come to my apartment at the Broadmoor Hotel tonight and bring me an armful of literature." Parten accepted the invitation. Jack Blalock, however, protested, warning Parten that they could not afford to be seen meeting with the controversial Long. "Certainly, we're going to go," Parten replied, "but only after dark. Nobody will see us."

Late that night, Parten and Blalock went to Long's three-room apartment in the Broadmoor Hotel. "All right, boys," Long declared, "you're the teacher, and I'm the pupil. Let me have it." As Parten and Blalock explained their reasons for opposing the Thomas and Disney bills, Long paced back and forth listening intently. Every few minutes Long would interrupt their presentation and make a brief but fiery speech based on the argument the two men had just made. After a couple of hours Parten and Blalock left Long with a large batch of literature against compulsory unitization and federal control of oil production, and Long promised to keep quiet unless he was needed. But if the bill made it to the floor of the Senate, he promised to "filibuster that God-damn thing till frost."[19]

The next evening, Jack Blalock, Parten, and Opal's sister, Mary Lynn, who had come from New York to visit her brother-in-law, were having cocktails in Parten's room at the Shoreham Hotel when Huey Long paid them an unexpected visit. Long asked if they wanted to go to dinner with him. Parten, not wanting to be seen in public with Long because of their lobbying effort, said that he would have room service bring them dinner. "Oh, no, let's go down to the dining room," Huey exclaimed, "I want to dance with Mary Lynn." Parten and Blalock offered every excuse they could think of to stay in the room, but Long insisted. They went downstairs to the hotel's dinner club, with Long's bodyguards taking positions outside the club's doors. Parten slipped the maitre d' some money and whispered, "Get us into the darkest corner you can find." When they finished their meals, the three men took turns dancing with Mary Lynn. Later in the evening, a beautiful woman wearing a red hat entered the club accompanied by two army colonels. Huey noticed her immediately. Grinning mischievously, he pointed toward her, telling Parten "I know that woman." Parten, worried about Long creating another one of his public scenes, which would land them all in the next day's newspaper, cautioned: "You better be careful Huey. Those colonels aren't going to like you cutting your eye around at that lady." Huey insisted, "I've got to dance with that woman tonight. I know her, if I can just place her." As Parten left to take Mary Lynn to the train station to catch the overnight train back to New York, he whispered to Jack Blalock to "take good care of the senator." When Parten returned from the train station after midnight, he went straight to bed. About three o'clock in the morning, Jack Blalock woke Parten up to report that he had "just turned Huey over to his bodyguards." Relieved that they had avoided being involved in another one of Long's notorious nightclub incidents, Parten went back to sleep. He received a phone call from Long about seven o'clock that morning. "The trouble 'bout you rich people," Long shouted through the receiver, "is that you sleep all day. Hell, I'm already in my office, and I've already gotten a half a day's work done. But I just had to call you up to tell you that last night after you left, I did meet and dance with that woman with that red hat."[20]

As events developed, Parten never had to call on Long's services in the fight against Thomas-Disney. He also never saw Huey Long again. Sixteen months later, the "Kingfish" was assassinated in the corridor of the state capitol in Baton Rouge. Parten later stated that although he never voted for Long, "I respected him as an able advocate. I jostled him once in a while for being such a demagogue, but I never found anything vicious about ol' Huey. But Huey had a lot of enemies, all right. That was the reason he was finally killed."[21]

Defeat of the Disney Bill

When Ickes found out that the oil-control bill was going to Rayburn's committee, the interior secretary decided it was time to go on the offensive against the "Blalock Crowd." At a press conference he declared that "these obstructionists . . . do not represent any legitimate oil interest. They are runners of hot oil. . . . These men constitute the crooked fringe. . . ." Despite evidence to the contrary produced by his own investigators, Ickes claimed that the three independents leading the opposition to Thomas-Disney "would make Ali Baba look like a Sunday school pupil. They are three in number, one in California [Keck], one in East Texas [Parten], and one in New York [Jones]." He argued that the bills proposed to do nothing more than give him clear-cut powers to make it possible to control the production of crude oil and hold it to actual market demand, for the benefit of producers and consumers alike.[22]

Meanwhile, Sam Rayburn let the Disney bill have a "prolonged airing out" in hearings that he managed to continue for a period of several crucial weeks. Testifying at the hearings on June 5, Parten defended himself against Ickes's charges, declaring that neither he nor his company had ever run hot oil. He vehemently denounced the provision in the Disney bill giving the secretary of the interior the power to set compulsory production quotas within states. This would lead to compulsory unitization and acreage prorationing, which were goals "sought by the Integrated Oil Companies for the past decade." He insisted that the hidden motive behind the Ickes plan was to eliminate competition.[23]

As Rayburn's hearings continued, Norman Meyers reported to Ickes that the committee members would pass the bill if Rayburn would let them vote on it. "There is no doubt that Rayburn intends to kill the Bill, " Meyers reported. Frustrated, Ickes confided to his diary that "the oil bill . . . is in bad shape." Ickes called upon the president to pressure Rayburn. Claiming that Rayburn was "deliberately choking this bill to death," Ickes complained that Rayburn was telling his colleagues that the president was not interested in the bill. Claiming that "95% of the oil industry wants this legislation," Ickes told Roosevelt that if he would ask Rayburn to report the bill favorably out of his committee, "it will so be reported." Roosevelt finally sent Rayburn a rather weak note wondering if it might not be time to report the bill out of committee. Rayburn believed, however, that Roosevelt's timidly made request meant that he really did not like the bill, so Rayburn continued to stall. He told Parten afterward that he had responded to the president's note by explaining that "this is a matter of such transcending importance that the fullest hearing possible is essential." Typically, Roosevelt had managed to leave the impression with both Ickes and Rayburn that each actually had his support. The president remained politically uneasy about the "oil dictator" concept. Even more important, however, Roosevelt was relying heavily on Rayburn's help to get his overall legislative plan through Congress, so the White House refrained from pressuring the Texas congressman.[24]

Rayburn's foot-dragging and Roosevelt's ambivalence encouraged Parten so much that he decided in mid-June that he could return to Texas to work in the upcoming state Democratic primary. While Rayburn sat on the bill, some of its supporters in the oil industry changed their opinion. J. Howard Marshall believed that "some people got unduly scared about the oil industry becoming a public utility. . . ." On June 14, 1934, Rayburn's committee voted twelve to five to reject the Disney bill. The committee recommended that the oil matter be investigated further during the summer and the findings reported during the next session of Congress. Delighted, Thompson assured Parten that he had "won a great victory for Texas." He added rather grandly that in terms of states' rights, it had been "probably the greatest fight that has been made since the civil war."[25]

CHAPTER 8

The "Boy Orator" and "Tom Foolery" Hunter

Jimmy Allred Runs for Governor

B efore Rayburn's committee killed the Disney bill in the summer of 1934, Parten had to leave Washington to tend to an important political situation in Texas. Jimmy Allred had announced his candidacy for governor the previous April and Parten was determined to do all he could to get him elected. He believed that moving Allred into the Governor's Mansion would be as important to his fight against the federal government as anything he could do in Washington.

During the preceding year, Parten had become Attorney General Allred's unofficial advisor on oil industry matters. Many of Allred's speeches on oil matters relied heavily on Parten's recommendations. Although they disagreed on a few specific issues, such as Allred's support of Prohibition, the two men shared the same general political world view. Allred is too often loosely described as a "liberal" and even a "progressive," but those terms are relative. He and Parten were far more conservative on many issues of public policy than most New Dealers. They were both fiscal conservatives and strong supporters of states' rights. Allred, for example, shared Parten's dislike of the NRA, which they both believed was an unconstitutional broadening of presidential power. Allred earned his reputation as a liberal governor mainly because of his antitrust views. It was their mutual hatred of business monopoly, in fact, that provided the most important basis for the Parten-Allred alliance. Allred also shared Parten's views about oil policy. Having the energetic and charismatic Allred in the governor's chair would be a powerful safeguard against any new moves to gut the Texas Railroad Commission's authority over the state's oil and gas industry. As a governor, Allred would also be an important ally in the battle at the federal level. "As Attorney

General, Jimmy had been instrumental in helping us fight federal control," Parten later explained, "so we owed him a real debt, and we paid it."[1]

When Governor Ferguson announced her decision in November 1933 not to seek reelection, Parten was among those who urged Allred to announce his candidacy, pledging his personal financial support and offering to raise additional money from his friends in the oil industry. A month after Ferguson's announcement, Allred told Parten that he would run, but he decided not to make a public statement until the spring. Parten spent a weekend in early March in Houston at the Texas State Hotel with Allred and a few of his other key supporters to plan the campaign. When Allred finally announced publicly that he would run for governor, Parten was too deeply involved in the fight against the Ickes oil-control plan to be of any immediate help. In May, while Parten was still in Washington, Allred sent word to him that he needed his help whenever he returned to Texas. He apologized to Parten for his absence from the fight against the Ickes plan, explaining that he was opposed to the Disney bill, but for reasons of campaign strategy he felt that he "ought not take any part in the argument at this time." It was this letter from Allred that caused Parten to return to Texas.[2]

Parten went to work for Allred immediately upon his return. Serving as the campaign's unofficial treasurer, he spent the summer in Austin raising money, advising on campaign strategy, and writing speeches. To serve as a financial committee to pay for the campaign, Parten organized a small group of independent oil men that included Jim Abercrombie, Dan Harrison, William Keck, Mike Hogg, Hugh Roy Cullen, and Jim West Sr. "I didn't do anything else that summer," Parten later recalled. "That was the most involved I'd ever been in anybody's campaign." Parten became Allred's closest campaign advisor. Ed Clark, who later served as Allred's secretary of state, recalled that Allred "deferred completely to Major Parten's judgement on campaign matters. The Major's word was pretty close to law as far as Jimmy was concerned." Ralph Yarborough stated that "when Jimmy was running that hard race in 1934, Parten was his main advisor, main money man, just the guru, you might say of the campaign."[3]

Although there were six other candidates for governor in 1934, Allred's main opponents were Tom Hunter, an independent oil man who had placed third in the 1932 governor's race; Clint Small, a state senator and unsuccessful candidate for governor in 1930; Edgar Witt, the current lieutenant governor; and Charles C. McDonald, a former Texas secretary of state and an ally of the Fergusons. Allred was undoubtedly the better known of the group because of his high profile as an activist attorney general and because of the publicity generated by his antitrust suit against the major oil companies, but each of his chief opponents had important sources of support. Newspaper polls designated Allred the early favorite, but it was almost a certainty that no one would win the majority needed to win without a runoff.[4]

Texas in the summer of 1934 was still in the grip of the Depression, although oil had somewhat alleviated the economic crisis, especially in Dallas, Fort Worth, and Houston. Agriculture, however, was still in a desperate condition much wors-

Jimmy Allred on the campaign trail, 1934. Parten, wearing a hat, can be seen to the right of Allred's feet. *CN 09597. Courtesy Parten Photograph Collection, CAH.*

ened by a severe drouth, leaving rural Texas, except for the oil regions, in bad shape. Despite eighteen months of the New Deal, tens of thousands of Texans were still on some form of work relief. The financial condition of the state government reflected the condition of the economy. Taxes were going uncollected and the state deficit was growing. Despite these enormous problems, none of the candidates for governor offered much that differed from those governors who had preceded them during the Depression. Nor did they differ much among themselves on such important issues as taxation, education, and social welfare. Allred's trust-busting record, however, which was more image than reality, attracted vigorous opposition from the major oil companies, still smarting from the defeats they had suffered in Washington and Austin as a result of the efforts of the attorney general, Ernest Thompson, J. R. Parten, and their allies. Small, Hunter, and McDonald attracted support from the major oil companies and many of the members of the Texas Oil and Gas Association. Small openly advocated stripping the Railroad Commission of its authority over oil and gas production. "The corporations of Texas would rather have had any of those men as Governor than Allred," Parten later claimed, "and we knew it was going to be a tough race. So we organized and went at it."[5]

Parten joined a small group of activists that included Ed Clark, Claude Wild, Myron Blalock, Ralph Yarborough, state representative and future Texas Supreme Court judge Robert Calvert, and Elbert Hooper, another one of Allred's assistants in the Attorney General's Office, to run Allred's campaign headquarters in Austin. As Allred campaigned around the state "like a mad man" in the searing summer heat, Parten raised money and gave Allred material for speeches about oil-related issues. A letter Parten wrote Allred on July 3 was typical of the advice he was giving the candidate. He told Allred that in his next speech, he needed to "state briefly the history of the Oil Monopoly's activity in seeking the special kind of oil control it desires; namely price fixing on refined oils and production control by 'acreage proration' and 'compulsory unitization of oil land'." He urged Allred to empha-size that "Texas has more than one-half of the nation's oil reserves, and Texas can . . . manage her own internal affairs." Taking a rigid states' right position reminis-cent of antebellum secessionists, Parten repeatedly urged Allred to emphasize that his record "has been on the principle . . . that Texans should rule Texas."[6]

Parten, like Allred, believed radio provided an essential tool for a statewide political campaign, especially in a state as large as Texas. Although American polit-ical candidates had made use of the radio for years, as late as 1934 it was still con-sidered an innovative campaigning technique in Texas and other areas of the South. Jimmy Allred, who had an excellent radio voice, used the medium to great effect. Accordingly, Parten arranged and paid for Allred's speeches over statewide radio networks during the campaign. Parten closely monitored preparations for these broadcasts and made certain that they were widely advertised.[7]

Although the oil issue was of profound importance to Parten and his friends and had real significance for the Texas economy, it was not an issue with which to stir the masses. The election campaign generally failed to attract much attention among Texas voters. A political columnist for the Austin *Statesman* reported that most voters were responding to the candidates with a "wide yawn." The field was so large and the candidates, including Allred, so similar in their platforms, that it was hard to generate much interest. They all opposed higher taxes while favoring old-age pensions and a thrifty state government. Nevertheless, as one campaign observer noted, Allred "had talent as an evangelist and an actor along with expert . . . political ability" and he was widely seen as the front-runner. As election day neared, Parten's confidence grew as he received optimistic reports from the field, such as one from a San Antonio radio station stating that its information indicated that "Allred will carry Bexar County by a substantial margin."[8]

To Parten's disappointment, however, Allred was forced into a runoff against Tom Hunter. Although he led Hunter by over fifty thousand votes, his five chal-lengers together attracted roughly four hundred thousand more votes than Allred. Former governor Jim Ferguson quickly announced in favor of Hunter, as did each of the other defeated candidates. Faced with the combined opposition of the can-didates from the first primary election and disappointed by his own vote total,

Allred and his campaign leaders rushed back to work immediately following the July election. Allred went on the road to conduct a whirlwind speaking tour while Parten and Myron Blalock functioned as unofficial campaign managers in Austin. After Allred opened his second campaign with a rally in Dallas, Parten told him not to worry about the Austin headquarters: "Myron and I will have that situation under constant supervision with one of us on the ground all the time. Your . . . address in Dallas has had a wonderful effect. . . . Texas now believes in you." Parten urged Allred to give Hunter "plenty to explain and at the same time keep your speaking campaign elevated . . . to the highest standard of statesmanship. . . ." Calling Hunter a "political lobbyist" for "big oil" Parten told Allred to "tie Hunter to the major oil companies" in his campaign.[9]

A few days after Allred's speech in Dallas, the Austin *Statesman* published a report about a campaign strategy meeting for Hunter involving some associates of Ferguson who had been charged with financial improprieties and others who were alleged to be Ku Klux Klan leaders. Reading the story in the Austin paper, Parten immediately saw an opportunity for Allred to make Ferguson himself an issue in the campaign. "Fergusonism" and the Ku Klux Klan would attract more attention than arguments about prorationing and unitization. Allred heard about the sensational story from a radio broadcast. He hurried back to Austin and conferred with Parten, Myron Blalock, Robert Calvert, and Claude Wild. Parten and Wild urged Allred to make Fergusonism a major issue. Parten had heard from sources close to Charles McDonald that after his defeat in the first primary, Hunter's backers had secured Ferguson's support by assuming responsibility for McDonald's campaign debt. He argued that Allred should play up this so-called Ferguson-Hunter "trade-off." Parten also urged Allred, who was calling for tighter restrictions on the governor's power to issue pardons to criminals, to resurrect the old charge that Ferguson sold pardons to criminals when he was governor. Allred agreed with Parten. When he returned to the campaign trail, as Parten later described it, Allred "tied Ferguson to Hunter's neck." Hunter quickly denied that he had made a deal of any kind with Ferguson, but Allred's charges kept Hunter on the defensive for the remainder of the campaign. Allred's new strategy also invigorated his own campaign and attracted widespread attention to the race. Political rallies drew much larger, and louder, crowds, and newspaper coverage increased noticeably.[10]

Jim Ferguson fought back, not only against Allred but against his chief supporter as well. In a campaign issue of his widely distributed newspaper, the *Ferguson Forum*, he printed a front-page story written in the form of a play, titled "With Apologies to Shakespeare (sic)." Allred and Parten, the main characters in Ferguson's "play," were shown in a plot to buy the election by promising jobs and cash to various political figures. Parten was identified as "Major Parten, a citizen of Louisiana, chief hot oil runner of Texas, advisor and financial backer of Allred's campaign." At one point, the "Parten" character declares ". . . since there is some talk about me being connected with the campaign, I changed my address on the hotel register from Shreveport, Louisiana to Houston, Texas." To which "Allred" exclaims,"Major, you're not such a bad politician yourself; you must be a relative of Huey Long." It was a classic Ferguson performance. In one brief and simple comedy sketch, he had alleged that Parten was a carpetbagging hot-oiler and associate of Huey Long's who was masterminding Allred's campaign and buying votes, presumably with his ill-gotten gains from East Texas. Despite the increasingly bitter campaign, Ferguson and his friends were always interested in making a "friendly little wager." Parten later claimed that Ferguson and his associates were "so confident that they would win it for Tom Hunter that they wanted a bet. We finally gave them one. There was a twenty five thousand dollar bet made, and the Allred group won it. That helped greatly in resolving the campaign deficit question."[11]

As the campaign heated up, Hunter counterattacked with charges that the thirty-four-year-old Allred was too young to serve as governor, often referring to him as the "boy orator," the "high school boy," and the "little boy with the big britches." Parten's reaction was to suggest that Allred declare that "youth is not a bar to places of trust and honor." Noting that Thomas Jefferson, Stephen F. Austin, Sam Houston, Columbus, and Martin Luther were as young or younger than Allred when they made their greatest achievements, Parten wrote, "but Tom Hunter says, on the authority of Jim Ferguson, that a young man cannot serve his country." Allred delivered a version of this speech on several occasions.[12]

Unfortunately, not all of Allred's rhetoric was so harmless. Stung by Hunter's charges that he had been bought by Parten and his group of independent oil men, Allred slipped into some shameful demagoguery when speaking extemporaneously. While campaigning in East Texas and referring to his opponent's proposal to combine the state bureaucracy into a cabinet managed by five gubernatorial appointees, Allred declared that Hunter wanted to "set up a Hitler government in Texas with Tom as dictator. Hunter doesn't believe in our form of government, so he wants to destroy it." On another occasion, Allred declared that "Tom Foolery" Hunter resembled the "missing link," therefore proving that "man descended from the monkey."[13]

As the second campaign reached its latter stages, Parten and other Allred advisors worried that the race seemed to be uncomfortably close. They and Allred gathered in Parten's apartment in the Stephen F. Austin Hotel to discuss strategy for the final two weeks of the second primary campaign and to identify an issue to carry Allred to the finish line. Parten later recalled that Allred's secretary came to the meeting with a letter she had discovered while reviewing her boss's correspondence files. Dated November 26, 1932, and signed by Tom Hunter, the letter urged Allred to support a general sales tax, "which would reach all of the masses to some degree. . . ." Parten recalled that when he and Allred saw Hunter's letter, "we knew we had something." During the campaign, Hunter and Allred had both insisted that they had always strongly opposed the general sales tax, but Allred claimed Hunter's stand was insincere. He charged that his opponent had hidden a sales tax in a complicated scheme he was proposing called the "blended tax." Allred had called the plan, which Hunter proposed as a substitute for the ad valorem tax, "more tax than blend." Parten had two dozen photographic copies made of the letter and gave one to Allred. He placed the original in a bank's safe-deposit box "for safe keeping." Parten and Allred agreed that Allred would announce that he now understood what a blended tax was, because he had a letter from Tom Hunter defining it. "Allred teased [Hunter] with that for a couple of days and had all the newspaper men asking [Hunter] what letter he was talking about," Parten recalled. Hunter declared that he had never supported a sales tax and demanded that Allred provide evidence for his charge.[14]

Hunter had fallen into the trap. Parten and Claude Wild quickly arranged an Allred rally in Corsicana on August 10, advertising that Allred would present a certified copy of the letter to Hunter's representatives. Their strategy not only put Hunter on the defensive once again, it created valuable publicity. Curious about the "mystery" letter and the entertainment promised by the formal presentation of the document to Hunter's people, the Allred rally drew one of the campaign's largest crowds. "I'll never forget that night," Parten, who was present, remembered later. "It was very dramatic. . . . Tom Hunter's friends were there in the audience, and they were ready to get the letter. But [Allred] chose to go on with his speech and give it to them at the proper time, and he made them listen to an hour's speech before they got the letter." Waving a sheet of paper above his head, Allred exclaimed: "Here's a letter Tom Hunter forgot all about." Allred charged that the letter proved Hunter wanted to place a "tax on poverty." Allred had the newspaper reporters file down the aisle to the platform to get a copy of the letter. "Tom Hunter remembered that he had written such a letter right quickly," Parten later claimed. The next day Hunter explained that though he must have dictated the letter, he had obviously not reviewed it, pointing out that the actual signer of the letter was his secretary. Allred countered that he never accused Hunter of signing the letter, he accused him of writing the letter. Parten recalled that "Jimmy just poured it on him, that issue beat Hunter." One historian of the campaign lends support to Parten's contention, arguing that "the public did not feel that Hunter had cleared himself of the suspicion of sales-tax leanings. . . ." Hunter quickly announced that he would veto any sales tax passed while he was governor. But it was too late— Hunter was wounded, the issue had "cut deeply into his . . . credibility."[15]

Allred beat Hunter by approximately forty thousand votes, sweeping most of the large urban counties except for Bexar (San Antonio). The election results await scholarly analysis, but it is probable that Allred's charismatic personality, better name-recognition, and clever use of Fergusonism and the tax issues proved decisive. The absence of substantive issues, typical of most Texas election campaigns since World War I, makes it difficult to determine with confidence the reasons for the outcome. Unfortunately, however, one must conclude that among the reasons for Allred's victory was that his demagoguery was more effective than Hunter's, which is another factor typical of campaigns for governor in Texas. Whatever the reasons for Allred's victory, Parten was overjoyed. The night of the election he sent Allred a telegram declaring ". . . you have acquitted yourself with glorious honor as the most distinguished statesman Texas has produced in this generation." Parten was proud that he had financed Allred's campaign without going into debt.

"Jimmy went in with a minimum of strings tied to him," he later claimed, "and when . . . people came around, wanting to help share in paying off his deficit, I took a hell of a lot of delight in saying 'there's not any.' He owed some campaign debts, so to speak, but not money wise."[16]

Texas being a one-party state, Allred easily won the general election in November. Although Allred, Parten, Myron Blalock, and their associates won the governor's office, they lost in their bid to get control of the Texas House of Representatives. In Texas, the lieutenant governor, who presides over the Senate, and the Speaker of the House possess far greater legislative powers than the governor, whose only effective legislative tool—the veto—is negative. The newly elected lieutenant governor, Walter F. Woodul, though independent-minded and more conservative than Allred, nevertheless expressed his eagerness to work closely with the new governor. But Allred also needed a friend in the Speaker's chair in the House. Coke Stevenson had served as Speaker in the previous session, but he had indicated to friends that he would not serve a second term. This news delighted Allred, Parten, and Myron Blalock. Stevenson was an ultraconservative rancher with reactionary Republican political views even though he ran for election as a Democrat. The Allred administration believed he would be an obstacle to the governor's legislative agenda if he retained the Speakership. He had strongly supported the attack on the Railroad Commission in 1933. Parten viewed him as a major oil company stooge masquerading as a simple country boy who believed only in truth and justice. "Stevenson was strictly a corporation man," Parten later charged, "you tell me where the big corporations were in any fight, and that's where Stevenson would be."[17]

State representative Robert Calvert, a thirty-year-old lawyer from Hillsboro, who had served as Allred's official campaign manager, agreed to stand for election for Speaker. Parten, Myron Blalock, Claude Wild, Ed Clark, and other Allred stalwarts lobbied the legislators on Calvert's behalf, arguing that Calvert was needed to ensure smooth passage of Governor-elect Allred's legislative program. By Christmas 1934, Calvert's chances to be elected when the Forty-fourth Legislature convened in January appeared to be excellent. Parten sent a telegraph to Allred, who was in Wichita Falls for the Christmas holidays, assuring him that the Speaker's race was "in good shape, but there remains a great deal of work to be done." Allred's plans were thwarted, however, when a delegation of anti–New Deal legislators went to Stevenson's ranch in the Texas Hill Country near Junction and convinced him to stand for reelection to an unprecedented second term as Speaker to serve as a legislative restraint on Allred. The result was a bitter battle in the House over the choice of Speaker, one that Calvert later characterized as being "quite vicious."

Parten, Myron Blalock, and Ed Clark organized a coalition of legislators, including Sarah Hughes, Roy Hofheinz, Franklin Spears, and Herman Jones to support Calvert. Standing on the floor of the House chamber, the fiery Hughes told her colleagues that they all knew a vote for Calvert would be a vote of confidence for Allred and a New Deal for Texas, while a vote for Stevenson would be a vote for a lackey of "the sulphur . . . and oil interests." Parten recalled that "it was quite a fight, but we lost." The vote was 80 to 68 in favor of Stevenson, making him the first Speaker in Texas history to serve two consecutive terms. Parten later admitted that it had been a tactical mistake to pressure the legislators to elect a Speaker supported so actively by the governor. Ironically, the Senate rather than the House eventually gave Allred the most trouble during his tenure as governor.[18]

Despite the defeat of the Allred forces in the Texas House, Parten looked forward to the new year with confidence. Allred's election as governor meant that the legislative threat to the oil-regulation authority of the Railroad Commission was over—at least for the next two years. In addition, a move was now underway among the governors of some of the major oil-producing states to create an interstate oil compact to control production through concerted state action. As governor of the leading oil-producing state, Allred would have to play a significant role in any agreement to create an oil compact. As Allred's friend, financial supporter, and closest advisor on oil policy, J. R. Parten was in a strong position to see that such a compact protected the interests of the independent segment of the oil industry.[19]

CHAPTER 9

Oil and Politics

"From Hell to Hog River," 1935

While the Texas gubernatorial campaign was being waged during the summer of 1934, large amounts of hot oil continued to be produced in East Texas, despite the best efforts of the Texas Railroad Commisson. Relief finally came in October when Harold Ickes invoked the authority granted to the Interior Department by subsection nine (c) of the NIRA to establish a Federal Tender Board in East Texas to issue permits ("tenders") to allow producers to transport oil out of state. To receive a tender, a producer was required to show proof that the proposed shipments were not produced in excess of legal allowables. The Federal Tender Board, whose efforts were helped by the refusal of the courts to issue injunctions against it, effectively curbed the flow of hot oil from East Texas.[1]

The success of the Federal Tender Board brought a quick end to the hot-oil crisis. With the problem under control by the beginning of November, many of those in the oil industry who had supported strong federal controls reversed their position. Harold Ickes's threat in a speech at the annual meeting of the American Petroleum Institute in Dallas on November 14, to make the oil industry a federally controlled public utility played a major role in changing some minds. His speech, which was delivered in the secretary's usual combative style, so upset the API's board members, that they reversed the board's official position on federal control, calling instead for an interstate compact to control production through state action. Charles Roeser and Wirt Franklin continued to argue for federal control, but they now found themselves in the minority.[2]

Inspired by the API's call for an interstate oil compact, Ernest Marland, the recently elected governor of Oklahoma, invited Allred (still governor-elect) and the governors of other oil-producing states to meet with him in Oklahoma in December 1934 to discuss the merits of creating such a compact. Prior to the meeting, Parten and Jack Blalock warned Allred that Marland wanted to strip the individual states of the power to regulate oil production. Parten urged Allred to oppose such a plan and to argue instead for the right of each state to regulate the oil within its own borders. As Parten and Blalock had warned, at the December meeting and at a subsequent meeting in January 1935, Governor Marland and the majority of his fellow governors argued that an interstate oil compact should have the power to establish market-demand proration quotas for each state. Objecting to Marland's proposal, Allred offered to bring an alternative plan to the next governors' meeting in Dallas in February 1935. At Allred's request, Parten and Blalock drafted a plan for an oil-policy compact with authority limited, in the main, to the areas of conservation and the policing of hot oil. Because Texas produced half of the nation's oil, no plan would work without the Lone Star State's participation, so Allred was able to force his fellow governors to accept most of the Parten-Blalock plan. Allred did agree, however, to add provisions creating a permanent interstate compact board to oversee the execution of future interstate agreements and to allow this board to recommend production quotas for those states requesting them. The final compact agreement directly reflected the views of J. R. Parten and Jack Blalock. In consultation with Parten, Blalock authored Article V of the compact (which Allred inserted without revision into the final document), prohibiting compact members from promoting the creation of oil monopolies or engaging in market-demand production controls. It was Allred's persistence and debating skills, however, that persuaded the other governors to adopt the Parten-Blalock plan. The Texas legislature subsequently ratified the compact in April 1935 without opposition.[3]

The Premier Oil and Refining Company

Despite his deep involvement in Jimmy Allred's gubernatorial campaign, the fight against the Disney bill, and related efforts, J. R. Parten still found time in 1934 not only to manage the overall activities of Woodley Petroleum, but also to create a new oil-refining company. In the spring of 1934, Sylvestor Dayson proposed that he and Parten build a refinery at Greggton, a few miles west of Longview. "Sylvester wasn't very busy with our little 2000 barrel plant out there at Baird," Parten recalled, "so he got ants in his pants to build a refinery at a little switch on the Texas and Pacific Railroad." Woodley was having difficulty getting dependable pipeline connections for its production in East Texas, so the company was forced to store a large amount of crude in steel tanks. Dayson proposed to build a refinery similar to the one at Baird and produce gasoline and fuel oil. Parten thought it was a good idea, but his fellow directors at Woodley disagreed. With nearly a hundred refineries operating in the East Texas field, they could not see how a new one could be profitable. They also worried that Woodley's participation in a refinery might associate the company with the hot-oil trade. Small, independent refineries had proliferated throughout East Texas providing a ready outlet for hot oil. "Every illegal runner of hot oil . . . gave a silent prayer of thanks for the independent refineries," noted one observer at the time, "had it not been for these nearby refineries, seeking to buy oil as cheaply as possible . . . there would have been comparatively little legal oil run in East Texas." This last worry did not bother Parten,

The Premier refinery in Longview, Texas, late 1930s. *CN 06646. Courtesy Dayson Papers, CAH.*

he had no intention of operating an outlet for hot oil. "I did not produce hot oil and I would not buy it and my colleagues knew that, so that was no problem as far as I was concerned."[4]

Parten was so taken by Dayson's enthusiasm for the Greggton refinery that he decided to build it without Woodley's participation. He and Dayson invited Joe Zeppa of Tyler, a colorful Italian immigrant whose Delta Drilling Company was drilling most of Woodley's wells, to join with them in a partnership to build and operate the refinery. Parten had met Zeppa in Arkansas when the latter was a crude-oil buyer in the Smackover field. At Dayson's suggestion, they named the new company the Premier Oil Refining Company. Parten became chairman of the board, Dayson was named president, and Zeppa vice president. Jack and Myron Blalock bought stock in the company soon after it was formed and also became members of the board of directors. Centex, the refinery at Baird, was made a subsidiary of the new company. The Premier refinery opened for business in December 1934 as a thermal cracking plant, processing over three thousand barrels of crude a day and producing gasoline, mainly for independent gasoline-station owners. One of the company's biggest markets was Detroit, Michigan, which had a large number of independent filling stations. Located on the Texas and Pacific tracks, Premier was able not only to ship gasoline wherever it could be sold, but also to sell the fuel-oil by-product to the railroad for use in its locomotives.[5]

Dayson built an attractive and comfortable house on the refinery grounds and moved his family into it. He later added a nine-hole golf course, a skeet range, and a lighted airstrip where Parten could land his airplane. Parten made frequent trips to the refinery and the Dayson house became a second home for the oil man. He enjoyed the fun-loving Dayson's company. The dapper little Frenchman seemed to be the only person who could get Parten to loosen up, relax, and take advantage of some leisure time. Childless and unhappy about it, Parten developed a fatherly affection for the Daysons' little girl, Suzette. Many years later, Suzette would remember how excited she would get when her parents told her that J. R. was coming to visit. One of her earliest memories is of Parten landing his Stearman on the landing strip near the refinery. She would stand and watch from the adjacent pasture, thinking that he "looked so glamorous in his scarf and goggles" as his plane touched down. As a child, she loved to sneak into his room and crawl into his bed to wake him up in the mornings. Although Parten brought Suzette a lot of little gifts, one gift in particular, her first pony, would always stand out as special in her memory.[6]

The Longview refinery was a highly successful business venture. By refusing to participate in the hot-oil trade and by working hard to create its own legitimate independent market, the refinery survived when the production of hot oil was finally stopped. Parten and Dayson made a good team. "It was a great combination," a friend of both men later noted. "Parten appreciated that Sylvester knew how to build and run a refinery. . . . The Major worked more on the financial situation and was a stabilizing force." Of the nearly one hundred refineries that had operated at the peak of the hot-oil days, the Premier refinery was one of only seven refineries still in operation in 1938. Later, Parten and Dayson bought an existing small refinery near Tyler, and built new refineries at Cotton Valley, Louisiana, and El Dorado, Arkansas. During World War II, the Cotton Valley plant was a highly profitable producer of hundred-octane aviation fuel and butadiene for synthetic rubber.[7]

By the begining of 1935, Parten's wealth had grown considerably as a result of the success of his new refinery at Longview, substantial production from oil properties in East Texas, and profitable stripper wells in Arkansas, Louisiana, and Callahan County, Texas. He had added eleven producing wells in East Texas to his inventory and was exploring new leases in South Louisiana. Financial success helped soften his formerly rigid opposition to prorationing of any kind. Because of the Railroad Commission's success in cutting the flow of hot oil from East Texas, crude-oil prices had risen to nearly one dollar a barrel in the last few months of 1934. In Woodley's annual report, Parten assured his stockholders that if the price of oil remained at the one dollar level "your company can make good profits. Should prices decline materially we have facilities to store most of our production." In a revealing statement indicating a growing appreciation for the results of prorationing, Parten admitted that "the restricted flow of wells [in East Texas] will greatly lengthen the flowing life of production and lessen producing cost of oil in that field."[8]

By the beginning of 1935, Parten had decided it was time for Woodley to move its company office to Texas. He was in Texas most of the time now, working with Dayson on the Premier refinery, monitoring Woodley's production in East Texas and Callahan County, or lobbying in Austin. With oil production declining in Arkansas and Louisiana and with promising new oil land in Texas, Parten realized that he and Woodley Petroleum would become even more active in the state in the near future. His choice for Woodley's new home was Houston, despite the fact that Dallas was the preferred location for many of his East Texas colleagues. A move to Houston had been on Parten's mind since 1930, when his brother-in-law had advised him to look for oil loans there. To Parten, it made sense to move Woodley's offices to the city where most of the nation's oil action was centered and where oil loans were more likely to be had. In addition, a move to Houston would put him close to Madisonville, where his parents and much of his extended family still lived and where he retained deep emotional ties. "It was a hard decision to make," Parten recalled, "but it was very clear to me that Houston was . . . where the action was." Parten's fellow directors agreed, officially approving the move on February 11, 1935.[9]

The move to Houston ended the business relationship between Andrew Querbes and J. R. Parten. The banker wrote to Parten that his decision to leave Shreveport was "a personal loss to me individually," but he conceded that it was probably a wise choice because Houston was a "more advantageous" business location. Querbes, who had been so important to Parten's business success, gave his departing protégé some sound advice to which the oil man would subscribe for the rest of his career. "The only thing I ask you to do," Querbes counseled, "is to follow the conservative policy that you followed from the day you took active control [of Woodley]. Always keep in mind that there are many people owning stock in your company that a loss would work a severe hardship on. If you keep that in mind . . . I know that you will not be carried away with the idea of trying to make the Woodley equal to the Gulf [Oil Company] all at once. You are young and have plenty of time to build upon a solid foundation." Parten assured Querbes that he would follow his advice "implicitly." Querbes died within a few years of Woodley's move to Houston, but his support and counsel left a lasting impression on J. R. Parten. Fifty years after he left Shreveport, Parten sent a letter to the First National Bank of Shreveport. He wrote that he had "met and done business with many commercial bankers, but I still regard Andrew Querbes as the greatest and noblest of them all." Enclosed in the letter was a personal check in the amount of two million dollars. Parten instructed the bank to issue him a certificate of deposit that paid only 6 percent interest (the current rate was 8 percent). He said that was all Querbes would ever charge him for a loan and he wanted to do something for the bank in memory of his old mentor.[10]

Woodley's decision to move to Houston resulted in significant changes in the company's management structure. Eugene Palmer retired as board chairman and Parten assumed his position while also retaining the company's presidency. William T. "Uncle Billy" Moran, a Woodley director who had moved to Houston from Shreveport a couple of years earlier, became vice president, replacing Rutledge Deas, who, like Palmer, had been a member of the group that had purchased E. L. Woodley's stock. Although these changes solidified Parten's control over the company's policies as well as its day-to-day operations, Moran's ascendancy created a future rival and source of contention within Woodley that eventually had an important impact on the company's development.[11]

The Connally Hot Oil Act

Several weeks before Woodley's move to Houston, a decision by the United States Supreme Court threatened to bring an abrupt end to the brief period of stability the oil industry was enjoying. On January 7, 1935, the Court ruled in the Panama Refining Company case that subsection nine (c) of the NIRA was unconstitutional. The Court declared that the regulation of interstate commerce was a power expressly held by the Congress and that it could not be delegated to the president. The Federal Tender Board, which regulated interstate oil shipments and had been created by an executive order, was therefore an unconstitutional delegation of power. This ruling rendered the Federal Tender Board powerless to take action against hot oil. As soon as he heard the news, Parten realized that the inevitable flow of hot oil from the East Texas field would encourage Ickes to make another attempt to bring the oil industry under federal control. Parten sent an urgent telegram to E. O. Thompson, who was on a train headed for Washington, to give him the bad news and to offer his help in the fight certain to result from the Court's decision.[12]

Soon after the Supreme Court decision, Jack Blalock joined Thompson in Washington to work for new legislation to restore federal authority to regulate the interstate shipment of hot oil. They soon learned that Sen. Tom Connally would submit a bill to restore federal authority over the interstate transportation of hot oil. Drafted by J. Howard Marshall and Norman Meyers, Connally's bill, known as the Connally Hot Oil Act, was basically a reworking of the old NIRA subsection nine (c) with a few modifications. The bill prohibited the transportation of hot oil, and the products made from it, from interstate and foreign commerce. Hot oil was defined as oil produced in excess of a state's production quota. The quota would be whatever the state said it was, with the federal government's role restricted to enforcing the state quota. Marshall and Meyers went about their task very quietly. They knew Ickes would oppose the bill because it gave no authority to the federal government to set state production quotas. Ickes's assistants were now convinced, however, that the Supreme Court would never support such a transfer of power from the states to the federal government. The very day they were drafting the bill, Meyers sent Ickes a memorandum informing him that "rumor has it that Senator Connally will have an oil bill on Thursday." The "rumor" certainly came from a well-informed source.[13]

After the Connally bill went to the Senate, Thompson returned to Texas to guide the Railroad Commission's effort to minimize the effects of the Supreme Court ruling, leaving Jack Blalock in Washington to continue the lobbying work.

Parten met Thompson when he arrived in Austin. Operating out of Parten's suite in the Stephen F. Austin Hotel, they spent several hours on the telephone, cajoling and pleading with key independents in East Texas to help the Railroad Commission's enforcement staff in their effort to control hot oil in the field. Thompson followed this personal appeal with a more effective tactic. He succeeded in getting temporary court injunctions restraining the shipment of hot oil out of state.[14]

In late January, despite opposition from Secretary Ickes, the Senate passed Connally's hot-oil bill. When the House began its consideration, Thompson sent a telegram to Jack Blalock asking him to make certain that the Texas delegation in the House understood that Connally's bill was acceptable to the Railroad Commission because it recognized "state sovereignty and . . . [a state's] exclusive right to control production within [the] state." Because of opposition from the railroads the bill bogged down in Cong. William P. Cole's committee. The Cole committee was waiting to see if Texas was going to take care of the hot-oil situation within its own borders. A few days later, Parten advised Blalock to tell Congressman Cole that "hot oil production is now as low as it ever was and that situation is still improving." Thompson followed this with a telegram to Sam Rayburn, asking him to tell the Cole committee that ". . . yesterday not a car of oil or products moved from East Texas without a Tender or a court order. We are getting better results every day in our enforcement. . . ." With crucial help from Rayburn, the Cole committee finally turned the Connally bill loose and the House approved it on February 22, 1935. The newly reconstituted Tender Board (renamed the Federal Petroleum Board) reopened its operations in East Texas with almost immediate results, aided by the federal courts' refusal to issue injunctions to stop the board's activity. Dozens of East Texas refineries dependent on illegally produced crude oil went bankrupt in the course of a few months.[15]

A Final Oil Battle

Just when Parten thought the fight against federal control was over, Harold Ickes struck again. In early April, he persuaded Sen. Elmer Thomas to submit a revised version of the so-called "Ickes bill" to the Senate. Parten was forced to gear up for yet another fight, buoyed by the advice of Carl Estes who urged Parten to "battle that bill to a cat-footed finish, from Hell to Hog River." A few days after the filing of the Thomas bill Parten decided to send a strong message to the White House that Ickes was causing severe difficulties for some of the president's best friends in Texas. The Democratic National Committee had assigned Myron Blalock, now chairman of the state Democratic Executive Committee, a fund-raising quota of fifty thousand dollars for Texas, and he had asked Parten to help him raise it. Parten raised thirty thousand dollars from forty donors, including independent oil men Sid Richardson, Clint Murchison, and Jim Abercrombie. Blalock made certain that this fund-raising effort was brought to the attention of a grateful James Farley, the postmaster general and Roosevelt's chief fund-raiser. Parten's work also attracted the interest of Harold Ickes, who complained to the president that it was obvious that the "Texas clique" had made the contributions in a blatant attempt to buy influence and defeat his oil-control bill. Identifying Parten as the person behind this gambit, Ickes told Roosevelt that he was the oil advisor of Governor Allred and Commissioner Thompson "[who] is strictly against any kind of Federal control. He seems to have a complex on that subject." When questioned about the thirty-thousand-dollar contribution many years later, Parten explained that it "was simply an investment in good government," adding that he wanted President Roosevelt to know "that he had good friends in Texas" who just happened to be from the independent segment of the oil industry.[16]

Parten also knew that he would have to use more direct tactics to defeat this second Ickes bill (Thomas bill). Now that Allred was safely past his election campaign, Parten decided to get him openly involved in this new fight. Allred's political status, personal charisma, and outstanding speaking ability made him a valuable ally. Although the new governor was hard pressed by the legislative session and other state matters, including a highly publicized anti-gambling and anti-vice campaign, Parten asked Allred to go to Washington with him to assume the public leadership against the Thomas bill. Appealing to his guilty feelings for not having helped in the previous fight against the Ickes plan, Parten told Allred that he would be able to attract far more attention to their cause than any other advocate. Allred was heavily in Parten's political debt, but he also strongly shared his oil-man friend's views on this issue, so he agreed to go to Washington. He and Parten flew to the nation's capital on April 15 to join forces with Thompson, Jack Blalock, and the new attorney general, William McCraw. As Parten and Allred walked down the ramp from the airplane after their arrival in Washington, they were met by a large contingent of reporters. Allred, shouting over the noise of airplane engines, declared to the newsmen that he had come to Washington to oppose the Thomas bill "because it is unconstitutional and . . . wrong in principle." Parten also had Sam Rayburn on his side. "If any hearings are to be held," Rayburn declared, "I will do all that I can to have our people heard."[17]

With Ickes advertising the Thomas bill as an essential part of the Roosevelt administration's legislative agenda and implying that it had the president's full support, the bill initially attracted substantial support in Congress. This was especially surprising in light of the fact that the API and the major oil companies refused to endorse it. Parten was worried that a majority of Congress would follow if the president was willing to lead. This even included Rayburn, who as a loyal member of Roosevelt's legislative team would find it difficult to break ranks with the president if he called for its passage. Complicating the situation was the fact that Texas senators Tom Connally and Morris Sheppard were pleading neutrality, concerned that if Roosevelt, who was enormously popular with Texas voters, came out strongly in favor they could not afford to be on the wrong side. Sheppard's behavior was especially disappointing to Parten. "He just looked out the window on us. 'Too many people want it,' was all that he would say."[18]

Parten and his associates realized that the Thomas bill would have to be defeated at the White House. Accordingly, Allred met with President Roosevelt on

April 17 to make his case. Allred told Roosevelt that Ickes's efforts to get control of the Texas oil industry was "illegal, unnecessary, and inadvisable" from a political standpoint. The latter point was an indirect reference to the thirty-thousand-dollar financial contribution. Allred and his associates were loyal Democrats who obviously put their money where their mouths were, and now they needed the president's support. Roosevelt flashed his famous smile and told the governor that his arguments were worthy of thoughtful consideration.[19]

Although encouraged by the president's remarks, Parten and Allred pressured him from another direction. They went back to work on Senator Sheppard, who was one of the president's most loyal supporters in the Senate. Parten had failed to move Sheppard, so Allred agreed to try. Sheppard admitted to Allred that he was unenthusiastic about the Thomas bill, but he did not want to cross the president. Seeing his opportunity, Allred reminded Sheppard that he was one of Roosevelt's most dependable supporters and that he had helped pass some of the president's favorite legislation. Allred argued that it was time for Sheppard to go to the White House on a confidential visit and call in a debt. After much discussion, Sheppard finally agreed to do it.[20]

Allred and Parten returned to Texas hoping their effort would pay off. As he had done the year before with the Ickes bill, Rayburn kept the Thomas bill locked up in his committee. On May 4, when Ickes appealed to Roosevelt to do something, the president sent a note to another member of Rayburn's committee. He explained that while he did "not want to cross wires with Sam Rayburn about this matter," he nevertheless thought that a bill should be passed "somewhat along the lines of the Thomas Bill. . . ." Roosevelt admitted that "the Texas people want no legislation at this session but, as I have pointed out to them, even if Texas carried out oil production limitation some other state like California might fail to carry out their share, thus wrecking the situation for Texas." When this approach resulted in no progress, Ickes wrote Roosevelt again. "I am profoundly convinced," he argued, "that . . . this legislation . . . will be forthcoming if Congress is convinced that you want it." Ickes told Roosevelt that he believed that "only a minority of the oil interests in Texas" were opposed to the Thomas bill and that its passage "would be . . . a popular move." Roosevelt finally sent a note to Rayburn: "May I talk with you in about ten days in regard to the oil legislation? I still think we have to do something!" Rayburn, however, found several excuses to avoid meeting with the president to discuss the bill and it languished in the Interstate and Foreign Commerce Committee.[21]

As the congressional session drew closer to adjournment with little hope that the Thomas bill would get out of Rayburn's committee, Congressman Cole and Senator Connally submitted their own bills to regulate the oil industry. The Cole bill called for "voluntary" production controls and ratification of the Oil States Compact, while the Connally bill also ratified the compact and made permanent the Hot Oil Act, which had to be renewed every two years. Ickes attacked both bills. He described the Cole bill as "thoroughly vicious" because it would remove oil matters from the Interior Department's jurisdiction. He told Roosevelt that

"no oil legislation would be preferable to the Cole bill." Distracted by other matters and apparently reluctant to pressure Rayburn or to alienate Sheppard,
Roosevelt gave up. The president told Ickes that he would leave the troublesome
issue of oil production control "strictly up to Congress." This was the final blow to
Ickes's plan. When Roosevelt's attitude became clear, Congress junked all the oil
bills and on August 27, 1935, simply ratified the Oil States Compact.[22]

"I've come to discover now that you saved it"

By the fall of 1935, Ernest Thompson could declare to the members of the
American Petroleum Institute at their annual meeting that federal control was a
dead issue. "The desire for federal control came from within the industry,"
Thompson reminded the oil men, "then the industry . . . found the price . . . too
high." In his annual report to Woodley's shareholders a few weeks later, Parten
announced that most of the over-production problems were now past. "State
administered proration was fully in place," Parten said, "and it was being applied
legally. Hot oil just disappeared." For good or ill, the federal government no
longer posed a real threat to the independence of the U.S. oil industry. And this
was largely due to the persistent efforts of Parten, Ernest Thompson, Jimmy
Allred, Sam Rayburn, the Blalock brothers, and the Keck-Elliott group in
California, as well as others. A regulatory system was in place that remained undisturbed, with some exceptions, for decades to come. Instead of a federal oil czar,
the industry continued to be regulated at the state level, where agencies such as the
Texas Railroad Commission limited and allocated production. Under the
Connally Act, the federal government policed hot-oil shipments and through tariffs and voluntary agreements controlled oil imports. And of course, sophisticated
private arrangements existed among the major companies which served to maintain market stability and to guarantee "reasonable" profits. The system greatly
strengthened private controls over production, distribution, and pricing.
Although conservation of a crucial natural resource was the stated rationale for
this system, its real purpose was to maintain higher prices, limit competition, and
increase profits.[23]

A number of economic, political, and social factors worked to defeat the
attempt to place the oil industry under federal regulatory control. Perhaps the
most critical of these was the deep fear of nationalization, which appealed to no
one in the industry. Another significant factor was the return of stable conditions
and higher prices. The more business conditions improved, the less appealing federal controls appeared. Certainly at the political level, the leadership and decisions
of key individuals also made a difference. For example, Sam Rayburn's firm opposition played a significant role in turning the president away from Ickes's plan.
President Roosevelt, of course, played the most critical role of all. His final decision against federal regulation of production stopped Ickes in his tracks and led to
a national oil policy based upon two goals everyone could support: stabilization
and conservation. To Parten, however, Ernest Thompson was the real hero in the
federal oil-regulation war. Parten explained to a fellow independent oil man that

"all independent operators should be most grateful to [Thompson]. . . . It has taken great and inspired courage to maintain his position [against federal control]."[24]

From within the industry, however, J. R. Parten was the person who played the most significant role in the fight against federal control. No one spent as much of his personal time, money, and energy in the effort as did Parten. He organized, led, and largely paid for the team of Jack Blalock, Myron Blalock, Claude Wild, and Bailey Hardy, which fought and won the majority of the legislative fights in Washington and Austin. He kept the Independent Petroleum Association of Texas alive and visible as an opposition lobby during the most crucial days of the oil fight. Parten's close relationship with Jimmy Allred educated, energized, and guided Allred's efforts on their behalf, resulting, for example, in Parten being able to write important provisions of the Oil States Compact. The friendship that he forged with Sam Rayburn played a role in keeping that important congressman on their side. Ernest Thompson came to rely on Parten's advice and support in his struggle to preserve the Railroad Commission's authority to regulate oil production in Texas. For a period of six critical years, from the early days of martial law in East Texas to the fight in Washington to defeat the last Ickes bill, Parten was at the center of nearly every important oil battle. If he could not be on the scene personally, one of his lawyers, Jack Blalock, was usually there for him.

Despite Parten's omnipresence in public policy deliberations throughout the national oil crisis, his critical role in the episode has gone largely unacknowledged by historians and other students of the industry. This is in large part due to the involvement in the story of such dominating and colorful historical figures as Harold Ickes and Sam Rayburn, whose presence has overwhelmed and subsumed the significant role played by lesser-known players. Also, unlike oil men such as H. L. Hunt of Dallas and Hugh Roy Cullen of Houston, Parten was not a self-promoter. In all of his activities, he always preferred to play the position of producer or director rather than leading actor. In future years, this characteristic also resulted in Parten's relative anonymity in other significant public policy episodes in which he played a key role. His industry opponents in the federal oil-control fight, however, knew Parten and understood his role very well.

A few years after the federal oil battle, J. Edgar Pew of the Sun Oil Company came over to Parten's chair during a break in a meeting of the National Petroleum Council. "He tapped me on the shoulder," Parten later recalled, "and he said, 'I want to make a confession to you and an apology. I was one of those misguided oil men that thought that you and your group were wrecking the oil business in 1933 and 1934. I've come to discover now that you saved it."[25]

Part Two

1935–1941

CHAPTER 10

"But I Can Sure as Hell Appoint You!"

Parten Becomes a University Regent, 1935–1936

Within weeks after Allred won his race for governor in August 1934, University of Texas faculty members and ex-students urged him to appoint J. R. Parten to the board of regents, a nine-member policy-making board of trustees with ultimate authority over every aspect of the university's programs. In the months before his inauguration in January 1935, Allred kept his own counsel about possible regental appointments.

Meanwhile, Parten joined with a small group of influential ex-students in a concerted effort to persuade the legislature to increase the university's appropriations in its upcoming session and to change the method in which that body managed the university's budget. Appropriations remained at late-1920s levels despite the university's rapid increase in student population. Because of the Depression, the legislature during the previous session had implemented deep salary cuts for all university employees. One problem was the legislature's use of the line-item appropriation, which specified exactly how much state money would be made available for every job and activity at the university. The legislative budget tied the hands of the regents and the administration by not allowing the transfer of funds from one line to another. The regents were requesting that the legislature appropriate its state support in a "lump sum," allowing the administration to distribute the funds as appropriate among its various programs as developments warranted. The university's alumni organization, the Ex-Student's Association, had been ineffective in its lobbying efforts, so several influential and politically active friends of the university, including Myron Blalock, Houston businessman Mike Hogg, and former Texas attorney general Robert L. Bobbitt, decided to wage their own lobbying campaign. They asked Parten to serve as their leader because of his friendship with Allred, his lobbying experience, and his obvious interest in the University of Texas. Parten chaired a meeting of this group in Austin on December 16.[1]

In December 1934, the news leaked out that Governor-elect Allred had decided not to reappoint Beauford Jester to the university's board of regents. Parten and many other ex-students considered Jester, who was an old friend of Parten's from student days, to be an outstanding regent. Worried that a new appointee might not be as active and supportive of the university as Jester had been, Parten went to Austin in late December to urge Allred to reappoint him. He also took the opportunity to lobby the governor on behalf of the university's request for a lump-sum appropriation. The governor readily agreed to support the budget requests, but Jester was another matter. Allred complained that Jester had "abused and defamed" him during the campaign. "I just can't accommodate him," Allred stressed. "But I can sure as hell appoint you." Taken by surprise, Parten replied that his official residence was Shreveport and the legislature was certain to object to his appointment for that reason. Allred knew that Parten planned to relocate Woodley's headquarters to Texas within the next few weeks. He told Parten that he would wait until after Woodley opened its office in Houston to announce the appointment. Parten accepted.[2]

Despite facing new business challenges as a result of Woodley's planned move to Houston, Parten accepted Allred's offer for reasons that he felt were compelling. To serve as a regent was (and is) the dream of every prominent former student with a strong interest in the university. Although regents serve without pay for six-year terms, the position is a prestigious one that provides an opportunity for its most influential and active members to shape and direct the development of the state's "flagship" institution of higher education. In the mid-1930s the University of Texas and Texas A&M, the state's land-grant college located near Bryan, were the primary state-supported institutions of higher education. Because A&M did not admit women students, required its male undergraduates to belong to a military corps, and viewed its mission largely as an agricultural and engineering school, the University of Texas was unchallenged and preeminent as the state's leading institution for an education in the liberal arts and for graduate and professional training. Accordingly, a position on its board of regents was among the most important appointments the governor of Texas could make. This was the case not only because of the dominant and influential status of the University of Texas as an educational institution with a multi-million dollar budget, but also because it had been embroiled in politics ever since it opened its doors to students in the fall of 1883.

As the main public university in a state where religious fundamentalism and a strong strain of anti-intellectualism have made their marks, the University of Texas has often been the target of those who feared change, free inquiry and expression, and "non-Texan" influences. The university's regents have often served as lightening rods for the highly charged attacks on the institution by these elements of reaction and fear. On the other hand, the regents must also deal with a frequently hostile faculty never satisfied with any budget. In addition, the

University of Texas has always been seen by a large percentage of state legislators as an unreasonable financial burden on the state treasury. Every two years, the university and the legislature engage in an often acrimonious struggle over appropriations. Those regents who have become leaders on the board usually serve as the institution's most important lobbyists in this exhausting battle. Service on the board, therefore, can be hard and thankless work for those regents who take a leadership role. For these reasons and more, regental appointments are important and call for careful consideration by the governor, who must nominate the candidates for approval by the state Senate. Traditionally, governors have appointed political advisors or large campaign contributors to the board, so Allred's appointment of Parten did not surprise anyone who knew about the oil man's close relationship to the governor, as well as his active interest in the university.[3]

Allred announced Parten's appointment on March 11, 1935. By then, Woodley had made its move to Houston. Parten's appointment received widespread approval, despite the fact that he was replacing the popular Beauford Jester. Describing Parten as "tall and soldierly-looking," the Houston *Chronicle* praised Allred's selection, noting that the University of Texas "is close to Major Parten's heart. He studies its needs and fights for its advantages. . . . He owns and pilots his airplane, making short work of a trip to Washington or Austin when the oil business has a governmental angle." When Parten's father-in-law wrote a thank-you note to the governor, Allred replied that he was "proud to have appointed JR on the Board of Regents. I think he is one of the greatest and sweetest characters I ever knew."[4]

During his tenure on the board, Parten would develop an understanding and a deep appreciation of freedom of expression and inquiry, and he continued to the end of his life to staunchly defend both. The years Parten spent on the board of regents would have a profound effect on his political views and would be indicative of the deep love he had throughout his life for the University of Texas. He would spend six hectic and eventful years as one of the most active regents in the history of the university, and his actions in regard to its oil and gas leases in particular would have a lasting and beneficial effect.

Parten's appointment to the university's board of regents gave Allred an opportunity to do something for his good friend. Allred also liked the idea of having Parten readily available as a member of his unofficial "kitchen cabinet." The governor knew he would be a tireless worker on behalf of the university and that this would make him a frequent visitor to Austin. He expected to make use of Parten's knowledge of the oil industry during his administration. Allred's expectations materialized. Parten later estimated that during the six years he served as a regent, he spent more than half of his working time conducting university-related business, much of it on legislative matters. He was a frequent guest for breakfast and dinner at the Governor's Mansion and he and Allred occasionally attended University of Texas football games together. Parten also participated in Allred's informal "kitchen cabinet" meetings with several university professors, Ralph Yarborough, Sec. of State Gerald C. Mann, and student leaders in the university's chapter of the Young Democrats, including Creekmore Fath and Robert C.

Eckhardt. Fath later observed that "there's no question but that Jimmy [Allred] had a very high regard for J. R. and turned to him for advice over and over again. When Jimmy was governor, it seemed like every time the Legislature was in session, I would see J. R. wandering around the corridors of the Capitol. Everyone understood that he was one of the University's and one of Jimmy's liaisons with the Legislature."[5]

As soon as Parten became a university regent he gathered all the information he could about the duties of the position. He especially wanted to know the proper role of a regent in relation to the university's administration and its faculty and students. Before his first regents' meeting, Parten visited the campus and talked to Pres. Harry Yandell Benedict and several faculty members. He met with leaders of the ad hoc ex-students group working on the university's budget problem. His work with them had already given him a thorough understanding of the budget process and the university's financial condition. Parten also conferred with some of his fellow regents. "As I went along," he noted, "I made up my own mind about what a regent ought to be interested in and what he ought to do. He ought not to run the academic departments. He ought not to try to do the work of the football coach. He ought not to try to fire faculty members."[6]

The University of Texas Board of Regents

The board that Parten joined was generally one of the most harmonious and stable in the university's politically turbulent history. Regents serve staggered terms with three positions up for reappointment every two years, but six of Parten's colleagues served as regents for the entire six-year period he was on the board, and a seventh member served for nearly five of those six years. This unusual degree of continuity was the result partially of Parten's influence with Allred, who reappointed several regents at Parten's urging. Parten got along well with all of his colleagues, but his closest allies on the board were Dr. George Morgan, Marguerite S. Fairchild, Leslie C. Waggener Jr., and Kenneth H. Aynesworth. Morgan, also a new Allred appointee, was the same age as Parten and had the most in common with him. Morgan was a geologist and independent oil man from San Angelo who had supported Allred during the governor's race. Marguerite Fairchild of Lufkin was another recent appointee. Only the second woman regent in the university's history, Fairchild's special interest was in the fine arts programs. Parten grew to respect her strong sense of fair play and her dedication to the university. Leslie Waggener, the fifty-nine-year-old son of the first president of the university, became Parten's close friend. Appointed to the board in 1931, Waggener was an officer of the Republic National Bank of Dallas, one of the largest financial institutions in the state. Kenneth Aynesworth, a sixty-two-year-old surgeon from Waco appointed to the board in 1933, was a scholarly bibliophile who accumulated a large personal library in literature and history. Aynesworth was primarily interested in the University of Texas Medical Branch in Galveston and in the university libraries.[7]

Those regents with whom Parten occasionally clashed, were Hilmer H. Weinert, Henry J. Lutcher Stark, and Edward Randall Sr. Weinert, a banker,

Some of Parten's colleagues on the University of Texas Board of Regents, 1935. Top, H. J. Lutcher Stark (left) and Marguerite Fairchild; bottom, Edward Randall (left) and Leslie Waggener. *CNs 05748, 04598, 09712, 09711. Courtesy Prints and Photographs Collection, CAH.*

lawyer, and oil man from Seguin, had been appointed a regent in 1933 by Miriam Ferguson. A gruff and headstrong former University of Texas football letterman, Weinert was more interested in the football program than anything else. The forty-seven-year-old H. J. Lutcher Stark was another football-minded regent. Heir to a vast Southeast Texas lumber, land, and oil fortune, and a 1910 graduate of the university, Stark had been appointed to the board of regents in 1919 at the age of thirty-one. With the exception of the two-year period between 1931 and 1933, he had served on the board continuously since his initial appointment. Not shy about interfering in the administrative affairs of the university, he had been embroiled over the years in several campus controversies, especially in the athletic department. "Lutcher was always considered kind of a spoiled boy," Parten later recalled, "and he dealt a little misery to the professors from time to time."

At seventy-five, Dr. Edward Randall was the oldest member of the board. Son-in-law of William Pitt Ballinger, a politically powerful and wealthy lawyer during Galveston's most prosperous era, Randall was an influential member of the Galveston civic establishment. A member of the faculty of the University of Texas Medical Branch since its opening, he had served as president of the city's John Sealy Hospital for more than twenty-five years, and had operated a private medical practice in Galveston for over half a century. Initially appointed in 1929 and then reappointed by Allred in 1935, Randall acted as though he were solely responsible for the university's Medical School. Irascible, arrogant, domineering, and politically conservative, Randall frequently disagreed with the board's other physician, Dr. Aynesworth, about Medical School affairs. John T. Scott, president of the First National Bank of Houston and a trustee of Rice Institute, was the only member of the 1935 board who was not reappointed before Parten left the board. Former state senator E. J. Blackert of Victoria, an Allred ally, replaced Scott as regent in 1937.[8]

The University's sixty-five-year-old president, H. Y. Benedict, was a more important influence on Parten as a regent than any of his board colleagues. Known affectionately as "Benny" by students, faculty, and other friends, Benedict was a native Texan who graduated from the University of Texas only five years after it opened in 1883. He earned his Ph.D. at Harvard in 1898 and came home the next year to join the university's faculty as a teacher of mathematics and astronomy. Benedict held several administrative posts before becoming president in 1927, including dean of the College of Arts and Sciences. A gifted academic administrator, Benedict was able to manage the university with a firm hand while retaining the love and respect of his faculty and students, a difficult achievement for any university president.[9]

J. R. Parten was among Benedict's greatest admirers. Soon after Parten was appointed to the board of regents, he visited with the president to get advice about the proper role of a regent. He learned from Benedict that the person he should not emulate was Lutcher Stark. During the mid-1920s, when Stark was chairman of the regents, he had interrogated Benedict about his religious beliefs during a regents' meeting when Benedict was still the dean of the College of Arts and Sciences. Stark, searching for any sign of atheism in the university's administra-

University of Texas president, H. Y. Benedict, early 1930s. *CN 09621. Courtesy Prints and Photographs Collection, CAH.*

tion, asked the dean if he believed in God. Without hesitation, Benedict replied, "Do you mean an anthropomorphic God?" Stark immediately adjourned the meeting to find a dictionary. The inquisition never resumed.[10]

A few days before Parten's first regents' meeting on March 30, 1935, Stark asked for his support in his attempt to be the new chairman of the board. With Benedict's advice fresh on his mind, Parten agreed to support Stark for chairman only after extracting a promise from him that he would treat Benedict and his fellow regents with respect and that he would not meddle in administrative affairs. Later, Weinert, Waggener, and Randall met with Parten and asked him to serve as chairman rather than Stark, arguing that the latter's habit of interfering in the daily affairs of the university would cause no end of trouble. Parten declined the offer on the grounds of inexperience and the fact that he had pledged his vote to Stark after getting his promise to behave himself. This answer failed to placate Weinert and his two colleagues who subsequently asked Governor Allred to pressure Parten not to vote for Stark. When Parten heard about this he called Allred and advised him to stay out of the board's internal politics. The governor readily agreed. Stark was elected chairman at the first meeting Parten attended as a regent. Weinert, Randall, and Waggener dropped their opposition only after Stark agreed to appoint Parten and Randall to the board's executive committee. Stark also appointed Parten to the regents' legislative, athletic, land, and medical committees, appointments reflecting Parten's experience and interests.[11]

The debt Stark owed Parten for supporting his bid for the chairmanship had to be called in much sooner than Parten had ever anticipated. A few weeks after assuming the board chairmanship, Stark ordered Benedict to dismiss Roy Bedichek, the head of the University Interscholastic League (UIL). The UIL is an agency of the University of Texas that governs all competitive events between public schools in the state, such as football, basketball, debate, and marching-band contests. Bedichek had ruled Stark's son ineligible to play football because of a violation of UIL regulations. Benedict reported this incident to Parten, insisting that Bedichek, who was a close friend of the president's, had done nothing wrong. Benedict explained that not only was Stark's behavior improper in this particular matter, it was also bad policy in general for a regent to meddle in personnel decisions, especially outside a formal meeting of the regents. "I jumped Lutcher at the next regents meeting," Parten recalled. He scolded Stark for breaking his promise and demanded that he leave Bedichek alone. Stark agreed to drop the matter and Bedichek's job was saved. He went on to become one of the cultural heroes of Texas as the author of the classic *Adventures of a Texas Naturalist* and as a member of a the literary triumvirate that included his close friends Walter Prescott Webb and J. Frank Dobie. Parten had gotten a firsthand lesson from Benedict about the proper role of a regent. It was advice he would need to draw upon in the future.[12]

"Putting a forty dollar saddle on a twenty dollar horse"

The first serious problem Parten had to confront as a regent was the university's inadequate funding. The University of Texas had made great progress since the discovery of oil on a large portion of its two million acres of land in West Texas in 1923. The earnings from these oil lands went into an endowment, called the Permanent Fund, of which the principal could not be spent for any purpose. Income from the endowment, however, went into another account, called the Available Fund, which could be used only for the construction of buildings. Money from the Available Fund was making it possible for the university to replace its wooden-shack classrooms and laboratories with substantial and impressive buildings, such as the new "Main Building" with its twenty-seven-story clock-tower that soon became the university's architectural symbol. Despite this windfall, use of the Available Fund was so narrowly restricted that faculty salaries and a wide range of important activities remained dependent on legislative support. Unfortunately, as income from the oil money increased, legislative appropriations were reduced, resulting in a situation where an underpaid and understaffed faculty was teaching to an ever-increasing student population in new and aesthetically pleasing buildings. As J. Frank Dobie later observed, it was like putting a "forty dollar saddle on a twenty dollar horse." This was a situation that the university's administration and many former students, including J. R. Parten, earnestly hoped to remedy. It was Parten's primary goal when he became a regent. As he learned more about his university and its potential for helping develop and modernize Texas, that goal increased in importance and served as the underlying motivation for most of his actions on the board.[13]

At the end of April, Parten spent two weeks walking the corridors of the state Capitol urging legislators to pass a university budget with substantive increases in salary and operational funds and to make the appropriation in one lump sum. In his hands were letters from faculty members detailing how difficult it was to sustain a university's educational mission on an inadequate budget. A letter from physics professor W. T. Mather explained that his laboratory had long been obsolete. He lamented that he found himself "wondering at times why we have to make such efforts to secure that which is essential for the work we are engaged to do." With the strong help of the university's legislative allies and support from key ex-students, Parten made much progress in his effort to secure an increase in appropriations. He got nowhere, however, in his attempt to get a lump-sum appropriation. Most of the legislators believed that the line-item budget was the only way to insure that the university would spend the state's money as the legislature intended. In this fight, Parten's chief nemesis was his old friend "Uncle Elmer" Pope, who not only believed that the state was spending too much money on the university, but that the legislature needed every means at its disposal to prevent "radicals" from taking over the faculty. A "dangerous" professor protected by tenure could be eliminated simply by removing his "line" from the budget.[14]

On May 13, Parten sent the happy news to his fellow regents that the legislature had passed a budget increasing appropriations for the main campus by two hundred thousand dollars. Although the legislature retained the line-item budget, it did agree to a modest increase in faculty and staff salaries. It also approved plans to furnish and staff a university museum in honor of the upcoming centennial of Texas's independence from Mexico. Most of the money for the building, however, had to be raised by the American Legion through the sale of commemorative centennial coins. Parten knew that Allred favored the new budget, but he was also aware of other pressures on the governor to keep overall state expenditures as low as possible. Parten wrote Allred from Houston on May 15 requesting that if he found any reason to cut an item from the university budget, he wanted "the privilege of talking to you about same before it is finally done." Allred, ignoring the demands to cut the budget, signed the appropriations bill intact.[15]

"Baghdad on the Bayou"

Although the university's legislative struggle was over (at least for the next two years), Parten still spent as much time during the summer of 1935 on other university matters as he did on his oil business. By then, Woodley Petroleum had established its new headquarters on the fourteenth floor of the Second National Bank Building in downtown Houston. J. R. and Opal had purchased a new house at 2515 Pelham Drive in Houston's prestigious River Oaks, an exclusive neighborhood for the city's wealthy. Opal welcomed the move to Houston. She was somewhat bored with her life in Shreveport and "Baghdad on the Bayou," as Houston's newspaper columnists liked to call their city, offered many more cultural opportunities. Houston, the boomtown of the South with over three hundred thousand residents, was by 1935 the largest city in Texas. Although it had its share of people suffering from the effects of the Depression, Houston was relatively better-off economically than most American cities because of its ties to the oil industry. The city had an exhilarating liveliness boosted by a boomtown ethos.

Opal lost little time getting involved in the River Oaks social scene. She and J. R. joined the "right" clubs such as the Houston Country Club and the River Oaks Country Club, both open only to the socially prominent, and they supported the cultural institutions favored by Houston's economic elite, such as the Museum of Fine Arts and the Houston Symphony Orchestra. Continuing an interest she had developed in Shreveport, Opal became involved in the Houston Little Theater, serving on committees and acting in several plays. Such diversions were important to Opal because J. R. was away from home more often than not.[16]

Accordingly, Opal's open affair with Dallas Sherman continued uninterrupted by her move to Texas. She and Dallas, who was now out of the army and employed by a flying service in Pittsburgh, took vacation excursions together whenever they had the opportunity, which was often. The first summer J. R. and Opal lived in Houston, Opal went with Dallas on an extensive tour of the historic sites in the tidewater region of Virginia while J. R. shuttled between Austin and the upper Texas Gulf Coast, where Woodley was busy hunting for oil. As an example of the open way this affair between his wife and the dashing pilot was conducted, Dallas sent J. R. a report on his and Opal's tour, saying that she "seemed to get a great bit of pleasure from all the sightseeing we did. We thought of you many times while at Mount Vernon, Jamestown, Yorktown, Williamsburg." Dallas invited J. R. to go with him and Opal to the National Air Races in Cleveland on the upcoming Labor Day holiday, explaining that "Opal has told me many times during the last year or so that she would like to see the races, and I have asked her to meet me in Cleveland, which I think she intends to do." J. R. replied that his schedule would keep him away from the air races, but he wished them both to have a good time.[17]

"The most important work I did for the University"

While Opal and Dallas toured, Parten immersed himself in University of Texas affairs. As chair of a special regents' museum committee, he negotiated a contract with the American Legion to plan and operate the centennial museum, eventually to be called the Texas Memorial Museum. He carefully inspected each of several proposed sites for the museum building and held meetings with architects, Legionaires, and university administrators to determine the best location.

Parten also helped recruit a new chairman for the Petroleum Engineering Department and met with the faculty to get their suggestions on how to improve the department. After studying plans for new student dormitories, he lobbied his fellow regents in an effort to include dining halls in the new buildings. Parten's time-consuming involvement in the details of campus planning that summer caused Hines Baker, his friend at Humble Oil, to compliment him on "the real seriousness with which you are considering all matters having to do with wise planning for more effective results at the University. . . ."[18]

Parten's efforts to improve the university's financial situation did not end with the passage of the appropriations bill. He also worked to improve the university's income from its oil lands, a subject about which he had a special understanding. The state constitution of 1876 provided for an endowment of approximately one million acres (later increased to two million acres) in West Texas for the support of the University of Texas. Until the early 1920s, this arid and rocky land stretching over nineteen counties was considered nearly valueless. The university had earned a small income from leasing grazing rights, but nothing substantive. In 1923 that situation changed dramatically when it was discovered that oil lay beneath much of the land. The university had earned a significant amount of money in oil leases and royalties since that date.

Parten had never acquired an oil and gas lease on university lands, but he had inspected most of it and knew its potential for oil production. He was convinced that the lands were capable of generating much more revenue for the university than they were doing at the time. In July 1935, he and George Morgan convinced their fellow regents to withhold some of the oil land from development and keep it in reserve because of the certainty that the price would increase dramatically in the near future. A few months later Parten persuaded the board to adopt a policy of leasing small tracts of 160 acres, rather than the larger tracts of land it usually leased. He explained to Aynesworth and Fairchild that the smaller tracts would "ultimately give greater benefit to the University where there are good prospects for oil." In this case, Parten was also opening the door wider for his fellow independents. Smaller tracts, which would be available for less cost than the much larger tracts, would attract more wildcatters.[19]

Parten also suspected that the university's method of selling oil and gas leases by sealed bids was the most significant reason for the relatively low level of income. As an independent, he knew that sealed bids favored the major companies because they had the financial and technical resources to explore potential leases fully, while most independents did not. In a sealed bid, a major company (or any prospective bidder) could keep its interest in a lease a secret and therefore avoid competitive bids, keeping the lease price low. The sealed-bid system also kept the bids rational and calculated. An open auction, on the other hand, always had the potential to set off a buying frenzy resulting in purchasers making higher bids than they had intended. Another problem was that sealed bids were subject to fraud. Parten and many other oil operators had suspected that the sealed-bid system for public lands in New Mexico had been rigged. As Parten later noted, a sealed envelope could be "sweated open" by insiders overnight and resealed before the next morning. Although Parten did not believe there had been any fraud involved in the Texas bids, he knew that many operators suspected there had been. The result was that these oil men refused to submit bids, which made the system less competitive.[20]

In the summer of 1935, Parten discussed his concerns regarding the university's lease and royalty income with Clarence Lohman, an attorney and new partner of the Blalocks who had recently moved to Houston to handle much of Woodley's legal affairs. Lohman, a graduate of the University of Texas, had done legal work for the Osage Indians in Oklahoma before his move to Houston. He suggested to Parten that the university should adopt the open-auction bidding system used by the federal government in selling leases on the Osage Indian lands in Oklahoma. Lohman argued that the method was practical, inexpensive, and should result "in enormous returns." Parten liked the idea immediately. He subsequently made trips to Oklahoma to observe the open auctions on the Osage Indian reservation lands and to Washington to confer with officials at the Bureau of Indian Affairs who administered the program. What he saw and heard convinced him that the university should abandon its sealed-bid method of leasing and replace it with open-bid auctions. During the previous sixteen years, the Osage Indians had earned more than four times as much a barrel for oil taken from their lands as had the University of Texas.[21]

On November 23, 1935, the board of regents formally accepted the proposal Parten and Morgan submitted calling for a change in the bidding system. Afterward, Leslie Waggener told Parten that he believed it was "one of the most important and far reaching recommendations made" since he had been a member of the board. The decision was not welcomed by everyone, however. When news of the change was made public, Parten received telephone calls from several oil company executives, including Hines Baker, urging a return to sealed bids. Baker argued rather lamely that the open auction would actually bring in less money for the university; an argument Parten could easily dismiss. These protests only served as further evidence to Parten that the change was necessary.[22]

The Attorney General's Office ruled that the change in leasing methods was constitutional, but that the university could not pay for an auctioneer's services with funds generated by the auction. Parten and Morgan decided to pay for the auctioneer out of their own pockets until they could get a bill passed in the next legislative session to allow the university to pay for the auction by charging fees to the lease buyers. As the regents prepared for their first lease auction, Lohman suggested to Parten that they hire Col. Jacob E. Walters, the man who had conducted the Osage auctions, to serve as auctioneer. The colorful Walters had been an army scout in the Indian wars, a deputy U.S. marshall, and a horse and mule auctioneer. He had an outstanding reputation as an oil and gas auctioneer because of his success with the Osage auctions. On Parten's recommendation, the board of regents hired Walters, who conducted the first auction sale of oil and gas leases on University of Texas lands on July 20, 1936.[23]

With a change to open bidding, the independents flocked to the auction. Previous auctions had attracted an average of three or four bids per tract. The new system attracted more than a hundred bids per lease, resulting in a doubling of lease income and enriching the Permanent Fund by three hundred thousand dollars. Parten was delighted. Advising his fellow regents that the oil companies "seem to be in a buying mood," he recommended that another auction be held within three months. The next auction, in October 1936, had the same spectacular results. Bonuses on mineral leases for the fiscal year 1936–1937 eventually totalled 1.1 million dollars, compared to 347,000 dollars the previous year under the sealed-bid system. The open auction had nearly quadrupled bonus income.[24]

The auctions had been hugely successful, but the major oil companies complained about the higher prices for leases. Parten feared that unless the new system was codified by an act of the legislature, the major oil companies might be able to stop it when new regents came on the board. He decided that the law governing University of Texas oil lands needed revision, especially to mandate open auctions and to allow payment of the auctioneer with money from the proceeds. Parten also believed that the law should require oil companies to submit to the General Land Office all of the information they gathered while exploring university lands. This information, which included the results of seismic tests and test drilling, would be made public. He believed that such information would give the university important information about the location of underground water for irrigation purposes in future agricultural programs. It would also attract more independent bids.[25]

In late August 1936, Parten quietly began the work to get his new law. At his request, land commissioner Jesse H. Walker produced a rough draft of a bill. Parten then sent it to Clarence Lohman for revision into a final version to submit to the legislature in January 1937. "It is imperative that this bill be whipped into shape immediately," Parten instructed Lohman, "as quick action is essential to success." He warned Lohman not to discuss it with anyone because he wanted to give the major oil companies as little time as possible to prepare a lobby effort against it. He also met with Allred, who agreed to submit Parten's bill to the legislature. Forced a few days later to go to New York for an extended trip to conduct Woodley business, Parten persuaded George Morgan to take Lohman's draft to the next regents' meeting to get the board to authorize the governor to submit the bill on the university's behalf. "I think this matter of greatest importance to the university and do not hesitate to say that it is worth your while to make a special trip to Austin to confer with [Commissioner] Walker," Parten wrote Morgan.[26]

The regents voted to submit the official request to Allred. After Parten returned from New York, he had a brochure printed at his own expense to explain why the legislation was needed. Claude Wild distributed the brochure to each member of the legislature when Allred submitted the bill to the Senate. Parten expected strenuous opposition from the major oil companies, but it never surfaced. As he noted many years later, because of the demonstrated success of the open auction, the major oil companies were unable to sustain their argument that it would bring in less money than sealed bids. They could ill afford to complain publicly that they disliked the new system because it made them pay higher prices for leases that benefitted the public welfare. Wild monitored the bill through the committees and it passed easily on April 12, 1937. It has remained in effect ever since.[27]

Parten's leadership in revising the oil-and-gas-lease process resulted in tens of millions of dollars in additional income for the University of Texas over the years. Bert Haigh, who managed the university's lands for many years, considered Parten's work to be "an enormous success." He believed the university received valuable bonuses for tracts of land that probably would never have been bid on in the old system. University regents who served long after Parten departed from the board have stated that Parten's leadership in this matter ranks among the most significant achievements in the institution's history. Parten himself later concluded that putting together the open-auction system and revising the law governing the university's management of the leases was "the most important work I did for the University while on the Board of Regents."[28]

A "Second" University Education

1935–1936

Befor his appointment to the University of Texas Board of Regents, J. R. Parten's involvement in public affairs had been narrowly dictated by his own business interests. He had little experience in dealing with issues such as academic freedom. On the few occasions before 1935 when he is known to have expressed a formal opinion on academic freedom, his views were decidedly intolerant and self-serving. Two years before his appointment to the board of regents, for example, Parten had complained to Jimmy Allred about a speech made by university economics professor, George Ward Stocking, who had called for compulsory unitization of oil fields. Outraged, Parten asked then Attorney General Allred why the state allowed university professors to "take sides on such a highly controversial question?" There is no record of an Allred reply and the matter seems to have ended there, but Parten's complaint indicates that his view of academic freedom was extremely narrow at this point in his life. As a regent of the state's most important institution of higher learning, however, Parten now had new opportunities to expand his intellectual and political horizons. His frequent meetings with university faculty members and administrators exposed him to ideas and perspectives vastly different from those to which he had been exposed in the oil industry. As a regent, Parten was also forced to confront and make decisions about controversial issues related to intellectual, economic, and political freedom, such as press censorship, race relations, and free speech. When he recalled his years as a regent many years later, Parten admitted that the experience caused him to look at the world in new ways. "I didn't get a degree," Parten said, "but it was really my second university education."[1]

"Dr. Bob" and Academic Freedom

Parten's initial confrontation as a regent with the issue of academic freedom came only four months after his first board meeting. The problem stemmed from public statements issued by a member of the university's Department of Economics, which in the 1930s and 1940s had a reputation as a haven for leftist ideologues and intellectual bomb-throwers. In his memoirs, liberal Harvard economist John Kenneth Galbraith recalled that during these years the University of Texas had "the most radical of the major economic departments in the United States . . . even active Marxists were tolerated." This is an exaggeration. In reality, anti-Communist New Deal liberals dominated the department. The most prominent of this group were Clarence Ayres and Robert Montgomery. Because these well-known economists were highly visible critics of laissez-faire capitalism and the conservative policies of the Republican Party, they were frequent targets of conservatives who accused them of teaching radical and even subversive economic ideas.[2]

Ayres, who was one of the nation's leading scholars in the field of economics, attracted much attention in Texas as a proponent of the income tax as a tool to redistribute wealth; while Montgomery was equally well known as a critic of monopolies. Montgomery's favorite target in his antimonopoly lectures and writings was the Texas sulphur industry and its lobbyist, Roy Miller. Montgomery was a master teacher and energetic political activist, but he was not as highly regarded a scholar as Ayres. The latter, on the other hand, was not as politically active as Montgomery. Although very liberal for Texas, neither man was a Communist. The reason for their radical reputations stems more from the attacks made upon them by their conservative critics than from their actual economic philosophies. Conservative Texans tended to categorize anyone espousing the ideals of the progressive wing of the national Democratic Party as a left-wing radical. If they happened to be professors at the university, that made them *dangerous* left-wing radicals.[3]

Robert Montgomery in particular seemed to cause many sleepless nights for the state's economic reactionaries. The popular teacher, known by his students as "Dr. Bob," was a scourge of the Texas business establishment. A student of Thorstein Veblen and Charles A. Beard, Montgomery's politics were firmly rooted in the progressive tradition. He was a primary influence in the lives of a generation of students who later became leaders of the postwar liberal wing of the Democratic Party in Texas, including political strategist Creekmore Fath and seven-term congressman Robert C. Eckhardt.

Montgomery was a gifted public speaker who often spoke at banquets and civic club meetings around the state. At a public meeting in Fort Worth on July 1, 1935, Montgomery gave one of his standard talks on taxation policy, arguing that inheritance taxes should be increased enough to redistribute the wealth hoarded by the nation's richest families. Two days after the speech, an acquaintance of Parten's living in Fort Worth wrote to the new regent complaining that

Montgomery's lecture had been "socialistic in the extreme" and that his demands for a "soak-the-rich" taxation policy might lead to "nationalization of the country as advocated by all true socialists." He asked Parten if he thought such men should be employed by the university.[4]

The complaint about Montgomery's speech was similar in substance to Parten's earlier criticism of Stocking. Parten's immediate reaction to the complaint revealed that his thinking had not changed during the intervening two years. Replying to his friend in Fort Worth that he had received "several complaints about Dr. Montgomery's speeches," Parten declared that he was "very sympathetic with the ideas expressed" about whether faculty members should be allowed to give speeches on public issues. He explained that the University of Texas followed the same rules of academic freedom adopted by other schools, but he believed "that there should be limitations upon this privilege which should require professors not to go so far as to advocate destruction of our form of government. . . ." Parten promised to "do all within my power to stop the activities of professors that might bring discredit to the University. . . ."[5]

Parten met with President Benedict to discuss the complaint. Benedict told him that as a political conservative, he disagreed with Montgomery's economic philosophy, and as an administrator, he preferred that Montgomery keep his political opinions to himself. Nevertheless, the president was a defender of academic freedom as that concept was broadly defined on most campuses in the 1930s and he supported Montgomery's *right* to speak out on political and economic issues. Benedict explained that the preservation of such faculty rights was essential to the university's mission to pursue truth and to extend the boundaries of knowledge. "I can't say that it made a deep impression right away," Parten admitted, "but Benny gave me something to think about."[6]

Determined to know more about Montgomery, Parten hired a stenographer to transcribe one of Montgomery's speeches. When he read the transcript, he was surprised to discover that Montgomery's economic views closely resembled some of his own. The economics professor had called for a federal tax on the profits of monopolies at a rate "as close as possible to 100 percent," arguing that such a confiscatory tax would stop monopolistic practices. "Remove monopolies and we shall have a democracy again," Montgomery declared, "we have none today!" He also charged that "grasping capitalists" were conspiring to produce less simply to drive up prices, an argument Parten had made during the proration fight. Parten also learned that Montgomery was a close ally of Jimmy Allred and that he had drafted the governor's bill to regulate public utilities, then making its way through the legislature. At the end of July, Parten met with "Dr. Bob" and determined that although the economics professor was too supportive of federal regulation of all business activities to suit Parten's taste, he shared Parten's views on trust-busting and the need to protect the "little guy" in business. Parten and Montgomery soon became friends and their relationship grew as Montgomery became more involved as an advisor to Governor Allred.[7]

J. R. Parten's change of opinion about Robert Montgomery did not indicate that he had developed a new understanding of the tenets of academic freedom. At this stage of his life, Parten's support for academic freedom applied to those whose opinions he favored, rather than to those who espoused an opinion with which he strongly disagreed. His behavior in a similar affair only four months after the Montgomery incident, is evidence of this unchanged mind-set. In November 1935, a headline in the campus newspaper, the *Daily Texan*, titled "Dr. Stocking Urges Federal Oil Control" seized Parten's attention. The story alleged that Stocking told the student "Social Justice Club" that he not only supported compulsory unified operation of oil fields, but that he also believed those fields should be controlled by the federal government. Stocking was quoted as saying that the oil industry "is conducted on the principle of robbery," the same statement that had so outraged Parten two years earlier when Stocking had made it in a speech to the American Economics Association. As soon as he saw the *Daily Texan* story, Parten called Jack Blalock and requested him to contact the paper and demand an opportunity to counter Stocking's statements. Parten believed that it would be inappropriate as regent for him to make a public statement on the subject. The *Daily Texan* subsequently published Blalock's statement against federal control. "The only ones who favor federal control today," Blalock declared, "are . . . Harold Ickes . . . and a few professors who know nothing about the oil industry." Parten complained to Benedict that Stocking was "championing one side of the highly controversial issue of 'Federal Control of Oil Production.' Such utterances . . . are calculated to do great harm to the University. . . ." Claiming that Stocking was a "propagandist" rather than "a seeker of truth," Parten wanted Stocking's head.[8]

As in the episode with Montgomery, Benedict counseled Parten to calm down and to get Stocking's version of what he had said. Parten agreed to talk to Stocking, but the meeting was postponed several times because of the regent's hectic schedule and Stocking's own professional obligations. Stocking eventually wrote a long letter to Parten explaining that he had given a lecture to the student group about issues related to the regulation of the oil industry and that he had carefully explained every side of the controversy. The problem occurred when a student asked him after the lecture what his personal opinion was and he gave it. "I do sincerely regret," Stocking wrote, "that the *Texan* account left the impression that I was appearing in the role of an agitator for any particular program for the control of oil." By the time Parten received Stocking's written explanation in May 1936, he was eager to put the incident behind him. This was partly because Benedict had educated Parten about Stocking's considerable talents as a scholar and teacher, but it also stemmed from the fact that Parten was angry with the *Daily Texan* for reasons having nothing to do with the Stocking story and he was more than willing to shift blame for the incident to the student paper. "This is just another instance of where the *Daily Texan* recently has been unfair with a member of the Faculty," Parten wrote to Stocking.[9]

As a result of the influence of Benedict, Montgomery, and others, Parten gradually developed an understanding about the importance of preserving academic freedom. But he also understood the problems academic freedom created for a highly visible public university funded by legislative appropriations. Most of the university's budget remained dependent on the good will of a legislature highly sensitive to complaints from constituents about radicalism at the University of Texas. Parten and his board colleagues were preparing another major effort to increase the amount of its state appropriation and Parten did not want the budget to get tangled in a political spider web. Accordingly, Parten's desire to keep the university out of politics and away from controversial public issues guided most of his actions in a series of episodes in which the board of regents were involved in the final weeks of 1935 and the first six months of 1936.

As Parten's understanding of academic freedom evolved, he devised a strategy that sought to protect the faculty while making it seem as though he and his fellow regents were sympathetic to those who complained about the politics of individual teachers. Typical of this strategy was the way Parten handled two incidents in December 1935 involving Montgomery. Earl P. Adams, the chairman of the State Industrial Accident Board, complained to the board of regents about a speech Montgomery had given to the university's Progressive Democrat Club. Adams claimed that the professor, who was on leave from the university to serve on the Federal Planning Board in Washington, was a radical who was "teaching class prejudices and hatreds . . . that men who have accumulated wealth are enemies of society. . . ." He demanded his dismissal. Replying for the board, Parten thanked Adams for not taking his complaint to the press and assured him that Montgomery's activities would be thoroughly investigated. Parten, however, actually did nothing and the matter was quietly dropped.[10]

That same month, Parten received a letter from J. O. Guleke of Amarillo, a member of the state Board of Education and the author of a recently published pamphlet titled "Federal Encroachment Upon the Field of Education in Texas." The pamphlet's basic theme was that federal aid to education would end individual freedoms and turn the innocent children of Texas into Bolsheviks. Guleke, who had sent Parten one of his pamphlets, warned the regent that there were certain left-wing faculty members who favored the idea of federal aid to education. He advised Parten to consult with J. Evetts Haley, a gifted writer of western history and a passionate political reactionary who was working as a Texana collector for the university library, to learn the names of faculty members guilty of harboring such subversive ideas. Two months later, after Parten had failed to respond to Guleke's suggestion, he and Haley went to Parten's office in Houston to press their case about the subversives on the university faculty. Parten listened politely to their accusations, which were aimed mainly at Bob Montgomery. Comparing federal control of education to federal control of oil production, Parten assured Guleke and Haley that he opposed it as much as they. His "pride" in Texas, Parten said, had prevented him from "going to Washington begging for Federal funds for anything." Parten's assurances about his own beliefs and his rhetoric about Texas pride satisfied Guleke and Haley that something would be done about Montgomery and some of his colleagues. Parten, however, had no such intention and he did nothing. "I figured that these people who were so riled up about these teachers would go on with their business once they had time to calm down," Parten stated.[11]

Parten generally ignored accusations concerning Communist subversion on campus because he knew that the faculty members always under attack were not Communists. He also rejected the idea that communism posed any domestic threat to the United States. Instead, he believed that a form of corporate fascism similar to that in Mussolini's Italy posed a far greater threat to freedom in the United States. A few weeks before Parten's meeting with Guleke and Haley, Governor Allred had given him a copy of Elizabeth Dilling's *The Red Network* with a request for Parten to let him know what he thought about it. Dilling charged that with the active aid of the Roosevelt administration, the "Communist-Socialist world conspiracy . . . is boring within our churches, schools, and government and is undermining America like a cancerous growth." Parten told Allred that he was unimpressed. "Personally," he declared, "I have little fear of Communism in this country. . . ." Instead, he warned Allred about the threat from the extreme right. Parten argued that "any time . . . capital comes into violent conflict with Communism it has and will take shelter under the cloak of Fascism . . . as a means to protect itself."[12]

Out of the Night

On January 10, 1936, Cong. "Uncle Elmer" Pope complained to reporters that "rank communism" was being taught at the university. He warned that the legislature would investigate the situation as soon as possible. When Parten met with his family's longtime friend a few days later, Uncle Elmer told him that it would be difficult to prevent the legislature from cutting the university's budget because of the "bolsheviks" on the faculty. Parten assured Pope that there were no Communist faculty members currently at the university. He told Pope that the university had nothing to hide and that it would not oppose a legislative investigation of the faculty if it was necessary to prevent a budget cut. His friendship with the Parten family made no difference to Pope in this matter. "'Uncle Elmer' just shrugged his shoulders," Parten recalled. "Hell, I knew what was going on. The old man just didn't want the University to get any more money."[13]

In mid-January, with Pope's threat hanging in the air and the university planning to launch another campaign for increased appropriations in the next legislative session, Parten and his regental colleagues were presented with a very unwelcome development in the form of a newly published book titled *Out of the Night: A Biologist's View of the Future*. Written by internationally famed geneticist Herman J. Muller, who was on a leave of absence from the University of Texas, *Out of the Night* was a vision of a future world shaped and governed by scientific practices known today as genetic engineering. Although disconcerting to many, Muller viewed such developments positively, predicting the eventual betterment of the human race through eugenics. Muller predicted, for example, that in the future women could be artificially inseminated. His opinions about eugenics meant little to the university's board of regents. What was bothersome about *Out of the Night* was not only the fact that Muller was working in Moscow when it was published, but also that the book included a section in which he praised "the great and solid actualities of collective achievement" in the Soviet Union. On the title page of his new book, Muller was identified prominently as a professor of zoology at the University of Texas and "member of the Academy of Sciences of the U.S.S.R."[14]

At a meeting in mid-January, President Benedict warned the regents that Muller's book could prove to be very damaging to the university. Benedict explained that Muller was a Communist Party member who had been actively promoting the party as a university professor. A legislative investigation of Muller would provide much ammunition for the university's enemies to use in their fight against an increased appropriation. Parten knew nothing about Muller, so Benedict gave him the background.

Muller, who was described by Julian Huxley as the world's "greatest living geneticist," was one of the most prestigious scientists ever to serve on the University of Texas faculty. He came to Texas as an associate professor of zoology in 1920 after earning his doctorate at Columbia University. Muller bombarded fruit flies with X-rays in his university laboratory in 1926 and discovered that radiation could change the structure of genes. For this discovery he was elected to the American Academy of Sciences in 1931 and he was eventually awarded the Nobel Prize. From all accounts, Muller was a shy and quiet workaholic who pushed his physical and mental abilities to the limit. Early in 1932, he apparently suffered a nervous breakdown. After disappearing for two days, he was found wandering in the hills west of Austin bruised and dazed. Muller's physician determined that he was suffering from "melancholia" and concluded that the geneticist had tried to kill himself. Muller quickly recovered. A few weeks after this incident, he learned that he had won a prestigious Guggenheim Fellowship for 1932–1933 to conduct research in Europe. The university granted Muller a year's leave of absence.[15]

In June 1932, prior to Muller's scheduled departure for Germany, an unauthorized student newspaper titled the *Spark* was distributed on campus. The four-page publication denounced the low wages paid to construction workers employed on university building projects, the impoverished living conditions of Austin's African Americans, and the reactionary activities of Galveston businessman Maco Stewart, who was trying to get the legislature to pass a law against "subversive speech." Appearance of the *Spark* caused an immediate uproar. The regents, led by Chairman R. L. Batts, quickly passed a rule against student membership in "secret political organizations" and student participation in the production and distribution on campus of anonymously published material. A few days after the appearance of the *Spark*, an agent of the U.S. Immigration Service made available to the regents photostats of papers seized in a raid in San Antonio that included a handwritten letter signed by Herman Muller that not only implicated him as being involved in the publication of the *Spark*, but also provided conclusive evidence that he was a member of the Communist Party of the U.S.A. Muller's party membership was not illegal, but university policy prohibited the employment of party members and it was cause for dismissal. President Benedict wanted to fire Muller, but Chairman Batts feared that Muller's mental condition might cause him to commit suicide if he was dismissed, resulting in "much unpleasant notoriety" for the university. The regents finally decided to keep silent about the matter and allow Muller to go to Europe for a year. "Almost anything can happen during a year," Batts advised a fellow regent.[16]

Muller proceeded to Germany unmolested by the regents. After a year in Berlin, the regents granted Muller an extension of one year to his leave of absence to continue his unfinished research. Unknown to Benedict, Muller was headed for Moscow to conduct research at the Soviet Institute of Genetics. After several months in the Soviet Union, the regents granted Muller an additional year's leave. Muller was still in Moscow at the Soviet Institute of Genetics when *Out of the Night* was published in late 1935.[17]

Publication of *Out of the Night* threatened to expose the heretofore successful effort to hide Muller and his activities in the hope that he would never return from Moscow. Benedict proposed to Parten and his board colleagues that he inform Muller about the evidence the university had about his Communist Party membership and his role in the *Spark* affair. He would tell Muller that his leave of absence would not be extended another year and that he would have to return to Austin by September 1 to be tried by a faculty committee on the charge that he was conspiring to produce a second issue of the *Spark* in violation of regents' rules before he went on leave. This charge was obviously flimsy and would be difficult to prove, but Benedict hoped that the specter of being subjected to a public hearing would persuade Muller to resign and remain in Moscow. A few days after the regents approved Benedict's letter to Muller, the situation took on some urgency when the *Daily Texan* spread the news of Muller's affiliation with a Soviet scientific institute in a front-page story about *Out of the Night*. To many Texans it was damning enough simply to be working in the Soviet Union, much less to praise its government in a book.[18]

Muller replied quickly to Benedict's letter. He denied that he had any association with the *Spark*, but he verified his belief in communism. Much to Benedict's relief, Muller also stated his intention to resign from the faculty. In a follow-up letter, Benedict assured Muller that if he resigned, the university would drop the matter and nothing would be made public. Accordingly, on April 3, Muller submitted his resignation to Benedict, stating that the official reason was that his position in Moscow gave him better opportunities for research. He added, however, that staying in Moscow also gave him "greater freedom . . . in expressing what I consider to be the cardinal truths which must require recognition by the world today." The regents authorized a press release claiming that the scientist had resigned to become "the national genetics expert of Soviet Russia." There was no hint of controversy. Parten later explained that Benedict "just figured that Texans were so provincial that they just could not tolerate this Communist on the faculty and he thought he was doing the best thing for the University and the best thing for Muller." The best thing for the university meant that Muller's resignation

Herman J. Muller in his laboratory at the University of Texas, ca. 1920s. *CN 09624. Courtesy Prints and Photographs Collection, CAH.*

would spare it from the inevitable firestorm of protest during the next session of the legislature.[19]

When Parten was asked years later if he had any regrets about the way the Muller case was handled, he answered: "Things have changed a whole lot from that day to this. I might not feel the same way now. But I went along with Benedict, and the whole Board did." Parten's support of Benedict's action stemmed from his fear that the university's legislative enemies would use Muller as a weapon in their effort to keep the university's budget from growing. It was easy to sacrifice a man who held another prestigious post and therefore would not be unemployed, who was several thousand miles away, who did not protest publicly, and who was a Communist. Parten eventually moderated his position, but in 1936 he did not believe a Communist Party member should hold a teaching position at a public university.[20]

Unfortunately, not all of Parten's and his colleagues' efforts to prevent political damage to the university were as successful as the Herman J. Muller affair. But in their zeal to keep the university out of politics and to keep peace with the legislature, Parten and his fellow regents made decisions that hurt the university's academic reputation. And in the end, despite these preventive actions, the university still had to suffer unfair and highly publicized political attacks from right-wing political critics.

The 1936 Texas Democratic Primary

"This is the most apathetic state campaign so far in history," the Austin *American* lamented during the Texas Democratic primary campaign in July 1936. The main reason for apathy was the lack of controversy in the contest for the state's highest office. Jimmy Allred was an overwhelming favorite for election to a second term as governor and the races for other state offices, including Ernest Thompson's campaign for reelection to the Railroad Commission, seemed to generate little popular interest. The political situation pleased Parten because he did not want to take an active role in the election campaign. As a regent, he feared that his visible involvement in a heavily contested state campaign might cause political problems for the University of Texas. With hot oil under control and with no evident threat from the federal government to the oil industry, he had little motivation for personal political action.[21]

Accordingly, Parten took no part in Allred's reelection bid other than to make a sizeable donation to Allred's campaign fund. The only other political campaign of strong interest to Parten, the Texas Railroad Commission race, seemed to be under Ernest Thompson's control, so other than to make a financial contribution to Thompson, Parten planned to stay away from the campaign. He continued to be a strong supporter of Thompson. He appreciated his help in the fight against federal regulation and his support of the independent segment of the oil industry, calling him "the greatest champion of the true interests of the people of Texas first and the independent oil men second. . . ." Parten believed that his friend would easily win reelection in the first primary and avoid a runoff. In late June, he wrote Thompson that he had just returned from an extended trip around the state and "it appears to be all Thompson. I have . . . found few people who know the other candidates in the race. Honestly, I can't call their names myself."[22]

Despite this optimism, Thompson's reelection faced more difficulty than either he or Parten at first realized. Thompson's successful effort to bring the East Texas oil field under control had made him some powerful enemies among those who had thrived on hot oil. In addition, his opposition to consumer rate increases had alienated many of the state's gas utilities, and his public criticism of some of the major oil companies during the federal regulation battle had made many of them hostile to the commissioner. Complicating Thompson's campaign was a personal feud that had developed between him and a fellow commissioner, Lon Smith, which Thompson's enemies exploited.[23]

Lon Smith's son, Langston, was an attorney who had built a prosperous law practice by representing clients at hearings before the Railroad Commission. Several months before the 1936 primary, Thompson and Judge C. V. Terrell, the other Railroad commissioner, had warned Smith privately that his son's activity created a potential conflict of interest and smacked of political favoritism. Smith refused to tell his son to stop, forcing Thompson to issue a ruling prohibiting

Langston Smith from representing clients in Railroad Commission matters. This resulted in a nasty personal feud between Thompson and Lon Smith. When Thompson announced his reelection bid, Smith publicly declared that he would support Frank Morris, a former district attorney. Smith's active involvement in the campaign on behalf of one of Thompson's opponents attracted more attention to the Railroad Commission race than would have been the case otherwise. Smith was able to rally support for Morrison from among Thompson's enemies in the oil industry. He wrote a circular letter to all the gas utilities, for example, to remind them of their problems with Thompson and to warn that he would certainly run for governor in 1938 if he won reelection to the Railroad Commission.[24]

In the final weeks of the race, Smith's activities had a significant impact on Thompson's campaign. Smith was so visible as he traveled the state attacking his fellow commissioner that some voters became confused and thought he was a candidate for Thompson's position. Thompson and his campaign staff, who had assumed that they would win without a runoff, suddenly feared not winning at all. After Thompson called Parten to share his anxiety about the free-fall his campaign seemed to be suffering, Parten went to Austin to help. On his way to Austin, he took a side trip to Madisonville, where he was surprised to find no organized effort on Thompson's behalf. Parten quickly recruited Madisonville attorney Joe Webb to organize a Thompson campaign in Madison County. Claiming that "a lot of these folks around here have considerable faith in what you tell them," Webb urged Parten to publicize his personal endorsement of Thompson in the local newspaper. Parten subsequently met with Andrew Knight, the editor of the Madisonville *Meteor*, and arranged a "news story" about Parten's support for Thompson and his hope that his "friend of twenty years" could carry his "home county of Madison."[25]

The results of the primary election on July 25 were much better than Thompson and his staff had feared. Thompson carried 243 of the state's 254 counties and received 278,000 votes more than Morris, who placed a distant second, but Thompson missed avoiding a runoff by less than ten thousand votes. As expected, Allred rolled on to a major victory over four primary candidates, winning 52 percent of the vote and avoiding a runoff. Reluctant at first, Frank Morris was persuaded to stay in the runoff with a promise of strong financial backing from a group of former hot-oilers, led by independent oil man Freeman Burford, who had fought bitterly with Thompson over prorationing. Despite Thompson's large lead over Morris in the first primary, he and his campaign staff now worried that Morris might pull off an upset. Runoffs in Texas usually attract many fewer voters than the first election, making the results notoriously unpredictable.[26]

Grover Hill convinced Parten that Thompson needed his help on a continuing basis, so he agreed to work almost full time during the runoff campaign. From his room in Austin's Stephen F. Austin Hotel, Parten contacted his political associates in the independent segment of the oil industry to persuade them to raise money and to get the vote out for Thompson. He pulled Myron and Jack Blalock and Claude Wild into the campaign, paying for air time for Myron to make a rousing speech for Thompson on Dallas radio station WFAA, a powerful "clear channel" station heard easily throughout Texas. Parten urged his managers in Woodley Petroleum and in his refining company to push Thompson with the employees. After he told his refinery manager in Baird that it was "imperative that every effort be made to get the vote out on election day and that all of the sustained interest possible be maintained," a group of workers from the refinery spread out over Callahan and Eastland Counties to urge people to vote for Thompson. Parten also asked Sylvestor Dayson to organize the refinery workers in Longview and "do all for Colonel Thompson . . . that you can." Parten established Thompson campaign organizations in Grimes and Brazos Counties and persuaded independent refiners Joe and Jack Danciger to contribute money and help the campaign in Fort Worth.[27]

In Austin, Parten busily drafted speeches and dispatched information to others who were speaking for Thompson. Parten urged Thompson to go on the offensive against Smith and to publicly reveal the real reason for Smith's opposition. Thompson rejected Parten's advice initially, but as election day drew closer, he agreed to make public the conflict-of-interest problem the Railroad Commission had with Langston Smith. In a speech drafted by Parten, Thompson exposed Smith's motives on a statewide radio hook-up from Dallas on August 17. "Lon Smith is nursing a . . . false grudge," Thompson charged, "no recourse is too extreme, no neglect of duty is apparently too gross, to feed that grudge. Smith not only lets himself be made use of by the oil pirates of East Texas but he plays the role of turncoat and plays into the hands of the utility . . . trust." Parten had dozens of copies of the speech printed and photostats made of Lon Smith's letter seeking support from utility companies. He mailed them to newspaper editors and oil-industry leaders with a cover letter stating that the material indicated the "extremes to which the opposition has gone in this campaign and to show . . . that Lon A. Smith has deserted the people of Texas and seeks to cut Ernest O. Thompson down by sinister methods."[28]

Thompson eventually won reelection by a three-to-one margin. Afterwards, he thanked Parten for his "untiring labor" in the runoff campaign. "I love you for what you are," Thompson told Parten, "a true friend and a patriot." One of Thompson's close friends told Parten that Thompson was convinced that the "splendid work" Parten did in the campaign "had much to do with his winning the race by such a large margin. When you get behind a candidate it seems that he invariably wins."[29]

"Leeches Don't Like Light": Censoring the *Daily Texan*

In early July, while Parten was working to help reelect Ernest Thompson, an editorial in the *Daily Texan* created a public controversy that ultimately led the board of regents to impose censorship on the student newspaper. On July 9 the *Daily Texan* published an editorial titled "Leeches Don't Like Light," which implied that the directors of the Lower Colorado River Authority (LCRA) were involved in graft and misuse of three million dollars. The editorial also referred to powerful Texas congressman James "Buck" Buchanan as the "pork barrel chairman" of the House Appropriations Committee. The regents were especially sensitive to any student or faculty criticism of Buchanan; not only because he represented the congressional district in which the university was located but also because his committee had control over Public Works Administration (PWA) appropriations. Buchanan had played a key role in the university's successful request for three hundred thousand dollars for the Memorial Museum. The university had several other applications pending for PWA grants to build dormitories and other facilities. To make matters worse, the LCRA's legal counsel was Alvin J. Wirtz, perceived by many to be the most influential lobbyist in the state capitol. Wirtz made it clear that the *Daily Texan*'s comments were offensive and he demanded an official apology from the regents.[30]

Almost as soon as Parten became a regent, he had realized how damaging the *Daily Texan*'s political editorials could be to the university's relationship with the Texas legislature. The various editors of the *Daily Texan* loved to single out individual legislators as prime examples of corruption, indolence, and ignorance. Inflaming the situation was the fact that copies of the *Daily Texan* were placed on the desks of legislators every morning the legislature was in session. What the representatives read in the *Daily Texan* did not predispose them to be generous to the university at budget time, which was a problem of overriding concern to J. R. Parten. During most of the spring semester of 1935, when the university was trying to coax additional money out of the legislature, Parten and his regental colleagues were forced to apologize to legislators for statements made in the student newspaper.

With the next budget fight in mind, Parten had made an unofficial attempt late in the fall semester of 1935 to prevent a repeat of the problems caused by the *Daily Texan*'s editorials. In early November of that year, he asked William McGill, the director of student publications, to explain to the *Daily Texan* editor and to other Student Publications Board members that their editorials and other published writings were damaging efforts to improve the university's financial condition. Accordingly, McGill met with *Daily Texan* editor Joe Storm and student association president Jenkins Garrett and reported back to Parten that "the Editor has agreed to put forth every effort to avoid printing material which might be harmful to the University." He also reported that the Student Publications Board had passed a resolution stating that the board "feels that the news and editorials can be presented without antagonizing state officials and without stirring up controversies. . . ."[31]

Seven months later, however, Parten discovered that his problems with the *Daily Texan* were far from over. After he read the editorial on the LCRA, Parten called McGill and told him to issue an official apology for it as soon as possible. McGill subsequently printed the apology in the July 23 edition of the *Daily Texan*, stating that the comment about Buchanan was "poorly phrased and that the *Daily Texan* knows of no blemish on the Congressman's . . . record." Parten and Benedict were not finished, however. "It appalls me to know that the editors of the

Daily Texan are guilty of gross misconduct," Parten complained to Leslie Waggener. "It evolves upon the administration to alleviate this condition."[32]

As soon as the first primary campaign ended, Parten decided to put an end to the *Daily Texan's* troublemaking. At Parten's suggestion, Benedict drafted a censorship policy and submitted it to the board of regents for discussion and action on July 27. At the meeting, Benedict offered the view that the *Daily Texan* was not a real newspaper but merely a practical journalism lab, a teaching tool. Therefore, Benedict explained, it needed direct faculty supervision. The newspaper should also restrict itself to harmless "campus" news. Such a restriction would not prevent the student journalists from learning the mechanics of writing and editing a news story. During the discussion, Parten reminded his colleagues that the university faced a difficult struggle in the next legislative session in its attempt to get increased state appropriations. Parten's old family friend Elmer Pope had already warned him that some members of the legislature were upset by what they were hearing about radical faculty members. They were also receiving complaints from other legislators and powerful lobbyists about *Daily Texan* editorials and stories. The Texas Gulf Sulphur Company was especially insistent that the regents muzzle the newspaper.[33]

Without dissent, the regents accepted Benedict's censorship regulation. The regents also created an editorial advisory committee of two faculty members and one student whose charge was to select an "agent" to screen the *Daily Texan* for any material containing "improper personal attacks, reckless accusations, opinion not based on fact." Also forbidden were articles on national, state, and local political questions and a whole range of transgressions including violations of "good taste" and "material prejudicial to the best interests of the University." This action, which was discussed and voted on in an executive session, was withheld from the public. The next day, Benedict called *Daily Texan* editor Ed Hodge into his office and handed him a letter announcing the regents' new rule. The president told Hodge that "the *Daily Texan* is not a newspaper, but it is an annex of the University." Referring to problems with the legislature, Benedict said that he did not want the university "to suffer when the paper forgets this." In a letter to Parten, Leslie Waggener referred to this regents' rule as a "censorship regulation," and censorship it was. Journalism professor Granville Price, who agreed to serve as the censor, immediately axed an editorial against a proposed state sales tax and another editorial critical of the Texas sulphur lobby. News about the censorship policy was likewise ruled off-limits.[34]

On July 30, the Austin *American Statesman* broke the news that the regents had placed the *Daily Texan* under official censorship. The wire services picked up the story and made it national news, bringing forth an avalanche of criticism from the press, educational leaders, politicians, and civil libertarians from around the country. Censoring the *Daily Texan* quickly became a public relations blunder that hurt the university's image far more than anything any student had written in the newspaper. The most vocal denunciation of the censorship policy came from Cong. Maury Maverick of San Antonio, who accused the regents of "nazifying" the University of Texas. "That my university should adopt the policies of communists and fascists in suppressing the freedom of speech and press is astonishing," Maverick declared. Other critical voices joined Maverick's. The pastor of the University Methodist Church denounced the regents' action in a sermon. Claiming that the censorship was "out of harmony with the trends in American university life," the Academic Freedom Committee of the American Civil Liberties Union urged the regents to reconsider their "extraordinary" action.[35]

Censoring the *Daily Texan* even brought forth the wrath of the state's conservative press. Influential establishment journals such as the Dallas *News* and the Houston *Post* condemned the regents' policy. The Houston *Press* published the editorials that had been censored out of the *Daily Texan* with the observation that "if they are anything more than thought-provoking without being in the least damaging to anyone except a few selfish vested interests, we do not know the meaning of the English language." Noting that "the University is not a kindergarten," the Houston *Press* demanded an end to "petty academic tyranny."[36]

Despite the storm of criticism, Parten urged his fellow regents to hold fast and reminded them that they had merely exercised their obligations as regents to ensure proper control of student behavior. When he heard that some of the students were calling on Governor Allred to intervene, he contacted his friend in the Governor's Mansion and explained why the regents had passed the new regulation. When the press asked Allred for a statement, he declared that "the censorship of the *Daily Texan* is the business of the University Board of Regents and none of mine."[37]

Members of the Travis County delegation to the State Democratic Convention refused to stay out of the controversy. They announced that they would ask the state convention to pass a resolution condemning the regents for censoring the student newspaper. Parten worked hard behind the scenes to stop the resolution. Fortunately for Parten, Myron Blalock was slated to serve as chairman of the state convention. Blalock, who exerted much influence within the state's Democratic Party leadership, argued that it was "not censorship for the regents to tell immature youths the point beyond which they may not go." He mustered enough votes to defeat the motion of condemnation.[38]

When school began in the fall, President Benedict met with student leaders and the editors of student publications, including the *Daily Texan*, to explain the censorship rule, which had been passed while most of the students were away from campus on summer vacation. He explained that the *Daily Texan* was "not an ordinary newspaper whose owners are entitled to the liberty of the press." Benedict told Parten after the meeting that he would grade the success of the meeting "at C+ or B-." He was afraid the issue would continue to simmer among the student activists. Benedict was also concerned about a rumor that students were trying to persuade members of the legislature to file a resolution criticizing the regents during the next session, which was scheduled to open in January 1937. He urged Parten to head off such a move.[39]

Parten contacted several of his allies in the legislature and urged them to suppress any attempts to condemn the regents. Parten explained that it was important that the *Daily Texan* be subject to faculty supervision. "For several years," Parten stressed, "the administration was rather lax in the enforcement of this rule." The *Daily Texan* staff had abused the rules often in the last two or three years. "I refer particularly to *Daily Texan* personal attacks on Congressmen and Legislators," Parten stated, "and the taking of strong sided positions on political questions that are highly controversial." The regents believed that "academic freedom does not imply license to damage one's fellows" and they were not going to allow "a partisan newspaper to be run on the campus . . ."[40]

The J. Evetts Haley Affair

While Parten worked to minimize the public relations damage resulting from the censorship policy, a controversy hit the university from another political direction. In early September, J. Evetts Haley announced to the press that, because of his opposition to Franklin Roosevelt's reelection, the board of regents was forcing him to resign his job as a collector of historical materials for the university library. While liberals such as Maury Maverick were criticizing the regents for "nazifying" the campus, Haley attracted newspaper headlines by accusing them of being leftist toadies for the New Deal.[41]

Haley's problems actually began the previous spring. Employed in the university's Bureau of Social Science Research, Haley had been an effective collector of archival materials and had done much to make the university's Texas history collection preeminent. He was, however, an impulsive and highly opinionated man who held extremely conservative political views and had become a vocal and active critic of the Roosevelt administration. Two of his colleagues in the library, archivist Winnie Allen and rare-books librarian Fannie Ratchford, were equally strong willed, temperamental, and opinionated. The result was a library staff in constant turmoil over the unending and unpleasant tension amongst them. This feuding resulted in widespread and troublesome rumors about illegal, unprofessional, and unethical activities within the library.[42]

The situation had eventually forced the regents' Committee on Grievances and Complaints (Aynesworth, Fairchild, and Waggener) to investigate. Finding a "deplorable situation" caused by the personality conflicts involving Haley, Allen, and Ratchford, the committee recommended that each of them should resign from their positions "at the end of . . . the present fiscal year. . . ." In July, the regents referred the problem to President Benedict with instructions to convey to each "the necessity of an immediate change in attitude if a relationship with The University of Texas is to be continued." The regents authorized Benedict to dismiss any one of the three who failed to heed his warning.[43]

In the meantime, Haley had been appointed chairman of the Jeffersonian Democrats, a conservative organization bitterly opposed to President Roosevelt's reelection. Haley's active involvement in the anti-Roosevelt movement came as no surprise to anyone who had paid attention to his activities as he traveled around Texas collecting historical material for the university. In recent months, whenever

J. Evetts Haley, about 1937. *Courtesy Haley Library, Midland.*

Haley had been on the road collecting diaries, letters, and other historically valuable items he often provided his services as an anti-Roosevelt speaker at political gatherings. The line between his political activities and his university duties had become increasingly blurred. Typical of Haley's days was August 24, 1936, when he appeared before the board of regents to introduce the family descendents of Texas pioneer James Harper Starr, who were there to donate Alamo martyr William Barrett Travis's diary to the university. During that same meeting, the regents also approved Haley's request to go to Saltillo, Mexico, in September or October to collect historical material for the university. After the regents' meeting, Haley presided over the public opening of the Jeffersonian Democrats' state headquarters in Austin.[44]

The same day he appeared before the regents, Haley submitted to President Benedict a request for a leave of absence of six months, explaining that he wanted to devote his "best energies to exposing the . . . dangers of the so-called New Deal." The two founders of the Jeffersonian Democrats, Wichita Falls businessman Orville Bullington, the Republican candidate for governor in 1932, and J. M. West Sr., a rancher and oil man from Houston, were paying Haley to run their anti-Roosevelt campaign full time. Haley was not a member of the faculty. His appointment was as a staff member in the Bureau of Social Science Research, a position he had held for about ten years. Because he was not tenured, Haley's appointment was based on the same annual contract as every other staff member. The contract was for a term matching the university's fiscal year, which began on September 1 and ended on August 31. When Haley requested his leave of absence, he had not yet been reappointed for the coming year, 1936–1937. The budget for the Bureau of Social Science Research was not to be acted upon by the regents until September 26, although all of the bureau's staff members were virtually assured of reemployment. Haley's reappointment, for example, had been implied when the regents granted him permission to travel to Mexico during the upcoming semester. Nevertheless, because he had no budget for the bureau, Benedict could not give Haley an official leave of absence for a period of time not yet authorized by the regents. Benedict therefore gave Haley a leave of absence for the few remaining days in the fiscal year and informed him that his leave after that depended on action by the regents on the bureau's budget.[45]

Haley had been looking for an excuse to leave the university and now he had one. He had stated in his request to Benedict that following his leave of absence, he would return to work for only one month so that he could finish his museum work. Haley was unhappy about the regents' investigation of the library and the accusations that he had contributed to its personnel problems. He also disliked many of the faculty members on campus, especially Bob Montgomery, whom he had characterized as being "as wild as a March-hare." Haley later confessed to J. Frank Dobie that "the more I saw of the average run of University people the more my soul rebelled, until, during the last year or so, I found them almost intolerable." Seeing an opportunity to make some political points and garner publicity for the Jeffersonian Democrats, Haley called a press conference and announced that his request for a leave had been denied, which was untrue. "It may be that in declining to grant me leave of absence to fight the Roosevelt regime the university has taken the easy course of firing me by inaction," he declared. "If so, that alone is an indication of the danger of the New Deal tactics. When a bushy-headed . . . economist [Bob Montgomery] is hired by the new deal to propagandize the farmers, that is merely in accord with planning. But when I take leave to fight for constitutional government on my own time and at my own expense, that must be partisan politics."[46]

The news of Haley's accusations was spread throughout Texas. Headlines implied that he had been "fired" because he opposed Roosevelt. This was a distinct shock to the regents, who had not even known that Haley had requested a leave of absence. Leslie Waggener sent Parten a Dallas *News* clipping about Haley's charges and asked him if he knew anything about it. Parten replied that he knew nothing

"excepting what I read in the papers. . . ." He told Waggener that "it is rather pitiful that this man should have placed himself in such a position of embarrassment.
. . . As I see it, there was no occasion for the statement he made. I can see no objection to the . . . policy allowing an employee a leave to fight the [Roosevelt] administration as a private citizen if he chooses to do it, assuming at the same time . . .
that the person so conduct themselves as not to reduce their usefulness to the
University. . . ." Waggener agreed with Parten. "I am disappointed in Mr. Haley,"
Waggener stated. "I do not believe that Mr. Haley was fair with President Benedict
or the Board of Regents. . . ." At Parten's suggestion, Benedict issued a statement to
the press that explained what had actually happened. "The . . . cause that Mr. Haley
is now championing had nothing to do with my action and is irrelevant," Benedict
claimed.[47]

For more than fifty years after the incident, Haley claimed that he had been
purged by the pro–New Deal liberals on the board of regents. The fact is there were
no "pro–New Deal liberals" on the board in 1936. For example, regents Edward
Randall and Kenneth Aynesworth not only agreed politically with Haley, they
admired the work he was doing for the university as a collector of historical material. After reading one of Haley's articles attacking the New Deal, Aynesworth told
Haley that his views "conform so accurately to my own line of thinking . . . that I
endorse every thing you say." Randall had conveyed the same opinion to Haley,
telling him that his attacks on New Deal agricultural policies were "fresh and stimulating" and had shown that Haley was a man of "sublime courage." Not even J. R.
Parten was especially fond of the New Deal at that time, although he later became a
Roosevelt enthusiast. Haley resigned, he was not fired, either overtly or by "inaction" as he would later characterize it. His resignation *was* political, but for his benefit, not for the benefit of the phantom liberals on the board of regents.[48]

For the next two months, Haley traveled across the state, attracting headlines
by attacking the university almost as much as the Roosevelt administration,
implying that the campus was awash with Communists and race-mixers. Haley's
accusations implied that the regents had either ignored the subversion on their
campus or had endorsed it. During the fall of 1936, therefore, one could either
consider the regents a band of fascists because of the censorship of the *Daily Texan*
or Communist dupes because of the Haley incident. It was the latter charge that
bothered Parten the most, because he knew that the legislature, which was scheduled to meet in special session in late September, was more inclined to see the
campus the way Haley saw it.[49]

"My God, Bob. They're accusing you of teaching communism"

Just as Parten had long feared, the day after the special legislative session
opened, Cong. Joe Caldwell of Asherton introduced a resolution calling for an
investigation of rumors that communism and atheism were being taught on the
campuses of the state's universities. Haley's campaign-trail rhetoric and the *Daily
Texan* editorials critical of the legislature helped to make conditions ripe for the
investigation, but Caldwell made it clear that his resolution was the direct result of

the activity of Bob Montgomery and the university's chapter of the Progressive Democrats of Texas. Caldwell declared that he had "conclusive documentary proof" that at least one professor was teaching communism and that he had "gathered about him a group of young zealots who have pledged to devote their lives to the cause."

Caldwell's demand for an investigation of the university was motivated by a series of attacks by the *Daily Texan* (before it had been censored) on the powerful sulphur lobbyist, Roy Miller. The *Daily Texan* had published documents revealing details of some of Miller's lobbying tactics. Miller, whose official position with the Texas Gulf Sulphur Company was "public relations director," was alleged to have spent the then staggering sum of $173,000 for "publicity" in Austin during a previous legislative session. Because there had been little evidence of Miller's "publicity" efforts, some of his critics charged that he had used the money to entertain and even bribe key members of the legislature. One of Montgomery's protégés, Creekmore Fath, has claimed that Miller reserved entire floors of the Stephen F. Austin and the Driskill Hotels. Any legislator could have a room and charge anything he wanted on Miller's tab. "That's how Miller took care of the Legislature," Fath charged, "it was the most outrageous thing in the world."

Just prior to the opening of the special legislative session, Fath and some other Montgomery protégés organized a free dance at Gregory Gym officially dedicated to "A Higher Tax on Sulphur." A huge crowd of students showed up. When Miller heard about the event the next morning, he erupted with anger, immediately blaming his nemesis Bob Montgomery, who had earlier pinned the title of "Sulfurcrat" on Miller. The lobbyist had frequently been the target of some of the economics professor's most scathing speeches. The next morning President Benedict called Fath and asked him to come to his office at once. When he arrived, the exasperated Benedict asked, "young man, what are you trying to do to the University? Do you know how much trouble you've caused me with your dance? [Lt. Governor] Woodul called me this morning and said Roy Miller was raising hell all over the Capitol." Fath replied that he had hoped it would cause trouble over at the legislature, not with the university. Caldwell's demand for an investigation soon followed this incident.[50]

Benedict asked Parten to check with his friends in the legislature to see if there was any way to stop the investigation. Parten persuaded a small group of legislators to make an attempt to kill Caldwell's resolution. One of them, Cong. Bryan Bradberry of Abilene, used Parten's information to charge that Caldwell's resolution was actually "the voice of J. Evetts Haley." He declared that Caldwell and Haley were trying to discredit the Roosevelt administration which had hired university professors to serve as advisers. Despite Bradberry's and others efforts to stop Caldwell's resolution through various legislative maneuvers—Roy Hofheinz of Houston tried to send it to oblivion in the Committee on Livestock and Stock Raisers—it passed on October 2 by a vote of 67 to 61. Speaker Coke Stevenson, whose rulings thwarted most of the efforts to kill the resolution, appointed Caldwell chairman of the special investigatory committee.[51]

The special committee opened its investigation on October 13, 1936, with testimony by Bob Montgomery and his former students Herman Wright and Otto Mullinax. When Montgomery received his summons to appear before the legislative committee he walked to Benedict's office to tell him about it. Benedict replied: "My God, Bob. They're accusing you of teaching communism. I'd be pleased if some of these old farts [on the faculty] taught anything!" When Montgomery appeared before the committee, Caldwell demanded to know if the professor favored "private profit." Montgomery smiled and replied "So much that I'd like to see it extended to where 120 million people could have it." As the audience roared with laughter, Caldwell quickly shifted gears. Ignoring the communism issue, Caldwell focused instead on attacks made by the university's Progressive Democrats on Roy Miller. A reporter for the Houston *Press* noted that the committee seemed to be concerned only about criticisms of Roy Miller by university students.[52]

The House of Representatives eventually tired of Caldwell's investigation, which failed to find anything subversive at the university. A majority voted on October 27 to disband the committee and to commend the university's faculty members for their "patience" and their "fine work." After the investigation ended, the reason for Caldwell's interest in Roy Miller rather than communism soon became apparent. A lobbyist named Hulen R. Carroll claimed that the Jeffersonian Democrats and unnamed investors in the Texas Gulf Sulphur Company had hired him to stir up problems for the university and Dr. Montgomery in the legislature. He told the *Daily Texan* that "the Sulphur company is out for Dr. Montgomery's scalp" because of his call for a tax on monopolies. Carroll also stated that Texas Gulf Sulphur wanted to discredit the university because of the company's fears that the plan to increase its appropriations might result in higher corporate taxes. The Jeffersonian Democrats wanted to discredit Montgomery for political reasons. He had worked as a consultant for the New Deal for several months in 1936 and they had hoped to tie the charge of communism to the Roosevelt administration by making it look as though one of its economists was a subversive. Of course, Evetts Haley, head of the Jeffersonian Democrats, also had personal motives for encouraging a legislative investigation of the university that he claimed had "fired" him for political reasons.[53]

With political controversy swirling about the university, Parten now searched for a way for the board to get out of the censorship debacle, one that would maintain some level of administrative control over the *Daily Texan*'s editorial page. He still believed that if the regents allowed the *Daily Texan* to print stories and editorials highly critical of legislators, it would doom their efforts to get increased funding for the university in the upcoming regular session. Accordingly, in early February 1937, Parten, Stark, Randall, and Benedict worked out a compromise with student leaders that allowed censorship to be lifted. Future editors of the *Daily Texan* would continue to be elected, but to be eligible, students had to meet certain grade-average and course-work qualifications. The editor could be removed at any time by vote of the Student Publications Board, which consisted of three faculty members and three students. The dean of Student Life had the authority to break a tie vote. It was agreed that the *Daily Texan* would "exclude . . . unduly violent and partisan material" from its pages.

A significant part of the new plan required that censorship had to remain in place until June 1, which meant the newspaper would be censored until the legislature adjourned on May 31. When student leaders accepted this reorganization proposal, Parten went to work on his fellow regents. He was so anxious to resolve the matter before it caused any problems with the legislature that he did not wait until the next board meeting to get regental consent. He contacted the regents by telephone and by mail, asking for their agreement to lift censorship, arguing that he believed it was necessary "to act on this plan immediately." The compromise plan was quickly approved.[54]

In later years, Parten admitted that the censoring of the *Daily Texan* had been wrong, not because of the public relations damage, but because of its violation of the principle of freedom of the press. "The *Daily Texan*'s editorials seemed to threaten the University's financial health," he explained. "But I was wrong, preserving freedom of the press, even for a school newspaper, is more important than any increase in a legislative appropriation."

CHAPTER 12

A $15,000 Football Coach and the Search for a New President

1936–1938

J R. Parten's activities as a regent of the state's leading public university were not restricted solely to dealing with such hot political issues as academic freedom and freedom of the press or with trying to alleviate the University of Texas's critical financial needs. As an activist young regent who enjoyed working on university matters, Parten found himself involved during his first two years on the board in a multiplicity of activities ranging from the construction of the McDonald Observatory on Mt. Locke in West Texas to negotiations for the university to acquire an extensive rare-book and -art collection from Lutcher Stark's family. No activity during the fall of 1936, however, took more of Parten's time than the football program, which became embroiled in a controversy that threatened to damage the university's efforts to maintain goodwill with its ex-students and with legislative leaders. The satisfactory resolution of that controversy, however, had a positive impact on the university's academic as well as its athletic program.

"Jack's a clean liver, and he's not chasing any women"

In the fall of 1936, the university's head football coach was John Edward "Handsome Jack" Chevigny, a young, dynamic, and hot-headed protégé of Knute Rockne, the legendary coach of Notre Dame University. Chevigny scored the decisive touchdown in the famous game against Army in which Rockne urged his team to "win . . . one for the Gipper." Soon after the university hired Chevigny as head football coach in January 1934, he and Parten became good friends. Parten gave several of Chevigny's new recruits summer jobs and he helped pay their tuition and school expenses, a practice Parten continued after he became a regent.[1]

Parten's aid extended beyond the immediate needs of the football program. Chevigny was a compulsive gambler embarrassingly prone to accumulate debts to local gamblers. On more than one occasion Parten helped Chevigny to pay off these debts.[2] When rumors about the head football coach's gambling problem eventually reached President Benedict, he went to Parten and declared that Chevigny should be fired. Although he had no evidence, Benedict was also convinced that Chevigny, who was a bachelor with movie-star good looks, was having affairs with coeds. Parten defended the coach. "There's nothing to that," he later remembered saying, "Jack's a clean liver, and he's not chasing any women." When Benedict nevertheless insisted that Chevigny had to go, Parten urged him to keep his feelings private until the football season was over. "Let the boys get through the season," he told Benedict. "I'll assure you that I will give a sympathetic ear to your complaint just as soon as the season's over." A few days later, Parten, Hilmer Weinert, and Lutcher Stark, members of the regents' committee on athletics, confronted Chevigny about his gambling, telling him that it could no longer be tolerated. Chevigny promised to stop.[3]

The personal flaws of a head football coach are usually forgiven or ignored by football-crazy alumni as long as the team is winning, but Chevigny's problems worsened during the fall of 1936 as his football team lost game after game. Following a loss to Rice Institute, a vocal group of Houston exes began a movement to get him fired. Living in Houston, Parten was forced to endure harangues from disgruntled ex-students who called him at Woodley's offices. Parten urged the unhappy football fans to stop their complaining until after the season when the university's athletic council would decide Chevigny's fate. Frustrated, he lamented to one ex-student that "for twenty years the failing of our alumni has been quite obvious in their refusal to support with any degree of unanimity any coach." Parten's pleas went unheeded.

Calls for Chevigny's scalp reached a peak the week before the university's big game in Minneapolis with the nation's top-ranked team, the University of Minnesota. On the Monday night before the game on Saturday, Chevigny met Parten at the Blackstone Hotel in Brenham, about halfway between Houston and Austin, and handed the regent the draft of a press release he had written announcing that he would resign as coach at the end of the season. "Jack, I want to give you a piece of advice," Parten said. "Don't think that you can quiet things down now, and then change your mind later. . . . If you release this statement, you're through as head coach." Chevigny replied that he had no intention of changing his mind. He announced his decision publicly at a banquet the next night in Austin, a few hours before he and the team boarded a train for Minnesota.[4]

The game with Minnesota was a major event for the University of Texas and the fans of its football program. A large group of Texans accompanied the team on the train, while Parten, the only regent making the trip, joined another contingent

Jack Chevigny, 1936. *CN 09628. Courtesy Parten Photograph Collection, CAH.*

taking a later train. The trip to Minnesota turned out to be an important one for Parten. He was impressed with the Twin Cities area and with the University of Minnesota. The memory of his positive reaction later played a part in his decision to enter into business in the area. In addition, at Benedict's request, Parten paid a courtesy call on Dr. Lotus D. Coffman, the president of the University of Minnesota. Coffman assembled a group of university administrators and faculty members to give Parten their perspective and advice about some of the problems the University of Texas was having in a number of areas, especially with the student newspaper, fraternity hazing, and faculty salaries and benefits. As Parten talked with the Minnesota academicians, he filled a thick notebook with information he felt would be useful not only to himself and his fellow regents, but also to Benedict. Parten was especially impressed with President Coffman, who counseled him to "ease up" on the *Daily Texan*. Parten's visit to Minnesota, though brief, allowed him to compare and contrast his university with a highly regarded public institution of higher learning in another state. Seeing what Minnesota had done with generous support from its legislature, he returned home more determined than ever to do whatever he could to build and improve the University of Texas.[5]

Unfortunately for Chevigny and his football players, the trip to Memorial Stadium in Minneapolis proved to be less successful. Led by their star quarterback Bud Wilkinson, Minnesota defeated Texas 47 to 19 in front of more than forty-seven thousand spectators, at the time the largest crowd ever to have seen a University of Texas football game.[6]

In early December, after the football season had ended, the university's Faculty Athletic Council announced that it had fired Chevigny as head coach and athletic director. The council's action outraged Parten, who termed it "grossly unfair" to Chevigny. He felt that Chevigny's previously announced resignation made a formal dismissal unnecessary. Parten and James C. Dolley, chairman of the council, had disagreed on several minor issues related to the athletic program and the two men were not friendly. Blaming Dolley for the council's action and aware of faculty complaints about the amount of money devoted to athletics, Parten complained to some of his fellow regents that Dolley and his council colleagues had proven themselves incapable of managing the athletic program. He urged the regents to become more deeply involved in the search for a new head coach and in the effort to develop a program "that will well serve the interests of the University."[7]

Angered by the way Dolley and his faculty colleagues had handled the Chevigny affair, Parten followed his own advice to the other regents, immersing himself in the search to find Chevigny's replacement. On one point Parten and Dolley agreed: they were both determined to bring the best coach available to the university, no matter the cost. This decision and the resulting strategy devised to make it possible had consequences far beyond the parochial affairs of one university's football program. The effort to bring a nationally famed coach to the University of Texas to build the school's football program eventually resulted not only in Texas becoming a national powerhouse in the sport, it was an important development in the evolution of college football as more of a business than a part of the academic enterprise. Bringing a new coach to Texas at a price unheard of at the time played a significant role in the salary escalation of collegiate athletic coaches throughout the nation, eventually reaching outrageous levels in the post–World War II era. In addition, the shrewd strategy Parten devised to get the state legislature and his fellow regents to acquiesce in the university's paying a football coach twice as much salary as its president—a shocking idea at the time— eventually boosted the salaries of the entire faculty as well as the president and materially aided the effort to recruit a nationally prominent educator to replace Benedict. Nonetheless, the affair raised important questions about the importance of athletics versus scholarship at the University of Texas and did much to create its "football school" image nationally.

Dana X. Bible (left), greeted as prospective coach by J. C. Dolley, chairman of the Faculty Athletic Council. *From* Daily Texan, *January 20, 1937. Courtesy Prints and Photographs Collection, CAH.*

"We cannot afford Dr. Hutchins. Can we afford Mr. Bible?"

From the beginning, the athletic council's first choice for head football coach was Dana Xenophon ("D. X.") Bible, the coach of the University of Nebraska football team. Dolley was a good friend of the forty-six-year-old Bible and he had long wanted to bring him back to the state in which he had first gained fame. From 1917 until 1928, Bible won five conference championships as head coach at Texas A&M. He found even more success at Nebraska, winning the Big Eight championship six times, and was widely regarded as possibly the best football coach in the country. Dolley met with Bible in New Orleans before the Sugar Bowl game on New Year's Day, 1937, and asked him to come to Texas. Bible replied that he would consider an offer from Texas, but he doubted that the university could afford him. Undaunted, Dolley and his colleagues on the athletic council informed Parten and Stark that they wanted Bible despite the problems they had to solve to get him. Dolley explained that Bible had faculty status and therefore a permanent job at Nebraska. He had recently built a new home in Lincoln and he had estimated that he would lose about five thousand dollars by having to sell it so soon in a bad market. Pleasantly surprised by the council's recommendation, Parten and Stark pledged to raise the money privately to cover Bible's real-estate loss. Indeed, Parten later persuaded the Houston exes who had attacked Chevigny to pay the five thousand.[8]

There were additional obstacles, however, and these were much more serious. Although the University of Texas had never given any non-faculty employee a contract of more than one year, Bible was demanding a ten-year contract. An even more problematic issue, however, was salary. Bible's annual pay at Nebraska was $7,500, but he required an annual salary of fifteen thousand dollars plus other benefits to come to Texas. President Benedict's salary was only eight thousand dollars. Dolley was afraid that the board of regents would never agree to Bible's terms, especially his salary demand. Regent Stark immediately brushed aside Dolley's concerns, declaring that he would bring Bible to Austin no matter what the cost might be and to hell with faculty feelings and public opinion. Parten, however, knew that Benedict, some of the other regents, and many of the faculty would object strongly to paying any football coach twice as much as the university's president. He was also concerned about the impact such a salary would have on the university's campaign to increase its legislative appropriations. Although the football coach's salary was paid entirely with money earned by game-ticket sales and other nonappropriated funds, he knew that paying a football coach that much money in the middle of the Depression when the average salary for a faculty member was only $3,500 would generate negative publicity. It might also invite yet another legislative investigation. Despite those formidable problems, Parten felt that Bible would bring much needed stability to the university's troubled athletic department and that he could build a winning football program, which would please many of the university's most powerful and prominent alumni. "Well," Parten finally said, "there's not a man in the nation who would do as much for the University of Texas as D. X. Bible. I would persevere, that's my advice."[9]

Parten's primary concern was about how Benedict would feel about hiring Bible. If Benedict objected, Parten would not support Bible's candidacy. Before meeting with the president, however, Parten came up with a strategy that he thought might get not only Benedict's support but might also help the university's budget. "I thought that maybe this was a chance," he recalled, "to demonstrate to the legislature that we had to have more money for faculty salaries. It might be a wise move to hire this man and pay him more than the University President was being paid. We could send a message to the legislature that we have got to raise the president's salary at the next session." Although shocked by Bible's salary request, Benedict was more receptive to the idea of hiring him than Parten had expected. "I think D. X. Bible is the best man in the United States for that job," Benedict told Parten. "Wherever he's been, he's worked closely with the faculty. In my opinion, he has had experience enough and education enough to take my job, but his price is pretty high." Benedict agreed to support Parten's legislative strategy but he still argued against paying Bible as much as he was demanding.[10]

With Benedict's blessing, Parten easily secured support for his salary plan from Governor Allred, Lieutenant Governor Woodul, and the newly elected Speaker of the House, Bob Calvert. Parten's next task was to persuade his fellow regents. He sent a telegram to Weinert, for example, arguing that Bible was the "one man who can definitely straighten out [the] aggravated situation of the

[Athletic] Department and run it effectively and thereby relieve much worry to you and me. . . ." While Parten lobbied his colleagues, Bible made his task more difficult by refusing to consider a salary of less than fifteen thousand dollars and by threatening to withdraw his name if the regents took much longer to make up their minds. At the January 16, 1937, regents' meeting, Parten presented his plan to use Bible's salary as leverage to raise faculty salaries and informed his colleagues that Allred, Woodul, and Calvert had pledged their support. Edward Randall agreed that Parten's strategy might "help instead of hinder" the cause for increased faculty salaries. Benedict, however, repeated his strong disapproval, not of Bible, but of the salary. After a lengthy discussion lasting most of the day, the regents decided to invite Bible to come to Austin for an interview.[11]

Information soon leaked out about the effort to bring Bible to Texas at a salary previously unheard of for a collegiate football coach. Reactions were generally negative, especially because of a rumor that a special student fee would pay Bible's salary. Although still under censorship, the *Daily Texan* was allowed to publish an editorial denouncing the idea of paying a football coach more money than the university president. The paper doubted that the regents would pay as much to hire Robert Hutchins, the nationally famed head of the University of Chicago, as president, and asked, if "we cannot afford Dr. Hutchins, can we afford Mr. Bible?" News of the negotiations soon appeared in newspapers across the nation, resulting in a number of unfavorable editorial comments questioning the educational priorities of the University of Texas. The salary demanded by Bible was double that of any other head coach in the Southwest Conference. It was also six thousand dollars more than any head coach in the Big Ten, the nation's premier football conference at the time. Ward Burris, a sports writer, noted that in the depression economy "there is a limit to everything else, so why not a limit on coaching salaries?"[12]

A Fifteen-Thousand-Dollar Salary

When Bible met with the regents in Austin on January 20, he stressed that he could not come to Texas for less than fifteen thousand dollars a year, guaranteed by a ten-year contract. Nor would he come unless his conditions were accepted unanimously, not only by the board of regents, but also by the five members of the athletic council, and the president. If one dissenting vote was cast, he would not accept the job. When Bible was asked what he would do if he did get the job, he laid out a detailed and impressive program that depended heavily on the hiring of the top high school coaches in Texas to serve as his assistants. "But don't think I can come down here soon and win any championships," Bible argued. "I can't do it. We'll get results in four or five years."[13]

The meeting went well until Weinert declared that he was "constitutionally opposed" to paying a head coach and athletic director more than seventy-five hundred dollars a year. "Well, that was it," Parten recalled, "Bible got up and said, 'I'm sure that you people don't need me. You'll find somebody to do just as good a job as I could do for you', and made his leave." Parten followed him out the door and stopped him outside in the hallway. "Now, D.X., " Parten said, "Weinert . . . doesn't mean that. He's upset with Dr. Dolley by the way he handled the Chevigny dismissal. Give me a chance to visit with you after your dinner tonight." Bible agreed to go for a drive with Parten that night to talk about the matter. Parten returned to the board meeting and the regents agreed to recess for dinner. Parten pulled Weinert aside and had a talk with him. "I reasoned with him for a long time," Parten remembered, "and I just made him see that his anger about Chevigny was going to hurt our entire athletic program." Weinert grudgingly agreed to withdraw his opposition "for the good of the University." When the board reconvened, Weinert announced that he supported Bible's hiring at the fifteen-thousand-dollar salary. President Benedict declared that he still believed that paying that much salary was "unwise," but he would not stand in the way. The regents asked Parten to meet with Bible that night and try to talk him into accepting a lower salary. If that effort failed, the board authorized Parten to offer Bible a ten-year contract at fifteen thousand dollars a year.[14]

Parten drove Bible around Austin in his car from 9:30 p.m. until 3:30 the next morning trying in vain to persuade Bible to accept a lower salary. The next morning an exhausted Parten told Weinert that his efforts to get Bible to accept a lower salary came "to exactly zero." Weinert agreed with Parten that they should give up and accept Bible's demands. After checking with the other regents by telephone, Parten offered Bible the job on Bible's terms. He accepted. Parten later admitted to Waggener that Bible's demands were "stiff" but he thought Bible's employment "was highly desirable in the interest of the University." Although he believed Bible's hiring could aid their effort to persuade the legislature to raise the president's salary as well as those of the faculty, Parten also knew that it could just as easily backfire.[15]

The backfire began almost as soon as the university announced Bible's hiring on January 21. Sen. L. J. Sulak, a former university regent from La Grange, declared that it was "ridiculous" to pay a football coach twice the salary of the president. Sulak threatened to stop the appointment by getting the legislature to refuse to pay Bible's salary with state money. Parten's earlier work with the governor paid off, however, as Allred soon announced his support for hiring Bible. The university did much to deflect Sulak's attack when it announced that Bible's salary would be paid entirely with revenue earned by ticket sales for athletic events. Concerned that Sulak's criticism might cause Bible to change his mind, Parten wrote to assure him that nothing would come of it. "I am certain that the disturbance is minor," Parten declared, "out of it will come more good than harm, in that both Texas and A&M are requesting the legislature for an increase in professor's salaries. This will cause more legislators to take an interest in the university program than they would have taken otherwise, and therefore we think it is most probably a 'blessing in disguise'."[16]

Bible moved to Austin and eventually transformed the University of Texas's football program into one of the most most successful in the country. His admin-

University of Texas football coach Dana X. Bible, about 1940. *CN 00205. Courtesy Texas Student Publications Photograph Collection, CAH.*

istration was free of scandal and it spared the regents from having to concern themselves with problems in the athletic program. Parten helped with recruiting for a few years, but Bible's efficient "Bible Plan" recruiting system made his personal involvement less necessary. After Bible became athletic director, Parten's relations with the athletic program were restricted mainly to serving as one of the university's representatives on the committee that organized the Cotton Bowl Athletic Association in 1940, which sponsored the annual Cotton Bowl football game on every New Year's Day in Dallas. An active member of the association's governing board in its early years, he remained on the board until the 1970s.[17]

Bible relinquished the head coaching position after ten seasons, remaining as director of athletics for another decade. Bible's arrival marked the beginning of the era of "big time" football for the university. Many years after Bible's coming to Texas, Parten stated that he had no regrets about the decisive role he played in getting the university to agree to Bible's extraordinary salary demands, claiming that hiring Bible did "a lot for the University of Texas in many, many ways." Nevertheless, Parten grew to dislike what he called the "professionalization" of intercollegiate football and basketball programs that eventually occurred, admitting that the Bible episode had played a role in that development.[18]

"Some of the University's Problems"

By the end of January 1937, J. R. Parten had lured D. X. Bible to Texas and he had blunted the mini-controversy that Bible's salary had created in the legislature. Nevertheless, key elements of Parten's overall budget plan remained unfulfilled: a substantive faculty pay raise and an increase in the president's salary to a level above the football coach's salary. The administration also wanted additional funds to create the position of vice president and to establish a few distinguished professorships, as well as money for an expansion of the university's Medical School— requests that Parten fully supported. In total, the University was seeking 1.9 million dollars, an increase of eight hundred thousand dollars over the previous biennium. Complicating the effort to secure this increase was the regents' decision to once again ask the legislature to replace the line-item allocation with a "lump sum" appropriation.[19]

After only two years' service as a regent, Parten had become the unofficial leader of the board. At the end of 1936, Edward Randall wrote Governor Allred that Parten's appointment had been "one of the outstanding accomplishments" of the governor's administration. The majority of the board seems to have shared Randall's view. Kenneth Aynesworth, for example, told Parten that with respect to university matters, he knew of no one "whose opinion . . . I value more highly than I do yours. . . ." Accordingly, the regents asked Parten to become chairman now that Stark's two-year term had expired. Pleading that Woodley and Premier needed more of his time, Parten refused the offer. He did agree, however, to serve as vice chairman and to retain his position as chairman of the board's legislative committee. On Parten's recommendation, the board elected Edward Randall to serve as the new chairman. Despite Parten's intention to pay more attention to his business affairs and less to the university, events in Austin soon conspired to draw the forty-year-old oil man even deeper into university affairs.[20]

Parten's efforts on behalf of the university's appropriation began on February 28 at a private breakfast with Jimmy and Jo Betsy Allred at the Governor's Mansion, where he secured Allred's pledge to support the university's budget request. With the governor's pledge in hand, Parten launched his public campaign two days later at a banquet in Houston, where he spoke to more than seven hundred University of Texas alumni. As a part of his strategy to rally the university's ex-students, Parten paid special attention to the Houston alumni, the state's largest and most influential group of university graduates. To attract a large crowd, Parten brought new football coach D. X. Bible with him. After Bible explained his plan to raise the football program to new heights of gridiron glory, Parten gave his sermon, which he titled "Some of the University's Problems." His speech was an attempt not only to gain support for increased funding, but also to prevent future political attacks on University of Texas professors. Charging that the legislature's recent investigation of Bob Montgomery was nothing less than an attack on academic freedom, Parten urged the ex-students to help protect the university from such attempts to "control education." Turning to the immediate task, Parten warned the Houston alumni that the university had reached a critical stage in its development. Faculty salaries, which were among the lowest in the nation, had to be raised or the university would lose its most gifted teachers. "Most of those who remain through loyalty to the school are woefully underpaid," he declared, adding that "there seems no greater need . . . than that these men and women should be paid a worthy wage."[21]

Parten's speech was distributed statewide by the university, attracting positive editorial commentary from the state's major urban newspapers. The Houston *Chronicle* called the speech "a thoughtful analysis of the problems of all universities." The praise that Parten appreciated more than any other, however, came from George C. Butte, his old professor of international law. Butte had left the University of Texas in 1924 after nearly defeating Miriam "Ma" Ferguson in the gubernatorial election. He had returned to Texas early in 1937 after a distinguished career as a colonial administrator in Puerto Rico and in the Philippines. Parten was surprised when he received a letter from Butte telling him that he was back in Austin and that he had read the text of his Houston speech. Parten's speech, Butte wrote, was "so full of hard common sense expressed in scholarly language that I would call it a classic in its field. I am proud . . . of the high place of leadership you have attained in guiding the destiny of our greatest institution."[22]

Not everyone was impressed with Parten's performance. One newspaper in particular was in an unforgiving mood. Despite the fact that an agreement had already been reached to lift censorship by June 1, the *Daily Texan* excoriated Parten in an editorial. It identified the regent as the person "mostly responsible (and he will admit it) for placing censorship on the *Texan*. . . ." The editorial accused Parten of hypocrisy because of his statement that the university "must have . . . courage to combat the attempts to control education." The paper declared that someone should "define the words 'controlled education' for Major Parten." The students never saw the editorial, however, because it was immediately censored.[23]

From the middle of March until the end of May, Parten abandoned Woodley business to spend most of his time in Austin to lobby for the budget. Operating out of his suite at the Stephen F. Austin Hotel, Parten talked to student groups, dined with legislative leaders, consulted with Governor Allred, House Speaker Calvert, and Lieutenant Governor Woodul, and visited individual legislators in their capitol offices; all the while cajoling, pleading, and arguing about the university's need for more money. Although he heard criticism about the high salary paid D. X. Bible to coach the football team, the football fanatics within the legislature (and there were many) thought it was appropriate to pay the coach a high salary if he could produce a winning team. Once they had accepted that premise, Parten was able to shame some with the contrast between Bible's and Benedict's salary, not to mention that of the average faculty member.[24]

As head of the regents' legislative committee, Parten testified before the Senate Subcommittee on Education on March 25 and the House Appropriations Committee on March 30. In the latter appearance, he reminded the representatives that in creating the University of Texas, the Texas Constitution had called for the establishment of a "University of the first class." Claiming that the school was a long way from being first class in anything, especially in comparison to the state universities of Michigan, California, Wisconsin, and Minnesota, Parten urged the committee members to join with the board of regents to carry out their responsibility to see that the university fulfilled the pledge of the state's constitution. He also attacked the "popular impression that the University is a rich institution," reminding the legislators that the school's income from oil land could not be used for faculty salaries. The House committee proved to be a hard sell, especially when asked to abandon the line-item method of allocating money to the university. After the hearing, Parten wrote Waggener that he had encountered more difficulty in the House Appropriations Committee in regard to the lump-sum request than he had anticipated. "We may yet make the grade, but it is extremely doubtful."[25]

On May 10, as Parten prepared to mount another lobbying effort to persuade the Appropriations Committee to "loosen the purse strings," he and the entire university community received some sad news. As President Benedict walked on Guadalupe Street on the way to a meeting at the Capitol to discuss the university's budget request, he slumped to the pavement suddenly; dead of a cerebral hemorrhage. His close friend Roy Bedichek later observed that the sixty-seven-year-old Benedict had "literally . . . died in the harness on a trip to the Legislature . . . in behalf of some project for the University." Benedict's unexpected passing stunned Parten. As a regent, he had respected and trusted Benedict's judgement in all academic matters and had relied heavily on his advice on a wide range of issues with which the board had had to deal. Calling the "shocking news" of Benedict's death a "a tragic loss to the University," Parten declared that he had lost a "loyal, sweet friend." He and Opal attended Benedict's funeral in Gregory Gym, which attracted a large crowd of students, faculty, and ex-students wishing to pay tribute to one of the most beloved presidents in the history of the University of Texas.[26]

Parten's work on behalf of the university's budget finally came to an end on May 22. As Parten had anticipated, the legislature rejected the lump-sum request. It did, however, raise the president's salary from $8,000 to $17,500; authorize and fund the new position of vice president; and create a new faculty category called Distinguished Professor, which provided the highest level of faculty salary. Parten was pleased most of all by an overall increase in faculty salaries, although it was less than had been requested. The appropriation raised annual state aid to the university by about five hundred thousand dollars. This was three hundred thousand less than had been requested, but it was one of the largest increases in the history of the university. Among the budgetary surprises was $17,500 to serve as a down payment toward the $35,000 purchase price of an extensive rare-book collection on Mexican history, owned by a private collector in Los Angeles. There was some concern that Allred might veto the latter item as a sacrificial lamb in response to demands to trim the budget, but Parten persuaded the governor to leave the university budget intact. A grateful Edward Randall wrote Parten that his effort was "one of the finest examples of public service that I can recall. You have borne the burden. . . ."[27]

"A job that many consider more important than that of governor"

With the budget battle finally over, Parten devoted his attention in the summer of 1937 to developing a gas field in Cotton Valley, Louisiana, and drilling exploratory wells in West Texas. The forty-one-year-old Parten spent much of the summer flying back and forth in his Stearman from North Louisiana to the far reaches of West Texas. It was an exhausting and hectic schedule. Benedict's unexpected death, however, resulted in yet another time-consuming demand on Parten as an influential regent, drawing him back to Austin and away from his wife and business to serve as the leader in the search for a new president.

Parten felt a strong personal obligation to find Benedict's successor. Several weeks prior to his death, Benedict had indicated his desire to retire. Lecturing Parten about the importance of finding the right person to head the University of Texas, he had urged the oil man to take a leadership role in that effort. In Benedict's view the university had a special opportunity, as well as an increased obligation, in the coming years as immense oil wealth transformed Texas rapidly from a society characterized by agriculture and rural life to one dominated by new urban centers and industrial development. Benedict believed that the university, by training the state's next generation of leaders, by conducting research relevant to the "new" Texas, and by disseminating knowledge through public outreach, was destined to play a positive role in leading Texas into an exciting era of prosperity and progress. The next president, Benedict told Parten, had to have vision and imagination and a proper understanding of the university's need to lead in the coming era of growth and sudden change. Parten had agreed with Benedict and now that Benedict was dead, Parten felt a special responsibility to find a new president who could see the future as Benedict had, and as Parten himself saw it. The Houston *Post* declared in an editorial that the regents had the task of filling a job that "many consider more important than that of governor . . . or any other state office."[28]

Before initiating their search, Parten and his colleagues realized that it was important to appoint an acting president as soon as possible; someone who would not be a candidate for the permanent job. Several influential ex-students and faculty members made a serious effort to persuade Parten to accept the job. A few days after Benedict's funeral, the Dallas *Morning News* reported that a campaign to draft Parten was under way. Styling Parten as "one of the more influential members of the board," the Dallas newspaper reported that he deserved "much of the credit" for getting the legislature to increase the university's budget. Hilmer Weinert proposed that Parten be appointed to the job permanently. Although flattered, Parten had no intention of serving as the university's president, either on an ad interim or on a permanent basis. Telling E. L. Woodley that he was "somewhat embarrassed" by the proposal, Parten declared it would be "very unbecoming for the Board to allow one of its members to be elected for this task." Besides, he argued, he was not qualified for the job. When his former university classmate, George Wythe, urged him to pursue the presidency, Parten replied that he would not. He told Wythe that he was discouraging the idea by treating it "as a joke." He later explained that "there's just one way to elect a president of a great public university, and that is by proper procedures, with the representation of all interested parties . . . especially the alumni on the one hand and the faculty on the other."[29]

In late May, with Parten refusing to accept the job, the regents appointed John Calhoun, the university's longtime comptroller, to serve as acting president. According to Parten, the sixty-six-year-old Calhoun was "a tough handler of money, very conservative. We called him 'Diligent John.' He was one man on the faculty that we all agreed we could safely put in this job and not have him politicking for the long range position."[30]

As soon as Calhoun assumed the duties of acting president, Parten and his colleagues issued a national invitation for nominations for the permanent job. Despite the inevitable political pressure to move quickly and appoint someone expedient, Parten persuaded his colleagues to go slow. "I wanted us to take our time and search the nation over, study the problem closely, and come up with some of the best names we could find for the job," Parten said. He was also determined to include faculty and ex-students in the search process. Accordingly, at the regents' direction the faculty elected an advisory committee chaired by H. T. Parlin, dean of Arts and Sciences. The Ex-Students Association was represented by a committee that included former state attorney general Robert Lee Bobbitt, former governor Dan Moody, and Hines Baker. Edward Randall chaired the regents' search committee, which included Parten, Waggener, and Aynesworth, but it was widely assumed that Parten would play the major role in the process. As former regent Robert L. Holliday pointed out when the search began, "the selection of the president . . . is going to be largely in the hands of one Major Parten."[31]

Parten viewed the presidential search as not only an opportunity to find new leadership for the university, but also an opportunity to study the successes and failures of other universities and to use those experiences to improve the University of Texas. He proposed to the search committee that it travel to several of the leading public and private universities in the Midwest and on the East Coast to meet with trustees, administrators, and faculties to ascertain, as Parten put it, how "the greater universities of the land 'tick'." He argued that he could "visualize great benefits for our program . . . because we will . . . acquire a knowledge of these institutions that would better enable us to solve our own problem." His colleagues agreed, but scheduling problems caused them to postpone the tour until the fall. In the meantime, nominations and applications for the job poured in with each day's mail for the rest of the summer.[32]

The letter to which Parten paid the most attention was the first one he received. Lotus D. Coffman, the University of Minnesota president who had so impressed Parten during his trip to Minneapolis, wrote as soon as he heard about Benedict's death. Coffman urged Parten to take a close look at Dr. Homer Price Rainey, a former president of Bucknell University, who was currently director of the American Youth Commission of the American Education Council in Washington, D.C. Coffman liked Rainey for the University of Texas presidency for a number of reasons. Not only did he have considerable experience as an academic administrator with a proven record of success, he also was a native Texan and only forty-one years old. Rainey knew the territory and he was young and energetic enough to keep up the hard pace of work needed in the effort to build the university. Rainey's youth attracted Parten, who had already decided that the next president should be "young enough in years to promise at least ten years of active and vigilant service. . . ." According to Parten, Coffman's letter "put Homer Rainey on our list." Rainey's involvement with the University of Texas would greatly affect Parten's views on the issue of academic freedom and would bring about changes in his political views.[33]

In September, as the search committee prepared for its fact-finding tour of university campuses, it received news that a special legislative session would meet from late September until mid-October to deal with a major deficit in the state budget. Especially troubling were rumors that a vigorous effort was expected in the Senate to roll back the university's funding increases. To cover the deficit, Allred called for an income tax and an increase in corporate taxes, especially on sulphur. Faced suddenly with the possibility of a significant cut in state funding, the regents' presidential search committee postponed its trip. Parten was forced to spend much of the early fall in Austin, fending off a legislative raid on the university's financing. The rumors proved to be true. The Senate tried to slash every increase in the appropriations made during the regular session, including faculty salaries and the president's new salary. Parten urged Allred to stop the Senate from destroying the gains made in the university's funding. Allred eventually invoked his constitutional authority to limit the issues that the legislature could consider during a special session, declaring that the special session had been called only to raise revenues, not to reduce appropriations. Allred's action effectively ended the threat to the university budget, but the episode forced Parten's committee to delay its fact-finding trip until after the first of the year.[34]

A Trip to Find the Best

Parten, Randall, Aynesworth, and Waggener finally departed Austin on January 29, bound for several campuses in the Midwest and on the East Coast. Their first stop was Birmingham, Alabama, where they met with Frank Graham, the president of the University of North Carolina, who had built his institution into one of the leading public universities in the South. Graham was high on the committee's list of candidates. Not only did they interview him for the job, the committee was also interested in hearing his thoughts about the future of the University of Texas. Parten was impressed with Graham, but Randall thought his politics were far too liberal for Texas. He feared Graham would be a political activist and cause the university no end of trouble with the legislature. At Randall's urging, Graham's name was removed from the list.[35]

The committee's next interview, on February 2 with Homer Rainey in Washington, D.C., proved more promising. Already attracted to Rainey by Coffman's recommendation, the committee found his combination of background, training, and experience especially appealing. Rainey had deep roots in the Lone Star State. Born and raised near the tiny northeast Texas farming community of Eliasville (coincidentally the childhood home of H. Y. Benedict as well), Rainey had attended Austin College in Sherman, earning his bachelor's degree in 1919. His wife, Helen, had been a student at the University of Texas at the same time as Parten. After Rainey received his doctorate from the University of Chicago, he taught briefly at the University of Oregon and served as president of Franklin College in Indiana for four years. At the age of thirty-five, Rainey became president of Bucknell University in Pennsylvania. After a distinguished tenure at Bucknell, Rainey was appointed director of the American Youth Commission in Washington, where the quality of his leadership was attracting national attention. Rainey had other attributes that the committee believed would help him in Texas if he became president. He was an ordained Baptist minister, a family man with two daughters, and a former athlete who had played professional baseball.[36]

Attracted to Rainey by his résumé, the committee was also impressed with his comments during the interview, especially in light of the fact that he had very little advance warning about the visit. Rainey recalled that "one afternoon I was asked if I was free for an appointment, and three regents . . . descended on me there in Washington and said they were looking for a president. . . . And that was the first time that I ever knew about any possibility of ever being President of The University of Texas." Rainey's view of the university's future matched the committee's, especially Parten's. He stressed that the future progress of the university and the state were interrelated; the University of Texas was destined to play a decisive role in the development of the state's "entire social, political, and economic fabric. . . ." It was the university's responsibility, Rainey argued, "to provide the research and intellectual leadership that will lay the scientific and cultural foundation for the . . . reconstruction of that entire section." The next president of the University of Texas would therefore be one of the key individuals in the state's overall development.

Rainey told the committee that he had been deeply impressed by University of Texas history professor Walter Prescott Webb's recently published book *Divided We Stand*, which presented an argument popular among liberal politicians, academicians, and journalists throughout the southern states at the time. Webb's book elaborated the theme that Texas and the other southern and western states were being plundered by a "colonial-style economy." The plunderers were the great monopolistic corporations with their system of patent controls, discriminatory pricing and railroad rates, restrictive licensing arrangements, and other methods of "economic imperial control." The Republican Party, Webb argued, served as the political agent for this economic oppression. Rainey told the search committee that he believed Webb's argument to be sound and that an upgraded University of Texas could help end the state's exploitation by northern monopolies. In a follow-up letter to the committee, Rainey reiterated that Webb's book pointed "very clearly . . . to the tremendous need in the South for an intellectual re-awakening that will result in the building of a new economic structure for that section of the country." The University of Texas, he argued, was in a position to produce and guide that "intellectual re-awakening." Rainey added that as "one who loves his native state and that section of the country," he would, if appointed, "undertake the leadership at the University almost with a religious zeal."[37]

Parten's reaction to Rainey's comments was strongly favorable. The educator's views about monopolistic domination, his reference to Webb (whom Parten admired), his general philosophy of administration, and his energetic enthusiasm made a strongly positive impression. Rainey easily made the committee's "short list."

After its meeting with Rainey, the regents' search committee went to New York City on February 8 to interview Dr. Luther Halsey Gulick, a forty-six-year-old professor of Municipal Science and Administration at Columbia University, who also

Dr. Luther Gulick, 1938. *CN 09630. Courtesy Prints and Photographs Collection, CAH.*

served as the director of Columbia's Institute of Public Administration. Gulick, a political scientist with a doctorate from Columbia, was a nationally renowned expert in the field of public administration. An articulate and self-confident man, Gulick's ideas about how a large state university should be managed also impressed Parten and his colleagues. Although Gulick lacked Rainey's Texas background (he had never even been to Texas), he had a more dynamic personality than Rainey and he had a superior record as a scholar. His recently published textbook on public administration had won widespread praise from his professional peers. To Parten, Gulick seemed to have more potential as a leader than did Rainey. Parten noted his experience in 1936 as a leading member of President Roosevelt's Committee on Administrative Management. His comments to the search committee about his work in Washington attempting to reorganize the bureaucratic structure of the executive branch gave Parten the impression that Gulick was no ivory-tower intellectual, but rather a politically savvy scholar who had "real world" experience. In his own mind, Parten immediately ranked Gulick as the number-one candidate. Although Gulick told the committee that he had no interest in the Texas job and strongly recommended Homer Rainey, Parten refused to take his statement seriously. He believed that if they could lure Gulick to Austin and show him the great potential of the University of Texas he would respond to the challenge.[38]

Parten and his colleagues left New York on February 9 with the feeling that they had two very strong and attractive candidates. The committee spent the remaining time of their trip touring a few of the leading universities in the Midwest. A highlight of this part of the trip was a campus tour of the prestigious University of Chicago and a meeting with Chicago's famous president, Robert Maynard Hutchins. Hutchins had become president of the University of Chicago in 1929 at the age of thirty. Prior to his move to Chicago, Hutchins had been the "child" dean of Yale Law School, where he transformed Yale into a center of experimentation in legal education. By the time Parten and his fellow regents met him in 1937, Hutchins was not only the brilliant "boy-wonder" of higher education, he was, as one observer has noted, "the storm center of American academic life." His attempts to reorganize the University of Chicago and to reform its curriculum, as well as his calls for fundamental changes in American higher education had attracted controversial attention not only within educational circles, but in the national press. He became a leader of those who believed that the most effective way of producing an educated person was through an emphasis on the liberal arts and he was an opponent of the view that education should be centered on the concept of "usefulness."[39]

Parten had met Hutchins briefly in 1936 when Hutchins had visited Austin to consult with Benedict on the McDonald Observatory, the astronomical telescope on Mount Locke in far West Texas owned by the University of Texas but staffed and operated by the University of Chicago. In a discussion that Parten and his colleagues found uplifting as well as irritating, Hutchins cast his vote for Rainey, the University of Chicago graduate (typically, Hutchins told the Texans that Rainey "had risen above his education at Chicago.") He told the committee that he knew Gulick well and that because he was a New Yorker, he would probably have the difficulty in Texas of being a "Damn Yankee." Hutchins dazzled the Texans with his strength of personality and his nontraditional, controversial views about the state of higher education in the United States. It was a performance of such tour de force that Parten never forgot it. In a letter to a friend after his return to Texas, he wrote "Dr. Hutchins . . . is certainly a delightful person, very keen of mind, and *very* pointed in conversation." In recalling that meeting years later, Parten said, "I was very, very favorably impressed with Hutchins. It was clear to me then that Bob had a brilliant mind."[40]

Hutchins swept Parten off his feet. Three years younger than Parten, and six feet three inches tall, Hutchins was a striking figure. Articulate, handsome, and cultured, Hutchins scorned pettiness, small-talk, and pretension, yet his intellectual arrogance and magisterial personal style were softened by his self-deprecating wit and his masterful use of the ironic. One associate described him as "debonair, fluent, logical, provocative, courageous, and handsome." Hutchins was also impressed with Parten, a rich businessman from Texas who appreciated the iconoclast in any field. Their meeting in Chicago in 1937 began an acquaintance that developed into a friendship lasting nearly forty years. In later years that friendship deepened and Hutchins involved Parten in the Fund for the Republic, which

Robert M. Hutchins,
1936. *CN 09629.*
*Courtesy Prints and
Photographs
Collection, CAH.*

brought Parten into contact with a wide variety of diverse ideas and causes that he referred to as his "graduate education" in the liberal arts.[41]

Gulick or Rainey?

Parten and his colleagues on the regents' search committee returned to Texas on February 15 convinced that either Luther Gulick or Homer Rainey would be the next president of the University of Texas. Parten played the dominant role in making the final choice. Edward Randall, who was exhausted by the strenuous trip, made it clear to his younger colleague that it was up to him to keep the process going. Aynesworth and Waggener were also willing for Parten to play the leading role in making the final choice. At this point, Parten was leaning slightly toward Gulick, but Hutchins's endorsement of Rainey had made a strong impression. He wrote Randall that his mind was "yet open on the question as to who the man is to be." The entire committee agreed that Gulick and Rainey should come to Texas as soon as possible to meet with the faculty and alumni committees.[42]

Gulick, however, was doing all he could to eliminate himself from the list. When Randall invited him to come to Texas, Gulick refused, saying he could not visit Texas if he did not think he would accept the job. Rainey, on the other hand, eagerly accepted Randall's invitation. He visited the campus in late March and had

191

lengthy meetings with the regents as well as the faculty and ex-student committees. During his visit, Rainey was impressed with how well Parten and the other regents worked with the faculty and alumni committees. He was excited also by the university community's optimism and confidence about the university's seemingly limitless future. Rainey later wrote that his visit to Austin convinced him that the University of Texas had "some outstanding opportunities to develop a unique place for itself in several special fields." During his meeting with the regents, Rainey again referred to Webb's new book and the insights he had gained from reading it. He agreed with Webb on the need for new industrial development in the South, predicting that the entire region was destined to "experience a very marked industrial and economic development in the immediate future." Rainey stressed to the regents that the university had a critical role to play in laying the "intellectual and scientific foundation" for this development. He explained that one of the most important steps the university could take to help fulfill this role would be to build an outstanding graduate school with its faculty actively engaged in research. He argued that the university's research function, if properly developed and supported, "will be bringing to the people of Texas financial returns many times greater than the cost of the institution to the people of the State." Rainey also told the regents and the faculty that the university's proximity to Mexico and South America, coupled with its excellent library resources on Latin America, presented an excellent opportunity for it to become the leading center in the country for the study of South American relations. Rainey believed that if the university explained these possibilities to the people through an effective public relations effort, the legislature should be willing to provide the money to make it happen.[43]

Rainey's arguments anticipated the role Texas played in the so-called "Sunbelt" economy of the 1970s, as well as the university's importance to the state in the post-petroleum era. They were ideas with which Parten strongly agreed. In a speech to the university's Phi Beta Kappa chapter a month after Rainey's visit to Austin, Parten argued that with an active program of research, the University of Texas could aid in spawning new local industries and other business enterprises to lower unemployment and expand the state's economy. As an example, he claimed that an adequately funded research program in chemistry might result in a vast increase in the number of usable products from natural gas, one of the state's most abundant resources. Parten's speech also repeated arguments that Hutchins had made in his lecture to the regents' search committee about the critical importance of a strong liberal-arts education. Parten had listened well to Hutchins. "A liberal education might include technical training," Parten stated, "but with it should come training of judgment, the storing up of wisdom, and self-knowledge." Such an orientation, he added, should shift the emphasis away from building the physical campus so that more attention could be paid to improving the "spiritual and faculty side" of the University.[44]

Parten was also enthusiastic about Rainey's argument for a major Latin American studies program. Walter Webb, Eugene Holman, Wallace Pratt, and others had already discussed with Parten the need for the university to develop such a program. Because Standard Oil and the Rockefeller interests were actively involved in South America, Holman had argued that Texas could cut a valuable educational niche for itself by providing specialized graduate training in Latin American studies to produce skilled people to work for U.S. companies south of the border. Holman also urged Parten to strengthen the university's Spanish-language program. Encouraged by Rainey's speech and the enthusiastic reactions to it on campus, Webb went to Parten during the summer and proposed a formal program to be called the "Latin American Studies Center." He told the regent that he believed start-up money could be provided by the Rockefeller Foundation, which was deeply involved in South America. Parten, agreeing that such a program should be initiated as soon as possible, told Webb that he would contact his good friends Gene Holman and Wallace Pratt at Jersey Standard to seek their help in arranging a meeting between Webb and Nelson Rockefeller. Parten also told Webb he would get acting-President Calhoun to support the historian's effort. Parten subsequently wrote Calhoun to urge him to give Webb released time and financial support to go to New York to seek funding from the Rockefeller Foundation. Parten made certain that the notoriously tight-fisted Calhoun understood his intentions. "My unqualified opinion is that it is a duty of all in authority to pursue this idea diligently," Parten emphasized. "Texas is the place for this Institute. That one will be established I have little doubt."[45]

"How fortunate we are to have such a team in charge!"

Despite Gulick's announced decision not to come to Texas and the favorable reception Rainey had received from the faculty and the regents, Parten refused to accept Gulick's withdrawal. Although Rainey had said and done the right things, Parten believed Rainey lacked Gulick's leadership qualities. He felt that as a result of Gulick's background as a political scientist and his extensive work as a government consultant, he would be more effective with the legislature, the arena where the critical battles most important to the university's future would be conducted. Parten had also been impressed when Wallace Pratt told him that Nelson Rockefeller and other prominent leaders in New York had assured Pratt that Gulick was a "high-standing" person of great ability. Pratt, who was actively promoting Gulick for the presidency, suggested that because the officials at the Rockefeller Foundation thought so highly of Gulick, he could probably get the University of Texas on the foundation's money "pipeline." Gene Holman was also a Gulick supporter, urging Parten not to give up on him. Both men had talked to Gulick and were doing their best to change his mind. Accordingly, Parten decided to continue his pursuit of Gulick. If he failed with the New Yorker, Parten considered Rainey an excellent second choice. In early April 1938, Parten told Edward Randall that he believed Gulick's heavy work load and the stress of a rapidly approaching deadline on a study for the State of New York had caused him to reject their overtures. Gulick's consulting project would be over in late April, so Parten suggested to Randall and his other regental colleagues that a decision on the presidency be delayed until he could meet with Gulick in New York while he was there in May on a business trip for Woodley.[46]

In the meantime, a couple of Parten's fellow regents, as well as some influential former students, pressured the search committee to speed up their selection process. Increasing the pressure was an Associated Press story on April 10 reporting that either Rainey or Gulick would be the next University of Texas president. On behalf of the search committee, Parten declared that the selection process was not complete and that several candidates were still being considered. In addition to the demands to hurry the appointment, regents George Morgan and Lutcher Stark insisted at a board meeting early in April that Parten's old army buddy, Paul McNutt, who was now high commissioner of the Philippines, should be approached for the job. Although Parten admired McNutt, he felt strongly that his political ambitions could create problems for the university. Because of the widespread belief that Roosevelt would not run for a third term, McNutt was being mentioned in the news media as one of the likely candidates for the Democratic nomination for president in 1940. The faculty search committee had expressed its opposition to McNutt for the same reason. The regents had fended off attempts to make a political appointment shortly after Benedict's death, and Parten and his colleagues on the committee had no intention of making that mistake.[47]

Randall and Aynesworth now pressed Parten to abandon his plan to try and lure Gulick. "The University is at a stand-still at one of the most serious epochs of history, and will continue to be so until the president is selected," Aynesworth wrote Parten. "We should act with decision and dispatch . . . without further delay." Aynesworth urged that the search committee proceed with Rainey as its first choice. Parten replied that he was "mindful of the fact that we are faced with the hazard of tiring of the tremendous responsibility that is on our shoulders." He understood the need to hurry, but he wanted the time to work on Gulick and to satisfy Stark and Morgan about McNutt. He pleaded with his colleagues to delay their decision until mid-August, arguing that he would need that much time to deal with McNutt in far away Manila and to arrange a meeting with the busy Gulick.[48]

Hoping to keep the mercurial Stark happy and out of respect to his friend Morgan, Parten contacted McNutt. Parten had maintained his relationship with McNutt ever since their army days, often visiting Paul and his wife on his many visits to Washington in the late 1930s, before McNutt went to the Philippines in 1937. Parten had a high regard for McNutt's abilities; he wrote to his sister Lucy who lived near Manila that McNutt was "one of the ablest men I know." But Parten was adamantly opposed to appointing to the presidency anyone active in politics. Parten had succeeded in getting Morgan and Stark to agree to drop their campaign for McNutt if it could be demonstrated that he wanted to make a bid for the Democratic nomination. Parten's letter to McNutt, therefore, was written in such a way as to allow Parten to fulfill his promise to make contact with McNutt, yet smoke him out about his political plans without letting him know that he was being talked about for the university post. Parten asked McNutt if he intended to run for president, because he wanted to do "whatever I can for you in Texas" if he did. Actually, Parten's statement was not false. If Roosevelt decided not to run again, McNutt was Parten's choice to replace him. He told McNutt about his involvement in the search for a new university president and asked for his recommendations. Parten's strategy worked. McNutt replied that in regard to the 1940 presidential nomination, "if I have a chance, I expect to take it." He also wrote that in his opinion "[Homer] Rainey would make an ideal head of the University of Texas. . . ." McNutt's answer convinced Stark and Morgan that Gulick and Rainey should be the finalists.[49]

The complaints of a right-wing faculty member further complicated Parten's push for Gulick. Perry Patterson, a professor of government at the university, sent letters to each regent charging that Gulick was a dangerous radical because of his work as a consultant with President Roosevelt and the New Deal. Patterson's charges worried Hilmer Weinert, who asked Parten if either Gulick's or Rainey's writings indicated any radical or subversive tendencies. Parten assured Weinert that he had personally read the writings of both men and that he could assure him that "they both measure up in conservatism. They both believe in our American institutions. . . ." When Randall asked Parten if Patterson's concerns had any merit, Parten's reply not only reiterated his confidence in Gulick, but revealed the transformation in his own thinking about the New Deal since his earlier fight with Ickes over oil regulation: "I . . . know Dr. Patterson is obsessed with the idea that anything Mr. Roosevelt does is wrong. . . . I must say that I don't agree with him at this juncture. There are a great many things Mr. Roosevelt has done and is doing that are in my opinion quite worthwhile." Reminding Randall about what Wallace Pratt and Nelson Rockefeller had said about Gulick, he advised Randall to "discount Dr. Patterson's criticism." Parten now believed that FDR's programs were saving free enterprise in the United States rather than destroying it. "Roosevelt was just a great liberal in the sense of Thomas Jefferson," Parten later declared, "and he was for free enterprise all the way."[50]

Parten's support for Gulick was further bolstered by a letter he received from Lotus Coffman at the beginning of May. Although Coffman had been the first to recommend Rainey, he now told Parten that the University of Texas would be taking "something of a chance" with Rainey. "If there is need for a two-fisted fighter, I should doubt whether Rainey should be considered," Coffman said. "I don't think he is a great man, but I do believe that he will grow bigger with any job he gets." He stressed that Gulick and Rainey "are unlike in many respects. Rainey is more self-effacing, the quieter and the less vigorous of the two . . . Gulick is the more robust . . . a little abler intellectually. Gulick is the more effective [speaker]." After Parten received Coffman's letter, he wrote Randall that "Gulick would get off more speedily in our . . . program than would Rainey. I still retain some hope of getting Gulick to come to our campus. . . ." Parten's fellow regents finally agreed to delay their decision until he had another opportunity to talk to Gulick in New York in June.[51]

J. R. and Opal went to New York on June 3 to talk to Luther Gulick, conduct some business for Woodley, and visit with administrators of the area's medical schools to gather information that could be useful in regard to the University of Texas Medical Branch in Galveston. After he arrived in New York, Parten received a letter from Randall thanking him for agreeing to gather the information for the Medical School. "I realize we are putting a great deal of work upon you," Randall wrote, "but a capable and willing horse must bear many loads." The Partens took the Gulicks to dinner a few days later. J. R. and Opal turned on their considerable charm, persuading Gulick to come to Texas sometime late in the summer and to give serious consideration to the University of Texas presidency. A delighted Parten telephoned his good news to Leslie Waggener. Parten was so convinced that he had hooked Gulick that he told Waggener to talk to their board colleagues about the idea of hiring Homer Rainey for the new vice president's job. He considered the search to be over. Waggener was elated, stating that "such a combination appears to me to be unbeatable." Waggener declared that he did "not know how the University . . . is ever going to show its appreciation to you and Mrs. Parten for this . . . effective work. . . . How fortunate we are to have such a team in charge!"[52]

The Colonel, the Major, and Pappy

1938

J R. Parten returned to Texas in mid-June 1938, satisfied that the prolonged search for a new president for the University of Texas was nearly over. With the presidential search in good shape, Parten turned his attention to an important political matter: the campaign to elect Governor Allred's successor. To Parten's disappointment, Jimmy Allred had decided against running for another term in office. Allred needed to revive his law practice so that he could pay off some personal debts. With Allred out of the race, Parten had joined others in urging his old friend and political ally Ernest Thompson to run.[1]

A Thompson gubernatorial administration appealed to Parten for strong reasons of self-interest as well as a sincere concern for a people-oriented government. As a close political ally and longtime friend, Parten knew that he would have influence in the Governor's Mansion with Thompson in residence. A dependable friend of the independents in the Texas oil industry, Thompson could be counted on to use the governor's veto power to defend the independents against a state legislature dominated by the major oil companies. In addition, Thompson was a former student of the University of Texas who would support the university's funding requests and who would be helpful in its ambitious effort to join the ranks of the nation's best state universities. Parten also knew that Thompson would support much-needed legislation to improve living and working conditions for all Texans. Thompson had announced his firm opposition to a general sales tax, declaring it a "tax on poverty." He had also endorsed salary increases for public school teachers, full funding of old-age pensions, lower utility rates, and an end of the widespread practice of warehousing the mentally ill in county jails. These were positions Parten also supported. Parten wrote one of his friends in Madisonville that he had "never seen [Thompson] take a side on any question that in my opinion wasn't the people's side. His heart beats on the side of the people."[2]

Parten was not eager to see Thompson leave the Railroad Commission, but his presence on that regulatory body was no longer a critical need. The East Texas crisis was now history. Crude oil prices had remained at a level between $1.00 and $1.18 a barrel and the regulatory system seemed to be working well. Thompson, who had long held gubernatorial ambitions, needed little encouragement to make the race. He announced his candidacy on January 1. At the beginning of the campaign, Thompson's chances for victory in the Democratic primary on July 23 appeared to be excellent. Most political observers believed that among the eleven other candidates, only Texas attorney general William C. McCraw, whose basic political views differed little from Thompson's, loomed as a serious threat. Tom Hunter, veteran of three other gubernatorial campaigns, was considered to be the only other candidate with much of a chance against Thompson.[3]

"Pass-the-Biscuits Pappy"

During its early weeks, the gubernatorial campaign had proceeded according to expectations. Thompson and McCraw both drew large crowds as they toured the state, but the similarity of their programs, the lack of any sensational issues, and the colorless way they conducted their campaigns resulted in a boring, spiritless race. For example, the "highlight" of Thompson's set speech on his "program for permanent prosperity" was a detailed report on his plans for soil conservation. In early June, former governor Dan Moody wrote to a friend that "there has not been a great deal of interest developed in the Governor's campaign . . . it's not the kind of a campaign that people have fist fights over."[4]

A continuation of this situation was what Parten had expected when he returned to Texas after his meeting with Luther Gulick. A few days later, Myron Blalock, who was serving as one of Thompson's advisors, gave Parten the disquieting news that a clownish flour salesman by the name of Wilbert Lee O'Daniel, who had entered the governor's race on May 1, was attracting massive crowds at his campaign rallies in Waco, San Angelo, and Abilene, and in small towns in the Panhandle and west central Texas. A flour-mill owner, O'Daniel had earned the nickname "Pass-the-Biscuits Pappy" as a result of a flour commercial on his popular country-and-western radio show. Declaring that his platform would be the Ten Commandments and his motto the Golden Rule, O'Daniel was waging a classic "outsiders" campaign against "Johnson grass and professional politicians." Thompson, McCraw, and most of the state's newspapers had refused to take O'Daniel seriously as he toured the state with his country-and-western band the "Hillbilly Boys and Texas Rose."[5]

By mid-June, however, O'Daniel's traveling hillbilly show could no longer be ignored. Blalock admitted to Parten that he and Thompson's other advisors were worried that O'Daniel might take enough votes away from Thompson to force him into a runoff with McCraw. No one expected O'Daniel to win, but some political observers were saying that O'Daniel was such an unknown factor that his

W. Lee O'Daniel campaigning for governor of Texas, 1938. *CN 09640. Courtesy Jimmy Dodd Collection, CAH.*

impact on the race would be impossible to predict. Blalock asked Parten if he could spare the time to come to Austin and help Thompson's campaign. It was an invitation Parten could not refuse. He packed his bags and headed for the state capital, a city that had become his second home.[6]

Setting up shop in his usual suite on the sixteenth floor of the Stephen F. Austin Hotel, Parten worked for Thompson's campaign for the last half of June and most of July. Houston independent oil man Jim Abercrombie, Claude Wild, Grover Sellers, and Myron Blalock frequently joined Parten for strategy meetings in his suite. John B. Connally, who was a senior and student-body president at the university, worked in Thompson's campaign as a campus organizer. He occasionally accompanied Wild to these meetings at the Austin Hotel and watched with fascination as the "tall and suave" Major Parten ("I called him Major . . . all my life," Connally said) mapped campaign strategy and analyzed the opposition. "These men were masters at the political art," Connally recalled in his autobiography, "which included a certain skill at fund-raising."[7]

Parten conferred frequently with members of Thompson's small campaign staff about tactics and daily schedules, he helped write some of Thompson's speeches, arranged and paid for his radio talks, and spent much time on the telephone or in personal meetings trying to raise money from his friends among the independents in the oil and gas industry. He soon learned, however, that many of the independents were reluctant to help because they did not want Thompson to leave the Railroad Commission. Parten refused to believe, however, that Thompson would not make it to the runoff against McCraw. Despite reports of huge crowds attending O'Daniel's rallies, he still did not take O'Daniel seriously, so he and Thompson's other advisors agreed that their focus should be on McCraw.[8]

"Where did the other seventy five cents go?"

Parten was concerned by the lack of any substantive issues separating Thompson from McCraw. "Thompson had no issue with McCraw," Parten observed, "they were mamby-pamby, slapping one another on the wrist." Because McCraw was the more dynamic of the two in person, Parten feared that voters, with no issues of importance to stir them, might simply choose the better speaker. Ironically, his fears proved to be well founded, but for the wrong candidate. To find an issue that Thompson could use to separate himself from McCraw, Parten hired a researcher to review McCraw's record as attorney general. The researcher uncovered information on McCraw's handling of hot oil that Parten thought might do the trick. There had been earthen pits scattered throughout the East Texas oil field containing in total several million barrels of hot oil, which could not be sold by the producers without violating state and federal laws. The legislature had passed an act requiring the attorney general to confiscate and sell the oil and deposit the proceeds in the public-school fund. Reviewing records from the Attorney General's Office found by his researcher, Parten determined that McCraw had sold several million barrels of confiscated oil for twenty to thirty

E. O. Thompson campaigning for governor of Texas, 1938. *CN 09631. Courtesy Thompson Photograph Collection, CAH.*

cents a barrel when the market price was well over a dollar a barrel. Parten discovered that McCraw had sold some of this hot oil back to the original producers, who were then able to sell it legally for the market price. He realized that Thompson not only could hit McCraw with the charge of helping hot-oilers but also accuse him of robbing the public-school fund.[9]

Parten persuaded Jimmy Allred to write a speech for Thompson about McCraw's handling of the hot oil. He was delighted to finally have Allred's help. Several weeks before, he had asked the governor to endorse Thompson as his successor, but Allred had refused. "There were differences between Thompson and Allred," Parten noted. "They both had high ambitions politically, and they just didn't gravitate to one another. I spent a good deal of my time removing difficulties between them." Allred, however, had an especially bitter and intense (and unexplained) dislike for Bill McCraw, even to the point of quietly encouraging Thompson to run for governor just to keep McCraw from winning the office. So when Parten asked for Allred's help with the speech, he was happy to do it just to have a shot at McCraw.[10]

Parten and Allred worked in the Governor's Mansion until three o'clock in the morning writing the hot-oil speech for Thompson to deliver at Wichita Falls the next night. "McCraw had sold all the school children's oil for twenty five cents a barrel, and the market price was a dollar," Parten recalled, "so the question our speech asked was where did the other seventy five cents go? Jimmy and I thought it was pretty good." A courier delivered the speech to Thompson as he was leaving Fort Worth on his way to Wichita Falls. "He got to Decatur and he had one of his associates call me and tell me that that speech was very hot," Parten later remembered, "he was wondering if he ought to use it that night, maybe put it off. Well, I didn't like that." Thompson proceeded to Wichita Falls, where Parten had arranged and paid for air time on a statewide radio network for him to deliver the hot-oil speech. Traveling with the railroad commissioner were Jim Abercrombie, an independent oil man from Houston, and Grover Hill, one of Thompson's close friends from Amarillo. "Abercrombie and Hill dissuaded Thompson from giving that speech," Parten said, "they were afraid of him opening the hot oil issue because too many people would ask Thompson, as a rail road commissioner, why he let it be produced in the first place. Well, of course, that was no question at all, because the reason that hot oil was still in those earthen pits was because of Thompson's enforcement of the law."

Thompson's refusal to use the speech displeased and frustrated Parten, but it deeply angered Allred who was not enamored with Thompson in the first place. He had already been irritated by a Thompson speech made earlier in the campaign that Allred felt had implied that he had not done much to get old-age pensions funded in Texas. "There was already a Thompson cocklebur under Jimmy's blanket," Parten later claimed, "but Jimmy really quit helping Thompson after he refused to make that issue with hot oil." Despite Thompson's reluctance to use Parten's hot-oil charge against McCraw in his speeches, Parten proceeded on his own to write and arrange for the printing of a large broadside that was circulated throughout the state charging McCraw with helping hot-oil runners in East Texas while he was attorney general.[11]

Another sensational charge against McCraw that Thompson's advisors dredged up not only had no impact on McCraw, it quickly became a threat to Thompson himself. Although it was no secret among politicians in Austin that McCraw had been a member of the Dallas chapter of the Ku Klux Klan in the early 1920s (a membership McCraw had long since repudiated), that information had not been publicized generally. Thompson, who ran a conservative, issue-dominated campaign, with only rare personal references to his opponents, finally agreed to mention in one of his speeches McCraw's involvement in the Klan. Thompson regretted his reference to McCraw's Klan membership almost as soon as he made it. Two weeks before election day, South Texas political organizer Sam Fore Jr. sent Thompson a telegram warning him that a circular had been distributed in the heavily Catholic counties south of San Antonio alleging that Thompson had joined the Ku Klux Klan in Amarillo in the early 1920s. Fore urged Thompson to issue a strongly worded denial as soon as possible: "this [is of] vital importance . . . don't fail us . . . we are still for you strong and bitterly resent such tactics." The Thompson campaign quickly had the archbishop of San Antonio, Arthur J. Drossaerts, issue a letter they provided to him from R. A. Gerken, archbishop of Santa Fe (who had been bishop in Amarillo when Thompson was mayor) declaring that the charge of Thompson's Klan membership was a falsehood and that he knew Thompson to be a "true friend of all religion. . . ."[12]

Thompson still had a problem, however. When the accusing circular finally reached Thompson's campaign office in Austin, Parten was shocked to see that it featured a photostatic copy of Thompson's signature on an application for membership in the Klan in Amarillo. The next morning Thompson, Abercrombie, Hill, and Parten met to discuss McCraw's circular over breakfast. Thompson denied ever being involved in the Klan in any way. Jim Abercrombie urged Parten to go to Amarillo as soon as possible to find out where the photostat had originated. Parten had sold his airplane, so he called Austin newspaper publisher Charles Marsh, who loaned him his small two-seat, open-cockpit biplane and a pilot. "It was a fast airplane," Parten later remembered. "I went up there after breakfast and got back to Austin before dinner." It had not taken him long to confirm from some of his friends in Amarillo that Thompson had indeed attended the first meeting of the Ku Klux Klan in the Panhandle city. They had seen the original application, which was now in McCraw's hands. "At dinner," Parten recalled, "Ernest [Thompson] and Grover [Hill] finally remembered that yeah, they did attend this first meeting but they hadn't intended to join anything. Ernest didn't know what in the devil he was doing, and forgot that he ever belonged. But that was his signature on the paper. McCraw had already spread the documents all over the German-Catholic country down there. That was a little embarrassing," Parten admitted. Parten realized that there was no way they could now make an issue of McCraw's Klan membership. "We just decided not to answer McCraw's charge. That's the only thing we could do." On his way to campaign appearances in East Texas, an equally embarrassed Ernest Thompson, appreciative of Parten's quick dash to Amarillo on his behalf as well as his other supporting activities, sent him a telegram: "I am eternally grateful for the work you have done and are doing in my behalf. The thing that pleases me is that it seems to be on your part a labor of love. . . . No matter what happens I love you for what you have done for me."[13]

"Flour; not Pork"

In the final days of the primary campaign, Parten and his colleagues in the Thompson camp realized that the O'Daniel campaign was a political phenomenon for which they and every other political activist in Texas had been totally unprepared. They had concentrated exclusively on McCraw and had paid no attention to "Pappy" and his hillbilly band. McCraw, however, had understood O'Daniel's threat by late June and had gone on the offensive against him. For example, in a much quoted speech in Fort Worth, McCraw—who was more of a street fighter than was Thompson—called O'Daniel the "banjo man" and asked his audience if they could "imagine the immortal [former governor] Jim Hogg standing on a wagon wearing two-toned shoes and with perfume back of his ears singing 'Josephine'?" McCraw's attacks proved to be completely ineffective against the mass appeal of a semievangelistic master of public relations who happened to have the most popular program in the history of Texas radio and who was promising the "common" citizens of the state everything without explaining how he would pay for it.[14]

By the campaign's late stage, other political observers could see how popular O'Daniel had become. The U.S. attorney for North Texas, Clyde Eastus, reported to Democratic Party chairman James A. Farley that he had just returned from a trip through most of northeastern Texas and "everybody in these parts is for O'Daniel. I am convinced that if this keeps up . . . O'Daniel will be elected Governor in the first primary . . . to me it looks like a landslide." Dan Moody told a friend that he had gone to O'Daniel's rally in Austin "and it was the biggest crowd I ever saw at a political speaking." Moody confided to former university regent Robert Holliday that O'Daniel "has been having tremendous crowds. . . . I suspect he has spoken to more people than any other candidate for Governor has ever spoken to in a like length of time. . . . he had a larger crowd at San Marcos last night than had assembled there since they had a Klan parade in 1922." Jimmy Allred later recalled that when he received "reports as to his crowds and, knowing, as I did, the appeal of his little sermonettes, gospel hymns, poems, etc., I soon concluded that he would lead the ticket. . . ."[15]

Parten was slow to appreciate O'Daniel's appeal. Caught up in Thompson's campaign organization and isolated from the popular response to O'Daniel, especially among rural voters, Parten refused to take O'Daniel seriously until a few days before the election. He realized his mistake while on a visit to see his sister in Galveston just prior to the election. When Parten heard that O'Daniel planned an appearance on the island the next day, he called insurance tycoon and civic leader Maco Stewart Jr., a Thompson supporter, and suggested they "go down and see how this Pappy O'Daniel is doing it. Let's just look at his crowd." When they arrived, Parten was amazed to see an enormous number of people. The atmosphere reminded him of a combination of the Confederate veterans reunions, county fairs, and the evangelical religious revivals of his youth. "O'Daniel had the hillbilly band with him, and his children were there, helping him, and it was colorful and incredibly corny." At one point, after O'Daniel had read one of his poems about motherhood and before the Hillbilly boys sang "That Old Rugged Cross," O'Daniel announced that it was time to finance his campaign. His children, Molly, Mike ("Mickey Wickey"), and Pat ("Patty Boy") went into the crowd to pass around miniature flour kegs with coin slots on top and the words "Flour; not Pork," printed on the side. People crammed dimes and quarters in the slots. When a keg came to Parten, Maco Stewart pulled it from his hands and, to Parten's surprise, stuffed a folded dollar bill in the slot. After the rally, Stewart turned to Parten and declared, "'You know what J. R.? That fellow's going to get elected and I'm going to support him.' Old Maco switched from Thompson, went with O'Daniel and became one of his closest advisors when he became governor."[16]

Finally aware of the trouble Thompson was really in, Parten, Myron Blalock, and Thompson's other operatives now hoped that Thompson could at least take second place and qualify to go against O'Daniel in the runoff. Parten believed that Thompson could expose O'Daniel as a political quack in a second campaign, but first McCraw had to be eliminated. The day before the election Parten and Blalock attended Allred's regular press conference, then met with Allred in his office to show him a copy of a special issue of the *Ferguson Forum* predicting that McCraw would lead in the vote and urging all Ferguson friends to support him. Parten told the governor that he and Blalock wanted to "tie old Jim Ferguson around Bill McCraw's neck to let the folks all over the state know that McCraw is the Ferguson candidate." They believed the best way to do so on such short notice was for Allred to talk to the press about Ferguson's endorsement. Newspapers around the state would be certain to print whatever Allred had to say about it. Allred was reluctant, he had refused to do anything for Thompson after his rejection of the hot-oil speech and he had refrained from openly endorsing any candidate. Parten told Allred that he did not have to predict that Thompson would win, because "everybody knows O'Daniel is going to lead." They just wanted him to tell the press that he did not believe McCraw was going to get in the runoff.

The discussion was continuing when Allred's secretary suddenly came in and told Allred that for some reason the press had returned and they were expecting to see the governor again. Blalock had told the journalists as they left the press conference to come back in thirty minutes because the governor would have an important announcement to make about the election campaign and the *Ferguson Forum*. Laughing and shaking his head, Allred gave in and went out to meet the press. A reporter asked him what he had to say about the *Forum*. "I reflected a moment," Allred later recalled, "and I thought Parten and Blalock have done everything in the world for me and it might help Thompson. . . ." Allred replied: "Yes. Ol' Jim Ferguson is just tryin' to get his man McCraw in the runoff but it won't work. According to what I hear, Colonel Thompson has conducted a nice, clean campaign and he will be in second place and ol' Jim's candidate will be a poor third. . . ." Some newspapers, however, misinterpreted Allred and reported his remarks as an endorsement of O'Daniel rather than an indirect one for Thompson as he and Parten and Blalock had intended.[17]

Pappy's Landslide

Texans voted for a new governor on July 23, 1938. No matter what Parten or Allred had intended, Thompson and every other candidate was swept away in an O'Daniel tidal wave. To Parten's astonishment, there would be no runoff. O'Daniel attracted 573,000 votes (51 percent of the total) and won the election outright, carrying 231 of Texas's 254 counties. Thompson was a poor second with 231,000 votes; McCraw came in third with 152,000 votes. When asked for a statement after the results were in, Thompson admitted that he "didn't even see O'Daniel. The first thing I knew he passed all of us and left me with a cloud of flour dust in my eyes."

The O'Daniel blitz was so unexpected that no one had really gone to any effort to find out much about him. Parten was as confused and uninformed about O'Daniel as everyone else. A few days after the election, he wrote to a friend in Madisonville that "O'Daniel will probably make a good Governor from all reports I have had. He seems to be a pretty level-headed business man." Edward Randall, who saw Parten and Aynesworth in Galveston the day after the election, reported to University of Texas acting-president John Calhoun that "we had a good bit of fun with Major Parten. He takes Thompson's defeat well with the solace that McGraw will not be the next Governor." Parten told Calhoun, who was worried about the next governor's views on higher education, that the "conservative element of Texas seems to be not at all disturbed about his election, as he is a successful businessman possessing a private fortune of his own making. Personally I regard his election as promising of material benefits to education generally in the state." In the summer of 1938, Parten still considered himself to be a member of the state's conservative business establishment. In the coming years, however, he discovered that his views and the views of "the conservative element in Texas" about education, government, civil liberties, and many other topics of importance to the public good were widely divergent. He also soon changed his mind about "Pass the Biscuits Pappy" O'Daniel. "It was a funny time," Parten said many years later, "O'Daniel just happened to come along with a flour sack, out of that jungle, beating those drums."[18]

Thompson's defeat was not the only unexpected news Parten received in late July. On the day of the Democratic primary, Parten received a letter from Luther Gulick stating that he would have to postpone his trip to Texas until the fall. "I really think you should ignore me and appoint someone promptly to proceed with your work," Gulick added. "I do not have any intention of encouraging your Board to think that I am available. . . ." Gulick emphasized that he would visit Austin simply as a favor to Parten. Parten and the other members of the presidential search committee rushed to Edward Randall's house in Galveston to discuss this unwelcome development. Aynesworth angrily urged Parten to forget Gulick, threatening to do "all in my power . . . to defeat his election. . . ." Randall agreed: "We have waited practically three months on Dr. Gulick's decision," he argued, "and after all our labors we have but one man left, namely Mr. Rainey. . . ." Randall warned that if the committee did not act quickly there would be intense pressure from other members of the board to appoint a politician or some local candidate. Parten, however, argued that even if Gulick did not want the job they should proceed with his visit with the thought that the regents could benefit from Gulick's appraisal of the university. Despite all evidence to the contrary, Parten was convinced that Gulick would change his mind once he saw the campus and understood the opportunity he would have to lead the university to greatness. Parten eventually persuaded his restless colleagues to wait until Gulick visited the campus before they made a final decision about the presidency.[19]

The Search for a New Medical School Dean

While they waited for Gulick's visit to campus, the board of regents concentrated on completing another important university job search. Dr. W. S. Carter, the dean of the Medical Branch in Galveston was due to retire on September 1, so the regents had assigned the task of finding his replacement to the regent's medical committee, consisting of Parten, Aynesworth, and Randall. Parten had been appointed to the medical committee because he lived in Houston, which allowed him to attend meetings in Galveston easily, and because it was well known among his colleagues that he had a strong interest in the school. His brother-in-law, Dr. Earl Cone, taught urology at the Medical School and his sister had nursed there for many years. Initially, Parten had thought that finding a medical school dean would be relatively easy compared to the search for a new university president. Because he was serving on the committee with two physicians who had long-standing relationships with the Medical School and who had intimate knowledge of its operations, Parten had decided early on to defer to his two colleagues in evaluating and selecting a candidate to recommend to the board. Parten would not get off so easily, however. As a member of the committee, he soon learned that Aynesworth and Randall had a significant difference of opinion about how the school should be administered and whether or not it had serious problems. The Medical School situation eventually became one of the most difficult problems with which Parten would have to deal as a regent.[20]

In August 1938, the University of Texas Medical Branch at Galveston—the only state supported medical school in Texas at the time—suffered from the results of years of neglect by the state legislature. Although the school was well regarded for the quality of its teaching and the high standards of most of its clinical departments, a report released in 1937 by the American Medical Association's Council on Medical Education indicated that the school was understaffed and its faculty poorly paid. In addition, its rankings in several educational categories were lower than in previous years. This report deeply alarmed Aynesworth, who saw it as evidence that the school was being mismanaged and that it was being hurt by an

unsound organizational structure. Aynesworth blamed most of the school's prob-
lems on the complex relationship between the University of Texas, Galveston's
John Sealy Hospital, and a local foundation that provided major support to the
Medical School and to the hospital.

In 1887, the University of Texas received fifty thousand dollars from the estate
of John Sealy I to construct, equip, and furnish a hospital building to serve as the
teaching hospital for the Medical School. The city of Galveston subsequently contracted with the university the facility's use as the city's charity hospital. In 1922,
John Sealy II and Jennie Sealy Smith established the Sealy and Smith Foundation
to provide continuing support for the hospital, which was named in honor of John
Sealy I. The Sealy and Smith Foundation made up the difference in operating
expenses between the city's contribution and the fees paid by patients. The hospital was administered by a five-member board of managers. The university regents
appointed two members, the city council appointed two members, and the four
managers appointed a fifth.

Over the years, the trustees of the Sealy Foundation had come to dominate
the hospital administration, which had an administrator answerable only to the
board of managers, not to the University of Texas. A situation had evolved whereby the Medical School dean and the hospital superintendent had conflicting lines
of authority. Complicating the situation was an executive committee of five faculty members elected by the general faculty, which managed the Medical School.
The dean therefore had little real authority and the University of Texas president
in Austin, as well as the regents, had usually rubber-stamped the executive committee's decisions. Although the university board of regents as a group had practically no control over the hospital and very little over the Medical School, one of its
individual members exercised a considerable amount of influence over both. Dr.
Edward Randall not only served on the regents' Medical School committee, he was
also a director of the Sealy and Smith Foundation and a member of the hospital
board. In addition, he had taught at the Medical School for many years and his son
was now a faculty member. In effect, Randall "ran" the Medical School with the
faculty executive committee. "Benedict had not been happy with the fact that a
regent was directly helping to run the medical school and not allowing the
President to have anything to do with it," Parten noted. This convoluted administrative set-up and its overlapping and competing lines of authority had allowed
Randall and a faculty clique to control the Medical School for years.[21]

Months before the search for a new dean began, Kenneth Aynesworth had
complained to Parten that, in his opinion, the quality of medical education at the
school was second-rate. In Aynesworth's view, the problems not only included a
lack of funds and quality faculty, but also inbreeding in hiring practices. He also
opposed the policy that allowed the Medical School faculty to teach part time so
that they could maintain an outside practice. Aynesworth wanted a full-time
teaching staff at the school. Parten agreed, but the university did not have the
money to pay the faculty a competitive salary, so they had to supplement their
incomes with outside patients. Aynesworth declared that the only way the

university could reassert its authority in Galveston and clean up what he claimed was "the mess" at the school was to recruit a new dean from the outside. He was especially opposed to allowing the Medical School faculty select their next dean. Aynesworth basically wanted to give more authority to the dean and the university president at the expense of Dr. Randall and his allies on the faculty executive committee and on the hospital board. "The Medical College needs some drastic reforms," he told Parten, "too long has the Medical College been left as an orphan child to run itself with little or no supervision. . . ." Although Randall did not oppose the idea of recruiting an outsider to serve as dean, for obvious reasons he was not so critical of the faculty nor did he advocate an administrative reorganization. He also differed with Aynesworth over such policy matters as whether or not the faculty should be allowed to have an outside practice. Aynesworth's and Randall's differences gradually escalated into a serious disagreement about the overall program of the Medical School, with Parten in the middle, forced to serve as mediator.[22]

In an attempt to reassert Austin's influence over the Medical School, President Calhoun, Arts and Sciences dean H. T. Parlin, and other administrators met with Parten in late May and urged him to consider Dr. Tom D. Spies, a professor of medicine at the University of Cincinnati, as a candidate for medical dean. A native of Bonham, Texas, and a graduate of the University of Texas who had received his medical training at Harvard, Spies was an internationally known expert on nutritional diseases—he had discovered nicotinic acid as a cure for pellagra, long a public-health scourge in the South. Not only did he have an impressive professional record, he also had no prior association with the University of Texas Medical Branch and its administrative clique. Parten submitted Spies's name to Randall and Aynesworth. To Parten's surprise, they both agreed that Spies should be interviewed. Their agreement and Spies's impressive record immediately made him the top candidate in Parten's mind.[23]

In early August, Tom Spies agreed to be interviewed about the deanship. After a tour of the Medical School in Galveston, Spies met in Austin with Parten, President Calhoun, and a few of the other regents. Spies told the group that he was flattered by the attention, but he really did not want to abandon his research to do administrative work. He recommended instead that the university interview his brother, John William Spies, a Harvard-trained cancer specialist who was leaving a medical post in India. Tom insisted that John was the superior administrator of the two.[24]

Although Parten and his colleagues were impressed with Tom Spies, they were intrigued by the background of his brother John, a forty-two-year-old bachelor who had received his undergraduate degree from the University of Texas in 1920 and who had been trained as an oncologist at Memorial Hospital (later to be renamed Sloane-Kettering) in New York City. After completing his postgraduate training in New York in the late 1920s, John Spies had been a student of Prof. J. Maisin, an internationally famed cancer specialist in Belgium. He subsequently administered a Rockefeller Foundation–sponsored cancer ward in Beijing, China, for four years. Since 1935, Spies had served as director of the Tata Memorial Hospital in Bombay, India. His training in oncology and his extensive administrative experience made him an attractive candidate to Aynesworth and Randall. Oncology was a field to which both regents wanted the Medical School to devote more attention. In mid-August, with Parten's and Aynesworth's support, Randall sent a cable message to John Spies in Bombay asking him if he would be a candidate for the position of Medical School dean. Spies replied that he would, so an interview was scheduled to be held in Galveston in late October.[25]

Randall went to New York on his own initiative, and without Parten and Aynesworth to interview John Spies when he arrived from India. He then accompanied Spies to Galveston, where Parten and Aynesworth met him at a luncheon for the faculty and staff at the Medical School on October 28. As Parten took his seat at the luncheon table next to Dr. Albert O. Singleton, the head of the Surgery Department and member of the faculty executive committee, Randall stood and made a surprising announcement. He thanked everyone for coming to the luncheon "to meet the next dean of the medical school." The luncheon guests were stunned to silence. "That got my attention, and Aynesworth's attention," Parten later recalled, "we weren't even consulted." Parten remembered that he could "just feel Singleton freeze as I sat there beside him." Ignoring the absence of applause, Randall proceeded with a talk about Spies's training and background. When he invited Spies to comment, the embarrassed oncologist declared that "I want you people to know that Dr. Randall's carrying me awful fast. I still don't know that I'm the man to be Dean of this medical school. I want to see more of it, and I want to get acquainted with the members of the faculty."[26]

After lunch, Parten walked down the street with Singleton. "Poor Singleton was just shaking, almost to the point of tears," Parten said. "He was plainly burning up." Parten explained to Singleton that the medical committee had not voted on Spies and that the other regents and President Calhoun had not been consulted. "If you people of the faculty don't like this move, let us have your opinion, and we'll still turn it around and fix it right. Spies is in no hurry to take this job, not knowing about it yet." Singleton answered that there was nothing Parten could do. "That's just the way Dr. Randall is." Singleton, the most influential member of the faculty executive committee that for several years had dominated the Medical School, never accepted Spies's appointment and became one of Spies's staunchest foes. "It was so unfair to John Spies," Parten said. "Randall's action turned Singleton and a lot of the faculty against Spies before he could even get started."[27]

Parten and Aynesworth were greatly impressed with John Spies despite Randall's imperious manner of handling his candidacy. They believed he was strong and energetic enough to take on the tough job in Galveston. President Calhoun agreed. Both of the Spies brothers had been former students of his and he remembered them well. He had been the first to suggest John Spies as a possible candidate. Calling him an "unusually outstanding man," Calhoun urged Parten to persuade the other regents to offer the job to him.[28]

"A dream fulfilled"

With the Medical School deanship apparently resolved, Parten turned his attention back to the university presidential search. His choice for the job, Luther Gulick, finally made his long-delayed visit to Austin in early November 1938. To Parten's delight, Gulick managed to impress everyone with his leadership style, his ideas, and his learned but common-sense approach to academic administration. Like Rainey, Gulick also saw a critical leadership role for the University of Texas in the future development of the state. He left Austin with the regents eating out of his hand. In a letter to Gene Holman after Gulick's departure, Parten declared that he had "little doubt" that the elusive scholar was "interested in the University from a standpoint of its great possibilities for development. . . ." He urged Holman to persuade Wallace Pratt and Nelson Rockefeller to continue lobbying Gulick on behalf of the university.[29]

Gulick's performance convinced Parten and his board colleagues that he was a much stronger candidate for president than Homer Rainey. During their November meeting a few days after Gulick's visit, the regents voted unanimously to offer him the presidency, giving him a deadline of December 1 to make his decision. They also voted to appoint John Spies dean of the Medical School. Spies accepted his appointment that day, but Gulick was another matter. Parten travelled to New York to deliver the regents' offer to him in person in late November. He returned to Texas confident that the New Yorker would be the university's next president. On December 5, however, Gulick informed the university that he would not accept the job. Disappointed, bewildered, and somewhat embarrassed by the outcome of his pursuit of Gulick, which had delayed the appointment of a new president for six months, Parten wrote his former candidate a brief letter stating that he regretted his decision. Perhaps understanding for the first time that he had blindly pushed Gulick's candidacy despite his openly stated lack of serious interest, Parten wrote that he realized that "only you were in a position finally to weigh the circumstances and reach a conclusion." He assured Gulick that his decision would not affect their friendship, and it did not. Parten did not know it at the time, but Gulick believed he was in line to become the next president of Columbia University and he feared going to Texas would eliminate him from consideration. He gambled that if he remained at his post in New York, the Columbia job would eventually be his. He lost the gamble.[30]

The regents now turned to Homer Rainey, despite the fact that Randall, Weinert, and Stark had their doubts about him. Randall quickly dispatched an offer to Rainey to become the next president of the University of Texas at a salary of $17,500, the highest compensation ever provided by the state of Texas for one of its officials. To Rainey, the university's offer was "a dream fulfilled." He accepted the offer on December 28, 1938. Because of Rainey's obligation to complete some projects for the American Youth Commission, the regents agreed to make his appointment effective June 1, 1939. Parten was more than satisfied to have Rainey as an alternative choice. Parten was responsible for Rainey being one of the two finalists and he had argued in his favor when Gulick turned down the job. Parten had been attracted to Rainey because of his being a protégé of Lotus Coffman, the president of the University of Minnesota, who had died three months earlier. "I think he has a great many of the qualities that Coffman possessed," Parten confided to a friend. "If he can have only half of them . . . that will be enough. . . ."[31]

Parten looked forward to 1939 as a year during which he would work closely with Homer Rainey and his colleagues on the board of regents to make the University of Texas truly a "University of the first class." He believed that the very future of his home state was at stake. If Texas was going to abandon its long-standing status as a backwater economic colony for northern bankers and industrialists and take its place among the more progressive and prosperous states of the union, the University of Texas would have to play a critical educational and intellectual role. Success would require leadership and money from the state, but Parten was optimistic that those would be forthcoming. Although he would have preferred to have Jimmy Allred or Ernest Thompson in the Governor's Mansion to help build the university, he believed O'Daniel would be a governor with whom the university could work. Economic conditions were improving statewide and royalty and lease money from its oil lands was pouring into its coffers. He believed the legislature might now be willing to help the University of Texas make the greatest leap forward in its history. Such a leap forward, however, obviously demanded significant increases in state support, which meant increased taxes. It also threatened to enhance the influence of teachers who advocated economic and social policies very much opposed by the state's conservative power elite. The corporate establishment, allied with Governor O'Daniel, had no interest in paying more taxes, nor did it intend to allow academic "agitators" at the university any opportunity to influence the state's public policies. A period of bitter conflict rather than peace and harmony lay ahead.[32]

CHAPTER 14

A "New Texas" and a New Chairman

1939

The regents of the University of Texas elected J. R. Parten chairman of the board on February 4, 1939. Explaining that Parten was the man most responsible for the selection of Homer Rainey to be the next president, the Houston *Chronicle* declared that his elevation to the board chairmanship was received with "much satisfaction among the university's friends and former students over the state." A majority of the regents shared that satisfaction. Edward Randall, who willingly gave up the chairmanship to his younger colleague, told Parten that his knowledge of the university and his "judgement and political flare could not be duplicated by any other man in the State." Kenneth Aynesworth admitted to Parten that he was "the most overworked" member of the board, "but you take to it like a duck to water, until we all now rely upon you to do the heavy work. . . ." The new president was pleased that Parten agreed to take the chairmanship. Of all the regents, Rainey had been most impressed with the tall, handsome, young millionaire from Houston. He looked forward to working closely with Parten to establish the progressive program they both wanted for the university.[1]

Parten had resisted earlier attempts to elect him chairman, but he now felt better prepared for the job as a result of the work he had done while serving as a member of the presidential search team. He wanted to be in the best position to do whatever he could to help the new president. The legislature would be conducting its biennial session throughout the spring and it was critical that the new president have sufficient financial resources to carry out his program to upgrade the university. Parten knew that much of the burden of dealing with the legislature would fall on him. He believed that the board chairmanship would enhance his stature with individual legislators and give him more authority in budget negotiations.[2]

Funding for a New Texas

As a result of the victories won in the previous budget fight in 1937, the university's immediate needs were less critical than they had been in years. Faculty and administrative salaries, although still not competitive with the nation's leading public universities, compared well with the best universities in the South. Money from the oil lands in West Texas was making it possible for impressive improvements in the university's facilities. What was needed now, Parten and his board colleagues and Rainey believed, was an investment by the legislature in the future of the university and, by extension, the future of Texas. The "new" Texas needed trained professionals, scientists, and technicians not only to provide the intellectual and skilled support necessary for the state to exploit and benefit from its own natural resources, but also to engage in research to develop new industries to create jobs and raise the overall standard of living of all Texans. Rainey, strongly influenced by Frank Graham's work as president of the University of North Carolina, had stressed this need and had cited the North Carolina model in his discussions with Parten.[3]

The few existing graduate programs in the sciences and engineering at the University of Texas were considered weak by any standard. Because of its lack of trained scientists, the university was in the embarrassing situation of having to turn the operation of its newly constructed state-of-the-art astronomical observatory in West Texas over to the Astronomy Department of the University of Chicago. For decades most Texans had been forced to leave their home state to get quality professional and postgraduate training. Surveys indicated that few of these new physicians, scientists, architects, technicians, and engineers returned to Texas after they received their training. To stem this "brain drain" Rainey, Parten, and most of the regents decided that the most important goal for the coming years was to expand and improve the university's graduate school in Austin and its Medical School in Galveston. The cornerstone of the university's legislative budget initiative, therefore, was a request for an appropriation of nearly nine hundred thousand dollars to fund research and to upgrade graduate education. A separate allocation was requested for a new Latin American Institute, which the university viewed as an integral part of their overall effort to expand graduate studies. To help in their request for more money for graduate and research programs, the regents decided to keep their request for general operating funds at the same level as in the previous biennium. Because of the growth in the student population since 1937, this decision meant a reduction in the amount of money allocated per student.[4]

Parten realized he faced an uphill struggle in trying to convince most members of the legislature—some of whom were vocally anti-intellectual—to provide money for something so "intangible." A major effort was needed to sell such programs to the legislature and to educate the general public about the importance of graduate education and academic research to the economic and cultural well-being of the state. Parten and Rainey therefore devised a public relations strategy to set the stage not only for legislative budget deliberations, but for Rainey's ascendency to the presidency in June.

Parten knew it would be futile to use abstract ideas about the betterment of mankind to justify their request for money to expand graduate education and basic research. Instead, he decided to push the economic argument that university research and graduate training could create new industries and jobs, alleviate unemployment, improve agriculture, and generally raise the standard of living for all Texans. To appeal to the rural-dominated legislature, Parten also stressed that university research could create new products for agriculture, which would raise incomes for farmers and halt the large-scale migration of rural Texans to the rapidly growing cities, which he believed had created the state's unemployment problem. To bolster his argument, he consulted with various faculty members involved in state economic and industrial studies to gather statistics showing the tremendous shift in Texas over the previous thirty years from an agricultural, rural economy to an urban, industrial one.[5]

A key component of Parten's strategy was to get editorial approval for the plan from the state's most influential urban newspapers. Parten sent word to newspapers in Dallas, Fort Worth, San Antonio, Houston, and other cities that he was available for interviews about the future course the University of Texas would take under its new president and new chairman of the board of regents. Several editors accepted Parten's invitation, which resulted in much favorable publicity for the university. The Houston *Chronicle*, for example, prominently featured Parten's views about the need to improve and expand programs in graduate studies as a key to the state's future economic vitality. At Parten's request, Homer Rainey visited Texas during the first week in February to help with the public relations campaign. Rainey met with prominent alumni, faculty, students, and members of the legislative leadership. He also met with Ted Dealy, the influential publisher of the Dallas *Morning News*, as well as with its popular columnist Lynn Landrum. After Rainey's visit to Dallas, Landrum noted in his column that Rainey had impressed everyone during the visit, declaring that "at last the man for the job and the job have been brought together." The highlight of Rainey's visit, however, was his speech to a joint session of the legislature on February 6. Parten, who had arranged the appearance, accompanied Rainey and Governor O'Daniel to the speaker's rostrum and presented Rainey to the lawmakers. Rainey, who was greeted with a standing ovation, used the opportunity to stress the critical role the university could play in expanding the economy of Texas and in enriching the lives of most of its citizens.[6]

Two days after Rainey's speech to the legislature, Parten presented the university's budget request to the House Appropriations Committee. Citing studies done at the university, Parten told the committee that the population shift from farm to city had worsened the state's unemployment problem because the urban economy had been unable to absorb the influx of rural people. "The only way in which this shift of population can be checked is to restore profitable income to the farm and smaller communities," Parten claimed. "Research activities to find new uses and markets for farm products and resources is the key to this solution. Only through a well-organized research program . . . can this problem be met." As an example of the benefits the state could reap from a well-funded research program, Parten explained that relatively small grants from foundations had allowed the university to find new uses for cotton and other natural resources. The amount of money the university was requesting for research was only half as much as that appropriated for university research by state legislatures in California, Illinois, and Michigan. Parten also once again called for a lump-sum appropriation. He explained that due to the efficient manner in which the university was administered and the fact that it was keeping its other budget requests at the same level as in the previous biennium, its per capita expense for educating students was a mere $200 per year, as compared to Michigan's $500 per year and California's $350 per year. Such a conservative financial record was proof that the university would not abuse the privilege of being allowed to shift state money from one program to another if unanticipated circumstances warranted it. Calling his speech a "masterly presentation of the needs of the university and the resulting benefits to the people of Texas," Waggener told Parten that "as usual I am proud of our chairman."[7]

Parten's presentation failed to excite some members of the legislature, however. Claude Wild, whom Parten had employed at his personal expense to help with the university's lobbying effort, reported that one senator was complaining to his colleagues that for nearly thirty years he had watched the professors at the university supposedly doing research when they were not in the classroom and he had yet to see any valuable discoveries. Wild also reported that he had heard a key member of the appropriations committee tell other members that he was "definitely against any [research] appropriation. He thinks that too many are going to college. . . ."

This attitude was soon evident in the legislature's reaction to the university's decision to hold its general-budget request to the level of the previous biennial allocation. Some members of the legislature wanted to reward the university's budget restraint with a rollback in faculty salaries and a cut in other operational allocations. There was a serious attempt to eliminate the entire budget for out-of-state travel by faculty members who needed to do research or give papers at scholarly conferences. Even worse, Governor O'Daniel announced a plan to streamline the administration of the state budget that included a proposal to abolish the university's Permanent Fund and place the income from the oil lands in the state's general revenue fund.[8]

While the budget fight continued in the state capital, Parten staged three impressive out-of-town public relations shows for the university and for Rainey. One was intended to raise awareness in the nation's capital that the University of Texas was beginning a new and exciting era; another publicized the university's plans to serve as an active force in the effort to upgrade public education in Texas; and the third served to demonstrate the university's intention to enter the exclusive club of the nation's first-rate state universities. All three events, of course, had the additional goal of educating the Texas public as well as the legislature about the importance of the university to the state's well-being.

Working directly with University of Texas alumni in Washington, D.C., Parten arranged a Texas Independence Day banquet on March 2 with Homer Rainey as the guest of honor. Not only was the banquet attended by several hundred notables in Washington, including most of the Texas congressional delegation, Parten also had Rainey's speech broadcast back to Texas over a network of twenty-three radio stations reaching nearly every corner of the state. Parten spoke briefly on the radio hook-up and introduced Rainey, whose speech repeated his and Parten's determination to "make the University of Texas the scientific and intellectual center for the economic, social, and cultural Renaissance of the South." Rainey's speech received much attention from newspapers throughout the state.[9]

Another event Parten helped conceive and arrange was a speech by Rainey to a commencement of more than two thousand high school seniors in Houston. For a brief period after graduation from Austin College, Rainey had played professional baseball for the Houston Buffs of the Texas League. Parten and some of the university's baseball-loving former students in Houston developed the idea of staging an event that brought Rainey back to Buffalo Stadium, the site where he had played baseball twenty years earlier, to address the city's graduating seniors and to demonstrate the university's intention of playing an active role in the educational life of the state at all levels. The event was a tremendous success. Rainey had a captive audience of more than twenty thousand people who crowded into the old baseball park in south Houston to watch the graduation ceremonies.[10]

"a mirror which reflects the stars"

The formal dedication of the McDonald Observatory, held a month earlier, proved to be the most successful event at attracting favorable attention for the university, not only in Texas and throughout the United States, but internationally. Upon his death in 1926, W. J. McDonald, a banker and land-speculator from Paris, Texas, gave the University of Texas a gift of eight hundred thousand dollars to build a telescope and astronomical observatory. Construction began in 1933 at an isolated site on Mount Locke (6,800-feet elevation) in the Davis Mountains in far West Texas. Because the university had no qualified faculty to operate the observatory and its eighty-two-inch reflector telescope, President Benedict had negotiated an agreement with University of Chicago president Robert M. Hutchins for Chicago's astronomers and other trained staff to operate the facility jointly with Texas. The basic agreement had been made before Parten became a regent, but Benedict had asked him to help with the negotiations on the final contract.[11]

The university had long envisioned the dedication of the observatory on May 5, 1939, as a special occasion to which prestigious astronomers from around the world would be invited, but Parten also saw the event as an opportunity to advertise the university's coming of age, its new leadership, and its potential for greater educational glory. The university made a major effort, therefore, to bring as many as possible of the leading names in astronomy and related sciences to the remote

"... a mirror which reflects the stars." Parten dedicates the McDonald Observatory, May 5, 1939. *CN 09638. Courtesy Parten Photograph Collection, CAH.*

From left to right, Dr. Gerald Kuiper, Dr. H. K. Aynesworth, and J. R. Parten at McDonald Observatory dedication, May 5, 1939. *Courtesy Parten Photograph Collection, CAH.*

location nearly five hundred miles from Austin. This effort succeeded in attracting forty internationally famous astronomers and physicists, including Nobel Laureate Arthur Holly Compton, who represented Robert Hutchins and the University of Chicago. Parten instructed University of Texas acting-president Calhoun to charter a special Southern Pacific train from San Antonio to Alpine to make it easier for university dignitaries, state officials, prominent alumni, journalists, and other guests to get to the Mount Locke area. Parten, who was an enthusiast for using the radio as a public relations tool, arranged for a twenty-three-station radio network to broadcast the dedication ceremonies throughout Texas. The presence of correspondents from every large-circulation newspaper in Texas as well as from the major national wire services ensured widespread press coverage.[12]

Parten traveled to Alpine on the special train from San Antonio. From Alpine, the party rode in buses to Fort Davis, the nearest town to the observatory with hotel accommodations. It was Parten's first trip to the observatory and he was swept away by the facilities and the impressive equipment. The eighty-two-inch telescope was the second-largest of its kind in use at the time. He was equally impressed by the celebrated group of scientists present, and especially with the brilliant forty-seven-year-old physicist Arthur Compton. As the official history of McDonald Observatory later noted, the group "probably represented the most remarkable galaxy of astronomical talent gathered together in any one place in the years between the two world wars."[13]

At the dedication ceremony held in the domed building housing the main telescope, Parten stood with Rainey, Compton, Edward Randall, and observatory director Otto Struve, on a platform above the crowd standing in the space below. As chairman, Parten made the acceptance speech on behalf of the regents. Gazing with wonder at the telescope, Parten declared that it was "a mirror which reflects the stars, an instrument which brings the dazzling reaches of the night into the ken of the average man. . . . This observatory should give the stars a nearness and reality heretofore undreamed of by most of us." When Parten recalled that moment many years later, he admitted that he was almost overwhelmed with pride, awe, and excitement. "As I stood there with Compton, Rainey, and the others," he said, "I truly believed that anything was possible as far as the University was concerned. The future was unlimited."[14]

After the dedication celebration, Parten drove with Rainey in a car back to Austin. As they traveled over bad roads during the long trip home, they chatted excitedly about the future. Caught up in their mutual enthusiasm, they discussed what should be done to maintain the momentum they felt had been created by the opening of the observatory. They decided to turn the presidential inauguration into an important public event symbolizing the beginning of a new and dynamic era for the University of Texas. The inauguration would extend over a period of days and feature a major conference on the role of the university in the state's future. They also agreed to delay the inauguration until December 1939—six months after Rainey actually assumed the duties of president. The extra time would be needed to line up speakers and other conference participants.[15]

Rainey had additional ideas for Parten to consider. He told Parten that he wanted to lure a famous scientist to Texas from one of the nation's more prestigious universities. Such a person would not only bring immediate stature to the University of Texas, he would also attract foundation money, private gifts, and promising young professors and students wanting to work with a leading scientist. Parten agreed that it was an excellent idea, but he questioned where they would get the money to pay someone of that stature. Because of income from the oil lands, the university could provide first-class facilities and equipment, but that money could not be used for salaries. The distinguished professorships that the legislature had approved in the previous session paid only sixty-five hundred dollars a year—a higher amount than a regular professor at the university but hopelessly inadequate as an inducement for an academic star.

Rainey had an idea. Why not use the newly created position of vice president, which paid fourteen thousand dollars a year, as the position to be filled by a nationally acclaimed academic? Administrative duties could be kept to a minimum, allowing the professor plenty of time to do research and some teaching. Arthur Compton, who had struck Parten and Rainey as someone who could fill an administrative job while continuing his research, might be the ideal candidate for what Rainey had in mind. Rainey also told Parten that the university needed an aggressive public relations program to educate the public about the critical role the university would have to play in making Texas one of the leading states in the union. Rainey wanted to hire a public relations specialist to carry out such a program, specifically Arthur Brandon, a former associate of his from Bucknell. Parten thought both proposals had merit, especially the one to attract a prestigious scientist to Texas, particularly if that scientist was Arthur Compton. He promised Rainey that he would sell the ideas to his fellow regents.[16]

Parten stayed in Austin almost continuously throughout the spring of 1939 lobbying the legislature to fund the university's special appropriation for research and fighting off cuts in the operational budget and raids on the university's Permanent Fund. For example, when Governor O'Daniel proposed to abolish the Permanent Fund, Parten had the university issue a strongly worded statement reminding the governor and the legislature that the revenue from the fund was pledged until 1944 to pay off capital-improvement bonds. He also made certain that the university's bondholders were aware of O'Daniel's idea. Nothing more was heard from the governor on this issue.

The legislature finally passed a university budget on June 21. Despite the efforts of Parten, Rainey, Wild, and others, the university's request for research funding was cut from $900,000 to a miniscule $25,000. The budget initiative was not a complete loss, however. The $25,000 appropriated for research was to be used to establish a University Research Institute. The establishment of the institute was a major step forward because it allowed the university administration to allocate the money as it saw fit. Previously, the legislature had restricted the university's research funds to specific projects. Parten and his allies also preserved funding for faculty out-of-state travel, stressing that such travel was necessary to prevent intellectual stagnation and provincialism. Nevertheless, these were minor victories that basically preserved the status quo. It was clear to Parten, Rainey, and their administrative colleagues at the university that they still had much work ahead of them if they ever hoped to convince the legislature to provide the level of support necessary to build a first-class university.[17]

Problems in Galveston

Despite the lack of support from the state, Homer Rainey was brimming with excitement and confident of the future as he assumed his official duties as president in June 1939. That confidence was tempered slightly, however, when he attended his first regents' meeting in Galveston and learned for the first time that the new dean of the Medical School was having problems. John Spies had begun his duties as dean in January with the old guard on the faculty openly hostile to him. Bypassed during the search process for a new dean, they felt Spies had been crammed down their throats. Aynesworth, Parten, and Calhoun told Spies when he was hired that they expected him to administer the school with a strong hand, which required the transfer of much authority from the faculty administrative committee to the dean. Spies, not one to shy away from a fight, took their request as a mandate for quick and strong action. This immediately led to a bitter administrative conflict with Dr. L. R. Wilson, superintendent of the John Sealy Hospital, and Dr. A. O. Singleton, the distinguished longtime head of the Medical School's Surgery Department.[18]

Singleton and his colleagues on the executive committee of the faculty had run things their way for so long that they had taken it for granted that they could ignore basic operational rules passed by the university's regents. For example, despite well-known, long-standing regulations, Singleton and his cronies frequently took time away from their administrative duties to attend professional meetings out of state without bothering to request permission from the regents as required or without informing their dean. When Spies insisted that Singleton and the senior faculty members had to follow university administrative procedures, they reacted with outrage. Spies later claimed that Singleton at one point marched into his office to inform him that he and Randall had run the Medical School for many years before Spies became dean and they would run it long after Spies was gone.[19]

The opposition to Spies also spread to the hospital, which Dr. Wilson had turned into his personal fiefdom. Responsible only to the hospital board, Wilson's authority conflicted with that of the medical dean. Severely complicating a badly confused situation was the fact that university regent Randall was a longtime friend and associate of Dr. Wilson's. The two men happily dominated the hospital board without opposition from other board members. Worst of all, however, Randall was also an ex-officio member of Singleton's faculty executive committee. Spies, therefore, found himself in a situation of unavoidable conflict when he attempted to reestablish the authority of the Dean's Office over all Medical School matters. Not a patient or tactful man, Spies's meetings with Singleton and Wilson frequently ended in profane shouting matches that echoed throughout the corridors of the Medical School's "Old Red" building.[20]

By the end of May 1939 the problems at the Medical School had become the subject of much public gossip in Galveston. When Parten heard about them, he asked Spies to report on the situation at the regents' meeting on July 15. Spies explained that the administrative-turf battle with Wilson was not his worst difficulty. The real problem, Spies claimed, was Regent Randall, who insisted that the dean had to share his authority over the Medical School with A. O. Singleton's faculty executive committee. Spies charged that when he attended the meetings of the executive committee, the three other members voted whichever way Randall and Singleton did. Every attempt he had made to reorganize the Medical School had been voted down by the committee. Spies, therefore, had only as much authority as the committee was willing to give him, which was very little. Spies further charged that Singleton had tried to sabotage every action he had taken outside of the committee's meetings, including his efforts to organize a new cancer program. Singleton, as chief of surgery at the hospital, had even gone so far as to prevent the dean from using the hospital's surgical facilities. Spies claimed that Randall had supported Singleton in all of these matters.

Randall had been unable to attend the regents' meeting and therefore was not available to answer Spies's accusations. However, because of information about the Medical School that he had received from his brother-in-law, a physician in Galveston, Parten suspected that the dean's claims were true. With his fellow regents approving, he asked Rainey to go to Galveston and investigate the situation. He also instructed him to tell the medical faculty that the board of regents had given him ultimate administrative authority over the Medical School and that the dean was his personal representative duly delegated to exercise authority on his behalf. The board of regents also approved Aynesworth's proposal to remove all administrative authority from the faculty executive committee and convert it into a dean's advisory council.[21]

Rainey met with the Medical School's faculty executive committee in Galveston on July 21. When he informed the committee that it no longer had administrative authority, Randall reacted angrily, charging that the action had been taken behind his back. He heatedly declared that he did not need to be a regent and that he could resign if that was what his colleagues preferred. Rainey assured Randall that no one wanted him to resign. Dr. Singleton then declared that neither Rainey nor Spies knew enough about the Medical School to know if any changes were in order. Singleton argued that he had been at the school for thirty years and that he knew that the executive committee could run the school better than any dean or president. Confident of strong regental support, Rainey refused to be intimidated. He explained to Singleton that the rules had been changed by the regents and they would be followed by everyone without exception. Rainey left Galveston not fully understanding that in Randall and Singleton he had made two powerful and unforgiving enemies.[22]

Atom Smashers and a Prized Physicist

Hoping that he had straightened out the situation in Galveston, Rainey followed through with the plan he and Parten had developed to lure a famed scientist to Austin to serve as vice president. Rainey had called Arthur Compton soon after he assumed his duties as president, but Compton was not interested in coming to Texas. Rainey now turned his attention to the West Coast, where the internationally renowned inventor of the cyclotron, University of California physicist Ernest Orlando Lawrence, was studying the nuclei of atoms. Rainey had learned from Compton that Lawrence was unhappy because the University of California had not built him a much larger cyclotron. That tip gave Rainey the idea to see if he could entice Lawrence to Texas by promising to build the cyclotron he wanted.[23]

With Parten's enthusiastic encouragement, Rainey went to Berkeley in early September 1939 and toured Lawrence's Radiation Laboratory. While they strolled through the building, Rainey congratulated Lawrence on the impressive equipment and facilities. Lawrence, who has been characterized as a master salesman living "from machine to machine," always pushing for a bigger and better cyclotron, replied that as impressive as the equipment was, he really needed the "great" cyclotron that could generate one hundred million volts. He complained that the University of California administration did not have the eight million dollars needed for such an undertaking, so he would soon go to the East Coast on a fund-raising expedition to seek help from the large foundations. He was not optimistic about his chances because a foundation would have to provide nearly the entire amount needed. In the privacy of Lawrence's office, Rainey told the physicist that the University of Texas was poised to become one of the leading state-supported universities in the nation. The institution was blessed with an enlightened board of regents and it had money. Rainey explained that during the last ten years the university had accumulated an endowment in excess of thirty million dollars from oil royalties and that the flow of money from its oil lands would accelerate greatly in the coming years. As president, he was determined to upgrade the university's faculty by using its substantial financial resources to attract the top academicians in the country to Texas. He stressed that he and the chairman of the board of regents, J. R. Parten, had agreed that the Medical School in Galveston, and the Physics and Chemistry Departments in Austin would be their primary focus. Because of that focus, he needed a top-ranked scientist to serve as his right-hand man and Lawrence was the man he wanted. Rainey offered Lawrence the new position of vice president and promised that his administrative duties would be light enough to allow the physicist to continue as an active scientist.

Lawrence was quick with an enticing reply. "Much as I am attached to California," Lawrence said, "I would certainly undertake the Texas post if it would be possible to build the great cyclotron there and . . . not possible to do so here in the next few years." Rainey shocked Lawrence by answering just as quickly that if he would come to Texas, the regents would seriously consider allocating funds to match whatever money Lawrence raised from a foundation for the "great" cyclotron. Lawrence assured Rainey that if the university built the cyclotron, the top physicists in the nation would come to Austin. He promised Rainey that he would give his offer serious consideration but that he would need some time to think it over. Rainey replied that he was in no hurry; Lawrence could take a year to make the decision if he needed to, but he did want him to inspect the campus at Austin and to meet J. R. Parten as soon as it could be arranged.[24]

Lawrence made quick and effective use of Rainey's offer. He told a colleague who was close to University of California president Robert G. Sproul about the Texas proposal. As Lawrence no doubt intended, the friend immediately sent a note to Sproul. "This is a matter of great concern to the State of California," Lawrence's friend warned, declaring that it would be a "calamity" to lose to "a state like Texas the leadership which we have established in the field of physical research." Meanwhile, Lawrence wrote to Rainey that he was "thrilled by your program for Texas. . . ." He told Rainey that if California agreed to build the cyclotron he wanted, he would stay at Berkeley. But since that was very uncertain, he had decided that he would accept his invitation to visit Austin. Lawrence also wrote to President Sproul. Not only did he explain Rainey's offer with unabashed enthusiasm, he also improved on what Rainey had actually said. Rainey's promise that the Texas regents would seriously consider funding the cyclotron suddenly became a firm agreement in Lawrence's letter. Rainey "almost took me off my feet," Lawrence wrote, "by saying . . . that . . . he could guarantee the necessary funds for such an undertaking *immediately*." Sproul's reply assured Lawrence that the University of California would do whatever it could to keep him in Berkeley. "For the duration of your consideration of the Texas offer," the president wrote, "my motto will be 'Lawrence must not go'."[25]

Lawrence visited Austin on October 18 to tour the campus and meet with Rainey, Parten, a subcommittee of other regents, and selected faculty. Prior to Lawrence's visit, Parten had circulated a letter to his fellow regents, telling them that they should feel "honored to have a visit from such a distinguished scholar," and asking for their consent to tell Lawrence that the cyclotron would be built. He realized that the university could get foundations to provide most of the funds and that the university's oil money could provide the remainder. When he met Lawrence in Austin, Parten promised that the university would build the cyclotron and provide him with any other special equipment and facilities he might need. Lawrence replied that if the university built the cyclotron, he would move to Austin and bring four of his brightest associates with him.[26]

After he returned to California in late October, Lawrence learned that the Rockefeller Foundation had decided to provide some support for the cyclotron project. He quickly informed Sproul and Rainey. It was now up to California or Texas to match the Rockefeller money. Lawrence's future, however, was soon decided by a powerful Houston banker. "One man finally broke it up," Parten later claimed. "E. J. Blackert (the newest regent) went down to Houston and talked to 'Judge' Jim Elkins about the cyclotron. Without any knowledge whatsoever of the circumstances, Elkins made the offhand remark to Blackert that the people of

Texas would run the Board of Regents out of the state if they did such a foolish thing." Elkins, a lobbyist and legal counsel for several large out-of-state corporations, was quick to oppose anything that might lead to an increase in state taxes and this "scheme" to build an atom-smashing machine seemed to have new taxes written all over it. He warned Blackert that his friends in the legislature would never allow the university to spend the money. When Blackert gave this unwelcome news to Rainey and the board of regents, some of Parten's colleagues on the board wavered. They knew well enough that Elkins had enough influence in the legislature to cause the university considerable difficulty at budget time. "I scolded Blackert about it," Parten later said, "we had the money in the available fund, we didn't need money from the state. Blackert was a damn fool for going and talking to anybody about a thing like that. How were they in a position to judge. . . ?"[27]

Parten tried to rebuild his board consensus but failed. When nearly a month passed without action from either California or Texas, Lawrence, in an obvious attempt to put more pressure on everyone, leaked the news to the United Press that Texas had made a "very attractive" offer and that he was giving it "serious consideration." Lawrence made it clear that he wanted California to build the "atom smasher," but if they would not, he would go to Texas. Much to Parten's and Rainey's displeasure, this news was immediately published in Texas newspapers, making it even more difficult for the university. Parten resented Lawrence's giving this information to the press. He and Rainey felt that the scientist was using Texas just to get what he wanted from California.[28]

Nevertheless, as late as February 1940 Rainey still believed that the university might be able to build the cyclotron and get Lawrence on the faculty. Because of opposition on the board to paying for the cyclotron with oil-land revenues, Parten and Rainey approached the trustees of the newly created and richly endowed Monroe D. Anderson Foundation in Houston for the funds but the effort failed. Lawrence called Parten and told him that he needed a firm pledge as soon as possible from Texas that the cyclotron would be built. After a consultation with Rainey, Parten called Lawrence back and told him that there was too much opposition in Texas to spending the money for the cyclotron. He wished Lawrence well with his project in California.[29]

The Rockefeller Foundation announced in early April 1940, that it would provide slightly more than one million dollars to Berkeley to build a 4,900-ton, 184-inch cyclotron. When he heard this news, Rainey wrote Lawrence that he regretted "very much" that the University of Texas lost the opportunity to share in Lawrence's good fortune. But he also implied that Lawrence had been using Texas as leverage to get what he wanted at Berkeley. "J. R. Parten," Rainey told Lawrence, "says that you ought to put my name upon [the new cyclotron] because of the part that we had in pushing it along." Several months later, Parten's oil-business friend Edwin Pauley, who was a member of the California board of regents, visited with Parten in Washington. "Oh, yeah, you were trying to steal our prize physicist," Pauley told Parten. "I picked up your trail. I want to tell you, we built the cyclotron and we did it largely with outside money."[30]

Rainey made one other attempt to bring a Nobel laureate to Texas. The 1934 winner of the Nobel Prize in chemistry, Harold Urey of Columbia University, spent two days in Austin touring the campus and meeting with Rainey, Parten, and faculty members. When Urey returned to Columbia, however, he sent word back to Rainey that an administrative job, no matter how light in responsibility, simply had no appeal to him. American entrance into World War II and lack of interest on the part of a new board of regents soon ended the university's attempt to lure a Nobel laureate to Texas. To Parten's deep disappointment, the university had missed its opportunity to build a world-class physics program headed by a Nobel laureate. The university would not land its Nobel laureates for another thirty years. Parten always regretted his and Rainey's failed efforts. "In those days," Parten recalled, "I was excited by the idea that the atom had been split and that it had opened up a whole new field of energy. Everybody that I knew visualized great gains would come to humanity from that fact." Parten soon lost his enthusiasm for nuclear energy, but he always believed that if they had been able to build a cyclotron and bring Lawrence to Texas, it would have had a positive effect on every department of the university, propelling the university into the ranks of the most prestigious institutions of higher education in the United States. It is one of the more intriguing "what ifs" in the history of the University of Texas.[31]

An Investigation in Galveston

While Rainey and Parten were still working to bring Ernest Lawrence to Texas, the war against Dean Spies resumed at the Medical School. In addition, the American College of Surgeons failed to approve the University of Texas Medical Branch for graduate training in general surgery or for surgical specialties. Parten and Rainey now realized that the university had a very severe problem in Galveston. Angered, Parten told Rainey and Aynesworth that "something can and should be done to remedy this situation." They agreed that a regental investigation should be conducted as soon as possible in Galveston.[32]

Parten knew that a remedy would not be found easily. Ely Thornton, a long-time acquaintance of Parten's who was Galveston's representative in the legislature and chairman of the House Appropriations Committee, warned Parten that the physicians at the Medical School who opposed Spies had strong connections with powerful business leaders who had their own complaints about the university's programs and the politics of some of the faculty. Thornton admitted that Randall in particular was stirring up trouble in the business community and in the legislature. After his meeting with Thornton, Parten decided to make a personal appeal to Randall to stop his lobbying against Spies. Emphasizing that they had "an honest difference of opinion" on an internal matter that did not warrant the involvement of members of the legislature, Parten reminded Randall that when they were searching for a new dean, he had agreed with his colleagues on the search committee that the Dean's Office had to be given more authority than in the past. Parten assured Randall that it had not been easy for him to disagree "with one whom I respect and esteem as highly as I do you."[33]

When the regents began their investigation in Galveston on October 7, Parten learned that his personal plea had had no effect on Randall. The regents and President Rainey suffered through three days of acrimonious hearings during which they listened to the contradictory testimony of more than thirty faculty and staff members. Parten confided to Marguerite Fairchild that he had "dreaded this meeting for a long time" because of his awareness that Dr. Randall was the chief source of most of the opposition to Dean Spies. At the hearings, Randall, Singleton, and Charles T. Stone (head of the Department of Medicine), accused Spies of being immoral, dictatorial, professionally incompetent, verbally abusive, and responsible for the suicides of two faculty members.

Determined to give Spies a fair chance to present his side of the affair, Parten asked Waggener to chair the hearings so that he would be free procedurally to question witnesses and raise points of order. His active role at the hearings resulted in frequent clashes with Randall. Whenever Parten felt Randall was being unfair in his statements and questions, he would challenge him openly, resulting in several heated exchanges between them. At one point, Waggener had to intervene to stop a vigorous and emotional argument between the two regents. By the time the hearings had finally ended, so had the friendship between Randall and Parten.[34]

The regents left Galveston emotionally exhausted and with frayed nerves. A week later, Aynesworth admitted to Parten that he was "just now recovering from the terrible mental, psychic, and physical ordeal of our three days in Galveston." Waggener wrote Parten that the meetings in Galveston had been "painful for me and I know that they were even more so for you and Dr. Randall." Parten told Fairchild that "it pained me without end that Dr. Randall was hurt, and more especially since my acts might have contributed to his disturbance of mind." Despite the hard feelings, Parten believed the hearings had been productive. He told Spies that what he had heard and seen at the Medical School had convinced him that the problems in Galveston dated "back to a time far before you became identified with the Medical School." He remained a Spies partisan.[35]

A few days later Rainey and Parten returned to Galveston to tell the faculty that the board of regents were absolving all charges against Dean Spies and that the president was assuming full responsibility for the Medical School. Spies would report directly to the president rather than (as had been the case traditionally if not officially) to the regent representing the Medical School, which for the past eleven years had been Edward Randall. If any of the faculty wondered how the school would now be managed, Rainey advised that they review a copy of the Board of Regents' Rules, which had been routinely ignored over the years. He promised that the faculty as a whole would have more influence and that faculty meetings would be more frequent than in the past. Parten, who earnestly hoped that the situation was at last under control, reported to a fellow regent that he believed these latest actions would produce "constructive results at Galveston."[36]

Parten's hopes proved to be false. Edward Randall told Aynesworth that if the board did not restore authority to the faculty executive committee, he would resign as a regent and carry on the fight not only against Spies but also his allies at the university—an implied threat to Rainey and Parten. When Aynesworth reported Randall's threat, Parten said he hoped Randall would not resign, but "to retreat from the position which we have taken would mean nothing less than a complete surrender to the small group in the medical faculty. . . ." The Singleton-led faculty faction in Galveston likewise had no intention of giving up the fight. For example, a few weeks after Rainey's speech at the Medical School, surgeons from around the state reported to Aynesworth that Singleton was sending out letters charging that Dean Spies was trying to destroy the Surgery Department. In addition, Parten heard that Randall and Singleton, who had trained some of the most prominent physicians in Texas, were urging their former students to complain to members of the legislature about the situation at the Medical School. The Medical School controversy was becoming intractable. By the end of November, as Parten was preparing for the university's major public celebration in honor of Rainey's inauguration, he confided to Lutcher Stark that "this matter has caused me a great deal of worry and grief. I am convinced that it is going to take sound thinking and wise action to thoroughly straighten it out." Parten resolved to settle the Galveston problem once and for all as soon as feasible after Rainey's inauguration.[37]

The Inauguration of Homer Price Rainey

Standing at the podium erected on the front steps of the university's Main building, J. R. Parten looked down the south mall of the campus toward the massive granite Capitol dome bathed in the bright sunshine of an unseasonably warm early December morning. Before him sat more than five thousand University of Texas students, faculty, staff, and alumni, state officials, the presidents of nearly two dozen universities from around the nation, and other guests. Sharing the stage with Parten was a group of dignitaries that included his fellow members of the university board of regents; Gov. W. Lee O' Daniel; Speaker of the House Emmett Morse; Lt. Gov. Coke Stevenson; Chester H. Rowell, former editor of the San Francisco *Chronicle*; and Charles A. Beardsley, president of the American Bar Association. Parten and Homer Rainey, the man who was to be inaugurated on this day as the university's twelfth president, had conceived of this event many months before as a symbolic beginning—not just of a new university president's administration, but of the emergence of the University of Texas as the institution that stood ready to lead Texas and the South into a glorious future.

As he gazed at the crowd around him, and as motion picture cameras recorded the event for later showing in high schools throughout Texas, Parten proclaimed into the bank of microphones connected to two statewide radio networks that "the University is today a handsome city set on a hill. The University has come a long way since its establishment," Parten continued, "but we hope and believe that the journey toward real distinction has only begun. When the regents started out two and one-half years ago to find a new president, we hoped to bring to the campus one of the outstanding educators of America." He turned to Rainey and declared, "you are considered exceptionally well fitted . . . to take over the office to which you have been elected." As Rainey rose from his chair to stand by his friend

"... you are considered exceptionally well fitted ... to take over the office to which you have been elected." Homer Rainey and Parten at Rainey's inauguration, December 9, 1939. *CN 09637. Courtesy Parten Photograph Collection, CAH.*

at the podium, Parten said, "I commit into your hands this high office, fully confident that . . . to the people of Texas your presidency will be a source of gratification and achievement." Rainey replied that he accepted the presidency "with a deep sense of gratitude." As the two men shook hands, the crowd responded with a standing ovation as "rebel yells" and "yahoos!" pierced the air.[38]

Rainey's installation as president on December 9, 1939, was the culmination of a three-day inaugural celebration which had featured a free concert by the Houston Symphony Orchestra and a major conference on the state's responsibility toward education and the role the University of Texas should play in the development of the state. When Rainey and Parten were planning the inaugural conference, they both agreed that it would present an excellent opportunity to educate the state's political leaders and the general public about how critical the university was to the overall cultural, political, and economic good health of Texas. "We were trying to answer the question," Rainey would say many years later, "why do democratic people pay taxes to support an institution of this sort? What do they want to get out of it?" Rainey had stressed to Parten that one conference session should emphasize how the university could help develop the state's natural resources, as Rainey said, "for the welfare of the people." Accordingly, several sessions were held on topics related to those themes, with speakers including Clarence A. Dykstra, president of the University of Wisconsin; John Erskine, arts critic for the New York *Times*; former Texas governor William P. Hobby; Harry C. Weiss, president of Humble Oil Company; Americo Castro, former Spanish ambassador to Germany; Herman James, president of Ohio State University; and others. Parten even prevailed on Luther Gulick to return to Austin to participate in the conference, and, Parten later admitted, "to get a glimpse of the opportunity he had missed."[39]

Rainey's inaugural address repeated the general theme that he and Parten had stressed since the public announcement of his appointment as president the year before: the university's critical importance as an active leader and shaper of the "new" Texas. He also made clear his strong belief in the principles of academic freedom and the responsibility of the university to the people of Texas as an instrument of democracy. Rainey noted that a "momentous decision" had been made by the regents to carry through with their constitutional mandate to build "a university of the first class." The achievement of such a worthy goal, Rainey said, would be possible only if the legislature provided adequate financial support and if "all hampering restrictions" on academic and administrative freedom were removed. The new president also declared that he would never forget that public institutions of higher learning "belong to the people. They are controlled democratically and are responsive to the commonwealth." The university was prepared to "train leaders for a democracy" and to help those leaders solve the social, economic, and political problems of the region and the state. Years later, when recalling his inaugural speech, Rainey said that he had come to "the simple conclusion . . . that the function of a university . . . was to improve people's well being. That's why the people want it; they use it as a great instrument to serve their needs in all of these various fields and aspects."[40]

Rainey's spirited defense of academic freedom and his advocacy for making the university an agent of social and economic change failed to bring forth any immediate reaction from elements hostile to such concepts. The Dallas *Morning News'* conservative writer Lynn Landrum, whose "Thinking Out Loud" column reflected the views of the state's conservative power-elite, praised the inaugural ceremony and Rainey's address. "The ceremonies of inauguration have been elaborate," Landrum wrote, "but they were in no sense out of proportion to the expectations which this whole region has centered in Dr. Rainey." Landrum predicted that Rainey was the man who could bring to realization the dream of making the University of Texas a first-class institution. Not surprisingly, J. R. Parten was equally enthusiastic about the event. "I was very proud of you at the inauguration," he wrote Rainey, "my opinion is that your inaugural address . . . points the way for a real educational program in Texas. . . ."[41]

CHAPTER 15

"How Do You Fire a Professor?"

J. R. Leaves the Board of Regents, 1940–1941

J R. Parten would remember the inauguration of Homer Price Rainey as the high point not only of the new president's tenure at the University of Texas, but of his own as chairman of the board of regents. Instead of greater glory and achievement in the name of the university, both men were to experience controversy, confrontation, and ultimately, defeat. The basic source of their problems was a conservative corporate and political establishment opposed to the vision Rainey, Parten, and others had of a "New Texas" led by the university, driven by economic and social reform, and paid for by higher taxes. Opponents of progressive economic change knew that, other than maintaining their political control of the Governor's Mansion and the statehouse, the most important action they could take to stifle the "New Texas" was to muzzle its new president and some of his meddlesome faculty. To achieve that goal, they had to gain control of the board of regents. That effort would be aided by the continuing controversy involving Dean Spies at the Medical School. Although fueled by issues essentially unrelated to the "New Texas" concept, the power struggle at the Medical School nevertheless played a significant role in the ultimate defeat of the Parten-Rainey initiative.[1]

"Cease this fight upon Dean Spies"

With Rainey formally installed as president, Parten decided that it was time to stop the fighting at the Medical School. As long as Dean Spies's opponents used John Sealy Hospital as a power base, they would obstruct the dean's effort to reorganize the Medical School and create a cancer-research program. That Dr. Singleton, as the hospital's head surgeon, had been able to ban the dean of the

Medical School from the hospital's operating rooms especially angered Parten. In early January 1940, Parten, Rainey, and Scott Gaines, the university's legal counsel, drafted a proposal for the regents to dissolve the board of managers of John Sealy Hospital and appoint a new superintendent who would be subordinate to the Medical School dean. The plan also called for the creation of a cancer clinic to be supervised by Dean Spies. "Most of the difficulty we are having in Galveston at the present time," the proposal declared, "arises out of the fact that the University does not control and operate its own hospital." The report also urged the Sealy Foundation to direct its financial support toward research instead of using it to pay the hospital's operational deficits. Parten wanted to lessen the influence of the foundation over the administration of the Medical School. He was confident that if the university re-assumed administrative authority over the hospital, the legislature could be persuaded to increase appropriations to cover the hospital's deficit. At its meeting on January 13, the board of regents accepted the proposal and instructed Rainey to move toward implementation.[2]

Two weeks later Edward Randall resigned as a regent. He admitted in a letter to Parten that his resignation "was not an impulsive one. For sometime, I have realized that . . . I had lost my hold on the Board and that my influence was negligible. My self respect demanded my resignation."[3] Randall's resignation did not end his involvement in the Medical School controversy. He remained as one of the university's representatives on the hospital board of directors as well as chairman of the board of the Sealy Smith Foundation. A politically powerful member of Galveston's civic elite, Randall also was capable of causing much trouble for the university in the legislature and with Governor O'Daniel. He was, for example, on the board of directors of the Galveston *News*, which served as an editorial outlet for the members of the Medical School's old guard in their fight against Spies. Within Randall's close circle of friends were Galveston title-insurance tycoon Maco Stewart Sr., one of O'Daniel's chief financial supporters, and state representative Ely Thornton, a leading member of the legislature. Randall knew that neither man was pleased with some of the university's liberal faculty members. Three weeks prior to Randall's resignation, Maco Stewart had complained to Ely Thornton about a speech Clarence Ayres had given to the Dallas Open Forum in late December in which he had called for a state income tax as a means to redistribute wealth. In response to Stewart's complaint, Thornton had written Parten a letter demanding that the regents force Ayres and other faculty members to "desist from the practices they are now engaged in under the guise of 'freedom of speech'." Parten knew that Ayres was no subversive, so after assuring Thornton that "every appropriate effort" would be made to persuade Ayres and other professors to act with "reasonable conduct in situations of this kind," Parten had let the matter drop. Maco Stewart was not so easily placated, however.[4]

Randall also knew that despite the seeming harmony among the regents, at least two members, Hilmer Weinert and Lutcher Stark, were displeased with Rainey. Stark had not favored Rainey during the search process. After Rainey became president, Stark's negative opinion intensified as a result of Rainey's refusal to remove Roy Bedichek as head of the University Interscholastic League. Rainey had made an enemy of regent Hilmer Weinert back in the early fall of 1939 for similar reasons. The president had refused Weinert's demand to remove J. C. Dolley as chairman of the Faculty Athletic Council. Weinert had harbored a grudge against Dolley because of the manner in which he had handled the firing of football coach Jack Chevigny. Weinert's unhappiness had deepened a few weeks later, in October 1939, when his brother, state senator R. A. Weinert, exploded over one of Clarence Ayres's public speeches calling for higher taxes on the wealthy. Senator Weinert complained that Ayres's statements were the "communistic mouthings" of a "demagogue." The senator warned Rainey that the activities of certain professors such as Ayres and Bob Montgomery were creating an "ever growing hostility to the university." Ominously, he added that both professors should be dealt with, because the university would "soon need its friends." Parten assured Senator Weinert that he could "safely say that. . . . a great majority of the University staff is conservative rather than ultra-liberal or radical" and that Ayres's statements did not represent the views of "any appreciable group of the University's staff." To Weinert's irritation, Parten refused to take the matter any further.[5]

After Randall's resignation from the board of regents, Hilmer Weinert and Maco Stewart lobbied Governor O'Daniel to appoint a regent who would help get rid of Spies and who could be counted on to help muzzle the politically progressive faculty members. Weinert met with Governor O'Daniel in late January to discuss the problem of "radical professors" at the university. In his letter requesting the appointment, Weinert declared that he did not believe the bill of rights gave faculty members the freedom "to attack the executive and legislative branches in the manner they do." During the meeting, Weinert asked the governor to appoint forty-four-year-old Fred Branson of Galveston to replace Randall on the board of regents. His request was supported by O'Daniel confidant Maco Stewart Sr., who happened to be Branson's employer. Accepting their recommendation, O'Daniel announced on January 30, 1940, that Randall's replacement would be Branson, a former state banking commissioner who was then serving as vice president of one of Maco Stewart's financial institutions. "I liked Fred Branson" Parten said. "But unfortunately, he was simply Maco Stewart's man on the board of regents and did whatever Maco asked him to do."[6]

In the meantime, Randall obstructed Rainey's attempt to regain control of John Sealy Hospital. In early February, when Parten and Rainey requested a meeting with the Sealy Smith Foundation's board of directors to discuss the foundation's relationship with the Medical School, Randall denied the request. He also informed Parten that on all matters related to the hospital, the regents had to deal exclusively with himself and local Galveston attorney Mart Royston, the other university representative on the hospital board, rather than with City of Galveston officials or Sealy Smith Foundation trustees. Randall complained to Parten that he and Aynesworth had been "misinformed" about what was really going on in Galveston and that Rainey "knew nothing about our institution . . . showing in my judgment a closed mind and a prejudiced attitude." He saw no reason for them to meet with the foundation until they had a better understanding of the actual state of affairs at the hospital. Randall urged Rainey and Parten to come to Galveston as soon as possible so that he could give them a tour of the hospital and give them the facts.[7]

Randall's behavior convinced Parten and Aynesworth that Randall and Mart Royston had to be removed as the university's representatives on the hospital board. Aynesworth wrote Parten that "Dr. Rainey has . . . been confronted with one of the most difficult of . . . problems: the long tenure and absolute control of an institution by a small group of powerful men who have resented every effort for betterment, who have always assumed that every suggestion . . . was a personal affront." Aynesworth argued that until the university took over the hospital, the Medical School would not be able to make "real and permanent progress."[8]

In early March, Parten accompanied Rainey on a tour conducted by Dr. Randall of the John Sealy Hospital. In every room and corridor, Randall seemed to have stationed staff members who were eager to pass on to their visitors every word of derogatory gossip circulating about Dean Spies. After an unpleasant day in Galveston, Rainey and Parten concluded that there was an organized effort by Randall, Singleton, and their allies to discredit Spies through a rumor-mongering campaign. Aynesworth had earlier complained that the rumor mill in Galveston was spreading lies about Spies's personal life throughout the state's medical community. With Parten's approval, Rainey wrote a letter to Randall declaring that during his and Parten's visit to Galveston "the air seemed to be filled with veiled accusations and innuendoes regarding Dean Spies' character. . . . None of these accusations, however, were supported with any concrete evidence." He urged Randall "to cease this fight upon Dean Spies." Randall countered that if Rainey and Parten had gotten the impression that "there is a very serious . . . revolt on the campus, it is exactly the impression we wished you to take home." Randall complained that when Spies was appointed dean, he had no "idea that [Spies] was going to have such revolutionary plans and I must confess . . . that we acted without sufficient investigation of Dr. Spies' record." Randall warned Rainey that the controversy threatened not only the future progress of the Medical School but also of "the University as a whole."[9]

Randall's warning took on added meaning a few days later at the next meeting of the board of regents. Lutcher Stark warned the board that the physicians in Galveston were lobbying powerful members of the legislature. He cautioned his colleagues that if Spies's authority was not cut back the legislature would surely conduct an investigation. Stark then shocked the board with an allegation that Spies had molested a woman during a physical examination. Parten immediately dismissed the accusation as a prime example of the attempt by Spies's enemies to ruin him by rumor and innuendo. Although no action was taken as a result of Stark's attack (he admitted that his anonymous source in Galveston had no proof), Aynesworth was deeply disturbed by the incident. After the meeting, he complained to Parten that Stark's accusation was the "refuge of low and debased minds and does not merit the consideration of the Regents." Aynesworth warned

Parten that Stark's behavior was evidence that Randall and his allies were focusing on individual board members in an attempt to divide the board. He feared that Spies's enemies in Galveston were influential enough to cause the university serious political difficulty. Aynesworth urged Parten to demand the removal of Randall and Royston from the hospital board and Singleton as head of the Department of Surgery. He also wanted the resignations of any other faculty members obstructing Spies. "If we delay definite action much longer," Aynesworth warned, "the attack will be made on the President of the University."[10]

Parten told Aynesworth that he realized that "the Board has quite a problem on its hands at Galveston." He warned Aynesworth, however, that a wholesale dismissal of staff would be an act of "panic and irrational conduct." Parten believed in the ultimate value of a cautious, diplomatic approach. He was surprised by Stark's attack on Spies, but he argued that they should have expected such behavior from the erratic and temperamental regent. Parten believed the other regents were firm in their support of Spies and that the overall situation was promising. Morale among the medical students was high and Spies seemed to have a strong following among them. Parten was confident that the attacks would soon end.[11]

The attacks on Spies grew worse, however. Rumors were spreading that the Medical School dean was a sex pervert, a thief, professionally incompetent, an anti-Semitic Fascist, and a Communist. A priest at the Shrine of the True Cross in Dickinson, a small town near Galveston, reported to the regents that he had confidential information that Spies had read Adolf Hitler's *Mein Kampf* in the original and was "pretty much in agreement with it." He demanded an investigation. Rainey described the campaign against Spies as "well planned, organized, and executed with a maliciousness that I have never seen before." Parten received a telephone call at his office in Houston one morning from a physician who said he had heard someone say at a cocktail party that Spies, who was a bachelor, was a "notorious homosexual." That same day at lunch, a business associate told Parten that the physician of one of his friends in Galveston had told him that Spies had been forced to leave India because of his lecherous behavior with the wives of his professional associates. A few days later, Parten received a letter from Randall quoting an unnamed doctor to the effect that Spies had been fired for unknown reasons while in India. Parten had heard enough. He wrote a scolding letter to Randall reminding him that during the search for a new dean, they had all agreed that bringing in a man from the outside would cause friction at the Medical School, but they had also agreed that it was necessary. He called on Randall to "desist in these activities which amount to nothing short of a deliberate attempt to persecute a University staff member by a campaign of gossip, innuendo, and . . . partial truths."[12]

Sick of Randall's tactics, Parten removed Randall and Royston from the hospital board in early April, replacing them with two Galveston people friendly to Spies. This action intensified the Randall clique's opposition. Lamenting that "there seems to be no end to this," Spies reported to Parten that Randall and his allies had persuaded Galveston congressman Ely H. Thornton Jr., chairman of the House Appropriations Committee, to work on their behalf in the next session of the legislature. Aynesworth told Parten that the situation in Galveston was "now probably more serious than at any time. The 'appeasement' policy has not brought peace and tranquility to the situation." He demanded that an emergency meeting of the regents' medical committee be held to consider the removal of Randall, Singleton, and their associates from the Medical School. Parten refused to call the committee meeting. He was leery of the board initiating discharge proceedings against any faculty member, no matter how vicious and unfair their criticism of Spies. Parten felt that it was Rainey's procedural responsibility to take whatever action was needed to end the fight in Galveston, including making recommendations to the board of regents if he felt a faculty member should be discharged. He believed that the fight against Spies would eventually dissipate on its own.[13]

"My God, J. R., we would have been hung by our necks from lamp posts"

The Medical School problem did not go away. Instead, it fueled a movement that would eventually cost Rainey his job and result in a major statewide controversy that would have a profound influence on Parten's political views. Parten later claimed that Edward Randall and his medical colleagues who were opposed to Dean Spies forged an alliance with conservative businessmen who were eager to purge liberal professors from the University of Texas. This businessmen's group included several men who had become Governor O'Daniel's chief advisors (such as Maco Stewart Sr.). The alliance included regents Weinert and Stark, who disliked Rainey for personal reasons. Their purpose, Parten believed, was to gain control of the board of regents so that each faction in the anti-Rainey alliance could achieve their individual goals. The old guard in Galveston could remove Spies and preserve their control over the Medical School; Weinert and Stark could settle accounts with Bedichek and Dolley; and the politically liberal troublemakers on the faculty could be silenced or purged. Rainey could either cooperate or lose his own job. The university could then be purged of those who had wild-eyed dreams of using the institution to promote a state income tax and economic and social reform. Subsequent events supported Parten's claim that such an antiprogressive coalition existed.[14]

One of the first strong indications of a concerted plan occurred in late May 1940, during the board of regents' annual budget meeting in Galveston. Parten arrived a day early to get in a round of golf with the newest regent, Fred Branson. While they were waiting to tee off, Branson suddenly asked Parten a disconcerting question: "How do you fire a professor?" Parten explained that the faculty-tenure rule made it very difficult and appropriately so. He asked Branson why he wanted to know. Branson confessed that his employer, Maco Stewart, had persuaded Governor O'Daniel to appoint Branson to the board for the specific purpose of getting some economics professors fired, especially Bob Montgomery. He told Parten that he and Lutcher Stark had agreed to support each other's motions to remove certain professors and staff members from the university budget. Shocked and angered, Parten asked Branson why he and Stewart would want to do such a foolish and improper thing. Branson admitted that he knew nothing about the professors, but that Stewart had insisted that they were dangerous subversives. Parten replied that not only was Montgomery no subversive, he was one of the best teachers in the university. With a shrug of his shoulders, Branson smiled and said, "you may be right, Major, but the boss says get the man fired. What else can I do?"[15]

At the board meeting the next day, Branson made a motion to strike a specific line of a specific page from the 1940–1941 budget. Lutcher Stark quickly seconded. Parten asked to what purpose the motion was directed. Neither Branson nor Stark would answer. Rainey, sitting at the other end of the table, his face flushed, declared that it was Bob Montgomery's position and salary. Parten immediately ruled the motion out of order on the grounds that it violated the regents' rules on tenure, which stated that a tenured professor could be dismissed only after a formal complaint was filed with the board and a hearing conducted which allowed the professor to defend himself against the charges. "That seemed to satisfy Branson," Parten said later. "He had acted as ordered and that was it. It really didn't seem to mean much to him either way."[16]

After Branson's motion was ruled out of order, Lutcher Stark began a harangue about the University Interscholastic League (UIL). His sons had not been allowed to play high school football their senior year because of a change in eligibility rules. Stark made a motion to eliminate the UIL's entire budget, but it failed to attract a second. Glaring at Branson, Stark then moved that Roy Bedichek and Rodney J. Kidd of the UIL staff be removed from the budget. Branson immediately seconded. UIL staff members were not protected by tenure. Forewarned by Parten, Aynesworth quickly offered a substitute motion to postpone the question until the next board meeting. Aynesworth's motion passed. "Lutcher was angry at Branson for not seconding his motion to destroy the UIL," Parten recalled, "but Fred told me afterward that his agreement had been to support the removal of Bedichek and Kidd, not to destroy the Texas high school sports program. He said, 'My God, J. R., we would have been hung by our necks from lamp posts if we had destroyed the UIL.' Fred and I were good friends," Parten said, "we talked later and laughed about it."[17]

"Peace and Democracy"

A few days after Parten had prevented Branson and Stark from dismissing Montgomery and the UIL staff, an event occurred at the university that played into the hands of those seeking to establish antiprogressive political control of the university. The source of the problem, the *Daily Texan*, was an all too familiar one to J. R. Parten.

Ernest Thompson, who had once again entered the governor's race against O'Daniel, gave a speech at the Texas National Guard post at Camp Mabry in Austin emphasizing the need for American military preparedness. The German Army had overrun Holland and Belgium; and France was near collapse. In light of the stunning events in Europe, Thompson, a full colonel in the National Guard, warned that it would be national suicide for the United States not to prepare as rapidly as possible for war. Thompson called for the University of Texas to make its contribution to preparedness by creating a Reserve Officers Training Corps (ROTC) program. Thompson denounced those students who opposed such a program on campus. On June 16, the *Daily Texan* printed student editor William Boyd Sinclair's bitingly sarcastic response to Thompson's speech. The editorial, an antiwar essay titled "Peace and Democracy," denounced politicians for taking political advantage of a war scare. Accusing Thompson of "depending on bullets for ballots," Sinclair wrote that the railroad commissioner and the others running for governor would "tell you how we have had a personal message from God informing us that He is on our side. Every time you knife somebody; God grins. All the candidates for governor are sorry that they have only about six million lives to give for their country."[18]

With most of western Europe rapidly falling to Nazi armies and Great Britain's very existence in doubt, reaction to the *Daily Texan*'s editorial was swift and emotional. Thompson was so upset by the editorial that he telephoned his good friend Parten and accused him and the other regents of allowing subversives to infiltrate the school and influence naive students like the *Daily Texan* editor. Parten told Thompson that he was sorry that the editorial had been printed and that he thought the student editor was "certainly guilty of impropriety. . . ." Parten later recalled that "Ernest was sore as hell, he was convinced that the campus had been infiltrated by Nazi agents and Reds."

The incident upset Parten, because he felt Thompson was also angry and disappointed that Parten had decided not to take an active role in the gubernatorial campaign. Parten had counseled Thompson against making the race.[19] He believed O'Daniel was unbeatable, despite an embarrassingly inept performance during his first term in office. "The people were just too easily swayed by that hillbilly music and O'Daniel's silver tongue," Parten lamented later. Parten decided to stay out of the governor's race because of his growing concern over the political tone of the Medical School squabble. He saw that Maco Stewart, who was one of O'Daniel's three closest political advisors, was working with Randall to make trouble for the university. As chairman of the board of regents, Parten did not want to do anything that might cause political problems for Rainey.[20]

The *Daily Texan* editorial and the hostile reaction to it received much attention from Texas newspapers. Rep. J. H. Goodman, who was in the middle of a difficult reelection campaign, grabbed headlines by demanding a "drastic house cleaning" to remove from the university faculty members responsible for "anti-American activities" and the spread of "Communistic and Nazi propaganda . . . among the students." The newspaper stories generated a large number of letters from other Texans protesting "un-American" activity at the university. Typical was one sent to Rainey by Mrs. B. M. Cummings of Austin. "I was not surprised to learn of the recent Communistic developments in your school as I have heard of such activities for many years," wrote Mrs. Cummings. She added, "And, while I am on the subject of Communists . . . I would like to refer to . . . your Dr. R. H. Montgomery. . . . I am hoping for a U. of T. house cleaning."[21]

As the controversy intensified, Parten rushed to Austin to consult with Rainey and meet with the *Daily Texan* editor, Boyd Sinclair. Assuming sole responsibility for the editorial, Sinclair assured Parten that he had not been influenced by any faculty members to write the editorial. He told Parten that he was sorry he mentioned Thompson by name, because he actually preferred Thompson over O'Daniel in the gubernatorial race. As Sinclair explained in a follow-up editorial after his meeting with Rainey and Parten, "I was not arguing against defense. I was arguing against . . . candidates making political pudding out of the current war. I was also maintaining that . . . fighting . . . really never settles anything. . . ." During the meeting with Sinclair, Parten and Rainey realized they were not dealing with some dangerous subversive, but rather with a sensitive young man who understood that he and others of his generation were facing an uncertain and dangerous future. Nevertheless, Parten urged Rainey to consider invoking the censorship policy that had been imposed in July 1936 and later lifted.

Parten elaborated this position in a reply to Carl Phinney, a Dallas attorney who had been among those who had protested the editorial. Parten told Phinney that it was his view that because the *Daily Texan* is published from the university campus, its editorial policy should be different from a privately owned newspaper. "It is my sincere hope that we can find a way to preserve a degree of freedom [with the *Texan*], Parten said, "and at the same time avoid outbursts that . . . take unfair position in controversial matters. Certainly the *Daily Texan* should not devote its columns to dealing in political personalities." Rainey, however, strongly disagreed with Parten on this point. He explained his position in a letter to Representative Goodman. While expressing regret that Sinclair had named "fine patriotic citizens" in his editorial, Rainey stressed his belief that in a democratic society "it would not be desirable for me . . . to tell the editor what he should or should not print. Among the things we have labored for and long guarded in this country are freedom of the press and freedom of speech. These are essentials in a democratic government, though it must be admitted they sometimes bring . . . difficulties."[22]

Parten eventually accepted Rainey's decision not to invoke the censorship rule, although for a few years he believed that the student newspaper of a state university should not be allowed to print editorials criticizing public officials or taking positions on controversial political issues. In July, he told Ernest Thompson that he still believed a rule should be invoked "whereby the *Texan* will for all time desist from entering into political controversies, especially political personalities. It certainly makes no sense for the *Texan* to argue pacifism in such a time as this when national defense is on the minds of all serious thinking Americans." Thompson had calmed down by then, however. Parten had organized a Thompson for Governor rally in Madisonville at the end of June, which had drawn a large and enthusiastic crowd. Delighted by the warm reception he had received in Parten's hometown, Thompson sent a telegram thanking Parten and assuring him that all was right between them. "Those good people are really helping me thanks to you my dear friend," Thompson said, adding that he was "not excited about the university and have said nothing to anyone but you about it. I meant no offense. Forgive me." Parten told Thompson not to "think for a minute that I worried a great deal about your excitement about the *Texan* matter." Parten assured Thompson that "it will not occur again. I met and talked to the young editor. . . . I don't think he is a bad boy." Despite Thompson's warm reception in Madison County, O'Daniel won reelection without a runoff, easily swamping Thompson (who came in a poor second), former highway commissioner Harry Hines, Miriam Ferguson, and several minor candidates. Thompson's hopes of becoming Governor of Texas were dashed forever. He remained on the Railroad Commission for another quarter of a century.[23]

The Trojan Horse in America

Soon after O'Daniel's reelection, Parten was surprised to read in the July 31st edition of the Houston *Post* that the so-called Dies Committee of the U.S. House of Representatives claimed to have acquired the secret records of the Texas Communist Party and that the records revealed the existence of a Communist "cell" at the University of Texas. Parten doubted that the committee actually had any evidence of the sort, but he realized that the accusation gave credibility to charges recently made by those who were outraged by the *Daily Texan's* "Peace and Democracy" editorial. Created in May 1938, the committee's official name was the House Un-American Activities Committee, but it quickly became associated with its chairman, Martin Dies Jr., an East Texas congressman. Its purpose was to conduct hearings on subversive activity by Fascists and Nazis, as well as Communists, but the latter quickly dominated the committee's concerns. The flamboyant Dies made the committee his personal forum. He garnered national headlines by conducting sensational hearings on alleged Communist activities in labor unions, the Federal Writers Project, the Federal Theatre, and the American Civil Liberties Union. By the summer of 1940, Dies, who had ambitions for the U.S. Senate, focused his attention on his home state.

Parten knew the university could ill afford to let Dies's claims go unchallenged. Unsubstantiated charges of Communist subversion had caused unending headaches for the university with the state legislature. Just a few weeks earlier, Parten's frustration with these never-ending rumors had led him to ask the FBI if it had any information about subversive activities on campus, but he never received a reply. "I wanted to end the matter once and for all," Parten said. "I figured that if the FBI would clear up the charges for us, that would do the trick. I now realize that J. Edgar Hoover was probably the man who actually gave Dies the idea about the University." According to one study of Hoover's practices, the FBI director was not especially cooperative with Dies himself because Hoover viewed him as a rival. Nevertheless, the FBI did leak selected confidential information from its files to members of Dies's committee and to the committee's investigators. Parten later believed that the FBI had been the source for Dies's accusations against the university.[24]

Parten feared that such charges in the hands of a demagogue as well known as Martin Dies could eventually result in a purge of the faculty and end the university's dreams of educational prestige. Parten sent a telegram to Dies asking him to share any information he had about communism at the university with the board of regents and President Rainey. "Rumors have been abroad for some time that there is communistic activity at the university," Parten's telegram stated, "but thus far we have been unable to locate evidence." He said that if Dies would give his information to the board, an investigation would be conducted.[25]

While Parten waited for Dies's reply, Robert Stripling and Wick Fowler, the committee's investigators, proceeded to Austin to conduct their "investigation." After interviewing a few students about communistic activities on campus, they met with Homer Rainey and announced that they had found no evidence whatsoever of subversive activities and were prepared to give the university "a clean bill of health." Rainey relayed that information to Parten. Dies then responded to Parten's telegram with a letter assuring him that his staff would soon provide a formal report of their investigation to the university. A week later, however, in a speech in Orange, Texas, Dies charged that there were two "small revolutionary groups active among Texas university students." He claimed that one group was composed of "Stalinists," while the others were "Trotskyites." At least one faculty member, Dies charged, met regularly with students to discuss Marxist theory. Dies also said that his investigators had found "communist literature" in a student's dormitory room at the University of Texas. Immediately after Dies made these vague accusations, he dropped the subject and left Texas to embark on his second round of hearings on communism and the movie industry. Parten, after sending more letters asking for the information, waited for Wick Fowler to make good his promise to deliver the "transcripts of interrogations of University of Texas students relative to un-American activities" to him in Houston. When he recalled the incident fifty years later, Parten smiled and said "I'm still waiting for those transcripts." [26]

Parten and the university were not entirely free of Martin Dies or his accusations, however. In January 1941, five months after Dies made his unsubstantiated charges about Communist activity at the university, the Texas Senate created a committee, dubbed the "Little Dies committee," to investigate subversion in all Texas colleges and universities, although the focus was on the University of Texas. While the "Little Dies committee" held hearings, the *Daily Texan's* Boyd Sinclair struck again. On March 27, 1941, the paper featured his scathing review of Dies's book, *The Trojan Horse in America*, in which he characterized the congressman's political views as "Fascism parading as Americanism." The same day Sinclair's review appeared in the *Daily Texan*, Rep. Joe Ed Winfree of Houston went to the floor of the House and attacked the university for not censoring the book review. He also charged that professors such as Bob Montgomery were teaching "nazism, communism, and fascism." Waving a copy of the *Daily Texan* above his head, Winfree declared that he "would rather close the university . . . than to ruin America from within. Those . . . teachings in the University of Texas have got to stop. If it doesn't, we'll shut her up."[27]

Urging Rainey to fight back, Parten told the president to release photostats of Parten's correspondence with Dies to show that the university had tried and failed to get the congressman's evidence. "I knew that Dies had nothing, that it was just all put up," Parten later recalled. "Martin Dies was a crackpot. He had no sense of morality or ethics. I was tired of hearing all of these rumors and accusations. It was time we called their hand." Rainey distributed the photostats of the Parten-Dies correspondence on April 2 at a press conference, where he also challenged the legislators who had made charges of subversive activities at the university "to put up or shut up." In his strongly worded announcement, Rainey declared that "if well-meaning persons who speak about harmful un-American activities have any real information and do not reveal it they are guilty of criminal negligence."[28]

Dies, who was preparing to run for the U.S. Senate in a special election to fill the vacancy created by Morris Sheppard's death, made a quick retreat. In a speech in Houston on April 8, Dies dismissed the affair as "a tempest in a teapot," declaring that "at most" there were no more than one or two Communists at the university. "That is nothing to be alarmed at," Dies said. "I am proud that the University of Texas has had so few Communists." Parten told Leslie Waggener that they had "finally smoked out" the congressman. "I believe this leaves the University's case in good shape." Parten added that Dies and "the group of ultra-conservatives who have been cheerfully applauding his actions" were simply smearing "persons and institutions broadly just for the psychological effect of inciting the people to hatred of communism. . . ." He warned Waggener that such tactics would undoubtedly be used to attack the university again "at some distant date."

His clash with Dies and his imitators in Texas left a lasting impression on Parten. "I saw the super patriot style first hand with Mr. Dies," Parten later recalled. "I learned that you have to challenge a demagogue or there's no end to it." This experience and others soon to follow would make J. R. Parten a vigorous opponent of McCarthyism and the red scare in the 1950s.[29]

The Houston Gag Conference

In August 1940, a few weeks after Martin Dies made his initial accusation that subversive activities were being carried out on the university campus, Ely Thornton Jr. visited Parten in his office in the Second National Bank building in downtown Houston to warn him about a conspiracy that conservative businessmen had organized to take over the governing boards of the state universities. Thornton claimed that he had recently attended a meeting in Houston with Governor O'Daniel and his largest financial supporters and closest political advisors, including Maco Stewart Sr., independent oil men Jim West Sr. and Dan Harrison, and state senator Tom Holbrook. Also in the group was former regent Edward Randall, still leading the effort to remove Spies as dean of the Medical School. Thornton stated that the main reason the group wanted to gain control of the governing boards was to purge faculties of so-called radicals. They also wanted to get rid of Spies and certain economics and government courses from university curricula. If Homer Rainey or any of the other state college presidents got in the way, he and they would also have to go.

Each of these men had his own particular reason for carrying out this plan,

Thornton told Parten, but in general, they all were concerned about the rhetoric coming forth from the University of Texas about the "new" Texas and the need for political and economic reforms and progressive taxation policies. Thornton claimed that Jim West had cited Parten by name as a person who had to be removed from the board of regents. According to Thornton, O'Daniel assured West and the others that Parten would not be reappointed as a regent. Thornton, who had known and worked with Parten for many years, told Parten that he considered him to have been one of the best regents in the university's history and that the criticism was unfair. He wanted Parten to meet with Maco Stewart and Jim West in particular to see if his removal from the board of regents could be avoided. Thornton asked Parten never to reveal the source of his information about the meeting, which would later be referred to as the "Houston Gag Conference." Parten agreed, but told Thornton that he would not talk to any of the participants because he refused to beg anyone for reappointment to the board. He also thought the whole thing was ridiculous and that it would never get anywhere. Parten told Rainey about Thornton's claim, but did not divulge the source of his information.[30]

A few weeks later, Fred Branson also warned Parten that O'Daniel would not reappoint him to the board of regents in January 1941 unless Parten engaged in a major lobbying effort. Branson offered to help. Parten replied that he had not expected to be reappointed because he had supported Ernest Thompson against O'Daniel in 1938 and 1940. "I didn't do anything to get the job the first time," Parten stressed, "and I'm not going do anything to get reappointed. I think it's unbecoming of a man to lobby to get a regent's job." Branson replied that it was too bad Parten felt that way because "everybody in Texas who knows O'Daniel and who is upset with the University is either lobbying for the job himself or for a friend." Branson then told Parten about the "Houston Gag Conference." Branson admitted that he did not attend the meeting, but that his boss, Maco Stewart did and that it was Stewart who had told Branson about it. Branson added that Hilmer Weinert and Edward Randall were allied with the O'Daniel group. Parten dismissed Branson's warning, just as he had Thornton's. For one thing, Parten knew that if O'Daniel had already decided not to reappoint him, there was nothing he could do to change his mind. He also refused to believe that Maco Stewart, Hilmer Weinert, Edward Randall, Dan Harrison, and Jim West—men he had known and liked and with whom he had worked for years—would actually try to purge the university and shut down academic freedom.[31]

The Death of Wayne Parten

Parten's deep involvement in family and other personal matters in the summer and fall of 1940 was one reason he paid little attention to the stories about the so-called "Houston Gag Conference." J. R.'s eighty-two-year-old father had suffered a major stroke in June that left him partially paralyzed and bedridden. J. R. had arranged to have a nurse stay with his father full time. He travelled to Madisonville nearly every weekend to be at Wayne's side. The end finally came on November 18, while J. R. was in Washington, D.C., on a business trip for the university. When he received the news, J. R. rushed back to Madisonville to comfort his mother and help with funeral arrangements. With Wayne Parten's passing, Madisonville lost a respected pioneer who had helped make the town a thriving agricultural and trade center. A few years before, when Wayne had turned his store over to one of his daughters and her husband, he had ended forty-seven years of continuous business in Madisonville. The funeral was a large affair, attracting Wayne's wide circle of old friends and his own large extended family.[32]

Parten Leaves the Board

As 1940 drew to a close and with his term on the board nearing its end, Parten remained optimistic about the university's future under Homer Rainey. Despite persistent rumors about the conspiracy to take over the state's system of higher education, Parten was confident that the effort to create the constitutionally mandated "University of the first class" would proceed unhindered. He also believed that Dean Spies was well established in Galveston and that he had weathered the worst of the storm. Several new and impressive medical faculty appointments had been made. Now that Randall and Royston were no longer members of the hospital board, an agreement was being negotiated that would return the hospital to university control within the year. Superintendent L. R. Wilson, one of the chief obstructionists, had resigned under pressure in late October 1940. Earlier in the fall, Parten had written John Spies's brother, Tom, who was now conducting research in Birmingham, that he could see "definite improvements in our situation at the Medical School. Of course there is still some friction," Parten admitted, "but this is definitely on the wane."[33]

As Parten had anticipated, Governor O'Daniel did not reappoint him to the board of regents. In early January 1941, O'Daniel announced that independent oil man Dan J. Harrison of Houston would replace Parten and that Orville Bullington of Wichita Falls would take George Morgan's place on the board. O'Daniel reappointed Fred Branson, who had served out the time remaining in Randall's term. J. Evetts Haley played a key role in getting Harrison and Bullington on the board of regents. Now the general manager of Jim West's ranching interests, Haley had lobbied his employer and former associate in the Jeffersonian Democrats to get O'Daniel to appoint Bullington and Harrison to the board.

Haley had political, academic, and personal reasons for wanting Harrison and Bullington to be regents. At the top of his academic agenda was a sincere and deeply felt belief that the university should do something significant in support of the field of Texas history. Haley had worked hard while on the university payroll to collect and preserve an extensive array of archival materials documenting local and state history. He was upset that the university had not given the attention to this valuable research collection that he thought appropriate, so he had joined with J. Frank Dobie, Walter Webb, and others to persuade O'Daniel to appoint regents who would be sympathetic to their request for a separate Texas history center to house the collection. Haley knew that Bullington and Harrison were, in his words, "real two-fisted, red-blooded Texas patriots," who would support the university's efforts to collect Texas history. Texas history was not the only interest they shared with Haley. Bullington (who had recruited Haley to run the anti-Roosevelt campaign in 1936), Harrison, and West shared Haley's opinion that several members of the faculty, especially certain economics professors, needed to be fired. Haley wanted heads to roll at the University of Texas as much or more than his wealthy right-wing friends who were giving instructions to the governor. Haley's hostility toward such New Dealers as Bob Montgomery was deep and intense. A few months after leaving university employment, Haley had referred to such professors as "perverted dogs" and "intellectual bastards" who were working to "destroy the ideals that have made us a virile race. . . ." Although he later denied that there was a conspiracy to get political control of the university, Haley openly admitted that Jim West, who was identified as being at the alleged "Houston Gag Conference," was the person who "told" O'Daniel to appoint Bullington and Harrison to the board of regents.

O'Daniel was happy to oblige. Shortly after O'Daniel's surprising victory in 1938, Bullington had been among those who had quietly joined the governor-elect's inner circle. The Wichita Falls attorney and businessman did not subscribe to Parten's and Rainey's vision of a "new" Texas led by a University of Texas full of "commies" and "perverts" and funded by higher taxes on corporations and the wealthy. Bullington had warned O'Daniel that the legislature was wasting a great deal of money by paying for unnecessary and even harmful programs and activities at the state's universities. In Bullington's opinion, the newly created fine arts program at the University of Texas, which Parten had strongly supported, was a prime example of the rampant waste. Bullington later declared that if the "dirt and paint dobbers" at the university wanted to study art, "they should go to a girls school or to Paris or some other 'furrin' seaport." Bullington told O'Daniel that if extravagances such as a fine arts school and research in the social sciences were eliminated it would be possible for the governor to reduce the state's higher-education bill by more than 50 percent. "Pappy O'Daniel collected a lot of rich men's money," Parten later observed, "on the ground that he would . . . save them a great deal of money." [34]

Several members of the Texas Senate were not as obliging as O'Daniel when it came to placing Bullington and Harrison on the board of regents. Both men were well-known Republican Party activists who had been fiercely and publicly critical of President Roosevelt. Texas in 1941 was still very much a one-party state and FDR was immensely popular. Only three months earlier, Roosevelt, who had defeated his Republican opponent Wendall Wilkie to win a third term as president, had carried Texas by an overwhelming margin. The dean and president pro tempore of the Senate, Clay Cotton of Palestine, and several of his colleagues were appalled, therefore, when O'Daniel nominated two vigorously anti-Roosevelt Republicans. Word soon spread that the Senate would stall or even reject the nominations. Complicating matters for Harrison and Bullington was the fact that the Senate had generally looked with disfavor on many of O'Daniel's nominees for state office in that session, eventually rejecting twelve of them, including J. Evetts Haley, who had been nominated for the State Livestock Sanitary Commission.[35]

With Harrison's and Bullington's appointments threatened, Houston attorney Steve Pinckney, who was a good friend of Harrison's, asked Parten if he would talk to his friends in the Senate to get O'Daniel's appointees confirmed. Pinckney knew that Parten was philosophically opposed to barring a person from being a regent for political reasons. Parten went to Austin and called on individual senators to persuade them to vote for Harrison and Bullington. With Parten's help, Harrison and Bullington were confirmed on January 29. Parten later admitted that if he had taken Ely Thornton's warning about the "Houston Gag Conference" seriously or if he had known what kind of regents Harrison and Bullington would prove to be, he would not have helped them. "But I didn't believe that Dan Harrison was up to anything," Parten explained, "and I didn't know Orville Bullington well enough. It was just the principle that I was operating on. I thought that political affiliation should not be the reason to turn these men down," Parten said.[36]

"His was a liberated mind"

Parten left the board of regents on February 1, 1941, after six hectic and eventful years. He had been one of the most active regents in the history of the University of Texas, and many thought he had been among the best. Among those who praised his accomplishments as a regent was the Houston *Chronicle*, which noted that his reform of the auction system for oil and gas leases on University of Texas lands had resulted in a significant increase in revenue that would have a multiplying effect for years to come. Similar praise appeared on the editorial pages of many other Texas newspapers. Even the *Daily Texan* praised his performance. Although Parten had helped in censoring the student newspaper, it nevertheless admitted that he had carried out his university duties with diligence and selfless dedication, noting that "'Jube' Parten . . . seems to place his University above his business."[37]

Parten's office was swamped with mail from individuals who wished to express their thanks to him for his work as a regent. Of all the letters he received, however, those he appreciated most were from crusty old John Calhoun, who had served as acting president during the eighteen-month presidential search, and Dr. Albert O. Singleton, one of Dean Spies's bitterest foes at the Medical School. The formal and reserved Calhoun told Parten that his record had been one of "constant, unselfish, intelligent, and effective service. The . . . agony you have suffered in regard to the Medical School should bring you a Carnegie Hero Medal. Your . . . labors have made The University of Texas your debtor for all time." Singleton wrote that "though we have not always seen eye to eye . . . I regret that you are not going to serve longer . . . I am not unmindful of the great service you have been to the University and can truthfully say that you have done more to secure more revenue for us than any one I know."[38]

The dramatic improvement in the university's financial situation was an accomplishment that gave Parten the most satisfaction during his years as regent. "Hell, I realize money's not the answer to everything, especially in education," Parten said. "It has to be spent wisely. But it is the essential base from which everything else must begin." Parten was also pleased with his role in persuading D. X. Bible to accept the job of football coach. Although it led to a vicious political power struggle in the coming years that would leave a legacy of bitterness and frustration for decades to come, Parten was equally proud of the appointment of Homer Rainey and the ambitious program he, Rainey, and others devised for making the University of Texas an instrument for progressive change in Texas.[39]

Parten's term on the university's board of regents had done much for him as well. The experience enriched him intellectually and spiritually. Friendships he formed with faculty and administrators such as H. Y. Benedict, Homer Rainey, Bob Montgomery, Clarence Ayres, Walter Webb, Frederick Duncalf, J. Frank Dobie, and others exposed Parten to new ideas, broadened his vision, and reshaped his politics. He left the board of regents a wiser and more tolerant person, with a deeper appreciation for and a keener understanding of freedom of expression and freedom of inquiry. Parten joined the board with no understanding of the concept of academic freedom and it had no special place in his personal value system; he left the board as a vigorous proponent and defender of academic freedom. He came on the board as a conservative Democrat with conventional views about the world in which he lived. He left with his political and intellectual mind-set very much in a state of flux that would continue to be shaped by new knowledge and experience as he grew older. "Major Parten had the best informed, most spacious intellect of any man who ever served as a regent," J. Frank Dobie, a studious observer and critic of University of Texas regents, claimed. "He comprehended the real purpose of a university in a democratic society. His was a liberated mind."[40]

"But you never hear him mentioned with any credit at all"

Parten was disappointed not to have been reappointed to the board of regents, but he realized that he had neglected his Woodley business during the last six years. He later estimated that he had devoted about half of his working time to the University of Texas during the period between 1935 and 1941. "If I had not given all that public service to the University," Parten said, "I might have made more money for Woodley." The company had not made any spectacular gains in that period, but it had held its own with more than 250 oil and gas wells, spread over five states and producing solid profits and small but steady dividends to shareholders. For most of the spring and summer of 1941, therefore, Parten immersed himself in Woodley and Premier business—supervising wildcat wells in Texas and Mississippi, selling off Woodley's leases and sixty-five stripper wells in the Woodson Field in Throckmorton County, Texas, and working with Dayson on Premier's refineries.[41]

Parten's departure from the board of regents did not remove him entirely from active involvement in the university's administrative affairs. In the weeks immediately after he left the board, Parten made several trips to Austin at Rainey's request to lobby the legislature to appropriate 1.7 million dollars to create a state cancer hospital and research institute. "John Spies decided that the state of Texas ought to have a great tumor clinic," Parten said. "I wore out a couple of pair of shoes trying to help him."

The legislature eventually tripled the Medical School's appropriation and passed a special allocation for five hundred thousand dollars for the University of Texas to establish a cancer-research center and hospital to be located wherever the board of regents wished. Spies thought Houston would be the best location for the facility. Working with a group of Houston physicians led by Dr. E. W. Bertner, Spies persuaded Parten, Hines Baker, and other prominent alumni to arrange a dinner at the River Oaks Country Club for the trustees of the M. D. Anderson Foundation. Spies knew that the university had been trying for two years to encourage the Anderson Foundation to provide a major gift to support one of the university's programs. He hoped to persuade the trustees that the cancer hospital would be an ideal project for them. The effort succeeded. The trustees proposed that if the university located the new hospital in Houston and named it for the late Monroe D. Anderson, it would match the state's half-million-dollar appropriation. The University of Texas eagerly accepted the offer.[42]

Unfortunately for Spies, his efforts to create the cancer hospital deepened the hostility of the Medical School's old guard toward him. "The whole city of Galveston just . . . revolted with the idea that Spies was going ahead with this cancer hospital and forming this alliance with the M. D. Anderson Foundation," Parten said. Many of the faculty perceived the hospital to be a dangerous rival for state appropriations. Others suspected that the real objective of Spies, Parten, and Bertner's group of doctors was to move the Medical School to Houston. Parten always denied that they had any such intention, but those fears added much fuel to the fire threatening to consume Spies.[43]

In July 1941, a few weeks after the Anderson Foundation made its proposal to the university, regents Orville Bullington and Dan Harrison traveled to Galveston at Edward Randall's invitation to conduct their own unofficial investigation of the problems at the Medical School. After their quick inspection tour, Bullington and Harrison told Branson, Stark, and Weinert that they were ready to join them in voting to remove Spies as dean. When Bullington informed Rainey that there was now a majority on the board against Spies, Rainey, to avoid subjecting him to a public dismissal, decided not to renominate him as dean.[44]

The news that Spies would not be reappointed resulted in a vigorous protest from the state medical association and from a large number of the Medical School alumni who feared that the school would lose its accreditation. The Houston *Chronicle* and other major urban dailies printed editorials severely critical of Spies's opponents. Parten was deeply concerned about this new effort to remove Spies, but by July he was becoming involved in the federal government's preparations for war. Nevertheless, when Dr. Aynesworth told Parten that his old friend Leslie Waggener was showing signs of giving in to pressure from some of

Bullington's powerful banker friends in Dallas, Parten persuaded Cong. Sam Rayburn to call Waggener and urge him not to vote against Spies. Dean Spies's parents were longtime residents of Rayburn's congressional district, and he had known the family for years. Dan Harrison complained to Bullington that Rayburn was "really putting the pressure to old man Waggener." He urged Bullington to "stiffen up [Waggener's] back bone a little." It was too late. Waggener decided to support Spies. The storm of public protest also caused Stark, Weinert, and Branson to retreat. Spies was reappointed to a two-year term. Parten warned Aynesworth that although Spies's job had been saved, difficulties would "still surround the Galveston situation" until Rainey had firm control over its administration. He urged Aynesworth to do whatever he could to see that Rainey took control. Otherwise, Parten feared that the fight would continue.[45]

Six months later, Parten's fear came true. Randall, Singleton, and their allies had continued their relentless effort against Spies by spreading rumors that he was a Nazi sympathizer. These rumors were used to persuade the legislature to investigate "Un-American activities" at the Medical School. On the morning of February 21, Parten, who was in the middle of a move to Washington, D.C., to serve in a war agency, received a telegram from state representative Jack Love, the chairman of the newly created investigating committee, urging him to give testimony at a hearing in Galveston that afternoon. The official purpose of the hearing was to determine if the Spies controversy was harming the war effort by adversely affecting the training of doctors who were destined for the fighting front. Deeply frustrated by the continuation of the internecine struggle in Galveston and mentally involved with the challenge awaiting him in Washington, Parten was inclined to wash his hands of the affair. However, as one of the regents who had hired Spies in 1939, Parten felt obligated to help Spies one last time.

At the hearing in Galveston, Parten assured the committee that Spies had been thoroughly investigated before being appointed and that the Medical School problem stemmed from the fact that the school had been run by a small clique for many years. He urged that the committee recommend to the regents that Rainey be given complete authority over the Medical School. After Parten left Galveston, Edward Randall appeared before the committee and challenged his former colleague's statement. Randall, the man who had unilaterally decided to appoint Spies, complained that Spies had not been investigated properly and implied that it was Parten's fault because he had been board chairman at the time of the appointment. The hearings continued for three days. One of the faculty members opposed to Spies reported to Orville Bullington that the hearings had exposed "the dean's . . . un-American methods of administration, his spy system, his star chamber dictaphone and his ruthless treatment of anyone who disagreed with him." The physician also complained that "Major J. R. Parten . . . powerful political friend of the dean and President Rainey . . . forcefully advocated the immediate and complete turning over of the entire management of the Medical School to . . . Rainey, investing in him complete authority to do as he sees fit." He urged Bullington not to allow Rainey to assume that authority.[46]

After conducting another round of hearings in Austin, where Spies was defended by Rainey and others, the legislative committee called for the immediate dismissal of Spies as Medical School dean. To the chagrin of the Medical School old guard, however, the committee also called for the removal of the faculty members who had refused to cooperate with Spies when he became dean. Criticizing the board of regents for being "grossly negligent" in allowing the controversy to continue, the committee recommended that the regents give Rainey complete authority over the Medical School. Three months after the committee's report, the Association of American Medical Colleges placed the Medical School on probation, citing a number of deficiencies including poor facilities, an insufficient research budget, several "obsolete" departments, and "administrative confusion." The American Medical Association soon followed with its own probation, declaring that the administration of the school had suffered an "almost complete breakdown."

With the Medical School now on probation and an end to the controversy nowhere in sight, the regents finally removed Spies as dean on June 5, 1942, and temporarily transferred all control over the school to Rainey. By this time, Parten was in Washington working seven days a week to alleviate the nation's oil transportation crisis. He was disappointed by the action, but he made no protest. He knew that Spies's enemies had succeeded in making his position untenable. Reluctantly, Parten had concluded that as long as Spies remained dean, the fight in Galveston would continue to disrupt the Medical School and hinder the development of the cancer hospital in Houston. One reason Parten issued no public protest when Spies was removed was that Rainey had reached the same conclusion. Rainey himself was beginning to come under fire from the new regents and he could no longer afford the crisis in Galveston.[47]

It is difficult from this distance in time to make a fair assessment of John Spies. In Parten's view, however, if it had not been for Spies's determined and persistent advocacy, M. D. Anderson Cancer Hospital might never have been built. "Spies was responsible for raising $500,000 and creating M. D. Anderson Hospital, one of the most prestigious cancer centers in the world," Parten declared. "But you never hear him mentioned with any credit at all."[48]

Like most Americans, J. R. Parten was soon drawn into the all-consuming vortex of a world conflict. The war rapidly required all his attention, taking him away from the University of Texas and the increasingly bitter struggle over its future direction. When Parten returned from the war, he found his beloved university in turmoil. As a result, his relationship with his alma mater, as well as his relationship with the state's conservative business and political establishments, would be profoundly altered.

Part Three

1941–1950

CHAPTER 16

Oil and War

1941–1942

O n June 19, 1941, J. R. Parten sat with fifteen hundred other oil company executives in the Department of the Interior auditorium in Washington, D.C., waiting for a presentation by Secretary of the Interior Harold Ickes, a man most of those in the audience feared and disliked. Ickes had called the leaders of the oil industry to Washington to hear his plans for the Office of Petroleum Coordinator for National Defense (OPC), which President Roosevelt had established in late May after declaring an unlimited national emergency because of the increasing likelihood of war. Roosevelt had announced that the OPC would serve as an independent agency to insure a ready and adequate supply of oil and gas in the event of war. Serious transportation problems experienced by the oil industry after the outbreak of war in Europe in September 1939 had underscored the need for a planning agency. A recent loan to Great Britain of fifty U.S. oil tankers had aggravated those problems. Parten and every other person in the room knew that the nation's oil production and transportation systems would be a vital part of any future U.S. military effort, so the creation of the OPC had been expected. To the horror of many in the oil industry, however, President Roosevelt appointed Harold Ickes—whom many of these same men had fought in the early 1930s over the issue of federal control of their industry—to head the new agency.[1]

Aware that his appointment had caused widespread unhappiness, Ickes had brought the leaders of the industry to Washington to clear the air. "Let us get one thing straight, right now," Ickes declared. "I don't want to run your industry. In this effort, the oil industry needs the aid of the Government, and the Government needs the aid of the industry." Explaining how the OPC would operate, Ickes divided the country into five districts with an OPC administrative office in each district staffed by professionals nominated by and recruited directly from the oil industry. Texas was placed in District Three, which included the area from Alabama to New Mexico. Houston would be the district's headquarters. The industry would create its own parallel organization with local committees to assist the OPC in each of the five districts. This committee system insured that the industry would have the dominant voice in OPC decisions. Basic policy would be formulated by these industry committees and later sanctioned by government. Promising to keep regulations to a minimum, Ickes would rely on the industry to act voluntarily to achieve the desired goals.[2]

Ickes's forthright approach worked. The advantages of the partnership were apparent to Parten and to most of his colleagues, who enthusiastically endorsed Ickes's plan. They were also aware that the alternative to the OPC was to have the military seize the industry or have it taken over by a powerful federal agency staffed by civil service bureaucrats. In reality, the OPC was an advisory agency with no compulsory power. The president had been careful to demonstrate to the industry that he was sensitive about their fear of federal regulation. By appointing Ickes as coordinator, Roosevelt also sent a warning to the industry that he was prepared to go further if voluntarism proved ineffective.[3]

Ickes, however, had no intention of alienating the industry. He had, in fact, modified his views, concluding that the industry should be "run on the principle of conservation and not directed by a policeman in the form of the Sherman Antitrust Act." In 1936, Ickes had written in his diary that "an honest and scrupulous man in the oil business is so rare as to rank as a museum piece." But Ickes saw the partnership arrangement as a risk that had to be balanced against the need for people knowledgeable and skilled in the oil business. Like Roosevelt, who would declare that in his administration "Dr. New Deal" had given way to "Dr. Win-the-War," Ickes too would explain that his job was to do his part to win the war. "After that," he stressed, "nothing else mattered." As for the dangers of allowing the oil industry to run its own show in the war, Ickes was certain that his tough-mindedness, his ability to handle men of power, and his incorruptible dedication to the public good would keep the industry in line. Accordingly, Ickes created an administrative structure that would involve the industry in the policy-making process. In June 1941 he appointed Ralph K. Davies, an executive with Standard Oil of California, to be deputy coordinator of the OPC. Ickes and Davies had decided to organize the OPC carefully along the same functional lines as a major integrated oil company, creating a division for each component of the industry's activity, such as exploration, production, transportation, and refining. They would recruit experienced oil men rather than "government bureaucrats" to run each division.[4]

In the weeks following the meeting, the oil industry proceeded to set up its own organization, composed of a general committee in each district, with subcommittees for production, transportation, refining, and marketing. Committee expenses were paid by industry contributions. The district committees collected the data for the OPC to use in determining supply-and-demand estimates for each district and the nation as a whole; they also executed the OPC's policies and served as the liaison between it and local industry, providing the federal oil agency with an efficient and timely means of obtaining the industry view of any proposed course of action. By the end of the war, over three thousand oil-company employees had served on the industry committees. Among them was J. R. Parten, who received an appointment to the marketing committee for District Three on July 12, 1941.[5]

The Tanker Control Board

Parten did very little work for the marketing committee, however, before he received a request from Harold Ickes in late August to serve on the newly formed Federal Tanker Control Board. Chaired by OPC deputy director Ralph Davies, this board assigned service schedules for all American oil tankers to maintain the flow of fuel to Great Britain, while at the same time insuring that a sufficient quantity of oil was delivered to the U.S. East Coast. Centralized control of tanker traffic worked to avoid costly and inefficient snarls in the entire delivery system. Prior to Parten's appointment, the Tanker Control Board had attracted much political heat from independent oil producers in Texas. Whenever oil tankers were withdrawn from normal Texas–East Coast delivery routes, independent producers lost access to their most important markets—the independent refineries and distributors on the Atlantic Coast. It was essential, therefore, that the board have a member from the independent side of the industry. Wallace Pratt, vice president of Standard Oil of New Jersey, recommended Parten to Ralph Davies as the person who would be most acceptable to all segments of the industry. With Ickes's approval, Davies subsequently offered the appointment to Parten. "I went there with some misgivings about Ickes," Parten admitted. "I didn't leave that fight in 1933 with a very good taste in my mouth for him."[6]

The Tanker Control Board was composed of representatives from the Maritime Commission and the U.S. Navy, as well as three oil-industry representatives from each one of the U.S. coastal districts. Parten, who represented the Gulf Coast, was joined on the board by his old friend Eugene Holman, now the president of Standard Oil of New Jersey, who represented the East Coast. The fuel crisis threatening Great Britain in the early fall of 1941 forced the Tanker Control Board to meet so frequently that Parten was forced to stay in Washington for several weeks at a time. The problem in Great Britain was serious. In mid-summer, the Royal Navy's fuel reserve had dwindled to dangerous levels. Ickes ordered Davies to do everything possible to supply the British with fuel, which meant diverting large numbers of oil tankers from the East Coast to the British Isles. Tank ships under the U.S. flag and under U.S. contract had been pooled with British tankers and were being operated out of London, but routing decisions were made by the Tanker Control Board in Washington in consultation with the British government. Parten and his colleagues struggled most of the fall of 1941 with the complex problem of providing the East Coast with ample fuel supplies while also getting enough oil to Britain to keep the Royal Air Force in the air and the Royal Navy at sea. In mid-October, Parten wrote Kenneth Aynesworth that "transportation presents quite a 'bottle-neck' due to our having turned over to Britain the use of 145 tank ships. Especially has this created a problem of supply for the East Coast, the largest consuming area in the world." Within a few weeks, however, the Tanker

Control Board had so improved the fuel situation that the British were able to return the fifty oil tankers they had borrowed from the United States.[7]

Pearl Harbor

In late November 1941, Ickes decided that the district committee system was too cumbersome, so he created a national oil-industry council to meet periodically with OPC officials in Washington. Originally called the Petroleum Industry Council for National Defense, it was soon renamed the Petroleum Industry War Council (PIWC). Composed of seventy-nine of the nation's leading oil executives, including Parten, the PIWC met at least once a month for the duration of the war to provide the OPC a rapid response from the oil industry on policy matters.[8]

Ickes scheduled the first PIWC meeting in Washington on December 8, 1941. Parten departed for Washington on the morning of December 7 on an American Airlines DC-3. Midway in the flight, the pilot announced that the Japanese had attacked Pearl Harbor.[9] After Parten arrived in Washington, he joined Sam Rayburn for dinner at the home of Cong. Lyndon Baines Johnson. Jimmy Allred had introduced Parten to Johnson in 1937 when Johnson was running for his first term in Congress. Four years later, Parten was spending the first evening of the war with the Johnsons and Sam Rayburn, wondering about the future. "Lyndon talked about leaving the Congress and going into the Navy," Parten said. "We knew that we were in a real war now."[10]

Parten also had a decision to make about his personal role in the war. At forty-six, he was too old to contribute on the battlefront. Having left the army twenty-two years before as a major, Parten could have received a commission at a high rank. Aware of the critical importance oil would play in the war, however, Parten decided that he could make his greatest contribution by helping Woodley Petroleum find more oil and by building an aviation-gas plant for Premier and getting it operational as soon as possible. In addition, he would continue his service on the Tanker Control Board. Because of his membership on the board, Parten was among a very small handful of people in the United States who understood that the oil transportation system upon which vital industries on the East Coast depended was highly vulnerable to a complete shutdown by German submarines. The Tanker Control Board would have a serious challenge on its hands in the coming months.[11]

Parten's work on the board took up much of his time in the weeks following Pearl Harbor. Almost as soon as Germany declared war on the United States on December 11, German U-boats targeted American shipping along the East Coast, causing serious disruptions in oil shipments and forcing the Tanker Control Board to make a number of difficult decisions about tanker allocations. Late in December, for example, the Soviet Embassy in Washington requested two tankers to deliver high-octane aviation gasoline from the Gulf Coast area to Murmansk as soon as possible. The Red Army was engaged in a counteroffensive to repel the Germans from the gates of Moscow and to break the siege of Leningrad. They were desperate for high-octane aviation fuel. Since August, the British had been sending small convoys of war supplies to the Soviets through the Arctic ports of Archangel and Murmansk. The Soviets asked that the aviation fuel be delivered in one of those convoys. In December, however, the Germans attacked the convoys from air bases in northern Norway. These attacks plus adverse weather conditions and ice packs made it difficult for the British convoys to get to the Arctic ports. As a result, the British representatives recommended that the Soviet request be rejected.

"We had a two-day debate over whether we'd put those tank ships in or not," Parten said. "The Russians told us that if it took all the ice breakers they had, they were going to keep that channel in Murmansk open. That convinced me but not the British, who continued to object." After much argument, Parten moved to end the discussion and to send the tankers to Murmansk. The ships arrived in Murmansk by the beginning of February. The fuel allowed the Red Air Force to remain in the air at a critical stage in the offensive. Parten observed that his service on the Tanker Control Board provided him with the first evidence he saw that there was "pretty deep friction between the Russians and the British." Parten was also shocked by the depth of anti-Soviet feeling in Washington. "There were a number of people in Washington, saying, 'Well, we don't like either one of them. Let's hope that the Germans kill all the Russians, and that the Russians will kill all the Germans.' That kind of talk was going on in the streets of Washington in those days."[12]

Oil and War

World War II was a war of oil. The war machines of every belligerent demanded fueling and lubrication at an almost insatiable rate. A few numbers will illustrate the demand: one destroyer burned an average of 3,000 gallons of oil an hour, a typical four-engine bomber consumed 250 to 400 gallons of high-octane aviation fuel an hour, and a tank needed 10,000 gallons of gas for every 100 miles driven. Oil played a key strategic role as both sides worked to increase their supplies, while simultaneously cutting off those of their enemy. Without oil, no military operation could have been implemented. Frequently the availability of fuel meant the difference between life and death, success and failure.[13]

The United States, which was producing 60 percent of the world's oil by 1941, had the responsibility for providing the Allied military forces with the fuel needed to wage war. Oil accounted for more than half of the total amount of cargo shipped overseas during the war. By the end of the war, the United States had contributed six billion barrels of petroleum to the Allied cause—80 percent of the total of Allied requirements. This was an amount equal to more than one-quarter of the entire U.S. oil production from 1859 until 1941. As one historian of the petroleum industry has noted, those who carried out a supply-and-distribution program of such magnitude and vital importance had taken on a "fearful responsibility."[14]

In the spring of 1942, however, it was far from certain that the United States was capable of meeting this "fearful responsibility." Prior to 1940, industries in the Northeast, which were vital to the war effort, received 95 percent of their oil supply by tanker ship. In the weeks following Pearl Harbor, German U-boats sank

Parten (center), J. Howard Marshall (left), and Ralph K. Davies, with the OPC, 1940s. *CN 09589. Courtesy Parten Photograph Collection, CAH.*

U.S. oil tankers off the Atlantic Coast between Florida and New York with alarming regularity. In February, when the U-boat wolf packs struck in force, Harold Ickes confided to his diary that the situation was "very serious . . . tankers are being sunk faster than they are coming off the ways." Declining production in the Illinois and Oklahoma oil fields complicated the situation, necessitating a greater reliance on Texas oil, especially from the Permian Basin in distant West Texas. This made the problem worse because of the difficulty of transporting the oil from West Texas to the East Coast. There were too few railroad tank cars and trucks to move crude oil and oil products overland to fuel the large eastern cities and their war plants. Too few pipelines connected the Atlantic Coast with the midcontinent and Gulf oil regions to take on the added load. As fuel inventories on the East Coast fell to emergency levels, Ickes concluded that the only solution was to build a large capacity pipeline from Texas to the East Coast to deliver the oil to where it was most needed. The pipeline idea, however, was controversial. Powerful interests such as the ship companies and the railroads opposed its competitive impact on their business. Others believed that it would use too much steel needed for other military purposes.[15]

By February 1942, Ickes and Ralph Davies faced a daunting problem. They had to get oil to the East Coast as rapidly and efficiently as possible with virtually no tank ships or pipelines and an inadequate supply of railroad tank cars. Yet they faced a difficult battle in their effort to win approval of a large-capacity pipeline. Because the OPC's Transportation Division had the task of solving this problem, Ickes decided that he should replace its director, H. A. Gilbert, with an oil executive who had no significant business ties to any type of oil transportation; this ruled out anyone from the major integrated oil companies. Davies subsequently met with OPC legal counsel, J. Howard Marshall, to discuss candidates to take over the crisis-burdened division. Marshall, the former legal advisor on oil matters at the Department of the Interior, had worked in San Francisco under Davies at Standard Oil of California before joining one of the leading law firms in California. Davies had recruited him for the OPC in the summer of 1941. Marshall recommended J. R. Parten, the man he had investigated for Ickes in 1933 during the hot-oil crisis. Davies subsequently checked him out with leading members of the Petroleum Industry Council and they supported Parten with enthusiasm.[16]

Ickes also liked Parten for the transportation job. Because of the fight Parten had given Ickes during the battle over federal oil policy in the early 1930s, the secretary felt that the Texan had the respect of the oil industry, and was tough and persuasive enough to rally support from every segment. Marshall subsequently called Parten at his office in Houston and told him that Ickes wanted him to take over the transportation job at the OPC. The offer created a mild dilemma for Parten, who was not eager to move to Washington to assume a full-time government job. He understood, however, that the nation was at war and millions of Americans had other things they wanted to do but could not. Parten was also unsure about his decision not to return to military service after Pearl Harbor. He later confessed to Ralph Yarborough, who had left his wife and son and a prosperous law practice to serve as an army officer overseas, that he felt "a little guilty . . . for not having gone in again." For these and other reasons, Parten told Marshall he would give the offer his serious consideration, but he first wanted to have a personal discussion with Ickes in Washington.[17]

When Parten met with Ickes to discuss the transportation job, Ickes was candid with him. The job was going to be arduous and thankless. The OPC had to get oil to the East Coast and Parten and his staff would have to figure out how to do it. He promised Parten nothing but hard work, long hours, and many headaches. "I don't see how you can turn that down," Ickes declared without a smile. Parten told Ickes that if he accepted the job, he would need Ickes's total support. He anticipated strong political pressure from Congress on behalf of various pork-barrel schemes as well as opposition from the trucking and railroad industries against the pipeline program. "If you don't back me all the way," Parten stressed, "I'm going to give the job back to you and I'm going to buy my ticket home." Ickes gave

Parten his word that he would stand behind him. "Despite some pretty rough times, I can honestly say that not one time did he ever waver in that commitment," Parten later claimed.[18]

With Opal's encouragement, and assurances from his managerial staff at Woodley that the company would be in good hands while he was gone, Parten accepted the appointment, effective April 6, 1942. Armed with Ickes's pledge of support, the stage was set for Parten to play a significant role in initiating a complete revolution in the petroleum transportation system of the United States and in performing one of the most spectacular jobs on the home front during the war.

Parten accepted his appointment with the promise that he would serve for at least one year, though he believed he could do the job in four to six months. Parten turned down Ickes's offer to work for the same salary he was receiving at Woodley, feeling this would create charges of conflict of interest. He took a leave of absence without pay from Woodley and Premier. "I wasn't taking the job for the money," Parten later said. The conflict-of-interest issue was a very real concern. Parten would make decisions affecting the operations of his competitors in the industry. He would be unable to do his job properly if there were any questions about his neutrality. He warned Ralph Davies, for example, that Premier would be negotiating with the OPC in the near future because of its new aviation-fuel refining operations in Cotton Valley, Louisiana. Although Parten assured Davies that he would not participate in those negotiations, he still felt that he should not be on Premier's payroll while the OPC had business with Premier.[19]

"It looks as though I shall be here for some time"

Parten reported to his OPC office in the Department of the Interior building in Washington, D.C., three weeks early, so that he could study the transportation problem and evaluate his staff. He and Opal closed up their house in Houston and moved into a rent house near American University. Parten's Transportation Division was responsible for expediting the movement of massive amounts of petroleum and petroleum products across the United States. To do this required a highly complex organization with eleven departments or "sections" individually responsible for such areas as military supply, domestic supply, rail transportation, and pipelines; each managed by professionals with experience in and knowledge of the various methods of oil delivery available. As he studied the situation, Parten realized that it would take much longer than he had thought to do the job. In a letter to Homer Rainey, he stressed that his new work was "both heavy and exacting . . . a matter of transforming a whole transportation program that embraces a change from sea to land in large volume. . . . It looks as though I shall be here for some time."[20]

Ickes had made it clear that pipelines would be the chief concern of the Transportation Division in the coming months, so Parten recruited as his associate director Ralph McLaughlin, vice president of the Texaco Pipeline Company and one of the top pipeline experts in the industry. The man upon whom Parten would rely the most, however, was George Wilson, a thirty-two-year-old lawyer on leave from Standard Oil of Louisiana. Officially a member of J. Howard Marshall's legal staff, Wilson served as principal attorney for Parten's Transportation Division. He became so valuable to Parten, however, that Davies eventually named him Parten's executive assistant. Wilson's ability to deal with the maze of legal obstacles within the federal bureaucracy was invaluable to Parten, especially when his division was trying to get the big pipelines approved and built. Wilson was also skilled with pen and paper. Parten relied on his talents as a writer to produce speeches and reports, not only for himself, but for Davies and Ickes when they needed material for public statements related to petroleum transportation. This was a valuable contribution because of the highly sensitive and politically controversial nature of the division's mission.[21]

Other than Parten himself, the person who played the most critical role in the Transportation Division was OPC deputy director Ralph K. Davies, to whom Ickes had delegated day-to-day operational responsibility for the federal government's entire petroleum program. A year younger than Parten, Davies had been with Standard of California (SOCAL) for nearly three decades before joining the OPC. With little more than a high school education, Davies had worked his way up from clerk to a position on the board of directors. In 1930, at the age of thirty-three, Davies became the youngest man ever elected a director of SOCAL. Ickes had first known him as a member of the National Marketing Committee during the NRA period. A member of the OPC's legal staff described Davies as "a very remarkable man, very bright, a perfectionist. He sure as hell ran a tight ship. Ralph wasn't one of the most popular guys in the world. He was reserved and tightly controlled, very few people got to know him well."[22]

Parten found Davies a difficult person to work for. This was the first time since leaving the army in 1919 that Parten worked as an underling subject to orders from a supervisor. He also found Davies to be inaccessible. On two or three occasions when Parten needed an immediate decision from Davies but was having no success getting past his secretary, he walked down the street and sent Davies a telegram. Parten, a workaholic who did not believe in vacations, also thought Davies was lazy. He was outraged when Davies took an extended vacation during the 1942 Christmas holidays, while the OPC was confronted with a major fuel crisis in the Northeast. "He'd always go to lunch or leave for the day on the exact minute the office closed despite whatever we had going on," Parten later complained.[23]

Another source of stress was Harold Ickes. As deputy director, Davies insisted, and properly so, on being the link between the OPC and Ickes. He met more often with the secretary—sometimes as many as four or five times a day—than did anyone, including the assistant secretaries in the Interior Department. As the months passed and the political heat resulting from fuel shortages intensified, Ickes bypassed Davies and dealt with Parten, hauling him to congressional hearings and referring to him as "Major Parten, my transportation expert." Some of his associates felt Davies resented Ickes's habit of dealing directly with Parten. According to one of their colleagues, Justin Wolf, lines of authority were often ignored at the OPC. "This was a very unusual government agency," Wolf recalled. "We had an organizational chart, but nobody paid any attention to it. Basically, division heads ran their own shops and they didn't want Davies bothering them—except when they needed his help. And when that happened they wanted his help today, not tomorrow."[24]

That Parten's Transportation Division, and the entire OPC as well, was staffed with employees of the oil industry was a point of contention with many New Dealers, who felt that it was a case of the "cat guarding the mouse" and feared that it would facilitate monopolistic practices within the oil industry. Of the multitude of war agencies, only the OPC and the Office of Defense Transportation were operated by officers of private industry. J. Howard Marshall, whose duties included dealing with the Justice Department's Antitrust Division, claimed after the war that the Justice Department was convinced that "whenever any oil men get together at any meeting they always try to fix prices and restrain trade, so Justice was certain that was happening at OPC." But Marshall also admitted that the oil industry did exercise a controlling influence over the OPC. "We exercised extreme care never to order the petroleum industry to do anything," Marshall said, "until we had explored in detail with the [PIWC] and its committees what we or they proposed to do. When we acted, we already had the concurrence of the industry as to what ought to be done. . . ."[25]

Ralph Davies was a symbol to old-line New Dealers that the agency had been taken over by the oil industry. Ickes was criticized severely by his liberal friends for selecting the vice president of Standard Oil of California to head the OPC. Davies had volunteered to sever all connections with SOCAL after his OPC appointment, including the waiver of his pension rights. Ickes had refused that offer and allowed him to continue to receive his salary from SOCAL. Davies subsequently removed himself from any OPC discussions involving his company. Ironically, he carried out his duties with such strict neutrality that he soon attracted bitter criticism from some major companies, including SOCAL. Many oil men complained that they got along better with Ickes than with Davies. One oil executive from California even called him a socialist. Davies was not the only member of the OPC's staff to be accused of treason against the oil industry. Marshall later said that his only serious problems as chief counsel "arose when some individual drawn from a particular company would lean too far over backwards against his former company in an effort to prove that he was more than honest."[26]

Several members of Congress were also concerned that the major oil companies were dominating the OPC. Sam Rayburn passed that concern on to Ickes, warning him to keep a close watch over Davies because of his background with the major oil companies. Rayburn complained that "the big oil men" were all Republicans "who hated the President." Ickes assured the Speaker that he had no illusions about the oil industry and that he was "on guard constantly." Ickes confided to his diary that he knew "the danger that there is in having anything to do with oil and I am safeguarding myself to the best of my ability." Parten was able to render a service to Ickes and Davies by assuring Rayburn, with whom he frequently dined while he was with the OPC, that the major oil companies were not running the oil agency. Rayburn told Parten that his presence in the OPC was all the evidence he needed to convince him that he no longer had to worry about the agency.[27]

A Worsening Crisis

Parten faced a serious challenge when he officially began his new assignment in Washington the first week of April 1942. Eastern newspapers were predicting an imminent fuel disaster. Mailbags full of letters from panic-stricken northeasterners fearful of freezing during the coming winter were stacked in his outer office. The Nazis had sunk U.S. tankers at a rate of more than one a day since December 7. A winding black ribbon of oil could be seen along the high-water mark on beaches from New Jersey to Florida, the only visible remains of more than fifty sunken oil tankers. Throughout the spring of 1942, residents on the Atlantic shoreline could look eastward at night and see the sky offshore aglow with the blaze of an oil tanker hit by U-boat torpedos. The attacks, which could not be prevented by a U.S. Navy unprepared for antisubmarine warfare, soon shut down East Coast tanker deliveries. The East Coast had had its fuel deliveries cut in half, and consumer rationing had been invoked by the time Parten arrived at his job. During his first official meeting with his staff, Parten learned that it would require a daily train of seven thousand tank cars, fifty miles long to replace by land the fuel that had been transported by sea to the East Coast from the Southwest. Parten subsequently wrote to Sylvester Dayson back in Texas that he must have been "insane" to take on the oil transportation crisis.[28]

There was one basic and unalterable fact of life for the OPC's Transportation Division. More than 90 percent of the oil consumed on the East Coast, which was 40 percent of the nation's total oil supply, had been delivered by tankers that were no longer available. Parten and his staff now had to deliver approximately one and a half million barrels of oil a day overland. Ickes had long since been convinced that two large-capacity pipelines should be built to transport the oil from Texas to the East Coast. Parten's highest priority, therefore, was to get the steel to build the big pipeline. But even if that request was granted quickly, his division still had to get oil to the East Coast by some other method until the pipeline was completed. Throughout April and May, Parten and his staff worked on both problems.[29]

In the meantime, Parten's office was a flurry of activity as a stream of special-interest lobbyists, politicians, con artists, and hustlers filed through trying to sell him on some surefire (usually harebrained) method of getting oil from Texas to the East Coast quickly, or seeking his help for a special break on some local oil transportation problem. Parten soon learned that he had to be tough in his dealings with these people and careful about what he said to them. Ruth Sheldon Knowles, a well-known writer for oil journals and a sometime lobbyist, asked Parten to endorse a proposal by the concrete industry to build concrete-reinforced barges to transport oil along the coast. At this point, Parten had no idea what methods of transport should be used to replace the tankers, although he did know that Ickes had been considering barges. Parten told Knowles that he could not endorse her project. Knowles said she understood, but would Parten object if she called a conference of oil producers and refiners in Washington to discuss the idea? Parten replied that she could do anything she wanted, but he could not endorse the project.

After the meeting, Knowles sent out telegrams to the oil industry implying that the OPC had endorsed a conference to study the use of concrete oil barges. When Ickes heard this he ordered Davies to tell Parten to watch his tongue. "Tell Parten that he must be strong enough to run his own show and not let Mrs. Knowles think she is in the saddle," Ickes said. "She is a good looking woman and knows her way about. She . . . goes after what she wants without any indication of timidity." Parten learned his lesson well. As one of his colleagues recalled, "J. R. got the message. He was sort of like old man Ickes. He had a tough exterior and you knew you had better not waste his time with some wild-eyed scheme." Parten soon got back in Ickes's good graces. By April 26, Ickes was noting in his diary that he had met with his oil staff to determine "what progress was being made . . . to bring oil to the Atlantic Coast. My impression is that Major Partin (sic) is doing a good job."[30]

Knowles was not the only person lobbying Parten. The real pressure came from elected officials—congressmen to Roosevelt himself—who managed to become attracted to one quick-fix solution after another. Parten had to devote much valuable time explaining why these quick fixes were unworkable or inappropriate for the job. For example, the lumber industry argued for plywood pipelines. They even got to the president, who told Ickes at a cabinet meeting that he understood that "in Russia they build pipelines of wood." Ickes told the president it would not work. When Roosevelt asked Ickes if laminated wood might not do the trick; the secretary had to confess his ignorance. After the meeting he called Parten, who prepared a lengthy report to explain why laminated wood was poor pipeline material. Several members of Congress joined with Knowles and other cement-industry lobbyists to pressure Parten to use concrete for pipelines. Parten's engineering staff, however, reported that the metal rods needed to reinforce the concrete would use more steel than all-steel pipe. Other unworkable ideas for steel substitutes included glass and vitrified tile.[31]

The Tulsa Plan

The same week Parten began his job at the OPC, pipeline executives from sixty-seven companies met in Tulsa to formulate a comprehensive national-pipeline proposal for the OPC's Transportation Division. The keystone of this proposed new pipeline system would be the largest pipeline in the world, running from Texas to New York. Ickes believed that only the federal government could afford to construct this so-called "Big Inch" line. He had urged this course on the president in December 1940, but FDR had taken no action. With Ickes's encouragement, however, a group of oil-company executives proceeded in early 1941 with preliminary planning for the route, size of pipe (twenty-four inches), and location of pumping stations. This private group also concluded that there would be a need for a second but smaller line to carry refinery products. This second line, to be constructed with pipe twenty inches in diameter and to run parallel to the Big Inch, was called the "Little Big Inch" initially, but that clumsy phrase was soon shortened to "Little Inch."

Ickes urged the White House to adopt the pipeline plan, but he ran into opposition from the railroads, Texas refiners, and their allies in Congress. The railroads persuaded state legislatures in the southeastern states to obstruct the acquisition of right-of-way for two pipelines. In July 1941, Congress responded by passing the Cole Act giving the federal government the power of eminent domain to acquire right-of-way for interstate pipelines important to national defense. Ickes worked with the oil industry in the summer of 1941 to conduct preliminary land surveys and engineering studies for the big pipelines. In the fall of 1941, as American involvement in the war neared, Ickes asked the Federal Allocation Board for steel to build the pipelines. The board twice denied his request. After the Japanese attack on Pearl Harbor, Ickes submitted another request for steel for the pipeline to the newly created War Production Board (WPB), which had legal authority to allocate materials and facilities in whatever manner it believed necessary for national defense. The WPB rejected the request on February 20, 1942, explaining that the pipelines would require nearly 650,000 tons of steel; enough to build large numbers of fighter planes, bombers, tanks, and other desperately needed weapons to fight the war.[32]

Parten knew that the Tulsa Plan would call for an ambitious pipeline-construction program that would include the Big and Little Inch lines. He had strong doubts about the two big pipelines, partly because of his fear as a refiner that it would destroy the refining business in Texas by moving all of the crude to the East Coast. Parten decided to get advice on the subject from the top experts in the field. He knew that one of the best was a short, fat, and grouchy Texas A&M graduate by the name of Bert Hull, a pipeline engineer and vice president of the Texas Company. Hull admitted to Parten that he had been "luke warm" on the pipeline proposal until the Germans began sinking tankers along the Atlantic seaboard. "Now I am definitely in favor of building both pipe line projects in a hurry," Hull declared. "I am convinced that it is the only means of meeting the situation with the greatest expediency." His opinion persuaded Parten that the Big Inch lines were essential to the war effort.[33]

The Tulsa conference ended on April 2 with an urgent call for the federal government to proceed with an ambitious ten-part pipeline program. The plan proposed an extensive modification of existing pipelines, which included reversing the flow of east-to-west and north-to-south pipelines (the directions most of the nation's lines flowed) so that as much oil as possible would move toward the East Coast. Because of the steel shortage, the plan also called for digging up the large number of abandoned or little-used pipelines in the Southwest for reuse in several new short lines between Texas and different points on the Mississippi and Ohio Rivers, where they would connect with barge traffic. The report declared that if all of these projects could be completed it would still leave the East Coast far short of its estimated minimum daily oil requirements.

Accordingly, the Tulsa conference concluded that the only feasible solution was to build two big pipelines from Texas to New York, a distance of fourteen hundred miles. The Big Inch pipe, with a branch to Philadelphia, would deliver 250,000 barrels of crude oil a day, while the Little Inch would deliver 200,000 barrels of refined products such as aviation and automobile gasolines. These projects would be large and expensive: the twenty-four-inch line had an estimated cost of ninety-five million dollars. The call for pipelines twenty-four inches and twenty inches in diameter was quite radical, because at the time nearly all pipelines were from two to twelve inches in diameter. Nevertheless, railroad tank cars and river barges required more steel per barrel of oil moved than did the pipelines, and operating costs were far higher. Economy, however, was not the basic reason for building the lines. There was simply no alternative in the absence of tankers.[34]

Problems with the War Production Board

After the OPC accepted the Tulsa Plan in early May as the blueprint for its transportation program, Parten began the sensitive job of preparing a new request to the WPB for the hundreds of thousands of tons of steel needed to build the Big Inch line. Severely limiting nonessential construction, the WPB prohibited the use of scarce materials without its prior approval. The OPC was required to make application to the WPB whenever it proposed a project involving construction or the use of restricted supplies and material. The WPB judged all such applications in light of total needs, placing priority ratings on projects. In recent weeks WPB chairman Donald Nelson and his board colleagues had emphasized that the manufacture of military equipment and weaponry had the highest priority for steel allocation. The U.S. military had been woefully underequipped when the country went to war and it desperately needed enormous amounts of everything from fighter planes to transport ships. The OPC's request for steel, rejected as recently as February, obviously faced an uphill battle.[35]

Parten spent long hours at the OPC during May working with his staff to prepare the request. A workaholic anyway, Parten spent twelve to fourteen hours a day, seven days a week, at his desk, in conference, or in committee meetings, many of which were held at night. A writer for the Pure Oil News who interviewed Parten observed that "the day he saw me I got in about 1:15 pm after a wait in his busy outer office. He had not had lunch and did not expect he would get the time for it. Many of his days are like that." In early May, Opal told a friend in Houston that "the big job at the moment . . . is the preparation of a report to be given the War Production Board . . . for the steel necessary for a pipeline from the Southwest to the Northeast. The fact that such a request has been turned down twice before makes the third request even more weighty."[36]

One approach Parten took with the WPB was to promise not to ask for new steel for any of its other pipeline projects. "We were going to use second-hand pipe," Parten later recalled. "But we told WPB that we absolutely had to have new steel for these two big-inch pipelines, because there weren't any twenty inch or twenty four inch pipelines that had ever been built. It had to be new." Donald Nelson was making it clear, however, that the pipeline would be a hard sell. In late April, in a meeting with Ickes and President Roosevelt at the White House, Nelson complained that the OPC was asking for too much steel. Ickes responded that without the pipeline the OPC could not supply the industrial Northeast with fuel. He insisted that oil was "indispensable, without it tanks and ships and airplanes . . . were useless." Nelson replied that there was no steel available. Ickes later complained that Nelson believed that "sufficient oil could be transported by other means but he didn't tell me what other means." As usual, Roosevelt was noncommittal for most of the meeting. Ickes saw a ray of hope, however, when the president brought up the subject of New England's fuel-oil situation. According to Ickes, Roosevelt "expressed real concern about the supply of fuel oil for next winter. He said that people could not be permitted to freeze."[37]

A shortage of steel was not the only problem the OPC faced in regard to the big pipelines. Midwestern oil producers thought that they would close them off from eastern markets, while midwestern refiners feared that only the section of the lines from Texas to Illinois would be built, washing away their markets with a flood of cheaply refined Texas products. Others worried about who would own the lines after the war. Some companies complained that the federal government would build the lines at taxpayer expense and then after the war sell them cheaply to one of their competitors. A few industry spokesmen expressed the belief that at the end of the war the pipelines should be filled with oil, sealed, and kept inactive as a storage unit for use in some future national emergency. As one historian has noted, however, it was obvious that "a $142 million investment could not be abandoned in this way."

This debate, which was largely an in-house argument within the oil industry, took a different turn when some pushed the idea that the pipelines in the postwar period could be converted to natural gas use. That suggestion, which attracted much favorable response throughout the oil industry, brought forth protests from the coal industry and the railroads. The availability of cheap and clean natural gas in the Northeast would mean the end of coal as one of the region's most important sources of fuel. Although fuel oil had displaced many of the coal-burning furnaces in homes and in much industry, coal was still being used in large quantities. The mine owners feared natural gas would reduce coal use to the point where coal companies would have to close the mines and lay off large numbers of workers. This prospect brought the powerful United Mine Workers out against the pipelines. Because the railroads transported the coal, they and their unions also opposed the pipelines. The railroads opposed *all* pipelines, and their lobbyists worked overtime throughout the war trying to persuade Congress to impede their development. "Those damn railroads were the big problem," Parten declared. "Not only did they fight the pipelines, they wanted to charge outrageous rates for us to ship oil in their tanker cars."[38]

Davies and Parten knew that lobbyists for the various interests opposed to the big pipelines were working hard to turn Congress against the proposal. Although it was the WPB's decision to make, it was understood that congressional support for the pipelines would send a helpful signal to the board. For one thing, Congress could pass legislation to create a government-owned pipeline company and require the WPB to allocate steel for it. Congressional opposition, on the other hand, could obviously have the contrary effect. To counter the opposition to their pipeline plan, Davies and Parten appeared before the congressional committees that had special responsibility for petroleum transportation. The most important of these was the so-called "Cole committee," the petroleum subcommittee of the House Committee on Interstate and Foreign Commerce, chaired by Rep. William P. Cole. Ever since the fight over federal control of the oil industry in the early 1930s, the Cole committee had been at the center of Congress's relationship with the oil industry. Parten began his lobbying with the Cole committee because he knew he would receive a fair hearing. Representative Cole had been the author of the law that had empowered the president to declare specific pipelines necessary to national defense and to delegate the right of eminent domain to any company constructing such a designated pipeline. The Cole bill had also authorized the president to construct with federal funds and to operate through federal agencies any pipelines needed for the national defense. It was this authority that allowed the OPC to propose the big pipelines.[39]

Parten testified for three hours before the Cole committee on May 20. He gave a detailed picture of the serious fuel shortage faced by the East Coast and explained that his office was currently trying to get oil to the Atlantic seaboard chiefly with railroad tank cars, supplemented by pipelines and inland barges. Despite an intense effort that was succeeding in getting eight hundred thousand barrels of oil a day to the East, deliveries were still falling short on a daily basis by as much as five hundred thousand barrels. Because transportation equipment and facilities were operating at maximum capacity, deliveries could not be increased by any significant amount. Parten explained that by implementing the Tulsa Plan— especially the building of the Big Inch—that shortfall could be made up in a matter of months. Other methods would take years or would require too much scarce material and skilled manpower. Two days later, Parten followed his House appearance with nearly three hours of testimony before a subcommittee of the Senate Committee on Commerce. "The war program on the East Coast is going to be injured until this pipeline is built," Parten warned the senators. When one senator declared that Rear Adm. Emory Land, chairman of the Maritime Commission, had claimed that the Big Inch pipeline would use enough steel to build 120 ships, Parten replied that the Big Inch could "do the work of 140 to 150 ships" and could be built in half the time.[40]

Parten's appearances did much to win congressional support for the Tulsa Plan. He was an effective speaker and he impressed the committee members with his preparation and straightforward testimony. After Parten's appearance before his subcommittee on May 22, 1942, Arthur Vandenberg, a Republican from Michigan who would become one of Parten's most important allies in the Senate, declared that it was "very reassuring to . . . find gentlemen of his ability, of his complete mastery of the situation in charge of [the Transportation Division]." Later, on the floor of the Senate during a discussion of the oil transportation problems, Vandenberg stated that Parten had appeared before his committee, "and, by the way, I think Major Parten is one of the ablest men I have seen come into the Government service in my time." Ickes noted in his diary that Parten "had been up as a witness and had made the strong impression that he does on everyone." One of the impressive things about Parten's performance is that he had been on the job for only two months and had mastered an extensive amount of statistical and technical information.[41]

The Florida Barge Canal

While Parten worked for adoption of the Tulsa Plan, competing proposals for alleviating the oil transportation problem continued to take up his time. Most of these proposals were unworkable, but a scheme to build a canal and a pipeline across northern Florida presented a serious threat to the Tulsa Plan. The proponents of the canal plan, led by Florida's influential Democratic senator Claude Pepper, argued that a canal across northern Florida would make it possible to ship oil on the intracoastal waterway all the way from Texas to Philadelphia, thus making the big pipelines unnecessary. The waterway, a dredged passage protected from the open sea, ran without major interruption along the Gulf from Corpus Christi, Texas, to Panama City on the Florida panhandle. On the Atlantic Coast, it stretched from Jacksonville, Florida, to Philadelphia. Too shallow for oil tankers on most of its course, the intracoastal was largely a water highway for barges. Cargo arriving at Panama City had to be unloaded and shipped by tanker around the tip of Florida or placed on railcars or trucks and hauled overland to Jacksonville. U-boat attacks had made the trip around Florida too dangerous and the land route was too slow and expensive. As a solution, Senator Pepper adopted a plan, promoted by port authorities along the waterway and business interests in northern Florida, which called for the federal government to deepen and widen the existing waterway from Corpus Christi to Florida and construct a forty-four-million-dollar canal to bridge the land gap between Panama City and Jacksonville. The entire project was expected to cost eighty million dollars.

Parten's transportation advisors persuaded him to oppose Pepper's plan. The canal would take at least two years to build, it would be an inefficient use of critical war materials, and the skilled manpower needed to construct it was not available. In addition, the canal would not be able to accommodate oil tankers, rendering it economically uncompetitive as a route for oil transportation after the war. Instead of a canal, Parten and his staff proposed to build a pipeline across northern Florida from Carabelle on the Gulf Coast to Jacksonville on the Atlantic to carry so-called "white" products such as aviation gasoline. Parten's opposition to the canal unleashed a fierce reaction from the powerful lobby backing the proposal. He soon learned from Bob Montgomery, who was working in a war job in the Agriculture Department, that the Texas Gulf Sulphur Company, led by its lobbyist

Roy Miller, was the main force behind the canal. Although Parten's opposition to the canal was based primarily on the factual arguments against it, he later admitted that his dislike for the canal intensified when he realized that Roy Miller and the sulphur monopoly were pushing it. Miller had caused much trouble at the University of Texas trying to get Montgomery fired when Parten had been on the board of regents. Miller was also vice president of the Intracoastal Canal Association, which had joined with the sulphur monopoly to ask Congress to fund the canal project. Parten realized that Texas Gulf Sulphur was using the fuel emergency on the East Coast as an excuse to get the federal government to build the canal, which could then be used to ship sulphur. Ickes subsequently wrote in his diary that "a syndicate has been organized that has a lot of money to spend, the idea being that although this barge canal would be built by federal funds later it could be grabbed off by private interests."[42]

Senator Pepper made frequent telephone calls and personal visits to Parten's office in an attempt to change his mind. "Claude Pepper gave me a lot of trouble over building a barge canal across Florida," Parten recalled. "I thought the canal just wouldn't help us because it would take too long to build. And it really complicated our request for steel because a hell of a lot of steel equipment would be needed to build that canal." Parten knew the canal proposal would not be so attractive if he could locate enough secondhand pipe to get the pipeline project started as soon as possible. Because of the Cole Act, he did not need congressional approval to build the pipeline. Parten eventually thought of Clint Murchison's old eight-inch Liberty pipeline in East Texas that had carried hot oil back in the early 1930s, but was now little used. Parten worked out a deal with Murchison's partner, Toddie Lee Wynne, and the pipeline was dug up, reconditioned, and moved to Florida. It made its first delivery of oil to Jacksonville on June 17, 1943. This action, plus a report from the Army Corps of Engineers confirming that the canal would take at least two years to build, persuaded the congressional delegation from the Northeast that the Florida canal would do them no good. The House version of the bill was sponsored by Rep. Joseph Mansfield of Texas. By early June, the Mansfield bill was stalled in committee and seemed certain to die there. Parten, however, had not heard the last of the Florida canal.[43]

Organizing the Big Inch

Parten completed the formal application to the WPB on May 25 for the allocation of new steel to build the Big Inch pipeline. Despite growing support from Congress, WPB director Donald Nelson still opposed the pipelines. Only three days before, Nelson told reporters that "the pipeline is out unless you want to give up planes and tanks." When he heard Nelson's statement, Ickes wrote in his diary that "hell will begin to break loose in northern Maine along about September and that hell will sweep south. . . . In the end, we will have to build the pipeline because of the pressure of public opinion. . . ." The situation seemed to be anything but promising when Parten made an important discovery: "I finally found out the War Production Board, in fact, didn't have the damn steel. The Army and Navy had it, so I just concentrated all of my effort with them." Armed with endorsements from the appropriate congressional committees, Parten negotiated with the Army and Navy to let the OPC have a portion of their steel allocation to build the Big Inch. He explained that the pipeline was doomed unless those departments told the WPB they could spare some steel for it. The Navy feared the Big Inch would take steel it needed for ships, but Parten convinced them that it would actually free up oil tankers for Navy use overseas. "That's the way I got the steel," Parten later explained.

Bolstered by the military's approval and backed by Congress, the War Production Board accepted the OPC's application on June 10, but only for the section of the Big Inch line that would run from Longview, Texas, to Norris City, Illinois. Although Ickes denounced it as a "half-loaf" decision, he felt confident at last that the entire program would eventually go through. On the same day the board announced its decision, Ickes and Davies appeared before it to argue for the rest of the steel, emphasizing that the primary purpose of the pipeline would not be for consumer consumption in New England, but for storage in Great Britain to be used in the future invasion of Nazi-occupied Europe. Without the oil, Ickes argued, the second front would run out of gas almost as soon as it began.[44]

Parten had no time to celebrate. Now that he had his steel, he had to organize the project. He brought to Washington the chief executives of the eleven largest oil companies that operated principally on the East Coast. He told the executives that although the government was prepared to build and operate the pipelines, the OPC had no objection to the industry owning and building them. "I had a personal preference for the industry to take the project over," Parten said, "because I felt that it would lead to the speediest possible building, and I was interested in time. But I didn't tell them my preference." The industry representatives decided that a government-organized and -financed nonprofit corporation should build and operate the pipelines for the duration of the war. At Parten's insistence, the eleven oil companies created a board of directors composed of their company presidents. It was also agreed that the presidents could not send representatives to board meetings. "It was essential that we have the Presidents— not the Vice Presidents—so that decisions would be easy to make," Parten said. "That expedited the matter greatly." After the issue of ownership was decided, Parten turned the matter over to Howard Marshall to put together a legal structure for the new organization.[45]

The new nonprofit public corporation organized to build and operate the Big Inch pipeline was named War Emergency Pipelines, Inc. (WEP). The formal contract signed between the federal government and War Emergency Pipelines on June 26 authorized WEP to construct and operate the Big Inch, but the federal government, which provided financing through the Reconstruction Finance Corporation (RFC), retained ownership. W. Alton "Pete" Jones, an attorney and chairman of Cities Service Oil Company and a longtime advocate of the Big Inch pipeline, was appointed president. Parten had little respect for Jones, whom he had known since their days in the El Dorado oil field nearly twenty years before.

He viewed Jones as a corporate bureaucrat and not "a real oil man." They would clash frequently in the coming months.[46]

With organizational matters decided, Parten opened construction offices in Little Rock, dispatched surveying parties to stake out the route, and ordered pipe from the mill. The most significant action he took, however, was to persuade Bert Hull to serve as the vice president and general manager of War Emergency Pipelines, with direct responsibility for pipeline construction. The Navasota, Texas, native had worked as an engineer for Texaco since 1905. Hull worked his way up the corporate ladder, eventually becoming president of the Texas Pipeline Company (a subsidiary of Texaco). By the time Parten tapped him for the Big Inch project, Hull was widely respected in the oil industry as the "dean of the old-time pipeliners."[47] Hull recruited some of the best technicians and most experienced laborers in the pipeline business, many of them veterans of pipeline construction in the deserts of the Middle East and in the swamps and hills of Columbia and Venezuela. Work on the Big Inch line finally began near Little Rock, Arkansas, on August 3.[48]

Confronting the East Coast Fuel Shortage

While Parten organized the Big Inch project, the fuel shortage on the East Coast became critical. Transportation problems forced the OPC to cut fuel deliveries to the region by 40 percent, obliging the Office of Price Administration to impose a rationing system on consumers. Parten and his staff had to devise a way to move an additional half million barrels of oil a day overland to alleviate the situation. Trucks could not be used because of a rubber shortage and the fact that, in delivering gasoline, trucks consumed too much gasoline. The only options available were railroad tank cars, pipelines, and barges, each with its own serious problems. After studying his staff reports, Parten concluded that until completion of the Big Inch, he would have to organize a highly coordinated system using all three options, with special reliance on the railroads. His division had total authority over pipelines, but not over the railroads or barge lines. They were governed by the Office of Defense Transportation (ODT), which was responsible for moving petroleum between the points designated by the OPC. It was Parten's job to prove to the ODT that the petroleum in question not only had to be moved but that a plan had been devised that would cause the least disturbance to other crucial military and civilian transportation needs. This was no easy task and it complicated any plan involving railroad equipment or waterborne transportation.[49]

Throughout the summer and fall of 1942, Parten and his staff devised a complex plan that included the reassignment of 70 percent of all the U.S. tank cars exclusively to East Coast duty; the movement of tank cars in so-called "symbol trains" highballing from the loading facility straight to only one delivery point rather than to many delivery stops as in peacetime; and the use of trucks rather than tank cars for short hauls of fewer than a hundred miles, thereby freeing some twenty thousand tank cars to deliver an extra two hundred thousand barrels of oil a day. After much negotiation, the ODT agreed to the plan. As a result, within two

A solid "symbol" train of oil tank cars moves oil to the East Coast, 1942. *CN 09612. PAW Photograph, courtesy Parten Papers, CAH.*

years the OPC increased deliveries to the East Coast from five thousand barrels a day to an average of eight hundred thousand barrels a day, or half of the total need. The railroads provided the necessary transport although three times as many passengers and twice as much freight were being hauled in 1943 as in 1940. The transport of oil over long distances on railroad cars was far more expensive than any other means of transportation, with the exception of oil trucks. To prevent the oil companies from suffering huge financial losses on the East Coast deliveries, Parten's transportation staff persuaded the Interstate Commerce Commission to reduce rates for rail transport charges. The OPC also persuaded the RFC to subsidize the transportation costs. "Jesse Jones and the RFC played a big role financing everything that we did," Parten said. "All we had to do was work out our problem and send our recommendation to Jesse. He would call me up the next day after he got the letter and say, 'I've got your letter, and I see your name signed on it. Are you still of the same opinion this morning?' I would answer, 'Yes, Mr. Jones, I need to do it.' He'd go ahead and spend the money. Once we got a plan approved by the National Petroleum Council, there was no problem with Jones at all."[50]

Pipelines, however, and not just the Big Inch lines, offered the only long-term solution to the East Coast fuel problem. Unfortunately, most of the pipelines in Texas, the source of supply for most of the East Coast, moved oil in a southerly direction to the Gulf Coast to be refined and then shipped on tankers. As recommended by the Tulsa Plan, Parten's team eventually reversed the flow of twenty-eight hundred miles of existing pipelines. An old line from El Dorado, Arkansas, to Port Arthur, Texas, for example, was reversed to flow from south to north. Some thirty-two hundred miles of abandoned or less important lines were pulled up and moved to other areas. Parten's Transportation Division also constructed four entirely new pipelines other than the Big Inch and Little Inch. One of the most important was the Plantation Line from Baton Rouge, Louisiana, to Richmond, Virginia, which delivered ninety thousand barrels of oil a day.[51]

The third and most problematic component of the Parten team's plan for alleviating the East Coast fuel shortage involved the construction and use of wooden barges. Parten opposed the use of wooden barges because of their strong potential for leakage, which created a dangerous fire and pollution hazard. President Roosevelt, however, continued to be fascinated by the idea that wood, which was plentiful, could be used to transport oil. Ickes had persuaded the president that wooden pipelines were a bad idea, but Roosevelt continued to argue for wooden barges. Parten finally agreed to the limited use of wooden barges, but only after Jesse Jones privately warned him not to ignore Roosevelt's views on the matter. Although one thousand wooden barges were authorized, only half that many were built, due to safety concerns and the problem of seawater contamination of the fuel. In November 1943, for example, while the Navy was shipping ten thousand barrels of special fuel oil in wooden barges from Port Arthur to Panama City, Florida, many of the barges developed leaks that resulted in serious saltwater contamination. When Parten reported this to Davies, he declared that "we may thank our lucky stars that we did not, from the beginning, place much dependence in this proposed method of transportation." Barge transportation had additional problems. The engines (made of steel) needed to power the barges were in short supply, it required twice as much power to deliver oil by barge than by pipeline, and the inland water route from Texas to Pittsburgh is twice as far as the direct pipeline route. Despite these severe problems, by 1943 the OPC was able to deliver by barge an additional one hundred thousand barrels of fuel oil per day to the East Coast.[52]

It took several months for these complex maneuvers to begin to alleviate the fuel shortage. For most of 1942, the OPC was unable to deliver the total amount of oil required by industry, the military, and consumers. The shortfall was usually about half a million barrels a day. Throughout that difficult year unexpected disruptions such as floods, train wrecks, and fires—as well as the fluctuating needs of the military—greatly complicated the problem.[53]

"Pork Barrel" Rivers, H. L. Hunt, and the Florida Barge Canal

In late June, as Parten struggled to implement the Tulsa Plan and alleviate the dangerous East Coast fuel shortage, the northern Florida barge canal (Mansfield) bill was revived by the House Committee on Rivers and Harbors. After passage by the committee, Rep. Mendel "Pork Barrel" Rivers of Charleston, South Carolina, broadened the bill with an amendment providing for a special appropriation to construct a new 580-mile pipeline from the Tinsley oil field near Yazoo, Mississippi, to Charleston, South Carolina, or to Savannah, Georgia. On June 17, the House passed the Mansfield bill with its new amendment.

This development deeply angered Parten. The Florida barge canal was a bad idea, but the Tinsley pipeline was worse. Parten's division had recently rejected an application to build the Tinsley line because it did not produce enough oil to warrant the use of the precious steel. Parten was well acquainted with the Tinsley field. Woodley had drilled some wildcat wells in the area and he knew that the field was in rapid decline after a peak production of eighty-five thousand barrels a day. Even in sharp decline, however, the Tinsley field produced more oil than could be absorbed by the sparsely populated and impoverished area around it. Parten knew that H. L. Hunt and his son, H. L. "Hassie" Hunt Jr., owned most of the field and that they were eager to have a pipeline—built with thirteen million dollars of taxpayers' money—through which they could transport their oil to sell to the Navy bases on the coast. Parten also knew that the Tinsley line was actually a major section of an even longer proposed pipeline that would originate in Wichita Falls, Texas. This was a project of Trans-American Pipeline Corporation, a company servicing independent producers such as the Hunts, and it, too, was being held up by Parten. In essence, Trans-American was not only trying to bypass the OPC, it was trying to get the federal government to pay for a major part of its route to the Atlantic Coast. When Aldace Walker, a vice president for Trans-American, met with Parten earlier in June to discuss the pipeline application, he had warned Parten that he would suffer "a great deal of political heat" if he did not approve the application. Parten had replied that "political heat" would have no bearing on his decision. Walker warned Parten that he would live to regret a negative decision in the matter.[54]

To Parten, the Mansfield bill was an outrageous attempt by a coalition of private-business interests, including Texas Gulf Sulphur, H. L. Hunt, and the Trans-American Pipeline Corporation, to use the war emergency as an excuse to plunder the public treasury. The bill also threatened the OPC's request for more steel to finish the Big Inch pipeline. Determined to stop the bill in the Senate, Parten appealed directly to his three strongest allies: Sen. Arthur Vandenburg; Rear Adm. E. S. Land, Maritime Commission chairman; and Gen. Walter Pyron in the War Department. Parten knew that the Army opposed the Tinsley pipeline because it required an enormous amount of steel to carry oil that could be transported with much less steel by the Trans-Florida pipeline. He persuaded Walter Pyron, who was on leave from the Gulf Oil Company, to produce a letter from Sec. of War Henry L. Stimson declaring the War Department's offical opposition to the Tinsley pipeline. Parten asked Pyron not to submit Stimson's letter to the Senate committee until after he had an opportunity to state the OPC's case. Admiral Land also agreed to submit a letter to the committee opposing the bill. On June 29, the Senate Committee on Commerce opened hearings on the Mansfield bill. Senator Vandenburg, a member of the committee, gave Parten the opportunity to testify against the bill.[55]

Parten's testimony emphasized that the barge canal could not be built fast enough to end the fuel crisis on the East Coast. As for the Tinsley pipeline, there was not enough crude-oil production at the Tinsley field to warrant it, nor was there any new steel available. Only by taking steel away from the Big Inch project could the Tinsley line be built. Parten was questioned heatedly by Senator Pepper and Representative Rivers. The latter, given the privilege to participate in a Senate hearing, warned Parten that he would oppose the completion of the Big Inch if the OPC killed the Tinsley line. The committee also heard testimony from the bill's supporters, including Roy Miller, Aldace Walker, and H. L. Hunt Jr., who was serving as a lieutenant in the Army Corps of Engineers. Hunt argued that the Tinsley field and the surrounding area had unlimited potential for oil production. Although Hunt admitted that his family owned much of the production in the field and that they were having difficulty finding a market for it, Sen. Burton R. Maybank of South Carolina, one of the bill's staunchest advocates, tried to persuade his colleagues that the Hunt family had no financial interest in building the pipeline.[56]

After the parade of witnesses in favor of the bill, Parten told Walter Pyron that it was time to play their ace card. Pyron dispatched a U.S. Army lieutenant colonel to read Secretary Stimson's letter to the committee. Stimson's letter was unequivocal: "The War Department is opposed to the . . . pipe line . . . to the Tinsley oil field." The building of the Tinsley line, the secretary warned, would take steel directly away from that required to produce "weapons needed by the Army and Navy of the United States." The letter had its intended effect. The bill's supporters on the committee remained silent. "The letter speaks for itself as far as I am concerned," Vandenburg declared. When Admiral Land also declared his strong opposition to the Florida barge canal, it became apparent that Senator Pepper had made a tactical mistake in linking his canal to the Tinsley pipeline. The bill was reported out of committee, but when it got to the floor of the Senate, Vandenberg and his allies inserted a passage stating that it was subject to the Cole Act. This meant that the act's provisions could not be carried out unless the president declared they were necessary for national defense. The president had delegated all such decisions relative to petroleum to the OPC. The bill subsequently passed and was signed into law by the president on July 23. Citing the new law and declaring that Congress had "directed" that the Tinsley Pipeline be constructed, Trans-American resubmitted its application to the OPC, which quickly rejected it. The canal, however, would come back again in a major way in the spring and summer of 1943.[57]

Nor were the people behind the Tinsley pipeline finished with Parten. That same summer, the State of Louisiana charged Premier with running "hot" oil through its refinery at Cotton Valley. Outraged when he heard the news, Parten called Sylvester Dayson, who admitted that he had purchased oil that had been produced in excess of the state allowable. He told Parten that Jack Blalock had given him a legal opinion that the oil was not hot because of a technicality in the regulations and because of confusion caused by the OPC's refining rules. Parten would later claim that he had known nothing about Dayson's decision. He had resigned his office with Premier when he went to work for the OPC. Dayson's action had been a clear violation of Parten's longstanding policy. When Dayson asked him to come to Shreveport to testify in his behalf at a hearing on the matter, he refused. He told Dayson that he had gotten in this mess by himself and he could now get out of it by himself. Later, however, when Parten had had more time to study what had happened at Cotton Valley, he agreed that the charge against Premier *had* been based on a complicated technicality. He also suspected that Premier had been set up by someone who subsequently reported them to the state authorities. Although he had no substantive proof, Parten believed H. L. Hunt's company, which had oil production at Cotton Valley, had been involved somehow, and that the action had been in retaliation for Parten's stand against the Tinsley pipeline.[58]

Parten's suspicions deepened on September 2. Aldace Walker of Trans-American Pipeline charged at a congressioal hearing that the State of Louisiana had indicted "J. R. Parten's refining company" for hot-oil running. He also charged that Premier was totally dependent on the major oil companies for supply and implied that Parten was a stooge for the majors. Walker accused Parten of working for the major companies when he opposed the Tinsley pipeline, because the line would mainly benefit small independents. He demanded Parten's removal from the OPC. When Davies asked Parten for a written response to Walker's accusations, Parten admitted it was true that Premier had been charged with buying hot oil, but that it was a questionable case. Premier's refinery in Longview had been surrounded by oceans of hot oil since 1934 but no one had ever accused the refinery of running hot oil. The charge that Premier was dependent on major oil companies for crude supply was simply untrue. The vast majority of Premier's oil purchases had always been from independents, with most coming from Woodley, his own production company. Anyone who knew J. R. Parten, knew that he was no stooge for any major oil company. That was the main reason the independents had supported his appointment as head of transportation at the OPC. Walker's testimony was ignored and nothing came of his accusations. Nor was his pipeline built.[59]

Mountains, Floods, and Jehovah's Witnesses

By late August 1942, work was proceeding rapidly on the first section of the Big Inch pipeline, and Parten's office was busily involved in the thousand and one things needed to coordinate the supply of material and monitor construction. There was much to do and there was a great deal at stake. Although no one but the president and those at the highest levels of the military knew when or where it would happen, everyone understood that the Allies would have to open a "second front" against Germany somewhere in Europe. This dangerous and complicated invasion would require a dependable source of enormous amounts of crude oil. The only dependable source for that crude was in Texas. This one pipeline, therefore, was being depended on to move most of the crude oil (five times as much oil as had ever been moved by pipeline) halfway across the continent. Parten's office was not only coordinating the laying of the pipe from Longview to a point east of Little Rock, Arkansas, and then across the Mississippi River to a terminal at Norris City, Illinois, it was putting together a complex system to feed oil from the fields in West and South Texas into the line. The original plan had called for the East Texas field to supply the entire amount of crude for the line, but the refineries on the Texas Gulf Coast depended on East Texas oil to produce automobile and aviation gasoline, butadiene, fuel oil, and other products critical to the military. Oil production was increasing rapidly in the West and South Texas fields, so it was decided to route that oil to Longview. Parten's team had to reverse existing pipelines and dig up and recondition secondhand pipe for use in the new feeder lines. In addition to the pipeline construction, new equipment had to be designed, special anti-corrosion treatments had to be developed, thirty-six pumping stations had to be planned and built to push the oil through, and energy sources had to be found to power the electric motors for the pumps.[60]

While Parten and his staff coordinated the project in Washington, Bert Hull and his team worked in the field with pipeliners with names like Gold Tooth Sam, Airport Slim, and Chew Tobacco Blackie, many of them veterans of pipeline construction in the deserts of the Middle East and in the swamps of Venezuela. Hull's crews worked around the clock to dig a ditch four feet deep and three feet wide to a length that would eventually stretch for fourteen hundred miles through hardwood forests and wet lands, over four-thousand-foot mountains and under thirty rivers and two hundred streams and lakes. The seamless pipe, delivered in sections forty feet in length and weighing two tons, had to be welded together, placed in the ground, and buried. In good weather and favorable terrain Hull's crews laid as much as nine miles of pipe a day. At Norris City, Illinois, the eastern terminus of the first section, one mile of loading racks and seven miles of railway track were built to load tanker cars with oil when the pipeline reached that point.

After the second leg of the line was approved, the mountains of Pennsylvania offered one of the sternest challenges to the builders. There the pipe had to be laid in solid rock and up steep grades in winter, and, in early spring, with snow, ice, and mud creating tremendous difficulties. At one location in the Allegheny Mountains, work crews laid pipe four thousand feet up the side of a mountain in a snowstorm in two days. The work was treacherous. Several large earth-moving machines tumbled down the slopes while the pipe was being laid. Mother Nature slowed the project in other, even more severe ways, especially at the river cross-

The Big Inch pipeline snakes over a ridge in the Appalachians, 1943. *CN 09602. PAW Photograph, courtesy Parten Papers, CAH.*

ings. Among the worst incidents was a flood on the Mississippi River that hit the pipe-laying barges at four o'clock in the morning, December 29, 1942, breaking the lines and dropping the pipe deep into the river mud. It destroyed weeks of intensive labor and damaged tons of new twenty-four-inch pipe. Amazingly, the pipeliners were able to pull the pipe up, repair it, and get it back on line within two days. Severe floods on the Arkansas River also caused extensive damage. One forced the pipeliners to lay a temporary seven-mile line of twenty-inch pipe on the surface of streets running through Little Rock, until the flood subsided and the repair could be made.[61]

A few man-made obstacles also interfered with progress on the line. One occured in Arkansas in mid-September 1942. Jehovah's Witnesses were holding their state convention on the grounds of the Brinkley Hospital, sixteen miles from Little Rock, when a mob including a number of men from Hull's pipeline crew broke into the grounds and savagely attacked many of the Witnesses for refusing to salute the American flag. Six members of the religion were hospitalized, two with gunshot wounds, while many others were seen the next day wearing bandages. The following day, September 19, a gang of pipeliners attacked some of the Witnessess who were camped near the pipeline construction site. Twelve were beaten badly enough to be hospitalized. Seven of the Witnesses were arrested by the local police, but the pipeliners were left alone. The police explained that the Witnesses were conscientious objectors who were obstructing the war effort, while the pipeliners who had initiated the riots and administered the beatings were doing war work. When Parten heard about the incident, which resulted in the loss of precious work time on the pipeline, he called Bert Hull and demanded a written report. Hull's report defended his men and blamed the "goofy-looking" Witnesses who had "made quite a nuisance of themselves, through distribution of copies of a crackpot publication called the *Watchtower*. Hull claimed that the Witnesses told the families of the pipeliners that they could no longer use the restrooms of the "tourist court" they shared with the religious group. "A lady Witness," Hull wrote, "tried to forcibly eject a pipeliner's daughter from the ladies toilet and the girl's mother shoved the Witness, rump first, through the seat. At this point . . . two bearded Jehovah's Witnesses intervened; one had half his beard yanked out by the roots, and the other was slapped in the face with a wet diaper." When the pipeliners returned home that evening, their wives told them about the toilet incident. Hull reported that the pipeliners reacted to this news with understandable indignation. Armed with three-foot lengths of rubber-covered copper cable, they "proceeded to administer a sound beating to every Witness they could outrun." Hull made no mention of the real reason for the beatings—religious bigotry and mindless "patriotism." Parten later admitted that the overwhelming desire to keep the pipeline on schedule, as well as the general hostility most Americans had for the Jehovah's Witnesses because of their refusal to take part in the war, blinded him and his associates to this brutal outrage.[62]

The Big Inch is Completed

As Parten coordinated construction of the first leg of the Big Inch and grappled with other transportation problems, he pushed the War Production Board to release the steel needed to continue the Big Inch from Illinois to the East Coast. When the War Department endorsed the request, Parten told Ickes that he was making the new application "absolutely impregnable" to Nelson's criticisms. Ickes, accompanied by Davies and Parten, made his formal presentation to the WPB on October 26. "I do not believe we can win the war without at least this one pipeline," Ickes stressed. He added that it was doubtful that the big pipeline would be enough; a products line (the "Little Inch") would likely be needed as well. The board approved the request with a unanimous vote. Two weeks later, the United States military spearheaded the Allied landings in North Africa, sending the availability of fuel for civilian use to even lower depths. The need for the Big Inch line was now greater than ever.[63]

Parten finally had the steel with which to complete the Big Inch. Hull could now traverse Indiana and Ohio, jump the Ohio River at the northern tip of West Virginia, and cross southern Pennsylvania to the eastern main-line terminal at Phoenixville, where the line would connect with two twenty-inch lines to Philadelphia and New York. The RFC agreed to finance the second segment for sixty million dollars and work began in late December. By then, Hull's crews had completed the first 531 miles of the Big Inch line in less than 180 days. On December 31, a fifty-mile-long "slug" of water raced through the first segment of the pipe as a pressure test for leaks. No major leaks were found—a remarkable achievement considering how quickly the pipe had been laid. The first Texas crude oil delivered on the Big Inch arrived in Norris City, Illinois, on February 13, 1943. More than a thousand railroad tank cars a day were filled with Texas crude and shipped to the East Coast while the second leg of the line was being constructed.[64]

By the end of 1942, the hard work devoted to the oil transportation crisis by Parten's office and others in the federal war bureaucracy was beginning to pay off. Daily average tank-car deliveries of oil to the East Coast had increased from 98,000 barrels at the start of 1942 to 741,000 barrels by the end; while pipeline deliveries had increased from 64,000 barrels to 159,000 barrels a day. The job Parten thought would take him away from Texas for no more than six months was now in its eighth month, with more work still ahead. With the Big Inch slowly moving toward the Atlantic Coast, an end to the crisis (if not the problems) in oil transportation could at least be visualized. Meanwhile, a more immediate, short-term transportation problem had to be solved to prevent people in New England from freezing to death.[65]

CHAPTER 17

Oil and War

1943

Fuel Crisis in Boston

On the bitterly cold Saturday afternoon of December 19, 1942, J. R. Parten sat in the back seat of a government car as it slowly made its way through the icy side streets of working-class neighborhoods in Boston. He had rushed to Boston to see firsthand the problems caused by the severe fuel-oil shortage. Two days before, Boston's fuel coordinator had declared an emergency because of low inventories of kerosene during an unusually long period of below-freezing weather. Supplies had been placed on a day-to-day, hour-to-hour status. The city's schools, churches, and government buildings were kept open and heated so that families completely without fuel could move in and keep warm.

Exacerbating the problem was an inefficient kerosene distribution system that depended largely on self-employed peddlers who hauled the kerosene around the neighborhoods and sold the fuel out of old dilapidated trucks. Whenever the peddlers were able to get kerosene at the main terminal, they rarely made it very far. Hundreds of housewives and children carrying cans and buckets and bottles mobbed the trucks and drained whatever kerosene the peddlers had. As Parten's car went from one neighborhood to another, he saw people, many of them elderly, standing in more than a foot of snow, in lines stretching in length for several city blocks, holding gallon buckets and bottles to fill with kerosene. No one knew how many people actually depended on kerosene (or "range oil") for cooking and heating in New England, but it was believed to be well over two million, most of whom were poor. In this first full winter of the war, these people were in the grip of the oil transportation crisis with which Parten and his colleagues had been grappling for nine months. The gasoline shortages affected more people, but the heating-oil and kerosene shortages carried more potential danger to human health and safety.[1]

As early as May, Ickes had confided to his diary that the "spectre of cold homes next winter looms ever larger in my mind." Accordingly, Parten and his staff spent much time during the summer of 1942 studying possible short-term remedies to prevent or at least alleviate the coming winter crisis. They determined that 90 percent of the kerosene in the United States was consumed within sixty miles of Boston. Parten also learned that the demand for heating oil was about two and one-half times greater on the East Coast during the winter than in summer. It had been essential, therefore, to build up a reserve during the warm months to provide for winter heating. The OPC imposed fuel-oil rationing on the Midwest so that the surplus could be diverted to northeastern storage tanks. Because of the shorter transport distance from Texas to the Midwest, it was easier to make up shortfalls there than in the Northeast. The OPC asked oil companies to cut their delivery of fuel oil to customers by 25 percent and urged fuel-oil users to convert to readily available coal. Many of the people using kerosene, however, had equipment that could not be converted. The installation of new furnaces was out of the question because there were none to be had, even if people could have afforded them.[2]

Throughout September and October, Parten monitored the delivery of fuel oil to storage facilities on the East Coast. Supplies were so tight that even the slightest hitch in the delivery plan could result in a dangerous shortfall. Inevitably, mishaps and mistakes did occur, resulting in less fuel being delivered than planned. One major problem was a high rate of mechanical breakdowns on tank cars. In September, two different trainloads lost 20 percent of their tank cars. The railroads mistakenly attached a large number of tank cars to regular trains rather than to the special symbol trains, thus slowing deliveries considerably. In October, Parten discovered that refineries had not adjusted their production schedules as planned to make less gasoline and more fuel oil for the coming winter. He complained to Davies, who immediately ordered industry refiners to adjust production accordingly, declaring that "the necessity for some action along these lines seems obvious."[3]

Despite all of Parten's plans and efforts, however, the Allied landings in North Africa in November and the continuing military campaign drained away much of the oil he had moved east. For security reasons, the War Department had not warned Ickes about the landings, so the OPC had not been prepared for them. In mid-November, Ickes complained in his diary that the Navy had informed him of its need for an extra hundred thousand barrels of fuel oil a day—fuel oil the OPC had counted on for heating use in New England in the fast approaching winter. "I am apprehensive of a very serious situation in the East coast," Ickes complained, "as I see it, people are really going to be cold."[4]

Parten and his staff worked to get more kerosene delivered to Boston but they continued to lose ground to the fuel needs of the Allies in North Africa. The kerosene supply fell to its lowest point on Christmas Day. Parten, at his desk throughout the holidays, asked the Navy if it had any fuel oil in storage at New

York harbor that it could spare for Boston. The Navy had been buying fuel oil and moving it to New York without telling the OPC how much it had or when it would be used. When Parten learned that the Navy could spare some fuel oil but that it would take a few days to make it available, he immediately ordered a withdrawal of oil from the civilian supply in New York, which could be transferred without delay to Boston. He would replenish New York's civilian supply with the fuel oil from the Navy. The situation was relieved but only temporarily. New England still had the worst part of the winter ahead and Parten could not depend entirely on oil from the Navy.[5]

As Ickes and Parten drove to a meeting at the White House on New Year's Eve, Ickes told Parten that he was distressed about the situation in New England. Ickes then mentioned that he had learned that oil was being sent to North Africa in steel drums. He wondered if kerosene could also be placed in steel drums and then shipped to Boston in boxcars, which were in ample supply. Parten replied that kerosene is nonflammable and that it could be carried in boxcars, but it would take an enormous supply of steel drums to make any difference. "If you got the drums," Ickes asked, "how much could you deliver?" Parten replied that if the boxcars ran a passenger-train schedule, fifteen thousand barrels could be delivered to Boston daily. Ickes wondered where the drums could be found. "The Army's got two great big mountainous piles of them over in Ohio," Parten answered. "They're planning to ship them eventually to the war theater." As the car pulled up to the White House, Ickes asked, "Major, how many drums do you need?" Parten said at least one million.[6]

Ickes and Parten went to James F. Byrnes's new office in the White House, where they were soon joined by representatives from the Army and the Navy. Byrnes had resigned from the Supreme Court in October to head the recently created Office of Economic Stabilization and coordinate the domestic side of the war effort. He had called the meeting because of the president's concern about the fuel-oil situation in Boston. Ickes announced that he and Parten had developed a plan to ship boxcar loads of fifteen thousand drums filled with kerosene every day from the Gulf Coast to Boston, but they needed an estimated two million drums from the War Department. Ickes's statement alarmed and surprised Parten. "I thought that was moving pretty fast," Parten said, "because I knew that he and Jimmy Byrnes were going to see Mr. Roosevelt after our meeting. I was far from certain that we could load that 15,000 barrels every day in Texas, even if we had the barrels. I moderated his statement as much as I could." Ickes, however, was pleased that Byrnes immediately pledged his support. "Jimmy has gotten a real grasp of the situation by now and wants to be helpful," Ickes wrote in his diary. "We developed the possibility of getting . . . refillable drums from the Army for the transportation of kerosene in box cars to . . . areas where there is a scarcity of kerosene."[7]

After the meeting, Parten called his experts in New York and Houston to see if the project really could be done. Humble Oil economist, Dr. Richard J. Gonzales, assured Parten that around eighty-five hundred drums a day could be loaded without any special effort, probably twice that many if they really worked at it. "I felt like kissing him over the telephone," Parten later remembered. After the cabinet meeting, Ickes telephoned Secretary of War Stimson and asked him for a loan of two hundred thousand steel drums with which to get the movement started. Ickes wrote in his diary that "everyone has been working very hard on this. We are leaving nothing undone to get over the hump."[8]

Three days later, Stimson released two hundred thousand empty drums intended for North Africa. The War Department also directed every U.S. Army post to use their tank trucks for gasoline transport, so that their steel drums could be sent in for the transport of kerosene. The pressure was now on Parten to get the drums unloaded in Boston and turned around quickly enough to keep the operation properly synchronized. He received little help, however, from some of his colleagues at the OPC, which had recently been renamed the Petroleum Administration for War (PAW). Ralph Davies told Parten that his promise to deliver fifteen thousand barrels a day by boxcar was the "most foolish thing he had ever heard of." When Parten asked the Petroleum War Council in January for help in setting up the kerosene project, Pete Jones refused to support the plan. Chairman of the PIWC's transportation committee, Jones complained that it would cost more to ship the kerosene than the kerosene was worth. Parten replied that he knew it was "out of the ordinary, but these are extraordinary times." Harry Weiss of Humble, however, supported Parten. So did John Brown, president of Socony Vacuum (Mobil) and chairman of the production committee of District One in New York. Weiss confirmed that fifteen thousand barrels a day could be loaded on the Gulf Coast, but the same amount had to be unloaded in Boston and the drums returned daily for the program to function properly. Brown promised that Boston would do its part. "The whole effort had to work like a pipeline," Parten recalled, "or we were going to have a hell of a lot of boxcars stacking up and interfering with other transportation." Over Pete Jones's strenuous objections, the PIWC finally accepted Parten's proposal and authorized Wiess and Brown to work out the details.[9]

Brown's engineers subsequently devised a make-shift invention for quickly emptying the drums, characterized by one observer as "a contraption that would have delighted Rube Goldberg, but it worked." With the Reconstruction Finance Corporation's agreement to pay the extra cost of transporting the kerosene, Parten pasted together a complicated system of loading in Texas and unloading in Boston. He also arranged a schedule of nonstop trains. On January 13, about two weeks after Ickes and Parten told the White House it could be done, the first shipment of 3,200 barrels of kerosene in steel drums left the Gulf Coast. Deliveries quickly built up to Parten's promised 15,000 barrels a day, peaked at 25,000 barrels a day in July, and eventually averaged 20,000 barrels a day. The Defense Supplies Corporation built an additional supply of new drums and by the end of the war, 7.2 million barrels of kerosene had been shipped to New England in steel drums in boxcars.[10]

Parten later said that the role he had played in getting the kerosene shipments to Boston was his most personally satisfying accomplishment at the PAW. The boxcar shipments of drummed kerosene prevented widespread suffering among the large number of people in New England who depended on the fuel for heating and cooking. After the program proved to be a success and received much public praise from New England's newspapers and political leaders, Ralph Davies and Pete Jones abandoned their opposition to the shipments. The first question Davies asked every day when he arrived in the PAW office was "how many box cars will move today?" The project became so popular politically that Parten was unable to stop it when the completion of the Big Inch pipeline freed enough tank cars to make the boxcar shipments unnecessary. In late August 1943, Parten drafted a directive to stop the shipments. Drum and boxcar delivery was costing fifty-five thousand dollars a day more than delivery by tank car and a quarter of the drums were needed now by the Army. The PIWC rejected Parten's directive, ironically because of Pete Jones's objections that the shipments were too popular with Congress to stop. Parten complained to Davies that a continuation of the shipments exposed the PAW to a "most embarrassing" charge of waste. Davies ignored Parten's complaint. Except for a few months in 1944, the shipments continued until the end of the war.[11]

"If anybody delays this pipeline now, it's not going to be me"

Despite the effectiveness of Parten's overall program, the military's rapidly increasing need for petroleum products resulted in continued transportation problems for most of 1943. The task of Parten's Transportation Division was to meet the military's fuel needs while also keeping industrial plants in operation around the clock. Until the completion of the Big Inch line from Texas to the East Coast, however, civilian use was restricted. Even the Big Inch would fail to help the domestic situation once the anticipated assault on France took place. Nevertheless, a number of members of Congress, responding to intense pressure from constituents, pressured the PAW and its Transportation Division to increase the availability of petroleum products for civilian use, particularly gasoline for private automobiles. Throughout the first half of 1943, Parten devoted much time responding to congressional suggestions about how to get more oil to the East Coast. The Congress pushed ideas such as transferring more tank cars from the West Coast to the East Coast (there were none to transfer); forming huge oil-truck caravans stretching from Texas to New York (a waste of gasoline, rubber tires, and manpower); and using concrete barges. Replacing steel with concrete in pipelines and barges was an especially popular idea, despite the fact that it required as much, or more, steel to reinforce the concrete as it took to build entirely with steel.[12]

In late January, as progress continued on construction of the Big Inch, Parten could see that the military's insatiable demand for oil products was not going to be anywhere near offset by the help received from the huge pipeline. It was time to ask the War Production Board (WPB) for the steel for the western section of the second big line, the so-called Little Inch products line, to extend from the refining region in the Beaumont–Port Arthur area in Texas to Little Rock, Arkansas, from where it would run parallel to the Big Inch all the way to Seymour, Indiana. A products line had been accorded a lower priority by the Tulsa Plan, and a shortage of construction equipment had made it impossible to build the Big Inch and Little Inch pipelines simultaneously. Construction of the Big Inch had now reached a point that would allow the release of heavy equipment for use on the western section of the second line, and on January 18 Parten submitted his formal request to the WPB. Now that Ickes was a member of the board, it approved the request in record time, just eight days after submission.[13]

As soon as it was announced that Parten had his steel for the western section of the twenty-inch line, railroad executives from the Southwest pleaded with him to reverse his plan and build first from the East Coast to the Midwest. The southwestern railroads were upset because of business they had lost because the Big Inch was built from the Southwest. After the western section of the Big Inch had been completed and while the eastern section was being built, oil from the line flowed into an enormous tank farm at Norris City, Illinois. At the tank farm the oil was loaded into railroad tank cars and rushed to the East Coast, cutting the rail haul by seven hundred miles. The southwestern railroads now argued that for the sake of equity, the first leg of the Little Inch should begin on the East Coast and stop in Indiana, where the railroads would transport products to send via the pipeline to the East. The railroads received support from pipeline owners, such as Wade Phillips of Phillips Petroleum, who owned an eight-inch products line running from Tulsa to Chicago and realized that if the twenty-inch pipeline was completed from Texas to Indiana and the war should end before the eastern section was built, it would make Phillips's eight-inch pipeline obsolete. Midwestern refiners joined the protest out of fear that refined products could be cheaply routed through the pipeline from Texas and sold in the Midwest, depriving them of their market.[14]

Parten wanted to build from the Midwest to the Southwest first, toward the source of oil rather than away from it. The southwestern link could also be built much faster than the eastern link because of the Appalachian Mountains. With the strong help of Harry Sinclair, however, the plan's opponents persuaded Ickes to make a new study to determine the best beginning point for construction. Parten objected, pointing out that Sinclair had a personal stake in the outcome—if the war ended early, the eastern section of the line would be available to move his South American crude from New York to his refineries in the Midwest. Parten also stressed that the industry committee had worked out the pipeline program after months of study and work crews were already stringing pipe from Beaumont to Longview. "If anybody delays this pipeline now," Parten declared, "it's not going to be me. But I'm damn sure going to let the world know who did delay it." Parten thought Ickes might demand his resignation, but Ickes replied: "Don't worry Major. We're not going to delay it. Just make another study and make sure you're right, but keep building the pipeline."[15]

While Parten's staff "restudied" the pipeline plan, the midwestern group attracted the attention of Sen. Harry Truman's powerful committee investigating the nation's defense program. The Truman committee held hearings on the controversy on February 17, 1943. B. L. "Barney" Majewski of Deep Rock Oil in Chicago, and C. R. Musgrave, vice president of Phillips Petroleum, charged that the PAW had not consulted with oil men in the Midwest about which segment of the Little Inch pipeline should be built first and claimed that they had learned about the final plan at the last minute. Parten denied these accusations. He presented documents showing that Majewski had participated in the original planning sessions in April 1942. Parten explained that there were not enough railroad tank cars in the Southwest to move the oil to the pipeline while it was being built from the East to the Midwest. In addition, the western section could be built much faster than the eastern, which would mean a quick increase of twenty thousand barrels of product a day delivered to the East Coast. When Sen. E. H. Moore of Oklahoma asked if the Big and Little Inch lines would hurt Oklahoma's economy after the war, Parten commented, "one can concern oneself greatly over what might happen after the war, but . . . we have a job to do and that job is to furnish petroleum when and where it is needed to help win the war." Ickes was pleased with Parten's handling of the issue, noting in his diary that Parten had made a "real impression" on the Truman committee.[16]

At the beginning of March, Parten told Ickes that his division had completed the new study of the Little Inch route and had found no reason to change the original plan. When Ickes and Parten appeared before the Truman committee again on March 3, Ickes distributed copies of the study and announced that it proved construction of the Little Inch would have to begin in Texas. "We are not going to change our decision," Ickes declared. After the hearing adjourned, Truman met privately with Ickes and Parten and told them that he would "handle the opposition in the Senate." Although Parten had objected to Ickes's request that he produce yet another study, he admitted later that "politically it was the wise thing to do." The controversy ended, however, when the WPB agreed on April 2 to release the steel to finish both sections of the Little Inch line. The pipeline would not stop in the Midwest.[17]

The Barge Canal That Would Not Die

Parten had little time to celebrate the news that the WPB had released the steel for the last section of Little Inch. Claude Pepper and his cohorts had breathed new life into the Florida barge-canal proposal. As a result, Parten was forced once again to deal with the issue. Fortunately, he continued to have Senator Vandenberg's support. In a debate on the canal in the Senate on March 5, Vandenberg declared that the Florida barge canal could not be justified as the best and most efficient use of critical materials and manpower. Acknowledging that Parten had given him "the official facts to date," Vandenberg concluded that "they obviously . . . collide with the Florida canal lobby—and so do I." The arguments Parten, Vandenburg, and their allies made against the Florida barge-canal project led to its narrow defeat in the Senate Appropriations Committee. As an example of the bitterness generated by these battles over domestic war projects, Florida congressman Joe Hendricks, one of the canal's most vocal supporters, declared that Parten's successful campaign to kill the project had resulted in "a worse disaster than Pearl Harbor" for the nation's war effort.[18]

Continuing Problems in Congress

New problems broke out in New England while Parten was dealing with the Florida barge canal. The boxcar kersosene shipments had relieved the heating shortage, but gasoline supply remained a serious problem. With warm weather, civilian gasoline consumption increased (despite compulsory rationing) and gasoline stocks plunged. On March 22, the Office of Price Administration reduced the value of gasoline coupons for the East Coast region by 50 percent because of falling inventories and increasing military demands. Congressional representatives from the northeastern states reacted badly to this reduction. Some blamed the PAW, especially its Transportation Division, for the gasoline shortage, despite the obvious external conditions and the absence of any PAW rationing authority. On April 12, Sen. Styles Bridges of New Hampshire charged that New England was being discriminated against in the allotment of fuel oil and gasoline. "A product shortage is one thing; transportation another," he declared. "If it is a question of transportation, then it is time the men responsible for the job either do that job or get out and let someone else do it."[19]

Parten did not respond directly to Bridges's attack. For one thing, he, Davies, and Ickes had made dozens of appearances before congressional committees, given speeches to a number of organizations, and provided as much information as they could about the fuel situation. For security reasons the PAW could not make public the estimates they were now receiving from the War Department about the enormous amounts of fuel the military needed for the war in the Pacific and for the cross-Channel invasion of France, now scheduled for the first of May 1944. By the spring of 1943 the U.S. Navy had driven most of the German submarines away from the Gulf of Mexico and the south Atlantic, but now those freed-up tankers would be needed to ferry the required fuel to the distant battlefronts. The best Parten could do in the way of a response to criticism about the continuing fuel shortage was his answer to Massachusetts congressman John McCormack about gasoline rationing. Parten explained that petroleum stocks on the Atlantic seaboard were at an "all-time low," and that it was imperative that they be restored to levels that would safeguard the essential petroleum requirements for the coming winter, both domestically and for offshore shipment to the fighting fronts. "Because of these factors," Parten declared, "we cannot at this time anticipate any relaxation in the present restrictions on gasoline and heating-oil consumption."

Political pressure on Parten's office continued throughout the summer of 1943. In June, for example, the representatives of the twelve eastern states most affected by the gasoline shortage organized an informal bipartisan caucus to devise ways of improving the fuel situation. Parten was called to appear before the caucus several times. At a meeting on June 10, Fred Hartley, a Republican congressman from New Jersey who had organized the caucus, told Parten that the PAW should order the movement of an additional two hundred thousand barrels of gasoline a day to the East Coast for civilian drivers during the summer. Parten replied that

A BREED SO RARE

there was no way he could get more gasoline for the summer, especially for pleasure driving. Although he admitted that supplies would be significantly increased
when the Big Inch and the Little Inch lines were completed in the coming months,
Parten warned that the military would soak up the extra fuel. Early in July, Sen.
Henry Cabot Lodge Jr. of Massachusetts demanded that the military seize some
refineries and a few oil fields to produce fuel for their use only and leave the rest
for civilian needs. Parten assured Lodge that his proposal would "harm rather than
help the situation." Boston congressman James M. Curley wrote Parten that the
Boston Automobile Club was demanding an investigation of the gasoline supply
problem. He wondered if a public hearing should be held in Boston at which
Parten could appear and explain the situation. Parten told Congressman Curley
that another hearing would do no good because the public could not be given the
figures on how much fuel the military really needed, and that was the essence of
the problem. "The estimates Ickes was getting from the War Department about
fuel needs for future offensive operations scared the hell out of us all," Parten later
recalled. "Obviously we couldn't tell this to the public. So naturally the people who
bore the brunt of the shortages weren't satisfied with our vague statements about
'unknown military needs'."[20]

"A man who can commit fraud to get steel for a . . . pipeline . . . shouldn't need my help"

Parten dealt with all these problems at once. His meetings with the northeastern congressional delegations over the fuel shortage coincided with his confrontation with the midwestern refiners over the Little Inch pipeline and with the Senate
debate on the Florida barge canal. As was true with most of the managers of hard-
pressed war agencies, Parten switched from issue to issue several times a day, while
simultaneously trying to keep Ickes, Davies, and his industry committees happy.
In addition, throughout the spring and summer of 1943, minor crises involving the
ongoing construction of the Big Inch and Little Inch lines as well as the smaller
pipelines, occurred on a weekly basis. Although there were no typical days at the
PAW, some are illustrative of Parten's task. On Wednesday, July 7, Parten began the
day with a Transportation Division staff meeting. He spent the rest of the morning
on the telephone trying to find a replacment for the director of transportation in
the PAW's office in Houston; talking to Congressman Hartley about the gasoline
situation; dealing with the PAW's draft office about a military deferment for his
assistant; setting up a meeting with the Army for the next day; and speaking with
John Brown in New York City about fuel supplies in his region. He passed up
lunch to work on his correspondence. The afternoon included another lengthy
telephone conference with John Brown about the situation in New York; a call to
the Army about the boxcar deliveries of kerosene; a discussion with a senator
about a proposed pipeline from Albany, New York, to Boston; and a meeting with
a staff member about a report on the heating-oil situation for the coming winter.
It was often tedious, frequently frustrating, always exhausting work—and Parten
thrived on it.[21]

290

Despite an occasional public criticism from people such as Senator Bridges or pipeline contractor Aldace Walker, Parten had the respect of most of the industry, military, and political leaders with whom he had dealings. Early in June, several members of the PIWC urged Davies to make Parten one of his three assistant deputy directors, with transportation and supply remaining as one of his responsibilities. Parten's boosters felt that as an assistant deputy director, he could also serve as an effective PAW liaison with Congress on matters not necessarily related to transportation. On June 8, the Fort Worth *Star-Telegram* reported a rumor that Secretary Ickes was going to appoint Parten to such a post. The newspaper stated that Parten had been credited "for much of the sucess which has been secured in moving oil to the East by rail." Parten, however, refused the job when Ickes offered it, explaining that he preferred to stay where he was and concentrate on finishing the big pipelines. Once that job was complete, he wanted to return to Texas.[22]

Parten also refused the appointment because of his increasingly strained relationship with Davies. Parten did not like the way Davies was running the PAW and he did not want to become a part of his office. Parten and Davies clashed frequently during the summer of 1943. For example, when Davies's inattention to a priority request from Parten resulted in another federal agency having to take the matter out of PAW hands, Parten complained to Davies that the incident was typical of the way the PAW was being managed. "Subjects drift from one department of PAW to another," Parten complained. "A state of indecision, delay, inefficiency, and chaos exists." He demanded that Davies delegate authority to deal with other federal agencies to an assistant because Davies's insistence that every request go over his desk was slowing work down to an unacceptable pace.[23]

Parten also had a confrontation with Davies over one of Pete Jones's projects. In early August 1943, Humble Oil president Harry Weiss informed Parten that Jones had just completed a sixty-five-mile-long pipeline, made of new steel, to his huge new Cities Service Refinery in Lake Charles without going through Parten's office as policy required. Parten was outraged. He had promised the WPB that no private projects requiring new steel would be initiated. Parten soon discovered that E. D. Cumming, director of the PAW's Refining Division, had included the Cities Service pipeline when he approved the new refinery. Parten complained to Cumming that he had not been informed about the Cities Service line and that the action appeared to be "very irregular."[24]

Parten believed that the application could not have gone through without Davies's knowledge. "I jumped Davies," Parten recalled. "He said he didn't know anything about it. I found that to be pretty incredible, because he and Pete were very, very close." Parten told Davies that the approval was "highly discriminatory and unethical. It makes us look like liars to WPB." Davies denied any involvement. Shortly thereafter, Jones went to Parten to ask his help in getting some tank cars released for his new refinery. "Well, you shouldn't need my help on a thing like that," Parten told Jones. "A man who can commit fraud to get steel for a . . . pipeline from Sour Lake, Texas, all the way to Lake Charles, Louisiana, shouldn't need my help." Jones stormed out of Parten's office. "That's what I wanted him to do," Parten said. "I wouldn't help him at all. Jones got over it, but he was surprised that I caught him."[25]

The incident angered Parten as an example of inside dealing and favoritism, something many independents feared would be all too prevalent in a PAW with a major oil company executive at its head. Parten later admitted that some favoritism did occur but that it was extremely rare. Some independents, of course, tried to bend the rules for personal gain. In the fall of 1943, Texas independent Eugene B. Germany, an ultra-conservative Democrat who spearheaded the anti-Roosevelt movement in Texas in 1944, led a group of investors who wanted to build a private pipeline across Florida. Germany and his partners tried to sneak a request for new pipe around Parten. "They knew it was against the policy of my department to approve new steel for private lines that had little or nothing to do with the war effort." Parten found out about the scheme when Sam Rayburn asked him if the Transportation Division was sticking to its policy not to approve requests for new steel pipelines. When Parten said the policy remained in force, Rayburn frowned and said: "'You mean there are no requests in your department for new pipe?'" Parten replied that he was not aware of any. "I could tell Mr. Rayburn was plainly disturbed," Parten recalled. "He gave me that withering scowl of his and said, 'You better go back and find out what's going on in your office. I've been told on good authority that a request for new pipe made its way through your shop.'"[26]

The next morning, Parten discovered that Gene Germany had gone around the Transportation Division and slipped his application to R. E. Allen, one of Davies's assistant deputies. Contrary to PAW policy, Allen approved the application and sent it over to the Defense Plant Corporation. Parten called the plant and learned that the application was there with Allen's signature for approval. Parten explained that the application violated PAW policy and should not have been approved. The request was returned to Parten's office and the pipeline was killed. "I went right back to see Mr. Rayburn," Parten later recalled. "I showed him the rejected application and thanked him for tipping me off." Rayburn explained that he had learned about the application when one of Germany's partners called his office seeking his help with Jesse Jones to get the application through the Defense Plant Corporation. Two pipelines were slipped around me that I know of," Parten later noted. "I stopped one, but Pete Jones' pipeline had already been built when I learned about it. Those were the only two."[27]

Problems with the Big Inch

As the Big Inch neared completion in the summer of 1943, Parten had to confront two developments that threatened to delay the project for months beyond its scheduled finish. On July 14, anticipating that the Big Inch would reach Philadelphia by mid-August, Parten ordered the first oil to be pumped into the Big Inch pipeline at Norris City, Illinois. In early August, Parten received the news that the Big Inch had crossed the Susquehanna River, its last major obstacle in

Parten leads a PAW inspection team on the Big Inch pipeline project, June 1943. *CN 09603. PAW Photograph, courtesy Parten Papers, CAH.*

Pennsylvania. Parten ordered an immediate increase in oil-flow out of Texas. A few days later, however, Parten learned that the Susquehanna had not been crossed. There had been a delay because of the need to blast a pipe trench through solid rock in the riverbed. A serious mess occurred at Norris City because more oil was coming out of the line than could be handled there. Parten transferred tank cars from other routes (causing disruptions throughout the entire delivery system) and rushed them to Norris City to take the oil and deliver it to the East Coast. On August 13, Bert Hull told Parten that the Big Inch line had crossed the Susquehanna River the evening before and that crude oil was moving east. On August 14, 1943, the world's largest oil pipeline poured its first crude into storage tanks at the Sinclair and Sun refineries at Marcus Hook, near Philadelphia.[28]

Only the branch line to New York remained for the completion of the Big Inch, and it was scheduled to be finished within a few weeks. On August 26, however, Hull gave Parten the distressing news that the branch had developed serious leaks. Because of an unanticipated shortage of seamless pipe, Hull and Parten had been forced to use electric-welded twenty-inch pipe on this section of the Big Inch as well as on the eastern section of the Little Inch. Some of the pipe was splitting at the joints because the seams had been improperly welded at the mill. The problem was so serious that the pipeline could not reopen until October. Parten was forced to re-route railroad tanker cars to carry the oil to New York, once again disrupting the entire transportation system. Newspapers immediately broke the news about the leaks, resulting in a wave of telephone calls from congressional offices wanting to know if the shutdown would affect the heating-fuel situation in the coming winter.[29]

Problems at Woodley

When Parten accepted his appointment in Washington, D.C., he created an executive committee for Woodley Petroleum composed of geologist Ernest Funkhouser, treasurer Joe Pope, and Howard Davenport to manage the company in his absence. The executive committee administered the day-to-day affairs of Woodley, but Parten delegated ultimate authority to Howard Davenport for overall company operations. Davenport had been with Parten since 1919 when he joined Woodley as a laborer in the Pine Island field. In July, while he was grappling with pipeline problems, Funkhouser sent word to Parten that the executive committee was breaking down—the victim of petty jealousy, personality conflicts, and internal power plays.[30] Funkhouser charged that his fellow committee members Pope and Davenport were inept managers who had bred "distrust, bitterness, fear, and suspicion" among the staff, with the result that "the morale of the entire organization" had been damaged. Deeply concerned, Parten flew to Houston on August 17 to order Davenport and Pope to patch up their differences with Funkhouser. The peace Parten thought he had imposed on his managers fell apart within days, however. In late August, while Parten was confronting the leak problem on the Big Inch branch line, he received a letter from Pope announcing his resignation effective in October. "I am now convinced that Ernest [Funkhouser] will continue to dictate the policies of the company," Pope declared. "Since I have no confidence in Ernest. I feel that the only fair thing for all concerned is to remove myself from the scene."[31]

With the Big Inch pipeline leaking all over eastern Pennsylvania and western New Jersey and members of Congress wanting to know why it had not been repaired, it was impossible for Parten to go to Houston to settle this latest in-house squabble. The situation soon grew worse. A Woodley directors' meeting broke up in disarray on September 9 as a result of a bitter argument that nearly resulted in a fistfight between Davenport and Bill Moran, a director and major stockholder. Despite being overwhelmed with pipeline problems, Parten had little choice but to rush to Houston to save his company from being torn apart by personal disputes between its managers. On September 18 he flew to Texas and met with Moran and the members of the management committee. Parten accepted Joe Pope's resignation and succeeded in getting a pledge from the remaining members of his mangement team that they would work together without further dispute. He promised to finish his PAW duties by the end of November and to reassume the presidency of Woodley as soon as possible after that. The knowledge that Parten would be reassuming control before the end of the year seemed to establish at least the semblance of harmony within the company.[32]

"He has done a real job"

In early October, Parten finally received some good news. Bert Hull's work crews repaired the leaks in the Big Inch and oil was flowing to New York. On October 8, the western section of the Little Inch to Norris City was completed and construction was well under way on the eastern section. The most important part of the transportation job had been completed. Fearful that his company was falling apart in his absence, Parten decided that this would be a good time to resign. The industry now had to produce enough oil to fill the pipelines and that was not going to be easy. By returning to Woodley to produce more oil, Parten would be working to solve the newest problem.[33]

Parten went to Fort Worth on October 14 to accept the Distinguished Service Award from the Texas Division of the Mid-Continent Oil and Gas Association for his work at the PAW. Harry Weiss, who had worked closely with Parten as chairman of the District Three industry committee, made the award presentation at the association banquet. Weiss described the man with whom he had worked so well for the last two years as a "determined, tenacious, ingenious man. Whenever he gets an assignment, he is satisfied with nothing less than a complete mastery of the task. He has done a brilliant job in the field of transportation." Because this award was given to him by people in the industry with whom he had often disagreed, and opposed politically, it pleased Parten as much as any recognition he would receive in the future. Among those who had made the decision to recognize Parten's work at the PAW were Charles Roeser, Hugh Roy Cullen, J. S. Bridwell, J. Edgar Pew, and John Pew—all men who had fought Parten, sometimes bitterly, in other arenas in the 1930s.[34]

Submitting his resignation to Ralph Davies on October 21, 1943, to be effective on November 20, Parten emphasized that the problems at Woodley required his return. "As serious as the calls are for my return [to Woodley]," Parten stressed, "I would hesitate to go were it not a fact that the transportation problem . . . is now definitely under control." Parten was also confident that George Wilson, whom he recommended as his successor, could direct the Transportation Division as well or better than he had. Davies agreed with Parten's assessment of the transportation situation. A few hours after his meeting with Parten, Davies declared at a congressional committee hearing that in the matter of transportation, he was "pleased—and I confess just a trifle proud—to be able to say that this, our first major problem in the [PAW], has been virtually solved. Generally speaking, we can move the oil that we have to the places where we need to move it." Parten's division and the transportation industry, Davies declared, had won a "transportation victory" by managing to increase oil shipments by rail from 5,000 barrels daily to more than a million; pipeline deliveries from 42,000 barrels a day to 385,000; and barge shipments from 64,000 barrels daily to 168,000. Parten and his division had succeeded in supervising the creation of a transportation system that would be able to provide the fuel for the coming invasion of France.[35]

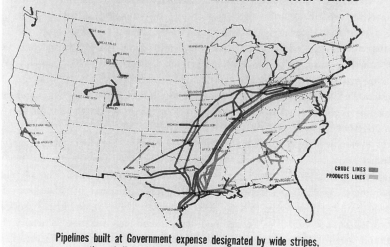

CN 09613. *From John W. Frey and H. Chandler Ides (eds.),* A History of the Petroleum Administration for War, 1941–1945 *(Washington, D.C.: Government Printing Office, 1946), ff 102.*

Humble Oil president Harry Weiss presents Parten with the Mid-Continent Oil and Gas Association Distinguished Service Award, October 14, 1943. *CN 09633. Courtesy Parten Photograph Collection, CAH.*

"People whose names are largely unknown but whose achievements were extraordinary"

The last major project Parten completed before leaving the PAW was to rearrange railroad tank car movements to carry oil products from the Little Inch terminus in Illinois to the East Coast. Although he hoped that the Little Inch would be able to carry those products by the time the last pipe had been laid in early December, Parten feared that serious leakage problems that had developed in the welded pipe of the Big Inch's twenty-inch crude branch-line would delay completion of the Little Inch. The railroad tank cars served as a back-up just in case they were needed; and, as it turned out, they were. On November 23, his last official day at the PAW, Parten informed Davies that more leaks had developed, mainly as a result of defective pipe. He added, however, that the large increase in tank car movements to the East Coast should prevent any serious difficulties. It was fortunate that the railroads were able to maintain shipments. During hydrostatic testing of the Little Inch pipe, ninety-five ruptures occurred in the welded portions of the pipe. In addition, eleven miles of pipe in the mountains of Pennsylvania had to be dug up and relaid. Because of these and other problems, the Little Inch line was not in full operation until March 1944.[36]

When the PAW announced Parten's resignation on November 22, 1943, the New York *Times* headline declared "Parten to Leave PAW, Wins Praise of Ickes." Ickes stated his "sincere regret that Parten is unable to remain. When we induced him to come to Washington, the PAW . . . faced the . . . complete rebuilding of the oil transportation system. . . . The problem was so acute and so formidable that there were many who doubted that it could be solved as long as the war lasted. But in twenty months, it has been virtually solved and I do not know of any individual who has worked more tirelessly or more effectively than Major Parten in bringing that solution about." Ickes's praise was sincere. In his diary, where Ickes never hesitated to make critical remarks about his associates, he noted Parten's departure and wrote that he had done a "splendid job."[37]

The work Parten did at the PAW received excellent reviews from the military and from the oil industry in general, including both majors and independents. General Pyron of the Army-Navy Petroleum Board expressed the military's view to Harold Ickes after Parten's departure. Parten's "cooperation with the Armed Services has been of the highest order," Pyron stated, "and this is the principal regret I have in his resignation. The oil industry certainly owes him a deep debt of gratitude for the splendid work he has done. . . ." James H. Pipkin, an executive with Texaco, expressed the view of one of the leading oil companies. "I truly believe that your contribution is one of the outstanding aids to the war effort," Pipkin told Parten, "and your accomplishments, under great pressure, should serve as an eternal memorial to your hard work and personal sacrifice." Praise for Parten's accomplishments also came from the chairman of the Texas Railroad Commission, Beauford Jester, who told the Houston *Chronicle* that "Major

Parten's energy and initiative enabled solution of the transportation problem in a remarkably short time . . . now we are moving more oil than ever."[38]

Parten also received praise from a number of congressmen. A letter from Oklahoma senator J. Elmer Thomas was typical of most. "[I am] sorry that one of the very few oil men in whom the entire oil industry had utmost confidence, has left PAW's staff," Thomas told Parten, "no man joined that organization more needed or more wanted than yourself. . . ." Parten's efforts were not universally praised, however. His opposition to the Tinsley field pipeline earned him, as well as Davies and Ickes, the enmity of Rep. Mendel "Pork Barrel" Rivers, chairman of the Petroleum Subcommittee of the House Committee on Naval Affairs. Rivers's subcommittee issued a report one month prior to Parten's departure attacking the PAW for "bungling . . . and its favoritism to the large oil companies." Parten later said that Rivers "was mad because we had stopped one of his pet projects—and for damn good reason. Undoubtedly our action deprived the Congressman of some income." Although Parten chose to ignore the Rivers committee's report, he would be forced to deal with it when he returned to government service during the Korean War.[39]

By the time Parten left Washington, he had played a significant role in initiating a complete revolution in the petroleum transportation system of the United States. Oil, which in prewar years flowed in all directions to meet the economic needs of individual companies had been made to move mostly north and east. Trucks had taken over almost all fuel delivery for distances of up to two hundred miles. And tank cars, barges, and pipelines had almost completely replaced ocean tankers in supplying the East Coast. In the pipeline field, Parten's team performed one of the most spectacular jobs on the home front of the war. His division supervised the construction or reconversion of more than ten thousand miles of pipelines. Of course, the Transportation Division's most visible successes were the Big Inch and Little Inch pipelines. Both lines were built at less expense than had been anticipated and both eventually performed beyond expectations. Jesse Jones later noted that "although many of the wartime projects inevitably failed to pay for themselves, quite a number turned in spectacular profits. Two of these were the Big Inch and Little Big Inch pipe lines. . . ." The Big Inch cost seventy-seven million dollars and eventually carried well over 245 million barrels of crude during the war; while the Little Inch cost sixty-five million dollars and delivered 102 million barrels of refined products such as aviation fuel and automobile gasoline. Together both pipelines carried about 379 million barrels of crude oil and products from Texas to the East Coast.[40]

The achievements of the PAW and its Transportation Division were underscored when high-ranking military officers from Germany and Japan cited the Allies' seemingly inexhaustible supply of aviation gasoline and other petroleum products as one of the chief reasons for their defeat. Even Joseph Stalin acknowledged the critical role played by United States oil. Offering a toast to Winston Churchill at a banquet in Moscow, the Soviet leader proclaimed: "This is a war of engines and octanes. I drink to the American auto industry and the American oil industry."[41]

Many years after the war, J. R. Parten was asked who contributed the most to this hugely successful wartime oil-transportation effort. He gave his answer without hesitation: "Of course, Harold Ickes is due most of the credit." He then looked out the living-room window of his home in Madisonville and was quiet for a long moment. Eventually, Parten turned back toward his interviewer and said that he would also stay with the answer he had given when asked that same question in an interview during the war:

> To my mind, a list of those who did the most would have to include the seamen who signed on again after having their ships blown out from under them, the pipe line crewmen who worked in bitterly cold weather and icy conditions laying pipe through the Allegheny mountains, the rail crews that kept the tank car movements on schedule despite the hopelessly crowded tracks, and the truck drivers and maintenance men who sometimes worked on twenty-four hour shifts to deliver critically needed fuel regardless of weather or road conditions. People whose names are largely unknown but whose achievements were extraordinary.[42]

CHAPTER 18

The Rainey Affair

1944

When Parten returned to Houston in December 1943, he acted decisively to end Woodley's operational problems. He reassumed Woodley's presidency, dissolved the contentious management committee, and hired Houston land-law specialist Marlin Elijah Sandlin as the company's new secretary-treasurer. Sandlin, a thirty-four-year-old graduate of the University of Texas Law School, also joined Woodley's board of directors. Woodley's oil reserves had been reduced and the company badly needed to find new oil production. Parten traveled throughout the southern sections of Mississippi, Alabama, and Georgia, overseeing wildcat operations and hunting for and buying leases.[1]

Parten's attention was drawn back to Texas in the fall of 1944, however, as a result of a serious dispute at the University of Texas between Homer Rainey and the board of regents. Since Parten's departure from the board in 1941, Governor O'Daniel and his successor, Coke Stevenson, had packed the board with conservatives who believed the university was overrun with politically subversive New Dealers, moral perverts, and other undesirables. The regents made it their mission to muzzle Rainey and his faculty supporters and to prevent the university from generating or providing the inspiration for economic, political, and social reform. Rainey's defense of the professors targeted for dismissal because of what the regents deemed inappropriate teachings convinced the regents that Rainey too should be purged. The highly publicized struggle that ensued dramatically affected the university's national reputation and polarized the Texas Democratic Party. It also profoundly influenced Parten's political views and the role he would play in state politics as a fund-raiser and campaign organizer.

"We want you to fire these men"

Ever since Parten's departure in February 1941, Homer Rainey had experienced increasingly serious problems with the board of regents, which had been packed with members whose view of the university and its faculty differed radically from that of Rainey and Parten. Regent Fred Branson had died of a stroke in June 1942. O'Daniel had been elected to the U.S. Senate, so his successor, Coke Stevenson, appointed conservative rancher Scott Schreiner of Kerrville as Branson's replacement. When regent E. J. Blackert resigned unexpectedly a few days after Branson's death, Stevenson appointed in his place Judge D. Frank Strickland, an attorney and corporate lobbyist from Mission, a town in the Rio Grande valley. Schreiner and Strickland immediately joined with Orville Bullington and Dan Harrison to form an anti-Rainey bloc of regents. Adding to Rainey's difficulties were his disputes with longtime regents Hilmer Weinert and Lutcher Stark over athletic matters.[2]

Led by Orville Bullington, this new board majority believed that the university was overrun with politically subversive undesirables who advocated such dangerous ideas as labor unionism, civil rights for blacks, federal fair labor standards and antitrust laws, and corporate and personal income taxes. They had no intention of allowing the state's dominant institution of higher education to be run by people who threatened the state's political, social, and economic status quo.[3]

The Bullington group began their work as soon as Schreiner and Strickland took their places on the board of regents. At the first meeting attended by the new appointees, in June 1942, Strickland handed a small card to Rainey with the names of four economics professors written on it. "We want you to fire these men," Strickland said, "we don't like what they are teaching." Rainey was not surprised to see that the list included Bob Montgomery and Clarence Ayres, but he was shocked by Strickland's matter-of-fact attitude about such a serious request. Rainey explained that the professors were tenured and could not be fired without going through the complicated process established by the regents' own rules. Since Strickland had no other charges than not liking what the professors taught, he reluctantly dropped the matter, but only after telling Rainey that the rules would have to be changed. Temporarily defeated by the tenure rule, the Bullington group attacked four instructors in the Economics Department who were not protected by tenure. Three months earlier, the four instructors had publicly criticized an antilabor rally in Dallas presided over by Karl Hoblitzelle, owner of an extensive chain of movie theaters and one of Strickland's clients. After the protest, Federal District judge T. Whitfield Davidson had complained to Bullington about the instructors. "It seems that we have a branch of our University . . . routing our children into the camp of State Socialism. . . ." He demanded a purge of the Department of Economics and Bullington was happy to comply. After a token hearing and over President Rainey's heated objections, the instructors were dismissed.[4]

At a subsequent meeting of the board, Frank Strickland introduced a motion to require all university employees to take a written examination designed to reveal disloyal beliefs. The exam included such questions as "do you believe in communism? would you fight for your country if asked? and do you support the US government?" Strickland explained that it was needed because of evidence he had of Communist activity among the faculty. When Rainey demanded proof,

Strickland explained that he had transcripts of Clarence Ayres's lectures in which he called for the federal government to issue millions of dollars so that people could buy consumer goods in times of depression. Rainey explained that this idea was Keynesian, not Marxist. Strickland's motion died for lack of a second, not because of Rainey's explanation, but because the other regents believed subversive faculty would not answer the questions truthfully.[5]

Rainey's spirited defense of the dismissed instructors and the Economics Department convinced regent Bullington that Rainey was among those who should be purged. Bullington confided to a friend that Rainey "does not believe . . . in our system of government" and that the president had to be removed as soon as possible before he stocked the university with more "radicals of his stripe." Bullington's concern deepened when he reviewed a batch of scholarly social science journals at the university library. He complained to John A. Lomax, the famed folklorist and prominent University of Texas alumnus, that "it is no wonder that many of our teachers are Bolsheviki when we see what kind of literature they are obliged to read in their journals." When Bullington confronted Rainey with the journals, he was shocked when Rainey explained that the articles were usually read aloud at professional meetings before they were published. The regent told Rainey that if that was what went on at professional meetings, then the faculty should not be allowed to attend them on state time and at state expense. Bullington's views on this subject soon became official board policy, once again over Rainey's strong objection.[6]

From that summer of 1942 until the fall of 1944, Rainey was involved in a constant struggle to protect the faculty and preserve his own position as president. Confrontation followed confrontation, as the president and the regents clashed over a variety of issues, including a highly publicized squabble that resulted in the removal of John Dos Passos's acclaimed novel *U.S.A.* from a list of recommended readings in the English Department. Bullington charged that the book was obscene and subversive. One of the most serious incidents occurred in January 1943, when Strickland followed through with his threat to change the university's faculty tenure rule. Strickland made a motion at a board meeting to delete the procedural clause in the tenure rule, which would, in effect, destroy tenure. Strickland told Rainey that the tenure system allowed the faculty to operate "a self-perpetuating feudal state." When Rainey warned that the removal of tenure would destroy the University of Texas because it would not be able to recruit good faculty members from other universities with sound tenure rules, Strickland responded that Rainey should not worry, he was certain they could find good patriotic Texans to teach at the university who were from smaller Texas schools that had no tenure. Regents Fairchild, Aynesworth, and Waggener were able to persuade their colleagues to postpone the action until they could hear other opinions.[7]

Parten had been deeply involved with PAW matters in Washington, D.C., when Rainey called him and asked for his help in the fight to preserve tenure. Parten subsequently persuaded Ex-Student Association president W. H. "Bill" Francis to call a meeting of Ex-Student Association leaders in Dallas in March 1943 to discuss Strickland's attack on the tenure rule. At the meeting, which Parten was able to attend, the association agreed to submit a resolution to the board of regents demanding that the tenure rule be preserved. The association also decided to mount a lobbying campaign against Strickland's proposal. Their efforts eventually succeeded in forcing Bullington and Strickland to abandon their frontal attack on tenure. Changing tactics, Bullington argued that the tenure rule was unconstitutional because the state constitution vested all power in the board of regents and the tenure rule delegated authority to the faculty that could not legally be delegated by the board. He and Strickland persuaded the board to submit the rule to Texas attorney general Gerald Mann to determine its legality. They were shocked when Mann declared that the rule was compatible with the Texas Constitution and that no changes were needed. Nevertheless, Bullington and Strickland persisted until they were able to get the tenure rule drastically revised and weakened by a committee of conservative faculty members.[8]

Distressed by the change in the tenure rule, Parten complained to J. Frank Dobie that the action was "bound to spell out two results: first, the loss of some of our best teachers. . . . and; second, serve as a positive deterrent to recruitment." He hoped that the Ex-Students Association would issue a strong public statement in support of Rainey and academic freedom. "While I am far away from the scene," Parten declared, "I . . . stand ready . . . to do my part. . . ." Dobie, who was convinced that the Bullington group wanted to remove Rainey from the presidency, told Parten that "a master plan has been operating in this state to expunge liberal thinkers . . . not only from the University of Texas but from other state institutions of learning . . . lots of us wish you were down here on the Board of Regents now." Dobie's claim that a political conspiracy was behind the attacks on Rainey and the faculty jolted Parten's memory. The earlier warnings from Ely Thornton and Fred Branson about the "Gag" meeting in Houston, which he had so quickly dismissed, now seemed plausible.[9]

"Plenty of rope [to] break his own neck"

Fearing that his administration could not survive if Coke Stevenson remained in office and appointed more regents like Strickland and Bullington, Rainey tried to recruit a progressive candidate to run against Stevenson in the 1944 primary. In early October 1943, he met with Attorney General Mann to see if he would be that candidate. Mann admitted that he was interested in making the race, but he needed financial support. He told Rainey that he would consider running if Parten would agree to support him and serve as his fund-raiser. Rainey sent this news to Parten, still in Washington completing his PAW service. "[Mann] told me quite frankly that his problem was financial," Rainey reported. "He is worried about already being in debt and hesitates to become further involved." Parten, who liked and respected Mann, also encouraged his candidacy. "I knew that we had to get that Stevenson crowd out of the Governor's Mansion if the University was going to make any progress at all," Parten said. "Jerry Mann was popular as hell, dynamic, and highly ethical. I think he could of pinned Coke's ears to the wall." Mann appreciated Parten's pledge of support, but he decided eventually that Stevenson was too popular and rich to beat, so he decided not to run. To Parten's and Rainey's disappointment, Stevenson won reelection easily.[10]

With Stevenson back in the Governor's Mansion and the conservatives firmly in control of the board of regents Rainey's presidency became untenable. His clashes with the regents over academic freedom continued throughout 1944. The majority of the board, now chaired by Southwestern Bell Telephone Company chief counsel, Judge John H. Bickett, made clear to the president their belief that academic freedom allowed professors to commit subversion without fear of punishment. Roy Bedichek and a group of faculty colleagues met with the the board in an attempt to explain the concept of academic freedom and its critical importance to research and intellectual inquiry. In response, Bedichek lamented, they received "a lecture from sweet-winded Chairman Bickett . . . about the glories of Southern Womanhood. It was like talking to a group of East Texas hog-raisers about Hindu philosophy: no contact. I don't believe the Regents (not a single one of them) knew what we were talking about."[11]

Events finally came to a head in September as a result of a speech Rainey gave in New York, which he titled "Fulfilling the Commitment of Christianity, Democracy, and Modern Science." Declaring that a "great gap" existed between the reality of economic and cultural conditions in America and the hopeful yearnings of Americans, Rainey warned that America had "a long way to go to realize its ideas." The speech received much attention in Texas. Some small-town newspaper editors labelled Rainey's call for social change communistic. The speech also disturbed the regents, especially Judge Strickland, whose dislike of Rainey was so intense that at least one regent feared Strickland might physically attack Rainey during one of the board meetings. While Rainey was still in New York, Strickland called Dr. Alton Burdine, the university's vice president, to complain about the speech and Rainey's frequent out-of-state trips. Strickland also told Burdine that he had information indicating that more than a thousand Communists had infiltrated the university during Rainey's presidency.[12]

Strickland's telephone call to Burdine convinced Rainey that a public confrontation with the regents was now inevitable. On October 12, 1944, before an assembly of four hundred of the university's faculty and staff, Rainey listed sixteen points on which he and the regents had differed during the previous months. These included the attack on tenure and attempts to fire tenured professors, the dismissal of three instructors in the Economics Department, the dismissal of Dean Spies and the general handling of the Medical School situation, an effort to stifle social science research and to intimidate the faculty, and frequent accusations by regents of subversive activities on campus. His basic charge against the regents, however, was that they had attempted to destroy academic freedom at the university and to impose a type of political control. The real question, Rainey argued, was "whether or not our state universities can be operated in ways that will guarantee their essential freedom from undue political interference. . . ." Rainey declared, however, that it was not too late for him and the regents to resolve their differences. He hoped a solution could be found by the next board meeting.[13]

Parten had not known that Rainey was going to challenge the regents publicly. When the news reached him while on a trip to Mississippi, he immediately sent a telegram to Rainey calling his action "a forthright and courageous step. It is my opinion that you have chosen the only course in the circumstances." Years later, however, Parten said in hindsight that Rainey should not have confronted the regents in such a public way. "I'm afraid it backed the Board into a corner," Parten admitted. "But Rainey . . . had an intolerable situation. He knew he had to bring them to toe, or else he was out." Parten also suspected that Rainey's allies on the faculty, as well as some liberal Democrats among the alumni, were urging him to force the board to fire him so that Rainey could run for governor and make his dismissal a cause celebre in the campaign. "There were a lot of wild-eyed people that had already talked to him about running for governor," Parten claimed, "some of those people were severely disappointed when Jerry Mann failed to run against Stevenson. I never advised Rainey to do that. The faculty wanted a New Dealer in the Governor's Mansion, but they knew nothing about what it took to get elected Governor."[14]

Rainey asked Parten to come to the next board of regents meeting in Houston on October 27 to help him work out his problems with the Bullington group. Surprisingly optimistic, Rainey explained to Parten that he had submitted a proposal to the regents in an attempt to "provide . . . all of us a new working basis and . . . get ourselves out of this difficulty." The proposal called for the creation of two committees composed of regents, faculty, administrators, and ex-students. One committtee would rewrite the administrative rules governing the board of regents. The other would revise the regents' policy on tenure and academic freedom to bring it in line with the best public universities in the nation. Rainey's optimism was contagious. Parten, who had not been close to the situation for nearly three years and who remained rather naive about the ultimate intentions of the Bullington group, believed that a compromise was possible and that Rainey's job could be saved. Assuring Rainey of his help, Parten added that he would organize an effort to persuade Coke Stevenson to appoint "one or more Regents from the liberal school of thought" to the board in January.[15]

There was no chance for compromise. Bullington had admitted to an associate as early as the summer of 1943 that he and his colleagues were going to get rid of Rainey by giving him "plenty of rope [to] break his own neck." By making his problems with the regents public, Rainey had slipped the noose around his neck. Bullington told his colleagues that their only options were to fire Rainey or turn the university "over to this would be dictator." Gene Hollon, a history teacher at the Schreiner Institute in Kerrville, Texas, reported to Walter Prescott Webb a conversation he had with regent Scott Schreiner (whose family had established the institute) a few days after Rainey's public criticism of the regents. Hollon claimed that Schreiner "started all of the old crap again (I have heard him tell the same thing dozens of times) about communism at the University and how it should be wiped out completely even [if] it took the whole economic and government departments with it. When you realize that there are several fellows on that board ... who are more narrow-minded than he is, it really makes you worried about the future of the University."[16]

Showdown in Houston

The regents held their first meeting after Rainey's speech on Friday, October 27, at the Rice Hotel in Houston. Members of special committees from the Ex-Students Association and the faculty, as well as others including American Association of University Professors general secretary Ralph Himstead, met with the board on that day in an attempt to resolve the dispute. Kenneth Aynesworth, one of Rainey's two remaining supporters on the board (Marguerite Fairchild was the other), died after a lengthy illness in Waco during the weekend. To allow the members to attend his funeral, the board recessed until Tuesday, October 31. Two days of intense meetings between alumni and faculty committees and the regents followed. A majority of the board had long ago decided to fire Rainey, but regent chairman Bickett, who was undecided, insisted on hearing the committees. Another reason for the meetings was that the Ex-Students committee was composed of some influential and highly respected alumni who could not be ignored, including Federal judge Joseph C. Hutcheson, powerful corporate attorney W. H. "Bill" Francis, former Texas attorney general Robert Lee Bobbitt, and Humble Oil executive Hines Baker. Because of assurances from Baker and Francis that chances were excellent for a peaceful settlement, Parten delayed his departure from Mississippi until November 1.[17]

When Parten arrived in Houston, however, he was surprised to learn that the regents had rejected every compromise proposal and that they were demanding that Rainey retract the entire statement he had issued on October 12. Deeply concerned, Parten met with Rainey and the Ex-Students committee to draft another proposal. After four hours of discussion, which included numerous meetings with individual regents, Parten and the other committee members wrote a final proposal that included a formal statement from Rainey declaring that he had not meant to criticize any regent personally or question anyone's integrity and that he would withdraw anything in his October statement "so construed."[18]

At 6:00 p.m., while Parten and his colleagues remained in their rooms, Judge Hutcheson delivered the final proposal to the regents, who asked Rainey to join them in executive session. During the lengthy and acrimonious meeting that followed, the regents rejected the new proposal and demanded a total retraction. When Rainey refused, Lutcher Stark made a motion, seconded by Scott Schreiner, to fire him. Stark's motion carried by a six-to-one vote, with John Bickett abstaining. Marguerite Fairchild voted against the motion, telling the regents that she "greatly" regretted their action. "I feel that a great wrong is being done a good man."[19] The regents appointed university professor Theophilus S. Painter, a nationally recognized expert in genetics, to serve as interim president. As they left

Daily Texan headline, November 2, 1944. *CN 01934. Courtesy Prints and Photographs Collection, CAH.*

the meeting, Hilmer Weinert, John Bickett, and Dan Harrison announced their resignations as regents. Weinert explained that his health did not permit him "to stand any more of this." Bickett and Harrison refused to give a reason for their resignations. Parten later said that all three had resigned "because they had done something they were ashamed of—like stealing eggs." As the regents left the meeting, a board spokesman announced to the reporters gathered in the hallway outside the meeting room that Rainey had been dismissed because of his speech of October 12, which had attacked the "motives and good faith" of the board of regents. No effort was made to refute Rainey's charges against the regents. When cornered by reporters, however, Bullington claimed ominously that if the public

University of Texas students march on the Capitol to protest Rainey's dismissal, November 2, 1944. *CN 09634. Courtesy Prints and Photographs Collection, CAH.*

only knew the real reasons behind the firing they would solidly support the regents' decision. This had the impact intended. Maybe Rainey was a Communist or maybe he had committed an immoral act. The rumor mill worked overtime, greatly abetted by dark hints and innuendoes made by Bullington and Strickland in the weeks following Rainey's dismissal.[20]

After the meeting, which had ended late in the night, Rainey woke Parten up with a telephone call and gave him the news. Parten went to the Rice Hotel's first-floor lobby, where he encountered acting-President Painter, who had also been asleep in his room when he received the surprising news of his interim appointment. Parten warned Painter that he was going to have a "very rough ride" because of the protest and acrimony certain to be unleashed by Rainey's dismissal. He advised Painter that the university's ability to function properly during the period in which the controversy would be played out depended largely on Painter's ability to remain neutral and treat faculty and students on both sides of the dispute fairly. "Remember that up to this moment you have been a university professor and what you had to say carried no weight of authority," Parten instructed Painter. "But now you are speaking as President, so watch what you say."[21]

Stunned and angered by the board of regents' decision, Parten sent a telegram to Governor Stevenson the next morning expressing his "deep shock" at the "precipitant action" of the regents. He urged Stevenson to replace the regents who had resigned with people who respected "freedom of expression and freedom of teaching and research. . . ." Parten told the governor that he would fly to Austin immediately and that he wished to meet with him to discuss the crisis at the university. The next morning, Parten rented a suite in the Stephen F. Austin Hotel near the Capitol and sent word to Rainey supporters on the faculty that he would be staying there for the duration of the fight to reinstate Rainey. "I'm going to stay . . . until we win," Parten told a news reporter. For the next month, Parten's hotel suite served as the informal headquarters for Rainey's reinstatement fight. Later that same day, Governor Stevenson met with Parten and heard him out, but he refused to tell Parten how he felt about the matter or what action, if any, he planned to take. Stevenson's noncommittal attitude did not surprise Parten, but he wanted to put Stevenson on notice that he was going to do everything possible to get Rainey reinstated. Later, when questioned by the press about his position on the Rainey firing, Stevenson told reporters that he had sat around enough campfires "to know that you can't drink coffee from a boiling pot."[22]

Rainey's firing made newspaper headlines and dominated radio news programs throughout the state on November 2. That same day the university faculty passed by an overwhelming majority a resolution demanding Rainey's reinstatement, and a large contingent of the university student body marched peacefully from the campus to the Capitol to protest the dismissal. At an emergency meeting, the Ex-Students Association passed a resolution calling for a new board of regents and the hiring of a new president, but not necessarily Rainey. At the Ex-Students meeting, Parten agreed to arrange and pay for radio time on the statewide Texas Quality Network, for Robert Lee Bobbitt to explain the association's demands and to present Rainey's side of the affair. Parten also agreed to draft Bobbitt's speech.

At Parten's request, Jimmy Allred went to Houston radio station KPRC (owned by former governor William P. Hobby) to buy time on the leading state network. Station manager Kern Tips refused their application, saying that the Texas Quality Network did not sell time for one-sided discussions of "controversial" issues. As an alternative, Tips offered free time for a ten-minute broadcast, but only if it was followed by a ten-minute statement from a student representative, and a ten-minute rebuttal from a representative of the board of regents. Allred rejected the offer because ten minutes was too little time to explain adequately what had happened to Rainey. Outraged by Tips's decision, Parten enlisted the help of Harris County judge Roy Hofheinz to buy time on the smaller Texas State Network and twenty unaffiliated stations. Bobbitt finally went on the air on November 9 to present Rainey's case.[23]

Parten now realized that he should have taken more seriously the observation Ely Thornton and Fred Branson had made concerning the secret 1940 Houston meeting—that conservative businessmen and other supporters of W. Lee O'Daniel intended to gain control of the university. He was convinced now that such a meeting had occurred and that the attacks on Rainey had been orchestrated. In response to a letter from University of North Carolina president Frank Graham expressing his outrage at Rainey's dismissal, Parten warned that the incident was "more than a local matter. When a group of politicians execute a designed plan to control education in any state, it is a matter for alarm nationally. This whole difficulty stems from the desire of a few to prohibit progressive teaching and research in the social sciences." Graham agreed with Parten's assessment. The Rainey affair, Graham declared, was "one of the most flagrant cases" he had ever seen of an assault "against freedom of universities."[24]

"Any other dirty thing about the university you want to volunteer?"

Rainey's enemies deeply resented Parten's visible and active leadership role on Rainey's behalf. History professor Eugene C. Barker, who had cooperated with the regents in the effort to weaken the tenure rules, expressed his fear to J. Evetts Haley, who was now ranching in the Texas Panhandle, that "the students are doing a lot of harm." A large number had attended protest rallies to denounce the regents. "They are supplied with abundant funds," Barker wrote Haley, "and are scattering thousands of circulars over the state to their parents and others and stimulating radio talks—all deliberately misleading or ignorant. I suspect that Parten is paying part if not all of the bills. He has not yet become reconciled to not being a regent, and, possibly with good intentions, is doing a lot of harm. . . ."[25]

Parten continued to do harm to the anti-Rainey cause. He helped persuade Sen. Penrose Metcalfe of San Angelo, chairman of the Texas Senate's Committee on Education and an old friend from his days as a regent, to conduct public hearings on the Rainey affair. Parten hoped the hearings would generate enough public outrage to force Stevenson to appoint more progressive-minded people to the three vancancies on the board of regents. He also hoped to put enough pressure on Bullington and Strickland to force them to resign. When Metcalfe announced the hearings on November 13, however, Lt. Gov. John Lee Smith and Sen. Houghton Brownlee, close friends and political allies of Strickland, Schreiner, and Bullington, challenged the committee's authority to conduct the hearings. When Metcalfe wavered, Parten persuaded Houston Harte, the influential owner and publisher of one of the state's largest newspaper chains and one of Metcalfe's financial backers, to advise the senator to proceed with the hearings. Despite the enormous pressure on Metcalfe to stay out of the affair, Parten and Harte persuaded him to request a ruling from Attorny General Grover Sellers about the legality of the hearing. Sellers ruled that Metcalfe could hold his hearing without permission from the lieutenant governor or anyone else. "I knew there was no damn way that Sellers could rule that a committee duly created by the Legislature could not meet any time its chairman wanted," Parten said. "But Metcalfe wanted some cover to run under and an Attorney-General's ruling gave him that cover."[26]

Metcalfe's education committee conducted hearings in the Senate chamber from November 16 until November 28. Witnessess included Rainey; regents Bullington, Strickland, Stark, Schreiner and Fairchild; Vice President Burdine; eight faculty members, including Webb, Dobie, Ayres, and Bedichek; Texas

Department of Public Safety director Col. Homer Garrison; and AAUP executive secretary Ralph Himstead. Representing the Ex-Students Association were Parten, Bobbitt, and Bill Francis. The hearings provided a public forum to air the issues involved in Rainey's firing and to counter rumors that were being spread against the former president. In a desperate attempt to smear Rainey and divert attention away from the real issues, Rainey's enemies launched a vicious rumor campaign that made full use of illicit sex, race hatred, and red-baiting—elements certain to insure the rapid spread of gossip. The Austin *American* reported a few days prior to

Orville Bullington, 1944. *CN 09632. Courtesy Prints and Photographs Collection, CAH.*

the hearings that the capital city was full of "anonymous, underhanded rumors" being spread by a "whispering campaign" that Rainey and his family were Communists and "race mixers." One completely false rumor claimed that Rainey's daughter, Helen, was having sex with a married black man who was a Communist. Other equally false allegations claimed that Rainey had run a homosexual ring on campus. These scurrilous rumors were so widespread and loathsome that Dr. Blake Smith, pastor of the University Baptist Church, received time on a local radio station to denounce them as un-Christian.

It is virtually impossible to discover the source of gossip campaigns, but Parten was convinced that in this case it was the work of Bullington and Strickland. "Both men," Parten would later claim, "were unprincipled bigots and mean of spirit. They were more than capable of such evil." When Bullington finally left the board of regents in 1947, Parten wrote Frank Dobie that Bullington's departure "with all of his viciousness" would "mark the end of the all-time low in University morale." Bullington's insinuating comment to the press the night of Rainey's dismissal was one reason for Parten's suspicions. He was also receiving from Webb and Dobie reports about the rumors that pointed directly back to the regents as the source. Webb for example, received a letter from Eugene Hollon claiming that Scott Schreiner had been busy "convincing the people of this town that Rainey is a communist negro lover, in league with all of the homosexuals at the University, and a very dangerous man in general. It is very depressing."[27]

During their appearances at the Senate hearing, Bullington and Strickland provided more evidence of their involvement in the "whispering campaign." Their testimony focused on the sex-race-subversion theme in a transparent effort to obfuscate the political reasons for their harrassment of Rainey and certain members of the faculty. Bullington was the first to inject the vice issue into the proceedings by charging that Rainey had purposely delayed telling the regents about an investigation of "a nest of homosexuals" at the university until it was too late for the regents to take action against those who had been accused. He claimed that Rainey had violated regents' rules in the matter and had probably made the homosexual problem on campus much worse. These charges were subsequently proven false. Colonel Garrison testified that Rainey had asked the state police to investigate as soon as allegations had been made to the president's office that a small group of faculty members and students were engaging in homosexual activity. Garrison stated that to protect the secrecy of the investigation as well as the reputation of those who may have been accused unfairly, he had instructed Rainey not to discuss the investigation with anyone—including the regents—until it was concluded. He emphasized that Rainey had cooperated fully and that he had handled the situation properly. Garrison also stressed that because the state police had determined that there was no such problem on campus, they had recommended that the investigation not be made public. Bullington's misleading and irrelevant statement, therefore, had been the first public announcement about the investigation. An obviously disgusted member of the Senate committee asked Bullington when he ended his testimony if there was "any other dirty thing about the university you want to volunteer?"

Bullington received a large amount of mail criticizing his testimony, and several newspaper editorials and columnists expressed shock at his behavior. The Austin *American*, for example, called for his resignation and declared that "what Orville Bullington said before this committee made an all-time low on the part of anybody connected with the University. . . ." The beseiged regent wrote John Lomax to explain that he had been forced to bring up the homosexual issue because he had taken an oath as a witness to tell the "whole truth" and that he would have committed perjury if he had not. This ignored the fact that no one asked him to testify about this episode. Bullington also complained that it was the fault of the newspapers for repeating his testimony without first verifying its accuracy.[28]

Frank Strickland, however, showed a little more finesse than his fellow regent Bullington by bringing up an issue that was more likely to be well received by the members of the Senate committee. He charged that Rainey had protected Communists on campus. Strickland testified that soon after the public announcement of his appointment to the board, his neighbors came to him to complain that their children "came home Communists" after graduating from the university. Strickland also claimed that students had come up to him while walking on campus to report that they were being taught communism. He became so alarmed by this information, Strickland said, that he had a conference with Rainey and urged him to conduct an investigation to root out the Communists on the faculty. Rainey refused to do it, Strickland claimed, explaining that it would alarm the faculty and lower morale. Strickland said that Rainey and Vice President Burdine subsequently fought against every request he made to crack down on Communist activity at the university. Strickland shrugged his shoulders and declared that one could draw only certain conclusions about Rainey from such behavior. When cross-examined, however, Strickland was forced under oath to admit that he had no proof that there were any Communists on the faculty or among the students.[29]

Strickland also accused Rainey of having radical opinions about race relations and of planning to allow blacks to enroll at the university. He referred to Rainey's involvement with the Southern Conference on Human Welfare and the fact that Rainey had given a speech to a racially mixed audience at Fiske University in Nashville as evidence to support his charge that Rainey sought to integrate the University of Texas. Strickland also complained that Rainey had given a speech in New Mexico in which he had declared the need to break down racial barriers in America. When Strickland confronted Rainey with a transcript of his speech, the regent testified that he had been shocked to hear him declare that "neither Christianity nor democracy made any distinction between races. . . ."[30]

Rainey and his supporters presented their side of the controversy and refuted Bullington's and Strickland's allegations. In his testimony, his voice hoarse from stress and tension, Rainey gave a thorough and detailed discussion of all the events that led up to his defiant October 12 speech to the faculty. He angrily denounced the attacks on his personal reputation and political beliefs. "I have no interest in Communism," he declared. "I regard myself as a liberal Democrat in the sense the term was used in the nineteenth century, as Woodrow Wilson used it." Vice President Burdine defended Rainey and denied Strickland's and Bullington's charges. As for the allegation that communism was rampant on campus, Burdine stated that he would "boil it down to about a dozen pinkish students with Utopian dreams." He told the senators that if he had known of a member of the faculty "who was an out-and-out communist, I'd want to get rid of him. . . ." J. Frank Dobie denounced Strickland's use of red-scare tactics, telling the committee that the "hysteria over Communism today [is] as rational as the hysteria of bobby sox girls over [Frank] Sinatra." He claimed that "most people don't know what a Communist is. This hysteria . . . is founded in distrust of Democracy—motivated by powerful interests." Dobie declared that "if any man in Texas has a liberal thought he is branded as a Communist by the special interests spokesmen. . . ."[31]

While the education committee was conducting its hearings, Governor Stevenson filled the four vacancies on the board of regents with Dallas attorney Dudley K. Woodward, Panhandle oil man David M. Warren, and physicians O. C. Terrell of Fort Worth and Judson Taylor of Houston. These appointments ended any doubts about where Stevenson stood in the Rainey affair. Each appointee was a conservative with ties to the Texas Regulars, the anti-Roosevelt Democrats in Texas. Woodward, for example, had publicly accused Rainey of promoting "radical and New Deal propaganda" on campus. Stevenson declared that the new regents were all well qualified to be on the board because they were successful physicians and businessmen. Whereupon Frank Dobie complained to Parten that "it is notable how some minds go backward. In talking about the qualities of his regents, it has never once occurred to Coke Stevenson to mention their *intellectual qualities*. Such are outside of his realm." These appointments also put an immediate end to the Ex-Students Association effort to persuade Stevenson to consult with them in selecting the new regents. The leadership of the association was unsure about what the organization should do now that the nominations had been made. Parten, however, had no doubt about what to do next. Stevenson had nominated four regents, but they still had to be confirmed by the Senate during the upcoming session opening in January 1945. Parten was determined to defeat them all and to restore Rainey to the presidency. He decided to organize an effort to accomplish both goals.[32]

On the afternoon of November 23, Parten hosted a luncheon in his room at the Stephen F. Austin Hotel for several university faculty members who agreed with him that Rainey should be reinstated as president and that Stevenson's regents should be kept off the board. They believed it was the only way the university could escape serious damage to its institutional reputation. Censure of the university by the AAUP and other professional groups seemed almost certain, which would make the recruitment of top-notch new faculty very difficult. In addition, several highly regarded University of Texas faculty members were already talking about leaving the state. Parten promised his faculty friends that he would work for Rainey's reinstatement. That same evening he brought together in his room at the hotel a group of Ex-Student Association members and other concerned people to discuss a future course of action. This group included Cong. Lyndon Johnson, Hines Baker, Myron Blalock, W. H. Francis, Robert Lee Bobbitt, and Marlin Sandlin. They agreed with the faculty group that Rainey should be reappointed as president. Lyndon Johnson stressed that he could not help the effort publicly, but he would work behind the scenes in Washington. Hines Baker was less enthusiastic about focusing the effort on Rainey because it personalized the controversy too much. He felt that a lot of people who disliked Rainey might be persuaded to support their effort to get new regents if he was out of the picture. Parten, however, argued that Rainey and his family had suffered a terrible injustice. They deserved better and restoring him to the presidency was the just thing to do. Baker finally agreed to support Rainey's rehiring.[33]

After his meetings with faculty and alumni, Parten testified before the education committee. He declared that the issues in the controversy were clear: "Shall academic freedom . . . be restored and respected by the board of regents? Shall undue regental interference with normal administration be practiced by the Board of Regents?" To answer the first question, Parten defined academic freedom as "freedom of expression, freedom of teaching, and freedom of research subject only to the rules of decent conduct. . . ." Parten then told the committee that the regents' firing of the three economics instructors and their attempt to abolish tenure were examples of their frequent violation of the principle of academic freedom. "No university," Parten declared, "can aspire to or maintain the rank of a university of the first class unless its governing board's policies respect academic freedom. . . ." Nor could a first-class institution of learning allow regental interference in its day-to-day operations. He cited Stark's attempt to fire Bedichek and Weinert's attempt to replace Dolley as head of the Faculty Athletic Council as examples of the regent's interference in the daily administration of the university. Parten also discussed in detail the problems at the Medical School, which Parten believed had provided much of the energy behind the effort to fire Rainey. Rainey had inherit-

Governor Coke Stevenson, 1944. *CN 02708.*
Courtesy Prints and Photographs Collection, CAH.

ed a very difficult situation not of his making, Parten argued, and he was now being blamed for it.[34]

Much of what Parten had to say about the background of the Rainey affair was well known to many of his listeners. Parten declared that in 1939 and 1940, conservative business interests in Texas had suffered from a "fear complex" that had resulted in demands that the boards of regents of state schools "rid the institutions of so-called radicals usually referred to by them as Communists." Parten said that when he was chairman of the board of regents, he received "literally dozens" of demands to fire Bob Montgomery and Clarence Ayres. "I was told that [Montgomery] was advocating subversive policies designed to overthrow the government. . . . Never was I able to determine more than that this teacher was a liberal thinker. . . ." He also discussed the Martin Dies incident and Fred Branson's attempt to fire Montgomery.

Parten stunned the committee and the audience, however, when he told them about the alleged meeting in Houston in 1940 between O'Daniel and his business supporters to plan a takeover of the University of Texas and other state schools and "to eliminate . . . all radical elements in the faculties. . . ." Parten explained that "a prominent Texas attorney" [Ely Thornton], whose identity he had promised not to reveal, told him about the secret meeting. He admitted that the attorney, who was now serving in the military, could not recall the incident when Parten contacted him before the hearing. "Thornton hoped to make a lot of money as a corporate attorney after the war," Parten later claimed. "He suddenly lost his memory when I asked him for the details." After news about Parten's testimony reached him, Thornton wrote Parten a letter denying that the so-called Houston "Gag" Conference had occurred, saying Parten must have confused him with someone else. Nevertheless, Parten refused to retract his statement. He told Thornton that his memory of their conversation about the "Gag" Conference was "as clear as if the conversation . . . were yesterday." Concluding his testimony, Parten called for Rainey's reinstatement as president and for the resignation of the three remaining regents who voted against him. They should be replaced, Parten declared, with people who loved the university and who were not associated with either faction in the controversy.[35]

The University of Texas and the Issue

Parten's testimony received much favorable response from newspapers throughout the state. The Austin *American*, for example, declared that "Major Parten's statement was the most detailed review of the roots of the university trouble yet presented." Typical of the letters Parten received after his committee appearance was one from Texas Democratic Party activist and Roosevelt loyalist Lillian Collier, who wrote that Parten's testimony had been "a masterpiece. How I wish that every thinking Texan could read it." From Washington, Lyndon Johnson wrote Parten that his statement to the Senate committee was "a gem." Johnson added that he had "brought it to the attention of others here who I think feel as you do about the matter and who I feel will be able to give some assistance to the position which we have taken." Among those contacted by Johnson was Harold Ickes. "I have heard you too often before Congressional Committees not to have a keen sense of your ability," Ickes subsequently wrote to Parten. "You know how to slug and the University of Texas situation calls for plain talking. You are quite right in remarking that freedom in education throughout the nation is involved in this controversy."[36]

Not all of the reactions to Parten's testimony were positive. Most of his critics focused on his accusation that Rainey's firing had been the result of a conspiracy by conservative businessmen. Parten's enemies called him a liar, while some of his friends believed he had been deceived. For example, Parten's former speech coach, Charles I. Francis, who was now a partner in Judge James Elkins's law firm, wrote to him that though he was "in absolute accord" about the injustice of the Rainey firing, he did not believe that a cabal had been formed to purge the universities.

One problem with the "Gag" Conference allegation was that every person accused of having attended the conference denied it strongly. Another problem was that Parten had no documentation. One of his sources denied having talked to Parten about it or of having ever heard such a story, and his other source (Fred Branson) was dead. Eugene C. Barker wrote John Lomax that the "most ludicrous part of Parten's story is his admission that the man who told him about the meeting later denied all recollection of the incident." Historians and others who have written about the Rainey affair have cited as evidence for the "Gag" Conference statements made by Parten, Bobbitt, Rainey, Dobie, and Clarence Ayres (not all of them made at the hearings). They have generally ignored the denials. Unfortunately, Bobbitt, Rainey, Dobie, and Ayres learned about the conference exclusively from J. R. Parten. John Lomax pointed this out to one of his friends. "Ex-Regent Parten seemed to be the sole source of the story. Presumably he passed it on to [Bobbitt and Rainey]. Not then nor since has any of these three men given to the public further details of the meeting." He called Parten's charges an "unproven vague rumor . . . too ludicrous for serious attention."[37]

Bullington's and Strickland's inept testimony at the Senate committee hearings were an obvious public relations disaster for the anti-Rainey forces. Hubert Mewhinney, a columnist for the Houston *Post*, wrote Walter Webb that when Strickland admitted in public that he was "unable to distinguish between the doctrines of Karl Marx and of the peer [Keynes] who advises the Bank of England—even after the differences are explained to him—he is convicted of incapacity to serve as a trustee for a first class kindergarten." The anti-Rainey regents and their associates realized that they needed to launch a counterattack. Scott Schreiner suggested to Bullington and Strickland that they commission a skilled researcher and writer to present their side of the story. Schreiner had just the right person to do it: J. Evetts Haley. The cowboy historian, who was operating a ranch near Canyon in the Texas Panhandle, had observed the unfolding of events with intense interest. His opinion of Rainey was the same as Bullington's and Strickland's. He was outraged to see Dobie and Webb defend a man whom he perceived as being the very embodiment of the academic type he loathed and despised: a communistic, "Negro-loving" academician. He accepted the assignment with eagerness.[38]

Haley worked rapidly, gathering information directly from Eugene Barker, John Lomax, and political reporter Alonzo Wasson of the Dallas *Morning News*. "Keep sending me your ideas," Haley wrote Lomax on December 23. "The job I have set myself is a big one. . . . I would like to . . . take . . . on for good measure, Bobbitt, Parten, Dobie, et al." Barker identified the general areas Haley needed to cover in his "expose." Especially keen to discredit J. R. Parten, Barker urged Haley to focus on Parten's "statement about conspiracy." Barker believed that Parten was bitter about not being reappointed to the board of regents and in a fit of spite told Rainey that he had been the victim of a conspiracy. Barker thought that was the reason Rainey had been unable to work with the new regents; that Parten's story poisoned his mind against them. Barker also told Haley he was certain that Parten had used his position as a regent to benefit his oil business. Erroneously, Barker thought that the university owned oil land in Madison County and that Parten, as a regent, had been involved in some kind of financial impropriety related to that land. He told Haley he suspected that J. C. Dolley knew about Parten and the alleged oil deal and that he should question Dolley about it. A few days later, however, Barker discovered his error and dashed off a note to Haley saying that "the university owns no land in Madison County. This is official." Nevertheless, Barker still believed Haley could find some information that could be used to embarrass

Parten. "The material facts [about Parten] are not necessarily altered [by the error about Madison County]," Barker wrote. "[I] hope Dolley talked." Haley, however, failed to find any hint that Parten had engaged in or been associated with any unethical or improper activity.[39]

Haley's series of articles defending the regents and attacking Rainey appeared in late January in the Amarillo *Times* and the San Antonio *Express*. The articles were also published and distributed widely as a pamphlet titled *The University of Texas and the Issue*. Unable to deny most of Rainey's charges against the board, Haley argued that the real issue in the Rainey affair was popular control of the university. Should a bunch of arrogant intellectuals, led by Rainey and supported by their "patron saint" J. R. Parten, run the state university as their own playground for radicalism, Haley asked, or should the people of Texas, speaking through "their" regents, have the final say about what goes on in an institution of "so-called" higher education paid for with their tax money? Haley also injected his personal resentment over his alleged dismissal in 1936. He charged that the "liberal souls" on the faculty who were defending Rainey on behalf of academic freedom were insincere and dishonest hypocrites. When the board of regents "fired" him in 1936 for "political reasons," Haley declared, none of the "liberals beat his sensitive breast, or tore his long hair . . . in denunciation of the board" for violating academic freedom. After Haley's articles appeared in the San Antonio *Express*, Gene Hollon complained to Walter Webb that he could "readily detect the smell of commercialism. It is an open secret here that Scott Schreiner had him write them. . . . I hope this hack writing backfires on both of them. . . ."[40]

"Jube, I have watched your intellectual development with great pride"

The Senate hearings did much to publicize Rainey's side of the affair, but the real fight was just beginning. Parten and the other pro-Rainey leaders in the Ex-Students Association decided to organize the alumni to put pressure on the state Senate to "bust" Stevenson's nominees. Everyone agreed that the key to this effort was the influential Houston chapter of the association. Accordingly, on December 15 Parten joined with a group of thirteen other prominent Houston ex-students, including Marlin Sandlin, Hines Baker, Charles I. Francis, cultural leader Ima Hogg, attorney Jesse Andrews, and Houston city librarian Julia Ideson, to sponsor a mass meeting of Houston-area alumni. The purpose was to discuss the issues in the Rainey affair and to pass resolutions Parten had drafted demanding Rainey's reinstatement and the defeat of the newly nominated regents. The president of the Houston-area Ex-Students Association was Otto J. Clements, manager of the Houston office of the Southwestern Bell Telephone Company and a crony of Judge Bickett, the telephone company's general counsel. After consulting with Bickett, Clements rejected the request from Parten and his associates to call an official meeting of the Houston chapter. Parten and Hines Baker issued a general call and held the meeting anyway. Clements organized a group of ex-students who supported the regents, including insurance tycoon Gus Wortham and Judge

Hutcheson, to attend this unofficial meeting and to counter the pro-Rainey effort.[41]

A crowd of five hundred people crowded into the auditorium at San Jacinto High School in Houston to determine what position the Houston alumni should take in the Rainey affair. Pro- and anti-Rainey speakers debated contentiously from 8 p.m. until midnight. The main debate, however, occurred late in the evening between Judge Hutcheson and Parten. While addressing the audience from the stage, Hutcheson pointed his finger at Parten, and angrily charged that Parten's agitation in support of Rainey was doing more damage to the university's reputation than Rainey's dismissal. The judge declared that he had tried to bring the regents and Rainey together during the board meeting in Houston, but Rainey had not cooperated. Rainey, Hutcheson argued, had refused to retract his provocative statement challenging the authority of the regents. Parten rejected Hutcheson's argument and called for the passage of a resolution demanding Rainey's reinstatement. He declared that much was at stake, not just for the University of Texas, but for higher education nationally. The manner in which the affair was ultimately settled, Parten claimed, would determine "whether our educational institutions shall be real schools for learning and pursuit of truth, or become institutions for propaganda, paid for by the tax payers but run in the interest of whatever powerful group may get control of the board of regents. . . ."[42]

Near midnight, William Loose, an attorney for Texaco, proposed that the Houston Ex-Students Association pass a resolution fully supporting the regents' decision to fire Rainey. Marlin Sandlin immediately offered a substitute resolution calling for Rainey's return to the presidency. At this point, another motion was made to adjourn without action and it won by a vote of 220 to 200. As the meeting broke up with shouts on all sides, a young attorney who supported Rainey grabbed the microphone on stage and declared that they were all cowards for not doing anything. A Houston *Post* editorial congratulated the Ex-Students Association for not taking a position, claiming that it had "set a wholesome example for all others who have the interest of the university at heart." Steve Pinckney, the Hogg family lawyer whom Parten had helped when he asked him to lobby the Senate to get Harrison and Bullington confirmed as regents in 1941, wrote Evetts Haley that "Judge Hutcheson made a fine talk and took Parten to a cleaning. Hutcheson . . . called him by name several times during the evening as he indicted him for the course he was following. If the issue had gone to vote, I am sure we would have licked them." Parten, of course, had a different feeling about the result, complaining to Bill Francis that the victory belonged to "the enemies of intellectual freedom." He wrote Marguerite Fairchild that it was now obvious, "that the ex-student groups of the metropolitan cities . . . are in the control of corporation lawyers and corporation people. . . ."[43]

Disappointed by the result of the meeting in Houston, Roy Bedichek wrote Frank Dobie that "the fight looks rather hopeless at present." He believed the outcome would determine "whether Texas youth are going to be taught in the future by intellectual geldings, or permitted contact with what Whitman calls the great seminal ideas of our time." Ralph Yarborough, who was serving as an army officer, wrote Parten a letter urging him not to give up, stressing that his "service to public education in Texas was never needed more badly than now. You are contending against the forces of bigotry, intolerance, and evil, no less than we in the armed forces." Parten assured Yarborough that he would not give up until he stopped the Senate from approving Stevenson's new appointees and forced the governor to appoint "open minded, unprejudiced people who have a real interest in higher education. . . ."[44]

About this same time, Parten received a letter from a realtor in San Antonio asking him to answer three questions. How could he defend the conduct of the three economics instructors who were fired? Did he believe that a professor should be able to ask his students to write a theme on the advantages of socialism in government? And did he believe Dos Passos's *U.S.A.* should be part of the curriculum? Parten's answer reveals how much his view of academic freedom had changed since he first joined the board of regents in 1935. In regard to the economics instructors, Parten declared that college teachers had the same right to protest as every other citizen "under our democracy and under the freedoms guaranteed by our constitution." On teaching about socialism, Parten stated that "in a university Socialism, Communism, Fascism and all other forms of government should be taught objectively." As for *U.S.A.*, Parten declared that "the issue of this book has no significance whatsoever in the university controversy other than . . . that the Regents made it an issue." These and all the other issues and incidents, Parten concluded, obscured the real reason for the controversy at the university. At the heart of the Rainey affair, Parten argued, was the effort by big business interests "to eliminate from the university the teaching of so-called New Deal economics. . . ." This was not the same J. R. Parten who in 1933 had complained to Jimmy Allred about Dr. George Stocking's endorsement of the unit operation of oil fields by asking "why should our college professors take sides on such a highly controversial question?" Frank Dobie, who had watched Parten closely for many years, wrote to him during the Rainey affair to say: "Jube, I have watched your intellectual development with great pride."[45]

Parten was not fighting this battle alone. Among his most active allies were a group of women who responded to Rainey's dismissal by organizing the Women's Committee for Educational Freedom. The committee's leaders included Lillian Collier, Minnie Fisher Cunningham, former Texas secretary of state Jane McCallum, former Democratic national committee member Clara Driscoll, and Democratic Party activist Marion Storm. The committee's purpose was to lobby for Rainey's reinstatement and for an end to political control of the university by the Texas Regulars. As one longtime liberal Democratic Party activist later observed, one of the few positive results of the Rainey affair was that it "got all of those wonderful women involved." Composed of pro-Roosevelt, Democratic Party loyalists, the committee eventually evolved into a component of the liberal Democrats of Texas in the early 1950s. Parten supported their efforts with money and moral support and helped recruit members, such as Marguerite Fairchild.[46]

A "new era of tranquility has begun"

On January 26, 1945, the university's board of regents met in the president's office in the Main Building. In attendance as observers were Homer Rainey and representatives of the AAUP and other professional organizations involved in higher education. Confident of winning confirmation despite the organized effort against them, Stevenson's nominees took their oath of office and participated in the meeting as regents. The new board included holdovers Bullington, Schreiner, and Strickland, who remained in office despite their previous pledge to resign. They selected Dudley K. Woodward, one of the nominees, to serve as the new chairman-elect. Woodward announced that the board would consider Rainey's reinstatement. Before the board could vote on the matter, however, Woodward took four hours to read a rambling, unfocused speech explaining why he would vote against Rainey. Remarking that he had never met Rainey prior to his appointment to the board of regents, Woodward declared that he therefore could have "no bias in his favor or prejudice against him." Woodward's declaration was less than honest, however. In letters that Woodward had written to John Lomax the previous October, the Dallas attorney had been outspoken in his denunciation of Rainey.

After Woodward's speech, which Parten would later characterize as "grossly unfair and injudicious," the board voted unanimously against Rainey's reinstatement as president. Although Rainey had tenure as a professor of educational administration, the board also refused to allocate money for his salary and voted against allowing him to teach classes. He was a professor without office, salary, or classroom. After the regents meeting, Bullington wrote Lomax that he and his board colleagues had succeeded in their goal "to prevent Rainey and his clique from destroying the University of Texas." He reported, however, that the faculty was still up in arms about the affair. "The faculty morons," Bullington complained, "are still raving about academic freedom which no one has denied or intends to deny. 'The wicked fleeth when no man pursuith'."[47]

Although it was now obvious that the battle was going to be lost, Parten persisted. On February 1, the day the Senate nominations committee opened hearings on the regental appointments, Parten spoke to an Ex-Students Association meeting in Fort Worth and implored the members to contact their senators immediately and urge them to vote against Stevenson's nominees. "We have no hope of getting the problem at Austin solved until we get a new board of regents," Parten declared. Reiterating his charge that a political conspiracy had captured the board, Parten offered to donate a thousand dollars to the local Red Cross if anyone could find more than one regent on the current board who was not a Texas Regular or a Republican. Concerned that his highly visible role in the fight to save Rainey was making the effort seem too much like a one-man show, Parten sent Marlin Sandlin in his place to the Senate hearings to testify against the nominations.[48] He was also able to recruit attorney Dallas Scarborough of Abilene and Angus Wynne of Longview, both well-known conservatives, to testify against the nominations. Wynn told the senators that he was "a very strong anti–new dealer and a Texas

Regular," but he opposed the effort to place the administration of the university under political control of any kind. The Texas Regulars, Wynn charged, "are trying to put the university . . . where it has no business being. He urged the Senate to defeat the nominees for the board, so that individuals could be appointed who would "try to build a university" instead of "always trying to get rid of somebody." The effort to stop confirmation, however, proved futile. The Senate confirmed the new appointees within a few days. Declaring that the controversy was now over, Strickland said that he was relieved because he would rather see a "Jap invasion" of the United States than have Rainey president of the university again.[49]

On February 16, 1945, Dudley Woodward reinforced Strickland's pronouncement by declaring on behalf of the board of regents that a "new era of tranquility has begun in the administration of the University." With Stevenson's nominees now safely confirmed and in total control of the university and Rainey's fate sealed, the Ex-Students Association voted to abandon their demand that Rainey be reinstated, and announced its intention to work with the new board to restore peace and to get on with the job of developing the university. In disgust, Frank Dobie wrote Parten that the Ex-Students "gesture of peace. . . . is pathetic to me. Hell, you can't do business with Hitler." Dr. T. S. Painter, an academician more to the conservatives' liking, eventually was installed as the permanent president, despite a pledge he had made to the faculty when he became acting president that he would not accept the permanent job if offered it.[50]

To some who had supported Rainey and who had fought for academic freedom, the defeat seemed to be total and—in hindsight—their effort appeared to have been quixotic. After all, Rainey was not reappointed and the Texas Regulars retained complete control over the board of regents. Parten did not share that view. Although he always believed that the affair seriously injured the university's reputation for years to come, driving away some of the better faculty and brighter graduate students, he also believed that the fight in support of Rainey had its positive side. "Hell, Rainey went down with guns blazing and it put the fear of God in some of the regents," Parten said. "It was a healthy thing, the fight we made. It had the effect, in the long run, of benefiting the University. I believe for several years after that it made the regents far more cautious about interfering in the day to day administrative affairs of the University. It may have saved the jobs of some professors, particularly Bob Montgomery and Clarence Ayres." Frederick Duncalf was among those who agreed with this view and who assured Parten that his fight had been worth the effort, despite the outcome. Duncalf wrote: "Jube, you can be proud of the part which you took in this struggle for a free university, and, be sure, that as time passes you will be even more proud of yourself for you will be vindicated in public opinion."[51]

Parten's role in support of Rainey won him the admiration and respect of Texans who identified themselves as political liberals and social progressives. The affair marked him as a rare breed—a wealthy and educated liberal Texas oil man— when the popular stereotype of the Texas oil man was the opposite of liberal or educated. Because of the Rainey affair, other politically liberal Texans took serious notice of Parten as someone who could be counted on to support many of the same progressive causes with which they identified.[52]

Although Homer Rainey was no longer president of the University of Texas, he was prepared to engage in a new struggle, but not for control of the university. The next phase of the Rainey saga would be a crusade for control of the Governor's Mansion—and again J. R. Parten would play a key role. A year intervened between the Rainey *affair* and the Rainey *crusade*, however. In the meantime, Parten answered the call to participate in another mission; this one took him to Berlin and Moscow.

CHAPTER 19

Mission to Moscow and the Dawn of the Cold War

1945

A s the war in Europe drew to a close in early May 1945, Parten received a telephone call from Ed Pauley, an independent oil man from California whom Parten had known since the days of the fight against federal control of oil production. President Harry Truman had recently appointed Pauley head of the United States delegation to the Allied War Reparations Commission, which was slated to convene in Moscow to negotiate German war-damage reparations. Pauley invited Parten to serve as the U.S. delegation's chief of staff. Parten reluctantly agreed to help Pauley organize the mission, but he initially rejected the invitation to go to Russia. He left the next day for Washington, and eventually accepted the job with the U.S. delegation though he knew almost nothing about the Allied War Reparations Commission or of the controversial circumstances behind Pauley's appointment. As the delegation's chief of staff, Parten would be one of the first American civilians to go into Berlin after the German surrender, he would view firsthand the destruction of Stalingrad, and he would serve on the U.S. delegation at the Potsdam Conference. Parten's experiences in the Soviet Union would make him a critic of the Cold War and an opponent of the nuclear-arms race. Although this would be Parten's only trip out of North America, it nonetheless contributed to his becoming a committed internationalist and an advocate for peaceful relations with the Soviet Union.[1]

"Someone as tough as Molotov"

When Franklin Roosevelt, Winston Churchill, and Joseph Stalin met at Yalta in the Crimea in February 1945 to discuss Allied plans for the postwar world, they agreed on the general concept that Germany should be made to pay reparations for the terrible devastation caused by the war it had initiated in September 1939. Little else about reparations had been agreed upon, however. The Soviet Union, having lost more than twenty million people and suffering the destruction of much of its industrial capacity, insisted that the Germans should be forced to pay the allies the equivalent of twenty billion dollars in reparations. Of that, half would go to the Soviet Union—in the form of industrial equipment, commodities, and forced labor. Great Britain opposed the Soviet plan with the argument that it would impoverish Germany and make it difficult for the Germans to take care of their basic needs. Although not wishing to create a new Germany capable of renewed military aggression, the British did want a Germany capable of working in concert with its neighbors as an integral part of the overall European economy.

Franklin Roosevelt was in the middle. The president and most of his advisors did not want to repeat the mistakes of the agreement ending World War I, which in effect resulted in the United States paying for Germany's reparations with loans. A stripped Germany, forced to pay twenty billion dollars in reparations, might end up being again supported by the United States. On the other hand, Roosevelt did not want to appear to be taking sides with the British against the Soviets. After all, as one historian of the period has noted, "the moral right in this case was . . . undeniably on the Russian side" because of the incalculable losses they had suffered at the hands of the Nazis." The Big Three finally decided to postpone settlement of the reparations issue. They agreed to establish a special commission, composed of delegations from the United States, Great Britain, and the Soviet Union, to formulate a detailed reparations plan. This commission was scheduled to meet in Moscow no later than six months after the Yalta Conference. With British insistence, Roosevelt and Stalin accepted the twenty-billion-dollar figure as a "basis" for negotiations. The reparations commissioners later disagreed strenuously on the meaning of that qualifying word.[2]

After his return to Washington following the Yalta Conference, Roosevelt appointed Dr. Isador Lubin, an economist, to head the U.S. delegation to the Allied War Reparations Commission. Averell Harriman, U.S. ambassador to the Soviet Union, temporizing with the hope of convincing Roosevelt of the need to use reparations as an economic tool to pry political concessions from the Soviets in regard to Eastern Europe, succeeded in delaying Lubin's departure for Moscow. Harriman knew how eager the Soviets were to reach an agreement on reparations and he believed a purposeful delay might serve as a diplomatic tool to help restrain the repressive actions taken by the Soviet authorities throughout the region occupied by the Red Army.

The week after Roosevelt's death, Harriman persuaded President Truman of the need to get tough with the Soviets and to use economic means—including Lend Lease, trade agreements, and reparations—as one way to exert pressure. In response to Harriman's advice, Truman replaced Lubin with his good friend, Democratic Party treasurer Ed Pauley. Pauley was given the rank of ambassador; while Lubin, who remained on the reparations commission, received the subordinate rank of minister. Truman told Pauley that he was to act as the president's personal representative on all reparations matters and that he was to report "personally and directly" to the president.[3]

Truman later said that he chose the tall, broad-shouldered, and talkative Pauley because he "wanted someone as tough as Molotov." Although Pauley's selection relieved the anti-Soviet hard-liners in the State Department, many observers were dismayed by the appointment. Pauley's only credentials seemed to be that he had played a critical role in the maneuvering at the 1944 Democratic convention that had resulted in Truman's selection to be Roosevelt's vice president. His appointment smacked of cronyism, but Truman, equally inexperienced in these matters, was more comfortable with having as his personal representative to the repararations conference someone he knew well and trusted. Some critics felt, however, that Truman should have selected someone better schooled in foreign affairs. Even some of Pauley's friends questioned the appointment. Upon hearing the news of Pauley's new job, Justin Wolf, former PAW legal counsel told geologist Everett DeGolyer: "Holy Jesus! Could it be that Ed has some inside dope to the effect there's oil somewhere in Europe and wants to get a first hand look-see? I am both amused and a little concerned. I would have been much happier if some one of greater stature had been appointed."[4]

Meanwhile, the Soviets were getting anxious about Truman's delay in getting the U.S. reparations delegation formed and dispatched to Moscow. Soviet foreign minister Molotov met with Harriman and Pauley in San Francisco during the United Nations meeting on May 7 and expressed his government's desire to get the process started as soon as possible. Harriman explained that the United States and Great Britain wanted to make France a member of the commission. The Soviets had refused initially to accept this proposal unless Poland and Yugoslavia were also included. Molotov now agreed to leave French participation open to further discussion and to drop the demand to include their Eastern European allies if the United States and Great Britain would come to Moscow and proceed with the commission's work. Satisfied that constructive work might be accomplished, Truman allowed Pauley to recruit the members for the U.S. delegation. Under the pressure of time, Pauley decided to get someone with known administrative talent whom he could trust to help him organize his delegation quickly. His first choice was J. R. Parten, whose administrative performance at the PAW had been admired throughout the oil industry.[5]

Staffing the Pauley Mission

Daunted by the complex nature of the reparations process, Pauley and Parten decided to recruit a staff of thirty experts to go on the mission to Moscow. These experts included businessmen to advise Pauley on the technical aspects of industrial equipment, plant facilities, and commodities. As a result of his experiences as a university regent and as a PAW administrator, Parten preferred the advice of experienced specialists over academicians on matters of business and industry. On the other hand, he was equally convinced that academicians were the experts on issues in the realm of human welfare. Because the commission would make decisions with far-reaching effects on the German people, Parten persuaded Pauley of the need to recruit social scientists to work on reparations-related social issues. He further advised Pauley to seek permission from Truman to allow the businessmen on the commission to serve without compensation ("dollar a year men"). That arrangement was necessary to recruit topflight industrial people because it allowed them to remain on their company's payroll. Truman approved the request.[6]

Ensconced in an office in the East Wing of the White House, Parten quickly assembled a staff for the mission. Some were personally recruited by Pauley, others by Parten. Pauley's selections included Dr. Robert Gordon Sproul, president of the University of California, who served as senior advisor on the "human aspects of reparations." Among Parten's choices were Dr. Luther Gulick, who served as advisor on governmental organizations, and Lt. Col. E. E. "Buddy" Fogelson of Dallas, an independent oil man who was a friend of Parten's from his days as president of the Independent Petroleum Association of Texas. Parten and Pauley both agreed that the commission's legal counsel should be their mutual friend, J. Howard Marshall, who had become president of the Ashland Oil Company.[7]

Pauley and Parten put together a staff drawn mainly from a pool of their own political and oil industry friends. Most of the members were qualified in their respective fields, but the delegation as a whole had little foreign affairs experience. George F. Kennan, Ambassador Harriman's chief foreign service officer in Moscow, thought the commission was too large. He complained to Harriman that the U.S. did not need "thirty experts to drive a bargain" with the Soviets. The delegation's size reflected Pauley's and Parten's belief in the value of specialists and their concern about being in the heart of the Soviet Union without adequate technical help. They also did not want to be dependent on the State Department for advice. Parten in particular distrusted the State Department, believing that it was dominated by Anglophiles who were under the sway of the British Foreign Office. Many of the problems dividing the Big Three he blamed on the British and their attempts to preserve the Empire. Parten also knew that the State Department opposed the idea of a reparations commission. "They wanted to handle that job," Parten recalled. "We didn't count on much cooperation from the State Department, and we didn't get much."[8]

As he recruited personnel for the reparations commission, Parten realized that Truman had created a problem by retaining Lubin as Pauley's second in command. The two men were stark contrasts in background, style, personality, and world views. Although Parten liked and respected Lubin, he feared that Lubin's presence would be divisive. This fear materialized as the commission staff gathered in Washington. It was clear to Parten that the staff was split between those such as Pauley, Marshall, and Sproul who were openly hostile to the Soviets and those such as Lubin, who viewed the Soviet Union as an ally and were determined to continue the policy direction set at Yalta by Roosevelt. "A good many of our people had little respect for the Russians," Parten recalled. "I knew that would cause some headaches." Parten soon found himself more in agreement with Lubin's accomodationist views than with Pauley's "get tough" stance.[9]

Parten had never perceived the Soviet Union as a threat to United States security. Quite the contrary, he shared Roosevelt's view that the Soviet Union was a valued member of the anti-Axis alliance and that it should be allowed to play an important role in shaping the postwar world. Parten felt that it was essential for the United States and the Soviet Union to maintain friendly and mutually beneficial relations after the war. Although opposed to communism, he nevertheless believed that the Soviet government and economic system were the exclusive concern of the Soviet people. These feelings were strengthened as a result of his work with the reparations commission.[10]

"He was on his way to Moscow"

As they worked to build the delegation, Pauley urged Parten to reconsider his decision not to serve as the mission's chief of staff. A few days before the delegaton was scheduled to leave for London, Parten reluctantly gave in to Pauley's pleas. Worried about the split between Lubin and Pauley, he believed he could serve a useful function as a referee between the delegation's factions. Sympathetic to Lubin's minority faction, he felt he could bring some balance to the delegation. "I got in trouble," Parten recalled. "I organized the damn thing, and then I had to make sure it worked." On May 15, 1945, President Truman announced Parten's appointment as the chief of staff of the U.S. delegation to the Allied War Reparations Commission.[11]

Before its departure for Europe, Pauley's delegation received no briefings from the State Department, which was unhappy about the mission, jealous of its turf, and uncooperative. Aware of the State Department's basic antipathy toward their mission, Pauley felt he needed someone "on the ground" back in Washington to serve as his liaison to see that communications moved smoothly from Moscow to the White House. For that job, Parten and Howard Marshall recruited Justin Wolf, their former PAW colleague who was now in the navy. After they began negotiations in Moscow, Parten cabled Wolf frequently. "We could get a message through to him any time," Parten said, "and he had the gumption to see that it got to its target." In a letter to Everett DeGolyer discussing his assignment, Wolf stressed that his job was to "watch for knives that might be thrown" by the State Department at Pauley's and Parten's backs. "I, apparently am to catch all such knives—and, if possible, stop there being thrown. Quite some fun, I assure you." Despite these arrangements, when it came to communications with Washington, Parten felt like they were, in his words, "down in the bottom of a deep, deep well" due to the State Department's delaying tactics whenever they tried to get timely information. After the Moscow meetings were completed, Pauley complained that while he was in Russia and Germany "there was no greater problem than maintaining satisfactory communications with Washington."[12]

After Parten agreed to go to Moscow, he had to return quickly to Houston to pack for the trip. Dallas Sherman was stationed in Washington with the Air Transport Command, so Parten requested that Sherman be recruited to fly him to

Texas. Sherman later recalled that his commanding officer asked if him if he would like to fly to Texas. When he said that he would, he was told that "we got a guy we need to take to Houston to get some clothes and bring him back. It was J. R. So I flew him to Houston in a twin engine beechcraft. . . . He grabbed his clothes and I flew him back. He was on his way to Moscow."[13]

Two days before departing for Europe, Pauley received his written instructions from Truman. The directive ordered Pauley to reach an agreement that would provide the Soviet Union with an appropriate, but unspecified, amount of reparations while limiting those reparations to a level that would allow Germany to remain self-sufficient in its basic needs. In other words, Germany would have to be able to provide for itself without dependence on "sustained outside relief" from the United States. Pauley's basic goal was to get the Soviets to back away from their demand for a twenty-billion-dollar reparations levy against Germany. That figure was considered excessive and likely to result in economic chaos in Europe. The United States had moved toward the position taken by Great Britain. George Kennan thought Truman's instructions were naive. He warned Harriman that neither Pauley nor anyone else could get a reparations agreement out of the Soviets that would be acceptable to the United States. "Reparations would simply be a matter of 'catch as catch can' in the respective zones," Kennan said. "The Russians could be depended upon to do just as they pleased in the area under their occupation, and would not be inhibited in this respect by any agreements with us." Harriman agreed, but he told Kennan to stop worrying about the Pauley commission. "Mr. Pauley's instructions are very firm and while we may not reach any agreement I have no fears about us giving in."[14]

On May 20, Pauley, Lubin, Parten, and most of their staff flew from Washington to London in a U.S. Army DC-4 specially outfitted for extra cargo. Accompanying them was a large amount of basic office equipment, everything they would need except desks and chairs, as well as approximately one ton of printed reports and background studies, raw data, and other research and background material. In addition, there were more than one dozen cases of whiskey, several hundred pounds of coffee, and a large supply of cigarettes; all paid for by Ed Pauley and intended for "diplomatic use." Parten carried his own "diplomatic" supplies: sixteen tubes of lipstick to give to hotel maids in Moscow. Harriman had sent word that Soviet women had rather have lipstick than diamonds.[15]

Parten and his colleagues arrived in London on the evening of May 21. It was Parten's first trip to Europe. The next morning, he joined some of his associates for a quick sightseeing tour of London, including stops at Buckingham Palace, St. Paul's Cathedral, and the Tower of London. In the afternoon they had a lengthy meeting with the British reparations representative Sir Walter Monckton and his staff, who urged the Americans to stay in London for awhile and let the Russians wait. Parten, however, was pushing Pauley to move quickly. Monckton asked Parten: "Why hurry? There's no necessity for rushing this thing, and the more time we'll take, the better off we will be, if we get a sensible agreement." Parten, already suspicious of British intentions, replied that they had no choice, the United States and Great Britain were obligated to carry out the Yalta agreement which specified a resolution of the reparations issue by August.[16]

The Pauley group left London for Paris on the afternoon of May 24 for briefings with Gen. Lucius Clay, who was slated to be military governor of the U.S. occupation zone in Germany. Pauley, Lubin, and Parten had lunch with General Clay at the Trianon Hotel in Versailles on May 25. From Paris, the delegation flew to General Eisenhower's headquarters in Frankfort. After a brief meeting with Eisenhower and his staff, the delegation decided to get some sense of the extent of the war damage to German industry and facilities. Using Frankfort as their base, they divided into six "teams" and traveled for nearly a week over much of the country. Parten's team, which included Howard Marshall and Luther Gulick, visited Heidelburg, Essen, Hamburg, and Leipzig. Parten was surprised that the damage in Germany was not as great as he and his colleagues had anticipated. "When we got to a plant," Parten later recalled, "we'd find that there was nothing in there that couldn't be fixed in two or three weeks. I thought that the bombing would be more devastating than that." The delegation's engineers estimated that the damage was not more than 30 percent of total production capacity and that with money and labor, the Germans could have restored their industry in about ninety days. Nevertheless, the destruction was bad enough. Parten wrote Opal that the trip had been a revelation. "The effects of the war upon this country cannot be pictured at home. Berlin was a sight but no more damaged than Koln or Essen or Manheim, if as much."[17]

The delegation finally departed for Moscow on the morning of June 11. En route, they made an unplanned landing in Berlin because of a misunderstanding with the local Soviet flight-control center. They remained grounded for about three hours. While the Soviet military authorities resolved the problem they provided the Americans with automobiles and escorts to guide them on a tour through the ruins at the center of Berlin. As a result of this bureaucratic hitch, Parten and his colleagues were among the first American civilians to enter Berlin after the German surrender. Soviet escorts drove the delegation down Wilhelmstrasse through the burned-out ruins of the capital city. As they toured Berlin, Parten and Pauley were struck by the contrast between how the Russians and the Americans were each handling their respective zones. The Russian Army had covered the walls of ruined buildings throughout Berlin with posters and slogans urging the Germans to cooperate, denouncing Nazism, and bolstering the self-respect of the German people. They also noted that the Soviets were publishing newspapers and posting them throughout the city and that large groups of Germans were reading them.

Parten and Gulick observed that the United States Army, however, had not initiated or even prepared a similar "reeducation" program. The only newspapers available in the U.S. zone were in English for the American soldiers and the only posters were ones featuring the word *verboten*. On the way to Moscow, they complained to Pauley that the Americans, unlike the Soviets, seemed to have no political program established. At Parten's suggestion, Pauley sent Truman a message as soon as they arrived in Moscow that the job "is not being done in American-occupied Germany. We have accomplished nothing towards convincing the German people that we can offer them a way of life better than the one they had." He urged the president to develop a political reeducation policy and proceed with its implementation as soon as possible. Pauley emphasized that the "military occupation of a once-great nation consists of something more than pointing a gun at its people."[18]

At one point during their visit to Berlin, the delegation walked through what remained of the Reichstag and Adolf Hitler's Chancellery. The highlight of their unplanned tour, however, was the opportunity to go down into the "Fuehrer Bunker" where Hitler had held out during the last days of the war. The underground building seemed surreal to Parten and "rather childlike and futile." Parten entered the quarters where Hitler had committed suicide six weeks earlier, surprised that the rooms seemed relatively undisturbed. The American visitors nevertheless could not avoid the temptation to grab souvenirs. Buddy Fogelson, for example, snatched a telephone from one of Hitler's offices. Parten, although disapproving of some of the petty looting, failed to resist temptation when he got above ground. After leaving Berlin, he wrote Sylvester Dayson to tell his daughter, Suzette, that they had found "scads of medals" in Hitler's Reich Chancellery. "I will bring her one as souvenir of this trip."[19]

Despite his interest in seeing the site of the Third Reich's *Gotterdamerung*, Parten's desire to proceed to Moscow safely proved more compelling. "I was in an awful hurry to get away," he later recalled, "because being an old flier, I wanted to get to Moscow before dark. We had a long way to go." The delegation finally received permission to leave and their two DC-4 airplanes took off from Berlin's Templehof Airport at 5:30 p.m. After a refueling stop in Poland, they landed in Moscow at 10 p.m., shortly after the late dusk of the Russian summer. They were met by Soviet officials who took them directly to the newly refurbished Hotel Savoy, which served as the delegation's home quarters for the duration of their stay.[20]

Moscow

The day after their arrival in Moscow, the Soviets took the Americans on a tour of the city, making stops at the Kremlin, Red Square, and Lenin's Tomb. Parten was deeply impressed with what he saw, especially the city's wide streets and the beauty of the Kremlin buildings. Nevertheless, his need for work and his impatience with leisure time pressed heavily on his feelings. He wrote Opal the evening after the Moscow tour that he was eager for the negotiations to begin; he wanted to get the mission accomplished and "our work done in record time."[21]

Before Parten could establish the delegation offices at Number 4 Stanislovsky Street, however, he, Lubin, and Pauley met with Ambassador Harriman at Spaso House, the U.S. ambassador's quarters in Moscow. Parten had never met Harriman and Pauley knew him only casually. Harriman gave the trio his strong views about reparations and the need to eliminate the twenty-billion-dollar figure as the basis for negotiations. He also stressed the severe problems Great Britain and the United States were having with the Soviets over Poland and the other Eastern European nations occupied by the Red Army. Harriman emphasized that he and the State Department saw no point in Pauley trying to reach a compromise with the Russians on the reparations issue, which he viewed as one of the bargaining tools to be used in settling the Polish problem and the larger problem of Eastern Europe. Harriman believed the reparations issue could not be resolved until Stalin, Churchill, and Truman reached an understanding on Eastern Europe. He saw little possibility of the Soviets accepting the U.S. position, which basically called for the Germans to pay reparations only after their production reached a level capable of maintaining German self-sufficiency. The Germans could not take care of themselves if the Soviets were allowed to strip them of the means to do so.[22]

Parten was impressed with Harriman's knowledge of the Soviet leadership and of conditions in the country, but he was upset by Harriman's general pessimism about the reparations conference. He left Spaso House feeling that Harriman was doing "a first-rate job as an ambassador . . . but he was being dictated to by the State Department. We were trying to get something done. We were trying to negotiate a fair settlement with the Russians who had lost twenty million people." Parten felt that the Soviets should be allowed to take as much from their German enemies as possible as partial compensation for their extraordinary losses and as an acknowledgment by their allies that they had borne the brunt of the war in Europe. He believed the Soviets had legitimate national security concerns in Europe and understood their need to make certain that Germany could never invade their country again. Parten was troubled by Harriman's report that the Soviets were already dismantling entire factories and removing them to the Soviet Union before an agreement had been reached, but he believed the United States and Great Britain were partly responsible for the Soviet actions. The western allies' purposeful delay in meeting with the Russians had given them reason to question their allies' intentions and to take unilateral action to meet their desperate needs. Parten knew, for example, that the United States had abruptly and without warning stopped Lend Lease shipments to the U.S.S.R. Although they had been restored by the time the reparations delegation arrived in Moscow, the incident had deepened Soviet suspicions about basic American intentions. "I thought the Yalta Agreement was a reasonable agreement," Parten said later, "and I thought we should abide by it."[23]

Parten was disappointed to learn that Pauley, in general, agreed with Harriman. Pauley was more confident than Harriman about his ability to talk the Soviets into a reparations agreement acceptable to the United States, but he shared Harriman's views about the need to be tough with the Russians. Parten did agree with the Truman administration's reparations goals as stated in the president's directive of May 18, especially to avoid a situation that would result in the United States paying for German reparations, but he disliked the unthinking anti-Russian "take it or leave it" attitude among most of the Americans and the British. He resolved to do what he could to encourage Pauley's sympathy for the Soviet's situation and his fair dealings with them at the negotiating table, but he understood that he had little chance for success in that area. If nothing else, he was determined to use his authority as chief of staff to ensure the respectful treatment of the Soviets, as allies who had suffered physical and human destruction far in excess of anything conceivable by the average American.[24]

Stalingrad

Parten's sympathetic feelings toward the Soviets and their reconstruction needs were strengthened the day after he and Pauley met with Harriman. The Soviets invited members of the delegation to go to Stalingrad to view the destruction wrought by the German Army. Pauley decided to remain in Moscow to continue his briefings at the embassy, but Parten accepted the invitation. When Parten, Buddy Fogelson, and a few other staff members boarded an American Lend Lease DC-3 with a Soviet Army flight crew, they were shocked when the pilot cranked on the engines and, to save fuel, began to taxi without allowing the engines to warm. As they taxied to their take-off position, Fogelson hurried up to the pilot's cabin and suggested to the crew that it would be an excellent idea to let the engines warm up before they took off. The Russian pilot glared at the American and said "What's the matter, Yank? Are you afraid to die?" Fogelson replied, "Hell no. I'm just not ready to die right now!" The Americans were much relieved when the plane landed safely in Stalingrad four hours later.[25]

On its way to Stalingrad, the plane flew over destroyed town after destroyed town. From the air, it seemed to Parten that the entire world had been crushed by some unimaginable force, as ruins and scorched earth stretched from horizon to horizon. As the DC-3 approached Stalingrad, it slowly circled the city at a low altitude. The first American civilians to see Stalingrad after the war, Parten and his colleagues viewed the ruins in awe of the terrible power of modern warfare. The city was utterly devastated. Parten was even more impressed on the ground. On the way to the site where the Russians were having a special banquet in honor of the Americans' visit, he sat in stunned silence in an open-air car as his driver slowly navigated through the rubble that had fallen on every street in the city. Stalingrad "was just levelled," Parten later said. "There wasn't anything standing in brick mortar higher than three feet. There wasn't a building, or the shell of a building, standing." He saw thousands of poorly dressed and malnourished Russians working without benefit of modern machines or tools, clearing by hand the smashed remains of their homes and buildings. Some of the workers waved and smiled as the cars passed. Parten recalled the letters he received from his fellow citizens while at the PAW, complaining about not being able to take the family car on picnics in the country on weekends. He wrote to Opal that he was profoundly touched by the spirit of the Russian people in the face of this mass destruction and death. "The people here have given a great deal . . . to win the war." He wrote to his mother back in Madisonville, living in what seemed now to be another world, that it was "obvious . . . that the Soviets have paid heavily." Noting their desperate need for food, housing, and clothing, it seemed to Parten that it was "the people of the USSR" especially who had "borne the cost of the war." These were feelings that J. R. Parten retained for the rest of his life.[26]

Parten and his colleagues eventually arrived at an open field where the Russians had set up a large tent, under which they had prepared a bountiful banquet. As they drove up to the tent area, Parten could see that the field was covered with people living out in the open, without shelter, using earthen ovens for cooking and for warmth at night. Nearby they were building a steel mill, which had priority over buildings for living quarters. The Russians had prepared "a rich man's lunch," Parten said. "Cheeses, wines, fruit, and fine sausages," which, according to the Russian interpreter, had been "generously furnished by the Germans." Amused, Parten asked Fogelson if he thought they should tell Pauley to be sure that the food was deducted from the total amount of German reparations due the Soviets. During the meal, there was much speech-making. One Soviet Army officer stood to make a toast, declaring that the Russian people "feel that we have a lot in common with you Americans" since both governments were products of popular revolutions. Parten and some of his colleagues also spoke, but it was Buddy Fogelson who delighted the Russian audience. Fogelson, a descendant of Russian immigrants, spoke with soul-stirring emotion about the great Russian Army and "that great heroine that killed so many Germans with a machine gun from her bunker" during the siege of Stalingrad. When he finished, a Russian soldier leaped to his feet, tore a medal off his chest, and, as the crowd roared, pinned it on Fogelson. After the banquet, the Russians took Parten and his colleagues to other sections of the city, but everything was the same—mind-numbing destruction.[27]

The Texas Fuehrer Parten

Parten was soon back to work organizing the large, auditorium-like delegation office, and making staff assignments for the upcoming negotiations. This preparatory work was conducted during the morning hours from June 15 until June 21. In the afternoons, many of the staff left the office to tour Moscow and its environs. The Soviets provided the Americans with cars, and with chauffeurs who were suspected of being KGB agents. On embassy advice, the Americans toured in groups, never alone. Rather naively, Parten thought the embassy was too cautious. He had second thoughts, however, when he and other delegates received telephone calls from seductively voiced women with heavy Russian accents, inviting them to trysts in Gorky Park. Parten, who assumed the women were KGB agents, lectured the staff against giving in to temptation or curiosity. The suspicion that they were under constant surveillance often forced the Americans to walk out of the hotel and into the street (there being little traffic) to converse. The knowledge that the hotel rooms were bugged inspired some age-old juvenile pranks. Fogelson and Marshall, after one evening of drinking the plentiful Russian vodka with Parten in his and Marshall's hotel room, talked directly to the surveillance "bugs" in the furniture. At one point, Fogelson kept repeating to one suspected microphone that "this is J. R. Parten talking. You are a son-of-a-bitch."[28]

The official negotiations finally began on June 22. Except for some preliminaries, little was accomplished before the conference adjourned on June 23 to allow the delegates to attend a parade the next day in Red Square in celebration of the Red Army's victory over Nazi Germany. June 24, 1945, was the fourth anniversary of Hitler's invasion of the Soviet Union. Accordingly, that date was selected as the long-awaited day when the Red Army would "return" to Red Square and parade victoriously before Marshall Stalin. Eyewitness accounts emphasize the grandeur and power of that event. It has been described as one of the most stunning ceremonial displays of military might in history, "comparable with the great . . . processions which passed through the streets of Rome in honor of the triumphant Caesars."[29]

The Soviets gave the U.S. delegation special seats on bleachers built next to Lenin's Tomb to view the great victory parade. Despite a continuous and heavy rainfall, Parten sat for hours, transfixed by the legions marching and riding past. The "grand spectacle," as he called it, left a lasting impression on him. "I saw those four Soviet armies, fully equipped, polished and shined, parade from ten o'clock in the morning until six thirty in the afternoon in a phalanx that was a quarter of a mile wide," Parten said later. It convinced him for the rest of his life of the need to maintain peaceful relations between his nation and the Soviet Union. A military conflagration between such mighty powers could result only in the destruction of both. Because he had read the secret provisions of the Yalta agreements, Parten knew that the Red Army was headed for Manchuria to fight the Japanese. Stalin had promised Churchill and Roosevelt at Yalta that the Soviet Union would declare war on Japan within three months after Germany's defeat, but that agreement was still secret. From his seat, Parten could easily see Stalin and his commanding general, Marshal Zhukov, as they stood together on Lenin's Tomb watching the Red Army march across Red Square with bared swords, saluting as they passed. At the end of the eight-hour parade, soldiers dragged through the square hundreds of brilliantly colored battle standards captured from the German Army, solemnly lowered them before Stalin, and then tossed them in a pile at his feet.[30]

The day after the parade, reparations negotiations finally began in earnest. Face-to-face negotiations were conducted for the Americans by Pauley and Lubin, while Monckton represented the British. Ivan Maisky, a veteran diplomat who had served as ambassador to Great Britain, led the Soviet side. As Harriman had predicted, the talks quickly bogged down over the critical issue of the twenty billion dollars in reparations demanded by the Soviets. Maisky insisted that the allies had agreed at Yalta to extract twenty billion dollars in damages from the Germans and that the Soviets were entitled to half that amount. Pauley sent a top-secret telegram to the State Department complaining that "Mr. Maisky keeps coming back to the 20 billion dollar sum . . . I have not officially resisted . . . in as much as Roosevelt, Stalin and Churchill agreed to use this as a basis of discussion at Yalta." Pauley's goal was to get Maisky to drop the dollar formula and replace it with a percentage plan. Once an accurate inventory of German factories, equipment, and other salvageable items was completed, each side would be entitled to their percentage of what was available.[31]

In addition to the difficult issue of the twenty billion dollars, the reparations commission also examined a number of complex issues related to the questions of which countries other than the Big Three should receive reparations, how much they should receive, and which of the Big Three would be responsible for seeing that they got it. At the heart of the entire reparations issue was Germany's ability to pay. Parten's staff, therefore, devoted much of its time estimating potential German agricultural output and the number of salvageable German factories and equipment available for reparations, as well as determining what new factories would have to be built to sustain the country and pay for imports.[32]

An especially vexing problem arose when Maisky declared that anything the Soviets had seized from the Germans in the course of fighting the war and in setting up their occupation was "war booty" rather than reparations and therefore should not be deducted from the total amount of reparations due them. The Red Army had already stripped large sections of the occupied areas of railroad rolling stock, heavy equipment, manufacturing tools, coal, tractors and other farming equipment, automobiles and trucks, household furnishings, and other valuable items. The Soviets viewed reparations largely as items to be taken from the western zones and as payments to be made in the future from new production and crops. Pauley and the British rejected the Soviet definition of war booty, arguing instead that war booty should be limited to the equipment and supplies belonging to the German armed forces. They also warned Maisky that to strip the Germans immediately of the ability to feed, house, and cloth themselves would force the United States to provide these essentials at their expense. Pauley stressed that such an arrangement was completely unacceptable. Truman later stated that "we did not intend to pay, under any circumstances, the reparations bill for Europe."[33]

As Pauley, Monckton, and Maisky debated these various issues, Parten coordinated the staff work necessary to provide Pauley with reports on the potential effects of specific actions and background information related to the different questions as they were raised. Unlike Monckton and Maisky, Pauley had no diplomatic experience, nor was he well informed on any of the issues. Although these shortcomings meant little because of his instructions to adhere strictly to predetermined general positions, they did mean that Pauley depended heavily on the staff to prepare the detailed information for his presentations and written responses. Pauley told Parten what he needed and Parten created committees to meet the requirements. These committees frequently conferred with their Soviet and British counterparts in meetings separate from the main negotiations. Parten also served as the delegation's petroleum specialist, occasionally cabling Wolf to get current oil information from Ralph K. Davies, who was still at the PAW. Parten was involved especially in discussions about petroleum production and about drilling and refining equipment in Rumania and Hungary and their availability as reparations. This was another contentious issue because U.S. and British companies had owned most of the petroleum-industry equipment in Rumania before the

Germans seized it. These companies wanted this valuable equipment returned. The Red Army, however, had already removed most of it to the Soviet Union as war booty.[34]

Like every job Parten had in his life, he took his assignment as chief of staff very seriously. He worked hard and expected everyone else to do the same. At the start of negotiations, Parten told the staff that they would adhere to a rigid six-day work schedule, with Sunday work likely. Because the Americans were short of clerical support and the Soviets were presenting large amounts of statistics and detailed projections that had to be analyzed quickly, Parten was often forced to keep his staff working for eighteen to twenty hours a day. Occasionally strategy meetings for the next day's discussions were held after midnight, usually with Ambassador Harriman in attendance. Because of the workload, Parten soon put a stop to the afternoon sight-seeing, complaining that a few of the delegates were more interested in goofing off than working. He also cracked down on anti-Soviet talk, which he viewed as unfair, unprofessional, and potentially damaging to the negotiation process. One of Parten's most troublesome problems was J. Howard Marshall, who found it difficult to hide his intense dislike of the Russians and his deep suspicions of their intentions. Marshall even questioned the loyalty of Isador Lubin, whom he considered to be much too friendly with the Russians. He believed Lubin was passing information to the Russians about the U.S. delegation's meetings. "Among us we had . . . many informers," Marshall claimed. "A good example . . . was our second in command [Lubin]." Friendships or not, Parten was determined to put a stop to the open hostility shown by some of his staff toward the Soviet delegation. He eventually persuaded Pauley to send six members of the delegation back to the United States.[35]

Parten apparently enjoyed the respect of most of his staff, but the fact that he had to be a policeman did not make him popular. One of the delegates composed a poem in honor of Parten's management style, "The Texas Fuehrer Parten":

> Let's raise a glass to Parten,
> Get off your ass for Parten,
> Don't urinate,
> or you"ll be late,
> Then you will hear from Parten.
>
> There's nothing will dishearten
> The Texas Fuehrer Parten,
> Like idle men, who sleep till ten—
> Beyond the time of startin'.
>
> There's no sense in your bleating,
> That there's no time for eating,
> Don't wail or weep, you don't need sleep—
> The Fuehrer's called a meeting.

So raise your glass to Parten,
Get off your ass for Parten,
The Chief Staff Aide, has now been made
The Texas Fuehrer Parten.[36]

A Night at the Bolshoi

There were respites from the hard work, however, even for Parten. In the evenings the Americans occasionally enjoyed Moscow State Philharmonic concerts, Bolshoi Ballet performances, and ethnic folk-dance presentations. Most memorable for Parten was a special evening at the Bolshoi. Parten went to the ballet with Ambassador and Mrs. Pauley and Charles "Chip" Bohlen, the State Department's Russian expert. The Russian vodka-drinking ritual had been observed prior to their departure for the concert hall and its effects influenced Parten, normally a man of rigid self-control, to do an uncharacteristic thing. Pauley had arranged for the beautiful star of the Bolshoi to receive two dozen red roses when she came onstage to take her bows. When the ballerina came out to acknowledge the ovation, she smiled and bowed toward Pauley and Parten. The two immediately argued about which one of them she was bowing to. Parten, not a betting man, bet Pauley one hundred dollars that she was actually looking at him. He told Pauley that he would prove it by taking the ballerina to an upcoming dance at Spaso House. Pauley readily accepted, saying there was no way she would go to Harriman's party. In the sober light of the next morning, Parten wondered "how in the hell I was going to win that bet." He decided to get help from Bohlen, who had excellent contacts in the Kremlin. Bohlen laughed, but told him he thought something could be arranged. Bohlen "pulled that off for me," Parten recalled. Parten and the star ballerina went to Spaso House. "My goodness, she was a wonderful dancer," Parten said. "Like all the other girls, she wanted to come to the States. I won that hundred dollar bet." J. R. wrote Opal a few days later that the ballet and opera had been "the chief amusement for our party. The ballet is most impressive. I wish they could tour the states."[37]

During the day, however, the tedium continued. "We'd meet almost every morning," Lubin recalled, "and we'd ask the Russians for a list of what they wanted and they'd come back and say we want so many billions of dollars. And we'd . . . argue the absurdity of it, and keep repeating it day after day—made no progress at all." In an attempt to get some kind of an agreement out of the conference, the State Department sent Pauley instructions advising him that the twenty-billion-dollar figure remained unacceptable, but the reparations agreement did not necessarily have to depend on a percentage formula. He was now authorized to propose a set figure of from twelve to fourteen billion dollars. Pauley felt he was getting contradictory instructions. He decided to stick by his original plan, ignore the State Department's new proposal, and inform Maisky that a plan based on a fixed-sum formula was the only kind the U.S. would accept. This guaranteed a deadlock. One of the American staff members, Richard Scandrett, later criticized Pauley's handling of the negotiations, charging that he had made no attempt to negotiate in good faith. Pauley's tactics and the attitude of the delegation, Scandrett argued, "clearly indicated to the Soviets that what he really proposed was to renegotiate the Yalta agreements." Lubin, however, had a different view. He believed the failure to reach an agreement was the result of a fundamental difference at the highest policy-making levels of the governments of the Soviet Union and the United States. "I don't think it would have made a bit of difference who represented us."[38]

Apparently as a result of Pauley's refusal to budge from his position, Maisky cancelled meetings "for reasons of ill health." Parten drafted an official letter for Pauley to send to Maisky protesting these frequent postponements and requesting that a schedule of daily sessions be maintained. The negotiations dragged on in this frustrating fashion until July 11, when the reparations commission finally gave up. They agreed to move the discussions to Berlin, where Stalin, Truman, and Churchill were scheduled to meet in the suburb of Potsdam. The issue of reparations had not been on the official agenda for the conference, so Parten drafted a cable to the State Department requesting that it be included. He prepared a similar letter for Harriman to send to Molotov. The Moscow reparations conference, hopelessly stalemated, officially ended on July 13.[39]

Ending the Moscow conference without an agreement or any sign of progress was a deeply disappointing experience for Parten. At the last session, the Soviets accused the Americans of reneging on the Yalta agreement. "I think there's some ground for the Russians to have felt that way," Parten said. "I left there with the feeling that if we didn't change our attitude, we would have a lot of trouble down the line with the Russians." Parten had seen that much of Russia had been destroyed by the Germans. When he arrived in Potsdam, he observed that the Soviets were engaged in the wholesale dismantling of German factories in their zone before any agreements had been formally reached. He believed the American intransigence at the reparations conference in Moscow was partly to blame. "The Russians decided that we were not going to let them have what they thought they deserved. They'd take complete plants, like a glass plant, or like an oil refinery," Parten said. "Although I didn't approve, I couldn't blame them for it, the way they'd been treated. They just wanted to let the Germans scratch out what they could."[40]

Chip Bohlen claimed in his memoirs, however, that the Soviets failed to prove that there were twenty billion dollars in capital goods and food that could be taken out of Germany without malnourishing and impoverishing its people for years to come. "After thirty-seven meetings with the British and Soviet representatives in Moscow," Bohlen has stated, "the American government had concluded that there was no basis for the Soviet claim." Bohlen's statement, however, fails to consider the fact that the Soviets were obviously using that figure as a bargaining chip. By rigidly refusing to discuss reparations in terms of monetary value and insisting on percentages, which were meaningless without an agreement on total value, Pauley gave the Soviets no real opportunity to scale down the amount in the negotiations.[41]

Although it has been well documented that the Soviets began their removal of factories and other industrial and agricultural material weeks before the reparations conference even began, part of the problem was one of definition. The Soviets believed they were entitled to this property as "war booty." Rejecting this argument, Pauley described their behavior as "organized vandalism." The Soviets probably did accelerate their removal program as a result of the deadlock in Moscow. However, the French were also "liberating" large amounts of the same type of material, but no one complained. One could well argue that these removals were necessary to reconstruct a nation desperately in need. Why not take what was needed from those who had created the need in the first place? Why starve while you waited for your former enemy to rebuild and prosper? Whether or not this argument was "right" or "wrong," obviously depends on one's own subjective perspective. Nevertheless, it was an argument with which J. R. Parten partially sympathized. He also agreed with Lubin's final judgement about the thirty-three days of hard work in the Soviet capital: "The mission to Moscow was a complete failure."[42]

Potsdam

On Saturday, July 14, the Pauleys, Lubin, Parten, Marshall, and Gulick flew to Berlin with Ambassador Harriman and his staff. They were taken to Babelsberg, the German movie colony halfway between Berlin and Potsdam, where they were given a large house overlooking a small lake. The next day, the entire U.S. contingent went to Gatow Airfield to greet President Truman and his new secretary of state, Jimmy Byrnes. Truman asked Pauley to ride with him to Babelsberg, where he was also staying. The president was eager to hear his old friend tell him about his experiences with the Russians in Moscow.[43]

Stalin did not arrive until the morning of the opening day of the conference, July 17. Churchill had arrived the previous day. The Soviet leader, who was serving as the host, officially opened the conference at the three-hundred-year-old Cecilienhof Palace in Potsdam, late in the afternoon of the 17th. Parten's spirits rose with the beginning of the conference. Not only was he excited about being a participant in such an historically significant event, but the new surroundings seemed to breath life into the reparations issue. Pauley told him that Byrnes was confident that a reparations agreement could be worked out and that he had some ideas about how to break the deadlock. He also noticed that the Soviets seemed more flexible. Truman, Churchill, and Stalin agreed to get the reparations talks back on track and referred the matter to the Foreign Ministers Committee, which subsequently established an economic subcommittee to continue the reparations negotiations. Will Clayton served as head of the U.S. delegation to the subcommittee, with Pauley serving as his chief advisor. Pauley immediately summoned most of the staff that had remained in Moscow, and Parten went back to work with his coordinating duties. Clayton also asked Lubin, Parten, and Marshall to attend the negotiation sessions and participate in the discussions. Maisky and Monckton continued to represent their respective countries.[44]

Parten's morale improved as he became more directly involved at Potsdam in the actual negotiations than he had been at Moscow. He was busy drafting memoranda and reports, participating in policy discussions, and attending the actual

Joseph Stalin and Harry S. Truman with advisors at the Potsdam Conference, 1945.
Photograph taken by J. R. Parten. *CN 09590. Courtesy Parten Photograph Collection, CAH.*

working sessions. In a letter to Opal, J. R. admitted that the assignment was "most interesting" but that the work day continued to be as long as fifteen hours. He was more optimistic than he had been in Moscow. "We are making some headway," he reported to Opal, "and hope to be through in August." The reparations discussions with Maisky and Monckton were going more smoothly than they had in Moscow. Each side seemed slightly more open to considering a variety of reparations options. Parten wrote Sylvester Dayson that "at last I feel we are getting a real grasp of our problems; it has been and is no easy task." Parten also felt that Pauley's performance had improved: "I have come to have greater respect for his ability," Parten told Dayson, "though I knew him mighty well before this trip."[45]

The evenings at Potsdam and Babelsberg were also more enjoyable than those at Moscow. Truman, Churchill, and Stalin tried to outdo each other in giving large and lavish banquets. Parten had a number of friends in the U.S. contingent. He visited frequently with his fellow Texan Will Clayton, whose house was next door to Parten's. One pleasant surprise was to find Dallas Sherman at the conference. Sherman had flown one of the American contingent's airplanes to Berlin. After dinner one evening, Parten told Sherman that except for a few medals, he had resisted the temptation to "liberate" any German military items for souvenirs. He had frowned upon his colleagues stuffing suitcases and lockers full of their own "war booty." He confessed, however, to wanting one souvenir. As a pilot, he would love to have some item from a Luftwaffe airplane. The next day Sherman went to an airfield and removed an altimeter out of a wrecked German fighter and brought it to Parten.[46]

On July 23, Parten accompanied Pauley to meetings with Byrnes, British foreign secretary Anthony Eden, and Molotov, where he participated in the discussion about reparations. He noticed that the Soviets were modifying their position, but Byrnes was not. Byrnes asked Molotov if it was true that the Soviets had already taken large quantities of material out of their occupation zone. Molotov said that they had taken war booty, but if that was a problem, he would agree to deduct the value of this material from the total amount of reparations requested by his government. When Molotov estimated the value of the material to be three hundred million dollars, Byrnes objected, claiming that the value of what the Soviets had already removed was far greater than that. Molotov offered to lower the Soviet half of the twenty billion by one billion dollars to cover the items already taken "and thus dispose of the question." Byrnes rejected this offer, insisting that nine billion dollars was still excessive. Parten was puzzled by Byrnes's increasing confidence and his unyielding attitude.[47]

As the conference entered its second week, Parten understood why Byrnes and others in Truman's immediate entourage seemed so newly confident and optimistic. It had nothing to do with any new plans or ideas. It had everything to do with news that the United States had successfully tested the first atomic bomb on July 16, the day after Truman had arrived in Germany. Truman and Churchill had decided at the time to wait a few days before giving this news to Stalin. On Tuesday, July 24, after the conclusion of that day's plenary session, Truman casually walked up to Stalin and told him that the United States had developed a new weapon of "unusual destructive power." He never used the words *atomic* or *bomb*, nor did he mention any plan to drop it on Japan. Truman and his close associates were surprised when Stalin showed little curiosity about this momentous development. He merely said that he was glad to hear the news and that he hoped it would be of use against Japan. No other questions were asked.[48]

Parten was not present at this plenary session, but he heard about the bomb an hour or two later from Pauley, who emphasized that it "would keep the Russians straight." It seemed to Parten that the news about the bomb changed the outlook on both sides at Potsdam. The Americans began to brag, Parten said, "about how much it would increase our power in handling Russia." When recalling the event many years later, Parten claimed that he could "tell right after it happened that Stalin's whole attitude towards the conference had changed. Stalin was a different man than what I'd seen of him the day before. You could see that. I thought the cold war started right there." Parten's colleagues talked openly about how the United States no longer needed Soviet help in the war against Japan and that, from then on, U.S. policy should be to build up Germany as a buffer to help contain the Red Army. Josiah E. DuBois, a member of Parten's staff at the Potsdam Conference later stated that he got "to know Pauley very well and he showed me a memorandum by the State Department . . . in effect saying . . . that our goal should be . . . rebuilding a strong Germany as a buffer against Communism. . . . It was not openly discussed—it was hush, hush."[49]

Parten became concerned about the resurgence of openly voiced anti-Russian hostility within his own group. Joseph E. Davies, a member of Truman's contingent, wrote in his diary: "The extent of the disparagement which one hears in our own delegation as to the Russians is alarming. . . . The Pauley Reparations Commission and Harriman [are] violently critical. It is disheartening." Chip Bohlen also noted the "animosity" and the deepening "reserve on both sides that symbolized basic distrust." One evening while dining among the delegates from the Soviet Union, Dr. Sproul began talking loudly about the Russians being inferior people. Parten scolded the university president and threatened to send him home. Parten reported the incident to Pauley, reminding him that Sproul, who had also been a problem in Moscow, had been Pauley's "mistake."[50]

By this time, Pauley, Clayton, and Byrnes had concluded that the only plan that had any chance of acceptance was one that allowed each country to take its reparations claims from its own zone. Since most of Germany's industrial capacity lay within the western zones, the United States and Britain would send some small percentage of the material in their zones to the Soviet zone, which was largely agricultural. The Soviets, in turn, would have to send a percentage of the agricultural output in their zone to the west. They decided to link this plan with a dispute over the permanent location of the German-Polish border. The United States would accept the border's location at the Oder-Neisse line as demanded by the Soviets if they would accept the zonal plan. Truman consented, and Byrnes made the proposal to Molotov, who agreed to take it to Stalin.[51]

On July 25, the day after the news about the bomb test, Parten and Marshall joined Pauley and Clayton in lengthy deliberations and arguments with Maisky and Monckton about this new zonal plan. The discussion centered on the question of how much the Soviets could have from the British and U.S. zones. Parten made a presentation on oil, emphasizing the need to transfer surplus oil from Eastern Europe to the Pacific to support allied military needs in the fight against Japan. Maisky interrupted Parten frequently. Marshall, keeping notes for Parten, could barely conceal his hatred for the Russians at this meeting. After Maisky made a conciliatory statement, Marshall wrote in Parten's notebook the words "Bull!" and "Actions speak a damned site louder than words!" When Maisky claimed that the Russians had been unable to find any surplus oil in Romania and Hungary, Marshall wrote "Bull Shit!" in the notebook.[52]

All negotiations were suspended for a day on July 26, when the British returned to London to await the outcome of national elections. As a result of the unexpected Labor Party victory, Churchill and Eden did not return. Clement Attlee, who had been attending the conference with Churchill, came back as the new British prime minister. While the British were in England, Parten accompanied Will Clayton and Pauley on a tour of industrial sites in Berlin. Although it did not appreciably lessen his sympathy for Russia's position, Parten did not like what he saw. He wrote in his notebook that "one gets the impression that sheer vandalism is running at high speed in [the] treatment of Germany. Not only are war plants being taken by [the] USSR before the Reparations plan is agreed on but as well all . . . light industry." He noted that stripping Germany of all manufacturing capacity without concern for future needs "means a tremendous problem of underemployment for Berlin and all of the USSR zone and to some extent the whole of Germany." The next day, Parten drafted a letter for Pauley reporting these observations to Byrnes.[53]

On July 28, Parten supervised the compilation of a report for Byrnes and Truman on the status of the reparations negotiations. There was little to report. Molotov strongly opposed the zonal plan and complained to Byrnes that the United States was trying to overturn agreements made at Yalta, claiming once again that Roosevelt had agreed on the twenty-billion-dollar figure. Byrnes explained that accepting something as "a basis for discussion" was not a sacred commitment. He told Molotov that "Mr. Pauley had been in Moscow for thirty five days" explaining that the figure was "not practical." This went on for four more days, with the Soviets desperately trying to make a deal that would establish a dollar amount to be taken from Germany as a whole, even to the point of lowering their demands to within one billion dollars of the amount estimated by the State Department as being fair. The Soviets needed the type of heavy industry located in the German Ruhr region and a zonal approach would keep them from getting it. Chip Bohlen, who was serving as an advisor and interpreter for Byrnes, recalled that "the discussions on reparations were endless, tortuous, complicated, and confused."[54]

On July 30, Parten came down with a virulent case of influenza and was confined to his bed for two days. As a result, he missed the meeting at which the Soviets finally accepted a plan. The United States, because of the bomb, no longer needing—or really wanting—the Soviets in the war in Asia, had made the last reparations proposal, a "take it or leave it" offer. Molotov's various compromises were rejected almost without consideration. On July 31, Byrnes told the Soviets that they had to accept the American offer or be left with nothing from the heavily industrialized western zones. No matter what the Soviets decided, Byrnes declared that he and Truman were leaving for the United States the next day. Stalin accepted the plan that same day, aware that he would get no reparations from the western zones if he left Berlin without an agreement. The Soviets would take their reparations from their zone in Germany and 25 percent (of an undetermined figure) of the total reparations in the other three zones. About half of the reparations to be taken from the other zones, however, would have to be paid for by food from the Soviet zone. There were no provisions for reparations to be paid from current German production. Reparations were to come exclusively from already existing material and food stocks.[55]

The Potsdam Conference ended on August 2. Officially at least, the difficult issue of reparations had been resolved, with the United States getting its way. Parten wrote to Sylvester Dayson that the reparations agreement was not exactly what he had hoped for, "but it is the result of a lot of very hard and painstaking effort. This has been a tough, tough job." Dayson replied with words calculated to get Parten home as soon as possible. "My friend, it looks like the Japs are calling it a day . . . I see plenty of reason for you to hurry back home so we both can get together and do some planning towards reconversion and the postwar economy."[56]

Pauley and Lubin returned to Moscow to finish some reparations business there, leaving Parten and the staff with the task of preparing interpretative directives for the implementation and monitoring of the agreement. Parten sent unneeded staff members back to Washington and moved the remaining staff to new offices at 9 Shillerstrasse in Berlin. While Pauley was in Moscow, Parten, Gulick, and Marshall drafted the interpretation of U.S. responsibilities under the Berlin Protocol. On August 11, J. R. wrote Opal: "We have this job about 90% finished—and we expect to slip into Washington and compile the Formal report—a lot of hard work for Gulick and . . . I fear for me."[57]

On August 14, Parten and his colleagues celebrated the news that Japan had agreed to surrender after atomic bombs had destroyed two of her cities. Pauley wanted Parten to stay in Berlin for a few more weeks to serve as his liaison with the U.S. Army, but Parten refused. He felt that the reparations agreement was so nebulous that there was nothing to liaison about. The U.S. military authorities would interpret the agreement in whatever way it suited American interests. As it turned out, less than a year after Potsdam the United States halted all further deliveries of reparations from its zone to the east because of Soviet treaty violations. This action effectively terminated the reparations agreement. Finally, on August 21, after more than one month in Berlin, Pauley, Parten, and the remaining staff closed the office and departed on an army C-54, arriving in Washington on August 22. Parten and Gulick took an office in the State Department building next to the White House, where they spent the next two weeks drafting the mission's final report.[58]

"The Russians are hard-headed businessmen, just like ourselves"

While Parten was in Washington working on the reparations report, he was interviewed by the Houston *Chronicle*. Because of public interest in developments in newly occupied Germany and the increasingly strained relations with the Soviet Union, Parten's interview was widely published by one of the wire services. Still a loyal member of Pauley's team, Parten placed the best light possible on the reparations negotiations. He stressed that the American public did not have to worry about the defeated enemy: "Germany will be stripped of her industry to the point where she will be unable again to wage war. The first aim of the reparations commission . . . was the demilitarization of Germany." He glossed over the deep divisions between the allies evident at Potsdam, stating that the Big Three had agreed on "a fair division of the movable industrial equipment and other German assets so as to compensate as far as possible for losses suffered by the Allied nations."

The *Chronicle* interview also gave Parten an opportunity to air his views about the Soviet Union. He remained upset by the behavior of many of his colleagues in Moscow and Berlin and their militant hostility toward the Soviets. He wanted to do whatever he could to maintain good relations between the two great powers. He especially believed that American businesses should be encouraged to trade with the Soviets. "The Russians are hard-headed businessmen, just like ourselves," he told the *Chronicle*. "They want to trade with us. They are very smart and well educated, and know what they want. They are very realistic." Parten believed that the Soviet Union "is friendly toward us and is going to be a good customer, willing to negotiate and pay for the things she buys." Knowing from personal observation how badly the war had damaged and weakened the Soviet Union, Parten downplayed any military threat. The United States, he claimed, "has nothing to fear from Russia."[59]

Parten wanted his fellow citizens, especially those in the business community, to understand the situation in which the Soviets had found themselves as a result of the brutal and mindless destruction wrought by the Nazi invaders. He even sent this message to his colleagues in the oil industry in Texas—not the most receptive audience. In October the *Texas Oil Journal* featured Parten's remarks about the Soviet Union with a story titled "Major J. R. Parten Sees Big Opportunity for U.S. Understanding With Russia." Knowing what his colleagues would understand best, Parten held out the promise of potentially lucrative business opportunities. He told his deeply conservative Texas friends that "there is no reason in the world why we should not deal openly and fairly with the Russians and have faith in them." Pointing out that the Russians had more undeveloped natural resources than the United States, he believed opportunities awaited American businessmen who were willing to put aside ideological differences. As a businessman, Parten stated that he admired the Soviet's frank admission of what they wanted and needed, and their sharp trading to get it.[60]

Parten was distressed by the negative reactions such statements were eliciting from his oil and gas friends, as well as the vitriolic anti-Soviet editorials he was reading in such newspapers as the Dallas *News* and the Houston *Chronicle*. Reflecting a hopeful if deeply naive view about the Soviet state—a view he shared with a wide range of American religious, political, and intellectual leaders during those first few months after the war—Parten wrote his journalist friend Henry Fox, the former editor of the Madisonville newspaper, that it was "very unfortunate that we in this country do not have more intimate knowledge of the people of the Soviet Union. Really, they are not a great deal unlike us. The fact is they like their system of government and are unable to understand why some of us in the U.S. dislike it so, in view of our long espoused principle that peoples of the world have a right to self-determination of government."[61]

Parten's opinions about the benign nature of the Soviet government completely changed with the outbreak of the Korean War and as the evils of Stalinism became more evident, but he never became a Russophobe, nor did he ever retreat from his basic belief in the need to maintain peaceful relations with the Soviet Union. His view of the proper relationship between the two superpowers was very similar to the detente policy later espoused by Richard Nixon and Henry Kissinger. Parten also never believed that the Soviet Union was solely responsible for the Cold War. Based on his own experiences, he felt that the United States deserved *some* share of the blame. Forty years after his trip to Moscow, Parten still held firm: "We are unfair when we claim that the Russians won't live by an agreement, when we ourselves did a great deal to tear up the Yalta Agreement. If you really try, I think you can make an agreement with the Russians. The trouble is, I don't think we've ever tried." Even in the darkest days of the Cold War, Parten's memories of Stalingrad and Moscow during that summer of 1945 continued to bolster his belief in the need to keep the peace. As the nuclear-arms race escalated to frightening dimensions, that belief became a dominant, overriding concern.[62]

While Parten and Gulick worked on the final report on the German reparations commission, Pauley urged Parten to continue as chief of staff for the Japanese reparations negotiations in Tokyo, which were scheduled to begin in October. Parten refused; he was eager to return to Texas to work on projects at Woodley. Because of difficulties in writing the final report for the Moscow conference, however, Parten was forced to commute from Texas to Washington almost weekly from October until December. When Gulick and Parten finally completed the report, they submitted it to the White House, where it was quickly buried and forgotten. "Neither Gulick nor I thought we had accomplished a lot," Parten admitted. Parten found the experience frustrating and a waste of time, leaving him with no desire ever to accept another government post, except on a temporary basis or as an advisor.[63]

"This is a destroyer of nations and people"

In December, while Parten was in Washington completing the reparations report, he attended a symposium on the effects of nuclear warfare. Among the panelists was Arthur Compton, one of the physicists Parten and Homer Rainey had tried to recruit for the University of Texas. Compton had been intimately involved in the effort to develop the atomic bomb. He and his fellow scientists explained the terrible power of the bomb and described in startling and vivid detail what it had done to the people of Hiroshima and Nagasaki. They also emphasized that there was no such thing as the "secret" of the atom bomb, every physicist understood how it worked; only the technical aspects of the firing mechanism was a "secret" and, being an engineering problem, it would not be a secret for long. They predicted that the Soviets could develop their own bomb within five or six years. Parten was sickened and frightened by what he heard that evening. He realized, as he said later, that "this is a destroyer of nations and people, and we must put this thing under international control."[64]

The revulsion Parten felt that evening about nuclear weapons stayed with him for the rest of his life. Over the years, that revulsion underpinned a deeply felt belief that the nuclear arms race had to stop; that nuclear weapons posed a grave threat to the very existence of life on this planet. By 1950, he was distributing to his business associates dozens of copies of a story about Albert Einstein's warnings against developing the so-called "super" or hydrogen bomb. The newspaper article was titled "Stop Fighting or Disappear From Face of Earth, Einstein Warns

347

Mankind." Parten wrote across the top, "Please note—Seems to me this is an IMPORTANT warning!!" Matched with his already strong views about Soviet-American relations, Parten's fear of nuclear war convinced him that everything possible had to be done to maintain the peace between the two superpowers possessing the capability of destroying the world. As the arms race escalated, the cause of peace became one of his burning passions.[65]

The Pauley Affair

In January 1946, President Truman appointed Ed Pauley undersecretary of the navy. Parten was pleased by this news, but many others were not. Pauley's appointment created a storm of criticism. At Pauley's Senate confirmation hearings, Harold Ickes testified that in 1944, Pauley, who was then serving as treasurer of the Democratic National Committee, had offered to raise three hundred thousand dollars in campaign funds from his California oil-industry friends if the federal government would not attempt to claim ownership of the submerged land ("tidelands") extending from the United States coastline. Pauley and his associates were exploring for oil at these offshore sites and they did not want to buy leases from the federal government, which would insist on higher royalties and bonuses. Pauley knew that more favorable financial terms for the oil companies could be arranged if ownership resided with the state governments of California and Texas, states that were certain to have extensive deposits of oil under their submerged coastal lands. Pauley denied Ickes's accusation, and President Truman defended Pauley. The subsequent furor began a chain of events that eventually led to Ickes's resignation as secretary of the interior.[66]

Actually, Pauley's appointment was not popular with many of the leaders of the oil industry, some of whom worried that Pauley, who had a reputation as something of a con artist, was a scandal waiting to happen. There was much uneasiness, for example, about the sanctity of the huge Navy oil reserve, which had been the object of scandal in the infamous Teapot Dome affair in the 1920s. The industry felt that it could ill afford the bad publicity sure to be produced by the confirmation hearings and the revelations that might surface about Pauley's alleged wheeling and dealing. Parten did not share this concern. He trusted Pauley and believed the California oil man was capable of being an excellent federal administrator. Nevertheless, Parten remained aloof from the controversy until the famed muckraking journalist Drew Pearson attacked Pauley in his nationally syndicated newspaper column. Pearson claimed that Pauley had mismanaged the reparations commission and had bungled the negotiations at Moscow and Potsdam. Quoting reparations commission staff member Richard Scandrett, Pearson charged that the men Pauley had selected for the mission were inadequate and unskilled for the job.[67]

Pearson's criticism, of course, stung Parten badly since he had personally selected some of the members of the commission and had been the person responsible for managing its affairs in Moscow. He sent a letter to Sen. David Walsh, chairman of the Senate Naval Affairs Committee declaring that Scandrett's accusations were "wholly unfounded." Parten pointed out that Scandrett was not present at Potsdam and was in Moscow for only a brief time. He claimed that Pauley's performance had been "intelligent" and "untiring" and "valiant." As for the staff that went to Moscow, Parten wrote that he "cheerfully" took his share of the responsibility "for the qualifications of the bi-partisan personnel of the American delegation" and that Pearson's criticisms of its members were "wholly unfounded." Parten deplored the fact that an international negotiation "of such far-reaching importance . . . has been injected into a partisan political fight." He urged the Senate committee to confirm Pauley's appointment. Nevertheless, on March 13, 1946, as the attacks by the press and Republican members of Congress mounted, Truman withdrew the nomination at Pauley's request.[68]

Parten's support of Edwin Pauley in 1946 is difficult to understand. The shadows of scandal trailed the California oil man for most of his adult life. Harold Stassen, Republican governor of Minnesota, once said of Pauley that his "sense of right and wrong is not fully developed." Nearly every student of the controversy has agreed that Ickes's charges against Pauley were creditable. Pauley, who became a special assistant to the secretary of the army after the naval appointment controversy (a special assistant did not need Senate approval), later admitted to making nearly one million dollars by speculating in commodities while a member of the Truman administration. Although he denied having benefited from inside information, a number of people accused him of unethical behavior. Pauley was later accused of questionable business activities in his oil dealings in Mexico and of having a financial conflict of interest as a regent for the University of California. Parten's support seems to have stemmed from a basic feeling of loyalty and a belief that Pauley had been falsely accused. He had worked closely with Pauley and he knew the accusations about his work in Moscow were unfair. When Pauley was forced to resign from his army post, however, Parten remained silent. Although they remained friends until Pauley's death, Parten eventually saw Pauley for what he was—a man with few scruples when it came to making money. As a result, Parten always rejected Pauley's seductive invitations for him to invest in his lucrative Mexican oil dealings.[69]

As for the reparations agreement, on which Pauley and Parten and their colleagues on the commission had worked so diligently in Moscow, in reality the Soviets got little beyond what they removed from their own occupation zone. The agreement, however, had far-reaching political consequences unforseen by the negotiators. Although the Potsdam protocol declared that Germany would be treated as one political and economic unit, the reparations agreement played a role in ultimately keeping the country rigidly divided between the Soviet zone in the east and the American, British, and French zones in the west. This division was a source of international tension and a threat to world peace for nearly forty-five years.[70]

CHAPTER 20

The Rainey Crusade

1946

Whole Parten was in Europe with the Allied War Reparations Commission during the late spring and summer of 1945, former University of Texas president Homer Rainey was preparing to run for governor. Although Coke Stevenson had not declared his intentions, it was generally believed that he would not run for a third term. In April, Rainey confided to one of his supporters that he had decided to remain in Texas to "see this fight through in whatever way I can. If it means ultimately that I am the one to become the leader of the liberal movement, I will not close my mind to it." Rainey's visibility as a public figure was given a boost when he began a daily statewide radio broadcast to present his commentary on current events and topics such as education, health care, and veterans affairs. The fifteen-minute radio program provided Rainey with an income and gave him a forum from which to launch a gubernatorial campaign. Former University of Texas students upset by Rainey's firing and liberal political activists eager to deny control of the Governor's Mansion to the conservative anti–New Deal faction of the Democratic Party began to organize "Rainey for Governor" clubs in several counties. Throughout the summer, Rainey worked to put together an organization. "I am making numerous contacts," Rainey wrote to one of his supporters, "and am carrying on a considerable correspondence and am keeping in touch with a great many people." The results of a statewide poll in August 1945, indicating that Rainey and Lyndon Johnson were the leading candidates for governor, provided Rainey with additional momentum.[1]

Parten had not shared in this enthusiasm for a Rainey candidacy. Before he left Texas to work with the reparations commission, Parten had tried to discourage Rainey from running for governor. He did not believe Rainey could raise enough money to wage a successful campaign against Coke Stevenson or whoever eventually became the conservative Democratic candidate. Instead, Parten was trying to talk Jimmy Allred into making the race, and Allred was listening. If

Allred eventually decided against being a candidate, Parten's second choice was Cong. Lyndon Johnson. Although Parten's lack of encouragement had not persuaded Rainey to stay out of the race, Rainey knew that Parten's support would be critical to the success of his campaign. In October 1945, while Parten was still in Washington, Rainey requested a meeting as soon as possible. "The time is rapidly approaching," Rainey said, "when I must make a decision about next year, and I don't want to make that decision without an opportunity to talk it over thoroughly first with you."[2]

Parten was unable to meet with Rainey until mid-December. By then, Parten's thinking had changed. Allred seemed to be losing interest in the governor's race and Johnson was sending out contradictory signals reflecting his very real ambivalence about the job. In addition, Parten was impressed with the popular response to Rainey's radio program, which was carried by nineteen stations and was generating about four thousand letters a week from farmers. Parten warned Rainey that it would be an exceedingly tough election campaign, but if Allred and Johnson really were out of the race, the former University of Texas president could count on the votes of the pro–New Deal majority in Texas. He promised his support, but advised Rainey not to announce his candidacy until late spring. The time would be needed to get an organization together and raise money. If Rainey did not declare his candidacy until late spring, Parten felt that he could continue to get free airtime as a "lecturer" for the speeches he would be making around the state. Parten's decision gave Rainey a great personal boost. He assured Parten that his support was "indispensable" and that he could not make the race without it. He had been told by a friend in Wichita Falls, for example, that "if Major Parten endorses your candidacy for Governor . . . I am sure that you will be able to carry North Texas."[3]

Once Parten made his decision to support Rainey for governor, he committed much of his working time in the early months of 1946 to organizing a "draft Rainey" movement to make it appear as though Rainey was responding to a groundswell of popular opinion when he declared his candidacy in May. Parten recruited former *Daily Texan* editor D. B. Hardeman to serve as Rainey's unofficial campaign manager, a title that became official after Rainey's announcement. Boyd Sinclair, who as editor of the *Daily Texan* had caused Parten and Rainey so much trouble because of his antiwar editorial, became Rainey's press officer. Marlin Sandlin served as Parten's liaison with Rainey's Austin staff, while Parten's personal secretary at Woodley provided a variety of clerical services to the unannounced campaign. Beginning in February, each month Parten personally sent a check for five hundred dollars to Hardeman to pay office rent and expenses.

Throughout February and March, Parten worked in Houston and Dallas to round up additional financial support. To avoid attracting public attention, he contacted only those persons he knew to be sympathetic to Rainey. These early recruits included Houston's Jesse Andrews, of Baker and Botts law firm, Judge Roy Hofheinz, and independent oil-operator Dick Hooper, and Dallas's Roland S. Bond, an oil man, and clothier Stanley Marcus. Sylvester Dayson pledged a large contribution, but Rainey was too liberal for Parten's attorneys Myron and Jack Blalock, who refused to help. In addition, Parten contacted the leaders of the Women's Committee for Educational Freedom and urged them to work independently at the grassroots level to prepare the way for Rainey's candidacy. Responding with enthusiasm, they organized "Rainey for Governor" clubs throughout Texas. These activities soon attracted attention. On March 6, the Dallas *Morning News* broke the news that Rainey had a covert "publicity" office in Austin managed by two former news journalists. Rainey refused, however, to admit that he was a candidate. He continued to travel the state giving "educational" lectures that were frequently broadcast on local radio stations, providing him with free radio time. Parten wrote "Lube" Lubin, who was now working for the movie industry in New York City, that the Rainey campaign was "getting along in fine fashion in the absence of a formal announcement by him. He is still talking daily on the radio simply lecturing on local, national, and international issues."[4]

Lyndon Johnson finally announced on March 27 that he would not be a candidate for governor and on May 18 Jimmy Allred did the same. "We knew Jimmy wouldn't run," Parten recalled, "but he helped us by making it a mystery. He delayed his announcement at my request. We felt that the threat of Allred being in the race might freeze some of our potential opposition." On May 21, Sen. W. Lee O'Daniel announced that he would not run. With the biggest names out of the race, others were quick to jump in. A total of fourteen people eventually announced their candidacy, but only four were considered to be major candidates. On the extreme right was Lt. Gov. John Lee Smith, whose supporters included Frank Strickland, Orville Bullington, Scott Schreiner, and Dudley Woodward. Also among the major candidates were former railroad commissioner Jerry Sadler and Attorney General Grover Sellers, both of whom were more moderate than Smith, but were still far to the right of Rainey. The candidate who concerned Parten the most, however, was his old friend Beauford Jester, who was now a member of the Texas Railroad Commission. Despite the fact that polls indicated Jester had the least support of any of the major candidates, Parten knew that most of the state's oil money would go to Jester, who would play the moderate alternative between the race- and labor-baiting lieutenant governor on the right and the liberal Rainey on the left. Parten was optimistic about Rainey's chances, however, because he believed that the four major candidates would splinter the conservative vote, while Rainey would attract a solid bloc vote from Roosevelt loyalists. With all the major candidates now in the open, Rainey announced his candidacy over a statewide radio network on May 23. One week later, Coke Stevenson, who had played the role of stalking horse in an attempt to scare Rainey from running, announced that he would not stand for reelection.[5]

"We are Wall Street's richest colony"

Rainey's announcement speech declared that Texas needed "a government run by real Democrats for the benefit of all the people. Too long our state government has been run by Texas Regulars and their fellow travelers, all posing as

Democrats, but actually as reactionary as any Republicans in our national life." Promising a crusade to "unshackle Texas from the powerful economic forces which today control our politics, our industrial life, and threaten our education," Rainey's opening speech was a ringing affirmation of his belief that a "New Texas" was possible, but only if it was rescued from the stranglehold of a colonial economy. Rainey declared that his opponents would be the "people who fear any change or progress; people who now enjoy special privileges; people who fear they will have to help foot the bill for better schools, better roads, better hospitals, and a better welfare program." Like Rainey, Parten believed the battle lines in this election were distinct and uncomplicated. "This is a . . . race of Liberalism against Reaction," he told a friend. "In this campaign essentially all of the Roosevelt people . . . are supporting Rainey enthusiastically, while all the antiRoosevelt people are opposing him with . . . vigor and . . . money."[6]

The issues of this campaign were defined by Rainey and Parten as being identical to the problems that they had hoped the University of Texas would play a leading role in solving in 1939. Walter Prescott Webb's book *Divided We Stand* and its concept of Texas as a "colony" of northern business monopolies served as the overarching framework for Rainey's campaign, just as it had served as an influential guide for his university presidential administration. Equally influential and intimately connected to Webb's thesis, were the economic ideas advocated by Bob Montgomery and Clarence Ayres. Montgomery called for an aggressive antitrust program to open up competition and to end corporate control of the state government. Ayres advocated an equitable and progressive system of taxation based on personal and corporate income taxes. In agreement with Ayres, Rainey argued that great wealth in Texas was going untaxed while the basic needs of the people were going unmet. He called for higher taxes on oil, sulphur, lumber, cigarettes, liquor, and gasoline to provide money for improved health services and education, pay raises for teachers, pensions for the elderly, and farm-to-market roads for farmers. A key part of Rainey's plan to make state government more responsive to the people was his call for the abolition of the poll tax. Initiated in 1902 to discourage people from voting for the Populist Party, the poll tax had been used to disenfranchise poor whites as well as blacks. Rainey emphasized in his campaign speeches that only 28 percent of Texans over the age of twenty-one voted in the 1940 presidential election, when the national average for non–poll tax states had been 71 percent.[7]

Rainey was launching a fullblown populist attack on the Texas economic/political establishment. He stressed this populist theme in a widely noted interview in the Washington *Post* published three days after his official entrance into the race. Claiming that an economic "clique" whose members resided largely outside of Texas controlled "every phase of the life of the State," Rainey charged that out-of-state companies owned or controlled at least 75 percent of the state's developed resources of crude oil and natural gas, and that about 96 percent of the utilities in Texas were controlled by out-of-state interests. Focusing on Montgomery's favorite target, Rainey also charged that a small group of wealthy Wall Street investors controlled almost 100 percent of the state's sulphur production. Rainey said that something was desperately wrong when 70 percent of the state's residents had incomes below the federal poverty line, despite the fact that Texas had a world monopoly on sulphur, over half of the nation's oil reserves, and tremendous amounts of natural gas flowing to the Midwest and the East Coast. Texas was the largest producer of cotton in the nation, yet only 5 percent of that cotton was processed in the state. "Why are we so poor?" Rainey asked, "because we don't own our own resources and the profits go elsewhere. We are Wall Street's richest colony. . . ." The result, Rainey argued, was that Texas had a poor standard of living, poor health, poor nutrition, poor schools, and low teachers' salaries. Rainey repeated and stressed these points in speeches throughout Texas. "I made a speech on the steps of the courthouse [in Stephens County] in which I raised all these questions," Rainey later recalled. "Stephens County was one of the great oil producing areas. . . . They had taken hundreds of millions of dollars of oil out of that one county and yet the county was just as poor as it practically had always been. Well, that was a classic example really of what the rest of the state was experiencing."[8]

J. R. Parten was in full agreement with Rainey's views. "It is a well-known fact," Parten wrote a friend in New York during the campaign, "that a majority of the ownership of many of the large resource industries such as oil, gas, and sulphur, as well as utility companies, et cetera, belong to absentee owners. Texas' raw materials are being drained away from the state at a very rapid rate with meager benefit left to Texas to support an adequate school system, welfare programs or health program." Near the end of the campaign, Parten was asked by an old friend in the oil business, why he was working so hard for Rainey when he was attacking the natural resource industries, especially oil, and calling for higher taxes on companies like Woodley. Parten replied that though he had no special desire to pay higher taxes, "as an oil man I should not object to paying more taxes if it is reasonably necessary for Texas to have a school system and a program of public health and preventive medicine supported by hospital facilities comparable to those enjoyed in such states as California and New York. I regard [Rainey's] program . . . as realistic and sound." In a private letter to one of his cousins in Madisonville, Parten wrote that a Rainey victory "would be the greatest thing for Texas that has happened in this century . . . because he really is the people's friend. . . ."[9]

A partial explanation for Parten's strong support of Rainey was that he obviously harbored a desire to help Rainey vanquish those who had harassed him and treated him so unjustly. But the reasons for Parten's vigorous support of Rainey ran much deeper than that. The wealthy oil man was not the same person who had railed against an active and powerful federal government in 1933. Unlike many who become more conservative and intolerant as they get older and wealthier, Parten had gone the other way. Friend of Rayburn and Ickes, admirer of Montgomery, Dobie, Webb and Ayres, shaped profoundly by his experience as a regent and broadened by his work in Moscow and Berlin, Parten had broken away from the intellectual straitjacket constraining many of his fellow oil men. He would continue to defend the overall interests of his industry; but he was now able to see beyond the narrow confines of greed and selfishness so characteristic of other oil men. At the age of fifty, Parten had become a strong adherent of the brand of liberalism symbolized by Franklin D. Roosevelt, a man whose memory Parten had come to revere. He declared in a speech for Rainey in Madisonville that he was "not ashamed that I believed in the program of the late President Roosevelt. I am proud to tell you that I voted four times for this great Democrat." The depth of his respect for FDR was matched by the intensity of his dislike of the Texas Regulars, and some of his motivation in the Rainey campaign clearly stemmed from a desire to hit them as hard as he could. Parten wrote Ralph K. Davies that Rainey's victory was necessary for "the preservation of democracy. The leaders of the opposition [Texas Regulars] two years ago turned heaven and earth and spent a mint of money in their efforts to steal the Texas vote away from the people." In a speech to his neighbors in Madison County, Parten emphasized that Rainey's program would mean "a better life for Texans freed from the clutches of corporations and their hirelings, the Texas Regulars."[10]

Rainey began the campaign as the leading candidate in the polls, but his rating was only 29 percent. Jerry Sadler was ranked in second place with 24 percent, John Lee Smith followed with 15 percent, and Grover Sellers and Jester were in a virtual tie with 12 and 11 percent respectively. Parten knew that it was highly unlikely that Rainey or anyone else could win a majority of the votes in the first primary. The goal was to make certain that Rainey made the runoff. Hopefully, Rainey would increase his percentage of supporters during the first primary and either Smith or Sellers would be his opponent in the second one. Parten believed that Jerry Sadler's supporters could be won over to Rainey if either or both candidates failed to make the runoff. Although heavily tainted with racism, Sadler espoused a strain of East Texas populism. Parten felt that Rainey's call for populistic-style economic reforms would appeal to Sadler's followers and that he could win the runoff by converting the Sadler vote.

This strategy made sense for a campaign dominated by substantive issues of public policy such as education, welfare, and tax reform. Unfortunately, the 1946 Texas gubernatorial race was not fought on such a high level. The campaign was dominated by the demagogic use of race, subversion, and sex. Robert Lee Bobbitt expressed this fear to Rainey in late March when he reported rumors that the opposition was planning to throw a lot of mud in Rainey's direction when the campaign began. "I hope and pray that in the days ahead, we can keep this campaign on a high plane." Bobbitt's hopes were soon dashed.[11]

"Rayburn was always nominating me for something"

A summons to a private meeting with President Truman briefly distracted Parten from the Rainey campaign in mid-June. The month before, Sec. of the Interior Julius Krug had appointed Parten, J. Howard Marshall, and ninety-eight other leaders of the oil industry to the newly created National Petroleum Council. Organized to continue the consultative relationship the PAW had developed between the federal government and the oil industry, the council scheduled its first meeting in Washington on June 21, the same day Truman asked Parten to the White House. Parten, who had already made plans to attend the meeting of the Petroleum Council, quickly accepted Truman's invitation, although he had no idea why the president wanted to see him.[12]

When Parten arrived in the capital the day before his appointment at the White House, he dropped in to have a drink with Sam Rayburn at one of the Speaker's famous afternoon "Board of Education" meetings. Held in a private hideaway on the ground floor of the Capitol, Rayburn's after-work sessions included a small group of his friends who would join the Speaker to "strike a blow for liberty" with some bourbon and branch water and to discuss the day's business. The participants in these sessions included whoever Rayburn invited that day and a few regulars such as Texas congressmen Wright Patman and Lyndon Johnson. Parten was among a small group of men who had a standing invitation to attend these sessions whenever he was in town.

Parten's friendship with Rayburn, which dated back to 1933, had deepened during the period Parten had served at the PAW. Rayburn was especially grateful to Parten for his help when the Texas Regulars made a major effort to defeat him in the 1944 primary and his efforts (not particularly successful) to persuade Texas oil men that Rayburn was not their enemy. Parten was grateful to Rayburn for his help in the fight against federal control of the oil industry in the early days of the New Deal and for his continuing defense of the oil-depletion-tax break. But his affection for the short, baldheaded, and stern-faced "Mr. Sam" was genuine, transcending self-interest. Parten especially admired Rayburn's honesty and his utter dedication to the public good. "You know, Rayburn didn't know anything but to tell the truth," Parten would later say. "It was foreign to him not to. Everything that Rayburn did as a public servant, he did in such a way that he wouldn't be embarrassed any way in the world if it was hung on the line tomorrow."[13]

Bernard Rapoport, a Texas insurance company executive and liberal Democrat who became a close friend of Parten's, noted that "if you were going to list the people in J. R.'s life who he would put on the highest pedestal, who he really admired the most, Sam Rayburn would be that person." As a twenty-seven-year-old Texas congressman, Lloyd Bentsen first met Parten at one of Rayburn's Board of Education sessions at about this time. He later recalled that Parten "looked like someone 'central casting' would have sent down to play the role of Secretary of State." Bentsen remembered that Rayburn "often turned to him for advice, not only on matters concerning minerals, but on questions concerning the military-industrial complex and foreign affairs." Rayburn advised Bentsen to become better acquainted with Parten, because he was "a broad-gauged man—a friend on which you could depend." This was advice Bentsen would act upon twenty years later when he ran for the U.S. Senate.[14]

It was at a Board of Education session that Parten learned what Truman had in mind. Rayburn told him that the president wanted him to serve as the first chairman of the recently created Council of Economic Advisors. The purpose of the council, authorized four months earlier by the Employment Act of 1946, was to analyze and interpret current economic developments and to advise the president on appropriate action to take to keep the national economy healthy in the postwar period. Composed of three members, the council was expected to have a dominating influence in the making of federal economic policy, and its chairman was slated to become the nation's chief economic planner. Rayburn explained to Parten that deliberations between the White House and the Congress over the persons to be appointed to the council had been bitterly contentious. Sec. of Commerce Henry A. Wallace had fought for the right of his department to select the nominees, but the conservative congressional leadership did not want Wallace, a liberal New Dealer, to have any influence over the council. Rayburn had warned Truman that Congress would never approve Wallace's nominees. In discussing his problem with Rayburn, Truman argued that he needed to placate Wallace's supporters by appointing a businessman with a progressive political reputation to the chairmanship. When Rayburn suggested Parten, Truman replied that the Texas oil man who had been so impressive in his appearances before Truman's Senate committee during the war was exactly the kind of man he wanted. "Rayburn was always nominating me for something," Parten later joked.[15]

Parten, however, did not want the job. He was committed to seeing Rainey through the Texas primary, he had no interest in returning to a government position in Washington, and, most importantly, he did not believe he was qualified for the job. Rayburn was disappointed but sympathetic. "Alright, J. R.," Rayburn responded, "but you need to tell Harry that yourself." The next morning, when Truman heard Parten's explanation, he replied that he understood, but he wanted to know if his decision had also been influenced by the treatment Ed Pauley had received from the Senate a few months before when Truman had nominated him to the post of undersecretary of the navy. Parten assured him that the Pauley affair had no bearing on his personal decision, but he did admit that he had been deeply angered by the episode.[16]

After Parten returned to Texas, he was surprised when the news broke that Truman had written a letter to Sen. Charles Tobey, the Vermont Republican who had led the attack on Pauley, implying that Tobey's behavior in the Pauley affair was the real reason Parten had turned down the chairmanship of the Council of Economic Advisors. Truman's letter charged that the senator's opposition to Pauley "had caused many good men, particularly oil men, to turn down government positions." In addition, after Parten had left the White House, Truman had complained to reporters that Parten's refusal to take the post was "another example of the fact that government salaries are too low to attract men of high ability into the government services." Although neither reason had anything to do with Parten's decision, he agreed with Truman's statements in the abstract and remained silent. [17]

"It really was an existential experience"

The 1946 Texas gubernatorial campaign began in earnest in June. With the primary scheduled for July 27, Parten essentially took two months away from

Woodley to work for Rainey. Although Hardeman managed daily affairs, Parten immediately became the dominant figure in Rainey's campaign organization. As Bernard Rapoport, himself a Rainey activist, recalled: "[Parten] was the angel for Homer Rainey in 1946, and he was really *the* angel. He was a stalwart . . . he was Rainey's primary support. . . ." Justin Wolf said that he was amazed at Parten's zeal in the face of intense hostility from his colleagues in the Texas oil industry. "J. R. took on the whole damn state of Texas over Homer Rainey," Wolf declared. During the first primary, Parten served as the major fund-raiser, chief campaign advisor, sometime speechwriter and researcher, and campaign organizer in Madison and Harris Counties. He persuaded E. L. Woodley to manage Callahan County, Sylvestor Dayson to manage Gregg County, and his cousin Ben Parten to manage Robertson County. In Houston, Parten organized a group of supporters that included Marlin Sandlin, Ima Hogg (socialite daughter of former governor James S. Hogg), Jesse Andrews, Burke Baker (president of American General Insurance), Roy Hofheinz, Roland Bradley (attorney), W. T. Moran, and Dr. Ray K. Daily (physician and liberal member of the Houston public school board).[18]

Parten's most important role, however, was as fund-raiser, a job that proved to be exceedingly difficult. He personally donated six thousand dollars to the general campaign fund and three thousand dollars for radio time, and was able to get another five thousand each out of Dayson and Dick Hooper. The owner of the Jacques Power Tool Company of Denison was Rainey's other important fund-raiser, donating three thousand dollars for radio time and five thousand for the general campaign. Finding it hard to raise money in Texas, Parten made an effort to raise funds outside the state. Pleading that "certainly we will need all of the help we can get," Parten asked Isador Lubin to seek financial help for Rainey from his liberal show-business friends in New York. Lubin was morally supportive, but little money came from his direction. Parten also tried to raise funds in Washington and California, but there was not much to be had. Nineteen forty-six was a tough political year for Democrats nationally and much money was being reserved for use in the fall campaigns, in the ultimately futile effort to keep control of Congress. The Rainey campaign raised a little more than fifty-six thousand dollars in all, half of that total from Parten, Jacques, Dayson, and Hooper. The other half came in small contributions of from one dollar to twenty-five dollars from hundreds of people such as labor union members and educators who felt that Rainey represented their best hope for the future. Faculty members from the University of Texas and other Texas colleges, for example, contributed a total of twenty-one hundred dollars in small donations. Rainey's campaign had the aura of a crusade about it, and it brought forth enthusiastic and dedicated support from people who could ill afford to make even a small financial contribution.[19]

Typical in their passion if atypical in the amount of their financial support were Bernard and Audre Rapoport of Waco. Although Bernard Rapoport eventually became a millionaire from his insurance business, in 1946 he was a struggling small-businessman. The Rapoports donated all of their savings (about two thousand dollars) to the Rainey effort and Audre worked as a county manager for the campaign. "We felt that the whole world rested on [Rainey's election]. And the truth is, we weren't all that wrong. Four years of Rainey could have done so much more for this state, because the state has never had the kind of commitment to higher education that it ought to have had." Essentially all of the big money, however, went elsewhere, mainly to Jester and Smith, and Parten could do little to match that.[20]

What the Rainey campaign lacked financially, it made up in human resources, especially with its women volunteers. Led by Marion Storm, Lillian Collier, and Minnie Fisher Cunningham, members of the Women's Committee for Educational Freedom, with support from a large number of student volunteers, performed most of the organizational work at the county level. One of these volunteers was Opal Parten, who was working for the campaign back in Washington. At J. R.'s request, Opal made expeditions to the Library of Congress to do research for Rainey position papers and to draft speeches. One of Opal's drafts compared Rainey to Woodrow Wilson, pointing out that after Wilson had been forced out at Princeton University he ran for governor of New Jersey. She wrote that in "both cases it is a story of conflict between Privilege and Democracy. Wilson felt . . . as Rainey feels today in Texas, that education should belong to the yearning, eager many and not to the chosen, wealthy few." Parten liked that idea. Declaring that the Rainey-Wilson comparison "could ring the bell in this campaign," he had one of Rainey's supporters read Opal's speech on a Rainey radio broadcast. Other behind-the-scenes aides included Rainey's former vice president Alton Burdine and rural newspaper editor Henry Fox. Burdine drafted position papers on a variety of topics, such as the need in Texas for more farm-to-market roads; while Fox, a former editor of the Madisonville newspaper who was recruited by Parten, wrote colorful anecdotes for Rainey's use in his stump-speaking. "We all came together in the Rainey campaign," Rapoport later recalled, "it really was an existential experience."[21]

An Appeal to the FCC

Parten also played a guiding role in formulating and directing Rainey's campaign strategy. During the first primary when he did most of his campaign work from Houston, Parten flooded Hardeman's office with letters filled with detailed advice about everything from publicity tactics to the contents of letters that the campaign office should send to newspaper editors. Few details escaped Parten's scrutiny. For example, after one of Rainey's radio talks he complained to Hardeman that Rainey had failed to mention his own name enough times. "I cannot emphasize too strongly," Parten said, "that the candidate should call his name frequently in a radio speech as well as elsewhere." On another occasion, Parten wrote a letter to the local Rainey organization in Tarrant County to remind them to buy ads in the local papers and spots on the local radio to advertise the various radio speeches scheduled for the last days of the campaign.[22]

Most of Parten's advice was followed to the detail. He urged Hardeman, for example, to devise a way to get a story in the sports pages about Rainey's days as a

Texas League pitcher—perhaps by opening his campaign with a speech at a baseball park. Rainey subsequently opened the campaign on June 4 at a baseball park near Sherman, where he had pitched his first professional baseball game. Rainey spoke over a microphone hook-up at the pitcher's mound and his press release emphasized that he was a former "preacher and pitcher." In May, Jester's opening campaign speech attacked Washington bureaucracies (and implied that Rainey was supported by Washington bureaucrats) and denounced federal regulation of business. Parten sent word to Hardeman that in 1933 his old friend Jester had been among the most fervent supporters of federal control of the oil industry. Jester had taken that position in 1933, Parten told Hardeman, because "all of the major oil companies favored it" and he now opposed it because the majors opposed it. Parten recommended that Rainey should use that information as evidence that Jester was the candidate of "Big Oil," advice that Rainey subsequently followed. Although he would point out the connections between his opponents and the big businesses that controlled the state's politics, Rainey nevertheless intended to take the highroad in the campaign. His basic strategy was to run on his reformist platform, traveling around the state giving professorial lectures full of details, statistics, and analytical evaluations. The idea was to build his base of support and get into the runoff, hopefully as the top vote-getter.[23]

The very first week of the campaign, Rainey and Parten were given a lesson about power and money and the intention of the business elite to do whatever was necessary to keep Rainey out of the Governor's Mansion. Parten had always been a strong believer in the importance of radio in a political campaign. An integral component of Rainey's campaign strategy was for him to make frequent use of the airwaves to deliver his carefully crafted speeches. As Rainey had already demonstrated on his daily radio program, his speeches, laced with facts and figures, were far more effectively delivered on the radio than on the stump. The most important broadcast hook-up in the state was the Texas Quality Network (TQN), which was comprised of the state's four powerful "all clear channel" radio stations covering most of the counties in Texas. Because there were few local stations in many sections of the state, TQN provided the most efficient method of reaching rural voters. When the Rainey campaign tried to buy airtime on the network, however, they were told that management had decided to initiate a new policy for the gubernatorial campaign. Airtime would not be sold to candidates until June 11. After that date and until mid-July, each candidate would be allowed to buy only one broadcast. During the last two weeks before the election, time would be prorated among the fifteen candidates.[24]

This new policy especially outraged Parten, to whom it symbolized the forces against which Rainey was fighting. Three of the four stations were owned by newspapers, including the right-wing Dallas *Morning News*, which had printed vitriolic editorials against Rainey's candidacy. Recalling the actions that the TQN had taken to prevent Rainey's supporters from presenting his case on the network in November 1944, Parten believed that the conservative managements of the four stations were now conspiring to deny him the use of his best campaign weapon by keeping him off the air. Believing that the policy violated the Federal Communications Act, Parten met with Rainey and persuaded him to send telegrams protesting the action to the Antitrust Division of the Department of Justice and to the Federal Communications Commission (FCC). The FCC responded four days later by requesting each station to provide an explanation. When it became clear that the FCC would do little else in the matter, Parten hired Leonard Marks, a former staff attorney for the FCC who was now in private practice representing Lady Bird Johnson's newly purchased radio station KTBC.

Marks filed a formal request for a hearing with the FCC, which agreed to hold a hearing in Dallas on July 10, only sixteen days before the election. Jimmy Allred and Austin attorney Everett Looney, assisted by Leonard Marks, represented Rainey at the two-day hearing. Most of the candidates testified, charging that Rainey's petition was a publicity stunt. They all claimed that the TQN had been fair in its policies. Jester held a press conference outside the hearing room to charge that Rainey's complaint against the TQN had been a "vicious" attempt to muzzle freedom of the press. Implying that Rainey was engaged in subversive activity, he declared that "everyone knows that the entering wedge of Communism is the breaking down of the confidence in the newspapers and radio." The hearing ended without any action taken, the FCC's investigator stating that he was only gathering information to take back to the commission. The FCC would not be heard from again for six months. In the meantime, although Rainey bought time on local stations and on a smaller statewide network, he was denied full access to the most important radio network in Texas.[25]

Race, Sex, and Subversion

The 1946 gubernatorial campaign deserves a place on any short-list of the dirtiest ever conducted in the Lone Star State. Few political campaigns in Texas history have been blemished so thoroughly by blatant demagoguery. And, as always, these demagogic tactics were used by defenders of the status quo as an effective smoke screen to obscure the real issues: an inadequate public school system (except for high-income areas), a shameful lack of public health and welfare services, the continuation of Jim Crow segregation laws, a feudalistic farm-labor system exploiting Mexican Americans, a civil code that treated women as children, an extractive economy not unlike those of the old European colonial systems, election laws structured in such a way as to disenfranchise a large segment of the population, a legal and business environment utterly hostile to the idea of collective bargaining for workers, and a regressive and inequitable system of taxation.

In 1946, challenges to the status quo in Texas were emanating from three main sources. One was the civil rights movement that was already beginning to dismantle the structures of racial segregation and exploitation for Hispanics as well as blacks. In 1944, the Supreme Court had ruled in *Smith v. Allwright* that the all-white Democratic Party primary was unconstitutional. In the middle of the 1946 primary campaign, a federal court ruled that Heman Sweatt, a black man who had been denied admission to the University of Texas School of Law, had been denied his constitutional rights. The State of Texas appealed the decision to the U.S. Supreme Court. Another challenge to the status quo came from the labor union movement, which had made tremendous strides in certain industries in Texas during the war years, especially on the Gulf Coast. The third challenge came not from an organized movement or group, but it scared the reactionaries who sought to preserve the status quo as much or more than the National Association for the Advancement of Colored People (NAACP) or the Congress of Industrial Organizations (CIO). And that was the challenge created by an educated citizenry, especially one exposed to the ideas and concepts of higher education. To many defenders of the status quo, the University of Texas, with its rabble-rousing faculty, was the source of much of the agitation behind the demand for social and economic reform.

Homer Rainey symbolized everything feared by the conservative power elite in control of the state in 1946. For reasons of political expediency, Rainey suppressed his true feelings about racial justice and downplayed his support of labor unionism, but his foes knew better. They understood what Rainey was all about and they would not stand for his election. To frighten and intimidate the electorate in a desperate effort to insure that Rainey would not be governor of Texas, his opponents focused on three of the favorite subjects of American demagogues: race, sex, and subversion.

Of Rainey's four major opponents, the most demagogic were John Lee Smith and Grover Sellers who concentrated their attacks on Rainey as a person, to the almost total exclusion of any substantive issues. Both men seemed to get special pleasure from the trumped-up issue of Rainey's alleged sponsorship of immorality while president of the University of Texas. The evidence at hand was John Dos Passos's *The Big Money*, one of the books in the trilogy *U.S.A.*, which Bullington had made such an issue of in his explanation for Rainey's dismissal in 1944. Despite Rainey's having had no involvement in the English Department's decision to use *The Big Money* on a recommended reading list, Smith and Sellers charged that as president Rainey was responsible for creating a campus atmosphere that allowed faculty members to expose young and innocent students to such "filth." Rainey's opponents reprinted passages from *The Big Money* and circulated them among the state's clergy as proof of the former president's personal "depravity." *The Big Money*, Homer Rainey, and immorality at the University of Texas soon became the subject of Sunday sermons in many of the churches in Texas.

Sellers took the prize for theatrics, however. He ended his campaign speeches with a request for the "little ladies" to leave, so that he could present his evidence about *U.S.A.* to the men. After the women departed, Sellers put on a pair of white gloves to protect his hands from contamination by the "filth" in *U.S.A.* He then read aloud "perverted" passages from the "degenerate" book. At the conclusion of the reading, Sellers would declare dramatically: "This is the sort of filth your daughters were required to read at Texas University when Dr. Homer P. Rainey was president." The *U.S.A.* stories were tied so closely to Rainey's name that many Texans who had never heard of John Dos Passos thought Rainey was the author.

When Rainey was riding in a taxi in Dallas one day during the campaign, the cab driver—not knowing his identity—asked him if he had ever read "that dirty book that Homer Rainey" had written.[26]

Initially, Sadler's campaign stressed his East Texas brand of southern populism, but as his poll ratings dropped, Sadler began to appeal to racial prejudice. After the district court's decision in the Sweatt case, Sadler charged that Rainey had encouraged the civil rights suit against the university. Sadler declared that if Rainey was so interested in educating "niggers," then when Sadler became governor he would be happy to appoint Rainey the president of a new "Negro" state university and J. Frank Dobie could serve as his vice president. Sadler declared that he was certain that Rainey and Dobie would enjoy working for an all-black board of regents. Newspaper reports noted that Sadler's audiences would react with loud cheers and much laughter at the thought of white men working for blacks. Grover Sellers and John Lee Smith also engaged in race-baiting. In his speeches Sellers frequently repeated the charge that Rainey would "herd white and Negro children into the same schools." Smith, whom Harold Ickes had once described as "clothed in the garments of patriotism but in the underclothing of self-interest," frequently charged that if Rainey won the election, he would go to the Governor's Mansion and hang pictures of "some kinky headed ward heeler of the CIO" on its walls. He also loved to titillate his audiences with the declaration that Rainey would have "white girls . . . taking dictation from Negro men" in the private offices of the state Capitol.[27]

The accusation Rainey's opponents made most frequently, however, was that he was a Communist or a Communist dupe. Although Red-baiting was nothing new to the American political tradition, in 1946 anticommunism as a political tactic was beginning to have a potency it had not had before. Perceiving fertile ground, Rainey's opponents beat the red-scare drum loudly and often. For example, one student of the 1946 campaign noted that John Lee Smith accused Rainey of having "Socialistic and Communistic tendencies" in more than thirty of his speeches. Smith charged that Rainey had filled the university faculty with Communists who were busy indoctrinating naive young Texan children. The charge of communism could be easily combined with those of race and immorality. Smith, for example, frequently claimed that not only was *U.S.A.* a dirty book, it was also part of the great international Communist conspiracy. At a Smith campaign rally at Fair Park in Dallas, Hal Collins, whose western band the "B. B. Bunch" was providing the musical entertainment, asked the crowd a question: "If Joe Stalin were voting in Texas, who would he vote for?" His band cried out "Rainey!" As an indication that the old traditional campaign style had not been abandoned completely, Collins and his band then gave a free bottle of hair tonic to every veteran in the audience and a free mattress to the most heavily decorated veteran present. Rainey's own campaign rallies were frequently marred by hecklers accusing him of being a Communist sympathizer. J. Evetts Haley provoked an incident in Amarillo on July 17 that ended in a mini-riot. Haley appeared in the audience and began to heckle and yell while Rainey was making a speech. At one point Haley interrupted Rainey and demanded to know why he supported academic freedom for "pinkos" and "sex perverts" but not for "red-blooded, two-fisted, pro-American men." Rainey ignored him, but a pro-Rainey leader in Amarillo yelled at Haley to shut up, whereupon Haley hit him in the face with his fist. A brief fight ensued, temporarily disrupting the rally.[28]

While Smith, Sellers, and Sadler were throwing mud at Rainey, Beauford Jester played the role of statesman, free to conduct a more moderate campaign aimed at getting his name before the voters, and stressing that he was a responsible choice between extremists on the right and left. Jester was able to announce near the end of the campaign that he was the only candidate with clean hands. His tactic paid off. With each passing week, he gained in the polls at the expense of everyone else, especially John Lee Smith and Jerry Sadler. Jester's percentage in the polls doubled in the month of June, while Smith's plunged from 15 percent to 8 percent and Sadler's from 24 percent to 17 percent. Rainey's poll ratings remained steady at about 30 percent, but it was apparent that his opponents' mudslinging tactics were preventing him from increasing that percentage.[29]

To avoid attracting even more attention to the vicious accusations of his opponents, Rainey at first tried to ignore them. Campaign workers in the counties, however, were reporting that the rumor of Rainey's communism and "Negro loving" were hurting their local efforts. The mayor of Somerville, a small town in East Texas, reported "much Negro rumor here [that Rainey] wants negroes in U. T." Another worker reported from Marshall that there had been "considerable talk" about Rainey's being a "Negro Lover." By the first week in July, Parten, Allred, and other advisors realized that Rainey would have to confront and deny some of those accusations publicly. They chose a campaign rally in Austin's Woolrich Park on July 5 as the place for Rainey to go on the offensive, especially against the accusations that he was a Communist. In a speech coauthored by Parten and Allred, Rainey noted that the campaign had been filled with accusations that he was sympathetic to communism. "That's nothing new," Rainey declared. "Desperate and frightened men, on the verge of being defeated at the polls, always yell, 'Communism'." The charge of communism was "just a smoke screen," Rainey declared, adding that his opponents [yell] "'Communism' at any man who dares to speak the truth about the needs of Texas." Stressing a point suggested by Parten, Rainey argued that FDR had been called a Communist whenever he tried to help the people. "The same was true here in Texas," Rainey declared, noting that in 1892 the Dallas News had "violently attacked Jim Hogg as a Communist for proposing a Railroad Commission." Rainey stated that Texas desperately needed better schools, more rural roads, more hospitals, and improved public-health programs. It was not communistic, he argued, to pay for these improvements by making corporations that were growing fat and wealthy exploiting the state's natural resources pay their fair share of taxes.[30]

During the final month of the campaign, Parten doubled his efforts to counter the charges against Rainey. Reacting to the accusation that Rainey was an atheist who had condoned immoral activities on the University of Texas campus, he recruited Jack Lewis, a former navy chaplain, to read a speech titled "A Christian Minister Looks at Homer Rainey" on a statewide radio hook-up. "I give you my word as a Christian minister . . . none of these foul accusations is true," Lewis declared. "Homer Rainey is not a Communist. Rainey is a man of God." Lewis called Rainey's opponents "morally depraved . . . monopolists" who were "captive to the coyotes from the canyons of Wall Street" and who would "stop at nothing to maintain their positions and gain their own ends." Parten also hired a researcher to search newspaper and magazine reviews of *The Big Money* for quotes to show that Dos Passos's book had been widely acclaimed by reputable reviewers when it was first published. He was delighted when the researcher discovered a laudatory review of the book by Oveta Culp Hobby that had appeared in the Houston *Post* in 1936. Oveta Hobby and her husband, former governor William P. Hobby, owned the Houston *Post*, which had published editorial attacks against Rainey. Parten had the review reprinted in a widely distributed Rainey campaign circular.[31]

Parten tried to deal with the racial issue by having one of Rainey's speechwriters draft a statement. He then persuaded Marguerite Fairchild to allow her name to be used as the author of the speech. Parten arranged to have the speech read by local women supporters in broadcasts from small-town radio stations throughout Texas. Fairchild read the speech herself on the TQN on July 15, two days after the network's moratorium on political advertising had ended. Emphasizing that Fairchild was an East Texan and "Southern housewife," the speech addressed the charge that Rainey wanted to allow blacks to attend the University of Texas. Fairchild declared that as a regent, she had known Rainey to be a "Christian gentleman and a real democrat" who was "a friend of all races," but she had never heard him advocate "the admission of Negroes to the University." Fairchild assured her listeners that Rainey supported the "separate but equal concept." Homer Rainey, Fairchild declared, "upholds the same Southern traditions that you and I uphold." Campaign workers such as future federal judge William Wayne Justice, reported to the Austin headquarters that Fairchild's speech had been "effective" and had done "lots of good," especially in East Texas.[32]

Some of Parten's more promising ideas never got off the ground. For example, in an attempt to counter the accusations that Rainey was an unpatriotic, disloyal citizen, Parten tried to get war hero and native Texan Audie Murphy to campaign for Rainey. Murphy, the most decorated American soldier in World War II, was studying acting in Los Angeles. Parten asked his friend Bogart Rogers, a prominent theatrical agent in Hollywood, to invite Murphy to return to Texas and make public appearances on Rainey's behalf. Murphy told Rogers, however, that he was too involved in his acting classes and that he was "not very interested in Texas politics." Parten also tried to get the Rainey headquarters to use the relatively new technique of raising funds through a direct-mail campaign. He asked Hardeman to contact Henry Hoke, a consultant in New York who was a pioneer in organizing direct-mail solicitations, but the sorely pressed and short-of-staff Hardeman was never able to follow through.[33]

Despite these and other efforts to counteract his opponents' smear campaign, Rainey's standings in the opinion polls continued to erode while Jester's ascended. A couple of weeks before the election, Parten received a disturbing letter from his sister, Lizzie Leonard, who was living in Madisonville. She had just returned from a visit to Nacogdoches in deep East Texas and had heard much about Homer Rainey while there. "I was appalled at the ignorance and misinformation," Lizzie reported. "Dr. Rainey has not reached the masses at all. They are ignoring the radio." She reported that several people had complained to her that Rainey was "a Red and . . . a negro lover." She also warned her brother that the average person in East Texas did not understand the concept of academic freedom. "They think you want the teachers to teach any thing from atheism to free love. It is pitiful. His enemies have truly done their work well mostly via an underground grapevine." She urged Parten to get Rainey's message "to the masses in a form we can assimilate."[34]

Spurred by his sister's letter, Parten called what D. B. Hardeman later described as a "council of war" to meet in Austin to discuss strategy for the last week of the campaign. Noting that the latest polls revealed that Rainey could not win a majority and that his opponents' mudslinging had hurt him badly, Parten urged him to cut back on the use of statistics and economic analyses in his speeches. Citing Lizzie's letter, Parten told Rainey that he needed to concentrate on the race and subversion issues, but not in such a way as to make it appear that he was trying to defend himself. For example, Parten urged Rainey "to state emphatically" that he was "opposed to negroes attending the University of Texas or any other white school in Texas. . . ." Accepting this counsel, Rainey incorporated a statement in his speeches declaring that he had "always opposed, I now oppose, and as your Governor will oppose admission of Negroes to our white schools."[35]

Rainey disagreed with Parten on one point, however. He argued that it was time to focus on the issue of political control of the University of Texas, which he had so far avoided on Parten's advice. Parten was deeply antagonistic to the idea. He wanted to keep the university as an institution out of politics. He also feared Rainey's campaign might seem to be a self-interested vendetta against those who had caused him to lose his job, rather than an attempt to bring the benefits of good government to all Texans. In the spring, the AAUP had placed the university on its censure list because of Rainey's dismissal. President Painter's charge that the AAUP had timed their announcement "to coincide with the Texas primary elections" was exactly the kind of accusation Parten wanted to avoid. Parten opposed Rainey's suggestion so vigorously that Rainey backed away. "Well, I yielded . . . to that advice," Rainey later lamented, "and I think . . . it handicapped me because . . . the University was actually in politics up to its ears. I think I lost some political power . . . by not going into it in the campaign."[36]

An incident that occurred during Rainey's appearance in Mineral Wells on the night of July 20, is an example of why Parten wanted to keep the issue of academic freedom out of the campaign. It is also an example of why Hardeman held his breath whenever Rainey answered questions from the audience after a speech. As Hardeman was later quoted as saying, "[Rainey's] so damned honest, if someone asked him his opinion on the circumcision of Indonesians, he'd give it." During a question-and-answer session following his speech, a reporter asked Rainey if his concept of academic freedom allowed atheists to teach atheism in class. Rainey answered that he frowned upon the idea of atheism being taught in the schools, but the "constitution guarantees it and we have to give even opponents of religion a chance to be heard." Rainey's opponents immediately seized upon this statement, citing it as an example of Rainey's atheism. Governor Stevenson, who had stayed out of the campaign, referred to Rainey's statement during a widely publicized press conference the day before the election. The governor declared that atheism was a "subversive doctrine" and that it was illegal to teach it in Texas schools.[37]

The Second Primary

As anticipated, no candidate won enough votes in the July 27 primary election to win the nomination. Beauford Jester won the largest percentage of votes with 38 percent of the total. Placing second, Homer Rainey won a spot in the runoff against Jester, but he received only 25 percent of the vote. Sellers came in a distant third, while Sadler and Smith slumped badly, placing fourth and fifth respectively. These were bleak results for Rainey because Smith and Sellers had campaigned against him rather than for anything in particular. Rainey could not expect to attract their voters. Sadler's virulently racist campaign, which had garnered only 9 percent of the electorate, could not be depended upon to produce many votes for Rainey either, although Sadler had been Jester's main critic.[38]

Despite this seemingly hopeless situation, Rainey told the press that "the fight has just begun." He, Parten, Hardeman, and his other workers made plans for a vigorous last stand. At this point, according to Hardeman and other Rainey activists, Parten took control of the Rainey campaign. His suite at the Stephen F. Austin Hotel became Rainey's unofficial campaign headquarters. Bob Eckhardt, one of Rainey's advisors, later recalled that Parten's suite was the site of constant commotion, where he and other Rainey activists went to attend strategy meetings, conduct telephone conferences, draft speeches, and consult with workers from the counties. In the middle of this swirl of activity was J. R. Parten, frequently with Jimmy Allred at his side. Parten brought in Claude Wild to help Hardeman, who Parten thought lacked experience. He also urged Hardeman to make better use of the women's committee to distribute campaign literature and to get out the vote. Parten and Marlin Sandlin felt the women's committee members were much more active and effective than the members of Rainey's other grassroots organizations. This involvement with the women's committee and contact with such leaders as Marion Storm, Jane McCallum, and Minnie Fisher Cunningham, influenced Rainey to take up and emphasize the issue of women's rights during the runoff campaign. On a statewide radio broadcast on August 13, Rainey gave a speech titled "To the Women of Texas." After an introduction by former Texas secretary of state Jane McCallum, Rainey declared that Texas women were "still relegated by law to the secondary and inferior roles of their mothers and grandmothers. The laws of Texas are still archaic, and women are not legally on the same basis with man. In many respects the law treats women as though they were children. . . ." He denounced the property laws in Texas as discriminatory and unacceptable, and promised to appoint women to state boards and commissions.[39]

Parten and Allred convinced Rainey that he had to alter his tactics if he was to have any chance in the runoff campaign. One major change stemmed from the fact that in the first primary Rainey was running for the position of governor rather than against any particular opponent. In a two-man race, that strategy had to change, especially now that Rainey was so far behind his opponent. Jester himself now became Rainey's target. Although Rainey had stressed in general terms his neo-populist economic themes in the first campaign, he now had to focus more on the contrast between his views and Jester's in areas such as tax policy. Jester was on record as supporting many of the programs that Rainey had advocated, such as road improvements and better schools and health services. The important difference in their programs, however, was in the way they would pay for them. Jester had hinted that he would support a regressive general sales tax to provide the necessary revenues. Rainey, on the other hand, declared that corporate and individual income taxes and increased natural-resource severance taxes would pay for his programs, thus throwing much of the tax burden on the wealthy and on consumers outside Texas.

Parten and Allred urged Rainey not only to hammer away at the difference in tax plans, but to paint a stark contrast between himself and Jester in simplistic and symbolic terms easily understood by the average Texan. Specifically, Parten recommended that Rainey should stress that Jester was "the rich man's candidate" and a stooge of "Big Oil" who favored an economic system dominated by business monopolies rather than a system of "true free enterprise." In contrast, Rainey should emphasize that he was in favor of "trust busting" and for the preservation of the small, independent businessman and farmer. Rainey subsequently incorporated these suggestions into his speeches. Parten and Allred had hoped that Rainey could make this economic contrast vivid in a series of face-to-face debates with Jester, but Jester refused to debate, saying he would not "embarrass" his friends by making them listen to Rainey's "subversive" economic theories.[40]

Parten perceived that Rainey had been badly wounded in the first primary by his opponents' mudslinging, so he persuaded him at the beginning of the runoff campaign to issue a press release declaring his opposition to the admission of blacks to white schools and his hatred of communism, atheism, fascism, Ku Kluxism "or any other 'ism' contrary to our democratic way of life." The race issue presented a special problem to the Rainey campaign. Privately, Rainey believed in racial equality and favored an end to racial segregation. He quietly sent word to black community leaders that he welcomed their votes and would address their problems if elected governor. Race relations had become an explosive issue, however, as a result of the NAACP's campaign to overturn legally imposed racial segregation through lawsuits in the federal courts. His opponents had denounced the Supreme Court decision declaring the state's all-white party primary to be unconstitutional, but Rainey did not. Parten was convinced that Rainey was hurting him-self unnecessarily by this stance, so they talked him into taking a "compromise" position. Rainey issued a statement declaring that as governor, he would propose a law to provide for racially segregated voting places for Negroes. Such a law would be in the spirit of the "constitutional principle of segregation." This compromise was hard for Rainey to accept. Hardeman later remembered that the idea of segre-gated voting was a "concept totally foreign to the thinking of Homer Rainey whose views on race relations were a generation . . . ahead of his neighbors."[41]

Parten also convinced Rainey that he needed to sling some mud of his own. A few days after the first primary election, the Rainey campaign learned that Phil Fox, the person in charge of Jester's account at a Dallas public relations firm, had been a leader of the Ku Klux Klan in Georgia and a close associate of KKK Imperial Wizard Hiram W. Evans. Fox had allegedly served time in a Georgia prison for a crime related to his KKK activities. Parten advised Rainey to use this information in his campaign to show that the vicious accusations being made against him came from bigots and haters who had once belonged to the Klan. Parten thought Jester's relationship with Fox might mean that Jester had been a member of the KKK, so Bob Eckhardt was sent to Corsicana (Jester's hometown) to see if he could find any evidence tying Jester to the Klan. Eckhardt learned from Rainey supporters in Corsicana that Jester may have wanted to join the Klan at one time, but he had been prevented from doing so. The Klan had blackballed him because of rumors that Jester's family was Jewish. Nevertheless, Parten urged Rainey to accuse Jester of having KKK sympathies because of his association with Phil Fox, a charge Rainey subsequently made in speeches in Waco on August 3 and in Nacogdoches on August 5. Rainey implied that if Jester became governor, the KKK would become a powerful force in state government. "Texas has no place for the Ku Klux Klan or any other hate organizations," Rainey declared. "I tell you that when Homer Rainey is Governor, every power of that great office will be used to prevent the return of the Klan or any similar hate organization. It must never come back to terrify and disgrace Texas."[42]

Rainey's attempt to smear Jester with the KKK was an unfortunate resort to the same guilt-by-association tactics that Rainey's opponents had used against him. Although Rainey's mudslinging is understandable given the viciousness of the unwarranted and unsubstantiated accusations made against him, it was never-theless a demagogic act. Unfortunately, it was not the only example of Rainey's resort to demagoguery. On August 8, in a speech in Abilene titled "Texas Regulars and Tokyo Rose," Rainey implied that the Texas Regulars had committed treason in 1944 by trying to deny Roosevelt a fourth term in office. By attacking the "com-mander in chief," Rainey declared, the Texas Regulars were guilty of "aiding and abetting the Nazis." In addition, Parten persuaded Rainey to criticize Jester for remaining on the Railroad Commission while he was running for governor, despite the fact that Parten had not objected to Thompson's doing the same thing when he ran for governor in 1938 and 1940. Denouncing Jester's action as being "morally wrong," Rainey even repeated one of the statements O'Daniel had made six years earlier against Thompson. "Any man who would run for another office while serving as Railroad Commissioner," Rainey quoted O'Daniel, "ought to be in the penitentiary." These accusations were rooted in desperation and stemmed from frustration among Rainey's advisors, including Parten, over their inability to overcome the opposition's scare campaign. Nevertheless, the use of these tactics denied Rainey any special moral advantage in the campaign.[43]

As election day drew closer, Parten continued to seek financial and other help from sources outside Texas. He contacted, for example, the politically liberal pollster Lou Harris in New York, an old friend from his PAW days, who indicated an interest in raising money for Rainey in the East. "We believe that we can win this fight," Parten told Harris, "if only we can get a little help from the outside to offset the big money which is being thrown behind Jester." Harris felt that the racist tactics used by Rainey's opponents would offend some wealthy Manhattan liberals, so he asked Parten to send him some news clippings documenting the racial charges. Parten did this and wrote Harris that the clippings "measure the very high degree to which racial hatred has been injected" into the campaign. Parten also called former vice president Henry A. Wallace on August 15, 1946, in an attempt to get help for Rainey from the Democratic National Committee (DNC), but the DNC refused to get involved in a Democratic primary.[44]

Jimmie Allred, who had feuded with Jester ever since his own campaign for governor in 1934, worked with Parten behind the scenes to help Rainey, but he had not made any public speeches or endorsements. Parten finally persuaded Allred in the last weeks of the runoff campaign to make his support for Rainey public. In his first speech on August 14 on TQN, Allred announced that he would vote for Rainey for governor because his campaign was for the small-businessman and farmer, the poor and the sick, the school children and the elderly. Jester, on the other hand, was the candidate of "the Big Uns"—the wealthy class, the monopolists, and the Texas Regulars. "Every man that hated, or tried to smear Franklin Roosevelt, is backing Jester," Allred declared. "The struggle between the 'Big Uns' for privilege and the 'Little Uns' for a fair deal never ends." Allred's public involvement and Jerry Sadler's announcement that he would also vote for Homer Rainey boosted Parten's hopes. In a letter to Stanley Marcus, Parten declared that "reports from all over the state indicate that considerable reaction has set in against the violent campaign of slander . . . conducted against Rainey . . . and there can be no doubt that Rainey is making substantial gains. Jim [Allred] and I still have confidence. . . ."[45]

A few days before the election, Parten went home to Madisonville to make his only public speech for Rainey. Addressing a large crowd in front of the Madison County courthouse, Parten announced that he was "ashamed and outraged at the slander and mudslinging . . . loosed against this good Christian man by the big corporations and their paid henchmen. . . ." Parten admitted that he was one of the few oil men in Texas backing Rainey, but he recognized that the state desperately needed economic and social reforms. He emphasized that his fight with Jester was not personal. "I went to school with Jester at the University of Texas," Parten stated. "I have no personal quarrel with him. I don't approve . . . of the crowd who backs him." The day before the election, Parten tried to be optimistic, but his deep concern showed in a letter he wrote to Ed Pauley, who had sent Parten a donation for the Rainey campaign. "The people go to the polls tomorrow," Parten told Pauley. "I have no doubt but what Rainey has gained a great deal in the past two weeks. The question which I cannot answer is whether he has gained enough. The alignment was simply the Roosevelt versus the anti-Roosevelt people with few exceptions. Unfortunately, most of the money was on the other side."[46]

Defeated in a Landslide

Winning every large city and all but seven counties, Beauford Jester overwhelmed Homer Rainey by a vote of 701,000 to 355,000. Historian George N. Green, in his analysis of the 1946 gubernatorial campaign, concluded that the results demonstrated the "underlying reality of conservative dominance" over the state's political structure. Green observed that "liberal hopes were dashed by . . . the vulnerability of low-income and laboring whites to racial and superpatriotic appeals." Austin journalist Stuart Long noted that the Jester campaign had pulled off an amazing feat. It had convinced a majority of Texas voters that an ordained Baptist minister was an atheist. Red-scare tactics had also taken their toll on Rainey's campaign, making the Texas primary a preview for the use of such tactics in the fall's general election campaigns throughout the country. Voters in every section of the nation were beginning to respond favorably to candidates who manipulated anticommunism and the fear of subversion to win election. In November, for example, a young war veteran by the name of Richard M. Nixon won election as a Republican congressman from California by red-baiting his liberal Democratic opponent, Jerry Voorhis. The election results in Texas also reflected a fundamental change in the national political environment. The New Deal era was over in Washington as well as in Texas. The general election in November resulted in a sweeping victory for the Republican Party, which took control of both houses of Congress for the first time in more than two decades.

Although Jester and the newly elected lieutenant governor, Allan Shivers, won election as Democrats, they had campaigned against the national Democratic Party and the Roosevelt legacy. The Democratic Party in Texas was now firmly under the control of conservatives who identified with the national Republican Party and who ran for office as Democrats only because Texas was still a one-party state. Parten fully understood the meaning of the election results. He wrote to a friend that he could now see "that post-war conservatism has a real grip on the people and it's just not the time to sell the progressive program." From his vantage point in Washington, Justin Wolf observed in a letter to Parten that "all in all it is clear that the postwar psychology is rather conservative. People have so much money, they just are not very concerned about anything very progressive even though it be education or public health."[47]

Despite Rainey's overwhelming defeat, Parten, Hardeman, Rainey, and a few others tried to hold together Rainey's supporters and organization in hopes of making another effort in the 1948 election. Nearly one month after the runoff debacle, Parten wrote to a friend that if Rainey's voting block could be held togeth-er, "Texas may still have a liberal administration in the not too distant future." Parten's plan for preserving the liberal group depended on keeping Rainey as its leader. To keep Rainey in Texas, Parten realized that he had to find a job for him; one that would not only provide financial support but would also keep Rainey's name in front of the voters and involve him in the public affairs of the state. While casting about for such a job, Parten heard a rumor from his Dallas friends that the Dallas *News* and its radio station (WFAA) might be for sale. Such a possibility seemed too good to be true. The owners of the newspaper been powerful foes of Rainey's campaign. Parten suspected that the Dallas *News* had been responsible for TQN's restrictive policy on political advertisements against which the Rainey cam-paign had filed a complaint with the FCC. If a liberal could be persuaded to buy the newspaper and make Rainey its leading political columnist and WFAA's lead-ing radio commentator, the liberal Democrats would have a powerful base from which to launch a major attack on the Texas political establishment in 1948. Stressing that it was "all important" to the liberal cause in Texas, Parten persuaded Rainey to contact Marshall Field, the department store millionaire and publisher of the liberal Chicago *Sun*, to try to interest him in the purchase. Rainey subse-quently wrote Field, arguing that "for any liberal movement in Texas to succeed . . . the problem must be attacked from many fronts. Certainly one of our greatest needs is for a first class liberal newspaper in Texas. Such a paper, we feel, ought to be located in Dallas." While Rainey and Parten waited for Field's response, Parten went to New York and met with a group of wealthy liberal businessmen to discuss possible financial backing for a liberal political organization in Texas that would be headed by Rainey.[48]

Parten's effort to create a Rainey-led liberal movement in Texas ended almost as soon as it began. Marshall Field turned down Rainey's proposal, pleading that he could not afford to own another newspaper. The meeting with the potential finan-cial backers in New York produced nothing. But the coup de grace was Rainey's decision to accept the presidency of Stephen's College, a private school for women in Columbia, Missouri. In late October, Rainey told Parten that the job was his and that he would probably accept it. An official announcement, however, was not made until early in December. By then, the Democratic Party had suffered its stun-ning defeat in the congressional election and it was clear that the old liberal move-ment associated with Roosevelt and the New Deal was dead or dying throughout the nation. Parten admitted to Leonard Marks that "in the light of political trends throughout the nation . . . I believe [Rainey] made a wise choice. . . ."[49]

The story of the Rainey campaign could not end, however, until the FCC ruled on his complaint against TQN. One month after Rainey's acceptance of the Stephens College presidency, and six months after the original complaint was filed, the FCC finally issued an official ruling, declaring that the evidence strongly indicated that the management of the TQN radio stations had conspired for polit-ical reasons to keep Rainey from making effective use of the public radio waves. Leonard Marks tried to put the best light on the ruling, telling Parten that the FCC criticism of TQN meant that they had "won." Rainey and Parten, however, were not pleased with the FCC's handling of the case. Not only was it too late to help Rainey, the commission essentially did nothing to TQN. The radio stations were not penalized, they simply promised never to misbehave again. As Rainey accurately expressed it to Parten, "they failed completely to meet the issue . . . and in the face of good evidence, they let them go scott-free."[50]

"Major Parten is something of an anomaly in Texas"

When D. B. Hardeman recalled the Rainey campaign in an interview in the 1970s, he declared that it was the most bitter political contest he had ever seen. "It really separated . . . people," Hardeman noted, adding that there was "still bitterness in Texas" three decades later. The affair resulting from Rainey's dismissal as University of Texas president and the subsequent Rainey campaign for governor were defining episodes for Parten and other Texas Democrats who remained loyal to the Roosevelt legacy and the national party. Split from the conservatives who opposed the national party and its more liberal agenda of civil rights, labor unionism, and the welfare state, the Rainey Democrats became the opposition party within the Democratic Party in Texas. Parten became one of the honored patrons of the liberal faction, earning the title among Texas's small band of progressive activists as the "*good* oilman." After Rainey's defeat, J. Frank Dobie praised Parten for his involvement in the cause. He told Parten that he was "one of the very few men with . . . money in this state who realizes the necessity for liberal minds, and . . . believe in something beyond a short range desire for more money." The reasons for Parten's intense involvement in the Rainey campaign had included nonpolitical motivations such as loyalty to a man he had been responsible for bringing to the university, but his belief in the liberal cause was sincere. As he told one of Rainey's supporters one year after the campaign, his fight had been "for liberal principles and especially an improved educational system for Texas." And he was in the battle for the long haul. He assured a friend that though Texas "is in the hands of the reactionaries at this time, the time will come when the liberals again will assert themselves with the approval of the people."[51]

Parten's identification with the liberal cause was not without cost, however. Because of the major ideological realignment and the bitterness that accompanied it, Parten lost his place among the state's political elite. He never again exercised the kind of influence in Texas he had enjoyed in the 1930s during the Allred years and his tenure as a university regent and as head of transportation in the PAW. Parten's New Deal philosophy was no longer the dominant view, and, as an unapologetic "Raineyite," he was very much a political outsider in Texas. The *Texas Spectator* noted at this time that "Major Parten is something of an anomaly in Texas, being both a wealthy oil man and a liberal." Parten's political move toward the left and his alienation from the power elite also had an effect on his personal relations. Parten admitted to Ralph K. Davies during the Rainey campaign that "as usual, most of my friends in the oil and gas industry are arrayed with the opposition. . . ." Many of his friends had become Texas Regulars or conservative

Republicans. Among them was Gene Holman, who was now chairman of the board of Standard of New Jersey. As Holman rose in corporate circles, his politics became increasingly conservative.[52] Parten, however, still retained influence in Washington as an active national Democrat, well known to the Truman administration. And, of course, he was a close friend of Sam Rayburn. He eventually served as an important political connection between Rayburn and the Texas liberal Democrats in the political struggles of the 1950s.[53]

Homer Rainey never forgot the help J. R. Parten gave him when it really counted. Twenty years after the campaign, Rainey wrote Parten that he could "never adequately express to you my profound appreciation for the support that you gave me." He told Parten that he was one individual who "understood the issues, and what was at stake, better than any other person in Texas. I have said many times that you were the best University Regent... that I have ever known...." Rainey underscored this opinion when he later told an oral-history interviewer that Parten was "the best public servant that I've ever had anything to do with."[54]

Parten never regretted the fight he made against the conservatives who fired Rainey from the university presidency. Although one result of Parten's leadership in that fight was that for nearly twenty years he would be persona non grata with the conservatives who controlled his beloved University of Texas, his stand on behalf of academic freedom and for a university free of political control inspired future leaders of the university. As Chancellor Harry H. Ransom assured Parten in 1969 in a personal note written during another period of political turmoil at the university: "The chapter in UT history entitled 'Parten' keeps encouraging me daily."[55]

CHAPTER 21

Divorce, Brimstone, and Remarriage

1947–1950

"They just decided to call it off"

The twenty-nine-year-old marriage of J. R. and Opal Parten ended in divorce in the spring of 1947. Their relationship, which had long been anything but traditional, entered its terminal phase in the final months of J. R.'s service with the PAW in 1943. In the early fall of that year he and Opal agreed to a trial separation. She remained in the house they were leasing in Washington, D.C., while J. R. rented rooms in the Shoreham Hotel. By the time J. R. left the PAW, Dallas Sherman had returned from overseas duty with the Military Air Transport Command and was assigned a desk job at the Pentagon. Opal remained in Washington with Dallas, and J. R. returned to Texas. During the Christmas holidays of 1946 Opal finally asked J. R. for a divorce. "Opal just couldn't continue to live like they were living," a friend of them both said years later. Dallas Sherman claimed that "after so many years of marriage without being together they just decided to call it off. There was no squabble."[1]

At Opal's request, J. R. persuaded their mutual friend Jimmy Allred, who had opened a law office in Houston, to serve as her legal counsel in the divorce proceedings, while Jack Blalock represented J. R. Although this arrangement obviously served J. R.'s interests, the divorce agreement appears to have been fair to Opal. According to Dallas Sherman, Opal felt that J. R. "bent over backwards to do everything fair and right." In February 1947, Opal wrote Claire Dayson that the divorce was "working out as nicely as anybody could wish. Jimmie [Allred] has been very kindly and conscientious. He is devoted to J. R. of course, and has plenty of reason for being. But he . . . has surprised me with his . . . fair-minded attitude." Their property, including the Woodley stock, was divided evenly. With half of their Woodley stock going to Opal, J. R. was no longer the single largest share-holder in the company. To protect his control over Woodley, Opal agreed to give J. R. legal authority to vote her shares at stockholder meetings for a period of ten years. Their marriage was over, but not their financial relationship or their friend-ship. Soon after the divorce, Opal married Dallas, who had left the Army Air Corps after the war to take an executive position with Pan American Airways in Washington.[2]

The Little Mothers

While Parten was working out his divorce settlement during the early weeks of 1947, he leased an apartment with Sylvester Dayson at the Dallas Athletic Club (DAC). Parten was spending much of his time in the booming North Texas city as a result of his appointment in January 1947 as chairman of the Federal Reserve Bank of Dallas. He had been with the bank since January 1944, after Marriner S. Eccles, chairman of the board of governors of the Federal Reserve System, per-suaded him to accept an appointment as a Class C director and deputy chairman. Parten and Eccles had become friends during J. R.'s tenure at the PAW.[3]

Parten's appointment as chairman required his presence in Dallas on a regu-lar monthly basis, but he soon discovered that the duties were not burdensome. Federal Reserve System policies are established in Washington, so the branch-bank chairman's job is mainly one of general oversight. In addition, the chairman-ship required that Parten attend general meetings of the Federal Reserve Board of Governors in Washington. These meetings gave the chairmen of the branch banks an opportunity to express their opinions to the board, "not that they listened a hell of a lot," Parten said. He remained chairman of the Dallas bank until 1955.[4]

At the Dallas Athletic Club, Parten and Dayson became members of an infor-mal group of oil men that included Buddy Fogelson, Cipriano ("Dick") Andrade, Roland S. Bond, Guy Warren, and Douglas Forbes. Organized by Fogelson and Bond in the early 1920s, the group was known as the "Little Mothers Club." The unusual name came from a story one of the members told about an Oklahoma preacher during World War I who, out of concern for the large number of preg-nant war brides in the congregation, decided to form a support group for them to share their common problems. The minister announced his plan from the pulpit one Sunday morning, inviting "all of the young war brides who would like to be 'Little Mothers'" to meet [him] at the rectory that afternoon." After hearing the story, the oil men agreed they now had an appropriate name for their "club." "The Little Mothers" met in their own large suite on the seventh floor of the DAC to play cards, exchange gossip, and make an occasional business deal.[5]

In March 1947, Dick Andrade brought Parten and his fellow Little Mothers together at the DAC to meet Bill Brady, an entrepreneur from Mexico who was on a desperate search for investors to provide working capital with which he and his two brothers could develop sulphur concessions in tropical Mexico. Parten was fascinated by what Brady had to say. Brady's story began four decades earlier in Mexico, with the discovery by an Englishman, Weetman D. Pearson (the future

Lord Cowdray), of what were believed to be at least four large salt domes on the Isthmus of Tehuantepec near the village of Jaltipan, just south of the Gulf port of Coatzacoalcos. Pearson formed a company called the Mexican Eagle to drill oil wells on the domes. He was disappointed, however, when he discovered sulphur instead of oil. Sulphur had little value because the world market for the yellow mineral was saturated with easily extracted and cheap sources from the U.S. Gulf Coast. This oversupply was the result of the work of a chemist by the name of Herman Frasch, who had developed a highly efficient and relatively inexpensive sulphur-extraction process that uses high pressure to force superheated water into well shafts drilled into salt domes to melt the sulphur underground. The sulphur is then pumped in a molten state to the surface, where it is stored in the open air to cool and harden. There being no market, Pearson did nothing with the discovery, eventually selling out to Royal Dutch Shell. Shell was interested only because a show of sulphur is often a sign that oil is nearby; the sulphur itself was of no interest to them either.[6]

Interest in the Tehuantepec salt domes remained dormant for nearly forty years. The Mexican government's nationalization of its oil industry in 1938 forced Shell out of the country. In June 1942 two Mexican citizens, Alfredo Breceda, a former revolutionary general and diplomat with excellent contacts in the Mexican government, and Manuel Urquidi, an engineer formerly with the Royal Dutch Shell Company, obtained concessions from the Mexican government to three of the salt domes. A concession in Mexico was legal permission to explore for sulphur or other minerals in a predetermined area and to extract any deposits found. Only Mexican citizens could legally hold such concessions. For two years Breceda and Urquidi tried without success to attract Mexican investors to provide the funds for exploration. Because their concession was only for five years, they soon faced the real possibility of losing it. In 1944 they forged a partnership with Bill Brady and his brothers, Ashton and Lawrence. Natives of Louisiana, the Bradys were economic adventurers who had wandered throughout Mexico for more than twenty years in search of oil and other minerals. They purchased 50 percent of the Breceda and Urquidi business enterprise. Unfortunately, the Bradys had little money of their own, so the new partnership failed to provide Breceda and Urquidi with the capital needed to begin exploration of the salt domes. They agreed, therefore, to give the Bradys a free hand to seek financial backers in the United States, where they had stronger connections than did the Mexicans. They signed a new contract allowing the Bradys to form their own company and assume all responsibilties. In return, Breceda and Urquidi were to receive royalties on whatever the Bradys produced in the future.[7]

The Bradys soon attracted enough small investors to drill some test wells, which eventually led them to the sulphur. This discovery allowed Breceda and Urquidi to get extensions from the Mexican government on their original concessions and to expand their size to three thousand acres. The Bradys subsequently formed their own company, Pan American Sulphur, and received permission from Breceda and Urquidi in January 1947 to continue exploration in these new concession areas. The Bradys quickly ran out of money and investors. To raise enough capital to exploit the sulphur deposits, Bill Brady went to the United States to find new investors. Among the first men he contacted was Dick Andrade, one of his previous investors, who told Brady that his sulphur project might be of interest to some of his friends at the Dallas Athletic Club. It was this chain of events that eventually brought Bill Brady to J. R. Parten and the other Little Mothers at the DAC on March 10, 1947.[8]

After Brady explained the history of the salt-dome concessions, he told Parten and his friends that he and his brothers needed financing to explore and exploit their concession. They were prepared to sell a portion of their company to raise the capital. To Brady's disappointment, most of the Little Mothers expressed their belief that his proposition was "wildly speculative." The financial risk did not bother the men so much as the fact that most of them had no experience in the sulphur business. There were other serious concerns as well. One problem was with the Bradys, who had a reputation as adventurers and con artists. Another was a concern about Mexico, a country that had confiscated the oil reserves and facilities of U.S. and European companies only nine years earlier.

J. R. Parten, who may have been the most cautious and financially conservative businessman in the group, surprised his friends when he declared a strong interest in Brady's proposal. Parten, an avid student of current international affairs, and as chairman of the Federal Reserve Bank of Dallas privy to the latest information about foreign investment conditions, was aware of new opportunities south of the border. He knew that Mexican president Miguel Aleman, who had taken office a year earlier after serving as governor of the state of Veracruz, where the concessions were located, had initiated an aggressive program to attract foreign capital. Parten had learned that the Mexican government was providing guarantees that foreign investments would be secure. President Truman had recently made a much heralded trip to Mexico City and relations between Mexico and the United States had never been better. Parten had also become interested in Mexico because of Ed Pauley, who had tried to persuade Parten to invest in some of his oil projects there. Because Woodley was having difficulty finding oil on its leases in Texas and Mississippi, the company was giving serious consideration to moving into Canada or Mexico for wildcat ventures. Ed Pauley's experience in Mexico demonstrated that even though the Mexican oil industry was nationalized, the government was eager to pay fair royalties to foreign exploration companies. There was a real possibility that once sulphur-drilling operations were underway in Jaltipan oil might also be found. Woodley would then be in an excellent position to take advantage of an oil discovery because of its investment in the Mexican sulphur company. "I thought I foresaw an opportunity for Woodley to back into Mexican oil by prospecting for sulphur on these known salt domes," Parten admitted later.[9]

There was another significant, but personal, reason for Parten's strong interest in the Brady proposal. Failure seemed to be stalking him from every corner in the spring of 1947. His divorce from Opal had affected him deeply, despite the fact that they had not really had much of a marriage for several years. He knew the responsibility for the failed marriage was his, not hers, and his sense of personal failure and loss was profound. The failure of the Rainey campaign haunted him, while Woodley's inablility to find new oil reserves created a specter of future business failure. Because of the loss of half of his Woodley stock to Opal, Parten was not even the biggest stockholder in the company that had been largely his own creation. And now he was fifty-one years old and without family. Parten was ripe for something new, especially an entrepreneurial venture that posed a number of interesting challenges in an entirely different field than oil. Mexican sulphur seemed to fit the bill and he was eager to jump in.[10]

Sylvester Dayson, Parten's dashing gambler buddy, was also excited by the idea. More familiar with the technical side of the sulphur-mining industry than his friends, Dayson explained that the Frasch process made the extractive operation very similar to the drilling of oil wells, work with which they were all well acquainted. Dayson also pointed out that because the sulfuric acid was a versatile chemical heavily used by the rapidly growing petrochemical industry, demand for the crumbly, nonmetallic, yellow mineral was certain to escalate. With Dayson's and Andrade's enthusiastic support, Parten persuaded his friends to join him in signing a sixty-day option to buy into the Bradys' company, Pan American. This gave them time to receive and evaluate "a more coherent statement" from the Bradys about their formal agreement with Breceda and Urquidi. It was also essential that they have guarantees from the Mexican government that the concessions were legal. Parten proposed to send a team of geologists and engineers to Mexico to evaluate the site at Jaltipan. Aware of the tropical terrain involved, Parten told the Little Mothers that he was particularly concerned about potential logistics problems. To help bring his associates with him on the deal, Parten agreed to make all the necessary arrangements and to pay for the site inspection. The other members of the Little Mothers accepted this proposal. If nothing else, it appealed to their gambling instincts.[11]

Parten hired geologists William A. Baker and John Myers to evaluate the site in Jaltipan. The geologists discovered that the site was actually one vast salt dome of about twenty-two thousand acres, rather than four smaller domes. They determined that an enormous amount of sulphur lay beneath the caprock of the dome, possibly one of largest deposits ever discovered. The geologists urged Parten to excerise his option with the Bradys and stressed the need to expand the concession to cover the entire acreage. They believed the success of the operation depended on being able to work the entire dome as one area. They also confirmed Parten's suspicion that oil might be found there. Parten now realized that he and his partners had an opportunity to exploit what might turn out to be one of the largest-known sulphur deposits on earth and maybe even find a large pool of oil. Unfortunately, the Bradys' concessions included only one-seventh of the total. Parten had heard a rumor that Texas Gulf Sulphur and other large companies were beginning to show interest in the area, so he resolved to keep the news about the size of the dome and its potential richness a secret, even from his partners. He feared that in their enthusiasm, one of the Little Mothers might indiscreetly leak the information. He swore Baker and Myers to secrecy and locked up their report and maps in his office safe.[12]

The Pan American Sulphur Company is Reorganized

In early April, the Little Mothers reassembled in Roland Bond's apartment at the Dallas Athletic Club to receive the site evaluation from Baker and Myers. Parten, however, had the geologists make an oral report because the written one revealed the potential magnitude of the sulphur deposit and Parten wanted that information to remain secret. After Baker and Myers discussed their highly favorable evaluation, Parten made his own pitch. He pointed out that the Jaltipan dome was near the railroad that cut across the Isthmus, connecting with an excellent deep-water port at Coatzacoalcos. Abundant water, which was an essential resource for the Frasch process, was nearby in the never-dry Chacalapa River, and relatively cheap fuel was available from the PEMEX refinery only twelve miles away. The consultants had determined that most of the sulphur was close to the surface, which meant that smaller amounts of heated water would be needed to extract it, lowering production costs considerably. This information, plus favorable political conditions in Mexico, convinced the Little Mothers to accept Parten's recommendation to join him in forming a syndicate to buy 75 percent of the capital stock in the Bradys' sulphur enterprise.

Andrade, Bond, and Fogelson each bought a 20 percent share of the new enterprise, while Parten assumed responsibility for the remaining 40 percent. Retaining one-third of his shares, Bond sold the remaining two-thirds to his Renwar Oil Company associates Guy I. Warren and Douglas Forbes. Parten's associates expected him to assume most of the responsibility for the management of the company. "Mr. Parten ran the show," one former employee later observed, "and the Little Mothers expected him to handle everything. Everybody had faith in him." Accordingly, Parten became president of the new company, which was to retain the name Pan American Sulphur Company. Roland Bond, who would be the most active and influential director other than Parten, agreed to serve as vice president and secretary-treasurer.[13]

Parten had assumed 40 percent of the syndicate's shares with the idea that Premier Refining and Woodley would buy most of them. Premier subsequently purchased half of Parten's Pan American stock, with Dayson personally acquiring a third of Premier's share. To Parten's surprise and irritation, however, Bill Moran persuaded his fellow Woodley directors during a board meeting in June 1947 that the Mexican sulphur enterprise was much too risky. As a result of the stock split caused by J. R.'s divorce, Moran was now the largest single Woodley stockholder and his new status increased his influence on the board. Parten countered Moran's opposition by arguing that Woodley was having little success in finding oil and that it would be smart to diversify. He also explained that it would give the company an opportunity to take advantage of any oil discoveries near the sulphur deposits. Moran, however, had invested in a Freeport Sulphur Company mine in Louisiana.

He warned that Freeport and the other companies that dominated the business would keep Pan American out of the world market. Moran's argument swayed his associates, who agreed that Parten should keep his investment for himself. As a result, Parten sold half of his share to Marlin Sandlin and to several of his friends at his cost. He eventually retained about a quarter of his original purchase.[14]

Moran's warning about the power of the major sulphur companies was no exaggeration. It was a concern shared by Parten, who was keenly aware of the daunting challenge faced by anyone who contemplated an entry into the sulphur market. In 1947 four U.S. companies controlled 99 percent of the total sulphur output from salt domes in Texas and Louisiana. The giant was Texas Gulf Sulphur which controlled 45 percent of the market, and the Freeport Sulphur Company, which had 30 percent. Two smaller companies, Jefferson Lake and Duval, supplied most of the remainder. These four companies produced more than enough sulphur to meet world demand and their reserves appeared to be adequate for future needs. In addition, the two largest companies were capable of exercising formidable political clout in the Louisiana and Texas legislatures.

Parten was well acquainted with the situation in the sulphur industry. To him, the sulphur companies—especially Texas Gulf Sulphur—embodied all the evils of monopoly his father had so vigorously denounced during family discussions at the dinner table forty years before: restraint of trade, price-fixing, political and financial corruption, subversion of the democratic process, and managerial arrogance. When he was on the University of Texas Board of Regents he had read Bob Montgomery's book *The Brimstone Game: Monopoly in Action,* which documented the sulphur industry's practices and its corrupting influence on Texas government. Parten also remembered the role Texas Gulf Sulphur's lobbyist Roy Miller had played in 1936 to initiate the legislative investigation of Montgomery. When Parten fought against the Florida barge-canal during his service with the PAW, he knew that the sulphur industry, led by Texas Gulf, was the major force behind the proposal. Many years later, he stressed that the main reason the Mexican sulphur enterprise attracted him was that he thought it was an outstanding business opportunity. But he also admitted that he was not displeased by the prospect of irritating Texas Gulf.[15]

It was this background that made Parten so cautious and secretive when he and his partners organized their new company. He believed that Texas Gulf was capable of doing almost anything to keep competitors out of the market. A major worry was that they might try to get the Mexican authorities to revoke Pan American's permits and take over the concessions for themselves. Parten's fears were well justified.

On May 18, Parten and Dayson travelled to Mexico to see for themselves the site of their new venture and to open an office in Mexico City. From the Mexican federal capital they proceeded to Jaltipan, about four hundred miles to the southeast, where they met the other Brady brothers. Upon their return to Mexico City, they organized a Mexican subsidiary, Gulf Sulphur Company de Mexico, S.A. (its name was changed in 1955 to Azufrera Panamericana, S.A.) and applied for a charter from the federal government, which was granted in September. Parten and Dayson remained in Mexico City long enough to negotiate an agreement with the Bradys giving their new Mexican subsidiary exploration and exploitation rights to their concessions. Intent on following the advice of Baker and Myers to get rights to the entire area covering the salt dome, Parten hired a local law firm, Hardin, Hess, and Suarez to seek as soon as possible an "amplification" (an increase in the amount of land) of their concession to include the rest of the salt dome. Only Parten, Sandlin, and now Bond, who had been briefed by Parten, understood the significance of this application. Parten had continued to suppress the information contained in the Baker and Myers report that indicated the potential size of the sulphur deposit and the critical need to gain control of the entire twenty-two thousand acres.[16]

Meanwhile, Texas Gulf Sulphur was also looking around in Mexico. Not knowing about the Parten group's activities, they hired Everett L. DeGolyer, who had worked in the area when sulphur was discovered, to evaluate the prospects in the region around Jaltipan. In early August, the president of Texas Gulf Sulphur, Wilbur Judson, urged DeGolyer to hurry with his report on the Tehuantepec salt dome. Judson had recently learned that "Major Parten and a group of big oil men in Dallas . . . are going to drill some sulphur test wells on Pontrerillos and Jaltipan." News of DeGolyer's activities got back to Parten, who grew concerned that his group had legal rights to only one-seventh of the area believed to be rich in sulphur deposits. If Texas Gulf discovered the actual extent of the deposits they might attempt to kill the Parten group's application for a concession amplification. All of their work and expense might result in having access to only a minor portion of the lode, while Texas Gulf picked up the remainder at comparatively little cost.[17]

The need for quick approval of their application for a larger concession took on new urgency. In mid-August, Parten rushed his brother-in-law, Carl Basland, and Marlin Sandlin to Mexico City to monitor the progress of the application. Gerald Blackburn, another Woodley employee on loan to Pan American, had been sent to Jaltipan a few weeks earlier to plan the exploration project at the concession site. Blackburn, who was appointed general manager of the Mexican subsidiary, had to solve the difficult logistics problem of transporting the drilling machinery by rail from Vera Cruz to Jaltipan. Parten also gave Basland the assignment of helping Blackburn in the field, especially in the important and sensitive task of labor relations. Basland, a native of South Texas, spoke Spanish fluently and was sensitive to the needs and expectations of the Mexican workers. John Myers, who was retained as the project's geologist, joined Blackburn and Basland at Jaltipan.[18]

Blackburn's crew began work on September 6, 1947, under extremely difficult conditions, his men forced to hack their way with machetes through the tangled vines of the jungle. In some locations the high overhead growth was so dense that spotlights had to be used even in the middle of the day to allow operations to continue. With a six-month rainy season, conditions were especially terrible for half the year as the rain transformed the work sites into swamps of quicksand. Despite these severe difficulties, exploration continued throughout the fall of 1947. Blackburn's crews drilled several test wells to outline the structure of the dome and to estimate the sulphur reserves. Meanwhile, Parten and the other Little Mothers could do little but wait anxiously while the Mexican government took months to consider their application for rights to the entire salt dome.[19]

Patsy

That fall as Blackburn's crew worked their way slowly through the Mexican rain forest, Parten was in Dallas making wedding plans. His bride-to-be was the glamorous Patsy Edwards Puterbaugh, a beautiful former Neiman Marcus model with big brown eyes and a dramatic voice. A thirty-seven-year-old graduate of Southern Methodist University, Patsy had grown up in Highland Park, the socially exclusive community in north Dallas. She was the widow of John L. Puterbaugh Jr., an engineer with the Sun Oil Company in Dallas, who had died in action as a fighter pilot in the war. John and Patsy had one child, Patricia, born in 1940. J. R. had met the couple at a football game in Dallas before the war and they became social acquaintances. After J. R. and Opal divorced, J. R. called Patsy during one of his visits to Dallas. After a whirlwind courtship, J. R. asked Patsy to marry him. The

J. R. and his new bride, Patsy Edwards, on their wedding day, at Sylvester Dayson's house in Longview, October 31, 1947. *CN 09635. Courtesy Parten Photograph Collection, CAH.*

wedding was held on Friday afternoon, October 31, 1947, in Sylvester and Claire Dayson's living room in Longview, with Sylvester serving as J. R.'s best man.[20]

J. R. and Patsy purchased a home at 1913 Sharp Place in Houston's River Oaks. Patsy's daughter, Patricia (nicknamed "Pepe") remained in Dallas with Patsy's mother, herself a widow, until the school year was over. J. R. and Patsy made a handsome and dashing couple. They joined the exclusive River Oaks Country Club and soon made the invitation list for every ball and party given by the River Oaks high society set. Although J. R. was an unenthusiastic and reluctant participant, Patsy loved the River Oaks social scene and she fit it well. As one friend later recalled, "Patsy had an incredible flair, very artistic. She was vibrant and one of the most attractive women I've ever seen in my life. I have never seen anybody who could get dressed and look more stylish, more fashionable, than Patsy." Another friend recalled that J. R. and Patsy were the center of attention that first year in River Oaks: "They made a wonderful couple, as far as looks are concerned, because J. R. was always dressed to the hilt. He wore the best clothes and always looked great, and she was really something to behold." Patsy's verve and style delighted J. R. He loved her and he was happy with the life they were leading. His happiness turned to pure joy in late spring of 1948 when Patsy learned she was pregnant. On January 13, 1949, one month away from his fifty-third birthday, J. R. became a father for the first time when Patsy gave birth to a robust baby boy. J. R. named his son John Randolph, but he would eventually go by the nickname of "Randy."[21]

7-J Stock Farm

Despite his deepening concern over the lack of progress on Pan American's application to the Mexican government for a larger sulphur concession, J. R. stayed away from Mexico and remained close to home throughout much of 1948. Not only was he anxious about Patsy's pregnancy for most of that year, in the early months he was also worried about his eighty-three-year-old mother, Ella, who was still living in the old family home in Madisonville. Her health deteriorating rapidly, she died on May 19.[22]

Parten also had business reasons for being a homebody. Woodley's frantic search for new oil, which had been the company's singular objective since the end of the war, had not been successful. While searching for oil prospects late in 1947, Parten and Bill Moran decided to purchase oil leases on the east bank of the Trinity River, about twenty miles from Madisonville in nearby Houston County. The potential leases were on the eleven-thousand-acre Murray cotton plantation. For many years, Parten had been aware of a noticeable bend in the Trinity River at one point in its flow through the western boundary of the Murray plantation. He had first noticed the bend when flying over it in his Stearman during trips from Shreveport to Madisonville in the early 1930s. Parten suspected that the bend was the result of a high spot of land and that oil might be trapped under it, but he did nothing to test his hunch. In 1947, Moran's geologist, John Ivy, showed Parten and Moran a pamphlet published in 1935 by the University of Texas's Bureau of

Economic Geology that also made note of the river bend. When Parten and Moran contacted the owners about leasing some acreage for a wildcat well, they discovered that the entire plantation could be purchased at a relatively cheap price. Once reputed to have been the largest cotton plantation in the United States, the Murrays had gone broke after root rot had destroyed the cotton crop. The Moody Bank in Galveston, which held the mortgage on the property, was on the verge of foreclosing.[23]

As a boy, J. R. had fished with his Uncle Oscar and his cousins at Patterson Lake, a natural body of water on the plantation that was the old riverbed of the Trinity, and he had always admired the land there. Although his

J. R. and his son, Randy, at 7-J Stock Farm, about 1951. *CN 09598. Courtesy Parten Photograph Collection, CAH.*

prime consideration was for whatever oil and gas might be hidden beneath the land, Parten was also attracted by the thought of converting the old plantation into a cattle ranch. So he and Moran formed a consortium of investors that included John Ivy, Woodley Petroleum, and Premier Refining to purchase the plantation from the Moody interests. Soon after the purchase, Parten and Moran drilled three wells in the area of the river bend called Fort Trinidad. One well showed enough oil to encourage further exploration. In the meantime, Parten, who became president of the company formed by his fellow investors, turned the plantation into a cattle operation. He bought his mother's cattle herd and his father's old "7-J" brand, moved them to the plantation (which was renamed the 7-J Stock Farm) and hired Nathan Colwell, husband of his youngest sister Alice, to serve as ranch foreman. Colwell built a ranch house and drained and cleared the land to create grazing pastures. Under Parten's careful and discerning eye, Colwell and his fellow workers soon turned 7-J into a showplace. With Greenbrier in Madison County and 7-J in Houston County, Parten was in the ranching business in a big way. Nothing he did in the future ever gave him more pleasure than working this land.[24]

The End of Premier

In the early spring of 1948, Sylvester Dayson surprised Parten with the news that he had a buyer for their refinery business, which then consisted of three plants: the old Centex plant in Baird, the Premier refinery in Longview, and the Octane Refining plant in Fort Worth. During Parten's service with the PAW, Premier had prospered as a result of its Cotton Valley refinery's production of highly profitable aviation gasoline, but that plant had closed as soon as the war was over. The Fort Worth refinery had been acquired in the spring of 1941 from the Ohio Oil Company. Parten and Dayson brought in Joe Zeppa as a major investor and the three of them quickly modernized and expanded the outdated refinery, which included a pipeline from the Ranger field west of Fort Worth. Fred Mayer, whose company financed the purchase, later observed that Dayson and Parten had "made a steal" when they bought the Fort Worth refinery. "It made a lot of money during the war," Mayer said, "it was a real bonanza for them."[25]

Parten had assumed that no one would want to buy such out-of-date equipment and that they would either have to invest large sums of money to upgrade the plants or shut them down. He was delighted when Dayson told him that a group of farming cooperatives in Minnesota and Illinois were eager to acquire the refineries. There had been much talk in the oil business about a possible gasoline shortage because of insufficient refinery capacity, so the cooperatives wanted to make certain they had a dependable supply to meet agricultural needs. Parten "got interested immediately" when Dayson told him that he believed the cooperatives would pay as much as nine million dollars for their refineries.[26]

After lengthy negotiations, the co-ops eventually agreed to pay eight and a half million in cash for the refineries. Elated, Parten explained to one of the minor stockholders after the sale that the price was "so attractive we couldn't resist the temptation to sell." Years later, when recalling the deal, Parten noted that eight and a half million in cash was "a hell of a lot of money for those largely obsolete thermal cracking plants. That put a lot of cash in our hands and we went out of the refining business." Although Dayson also sold all of his stock, he agreed to remain at the Premier refinery in Longview as the general manager.[27]

The refinery sale severed Parten's last business connection with his former father-in-law, E. L. Woodley, who was still managing the Baird plant. Woodley retired and moved with his wife to Brownwood, their original hometown, ending his nearly thirty-year business relationship with Parten. As one of the large stockholders and thus a major beneficiary, E. L.'s daughter Opal was also affected by the sale. Writing to her ex-husband from New York only seventeen months after their divorce, Opal's letter revealed no resentment or anger toward J. R. To the contrary, Opal's letter evidenced her continuing affection for her ex-husband. "As one of your little flock," Opal wrote, "[I] am keenly grateful and appreciative. I wish also to thank you for your unfailing kindness to my dad. . . . We are all indebted to you . . . for opportunities you gave him late in life, and which for that reason especially

Left to right, Gov. Beauford Jester, Sylvester Dayson, and Myron Blalock at Dayson's house in Longview, late 1940s. *CN 09636. Courtesy Dayson Photograph Collection, CAH.*

meant a great deal to him. These few lines do not cover the genuine appreciation I feel for the many things you did . . . but please know anyway that I speak from the heart."[28]

"This thing is as big as all outdoors"

During the spring of 1948, Parten began to have doubts about the future of his sulphur enterprise in Mexico. Pan American's application for new concessions had been trapped in the Mexican bureaucracy for nearly two years without a decision. In April, Parten and his Pan American partners finally learned the reason for the delay. As Parten had suspected, Texas Gulf Sulphur Company had quietly moved into Mexico and blocked Pan American's request with the Mexican government. Not only had Texas Gulf interfered with Pan American's application, they had hired, without Parten's knowledge, Pan American's own law firm in Mexico City to persuade the Mexican government to grant *them* the concessions to which Pan American had applied. Parten received this shocking news from his brother-in-law Carl Basland, who had heard it from Perry Allen, an attorney for Hardin, Hess, and Suarez. Allen, whose sense of legal ethics had been offended by his firm's involvement in an obvious conflict of interest, subsequently resigned from the firm. Parten rewarded Allen's loyalty by appointing him president of Pan American's Mexican subsidiary.[29]

387

The future of their Mexican investment now looked very bleak to most of Parten's fellow Little Mothers, some of whom were openly critical of Parten's stubborn insistence that rights to the larger concession had to be acquired before they could move ahead with exploration and mining operations. A few of his partners talked about selling out to Texas Gulf, but Parten refused to give up. Although the Mexican government had frozen Pan American's application, it had not yet granted the concession to Texas Gulf. Parten persuaded his colleagues to hold out while he and their associates in Mexico fought back. That fight would last another fifteen months.[30]

Parten decided that one of the most important steps he could take in his effort to win the government's favor would be to sell a large amount of Pan American's stock to influential Mexican investors. "I spent several weeks down there in the early summer of 1949," Parten later remembered, "walking the streets of Mexico City, trying to get some local stockholders in with us, but I had no success." Frustrated by his inability to attract Mexican investors, Parten decided to use some old-fashioned political lobbying techniques to get a hearing with the government. He knew that Carl Basland had made some powerful friends in Mexico City, including Pancho Cardenas, the younger brother of former president Cardenas, and Gen. Antonio Bermudez, the head of PEMEX, the government oil company. Parten had Basland get his friend Pancho Cardenas to arrange a meeting for Basland with ex-president Cardenas. At that meeting, Basland persuaded the former president, as well as General Bermudez, to intercede with President Aleman in favor of Pan American. Cardenas and Bermudez did so, allegedly stressing to Aleman that Texas Gulf was a North American "monopolista" that for decades had suppressed the development of Mexican sulphur in an effort to control suppy and maintain high prices.[31]

The government's delay in granting the concession forced Pan American to suspend operations and lay off its work force in July 1949, sending shock waves through the economy of the state of Veracruz. With some prompting from Pan American agents, local businessmen, ranchers, bankers, and government officials joined together and sent a delegation to Mexico City to demand that Pan American's application be granted. Although the delegation was given a hearing, no official reaction was announced.[32]

As the months dragged by without any decision from the government, Basland and Perry Allen learned from their Mexican contacts that the Bradys, without telling Pan American, had attached to the original application their personal request for a separate and even larger concession surrounding the twenty-two thousand acres in which Pan American was interested. Basland's and Allen's contacts in the Mexican government felt that this unauthorized addition to Pan American's application had contributed to their problems with the government. Outraged by this deception, Parten and the other Little Mothers confronted the Bradys with this charge in a meeting in Dallas on March 10, 1950. The Bradys admitted that the charge was true and refused to withdraw their application. The following month, Parten maneuvered Lawrence Brady's removal from Pan

American's board of directors and William Brady's removal from the board of the Mexican subsidiary. Pan American subsequently gave formal notice to the Mexican government that it had disassociated itself from the Bradys and thus was not involved in their separate application for a concession. Despite the formal break with the Bradys, Pan American's original contract with the brothers guaranteeing them royalties from future sulphur operations remained in force.[33]

After the break with the Bradys in the spring of 1950, Parten returned to Mexico City to make another attempt to get the application (now delayed for more than two and a half years) approved. On Perry Allen's advice, Parten hired another former Mexican president, Portez Gil, to serve as a special counsel to work with Allen. As an ex-president, Gil was able to go directly to Aleman to discuss the applications. The president informed Gil that what he heard in his earlier meetings with Cardenas and Bermudez, as well as the protest from the citizens' delegation from the Isthmus, had convinced him to issue an executive order to the minister of the economy directing him to grant the concessions. The news from Portez Gil was obviously welcome to Parten, but several weeks passed without a formal announcement. Finally, in September 1950, three years after the application had been filed, the Mexican government issued the concession. "We were never told why it took so many years to get that application approved," Parten later said, "but it was pretty clear to everybody that more than bureaucratic inertia was involved, even if it was in Mexico. But there was no doubt in my mind that we had double trouble: the Texas Gulf Company and the Brady boys."[34]

Parten's enjoyment over winning the concession was cut short when he learned of yet another serious threat to the company. This time not only was the additional twenty-two-thousand-acre concession at stake, the entire project, including the original concession was in danger. Having lost in their effort with the government, Texas Gulf Sulphur went directly to Urquidi and Breceda, the Mexican citizens who were the legal holders of Pan American's concessions, and offered them fifty thousand dollars in cash plus future royalties and fees from the sulphur operations for their concessions. Struggling with financial difficulties and desperate for cash, Urquidi and Breceda found Texas Gulf's offer extremely attractive. During a meeting with Marlin Sandlin and Perry Allen in Mexico City on October 13, 1950, they announced that they had decided to repudiate their contract with Pan American. As he left the meeting, Urquidi turned to a despondent Marlin Sandlin and explained, "I hate to do this to you Marlin, but we just have to have the money. We're both broke."

The next morning Sandlin and Allen hired Tomas Noriega, one of the most prestigious trial lawyers in Mexico, to negotiate with Urquidi and Breceda. Noriega, a close friend of the Urquidi and Breceda families, eventually negotiated a new agreement, which all parties signed on December 21, 1950. The Mexican government approved the assignment of exploitation rights from Urquidi and Breceda to Pan American on April 9, 1951, nearly four years after the legal process had been initiated. Pan American now had rights to the entire twenty-two thousand acres originally recommended by John Myers.[35]

Myers soon began an intensive exploration of the newly expanded concession to determine the perimeters of the salt dome. The geologist made some spectacular discoveries. The sulphur was richer and thicker—150 feet thick in some locations—than any deposits Myers or his sulphur drillers had ever seen. Astounded, Myers eagerly reported to Parten that "this thing is as big as all outdoors." The geologist's estimates of the size of the find, which were considered excessive by some of his colleagues, proved eventually to be too conservative.[36]

These developments came at a propitious time. In early March, Parten had reported to Galveston businessman Ike Kempner that a widespread shortage of sulphur had "every chemical concern in the country . . . seeking new sources of sulphur supply." During the long delay in getting the concession, an enormous global expansion of the chemical industry had lowered reserves of the yellow mineral significantly. The outbreak of the Korean War during the previous summer made supplies even shorter, pushing demand to more than 150 percent of the peak years of World War II. Despite a vast increase in domestic production, American producers could not meet the growing world demand. The U.S. Gulf Coast had been explored thoroughly, so there was little prospect of new sources being found there, which suddenly made Mexican sulphur more attractive. The price of sulphur had risen sharply as a result, making Pan American's holdings many times more valuable than Parten or any one else had dared dream four years earlier. Parten's years of dogged persistence were going to pay off handsomely for him and his fellow Little Mothers.[37]

The outbreak of war in Asia in June 1950, however, had also had an impact on the American oil industry and its relationship with the federal government. As a result, J. R. Parten was called back to Washington in September 1950. It is to that story that we now turn.

Part Four

1950–1961

CHAPTER 22

Oil for Korea

The Petroleum Administration for Defense, 1950–1951

On June 25, 1950, the army of Communist North Korea crossed the Thirty-eighth parallel into South Korea, smashing its way south across the Korean peninsula. On Tuesday, June 27, the leaders of the South Korean government fled Seoul as the city burned around them. Like most Americans, the unfolding events in east Asia alarmed Parten. His worries were exacerbated by his intimate knowledge of the serious aviation-fuel problem the nation would face if the conflict developed into a full-scale world war. In 1947, as the Cold War between the United States and the Soviet Union escalated, the federal government established the Military Petroleum Advisory Board to propose a program for meeting petroleum needs in a national emergency. Parten was among a group of oil men who had served on the board, and with the PAW. As a result, he knew that the United States did not have enough high-octane aviation gasoline to keep its air force flying during a protracted military conflict.[1]

The fuel shortage was the result of a number of factors, but the most critical was the lack of production facilities. Most of the high-octane aviation refineries had been disassembled immediately after the Japanese surrender. Premier's Cotton Valley refinery had been among them. Built in haste and stocked with mostly obsolete equipment to meet the war crisis, most of these refineries could produce aviation gas only at a very high cost. Those that had not been demolished had been converted for use as petrochemical plants. Another problem was that by 1950 Americans were driving automobiles that used much higher grades of gasoline than had been the case during the war. During World War II civilian gasoline use had been severely rationed and the octane grade drastically lowered as part of the effort to supply gasoline to the military. Because of the rapid increase in automobile production in the postwar years, tetraethyl lead, the prime ingredient used to boost the octane value of gasoline, was in short supply. Oscar Chapman, the genial career civil servant and Democratic Party bureaucrat whom Truman had appointed secretary of the interior in December 1949, later admitted that the war created "a crisis all around, far more so than the country knew. And we couldn't tell [the public] or else they would have been scared to death if they'd have known what a close picture we were in . . . with the lack of fuel oil and gas . . ."[2]

Because the Korean conflict presented problems of supply and transportation not unlike those of World War II, Chapman sought the advice of Ralph K. Davies, who counseled him to create another PAW. He warned Chapman that the federal government must "direct and correlate [industry] rather than . . . inject itself into operations as such." The PAW had succeeded so well, Davies argued, because it had been managed by oil-industry representatives and councils, which had alleviated the industry's fear of federal control. Chapman was persuaded by Davies's argument, but he knew the oil agency could not be independent of Interior Department bureaucracy like the PAW had been. The Justice Department had criticized the PAW during the war, charging that it fostered antitrust practices within the industry. Justice was putting great pressure on Chapman to make any new oil agency another division of Interior, under the tight control of federal officials. He asked Davies to head such an agency, but he declined, instead recommending J. R. Parten. Chapman knew Parten well and thought he was an excellent choice, one who would help quell industry suspicions about the government's intentions.[3]

At a cabinet meeting on July 14 held to discuss the Korean crisis, the Truman administration decided to confront the North Korean challenge head-on, ordering an immediate expansion of the military and huge increases in the military budget. Chapman told Truman that it would be necessary to create a federal oil agency to address the military fuel shortage and to confront other problems. He wanted J. R. Parten to head it. Truman was not unfamiliar with the history of federal oil policy. He had learned much about the PAW, and the oil industry in general, in 1943 and 1944 as chairman of the Special Senate Committee to Investigate Defense Expenditures. Parten was also Truman's choice to organize and head such an agency. Having failed in two previous attempts to lure Parten back into federal service, the president told Chapman he would contact Parten personally to offer him the job. "Mr. Truman asked me to come up there," Parten later recalled. "He said that he needed me to help Chapman organize the new oil administration." Parten also heard from Chapman and Sam Rayburn, who had been asked by Truman to help persuade Parten to come to Washington. Parten agreed to organize the agency, but not to run it, and persuaded two of his former colleagues at the PAW, J. Howard Marshall and Justin Wolf, to help with legal and organizational problems.[4]

Organizing the PAD

Parten arrived in Washington in time to confer with Chapman and his staff before the July 26 meeting of the National Petroleum Council. Chapman's subsequent presentation to the council resulted in what one participant described as "a spirited session." It was obvious from the heated comments that there was deep disagreement among the refiners in the industry about how the aviation-gasoline shortage should be alleviated. On one side were refiners advocating the lowering of octane for civilian gasoline, some of them having trouble competing for the high-octane gasoline because of inadequate plant facilities. A lowering of octane would help their competitive situation. On the other side were the refiners with modernized facilities who wanted to retain their competitive edge. In the middle were the tetraethyl manufacturers who knew they had too little product to maintain high-octane grades in civilian gasoline while trying to meet military needs, but who, like most of those on either side, were deeply suspicious of any federal effort to control production.[5]

There was a strong consensus on one issue, however. A new federal oil agency would have to be responsible for the full range of the oil industry, not just refining. The Petroleum Council insisted that the agency report directly to the secretary of the interior rather than through department channels. Otherwise, the council feared that the agency would be at the mercy of the department's career bureaucrats, who might be tempted to interfere with the oil industry's "free enterprise" prerogative. Above all, the council demanded that Chapman not combine the oil agency with any centralized mobilization bureaucracy. An independent oil agency managed by industry personnel, such as the PAW had been, would allow the industry to continue to manage its own affairs. The Petroleum Council meeting ended with its members assuming that a new oil agency would have to be created soon, but deeply concerned about who was going to control it and what powers it would have.[6]

In the following weeks, while Parten and his colleagues consulted with Chapman on the structure of the new federal oil administration, Chapman made a formal request to the refiners to voluntarily increase their production of aviation gasoline. This request was almost universally ignored. As a result, Parten concluded that the only way to secure enough aviation fuel for Korea would be through government control or direction. On Parten's recommendation, Chapman called a meeting of the Military Petroleum Advisory Board to receive the report from its Aviation Fuels Committee. Parten wanted the committee's conclusion on the table when the National Petroleum Council met again in September, in order to show the oil industry that only a new federal agency with power to order directives could secure the needed aviation fuel.[7]

At its meeting in Washington on September 19, the Military Petroleum Advisory Board recommended the creation of a new agency. After the meeting, Parten warned Chapman that the oil industry would not support the creation of the agency unless the secretary of the interior assumed the job as oil administrator and appointed an industry man as deputy administrator to direct it. Parten emphasized that the oil industry was too complex to be coordinated by anyone but expert oil men. Accepting Parten's advice, Chapman later explained that he had no choice, otherwise he would "never have gotten [the oil agency] organized. I didn't have the time . . . to talk and visit and . . . twist the arms of all these oil people to get them to stop squabbling. . . . No human being could have done that." Chapman knew that he would be "politically crucified" by his "so-called liberal friends . . . for working so closely with the oil industry." He understood that the PAW had succeeded politically because of the formidable reputation Ickes had among progressive Democrats. Although a liberal himself, Chapman was no Ickes and he faced a much different political situation than had Ickes. The Truman administration refused to call the Korean conflict a "war." Truman himself labelled it a "police action." As perceived by the public, the invasion of South Korea was not Pearl Harbor, and much confusion remained about the seriousness of this crisis. Although the country was deeply involved in a very serious military conflict, a war environment did not exist on the domestic front. Accordingly, Chapman knew that it would be difficult for the public to accept government control of the oil industry.[8]

Chapman felt it was essential, therefore, that he appoint an oil man with well-established liberal political credentials, preferably an independent, to run the new oil agency. Because of his fear that the agency would be especially vulnerable to charges of corruption, the secretary knew that he had to appoint a person who was as "honest as I could find." Chapman felt strongly that J. R. Parten was the honest, liberal, and independent oil man he was seeking. He leaned hard on Parten to run the proposed agency, pleading that his outstanding record at the PAW was recognized within the industry and that his pro–New Deal political sympathies were equally well known within Democratic Party leadership circles. Chapman argued that there were few men with that combination of credentials available. Parten firmly resisted Chapman's pleas. He simply had no desire to head a government bureaucracy of any kind, even one staffed by oil-company employees. In addition, the Mexican government had approved Pan American Sulphur Company's application for a larger concession only a few days earlier and the company was entering a critical stage in its development. Parten did agree, however, to serve as the secretary's special consultant for a period of at least three months to help organize and staff the agency.[9]

At the meeting of the National Petroleum Council on September 28, 1950, Chapman announced his decision to recommend to President Truman that the new oil agency be independent of the existing federal bureaucracy. He then turned the floor over to Parten, who was introduced as his chief adviser in the establishment of the new oil agency. Parten assured the council that he would make the proposed agency a carbon copy of the PAW. He asked the council to submit a list of nominees for the post of deputy administrator and for positions at every level of the organization. "I hope this council . . . takes the job seriously and gets something done about it before you leave here today," Parten said, "because this organization . . . should be set up and set up now."[10]

After the meeting, Parten told the New York *Times* that the civilian gasoline supply was secure and that rationing would not be necessary in the immediate future so long as the oil industry cooperated with the government's efforts to produce more aviation fuel. He emphasized that it was only the matter of gasoline quality rather than quantity that had yet to be determined, because octane would have to be lowered for civilian use in order to produce the higher octane "avgas."

He warned that his views were based on "today's known demands"; a widening of the war would change everything.[11]

Parten's appointment had the public relations effect Chapman had intended. The *National Petroleum News* applauded Chapman's decision and declared that Parten, "likeable as he can be tough," was a "recognized master of convincing argument and back-scenes strategy." The *Texas Oil Journal* declared that when Parten agreed to organize the new oil agency "the oil and gas industry of the nation breathed a deep and comforting sigh of relief. The oil industry is in good hands."[12]

With the oil industry on board, Parten, Marshall, Wolf, and their associates organized and staffed the agency. Late in the summer, Congress had passed the Defense Production Act of 1950, conferring sweeping powers on Truman to mobilize the nation for the defense of Korea. The legislation also gave the president wide-ranging authority over the country's natural resources. Accordingly, Truman issued an executive order delegating authority to the secretary of the interior to coordinate the oil and gas industries for defense needs. Chapman subsequently issued his own order on October 3, 1950, creating the new oil agency and naming it the Petroleum Administration for Defense (PAD).[13]

As he had promised, Parten organized an agency almost exactly like the PAW, but much smaller in size and scale. The PAD's task was to allocate petroleum products, to arrange transportation, to make forecasts for anticipating future needs, and to establish priorities for the domestic oil industry. It was given the power to order the oil industry to produce certain products and refrain from producing others. These powers were rarely invoked, however, because the agency was usually able to operate through negotiation and persuasion. A committee of the National Petroleum Council, chaired by W. Alton "Pete" Jones, Parten's former colleague in the Big Inch pipeline project, helped Parten select the personnel for the PAD's key management posts. Each manager came directly from the oil industry and served on a temporary, rotating basis, to insure that no one company had to provide more than its share of people. The perception that some companies had to give up more of their key personnel than their competitors had been a major complaint about the PAW within the industry. Of the nearly four hundred technicians, executives, and general consultants who served with the PAD during the four years of its existence, the overwhelming majority were employees of or were associated in some other direct way with the oil industry.[14]

Before he could return to Texas, Parten had four specific goals to carry out as part of his general work to organize the PAD: (1) establish the PAD as an independent agency reporting directly to the secretary of the interior; (2) recruit an outstanding leader from the oil industry to serve as the deputy administrator; (3) exempt the oil industry from federal antitrust action for any pooling activities in which it had to engage to carry out its defense job; and (4) persuade President Truman to waive the federal requirement that industry leaders who worked for the PAD had to take a leave without pay from their companies.

The most important of these goals in Parten's mind—PAD independence— was the first to be accomplished. Instead of the PAD reporting to Interior's Oil and Gas Division, the latter reported to the PAD. Except for the hot-oil act enforcement staff (which had to stay independent for reasons even the leaders of the oil industry could understand), the staff of the Oil and Gas Division were transferred temporarily to the PAD. With this action, it was obvious to everyone that the PAD was the industry's agency, directed by the industry. Parten reconfirmed this perception in an interview in a trade journal. "I want to stress that the petroleum industry is the best policeman of its own job," he was quoted as saying. "Secretary Chapman has made it clear that he wants the petroleum industry to do its own job with the least possible interference from government." The industry's satisfaction with and approval of these administrative arrangements was vividly demonstrated when Parten sent a telegram on October 4 to thirty refiners asking them to voluntarily refine more aviation gasoline. The refiners complied promptly with Parten's request.[15]

Parten accomplished the goal of recruiting a deputy administrator the first week in October when he persuaded Bruce Brown, president of Pan-American Southern Company in New Orleans (a subsidiary of Standard Oil of Indiana), to take the job. Parten selected Brown, who was also the first choice of Jones's personnel committee, because he was a highly regarded petroleum-refining engineer. The PAD's most difficult problem was the aviation-gasoline shortage, which was a refining issue. Although Brown was a Republican and Chapman preferred a Democrat, Brown's management of the PAW's refinery division had been widely praised. Chapman readily accepted Brown's selection.[16]

Parten's remaining two goals, antitrust exemption for the oil industry and a "work without compensation" status for the PAD's oil industry staff, were closely related. Because of strong opposition from the antitrust staff of the Justice Department, they were also the most difficult goals to accomplish. Antitrust protection, the most important of the two, was crucial to the creation of an industry committee system similar to the one used in the PAW. Under existing antitrust statutes oil company executives of different companies could not meet and make decisions that had industry-wide implications.

Because of the pressing need to recruit PAD staff, Parten first tackled the issue of leave without pay. He knew that it would be exceedingly difficult to secure the help of the best people in the industry if they had to give up their salaries, most of which were much higher than the corresponding government salaries, pension contributions, and other benefits. He and Marshall prepared a formal request to the Justice Department to allow oil industry personnel to serve the PAD as "dollar-a-year" men without compensation ("WOC's") so that they could remain on the payrolls of their respective companies and protect their jobs and fringe benefits. Bruce Brown, for example, had accepted his appointment to serve as the head of the PAD on the strict condition that he could serve as a WOC. Other executives were asking for the same arrangement.[17]

Congress had granted authority to the president in the Defense Production Act of 1950 to hire defense personnel on a "without compensation basis," but Truman had not issued the necessary executive order to implement it. Until the president issued such an order, no one could serve in the WOC category. Soon after the legislation had passed, Truman sent a draft of the order to the relevant agencies for the usual revisions and comments, but it had disappeared in the Justice Department. Marshall advised Parten that the department's Antitrust Division, which opposed the WOC hiring arrangement on the theory that it aided antitrust activity, was holding up Truman's executive order in its offices. In the meantime, Brown and other oil company employees who had agreed to work for the PAD on a WOC basis, came to Washington, confident that their employment status would soon be made official.[18]

Problems with the Gas Industry

In early October, while Parten waited for President Truman's executive order, he learned from Chapman that the natural gas industry had requested their own federal agency, separate from the PAD. Several companies were building large-capacity pipelines requiring a substantial quantity of steel, which was in short supply. Before the Korean War broke out, the gas transmission-line companies had cornered the market on large-diameter pipe with long-term advance orders and they feared that the PAD would reallocate some of their pipe to the oil and refining companies. They could get the steel they needed if they had their own agency. In addition, in the five years since the end of World War II, the Northeast had converted much of its fuel use from coal and kerosene to natural gas. The competition to hook up gas fields in the Southwest to the vast new energy market in the East had become fierce and bitter. The gas-transmission companies were deeply suspicious of any government attempt to allocate pipe, fearing that one company might get an unfair advantage over another because of defense priorities. This was a particular concern of the Tennessee Gas Transmission Company (Tenneco), which was locked in a struggle for northeastern markets with the Texas Eastern Gas Transmission Company, owners of the Big and Little Inch pipelines. Parten felt that it would cause "no end of headaches" if he let them have their own agency. "It will be very foolish to divide the administration of oil and gas" he said. "A great deal of this gas comes out of the same wellhead that oil does and petroleum gas is related to petroleum all the way." Chapman accepted Parten's reasoning, but hoping to avoid a confrontation, he sent an equivocating letter to the American Gas Association stating that he would take their request "under advisement." For the time being, the gas industry kept out of the PAD's way, erroneously thinking that Chapman's reply meant that he was considering their request.[19]

"I want them on my desk before noon"

On October 30, Bruce Brown had been on the job for nearly one month, but he could not assume his official position until the executive order governing employment of industry personnel had been issued. Parten explained to Chapman that most of the work that had been done up to then had been performed by a small group of industry experts serving as consultants without compensation. He reminded Chapman that the aviation-fuel problem had not been solved and that if the war spread to other countries the military would be in seri-ous difficulty. In addition, Parten's office was being deluged with requests from various oil and refining companies for permission to procure steel and expand facilities. Until the PAD was able to hire more staff, they would be unable to process most of these requests. Pete Jones's Petroleum Council committee had slowed its effort to find suitable personnel. "I cannot overemphasize the urgency," Parten wrote, "the work of PAD is rapidly approaching a standstill. . . ." He urged Chapman to go to Truman and ask him to get the order out.[20]

Nearly three weeks passed and there was still no executive order. Because the order was needed for the federal government's entire mobilization effort, every defense agency was affected. Only one of the top mobilization jobs had been appointed, that of the head of the National Production Authority, and it was filled by a retired telephone company executive. "It is my considered opinion," Parten stressed in another letter to Chapman, "that there is nothing more important to the defense program than the prompt issuance of these regulations." Because it was known that Truman supported the WOC arrangement, Parten concluded that the "continuing delay in the issuance of these regulations is due to the action of persons in the executive offices who are not carrying out the President's inten-tion." A few days later, however, Chapman confessed to Parten that he could not determine where the draft of the WOC order had been held up. The Justice Department claimed that they had sent it on to the Bureau of the Budget, but the bureau knew nothing about it. With the president facing so many other problems, Chapman hesitated to press him about the matter.[21]

"My friend Parten was getting madder and madder" about the lack of action on the WOC matter, Bruce Brown later stated. "Brother Parten . . . could and did speak his mind forcefully. He pounded the pavement daily, calling on several top executives in the White House as well as leaders in Congress to reemphasize the tragic delay in the mobilization program. . . ." Eventually, Parten discovered that the executive order was stalled in the Justice Department on the desk of Peyton Ford, the assistant attorney general in charge of the Antitrust Division.[22]

Parten took his problem to Stuart Symington, chairman of the National Security Resources Board and a protégé of Truman's. Symington took Parten's problem directly to the president . Parten later recalled "that President Truman just called Ford up and asked, 'Where are those regulations for the Interior Department to enable them to hire some dollar-a-year men on this petroleum business?' And Ford replied, 'They're on my desk.' And the President said, 'Well, I want them on my desk before noon.'" Truman issued his executive order on November 21 authorizing the PAD and other mobilization agencies to hire person-nel on a "without compensation" basis. Bruce Brown assumed his post and Pete Jones reconvened his personnel committee. The staffing of the PAD began to take final shape. Jones told Parten that his effort entitled him to "the Medal of Merit, the Congressional Medal and all other things." Bruce Brown later declared that he had "often wondered just what would have happened to the mobilization program

. . . if J. R. Parten had not been so determined to force a sensible conclusion out of the administration [about WOC's]."[23]

"Parten has explained this thing to me and I have total confidence in his integrity"

By the first of December 1950, Parten had devoted most of five months to the PAD and he was eager to return to Texas, but one goal remained unfinished. Chapman had not yet submitted the PAD's industry-committee plan to the Justice Department for an antitrust clearance. Nevertheless, now that the WOC problem had been resolved and Bruce Brown was in control at the PAD, Chapman told Parten that he could go home. Brown could finish the job. At Chapman's request, however, Parten retained his appointment as a special consultant and he agreed to return to Washington whenever Chapman or Brown needed him, especially if the industry-committee plan ran into trouble.[24]

Parten was in Texas for only a few weeks before Chapman and Brown called him back to Washington to help with a problem, but not in the Justice Department. In December, Brown had made a request to the natural gas companies for information on the pipelines they had under construction or were planning to build. Brown's request set off an alarm throughout the gas industry, which had continued to assume that Secretary Chapman was looking for a way to give them their own agency. At Chapman's request, Parten returned to Washington to help him face the angry gas company executives. Parten assured them that the PAD had no intention of running the gas industry any more than it would run the oil industry. The problem was steel. There was only one supply of steel and the same mills made the pipe for the both the oil and gas industries. Without central coordination over material, there would be chaos in the pipe supply with the result that both industries would suffer and the mobilization program would be adversely affected. Rejecting Parten's argument, the gas executives declared that they would not allow any oil man to have supervision over the industry.[25]

When Chapman was given this troublesome news, he met with Parten and Bruce Brown to discuss his next move. Parten argued that under no circumstances could the secretary give in to such a threat, especially during a military crisis. Brown agreed, but he suggested a compromise. Although gas would have to remain under PAD authority, the industry could be allowed to form its own advisory committee, parallel to the National Petroleum Council, which would select personnel for the PAD's Gas Division. Such a compromise would allow some of the gas company executives who felt less strongly about the issue to cooperate openly without seeming to break ranks. Parten and Chapman felt that this was a reasonable solution, but they worried that the Justice Department would object. They were already concerned that the antitrust staff at Justice might fight the oil industry committee. Chapman was planning to submit the PAD's industry-committee plan to Justice in a few days with a request that the department grant antitrust protection to it. The Justice Department's behavior in the WOC matter indicated that the industry-committee plan was unlikely to be looked upon with favor. Chapman nevertheless decided to follow Brown's suggestion. He called the gas executives together on January 26 and announced that the gas industry would remain under PAD administration, but that he would form a separate gas industry committee to nominate personnel for the Gas Division and to advise the PAD on gas matters.[26]

The gas industry representatives accepted Chapman's decision and proceeded to identify executives to serve on the PAD's gas committee. On February 2, however, just a few days after Chapman's announcement, Bruce Brown received a notice from the National Production Authority that in less than a month the PAD had to submit a list of material needs for both the oil and gas industries. Because of the long delay in getting the gas industry's cooperation, the PAD had no information to use in putting together the gas industry's allocation request. Brown realized that he did not have time to wait for the gas industry to form its committee, so he decided to find some well-known gas company executive who could come to Washington and help the PAD prepare the material request for the industry. Brown called Parten, who recommended one of his old friends from Shreveport, Texas Eastern Corporation president Reginald Hargrove. Brown was able to persuade Hargrove to serve as the PAD's "Acting Assistant Deputy" on gas matters until the material-allocation request was completed and until someone else was recruited for the permanent job.[27]

After the announcement of Hargrove's appointment, Gardiner Symonds, president of the Tennessee Gas Transmission Company, informed Chapman that Hargrove was totally unacceptable because his company (Texas Eastern) and Symonds's company were locked in a desperate competition for markets in New England. Symonds could not tolerate having his chief competitor in charge of the PAD's Gas Division. Republican senator Charles Tobey of New Hampshire, who was supporting the Tennessee Company's bid to serve as the gas supplier for New England, threatened to cause Chapman trouble in the Senate if he followed through with the Hargrove appointment. Although a Republican, Tobey, as Chapman well knew, was a close friend of President Truman's. To make matters worse, Chapman's former boss, Harold Ickes, also asked Chapman to reconsider Hargrove's selection.[28]

These protests nearly frightened Chapman into withdrawing Hargrove's appointment, but Brown and Parten talked him out of it. They argued that Symonds's concerns were unwarranted because no one in a decision-making position at the PAD had any involvement in the politics of the gas industry. Parten was especially adamant about sticking with Hargrove, telling Chapman that Hargrove was "a first-class gentleman who has been in the gas business four times as long as anybody connected with Tennessee Gas, particularly Gardiner Symonds." Brown and Parten offered to talk to Senator Tobey. Parten also promised to "pull Ickes off" Chapman's back. Parten explained to Ickes the pressing need for expert advice on the material-allocation request and iterated that Hargrove was not going to be in a position to help his company at Symonds's expense. Ickes subsequently called

Chapman to withdraw his objection, stating that "Parten has explained this thing to me and I have total confidence in his integrity."[29]

Neither Parten nor Brown had any success with Senator Tobey, however. Parten advised Chapman to proceed with Hargrove's appointment despite the senator's threats. Chapman felt, however, that Tobey and Symonds could not be ignored, so he decided to take care of their suspicions by asking Symonds to come to Washington with Hargrove and the two bitter rivals could serve as co-assistant deputies for gas matters. Symonds refused to work with his competitor from Texas Eastern, but he did agree to send his assistant, Dick Freeman, to serve as his representative. Bruce Brown subsequently appointed Freeman the acting director of the PAD's Gas Division, reporting to Hargrove, who remained as acting assistant deputy. This arrangement seemed to satisfy Symonds, and Brown proceeded to establish a gas-industry advisory committee.[30]

The Last Goal is Achieved

On January 29, 1951, Chapman submitted to Peyton Ford, head of the Justice Department's Antitrust Division, Parten's plan for the organization of industry advisory committees in the oil and gas industry. Securing approval of this plan had been Parten's fourth and last goal as Chapman's special consultant. In the cover letter to Ford, Chapman emphasized that because the plan had been based on the PAW model, it had been "tried, tested and proved in the bitter experience of war." Chapman asked Ford for Justice Department clearance in regard to antitrust law.[31]

Ford rejected the plan with the argument that the PAD's industry advisory committees had to be under the direct control of the government with each committee chaired "by a full-time government employee." Industry committees would not be allowed to meet on their own initiative nor could industry representatives control the agendas of meetings. Ford also warned against granting Bruce Brown the authority to delegate governmental powers to industry committees. Such delegation, Ford declared, would have "serious and far-reaching implications from the standpoint of enforcement of the antitrust laws." Ford also complained that Chapman's plan had "no requirement for representation of 'independent' small business enterprises or for 'fair' representation generally." The assistant attorney general was not impressed by Chapman's explanation that the PAD's organization was patterned after the PAW. "I must advise you that substantial questions of antitrust violations were raised as a result of the operation of these committees [under the PAW]," Ford wrote. "It is clear to us that . . . fundamental questions of basic policy were initially resolved by these committees and that resulting government action amounted to no more than giving effect to decisions already made by such committees." He argued that functions had been delegated to the PAW committees which "properly must reside exclusively in government officials." Ford declared that "the root of most of the complaints" received by Justice during the war was "this intermingling of government functions with private groups." He claimed that the industry committees had committed "abuses" during the war to the extent that they were cited by the petroleum subcommittee of the House Committee on Naval Affairs in October 1943.[32]

Ford's refusal to approve the industry-committee plan and his scathing criticism of the PAW stunned the secretary of the interior. He sent a copy of Ford's letter to Parten with a request for help in drafting a reply. Parten, however, was too deeply involved in the Pan American Sulphur Company negotiations in Mexico to give his immediate attention to Chapman's request. In late March, Parten finally enlisted the aid of Justin Wolf and J. Howard Marshall and the three men drafted a reply for Chapman, who sent it unchanged to Ford in mid-April. "Frankly, I was shocked and surprised at the nature of your criticisms," Chapman's letter to Ford declared. "Your charges are at complete variance with the facts as I know them and as they are generally accepted." The letter claimed that "the character and integrity of Secretary Harold Ickes, of . . . Ralph Davies, and the patriotic . . . executives who staffed PAW" refuted Ford's accusations; that PAW committees were always advisory and had no power to compel action against or for any oil operator; that all PAW actions "were the result of the Government's own decisions" and the PAW had not allowed antitrust activity. Quoting laudatory statements from several congressional committees, President Truman, and the military about the PAW, Chapman argued that the official records would show that it had worked closely with the Justice Department's Antitrust Division throughout the war. He stressed that the petroleum industry's complexity and the government's lack of expertise in supervising its operations required the active involvement of industry personnel in the PAD's management.[33]

Ford's rigid opposition to the industry-committee plan raised in Parten's mind the hated specter of federal control of the oil industry. One of the reasons he had gone to Washington to help set up the PAD was to make certain that the oil industry would remain free from federal regulation during the Korean crisis. Deeply concerned by this troublesome development, Parten went directly to Speaker of the House Sam Rayburn. Parten complained to Rayburn that Ford's insistence that federal bureaucrats had to serve as the chairmen of the industry committees threatened the oil industry's independence. He urged Rayburn to get the Justice Department to back down.[34]

When nearly two weeks passed without any action by Chapman to get the president involved, Parten went to the White House himself on May 15 and asked Truman to overrule Ford. Truman said that Rayburn had also brought the problem to his attention and that he had given it some thought. He explained that there were complicated political dimensions to this problem, and promised to work out a compromise that would be acceptable to both sides. Truman eventually forged an agreement leaving Parten's industry-committee structure intact as originally proposed, but prohibiting the committees from making specific recommendations on allocations of supplies and equipment among individual oil firms. Some of the independents had complained that their competitors who were on the industry committees were in a position to direct allocations unfairly. The agreement also declared that the industry committees were strictly "advisory" and that the minutes of the committee meetings had to be submitted for review to the attorney general. The crucial point, however, was that this "compromise" allowed the industry committees to remain under the control of the oil industry. Parten's fourth and last goal as Chapman's consultant had now been achieved.[35]

Parten had completed most of his work with the Petroleum Administration for Defense by late spring 1951, but he continued as Chapman's official advisor until he resigned on January 14, 1953, as the Eisenhower administration prepared to take over the agency. Eisenhower eventually terminated the PAD with an executive order on April 30, 1954, ten months after an armistice was signed ending the conflict in Korea.[36]

The Justice Department won the battle but lost the war in its dispute with the oil industry, which continued to control the PAD through the National Petroleum Council and its committees. Although in theory monitored by the secretary of the interior, the PAD as a government agency seldom did more than ratify the decisions already reached by the industry's representatives. Chapman's political biographer has argued that the secretary's "willingness to turn most of the day to day operations of the PAD to industry representatives . . . raised serious questions about how well the public interest was protected. The industry's rising profits suggested that it received maximum advantage from the war emergency with minimal sacrifice." The perception of the PAD as the oil industry's private federal agency caused some friction with other departments and agencies of the government. There were clashes between the defense-production staff in the Interior Department and the PAD staff, who were viewed by the former as nothing more than lobbyists for their individual corporations. And there was deep resentment in the Justice Department over the easement of antitrust liability. In addition, other industries felt that oil and gas had an unfair advantage in the fight over the allocation of controlled materials.[37]

Nevertheless, the record indicates that the PAD performed the job for which it had been organized and it did so free of scandal, all the while under the close surveillance of the Antitrust Division of Justice. Aware of the microscopic scrutiny under which the PAD operated, Parten was especially careful to do nothing that smacked of conflict of interest. In September 1951, for example, Bruce Brown learned that Parten was preparing a request to the PAD for permission to obtain some tubular steel for Woodley. When Brown related this to Chapman in his weekly report, he wrote that Parten was going to "ask a very special favor" of the PAD for material. "I wish he would not," Brown added, implying that Parten was taking advantage of his role as consultant to seek special privileges. Parten, however, was simply making a routine and ordinary request for material through official channels and according to policy guidelines. Parten was deeply offended by Brown's implication. Sensitive about the PAD's image, he was even more protective of his well-earned reputation for integrity. He confronted Brown, who immediately apologized and issued a written correction for the record. "I am very sorry about this whole thing," Brown wrote. "J. R. has yet to 'ask a very special favor' of the PAD and, knowing him, I doubt that he ever does."[38]

The PAD ended the aviation-gasoline crisis quickly and the military's total fuel needs were met with few problems. Like the PAW earlier, the PAD earned a reputation (even from some of its critics) as one of the most efficient emergency agencies in the federal government. The fact that oil profits rose during the Korean War is no indictment of the PAD. Overall profits for most American industries climbed rapidly during this period because of vast increases in military spending and other factors. There is no reason to think that the oil industry's revenues would have been significantly different if the PAD had not existed. That the oil industry essentially threatened not to cooperate with the war effort unless the federal government organized the PAD as an industry-controlled agency is, of course, another matter. The industry's bluff, if it was one, was never called. Chapman's reluctance to challenge the oil industry, combined with the administrative and political skills of Parten, Marshall, Wolf, and Brown, prevented such a confrontation. It likewise averted a possible constitutional crisis and a national controversy similar to the one that occurred when Truman was forced to seize control of the steel industry in April 1952—a presidential action ultimately ruled unconstitutional by the Supreme Court. What mattered most to those on the front lines in Korea, however, was that they had the fuel to keep their airplanes flying, their vehicles moving, and their ships sailing. J. R. Parten was among those who were responsible for the PAD's success at fulfilling those important missions.[39]

CHAPTER 23

Shivercrats and Mavericks

1951–1952

O n March 15, 1951, Marshall O. Bell, a Democrat from San Antonio,
introduced a resolution in the Texas House of Representatives accusing University of Texas professor Clarence Ayres of being a
Communist and of engaging in subversive activities. Ayres had
attracted Bell's anger by testifying at a committee hearing against the legislator's
proposed Texas Communist Control bill. Bell's resolution, which passed the
House by a vote of 130 to 1, ordered University of Texas chancellor James P. Hart to
inform the legislature within ten days if he intended to reappoint Ayres to the faculty. In support of Bell's resolution, Rep. Sam Hanna declared that "punks, riff-
raff, dirty skunks, and screwballs" such as Ayres should be "run out of the
University and out of the state." A fervent defender of academic freedom,
Chancellor Hart refused to give in to the pressure.[1]

Denouncing the attack as "wholly unjustified," Parten telephoned several
influential university ex-students to urge them to oppose Bell. Parten was shocked
by the reactions to his calls. Most agreed that the attack on Ayres was outrageous,
but they warned that unless Parten wanted to be accused of being a "commie"
dupe, he had best stay out of the affair. They advised Parten that the nation's political environment had changed, making it an especially dangerous time for anyone
accused of subversion or of being sympathetic to communism. Accusations such
as those being made against Ayres could have far greater consequences for the
accused (and his defenders) than had been the case in earlier years.[2]

Although preoccupied with his business and his work with the PAD, Parten was
not unaware of the larger developments shaping the American political culture. He and
millions of other Americans followed the disturbing national and international events
of the postwar era, including the development of the atomic bomb by the Soviet Union,
the Communist victory in China, the Soviet occupation of Eastern Europe, and the
seemingly never-ending accusations that subversives and Red spies were ensconced in

the federal government. Although he was concerned about the increasingly dangerous international environment, Parten did not believe that communism posed any threat to domestic institutions. He had watched the activities of Republican senator Joseph R. McCarthy and the House Committee on Un-American Activities with disgust as they hurled unsubstantiated charges against their fellow citizens. Nonetheless, the attack on Ayres and the frightened reactions of his friends made these developments more personal to Parten, forcing him to take closer notice of the nation's increasingly poisoned political atmosphere.

Parten now realized that the country was in the grips of a powerful "red scare," a widespread series of actions by individuals and groups whose intentions were to frighten Americans with false and highly exaggerated charges of Communist subversion for the purpose of political, economic, and psychological profit. The usual tactic employed by those carrying out the red scare soon became known as McCarthyism: the use of indiscriminate, unfounded accusations, inquisitorial investigative methods, and sensationalism ostensibly in the suppression of communism. Joseph R. McCarthy, the Republican senator from Wisconsin whose witch-hunt tactics provided a name for the principal red-scare technique, was the most famous of the anti-Communist crusaders. Although Senator McCarthy and his accusations of treason in the federal government embodied the phenomenon nationally, the postwar anti-Communist movement actually permeated all levels of society, affecting nearly every facet of American life for almost ten years. Opposition was nearly nonexistent at its height and what little did exist was generally ineffective.[3]

Ironically, the corporate power structure that had defeated Parten and Rainey and that now dominated the university's board of regents generally ignored these anti-Communist attacks. By 1951, the university was slumbering through a self-styled "era of tranquility," comfortably resting on the AAUP's blacklist, controlled by a safely reactionary board of regents, and administered by a president much admired by the state's conservative establishment. As a result of the changed power-structure at the university, as well as Chancellor Hart's strong support of Ayres, the legislature backed off from the confrontation and the economics professor remained on the faculty. The red scare in Texas in the 1950s instead centered on the public schools, churches, libraries, art museums, and the state legislature. The university community, emasculated by the Rainey debacle five years before, would generally be a passive observer of the hysteria raging around it.[4]

Marshall Bell's unsuccessful attack on Clarence Ayres alerted Parten to the political madness threatening the Bill of Rights. Because of Parten's past experience with Congressman Dies and his involvement in the Rainey affair, he had experienced firsthand the early stages of the political nightmare now descending upon the land. Bell's attack also renewed Parten's contact with the group of politically progressive women activists with whom he had worked during the Rainey affair. These activists soon lured him back into the factional warfare of the Texas Democratic Party.[5]

Allan and the Shivercrats

By 1951 the Texas Democratic Party had fallen under the control of Texas Regulars, Dixiecrats, and other conservatives opposed to the domestic and foreign policies identified with Roosevelt and Truman. Their leader was Allan Shivers, who had become governor after Beauford Jester's death in 1949. Parten had met, and liked, Shivers when he was a regent and Shivers was a young state senator from the heavily industrialized Port Arthur area. As a senator, Shivers had a moderate voting record. On his election to statewide office, however, Shivers joined forces with the conservative, anti-Truman, Dixiecrat, corporate power-elite in Texas. Many of Shivers's closest allies and supporters had fought against Rainey in 1946. To Parten, Shivers and his allies were closet Republicans who were subverting the "true" Democratic Party in Texas and were encouraging the state's blossoming red scare.[6]

At the state convention in Mineral Wells in September 1950, Shivers had purged pro-Truman Democrats from party offices and taken firm control of the party organization. By the summer of 1951, Shivers was criticizing almost every facet of Truman's domestic and foreign policies. When the governor signed a bill allowing cross-filing of candidates in elections (a candidate could run both as a Republican and as a Democrat), Sam Rayburn complained to Parten that Shivers was destroying the Texas Democratic Party. Parten and others worried that if Shivers managed to control the Texas delegation to the 1952 Demorcratic convention and then led a revolt against the party's presidential nominee, the Republicans would have an excellent chance of winning the state's electoral votes. This scenario had been narrowly averted at the 1948 Democratic national convention when the Texas Regulars and Dixiecrats had been thwarted only by Governor Jester's reluctant decision to stay in the party. To prevent a Democratic debacle in Texas in 1952, Parten and other Democrats loyal to the national party joined in an effort to wrest control of the state party from the so-called "Shivercrats."[7]

In July 1951, Lillian Collier, Margaret Reading, and Minnie Fisher Cunningham—the leaders of the newly organized Texas Social and Legislative Conference (formerly the Women's Committee for Educational Freedom)—persuaded Parten to meet with the Democratic National Committee (DNC) leadership in Washington to seek their help against Governor Shivers. They wanted to know if the DNC was concerned enough about Shivers to encourage them to create a loyal Democratic faction in Texas. The DNC's response to Parten's mission was unenthusiastic, mainly because of the lack of support from Lyndon Johnson, who feared Shivers as a potential political opponent. Rayburn, however, encouraged Parten to urge the women to proceed with their plans to organize a loyalist group to oppose Shivers at the county level.[8]

When Parten returned to Texas in August, he gave Rayburn's message to the national party loyalists and provided money to get their organizational effort started. Parten also tried to recruit some of his friends in the independent segment of the Texas oil industry to help take the state party machinery from Shivers. "I think it is time for real Democrats to get together," he explained to one friend. Parten's attempt to persuade some of the independents to join him in support of the loyalist cause was derailed, however, by an emotional and contentious issue: the dispute over ownership of the oil-rich, offshore lands called "tidelands." Texas oil interests argued that the tidelands, which extended nearly eleven miles from the Texas shoreline, were owned by the state, while the federal government, armed with supporting decisions from the Supreme Court, argued that the land was federal property. The dispute was not trivial; at stake was the amount of money the oil companies had to pay in leases and fees. On federal land the oil companies paid a royalty fee 25 percent higher than that set by the state. The federal government stood to lose millions of dollars in revenue if the land was judged to be state property. The emotionalism of the argument stemmed from its connection to the public schools of Texas. The revenue the state derived from its control of the tidelands went into the public-school fund. Although the amount of money earned to support the schools was small—it amounted to a fraction of one cent per child—the connection allowed the oil interests and their political representatives to charge that the federal government was attempting "to rob the little school children" of Texas. This rhetoric, coupled with the standard cry of states' rights, allowed oil industry leaders to avoid the real issue—the protection of their pocketbooks.[9]

Parten, of course, had fought against federal controls for many years and he vigorously supported the federal oil depletion tax allowance, but he had little interest in the tidelands dispute. The cost of operation offshore was "well beyond the reach of 99 percent or more of the independent oil men," Parten said. "I was very happy to leave [offshore drilling] to the large oil companies." He admitted that the argument that the tidelands belonged to the state had merit because of provisions in the 1845 Annexation Treaty by which Texas had entered the Union, but he felt that it was a relatively minor problem that politicians were manipulating for their own personal advancement. "I thought the tidelands thing was filled with a lot of emotionalism that caused a lot of people to do some very irrational things," Parten said. Unfortunately for the Democratic loyalists in Texas, Truman vetoed congressional legislation certifying state ownership of the tidelands, thus providing the state's anti-Truman forces with an effective issue to use against the Texas loyalists.[10]

In late October 1951, encouraged by Rayburn's message and boosted by Parten's money, women activists from the Texas Social and Legislative Conference joined with other disaffected national Democrats to form the "Texas Loyal Democrats." Their immediate goal was to work for the selection of pro-Truman delegates to the 1952 Democratic national convention in Chicago, delegates who would remain loyal to the Democratic ticket in the fall election. The loyalists elected Dickinson banker Walter Hall as their chairman, Austin attorney and former state representative Fagan Dickson as executive director, and Margaret Reading as secretary. "It was a loose-jointed organization with no constitution," Creekmore Fath, one of the organizers, later recalled, "but it had a consensus on purpose: to regain control of the Democratic party machinery for the real Democrats." Too

swamped by work to serve as an officer, Parten nevertheless pledged financial support and agreed to serve as a political advisor.[11]

Parten's involvement with the Loyal Democrats of Texas widened his circle of
political friends and led to his participation in the creation of an alliance among
the handful of liberal activists in the state who were willing to carry out the faction's political agenda. This group initially included Walter Hall, Fagan Dickson,
John Cofer, Creekmore Fath, Maury Maverick Sr., Minnie Fisher Cunningham,
Lillian Collier, and the remarkable Navarro County judge, James "Tiger Jim"
Sewell, a navy veteran blinded in action in World War II. Many of these activists
were veterans of the Rainey gubernatorial campaign.[12]

Parten knew most of the loyalist leadership. Maury Maverick was a former
university classmate, Creekmore Fath had been one of Bob Montgomery's student
protégés, and John Cofer had served as one of Lyndon Johnson's attorneys in the
legal battle with Coke Stevenson after the 1948 election. Parten had known Lillian
Collier and Minnie Fisher Cunningham since the days of the Rainey affair in 1944.
Walter Hall and Fagan Dickson were only slight acquaintances who were to
become Parten's close political allies for many years to come. Dickson, a forty-
eight-year-old attorney from Austin, was a liberal Democrat with a passion and a
capacity for outrage, traits that appealed greatly to Parten. These individuals provided much of the leadership for the liberal Democratic faction in Texas throughout most of the 1950s.[13]

Recruiting an Opponent for Shivers

Parten was valuable to the Loyal Democrats of Texas for reasons other than
money. He was their link to Sam Rayburn. Rayburn detested Shivers on a personal level, but he was wary of a public fight with the popular governor and did not
want to be openly identified with the loyalist organization. He knew that it was
going to be difficult for the Democratic presidential candidate to carry Texas, and
that they could ill afford Governor Shivers's active opposition during the campaign. The party had to be held together to avoid a catastrophe in November. Not
only was the presidency at stake, but also Democratic Party control of Congress
and Rayburn's speakership. Rayburn, however, did not want to give Shivers an
excuse to support the Republican nominee. He was prepared to hold his nose and
let Shivers and his delegation into the convention for the sake of party solidarity,
but Shivers would have to promise not to walk out of the convention or to campaign against the Democratic nominee.

Although Rayburn refused to oppose Shivers openly, he was willing to engage
in some subterfuge to help the loyalist cause. He asked Parten in January 1952 to
help him recruit an opponent to run against Shivers for governor in the
Democratic primary. Rayburn doubted that Shivers could be beaten, but it might
help the Texas loyalists in their effort to regain control of the party if Shivers was
forced to spend as much time as possible working on his reelection campaign.[14]

For an opponent for Shivers, Parten suggested Ralph Yarborough, a friend of
his from the days when Jimmy Allred had served as Texas attorney general.

Yarborough was a former district court judge who was practicing law in Austin after having served in the army in World War II. Parten knew Yarborough as a fighter for economic and social justice and as a firm believer in the principles of Jeffersonian democracy. He was the embodiment of the post–New Deal liberal spirit in Texas, and to Parten, he was the logical heir to the Allred-Rainey political tradition. Unlike many of the national Democrats in Texas, Yarborough was a friend of the independents in the Texas oil industry. Rayburn subsequently sent an emissary to Yarborough to ask him to run against Shivers. Believing that he could not raise enough money to run against the governor, Yarborough declined the invitation. He planned instead to be a candidate for attorney general.[15]

Another Request from Truman

As part of Rayburn's overall strategy to ensure his influence in the upcoming presidential campaign and to protect his flanks against the Shivers forces, he persuaded President Truman to offer Parten the post of treasurer of the Democratic National Committee. Rayburn made this request without Parten's knowledge. One of Parten's friends in Washington, however, warned him about the president's forthcoming offer. Forewarned and unwilling to accept the post, Parten prepared an excuse to save face for everyone.[16]

When Truman offered him the party post during a private meeting in the White House on February 14, 1952, Parten explained that he had recently applied to the Export-Import Bank for a seven-million-dollar loan to build a Pan American sulphur-extraction plant in Mexico. If he and his partners received the loan, the Republicans might charge that he had received it as payment for agreeing to work in the campaign treasurer's post. With the Republicans already accusing the Truman administration of gross favoritism and cronyism, Parten told Truman that he did not want to hand one more issue to the opposition. This was the third job offer from the president that Parten had turned down. "You know, Major, I've always admired you," Truman said, "and I admire you the more for this. You're absolutely right." It was Parten's last meeting with Truman as president. In March, Truman announced that he would not be a candidate for renomination.[17]

Parten could not help Rayburn by taking the party treasurer's job, but he did accept another mission for the Speaker a few weeks after his meeting with Truman. Rayburn asked Parten to organize an effort to have Houston oil man Wright Morrow removed as a Democratic national committeeman. A leader of the anti-Roosevelt Texas Regulars in 1944, Morrow was hostile to Rayburn, and the Speaker knew that he would not support the Democratic Party's nominees in November. Parten agreed to lead a quiet effort to kick Wright off the DNC. He wrote a letter to party chairman Frank McKinney asking him to demand a public pledge from Morrow that he would support the party's national nominees in 1952. If Morrow refused to make the pledge, Parten demanded that McKinney appoint someone in his place. McKinney, however, refused to demand a loyalty pledge from the committeeman. Thwarted by McKinney, Parten presented the petition to Morrow and demanded that he take the loyalty pledge or resign. Refusing to sign the loyalty pledge, Wright told Parten that he would not resign under any circumstances. With Rayburn remaining silent, Lyndon Johnson avoiding the issue, and McKinney uncooperative, Parten abandoned the effort to remove Morrow.[18]

After the venture against Morrow failed, Parten worked hard to raise money to fight Shivers. His activities soon attracted the governor's attention. In late April Weldon Hart, a Shivers aide, called Lyndon Johnson to ask if it was true that Parten was "trying to raise $300,000 in Houston to put an opponent in against Shivers." Johnson told Hart that the rumor was "completely unfounded." He and Parten had recently been on the same flight from Texas to Washington and they had discussed Shivers. Johnson saw no sign that Parten was trying to find an opponent for Shivers. Unconvinced by Johnson's argument and suspecting that Parten had traveled to Washington to get Rayburn openly involved against Shivers, Hart asked Johnson to assure Rayburn that Shivers would not bolt the party. "Ask Rayburn what he wants," Hart said, "does Mr. Rayburn want to be friends about this or not?" Johnson replied that he had already assured Rayburn that "there would be no embarrassing situation in Texas and that Shivers would go along for him."[19]

Hart had guessed right. Parten went to Washington to persuade Rayburn and other Texas Democrats to thwart Shivers's plan to control the Texas delegation. Truman's withdrawal just four months prior to the national convention had set off a wild scramble for the nomination. Tennessee senator Estes Kefauver *was* now the leading contender in a field that included Vice Pres. Alben Barkley, Sen. Robert Kerr of Oklahoma, and Sen. Richard Russell of Georgia. Rayburn told Parten that with Truman out of the race, he preferred that the Texas delegation not be pledged to any candidate. Rayburn hoped that an uninstructed delegation would vote for Senator Russell for president. Parten, however, preferred a delegation committed to Rayburn. He suspected that Rayburn coveted the nomination but would not admit it, not even to a close friend like Parten. Parten agreed to support an uninstructed delegation, but warned Rayburn that he would oppose an attempt by "closet Republicans" to control the Texas Democratic Party.[20]

During his meeting with Rayburn, Parten gave the Speaker a copy of a speech Shivers had made at a State Democratic Executive Committee meeting in New Braunfels in April in which Shivers had declared that he would not take a pledge to support the Democratic ticket. After reading Shivers's speech, Rayburn began to waver. He called Johnson and stated his fear that Shivers would not be able to control "some of the extremists" in his delegation and that he would probably abandon the party's national ticket. "You know those wild men," Rayburn complained, "you can't do a damn thing" with them. Johnson once again assured Rayburn that Shivers would support the national ticket. Following his talk with Rayburn, Johnson called Weldon Hart to warn him that Parten was working against Shivers after all. Johnson assured Hart that he had persuaded Rayburn not to oppose the governor's delegation in any challenges from Texas liberal Democrats at the convention, despite Rayburn's serious reservations about Shivers's ultimate intentions. He warned Hart, however, that Parten believed that Shivers was "not wedded to the party, does not give a damn whether his future is with the Democratic Party [and] is likely to be lead by the people who have never supported the party."[21]

There was one thing, however, that Johnson apparently did not know. While Rayburn might not deny Shivers a seat at the national convention, he was still encouraging Parten to persuade Yarborough to run against Shivers in the primary. Three months had passed since Yarborough had indicated that he would run for attorney general, but he had still not filed for the race. The Shivers political machine had anointed John Ben Shepperd, a conservative from West Texas, as its choice for attorney general. Yarborough later claimed that Shivers's representatives offered Yarborough a seat on the Texas Supreme Court in exchange for not running against Shepperd. When he refused, Yarborough alleged, Shivers's operatives scared off his potential financial backers. "My money pledges disappeared overnight," Yarborough said.[22]

Broke and frustrated by the power of the Shivers political organization, Yarborough planned to withdraw from the race for attorney general, but a meeting with Parten in Houston on April 30 changed his mind. Handing him a check for five thousand dollars, Parten told Yarborough that he would raise an additional fifty thousand if he would run against Shivers. Yarborough would also have Jimmy Allred's public endorsement as well as the covert help of Rayburn, who could not make a public endorsement. Yarborough announced his candidacy for governor the next day, declaring that his campaign would be "an extended struggle against the political octopus now strangling free governmental decisions in Texas." Yarborough's announcement confirmed Shivers's worst suspicions about Parten's intentions. He soon made plans to retaliate. Meanwhile, the loyalist faction prepared to challenge Shivers at the upcoming state convention in San Antonio.[23]

"Let us go"

The loyalist faction knew that they could not defeat Shivers at the precinct conventions or at the state convention in San Antonio on May 27. Instead, they decided to attend the state convention and as soon as the Shivers forces elected the Texas delegation to the national convention they would bolt the meeting and hold a rump session at a nearby hall and select an alternate delegation. This "loyal" delegation would go to the national convention in Chicago and challenge the credentials of the Shivers delegation. Loyalists hoped that the party's national leadership would accept their challenge and throw the Shivers group out of the convention. At Parten's urging and to please Rayburn, the loyalists even agreed to make their alternate delegation an uninstructed one, but one whose delegates had taken the loyalty pledge. Maury Maverick Sr. agreed to lead the San Antonio walkout and to direct the subsequent challenge to the credentials of the Shivers delegation. Maverick told Parten that even though they could not control the state convention, "human decency" demanded that they do whatever they could to harass "that snake" Shivers.[24]

Before the convention opened on May 27, Maverick rented a hall at La Villita, the block of historic buildings near the San Antonio River that he had been

"Let us go." Maury Maverick Sr. at La Villita in San Antonio, May 27, 1952. Parten, with handkerchief, can be seen just above Maverick's head. To Parten's left is Lillian Collier. *CN 09625. Courtesy Maury Maverick Photograph Collection, CAH.*

responsible for restoring twenty years earlier. The hall would serve as the place where the loyalists could hold their rump convention after the walkout. Parten won a place as a loyalist member of Madison County's delegation to the state convention. Rayburn asked him to be his "eyes and ears" at the convention and to do whatever he could to avoid the walkout. He feared a split would give Texas to the Republicans in the upcoming presidential election. Parten told Rayburn, however, that a walkout was unavoidable.[25]

In the opening session of the convention, held in San Antonio's Municipal Auditorium, Parten and his fellow loyalists were defeated when they attempted to deny credentials to pro-Shivers delegates from twenty-eight counties. The Shivers faction also defeated loyalist demands that the Texas delegation pledge support for the winner of the party's presidential nomination. Maury Maverick went to the convention podium and denounced Shivers and his supporters, ending his speech with the call of "Let us go." Nearly seven hundred noisy loyalists, including Parten, walked out of the auditorium to La Villita. Maverick led the loyalists in singing songs, including "Happy Days Are Here Again," "I'm Just Wild About Harry," and "The Eyes of Texas." Parten sat next to Lillian Collier at the head table as Maverick denounced Shivers in a fiery, arm-waving speech. "There wasn't a great deal done there, it was just a lot of hoopla," Parten admitted, "but Maury did make a hell of a speech and it was spontaneous." The loyalists elected their own delegation with Parten and Maverick as the cochairmen.[26]

With little hope for success, Parten nevertheless worked hard for the loyalist cause and for Yarborough. In early June, the loyalists launched a campaign to be recognized as the legitimate Texas delegation at the Democratic convention. When Parten sent Frank McKinney a five-thousand-dollar contribution, he explained that it was for the DNC rather than the State Democratic Committee, to serve as a tangible demonstration of his loyalty to the national party. Parten joined with Walter Hall to finance the printing of a booklet written by Fagan Dickson and Creekmore Fath titled *The Texas Story* to explain why the loyalists had bolted the state convention and to expose "the whole Shivers delegation as Dixiecrats of the first order." The loyalists mailed a copy of *The Texas Story* to each one of the thirty-five hundred delegates to the Democratic national convention. Parten also made a final attempt to enlist Rayburn's overt help. "It is simply unthinkable," Parten argued, "that a delegation should enter the convention threatening in advance not to be bound by majority rule." Urging Rayburn to become a candidate for the presidential nomination, Parten promised that the loyalists would give him their unqualified support if recognized as the official Texas delegation.[27]

Meanwhile, Shivers worked effectively behind the scenes to solidify his position with Rayburn. Aware of Rayburn's quiet yearning for the presidential nomination, Shivers sent Parten's former college debate coach, Houston attorney Charles I. Francis, to the Speaker to tell him that Shivers planned to back Rayburn for the presidency if his nomination became a possibility. Francis assured Rayburn that Shivers "had every intention of supporting the ticket . . . regardless of the candidate."[28]

"Parr, Parten, and Parlor Pinks"

Parten's efforts to thwart Allan Shivers at Chicago and to defeat him in his reelection bid were well noted in the Governor's Mansion. In a speech in Houston on July 15, Shivers charged that President Truman had sent a "Houston oil man who spends a lot of time in Washington and who is well-known in ultra-liberal circles" to Shivers to tell him to cease his criticism of the national Democratic leadership. Shivers alleged that Truman's emissary threatened to recruit and finance a "strong" candidate to oppose Shivers if he did not cooperate. "I've known this gentleman—and I use the word gentleman in the broad sense—for twenty years," Shivers declared, adding that he told him just where to go with his warning. "I'm tired of a lot of ultra-intellectual parlor pinks and so-called liberal crackpots running the Democratic party," Shivers complained. The Governor did not mention Parten by name during his speech, but he told a group of reporters as he left the stage that the Texas loyalist faction was being controlled by "[Duval County boss George] Parr, Parten, and Parlor Pinks."[29]

The next morning, Parten was shocked by a headline in the Houston *Press*: "Claims Parten Warned: Lay Off New Deal." Outraged, Parten immediately sent a telegram to the governor expressing surprise at his "fantastic" statement. Parten declared that he had never "even heard the President mention your name," nor that of Yarborough's. "I realize, Governor, the terrific strain you suffer in your des-

perate eleventh hour bid for votes," Parten wrote. "Governor, you . . . are a pro-
fessed churchman. . . .Would you give me an opportunity to hear from your own
lips the regret I know that you must already feel at having made this false accusation?" Shivers never replied. Parten told Yarborough that Shivers was "desperate"
to have made such a charge. "He can't find anything bad to say about you . . . so he
jumps on your friends."[30]

"Shivers was in the saddle"

When Parten arrived in Chicago on July 19, he joined the other Democratic
delegates and party officials flowing through the city's major hotels, being lobbied
and lobbying for the several possible nominees to be the party's standard-bearer in
the upcoming presidential campaign. In their own tumultuous convention two
weeks earlier, the Republicans had nominated World War II hero Gen. Dwight D.
Eisenhower as their candidate and had selected a young senator from California by
the name of Richard Nixon to serve as Eisenhower's running mate. Every
Democrat knew that the Republicans had forged a powerful team that presented
them with a formidable challenge. For the first time in twenty years, the
Democrats would not have the advantage of having an incumbent running for
reelection to the presidency. Although Sen. Estes Kefauver had cornered the most
delegates during the presidential primaries, Rayburn and other party leaders
opposed his candidacy. Close behind Kefauver were Senator Russell and New York
governor Averell Harriman. Russell was strongly opposed by the northern liberals,
while Harriman was unpopular with the southern delegations.

A deadlock was likely, which gave Rayburn some hope that he might be drafted as a compromise candidate. Many Democrats, however, were already talking
about how they should make Eisenhower's age a campaign issue. A Rayburn candidacy would deny them that opportunity since both were past the age of seventy.
Parten supported Rayburn out of loyalty, but he felt that Rayburn would make a
more valuable contribution to the nation if he remained as Speaker of the House.
Russell was far too conservative for Parten, who also did not care for Russell's
uncompromising stance against civil rights. Parten's personal favorite was an official "non-candidate," Adlai Stevenson, the popular governor of Illinois.[31]

When he arrived in Chicago, Parten made a last-minute appeal to Rayburn
on behalf of the loyalists, but it was too late. Shivers had already met with
Rayburn and given his word "as a man and as Governor of Texas" that he would
stay with the party and support the nominees if the credentials committee agreed
to seat his delegation. Because of Shivers's promise, Rayburn had to recognize the
Shivers group as the official Texas delegation. Rayburn served as permanent
chairman of the national convention and, as Shivers later noted, he "could have
had us kicked out of the convention, or kept us from getting into the convention,
if he'd wanted to."[32]

Practical reasons also dictated Rayburn's decision. He and the other members
of the national party leadership were certain that Shivers would abandon the party
if he was turned away at the convention. Allowing Shivers into the convention

denied him the excuse that he had been cast out of the party. By forcing Shivers to make a loyalty pledge, there would be no doubt about which side had broken its promise if the governor subsequently campaigned for Eisenhower. In addition, Senator Russell threatened to lead the Georgia delegation out of the convention if the leadership recognized the Maverick delegation. This threat terrified the party leadership, which was desperately seeking to avoid a repeat of the Dixiecrat walk-out of 1948.[33]

The convention credentials committee voted thirty-six to thirteen in favor of the Shivers delegation, but northern liberals led by William Proxmire challenged the decision from the convention floor. After a stormy debate, Shivers went to the podium and assured the convention that he had always voted Democratic and he promised that the party's nominees would be on the ballot in Texas. "Shivers was in the saddle," Parten noted, "and he had the votes." After the loyalist delegation's defeat, Rayburn told Parten that the loyalist challenge had been beneficial because it had forced Shivers to make the pledge in the open, in front of the delegates. Doubting that Shivers would keep his promise, Parten told Rayburn that Shivers was "the type who would suck stolen eggs and then hide the shells."[34]

After watching the party nominate Adlai Stevenson on the third ballot, Parten rushed back to Texas for the state's Democratic primary, which was held on the last day of the national convention. Yarborough had waged a spirited fight with the strong financial support of Parten and Walter Hall, but his campaign made little progress against the incumbent governor's powerful political organization. Largely ignored by a hostile press, Yarborough attracted only 488,345 votes to Shivers's 833,861. Parten encouraged Yarborough to make another attempt in 1954. "It is still my earnest hope that one day you may be called upon to make Texas a good governor," Parten stated. "It seems to me that the time will soon come when the people will demand it."[35]

Parten's suspicion that Shivers would not support the Democratic presidential nominee was confirmed in late August when the governor announced that he could not support Adlai Stevenson because of his opposition to Texas's claim to ownership of its tidelands and because of his pro–civil rights stand. Stevenson's position on both issues had been well known long before his nomination. Shivers declared that he would campaign for Eisenhower, who had promised his support for state ownership of the tidelands. The Texas governor argued that he had bro-ken no promises; he had promised to place the nominees on the ballot, but never to support them. "It was a pretty shifty act," said Parten, who was quick to point out to Rayburn that "Shivers has found an excuse to withdraw his support from the Democratic ticket. It appears to me very unfortunate that . . . oil companies have inspired Governor Shivers to make a national issue of Tidelands." Embarrassed by Shivers's betrayal, Rayburn could only reply that Shivers had taken the pledge in Chicago and that if he persisted in his stand against Stevenson, "the people of Texas are going to think that he has not been frank or candid with them and I will certainly be one that will help scatter this propaganda. . . ."[36]

"To hell with Texas Gulf; we'll operate it ourselves"

After the convention, Parten thought he could take a break from politics for a couple of months to tend to important business with Pan American Sulphur, but he soon discovered that his political and business activities were not so easily separated.

In March 1952, the Export-Import Bank had notified Pan American Sulphur that it would loan the company half of the seven million dollars it needed to build an extraction plant and auxiliary facilities. The loan was contingent on Pan American raising the other half in cash to put into the plant as equity. Daunted by having to find three and a half million dollars relatively fast, Parten advised the Little Mothers to sell their holdings and get out with a fat profit. Most of his partners, preoccupied with their own oil operations and having no desire to run a sulphur company, agreed with Parten that it was time to find a buyer.[37]

After negotiations with Freeport Sulphur failed because of its reluctance to become more involved in Mexico, Parten and his associates had no choice but to offer Pan American to their hated rival, Texas Gulf Sulphur Company.[38] In a meeting with Texas Gulf president Fred Nelson in late July, Parten offered to sell Pan American for fifteen million dollars of Texas Gulf stock, contingent on an evaluation of the concession by Texas Gulf's geologists. Accepting Parten's offer, Nelson sent fifteen of his company's experts to the Jaltipan site to appraise the sulphur potential. The geologists confirmed that Pan American's concession was rich in easily extractable sulphur. At their next meeting in August, however, Nelson declined Parten's offer and, instead, proposed a partnership. Initially, Parten suspected that the "sulphur monopoly," in consort with Freeport, was trying to force Pan American into selling out for much less than it was worth. But Parten eventually learned that Fred Nelson, unaccustomed to taking chances because of his company's longtime domination of the industry, had decided that the venture was too risky. Nelson later told the *Wall Street Journal* that Pan American's project was "still rather speculative."[39]

Rebuffed by Nelson, Parten recommended to his partners that they withdraw their offer to Texas Gulf, reopen negotiations with the Export-Import Bank for more money, hire some full-time sulphur experts with executive ability, and create a real sulphur business that would "pin Texas Gulf's ears back." His associates accepted Parten's recommendations as well as his suggestion that Pan American go public with a large issue of common stock to raise the cash to match the Export-Import Bank loan. As one participant stated, the Little Mothers all decided "to hell with Texas Gulf; we'll operate it ourselves."[40]

Parten's feud with Gov. Allan Shivers, however, soon intruded on Pan American's effort to raise cash. During a trip to Austin to get Pan American Sulphur Company's issue of stock cleared under Texas law, the company's attorney paid a courtesy visit to Governor Shivers, an old friend, and discussed Parten's plans. "I thought that was a real mistake," Parten later complained, "but [the attorney] just did it on his own and that's the way Shivers got wind of this whole damn thing." Parten claimed that Shivers warned Pan American's attorney that he would try to prevent Pan American Sulphur Company from offering its stock in Texas. At the next Pan American board meeting in Dallas, the attorney announced that he had been surprised to discover that Shivers had "a lot of venom for Parten" and that he had threatened "to put anybody in jail for selling Pan American stock in Texas." He advised Pan American's directors to issue the stock outside Texas. "Over half our stockholders were Texans," Parten said later, "but because of the Governor's threat, we couldn't even write them a letter to tell them what was happening."[41]

Pan American eventually issued its stock through the Wall Street brokerage house of Kuhn, Loeb, and Company, which held the stock meeting in New York, out of Shivers's reach. The response to the stock offering exceeded expectations. "By that time, it had gotten around that we had discovered sulphur," Parten recalled, "and the money just came swooping in." By the beginning of October, Pan American had raised more than enough money for the loan equity requirement.[42]

"No idea how to run a state campaign"

Shivers and his allies completely controlled the September convention of the Texas Democratic Party in Amarillo. Although unable to list Eisenhower on the state ballot as a Democrat due to legal restrictions, the Shivercrat-controlled convention officially endorsed the Republican ticket—an historical first for Texas. Denied the help of the Texas Democratic Party's campaign apparatus, the Stevenson campaign floundered with essentially no statewide organization. When most of the state's Democratic officeholders refused the job, Speaker Rayburn, obviously humiliated by Shivers's treachery, stepped in to direct Stevenson's effort in Texas. Rayburn, however, had no experience at managing a statewide campaign and no money with which to support it.[43]

Resolving to do what he could to help, Parten donated Marlin Sandlin's time to serve as the treasurer for Stevenson's Texas campaign. Parten also agreed to chair the steering committee for the Stevenson campaign in Harris County. The committee's most pressing task was to coordinate Adlai Stevenson's upcoming visit to Houston. Working closely with Judge Roy Hofheinz, Bob Eckhardt, and others, Parten and Marlin Sandlin made the arrangements for the candidate's appearance in Texas's largest city. On October 18, Adlai Stevenson arrived in Houston, a city critical to his effort to win Texas's electoral vote. Eisenhower was touring the state at the same time, and Stevenson's leaders in Texas hoped to attract crowds at least equal in size to his. Parten and his reception committee met Stevenson and Sam Rayburn at Houston's Hobby Airport. Following a brief welcoming ceremony, the Stevenson entourage and the committee drove in a motorcade to downtown Houston, where the presidential candidate spoke to a crowd of about fifteen thousand gathered in front of the city's Music Hall. Parten was by Stevenson's side much of the time, introducing him to individual reporters from Texas newspapers and to city officials. Stevenson and his staff left the city feeling good about the enthusiastic crowd and the warm reception given them. Rayburn later told Parten that he felt the Houston visit was one of the highlights of Stevenson's Texas tour.[44]

Another Personal Attack by Shivers

Parten's prominent role in Stevenson's Houston appearance soon led Governor Shivers to launch a second attack on Parten, this one far more personal and serious than the first. In late October, the Export-Import Bank announced that Pan American Sulphur Company had met its equity requirement of three and a half million dollars, and would therefore receive a matching loan for that amount to build its plant on a twenty-three-thousand-acre site on the Jaltipan salt dome. Construction of the plant was scheduled to begin February 1, 1954, with a tentative completion date of August 1954. In an obvious attempt to embarrass the Stevenson campaign in Texas by discrediting one of its prominent leaders, Shivers issued a press release on October 30 charging that the Export-Import Bank was lending the money because of Parten's "sizable contributions to Democratic political campaigns." The governor declared that it was a "strikingly strange" coincidence that the loan had been made just before the election. "Mr. Parten is a well-known Texas millionaire and is fully able to spend three million dollars of his own personal money," Shivers stated, ignoring the obvious fact that Pan American was a corporation owned by thousands of stockholders and that no director of a corporation would use his or her personal money to help build a company plant. "I don't believe that . . . tax money, people's money," Shivers continued, "should be used . . . where the head of a company is financially able to do it personally."[45]

Parten was not surprised by Shivers's personal attack. He immediately issued a statement denying the governor's charges. He pointed out that arrangements for the loan had been made in March, contingent upon Pan American's raising the required equity. "I called [Shivers] a liar in polite language some months ago," Parten said. "This statement of his is going to cost Eisenhower some votes. Seventy-five percent of the Directors of the Pan American Sulphur Company are Dallas oil men who are supporting Eisenhower." Parten claimed later that the loan "had nothing in the world to do with politics. My God, we had to match it with more than three million dollars of our own cash." Parten sent a copy of the news story about Shivers's attack to Rayburn. "I told you of this loan last August which was your first knowledge of it. Shivers says I used political influence. . . . The truth is we never called upon any congressman or senator to intercede for us at any time." Rayburn replied that "the reason why [Shivers] picks on you is that you are a Democrat and tell the truth every time you speak and some people don't."[46]

Eisenhower rolled on to an impressive victory in November, pulling with him a majority of Republicans into both houses of Congress. Despite the enormous problems faced by the Stevenson campaign and the popularity of his war-hero opponent, Stevenson lost Texas by only 133,000 votes out of the two million cast, a far better showing than anyone had expected. After the defeat, Parten wrote Stevenson: "It was not the year for the Democrats to win. We saw the greatest demonstration of the power of money translated into propaganda through radio, television, and the press which has ever been seen in this country. I think you fought a good fight and that you made the most forceful campaign that any Democrat in the nation could have made in the circumstances."[47]

J. R. Parten and his colleagues among the Democratic loyalists had suffered defeat on every front in 1952, but they had emerged as an organized faction, prepared to provide Texans with an electoral alternative to the powerful and well-financed conservative political establishment. The bitter contest for control of the Texas Democratic Party would continue and Parten would play an important role in that political struggle.

CHAPTER 24

Fighting the Red Scare

Robert Hutchins and the Fund for the Republic

I
n late August 1952, Parten received a telegram from Paul Hoffman, president of the Ford Foundation, inviting him to become a charter member of the board of directors for a new organization called the Fund for the Republic. Hoffman was the former head of the Studebaker Company and had become an international figure as a result of his successful tenure as director of the Marshall Plan in Europe. He and Parten met in Washington during the war, and had become casual friends. Parten had little interest in Hoffman's invitation. His political work with the Texas loyalists during the last six months had caused him to neglect his business affairs yet again. Pan American Sulphur had reached a critical stage in its development and he needed to devote more time to the company.

The next day, Parten received a telephone call from another old friend, Robert Maynard Hutchins,who had retired in 1950 after twenty-two years as president of the University of Chicago to become the associate director of the Ford Foundation. Hoffman had enticed Hutchins to the foundation, at that time the largest private philanthropic agency in the world, with the lure of having "the biggest blank check in history" to spend on projects for the advancement of human welfare and for the protection of civil liberties. Hutchins, who had grown restless in his position as university president, was alarmed by what he viewed as increasing government suppression of civil liberties, motivated by the hysteria over Communist subversion. Hoffman's invitation proved irresistible to Hutchins. He and Hoffman, along with other associate directors and support staff, subsequently established the Ford Foundation's new offices in Pasadena, California, on January 1, 1951. A few months later, Hutchins and a public relations adviser to the foundation, Wilbur Hugh "Ping" Ferry, developed the idea of the Fund for the Republic in direct reaction to the red scare raging throughout the country and Sen. Joseph McCarthy's demagogic accusations of Communist subversion in the federal government.[1]

In his telephone call to Parten, Hutchins urged the Texas oil man to accept Hoffman's invitation. The Fund planned to be a boldly activist division of the Ford Foundation that would provide grants to groups involved in civil liberties work, defend individuals whose rights were being trampled, and conduct studies and publish reports related not only to civil liberties and First Amendment issues, but to problems involving racial and religious discrimination. Unafraid of controversy, Hutchins repeated to Parten what he had told the Ford Foundation's trustees: that the Fund would "deal almost wholly in unpalatable causes." Accordingly, he cautioned Parten that joining the Fund's board would "be a rough ride. We are in for a battle and we need battlers. I need good men who are willing to stand up." Parten begged off, explaining that he had recently turned down President Truman's request to serve as treasurer of the Democratic National Committee and that he had pressing business concerns. Hutchins knew how to appeal to Parten, however. "This is going to be very important," Hutchins responded. "We are going to see if we can preserve the First Amendment. . . . Believe me J. R., you don't want to miss this." He asked Parten to think about it until Paul Hoffman had an opportunity to call.[2]

When Hoffman called, he explained that because the Fund planned to be involved in the areas of civil rights and race relations, the board had to have representatives from the South who had impeccable reputations. He also repeated Hutchins's warning that the Fund's directors would be the targets of racial bigots and McCarthyites, so the people who agreed to serve not only had to be willing to take the heat, they also had to be invulnerable to economic retaliation. Outraged by the political vigilantism sweeping the nation, Parten agreed to join the board. "Hoffman and Hutchins twisted my arm real hard," Parten later admitted, "and I finally went along with it."[3]

Parten felt that the Fund might give him an opportunity to fight the red scare. He thought not only about the recent attack on Clarence Ayres, but also his experience as a regent with Cong. Martin Dies, who had used the fear of communism as a weapon to advance his personal political ambitions. The Rainey affair and the racist and anti-Communist demagoguery of the 1946 gubernatorial campaign were also fresh on Parten's mind. He had warned his friends after the 1946 election that a right-wing political reaction posing a dangerous threat to civil liberties was falling upon the nation. His prediction was coming true. No matter what the demands of business might be, Parten finally decided, he would make his stand with a man he admired as much as any man, a man on whom he had conferred the nickname "'Battlin' Bob:" Robert Maynard Hutchins.[4]

Parten would come to take great pride in his lengthy association with Hutchins and the Fund for the Republic. Parten's role as one of the Fund's most influential directors and his support for the Fund's Center for the Study of Democratic Institutions would help bring meaningful public attention to social issues and raise the level of public discourse. The Fund and the Center would make numerous contributions to the civic good, including John Cogley's *Report on Blacklisting* and Michael Harrington's *The Other America*, which would inspire

424

LBJ's War on Poverty. Parten's involvement with the Fund would also bring him into contact with a wide variety of diverse ideas and causes that appealed to his love of learning and his dedication to the principles of the Bill of Rights.

Fifteen Million Dollars for Civil Liberties

The Ford Foundation had established the Fund for the Republic in October 1951 with a warning to the Fund to avoid any "precipitous involvement" in controversy. Nine months of nervous wrangling followed, with Henry Ford II, the powerful chairman of the foundation's board, especially uneasy about the Fund. Several members of Congress were demanding an investigation of foundations involved in so-called "controversial" activities. Hutchins's plan for the Fund for the Republic, which openly proposed to examine federal loyalty and security programs, seemed certain to invite congressional wrath. Ford and his fellow trustees eventually allocated up to fifteen million dollars for future programs, but they required that the Fund be operated as a semi-independent corporation with its own board of directors and officers. The Fund's headquarters even had to be separated physically from the Ford Foundation and located "in some eastern city" as far as possible from Pasadena. The largest foundation-sponsored corporation ever created to focus on civil liberties and civil rights had been given access to a huge amount of money and then "told to go away and spend it—carefully."[5]

The Ford Foundation provided a start-up grant of two hundred thousand dollars, but withheld additional funds until it could screen Hoffman's nominees for the Fund's board of directors and evaluate the new board's program. In July 1952, Hutchins and Ferry, in consultation with Hoffman, began the difficult task of selecting fifteen directors. Hutchins wanted a board composed of conservatives who could "present an impeccable front to the public because we all knew that [the Fund] was bound to get into trouble." After two months debating the names of more than two hundred individuals, Hutchins and Hoffman reduced the list to twelve names, including Parten's. Parten was one of Hutchins's personal selections. Hutchins had known him for sixteen years and had been deeply impressed by his stalwart defense of Homer Rainey and of academic freedom at the University of Texas. "Parten will be the best man on the Fund's board," Hutchins told the Ford Foundation staff. "He stands up for what he believes." After Parten agreed to join the board, five more members were selected by mid-September.[6]

Parten met his fellow directors for the first time at the Fund for the Republic's board meeting on January 29, 1953. They were a respectable and impressive group of business and professional men and one woman. From the West Coast were shoe manufacturer and retailer William Joyce Jr. of Pasadena, California, and James D. Zellerbach, president of Crown Zellerbach of San Francisco. From the Midwest were Russell Dearmont of St. Louis, president of the Missouri Pacific Railroad; Eleanor Stevenson, wife of the president of Oberlin College in Ohio; and Richard Finnegan, editor of the Chicago *Sun-Times*. Eight members were from the East Coast, including George N. Shuster, president of Hunter College in New York City; public opinion analyst Elmo Roper of Washington, D. C.; Charles W. Cole, president of Amherst College in Massachusetts; and Erwin N. Griswold, dean of the Harvard Law School. CBS news commentator Eric Severeid described the group as being among "the most responsible, respectable and successful business and professional men in the country." Severeid declared that they had "banded together in a Herculean effort to roll back the creeping tide of . . . McCarthyism . . . ." Hutchins hoped the board was as strong as the CBS newsman claimed, but he knew the kind of pressure all of them would soon be under. "It is a pretty good group, worried about civil liberties, and also worried about its respectability," Hutchins confided to a friend. "I do not know which worry will win."[7]

At Parten's first board meeting, Hoffman, Hutchins, and Ferry presented their views on the Fund's purpose, identifying the red scare and its threat to civil liberties as one of the most important areas in which the Fund could be involved. The first decision Parten and his fellow directors made was to appoint Paul Hoffman to serve as chairman of the Fund. Hoffman had resigned as president of the Ford Foundation a few days earlier because of internal politics at the foundation. The board deferred other decisions until the next board meeting, when Dean Griswold would present the draft of a plan for the Fund's future program and staffing. "We weren't going to be rubber stamp directors," Parten recalled. "Our idea was that we were going to design a program and then staff the Fund and have them do the work."[8]

After the board meeting ended, some of Parten's fellow directors admitted their surprise to find a Texas oil man with liberal political views and a concern for civil liberties. They had thought every oil man from Texas was as right-wing politically as Clint Murchison, H. L. Hunt, and Hugh Roy Cullen. All three had attracted much attention nationally by donating large sums of money to conservative Republican congressional candidates throughout the country. Some of Parten's new colleagues shared with him their belief that the oil depletion allowance should be removed from the tax law because they believed it was giving right-wing oil men money to use in support of red-scare demagogues such as Joe McCarthy. Talk of that sort sent cold chills down Parten's back. He had been appalled only two weeks earlier to see headlines in the Houston papers identifying Hugh Roy Cullen as the single largest contributor to McCarthy's successful campaign for reelection to the U.S. Senate. Parten had written a letter to Sam Rayburn recently to complain about Cullen's political activities and his outrageous public statements. Rayburn had been one of Cullen's unsuccessful targets in the 1944 campaign for Congress. Parten told Rayburn that he feared that "the conduct of some of the tycoons of the oil industry" would lead to the elimination of the oil depletion allowance. The Speaker confirmed Parten's fears, replying that if the oil depletion allowance ever came up for a vote in the House it would be in serious trouble because of the actions of men like Cullen, "who are trying to tear everyone to pieces who have been their real friends in the past. Many of them have no judgment whatever." Parten later admitted that his desire to demonstrate that not every Texas oil man was a political reactionary was one of the minor reasons why he had agreed to serve as a director of the Fund for the Republic.[9]

At the next Fund for the Republic board meeting on February 18, Parten and his colleagues approved Dean Griswold's report identifying general areas the Fund should explore. Bold and far-ranging, the report identified such ultra-sensitive topics as the scope and procedure of congressional investigations, specifically naming the House Un-American Activities Committee and the Senate Internal Committee as targets for "study." The Griswold report also named as potential topics for study federal, state, and local government loyalty and security programs; the extent and nature of domestic communism; censorship; blacklisting; academic freedom; racial discrimination in public accommodations; restrictions on the right to vote; immigration laws; freedom of religion; and the problems of Native Americans. This program, however, had to be approved by the Ford Foundation. Because Parten and his colleagues knew that the foundation directors were unlikely to accept a program with as much potential for controversy as the one they were proposing, they decided to ask them to approve in one lump sum the fifteen million dollars promised at the time the Fund was established. The Fund could then terminate its affiliation with the Ford Foundation and operate free from political pressure for five or six years into the future. "We knew that the Ford trustees were influenced by the Ford Motor Company," Parten later declared, "and we knew how susceptible the Ford Motor Company was to complaints from its car dealers throughout the United States."[10]

At stake was the Fund's future, because the Ford Foundation's support was far from certain. As one observer later noted, the Fund's directors feared the Ford trustees had already decided to strangle the Fund in its cradle. To present the Fund's request at the critical foundation board meeting in Pasadena, the board selected Parten, Erwin Griswold, and Bill Joyce, perceived by their colleagues to be the most prestigious and effective of the group. Bethuel M. Webster, the Fund's legal counsel, and Paul Hoffman would accompany them. It was the duty of this delegation to make the argument for money and independence.[11]

On February 24, Parten and his colleagues presented the Fund's case to Henry Ford and the other trustees at the Ford Foundation headquarters in Pasadena. Erwin Griswold, the most eloquent member of the delegation, made the key presentation, followed by Parten and Joyce. "We made it clear that we couldn't do this job with them looking over our shoulder," Parten said. He told the Ford Foundation that fifteen million dollars would give the Fund an opportunity to make a real impact in the effort to preserve civil liberties in this country. The presentation made by Griswold, Parten, and Joyce made a strong and decisive impression, changing the minds of some of the trustees who were inclined not to support the request. As a result, the trustees passed Henry Ford's motion to give the Fund 14.8 million ($200,000 had already been granted as start-up money), with three million dollars to be released immediately. If the Fund ever lost its tax-exempt status, it would have to return any uncommitted money. "We also got a lot of cautioning from the Ford trustees against hiring any communists," Parten recalled. "We gave them an absolute assurance on that and made the deal." Paul Hoffman quickly sent a telegram to the other directors: "Delighted to report that

427

the presentations of . . . Griswold, Joyce, and Parten was so persuasive that . . . Ford Foundation made a grant of a total of 15 million dollars. . . ."[12]

The news that the Ford Foundation had given fifteen million dollars to an organization dedicated exclusively to the defense of civil liberties at a time when those liberties were under a massive assault attracted national attention. The Fund for the Republic was recognized as an unprecedented attempt by an American foundation to become involved in the nation's legal and political crisis. One of Parten's friends from his Shreveport days, now teaching at Sarah Lawrence College in New York, saw his name in a New York *Times* story about the Fund. He wrote Parten that he was delighted by the news: "With Messrs. Velde, McCarthy and Jenner breathing down our necks, some of us teachers need the kind of spine stiffening the Fund can give us." New York publisher Alfred A. Knopf, who was a Woodley stockholder, and Frieda B. Hennock, a Federal Communications commissioner, were among the many who also sent thanks to Parten for agreeing to serve as a director of the Fund. "I hope that we can accomplish something in the interest of preserving the freedoms that have made this country great," Parten told Hennock.[13]

Not all reaction was so favorable. Sen. Joseph McCarthy urged Paul Hoffman to come to Washington "as soon as possible" to answer questions about the Fund. McCarthy also demanded a list of foundation personnel. Hoffman did not go to Washington, but he sent the list to McCarthy. J. Edgar Hoover was also paying close attention to the Fund. The FBI director asked his agents to produce a complete report on the background of each member of the Fund's board of directors. Among those produced was a poorly done biographical sketch of J. R. Parten. Of special notice to the FBI was Parten's trip to Moscow as chief of staff of the Pauley Mission in 1945. That information and the material indicating that he was a director of the Fund for the Republic was heavily underlined in ink. The report also stressed that Parten was reputed to be "a close personal friend" of Supreme Court judge Tom Clark. There was no mention of the Rainey affair in Texas with its allegations of Communist subversion at the University of Texas. Hoover was undoubtedly disappointed, not only by Parten's file, but by the files of his Fund colleagues. Hutchins's and Hoffman's decision to stock the Fund's board of directors with respected business and academic leaders had proved to be a wise one.[14]

Now that the Fund had its money from Ford, the next order of business was to find a president to manage its daily operations. In April 1953, Paul Hoffman suggested to his board colleagues that they should consider Cong. Clifford P. Case, a forty-nine-year-old Republican from New Jersey, for the job. Case, who had played an active role in Dwight Eisenhower's presidential campaign, had a solid reputation as a defender of civil rights. Parten was unable to attend the meeting in which Hoffman had nominated Case for president, but as soon as he learned about it, he visited Sam Rayburn to get his evaluation of the congressman. Rayburn thought well of Case, which was good enough for Parten. In May, the Fund announced that Case had accepted the position of Fund president and that he would resign from Congress in September. The lapse in time between Case's appointment and his official assumption of duties meant that the Fund was relatively inactive throughout the summer of 1953.[15]

Unfortunately, the red scare was reaching its peak just as the Fund for the Republic seemed to go into hibernation. The newly installed Eisenhower administration revised the federal security program, greatly broadening the rules for determining security risks among federal employees. Federal department heads were given the power to fire an employee accused of being a security risk without giving the dismissed employee any right to a hearing or an appeal. The House Un-American Activities Committee embarked on a lengthy investigation of Communist infiltration of public schools; while the Senate Judiciary's Internal Security Subcommittee, led by William Jenner, a Republican senator from Indiana, conducted hearings on Communist subversion in the federal government. Joe McCarthy was grabbing headlines with his sensational charges that traitors dominated the staffs of the State Department and the Voice of America. By the end of the summer, McCarthy was turning his attention to alleged treason within the United States Army. Rarely had the Bill of Rights been under such an unrelenting and effective attack. The Fund for the Republic had been created to contest the very forces now trampling the rights of thousands of Americans, yet it was doing nothing. In deep frustration, Ping Ferry complained to Roper and other board members, "for God's sake let's get something started. You've got all this money and lots of expectations are being built up here. . . ." Ferry later told an interviewer that "[Case] just farted around and farted around, read memoranda, and when he couldn't think of anything else to do, he'd call somebody up and get another memorandum written."[16]

Dr. Ebey and the Minute Women

The red scare was also peaking in Parten's hometown that summer of 1953. Because of his involvement in his various out-of-state business enterprises, he had paid little attention to events in Houston. The city's public schools were the target of a vicious attack by the Minute Women of the U.S.A., Inc., the American Legion, and other local red-scare activists. In July, they had pressured the Houston school board into firing Dr. George W. Ebey, the deputy superintendent of schools. Ebey was accused of having had subversive affiliations in the years prior to his coming to Houston in 1952, despite being cleared of the allegations by an independent team of former FBI agents. This so-called "Ebey Affair" symbolized much of the anti-Communist hysteria and resulting vigilantism affecting the country in 1953. When Parten returned to Houston for a brief stay in October, he was shocked when he read about the Ebey affair and its associated incidents in an eleven-part series of articles in the Houston *Post*. Written by reporter Ralph O'Leary, the series was a hard-hitting expose of the Minute Women's "reign of terror" in the city's schools, churches, and universities.[17]

Two days after the last of O'Leary's stories appeared in the *Post*, Sam Rayburn spent the weekend at the Partens' home in Madisonville, which the hard-pressed

Speaker later described as "the only vacation I have had this year." While they fished at Lake Patterson on the 7-J ranch, Rayburn tried without success to persuade Parten to accept an invitation from Democratic Party chairman Stephen Mitchell to serve as party treasurer. Rayburn did get Parten's promise to raise money for the 1954 congressional campaigns. Parten gave Rayburn two thousand dollars while he was still in Madisonville. When Parten returned to Houston, he got three thousand dollars from Will Clayton, another three thousand from George and Herman Brown (the contractors for Parten's Jaltipan sulphur plant), and a total of three thousand from Charles I. Francis and several other donors. When he sent the money to Rayburn, the grateful Speaker replied: "Thanks a thousand times. I knew you would do it. This is the finest thing that has come along. We will add to it up here in North Texas."[18]

During Rayburn's visit to Madisonville, the subject of the red scare also took up much of their conversation time. When Parten showed Rayburn the O'Leary series, Rayburn encouraged him to have it distributed nationwide. The behavior of Joe McCarthy and his allies in the Congress had thoroughly disgusted the Speaker. He told Parten that he believed the activities of McCarthy's followers in Texas had been encouraged by the Dallas *Morning News*, a newspaper often critical of Rayburn. "The Dallas *News*," Rayburn told Parten, "likes [McCarthy's] ranting and raving and accusing everybody in the US that does not agree with him of being traitors and communists. The Dallas *News* likes that kind of talk."[19]

Parten, who saw strong similarities between the Ebey dismissal and the attack on Homer Rainey nine years earlier, sent a copy of the O'Leary series to David Freeman, secretary of the Fund for the Republic. "So far as I know," Parten wrote, "this is the first time that any metropolitan newspaper in Texas ha[s] made any effort toward giving pitiless publicity to some of the political activities which have for so long tended to smother the educational system in this state." He asked Freeman to distribute copies to his colleagues on the Fund board. Parten also sent the O'Leary series to Robert Hutchins. As an associate director of the Ford Foundation living in California, Hutchins no longer had an official connection with the Fund. Nevertheless, he had closely monitored his brainchild's progress and he was extremely frustrated by its lack of action. The Ebey affair served as a further reminder to Hutchins of the Fund for the Republic's inactivity. In his reply to Parten, Hutchins expressed his impatience; complaining that it was long past time for the Fund to get moving. Hutchins felt that Paul Hoffman was more concerned with getting the Fund's tax exemption and the balance of the money due from the Ford Foundation than he was with the program. The O'Leary series gave Hutchins an idea. He proposed to Parten that they ask the Fund to give them grants to create local organizations similar to the Fund in Southern California and in Texas, "the two regions that need it the most." With his sulphur plant in Mexico under construction, Parten could not spare the time he thought it would take to create a local organization. He also felt that the red scare was a nationwide problem that deserved the Fund's full attention.[20]

The O'Leary series was discussed at the Fund's next board meeting in New York City on November 18, 1953. The board authorized president Case to determine if the Fund should disseminate the series in pamphlet form or support a major study on the subject of "the intellectual security of teachers." Case told Parten that "Houston's experience . . . holds a great many valuable lessons as to effective ways of approaching problem situations" relating to the red scare. Two months later, an evaluation by Harold C. Hunt of the Harvard University Graduate School of Education cooled the Fund's enthusiasm for the O'Leary series. Hunt concluded that O'Leary's research was shallow and that the situation in Houston was more complicated than the journalist had shown it to be. He argued, correctly, that the situation in Houston revolved "around personalities, ambitions, jealousies, and the ebb and flow of power over many years." Hunt advised against the Fund's distribution of the series, recommending instead that it do the research and publish its own pamphlet about the national crisis in education. Case told Parten that he agreed with Hunt, adding that he feared "wide publicity might actually help the Minute Women."

Although he disagreed with Case, Parten did not push the O'Leary series with the board. He did believe, however, that the Fund needed to study political fear in education. He urged Case to initiate a major national study on the subject, but Case did nothing. In addition, Parten and several other directors told Case that the Fund needed to investigate the entertainment industry's covert practice of blacklisting. Entertainers and others working in the industry were being subjected to a system of political repression that denied jobs to anyone who had been accused (usually without proof) of harboring "controversial" political opinions. After fourteen months of existence, however, the Fund under Case followed the path of inaction while McCarthy, HUAC, and others continued their assault on the First Amendment.[21]

The situation at the Fund quickly changed, however, when Case resigned as president on March 5, 1954, to run for the U.S. Senate from New Jersey. For his replacement, Parten and his fellow directors turned to Robert Hutchins, who had chafed at Case's timidity. Of the Fund's directors, Parten, Roper, and Joyce, in particular, were eager for action and they knew they would get it with the iconoclastic Hutchins. The educator, who had openly challenged the legality of the Nuremberg War Crime Trials and who had questioned the morality of the atomic bombing of Japan, had never been reluctant to confront unpopular causes. "We brought Hutchins in for the reasons that we knew he was fearless and that he could hit the ground running," Parten said. "And it worked that way, because Hutchins took hold of these things fast." Hutchins dismissed Case's staff and replaced them with his own group of firebrands, including the abrasive Ping Ferry, who became vice president. During the summer of 1954, within weeks of assuming the presidency, Hutchins had the Fund involved in a controversial investigation of the federal government's loyalty/security program, an investigation of the legal rights of aliens, and a program on racial relations in Chicago.[22]

431

"To strike a blow against McCarthy"

While Hutchins finally had the Fund on the move, Paul Hoffman was busy with a lobbying project that had to be independent of the Fund. Senator McCarthy's accusations and reckless behavior in attacking the U.S. Army as a hotbed of subversion had finally outraged President Eisenhower and enough of McCarthy's colleagues in the Senate to result in an effort to reprimand the Wisconsin Republican. On June 30, Republican senator Ralph Flanders introduced a resolution to condemn McCarthy for actions which were contrary to senatorial traditions and which tended to bring the Senate into disrepute. Within days, Hoffman recruited Parten as a member of an ad hoc group called the National Committee for an Effective Congress to support Flanders and to attack McCarthy. He asked Parten to help him raise money for a lobbying effort in the Senate. Parten immediately sent a large financial contribution to Hoffman.[23]

On July 17, Hoffman reported to Parten that there were "excellent prospects that the Senate . . . will go clearly on record on the issue of McCarthyism before the end of this session." He urged Parten to allow his name to be listed with twenty-two other prominent Americans on a telegram to be sent to every senator urging bipartisan support of the Flanders resolution. Parten consented enthusiastically, telling Hoffman that he was honored to be given a chance "to strike a blow against McCarthy." Hoffman's telegram gave Parten his second opportunity to criticize McCarthy publicly. In May, *Fortune* magazine had published an article on the relationship between McCarthy and Texas businessmen because of McCarthy's avid (and lucrative) friendships with oil men H. L. Hunt, Hugh Roy Cullen, and Clint Murchison. The *Fortune* article cited Parten as being one Texas oil man who was strongly opposed to the Republican senator.[24]

Hoffman's telegram was widely distributed and received much publicity nationally. Included among the signers with Parten and Hoffman was their Fund for the Republic colleague Erwin Griswold, as well as Will Clayton, movie mogul Samuel Goldwyn, paper-product magnate J. D. Zellerbach, Atlanta newspaper publisher Ralph McGill, theologian Reinhold Niebuhr, and labor-union leader Walter Reuther. The telegram declared that "the issues posed by McCarthyism override all considerations of party advantage or expediency. At stake are the integrity, dignity, and authority of our highest legislative body." A New York *Times* editorial called the group a "blue ribbon grand jury" composed of men "McCarthy can't ignore" who were totally immune from charges of being subversive. "If McCarthy was a sensitive person," the New York *Times* declared, "he would quail before a rebuke from such citizens as these. . . ."[25]

The Senate eventually censured McCarthy in December 1954, by a vote of 67 to 21, bringing to an end McCarthy's influence, both in the Congress and in the nation at large. The country was free of McCarthy, but it was not yet free of the red scare. As a result of his public stance against McCarthy, Parten received a large amount of hate mail denouncing him as a "commie dupe." Not every reaction was negative, however. His stance won him a reputation outside Texas as an unusually enlightened and liberal oil man. Journalist Robert Engler, writing in the *New Republic* about the reactionary role oil money was playing in the nation's political life, stressed that "no claim is being advanced that all oil producers behave this way. There are also those like Texan J. R. Parten who have been bluntly anti-McCarthy. . . ."[26]

The Academic Mind

Parten was delighted by the effort Hoffman was making against McCarthy and by the decisive manner in which Hutchins was now operating the Fund. He was especially pleased, however, when Hutchins resurrected the long-dormant "fear in education" project that Parten had urged on Case. On September 14, 1954, Parten and his fellow board members approved funding for Columbia University professor Paul Lazerfield to conduct a scholarly study of fear among faculty members and teachers who were under fire for "controversial ideas." When Lazerfield's work was published in 1955 as *The Academic Mind: Social Scientists in a Time of Crisis*, it provided hard evidence in support of the charge that higher education was being severely affected by the red scare.[27]

The directors also approved Hutchins's request to investigate blacklisting in the entertainment industry, another project that had Parten's vigorous support. Hutchins told the board that there had been "many flagrant cases" in which persons in the industry had lost their jobs because of "charges, often unfounded, about their political opinions." He explained that there were rumors of the existence of some type of system operated by a right-wing group which charged actors and other industry workers large sums of money for a political clearance to allow them to work. Two days after the board meeting, Hutchins hired John Cogley, the thirty-eight-year-old editor of the liberal and independent Catholic journal, *Commonweal*, to serve as project director for the blacklisting study. For his assistant, Cogley brought in the brilliant young Socialist writer Michael Harrington. Because of his strong interest in the subject, Parten agreed to serve as the board's liaison with the project. "I really didn't know much about this blacklisting racket," Parten admitted, "but I was assured it was real by Hutchins and Elmo Roper. I found the idea of such a system to be offensive and unacceptable and I wanted us to . . . expose it to daylight." Parten monitored the project closely as it proceeded during the coming eighteen months.[28]

The Fund for the Republic's board approved all of Hutchins's ambitious proposals during the lengthy September 14 meeting. They balked, however, at his bold request to launch an investigation of the FBI. Parten, and most of his colleagues, felt that such an investigation was unwarranted, not to mention possibly dangerous to the continuing existence of the Fund, which was vulnerable to having its tax exemption withdrawn. "This was long before we really understood what kind of bad character [FBI director] Hoover really was," Parten later explained, "but Bob Hutchins—as usual—was way ahead of us on that one."[29]

Great Northern

lthough J. R. Parten experienced nothing but losses in his political endeavors, his business enterprises saw significant gains in every respect. Woodley, which for years had searched in vain for a good source of oil to replenish its declining reserves, finally hit it big with a new oil field. Pan American Sulphur, which had experienced a long delay in developing its property in Jaltipan, received its loan from the Export-Import Bank and finally began the process of extracting sulphur. In addition, a new refining-company endeavor created by Parten, with Sylvester Dayson and others, and stagnant now for a number of months, was also rescued by Woodley's oil discovery.

"Seems we have two good wells in Canada"

Woodley's new oil field was in western Canada, a region in which Gene Holman had long urged Parten to explore. He had finally followed Holman's advice after important oil discoveries were made near Edmonton, Alberta, in the fall of 1948. In early 1949, Parten opened a Woodley office in Calgary and purchased a majority of the stock of a Canadian company called Western Prairie Exploration Company, Ltd. This acquisition included exploration rights to one and a half million acres in Williston Basin, located 150 miles west of Regina in the province of Saskatchewan, and a half interest in several thousand acres in Alberta. To finance the exploration of this property, Parten sold partnerships in Woodley's Canadian company to the Danciger brothers of Fort Worth (20 percent) and to Standard Oil of New York (50 percent). Exploration began that summer, but the initial results were not promising.[1]

Woodley's exploration activities continued for nearly three years without success. In late March 1952, J. Howard Marshall, who had become vice president of Signal Oil and who had made an investment in one of Parten's projects in Minnesota, opened a telegram marked "urgent" on its envelope. "Seems we have two good wells in Canada," the message inside read, "please call me Madisonville." This welcome and exciting news was from J. R. Parten. Woodley had hit a large pool of oil in the Williston Basin in Saskatchewan, one that eventually developed into four different fields. Parten was ecstatic for more than one reason. During the previous summer, Woodley had finally discovered oil in the Woodbine sand under the Fort Trinidad field near 7-J Stock Farm. From all indications, that field was also going to be a good one. The Canadian discovery plus news of the Fort Trinidad find more than doubled the value of Woodley's common stock, increasing Parten's wealth significantly.[2]

The Canadian discovery was welcome for another reason that had roots going back nearly two years. In the fall of 1950, while Parten was still in Washington organizing the Petroleum Administration for Defense, Sylvester Dayson had proposed a new refining venture. Because of the nationwide shortage in refining capacity, the federal government had allowed the owners of new refineries and other manufacturing facilities important to the war effort to amortize the cost of construction over a five-year rather than a ten-to-fifteen-year period. Dayson argued that this accelerated amortization program, which made it possible for a refinery to pay off its construction costs quickly, was too attractive an opportunity to let pass. At the time, he and Parten had been well aware that Imperial Oil of Canada was without a market for its large pool of Alberta oil. Dayson had argued that the rapidly growing region surrounding the "Twin Cities" of Minneapolis and Saint Paul in Minnesota was an obvious place to build a refinery to convert Alberta crude into gasoline for the local automobile market. Dayson suggested that he and Parten apply to the National Security Resources Board for a certificate of necessity and convenience to build such a refinery. Parten subsequently commissioned a market study, which confirmed Dayson's belief that Minnesota's largest metropolitan region was a prime site for a refinery. Imperial also seemed interested in making its Alberta oil available to the proposed refinery.[3]

By early February 1951, Parten and Dayson had assembled an investment group, which included J. Howard Marshall, refiner Barney Majewski, and oil man John Manley, to create Great Northern Oil Company as the corporate vehicle for their refinery enterprise. Ironically, Majewski had been one of Parten's strongest foes in the PAW dispute over which half of the Little Inch pipeline to build first. After Great Northern had been incorporated, however, Imperial refused to sell its Canadian crude at a price Parten thought fair. "That left us in the air," Dayson recalled, "so then we didn't have nothing left to do because we cannot run the refinery without crude." Great Northern continued to exist but only on paper.[4]

Woodley's Canadian discoveries in 1952 suddenly gave new life to Great Northern. The crude in Woodley's Canadian field was poor-quality, high-sulphur, heavy-gravity oil. Parten had originally planned to sell whatever crude oil Woodley ultimately found in Saskatchewan to a British-American refinery at Moose Jaw, but the sulphur in this new oil ended that plan. The Moose Jaw refinery was a technically obsolete plant that could not refine Woodley's poor-quality oil. Dayson had a better idea, however. He proposed that Woodley sell its Saskatchewan oil to Great Northern for the planned refinery in Minnesota. The refinery could be outfitted with special equipment to handle the high-sulphur crude. With Parten's enthusiastic approval of Dayson's plan, the Great Northern project was reborn.[5]

"We have arrived at the crossroad of our friendship"

While Great Northern struggled to resurrect itself with Woodley's Canadian oil during the summer and fall of 1952, Parten and his partners in the Little Mothers club—armed with their loan from the Export-Import Bank—established a management structure and recruited a professional staff to make Pan American Sulphur an operational company. That process began with Douglas Forbes taking Parten's place as president of Pan American. As Pan American became operational, Parten, who retained his position as chairman of Pan American's board of directors, could no longer do both jobs. Unfortunately, Forbes's appointment as president caused hard feelings between Parten and Sylvester Dayson, who had long coveted the position. Parten and his colleagues on the Pan American board had rejected Dayson's bid for the presidency because they felt that he was too reckless to be trusted with the company at such a critical phase of its development.[6]

Dayson was hurt by Parten's refusal to support him. He suspected that his relationship with Parten was being affected adversely by some of Parten's associates, especially J. Howard Marshall and Marlin Sandlin. Neither Marshall nor Sandlin liked or respected Dayson and they did little to hide it. Marshall, whom Parten had known almost as long as he had known Dayson, had invested heavily in Pan American stock and in Parten's Canadian operations, and he was deeply involved in Great Northern. Since joining Woodley in January 1944, Sandlin had become Parten's right-hand man and his closest advisor. Sandlin excelled in those areas for which Parten had little patience: detail work, bureaucratic maneuvering, and negotiations. Parten had needed someone to serve as a "front man" back in the office, someone he could trust and who could meet with people while he stayed in the background. Sandlin had filled those needs well.[7]

Sandlin had also become Parten's ambassador to the outside business world. Parten, who had no gift for small talk or idle chatter, was "discomfited by the cigar smoking 'hail-fellow, well-met, back-slapping' type," noted one of his longtime business associates. "Sandlin was . . . far more comfortable operating in that atmosphere, so he became the hand-shaker and socializer who took that burden off of Parten. He was the one that took everyone to dinner and out for drinks." To some of the businessmen who dealt with Parten and Sandlin, the two seemed to have developed a classic form of the "good cop/bad cop" routine for business negotiations. Fred Moore, a Texan who was an executive with Mobil Oil, claimed that in dealing with Woodley, Parten always played the role of statesman who gave the hard job of negotiating to Sandlin, whom Moore called "J. R. Parten's hatchet man."[8]

Dayson also believed that Patsy Parten was turning her husband against him. Within months after J. R.'s marriage to Patsy, Dayson and his wife felt that Patsy was creating a whole new atmosphere around her husband, one that was more formal and snobbish and that seemed to be cutting them out of the Partens' inner circle. The Daysons felt like outsiders around Patsy, although the two families continued for several years to meet for lunch on New Year's Day at the Dallas Athletic

Club before attending the annual Cotton Bowl game. Intimidated by Patsy's "aristocratic" ways, Dayson's wife felt Patsy was "pushing" her and Sylvester away from J. R. "Patsy probably thought Daddy was crude," their daughter Suzette said, "he cursed terribly and some women objected to that."[9]

A few days after his bid for the Pan American presidency had been rejected, Dayson expressed his anger and suspicions in a hastily scrawled note to Parten. "At long last," Dayson wrote, "we have arrived at the crossroad of our friendship. For the past few years your new acquired fair whether (sic) friends . . . and Mrs. Parten have been successfully working towards this end; accomplishing their mission according to plan. What a shame!! What a disgrace!! What a misfortune!!! — for both of us—." For personal and business reasons, Parten ignored the note and acted as though he had never received it. Not only did he not want to break off his friendship with Dayson, he was also depending on Dayson's expert help with Great Northern's plan to construct and operate an oil refinery. Relations between them, however, continued to deteriorate during 1953 as they squabbled over issues such as Dayson's expense accounts (Parten and Marshall thought them excessive) and whether Dayson could serve as the sole negotiator for Great Northern's crude-oil contracts.[10]

"The Devil uses it": Pan American Produces its First Sulphur

Over the next several months, Parten and Forbes recruited a management team with solid experience in the sulphur industry to take over Pan American's daily operations. Aware of the essential need to market the sulphur before it was actually produced, the first job Parten filled was vice president for sales. His choice was J. Leonard Townsend, legal counsel for the Federal Reserve Bank in Washington, whom Parten had met when they worked together to solve a minor labor dispute at the Dallas Federal Reserve Bank during the late 1940s. Parten thought that Townsend, a gregarious "hail-fellow, well met" type who subscribed to an antitrust economic philosophy, could be the kind of salesman Pan American needed as it attempted to break into the world sulphur market. Townsend knew his way around the federal government's various loan agencies, which would be useful in Pan American's dealings with the Export-Import Bank and the Securities Exchange Commission. When Parten asked him to become Pan American's first paid officer, Townsend protested that the only thing he knew about brimstone was that "the Devil uses it" and he had no intention of meeting him any time soon. Parten laughed and replied, "don't worry about it Leonard, I'll give you a book to read."[11]

Parten's choice to build Pan American's plant and to start sulphur production was Harry C. Webb, a forty-eight-year-old vice president of Texas Gulf Sulphur with twenty-five years of experience in the field. Webb had a reputation as a highly skilled manager who knew the sulphur business from top to bottom and was energetic and aggressively competitive. He became Pan American's executive vice president on May 1, 1953, with the understanding that he would replace Doug Forbes as president within a year, a promise that was subsequently fulfilled.

437

Once the two most important executives were appointed, Parten and the original Little Mothers expanded the board of directors to include two powerful Wall Street brokers who had purchased a large amount of Pan American stock during a recent public offering. One of the new directors was Mark Millard, a senior partner of the prestigious Wall Street investment firm of Loeb, Rhoades, and Company. The other was Hugh Knowlton, a senior partner of Kuhn, Loeb, and Company, another major New York investment firm. In addition, Parten's good friend and longtime legal advisor, Jack Blalock, was made the third new director. Doug Forbes assumed the chairmanship of the board's executive committee and Parten retained his position as chairman of the board of directors.[12]

With Pan American's top management structure in place, Parten and his colleagues turned the company over to Webb, with Marlin Sandlin serving as Parten's representative in the company's management. It was soon evident that Webb had been an excellent choice. Passed over for promotion at Texas Gulf, Webb was determined to show the sulphur monopoly what he could do. His most pressing problem was to finish the exploration of Pan American's concessions before the rainy season began in September. The concession contract required the company to complete all exploration and build a plant by September 1956. Any areas left unexplored by that time would have to be returned to the government. Only a small section of the dome had actually been explored with wells, so Webb was forced to embark on a crash-drilling program. He rounded up equipment scattered from Texas to California and personally supervised its transport by ship and rail car to Jaltipan. After enduring and solving a number of exceedingly difficult logistics problems, including a train derailment, Webb succeeded in completing the exploration in two and a half months, just prior to the onset of torrential rains.

Webb's quick work at completing exploration made it possible to begin the construction of Pan American's Jaltipan extraction plant in September 1953 on approximately one thousand acres of jungle cleared by bulldozers. Most of Pan American's workers were unskilled peasants who had never handled a wrench, much less power tools. After assessing the local situation, Webb flew to Houston and conferred with Parten and Sandlin to determine how to solve the labor problem. They decided that their only recourse was to train the local workers. By making that decision, Parten and his associates initiated a program that transformed the town of Jaltipan.

Under Webb's personal supervision, Pan American cleared additional land and erected a large building to serve as headquarters, meeting place, and motion picture theater. The company built a school and brought in agricultural agents to teach modern farming techniques to the local peasants and instructors to teach the company's local workers how to read and write, in English as well as in Spanish. Scores of peasants, whose only tool had been a machete, learned intricate industrial skills. Pan American paved Jaltipan's principal streets and provided funds for the restoration of its seventeenth- century church. The sulphur company's payroll and purchases of local fuel from PEMEX began to pump over one million pesos a month into the local economy.[13]

Webb recruited some of the best sulphur managers and engineers in the country and sent them to Mexico. With the help of an unusually dry rainy season, Webb's restless determination, and a skilled staff, the Jaltipan plant was completed months ahead of schedule. So long delayed, the operational side of Pan American was finally materializing. Pan American's Jaltipan plant produced its first molten sulphur on September 24, 1954. Parten had dared to hope when the company broke ground for the construction of its plant that it could produce at least enough sulphur to meet Mexico's annual needs, which was about thirty-eight thousand tons. After eighteen months of operation, however, Pan American was producing one and a half million tons of sulphur a year. The sulphur cartel, fat and complacent, had a fight on its hands.[14]

The Great Northern Refinery

Unfortunately, Parten's work with Great Northern did not go so smoothly. Standard of New York (Mobil), which owned a majority percentage (50 percent) of the Williston Basin wells, balked at selling crude to Great Northern, putting Dayson's plan for the refinery on hold for more than a year. Woodley and its partners had completed nearly one hundred oil wells and a few gas wells in the Fosterton oil field in the Williston basin in southwestern Saskatchewan, but most were shut in for lack of a market. Woodley, which owned 30 percent of the production, sold a very small quantity of its share by shipping it on railroad tank cars to Regina and Moose Jaw. The local demand for this heavy-gravity, high-sulphur crude oil was too limited to make much difference. The logical and the only dependable market for Woodley's Canadian oil would be through the proposed Great Northern refinery in Minnesota. Mobil, however, refused to cooperate.[15]

In early June 1953, Parten finally persuaded Mobil president Brewster Jennings to agree to negotiate a sales contract to provide Great Northern with the oil it needed to operate a refinery. Working out the agreement, however, proved to be a time-consuming and frustrating task. Parten insisted that Mobil agree to provide its oil to Great Northern's refinery for ten years, but Mobil was reluctant to sign a long-term contract. Mobil and Great Northern also squabbled over transportation costs on the refined products.[16]

Negotiations dragged on for several months. In September 1953, Sandlin finally reached a basic understanding with Mobil, which agreed to supply twenty thousand barrels a day to Great Northern for a period of ten years. Great Northern could now plan its refinery. Woodley, Mobil, and their other partner, Southern Production Company, agreed to construct a pipeline to carry their oil from Fosterton to Regina, where it would connect to the Canadian Interprovincial pipeline. The oil would then flow from Regina to Clearbrook, Minnesota, where it would be taken by another pipeline (to be built by Woodley) to South Saint Paul, the site of Great Northern's refinery—a total of 856 miles from well to refinery.[17]

After Mobil signed a letter of intent for the agreement, Parten reorganized Great Northern to improve its ability to secure financing for the thirty-thousand-barrel-capacity refinery and the connecting pipeline, which were expected to cost twenty-five million dollars. Parten persuaded Southern Production to join Woodley in buying out the original Great Northern investors, which totalled approximately 40 percent of the company's stock. Of the original group, only Marshall and Dayson kept their personal investments—each had one-sixth of the stock. Parten retained his financial influence in Great Northern through his control of Woodley stock. Marlin Sandlin became vice chairman of the board and secretary of Great Northern, replacing Marshall, who became the new vice president. Despite the bad feelings between the two, Parten gave Dayson the presidency and retained his position as chairman of the board. This reorganization left Woodley and Southern Production as Great Northern's principal stockholders.[18]

The problems between Parten and Dayson soon worsened. When Dayson assumed the presidency of Great Northern, it was with the understanding that he would move to Saint Paul to supervise the construction and operation of the refinery. Dayson, however, had no intention of moving. He had purchased a beautiful property with its own lake near Tyler that he called Holly Tree Farms, and he planned to stay there. Dayson informed Parten that he would commute to Minnesota in his plane whenever necessary and that he would keep an apartment in Saint Paul. Parten insisted that Dayson needed to be at the refinery nearly every day. "The Major was absolutely right," noted Fred Mayer, who was a friend of both men. "That Minnesota refinery was much larger than anything Premier had operated and it needed a full time president. He and the Major had a very bitter argument about it. . . ."[19]

Dayson's resentments came to the surface on the morning of October 14, 1953, when he joined Parten and Marshall for breakfast in Chicago prior to the closing of the loan. He told them that he would stay in Texas. He also demanded a salary of $50,000 per year as president and a package of lucrative stock options worth $225,000 dollars, which was his commission for conceiving Great Northern originally and for all the work he had performed in getting it started. Parten rejected Dayson's demands. A few days later, Parten learned that Dayson had contacted some of Great Northern's stockholders to seek their help in removing Parten as chairman of the Great Northern's board of directors. Two weeks later, Dayson gave an interview to the Minneapolis *Morning Tribune* that served as the basis of a major story about Great Northern's refinery, providing details about its location, source of crude, and other information that Dayson's associates had hoped to keep confidential until the contract with Mobil was signed. The newspaper identified Dayson as the company's "spokesman" even though he had no authorization from Parten and his partners to serve as such. One of Parten's friends in Minneapolis sent him the clipping with a cover note stating, "Apparently your boy friend is up to something. Hope the publicity doesn't hurt the project."[20]

At the next Great Northern board meeting on December 9, the directors unanimously accepted Parten's motion to terminate Dayson's official relationship with Great Northern. Also at an end was Dayson's friendship with Parten. Embittered by the episode, Dayson filed suit against Great Northern in a federal court in Delaware in June 1956 for breach of contract with a request for 2.7 million dollars in damages. The suit was eventually dropped without resolution.[21]

After Dayson's removal as president, Parten selected as his replacement William J. Carthaus, a chemical- and mechanical-engineering graduate of MIT with experience in the refining of oil. Construction of the Great Northern refinery finally began in the summer of 1954 and was completed in August 1955. Great Northern built its refinery—the largest in Minnesota—on the west bank of the Mississippi River adjoining the tracks of the Chicago and Great Western railroad in Rosemount Township, about fourteen miles south of Saint Paul. Parten and his partners organized the Saskatchewan Pipeline Company and the Minnesota Pipe Line Company to construct and operate the pipelines from the Williston Basin to Saint Paul. By July 1956, the lines were delivering thirty thousand barrels a day of Canadian crude oil to the refinery near Saint Paul.[22]

The fact that Woodley now had a market for its Canadian crude meant a substantial increase in its revenues. With Pan American's production exceeding all expectations, Parten's financial situation had never been better nor ever looked brighter.

"My heart … feels heavy"

The split between Parten and Dayson over Great Northern kept them apart for the rest of their lives, although the bitterness diminished with the passage of time. J. R. and Sylvester never rebuilt their friendship, but the Parten and Dayson families continued to maintain a relationship. Sylvester forged a friendship with J. R.'s son, Randy. "He was such a colorful character," Randy recalled. "He would always try to get me to come up to Holly Tree Farms, which I did a couple of times—something I never did with my father's other friends." During this same period, Dayson's daughter, Suzette, by then married to a prominent Dallas architect, wrote J. R. a letter pleading with him to visit Holly Tree Farms: "My heart just feels heavy thinking about all the years we've wasted not being close. You are truly my 'family' and you always have been."[23]

CHAPTER 26

"You, Not I, Are the Bulwark of the Democratic Party in Texas"

The Gubernatorial Campaign of 1954

Almost as soon as he had lost to Shivers in the gubernatorial election of 1952, Ralph Yarborough began to think about making another bid in 1954. The year after his defeat he kept his name in the newspapers by issuing press releases critical of the governor's actions (and inactions) since his reelection. He also maintained contact with his most important financial backers, especially J. R. Parten. In August 1953, when Yarborough met with Parten to seek his help and active involvement in the 1954 gubernatorial primary, Parten assured him of his support, but urged him not to make an announcement until the spring of 1954. It would take that much time to gather enough financial pledges to allow him to mount a serious challenge to the well-financed Shivers. Yarborough accepted Parten's advice.[1]

The national Democratic Party was also making plans for the upcoming congressional races as well as the 1956 presidential election. On February 1, 1954, national party chairman Stephen Mitchell appointed Parten to the Texas Democratic Advisory Council (DAC), an organization that Mitchell and Sam Rayburn created to provide leadership for Texans who remained loyal to the national party. Rayburn intended for the DAC to lead the effort to regain control of the state party from Allan Shivers. Parten, however, did not accept the appointment immediately. He knew that Rayburn had also created the DAC as an alternative organization to the Loyal Democrats of Texas, which Rayburn felt was dominated by liberals. Rayburn felt the liberal leadership had been unnecessarily strident in their public attacks on Shivers and, uncompromising in their tactics, had frightened off moderate Democrats who would not otherwise have followed Shivers.[2]

Parten was more than willing to follow Rayburn's lead on any political matter, but he feared that the DAC might not support Ralph Yarborough for governor. Parten had pledged his support to Yarborough and he did not want to accept the DAC post if it meant later having to resign over a Yarborough candidacy. He also did not want to encourage an organization that might split Texas loyalists between liberals and moderate conservatives and thus guarantee another Shivercrat victory in 1954. Rayburn told Parten that the purpose of the DAC was to unite party loyalists in Texas, not to create another faction, and that it would not oppose Yarborough. D. B. Hardeman, who was DAC secretary and Rayburn's personal representative on the council, also assured Parten about the DAC's intentions, saying that they were determined to make it "genuinely representative of all shades of opinion among those who have been faithful to the Party." Members included liberal Judge Jim Sewell (chairman), as well as Will Clayton, Jesse Andrews, and Mexican American civil rights leader Hector Garcia. Persuaded that his membership would not interfere with his plan to help Yarborough, Parten accepted the DAC appointment.[3]

After much speculation in the press, on April 20 Governor Shivers announced his intention to run for a third term. As Parten had advised, Yarborough waited until April 30 to announce his candidacy. Parten sent a copy of

Ralph Yarborough on the campaign trail, 1954. *CN 09622. Courtesy Russell Lee Photograph Collection, CAH.*

Yarborough's announcement speech to Rayburn, urging him to support another fight against Shivers. Unlike 1952, Parten was unsure of Rayburn's support because of the Speaker's negative feelings about the Texas liberals. "Ralph Yarborough has a lot of fine qualities," Parten reminded Rayburn. "He is a lifelong friend of mine and I think he would make a fine governor. It is my belief that he has the cards to beat Shivers, if he will play them right." In a reply that reflected his low regard for the liberal faction in Texas, Rayburn agreed that Yarborough did have a chance to beat Shivers, but only if "he doesn't let too many crackpots give him too many crackpot ideas. Somebody should tell Yarborough that he should keep such people as Creekmore Fath . . . and Fagan Dickson 'on tap, but not on top'," Rayburn argued, stating that he had heard from some conservatives in Texas who did not want to support Shivers, but who would not follow a candidate led by Fath and Dickson. Rayburn warned Parten not to let either man "write letters or give out statements for [Yarborough]." Marlin Sandlin shared Rayburn's view of the liberal leadership. He urged Parten not to waste his time or money in a hopeless cause. "Regardless of what he may say or do," Sandlin said, "[Yarborough] has been labeled as a Loyal Democrat (so-called) and I do not believe he can attract enough middle-of-the-road and conservative support to be elected."[4]

Despite Rayburn and Sandlin, Parten remained optimistic about the fight against Shivers. Parten believed that Shivers's attempt to break the two-term tradition for Texas governors would not play well with many Texas voters. More important, the Shivers administration had been tarnished by an insurance scandal that grabbed headlines in the early months of 1954. Although no evidence ever came to light directly tying the governor to the scandal, it left him open to charges by Yarborough that he had allowed the "fixers and influence peddlers in to operate in Austin."[5]

"That $425,000 was his payment"

Early in the campaign, Parten received some unexpected information that greatly boosted his optimism about Yarborough's chances. Garland Smith, chairman of the Texas Insurance Commission and an attorney from the Lower Rio Grande Valley in South Texas, gave Parten a court deposition that Allan Shivers had given in September 1952 as a result of a valley land-fraud suit in which Smith's law firm had been involved. The deposition seemed to indicate that Shivers was deeply involved in a land swindle with South Texas land developer Lloyd M. Bentsen Sr. (father of future U.S. senator Lloyd M. Bentsen Jr.). While he was campaigning for the Democratic nomination for lieutenant governor in May 1946, Shivers had acquired with a promissory note of $25,000 an option to buy 13,500 acres of brushland west of the valley town of Mission from Bentsen's development company. Seven months later, he sold this option back to another Bentsen company for $450,000—for a clear profit of $425,000. The Bentsen company paid out $25,000 a month in installment payments for eighteen months to Shivers, who by this time had been inaugurated as lieutenant governor. The Bentsen note was secured by a deed of trust that Shivers never bothered to file in the county courthouse.[6]

Three months after Shivers became governor, the State Board of Water Engineers gave permission to the Bentsen company to use water from the Rio Grande for irrigation of the land it had purchased from Shivers. This was the first water permit issued in the valley since the early 1930s. The value of the land soared from a little more than thirty-three dollars an acre to five hundred dollars an acre immediately after the permit was granted. Bentsen's company subsequently subdivided the land and named it "Texan Gardens." Unfortunately for the future purchasers of land in Texan Gardens, the water permit turned out to be nearly worthless. The water to which they had rights in the spring and summer existed only during rare flood conditions. Not long after he sold the tracts to farmers, a series of lawsuits were filed against Bentsen, charging that the land values had been misrepresented to the purchasers. Shivers gave his deposition as a part of these lawsuits, though he was not a defendant. The suits had been settled out of court in February 1954 and Shivers's deposition had remained sealed from public view. Garland Smith had retained a copy as one of the attorneys who had taken the deposition. There was no "smoking gun" in the deposition to indicate that Shivers had done anything illegal, but the entire transaction had the appearance of gross impropriety on his part. There was more than a hint of political influence-peddling in the matter of the state water permit. To Parten, however, the entire arrangement had been a "fraud for the purpose of selling land." Parten believed that Lloyd Bentsen Sr. had bribed Shivers for the water rights: "that $425,000 was his payment."[7]

Convinced that he had the weapon to ensure Shivers's defeat, Parten took the deposition to Yarborough and urged him to file a request with the court to make it public. He was optimistic that the deposition would be released because the judge who had jurisdiction in the matter was Jimmy Allred, appointed by President Truman in 1949. Yarborough agreed that the deposition raised grave questions about Shivers's ethics. Yarborough's staff subsequently persuaded Charles Landergott, one of the persons who had sued Bentsen, to file a request on May 17 in Allred's court for the deposition to be opened. Shivers's attorneys immediately filed a request to keep the deposition sealed "for the reason that the plaintiff might want to use it for other than judicial purposes." Because it was well known that he and Shivers were not friendly, Allred asked Judge Thomas Kennerly, the senior judge at Houston and a conservative with a reputation for high ethical standards, to hear the case.[8]

Judge Kennerly heard the case in Brownsville on June 23. Representing Shivers was the law firm of former regent and Homer Rainey nemesis, Judge D. F. Strickland. After listening to arguments from both sides, Kennerly surprised Shivers's attorneys by criticizing the governor for wanting to keep it sealed. He ordered it released to the public. Yarborough was free to make the land deal an issue. Parten believed that if Yarborough handled it correctly, Shivers's involvement in the affair could become the focus of the campaign. He told Yarborough that he needed "to find some way of picking an argument with Shivers ... that will enable you to get better coverage . . . in the daily newspapers," and advised

Yarborough that if he repeatedly raised questions about the Shivers-Bentsen land deal the newspapers eventually had to print it. To Parten's dismay, however, Yarborough hesitated to push the issue. Creekmore Fath, who continued to be one of Yarborough's chief advisors and speech writers, later recalled that Yarborough thought the issue was "too complicated" for the average voter. "We worked up a speech that I thought was perfectly clear on the thing," Fath recalled, "but Ralph said that no one would be able to understand it."[9]

Yarborough did release a statement to the Associated Press charging that the deposition revealed "a scandal" that Shivers needed to explain to the voters. The major urban daily newspapers in Texas, all of which were actively supporting Shivers, buried the news in their back pages. Shivers declared that Yarborough's charges were "just so much political poppy-cock . . . there wasn't one thing illegal, dishonest or unethical about the selling of that land. . . ." Playing on his insinuations that Yarborough was a "leftist," Shivers told reporters that Yarborough's charges proved that he must think there was something "wrong with this great American system of profit making."[10]

The issue of the Shivers-Bentsen land deal boosted hopes in the Yarborough campaign headquarters. The results of a statewide poll released prior to Judge Kennerly's ruling revealed a serious erosion of support for Shivers, and indicated that Yarborough was within striking distance. Hardeman, working in Austin for Yarborough, wrote to Parten that he was "very much encouraged about Ralph's chances. A month ago I was not in the least optimistic, but . . . if Ralph runs a smart race and we don't get over-confident, I think we can take the arrogant gentleman to the cleaners." Parten gave the campaign another boost in late June—a badly needed infusion of cash. The contribution came when Yarborough was nearly out of money, enabling him to continue during a critical time in the campaign. Parten also brought in substantial contributions from Howard Marshall, Will Clayton, Bill Moran, and even Marlin Sandlin, who gave Parten two thousand dollars. Parten's fund-raising made it possible for Yarborough to buy campaign ads in newspapers.[11]

His campaign in trouble, Shivers used racial and red-scare demagoguery to divert attention from his tangled business affairs and the charges of corruption in his administration. A few weeks before the campaign, the governor had attracted nationwide attention by proposing that the legislature outlaw the Communist Party in Texas and punish party membership with death in the electric chair. Although the legislature did not enact the death penalty, it did pass a tough new anti-Communist law. In his campaign against Yarborough, Shivers stressed (without proof) that Texas had been under imminent danger from communism, but that he had lessened that threat by his anti-Communist legislation. Shivers implied that a Yarborough victory would bring the Communist threat back to Texas. He charged that Yarborough's candidacy was sponsored by labor unions, the NAACP, and "those who do not approve of being tough on Communists." The Dallas *News* adopted a similar approach. In an editorial endorsing Shivers, the conservative Dallas newspaper declared that the Yarborough campaign represented "grafters,

Gov. Allan Shivers campaigning for reelection, 1954. *CN 09623. Courtesy Russell Lee Photograph Collection, CAH.*

perverts, and godless Communists who masquerade as Democrats. . . ." Shivers's anti-Communist rhetoric attracted the foot soldiers of the red scare to his campaign. Activists from such organizations as the Minute Women and the Americanism Committee of the American Legion flocked to the Shivers campaign headquarters in Houston, Dallas, and San Antonio to help the governor protect the state from Yarborough and his band of dangerous subversives. A group of Minute Women formed an organization called Women for Shivers, which provided volunteers to staff campaign offices and do much of the day-to-day grassroots election work.[12]

Disgusted with Shivers's tactics, Rayburn complained to Parten that "Shivers says that the Pinks and Communists are going to all vote against him. Why doesn't Yarborough challenge him to name one Communist in the State[?] . . . if [Shivers] knows Communists, he should be willing to name them. . . ." Parten passed Rayburn's advice on to Yarborough, stressing that "there is a lot of value in this suggestion." Recalling O'Leary's exposé of the Minute Women's activities in Houston, Parten told Yarborough that he should use the O'Leary material in an advertisement against Shivers. Yarborough followed this advice, purchasing (with Parten's money) full-page advertisements in all three of Houston's daily newspapers, accusing Shivers of being a "Minute Women candidate." Featuring quotes from O'Leary's exposé emphasizing the damage the organization had done to the local schools and churches, the ads asked in large type, "Why Are *Minute Women* Fighting So Frantically to Keep Shivers in Office?"[13]

"You have been a pillar of strength and light in this state"

As election day approached and the polls indicated that the race had tightened, Parten pleaded with Yarborough to focus on the Shivers-Bentsen land deal. Yarborough, however, still believed that it was too complicated for most voters to understand. Nevertheless, as a concession to Parten, Yarborough briefly discussed the land deal during a statewide television broadcast two days before the election. He quoted a portion of the Shivers deposition on the air and implied that Shivers had been paid $425,000 to influence the granting of a water permit. It was not the full and sensational treatment Parten had been urging. Yarborough explained to Parten that Shivers had been accusing him of dirty politics and he feared that if he emphasized the land-scandal issue too much the voters might interpreted it as mudslinging.[14]

On July 24, Yarborough stunned Shivers and the Texas Democratic establishment by forcing him into a runoff.[15] Shivers and his associates now had a serious problem. Every incumbent governor in Texas history who had been forced into a primary runoff had been defeated. The governor responded with a runoff campaign that was even more viciously demagogic than before. Manipulating the twin fears of Communist subversion and racial integration, Shivers and his advisors pulled all stops, stooping to such tactics as retouching a photograph of Yarborough to make him appear to be an African American and then distributing it to the state's newspapers for publication. The Shivers campaign also distributed a motion picture about the CIO's attempt to organize retail-store workers in Port Arthur in the fall of 1953. Titled the "Port Arthur Story," the movie charged that the strike was an attempt by the Communist Party to take over an entire Texas city. The business district in Port Arthur was filmed on a Sunday morning to make it appear as though the city had been turned into a ghost town by the union. Photographs were faked to show African American men picketing stores alongside white women. In his campaign speeches, Shivers declared that Yarborough's most enthusiastic supporters were "Reds, radicals, Communists, and goon squads." One of Shivers's aides later explained that "Allan really doesn't like to demagogue, but he was about to lose the race."[16]

Shivers's race- and red-baiting, coupled with massive numbers of newspaper and radio advertisements threatened to overwhelm Yarborough, whose chances were not helped by his own vacillation on racial integration. Although he tried to evade the emotional issue, he was eventually forced to declare his opposition to "forced commingling" and his support of separate but "genuinely equal" schools. He added, however, that he would not fight in the courts to preserve racial segregation in the schools. As aware as anyone else that the U.S. Supreme Court's recent decision in *Brown v. Board of Education* had ended legal racial segregation in the public schools, Yarborough was essentially trying to have it both ways with the voters. His tactics attracted few conservatives, to whom Shivers had promised to enforce segregation, and hurt him with liberals, who were disappointed by his support for racially separate schools.[17]

Characteristically, Parten remained hopeful about Yarborough's chances during the second primary campaign. He continued, however, to harp on the Shivers-Bentsen land deal. In the middle of the runoff campaign, Parten arranged and paid for a full-page advertisement in the Dallas *Morning News* for Yarborough to counter the *News*'s editorials against him and play up the Bentsen land scandal. Jim Wright, the future Speaker of the U.S. House of Representatives, who was running for his first term in Congress, had purchased a similar ad in the Fort Worth *Star Telegram* in July to counter its editorials against his own candidacy. Parten saw Wright's ad and liked it. It had been written by Fort Worth journalist Boyce House, an old acquaintance of Parten's who had written several books about the Texas oil industry. Parten hired House to draft an "open letter" from Yarborough to the Dallas *Morning News*. Not above playing a dirty political trick himself, Parten also had House draft a letter to Shivers, supposedly written by one of his supporters, accusing him of secretly supporting legalized racetrack gambling in Texas. Earlier in the campaign, Shivers had made the false claim that he had always opposed racetrack gambling in the state, and the letter cited his record of opposition as a state senator to Governor Allred's attempt to outlaw such gambling. Parten also found "a country preacher" to sign the letter. He sent the letter to several newspapers, but none of the major papers would print it.[18]

Boyce House's text appeared as a full-page advertisement in the Dallas *Morning News* two days prior to election day. Parten personally wrote and inserted into the text a description of the deal that Shivers had made with Lloyd Bentsen Sr. He concluded with a straightforward accusation: "Do not these oddities suggest this transaction was not at 'arms length' but was an inside deal to cover up a legal fee of $450,000 for political assistance in obtaining a water permit?" The advertisement caused a minor sensation in North Texas political circles and attracted much public attention, but it was too little and too late. When the second Democratic primary election was held on August 28, Shivers beat Yarborough by approximately ninety-two thousand votes. Yarborough was unable to overcome a Shivers juggernaut nourished by bigotry and the manipulation of red-scare issues, endorsed by nearly every major newspaper in Texas, and fueled with an unprecedented amount of money that had made it possible for Shivers to launch a massive media blitz.[19]

Yarborough's defeat was dispiriting to Parten. He complained to a friend and fellow Yarborough supporter in East Texas that it had taken "all of the race hatred and prejudice that could be generated by . . . active leaders of the opposition, to beat Ralph Yarborough." Angry, frustrated, and depressed, he flew to New York to attend a Fund for the Republic board meeting. He arrived two days early to have dinner with Opal and Dallas at their new apartment on Park Avenue. After dinner, as J. R. prepared to leave for his hotel, Opal slipped an envelope into his hand and asked him not to open it until he got to his room. When he did open the envelope, he found a sizeable contribution to help Yarborough pay off his campaign debt. Attached was a note from Opal that picked up Parten's spirits: "Dallas and I want you to know that we were with you . . . during the Texas campaign and we admire you very much for the way you continue to stick by your principles in what must often seem a discouraging situation. We may live in Yankee-land but we are still sho'-nuff Democrats."[20]

After his return to Texas, Parten received a gracious letter from Yarborough that also improved his mood. Declaring that he had lost a campaign he "should have won," Yarborough stressed to Parten that his advice "was always good, always the best received, always helpful. Had I been able to carry into execution all that you gave in the runoff, I think the disaster . . . might have been averted." Despite his loss to Shivers in a bitterly contested campaign, Yarborough claimed that he was optimistic about the future. He hoped Parten would stay with him. "When others were joining the forces of reaction," Yarborough told Parten, "you have been a pillar of strength and light in this state for all who believe in decency and Democracy. My campaigns of 1952 and 1954 are both indebted more to you than to any other one person. . . . Without your pledge I would not have been able to have announced either year. You, not I, are the bulwark of the Democratic Party in Texas."[21]

The *Texas Observer*

As he pondered yet another defeat at the hands of the conservative forces that had ruled the state since the 1938 election of W. Lee O' Daniel as governor (it had been Parten's fifth straight defeat in a gubernatorial election in which he had participated directly), Parten became convinced that Texas desperately needed a major news journal to disseminate the political and public-policy information that the state's conservative newspapers either refused to print or distorted for partisan purposes. Ever since his experience in 1946 when the largest state radio network refused to sell air time to Homer Rainey's campaign and most of the state's major newspapers actively opposed Rainey's election, Parten had hoped that a loyal Democrat would either purchase one of the urban newspapers or create a new one. Parten's view was shared by those in the liberal faction who were particularly bitter about Yarborough's defeat. "That 1954 campaign had a transforming emotional impact on Texas politics," one of them later noted, "the 'Loyal Democrats' of Ralph Yarborough decided the political process had been purchased by the Tories, who had manipulated the media, deceived the voters, and sabotaged the democratic idea."[22]

As a direct result of their collective experience in the Yarborough defeat, several of the more affluent and prominent leaders among the liberals decided in September 1954 to underwrite their own news journal. Led by Frankie Carter Randolph, an heir to a lumber and banking fortune and a dedicated progressive, the group included, among others, Parten, Jesse Andrews, Lillian Collier, attorney Franklin Jones, and Nina Cullinan (the daughter of a founder of Texaco). Will Clayton had introduced Parten to the extraordinary and formidable Randolph in

Frankie Randolph and Creekmore Fath, 1956. *CN 09617. Courtesy Parten Photograph Collection, CAH.*

November 1953. Working mainly through her own group, the Harris County Democrats, Frankie Randolph had played a major role as an organizer and worker for Yarborough in Houston. Randolph, Parten, and their associates agreed to provide the necessary funds to buy and upgrade the old *State Observer* from liberal publisher Paul Holcomb to create a new weekly journal to be called the *Texas Observer.*[23]

The *Texas Observer* group knew nothing about running a newspaper, so their first task was to recruit an editor. Lillian Collier suggested that they interview Ronnie Dugger, the former editor of the University of Texas newspaper, the *Daily Texan.* Only twenty-four years old, Dugger had written a "progressive" political column for the San Antonio *Express* while attending graduate school at Oxford University. He had recently returned from England and might be available. Parten had never met Dugger, but he knew of his work as a *Daily Texan* editor. When Dugger met with Randolph, Parten, and other members of the group in October, he was on his way to Mexico to work on a fishing boat in Tampico and write a novel, so he was not keen on taking the job. When he was offered the position of editor, Dugger agreed, but only if he had exclusive control of the contents of the journal. After some discussion, the group accepted his terms. Dugger went to work almost immediately and was able to get the first issue of the *Observer* out on December 13, 1954.[24]

The *Texas Observer* soon became the iconoclastic voice of liberal politics in Texas, featuring Dugger's passionate and incisive editorials and investigative reports on important topics that establishment newspapers preferred to ignore. In time, the *Observer*'s influence extended far beyond the borders of Texas, especially with the ascent of Lyndon B. Johnson to national power. Parten himself did much to help spread the word about the *Observer* among important opinion-makers outside the state. He regularly sent issues to Bob Hutchins, Ping Ferry, Elmo Roper, and his other colleagues at the Fund for the Republic and they also grew to appreciate Dugger's work. After receiving an issue in March 1955, Ferry wrote Parten that what he read in the *Observer* "makes me think that we ought to send a task force into your state . . . you rightly observe that Texas has California skinned without even trying. Keep the dope on Texas coming."[25]

Dugger eventually recruited to the *Observer* writers such as Willie Morris, Larry Goodwyn, Billy Brammer, Molly Ivins, Kaye Northcott, and Jim Hightower, among many others, who made the paper required reading for Texas politicians from every point on the political spectrum. Never a profit-maker, the *Observer*'s early financial losses were largely subsidized by donations from Randolph, Parten, Jesse Andrews, and Nina Cullinan. Parten, who forged a warm friendship with Dugger, was for a period of more than thirty-five years a steadfast member of a group of five or six of the largest financial backers on which the *Observer* could depend to save it from one of its frequent financial crises. At one point in the 1970s, Parten and Walter Hall made a loan to the *Observer* that rescued the journal from certain bankruptcy.[26]

Randolph, Andrews, Parten, and the other members of their group, also fought off frequent demands from politicians, business leaders, and others (some of them liberals) to control Dugger's editorials. Recalling Parten's stalwart support for the journal's editorial independence, former *Observer* editor Larry Goodwyn stressed that Parten "really was a democrat with a little 'd.' He was a 19th century Republican in the very finest sense of the word. The kind of man that Jefferson would have admired and gotten along with." In a 1981 interview in the Dallas *Morning News*, Parten admitted that he did not agree with everything printed in the *Observer*, "but I do feel strongly that both sides of any major issue should be heard. And since most Texas newspapers are editorially conservative, there is a need for the *Observer*."[27]

With one important exception, Parten's disagreements with the *Observer* were minor. The exception was over federal regulation of the oil industry in general, and the federal oil depletion tax allowance in particular. To the *Observer* and to most liberals, the oil depletion allowance was a symbol of the oil industry's power over public policy. The tax break was seen as an enormous give-away program to an industry that was making excessive profits. In addition, the highly publicized political activity of right-wing oil men such as H. L. Hunt and Clint Murchison convinced the liberals that the depletion allowance was diverting tax revenue from the federal treasury to the bank accounts of reactionary politicians and to the coffers of red-scare organizations. The *Observer* demanded that the oil depletion allowance be ended and that the federal government impose strict antitrust regulations on the industry. Dugger and Goodwyn later recalled that Parten was very unhappy about the journal's editorials against the oil depletion allowance. "It was highly predictable," Goodwyn said. "That was the one thing that the liberals wanted to do that J. R. didn't want to do."[28]

"Governor Shivers is no problem of mine. He is a problem of Texas"

Parten's differences with the liberals over federal oil policy, his deep respect for Sam Rayburn, and the frustration he felt over the string of bitter election defeats he had suffered since Pappy O'Daniel's victory over Ernest Thompson in 1938, caused him in 1955 to shift away from the liberals and move toward the so-called Rayburn-Johnson "moderates." Only the latter group, Parten now believed, was capable of defeating the despised Shivercrats. In addition, Parten was pleased with Johnson's defense of the oil depletion allowance in the Senate and his efforts in the winter of 1955 to pass a natural gas deregulation bill that Rayburn had carried through the House. Eisenhower ultimately vetoed the latter bill because of allegations that some senators had been offered bribes to vote for it. Nevertheless, Johnson's (and Rayburn's) efforts on behalf of the oil industry gave Parten even more reason to move toward the senator's camp.[29]

Actually, evidence of Parten's tactical shift away from the liberals was apparent as early as September 1954, when Jim Sewell asked Parten to raise money on behalf of the DAC for the congressional campaigns that fall. Parten accepted the fund-raising assignment, but warned Sewell that the DAC's close identification with the liberals would hamper his efforts to raise money from his oil and other business contacts in Houston. He decided, therefore, to pitch his appeal as one coming directly from Sam Rayburn, asking that contributions be sent directly to Rayburn rather than to the DAC. This tactic worked well, and Parten raised nearly twelve thousand dollars. He sent the money directly to Rayburn, informing Sewell that his donors were "much more prone to become interested from a standpoint of helping Sam personally." Parten also knew that Lyndon Johnson, for his own political needs, was working to bring Shivers back into the party fold. Accordingly, Parten felt that he should maintain a low profile in DAC affairs. His well-known personal feud with Shivers, which Parten refused to disregard just for the sake of party unity, might hamper this effort to bring the governor back into loyalist ranks. Parten also admitted many years later that he did not want to take a leadership role in a reunited state party if it meant having to work with Allan Shivers. "I had better things to do" he said.[30]

At first, the press of his diverse business enterprises gave Parten a legitimate excuse to remove himself from active participation in the DAC, which, despite Rayburn's intentions, had become strongly identified with the liberal faction.

Left to right, Sam Rayburn, Lyndon B. Johnson, and Adlai Stevenson at the LBJ Ranch, September 1955. *CN 09609. Courtesy Jimmie Dodd Photograph Collection, CAH.*

Parten's work load, for example, was the primary reason he had turned down a reappointment to the Federal Reserve Board in Dallas (a position he had much enjoyed) in January after eleven years of service. When Wright Morrow was finally ousted as a Democratic committeeman from Texas in the summer of 1955, Parten invoked his business responsibilities as the reason for turning down an offer to serve as the "liberal" candidate to replace Morrow. Although Parten's business activity was especially heavy, he was glad to have a reasonable excuse that allowed him to avoid close involvement with the liberals. Most of the liberal leaders were good friends of his and he had no desire to alienate any of them on a personal level.[31]

For the same reasons, in September Parten (who was the honorary chairman) also declined to succeed Jim Sewell as the working chairman of the DAC. He ignored fervent pleas from liberal friends such as Lillian Collier ("We need you—Major—please!") for him to take the job to help preserve liberal influence in the DAC. Parten told Collier that his work in Minnesota would not allow him to devote much attention to the job, but he also added that there were "many good Democrats who see a value in trying to get . . . Shivers . . . back in the Democratic ranks. I think that my relationship with Governor Shivers, wherein I have openly challenged his integrity, would disqualify me for such a position."[32]

The Johnson-Rayburn group's attempt to court Shivers for the sake of party unity for the presidential election campaign in 1956 surprised Adlai Stevenson, who was watching developments from Illinois while he contemplated another run against Eisenhower. "I keep hearing bewildering political reports from Texas and I think I shall forego further efforts to understand what goes on there," Stevenson wrote Parten in November. "But that is not to say that I will not eagerly welcome any counsel you have there for me." Parten replied that it was "true that our political situation in Texas is somewhat confused" and that it might be very difficult to get the Texas delegation to support his nomination at the convention in 1956. Nevertheless, Parten assured Stevenson that if he decided to run again ("and I certainly hope you do"), he would get the nomination despite whatever Texas did at the convention. He believed Shivers had been greatly weakened and that he would not dominate the state party convention in 1956 or lead the Texas delegation to the national convention. Parten did warn Stevenson, however, to avoid any confrontations with Shivers in the press while Johnson worked either to bring the governor back to the party or to neutralize him altogether. He recommended to Stevenson that if the press asked him any questions about Shivers, he should simply say that "Governor Shivers is no problem of mine. He is a problem of Texas." In his reply to Parten, Stevenson declared that his remark that Shivers "'is no problem of mine' is a solution of that interminable question which I wish I had had long since!"[33]

By the end of 1955, Parten had moved quietly into the Rayburn-Johnson faction while still retaining his strong contacts with the liberals. In this effort, he had the encouragement of Sam Rayburn, who needed Parten to continue to serve as his link with the liberal faction during the upcoming fight to take the Texas party away from the Shivercrats.[34]

CHAPTER 27

Confrontation with the House Un-American Activities Committee

1956

While the faction-ridden Democrats prepared for the 1956 primaries, Parten turned his attention to another internecine struggle, this one in New York, where an attempt was being made to remove Bob Hutchins as president of the Fund for the Republic. In the eighteen months since his appointment, Hutchins had involved the Fund in a wide range of social-change, civil rights, and civil liberties activities that had stirred up an equally wide range of hostile critics. In the past year alone, the Fund had given significant amounts of grant money to support such projects as a study of the censorship practices of the U.S. Post Office; a report on legal problems encountered by Mexican farm workers; a study of the impact on labor unions of loyalty/security programs; an investigation of the abuse of civil liberties in the military's personnel security program; and a report on legal problems related to racial desegregation. The Fund had given twenty-five thousand dollars to help Georgia teachers fired by school boards because of membership in the NAACP; forty thousand dollars to church groups to promote racial integration; and five thousand dollars to the (Quaker) Monthly Meeting in Plymouth, Massachusetts, for its "defense of democratic principles." Parten had supported every one of these initiatives and grants.[1]

The Fund's program had attracted criticism, but it was the grant to the Quakers that had enraged red-scare activists in Congress. The Fund had made the grant because the Quakers had refused to fire their librarian, Mary Knowles, despite heavy pressure from right-wing McCarthyite groups for them to do so.

Knowles had invoked the Fifth Amendment in 1953 when she had been called to testify before a Senate committee investigating Communist subversion. The Quakers investigated the matter thoroughly and determined that she was a loyal American, and when the Fund rewarded them for their support of her constitutional rights, it attracted the attention of right-wing radio and television personality and newspaper columnist Fulton Lewis Jr., one of the most widely followed political commentators in the United States. Lewis had mildly criticized the Fund for the Republic since its founding, but the Knowles grant hit a raw nerve. Beginning in the summer of 1955, the popular commentator made the Fund public enemy number one, denouncing the organization in at least sixty different radio broadcasts over a nationwide network of 214 stations.[2]

Lewis's attacks inspired a wave of hate mail to Parten and the other directors. One man wrote Parten, for example, that the Quaker grant was "funny business for a resident . . . of what was once the Lone Star State. Communism is treason. Americans who aid communism are worse than traitors." Many of the writers denounced Parten, the millionaire oil entrepreneur, as "a traitor to his class." Parten's reply to one such letter writer was a carefully written explanation for his association with the Fund. "It is fundamental with me that the capitalistic system and competitive free enterprise require preservation of the freedom of thought, freedom of expression and freedom of inquiry," Parten explained. "The Fund . . . is dedicated to the . . . proposition that in our struggle with world Communism our greatest strength lies in the jealous preservation of constitutional liberties. . . ." Parten saw no conflict between his work with the Fund and his status as a businessman because "the welfare and destiny of Woodley Petroleum Co. are so dependent upon . . . the individual liberties guaranteed by our Constitution. . . ." Addressing the charge that the Fund was too "controversial," Parten argued that no one could work in the field of civil liberties without getting into controversy. "Let us not forget," Parten wrote, "that many of our most . . . revered persons of action have been characterized as controversial, including Thomas Jefferson, Abraham Lincoln, and Sam Houston."[3]

Despite the criticism, Parten remained steadfast in his support for Hutchins and the program he had launched. Not all of Parten's colleagues were so supportive. Many of the directors "just didn't like the heat of public controversy," Ping Ferry recalled. "When you'd point out to them [that] the controversy arose from their own actions, it made them even more sore." Regarding the Knowles affair, Ferry claimed that some of the board members implied that "Hutchins and I had just contrived this project to embarrass them. The St. Louis *Post-Dispatch* described this board as 'the fifteen most courageous men in the U.S.' This was the biggest belly laugh I ever had. . . ." Parten was not among those who reacted badly to the attacks. When Ferry referred to Parten's "good support" in a letter written at the time, he added, "I don't know what we would have done without it."[4]

On December 6, 1955, the Fund received an especially damaging blow when Fulton Lewis read over the radio a letter that he had received from Henry Ford, expressing Ford's dissatisfaction with the Fund. "Some of its actions," he declared, "have been dubious in character and inevitably have led to charges of poor judge-ment." Ford's public criticism stung many on the Fund's board of directors, par-ticularly Arthur Griswold, who had been openly displeased for several months with Hutchins's administrative style and the controversies resulting from the Fund's activities. Calling for Hutchins's removal as president, Griswold charged that his combative and provocative style and his inflexible views on civil liberties had created unnecessary problems for the Fund and its directors.[5]

Parten attended a board meeting on January 6, 1956, to discuss Griswold's charges. He continued to be steadfast in his support of Hutchins, teaming with Elmo Roper and Eleanor Stevenson to defend the controversial educator. Roper later recalled that "if Parten or Stevenson or I had wavered at any time in our belief in Hutchins, he would have been gone. We had no intention of wavering." Griswold was especially upset by Parten's vigorous defense of Hutchins. The two men had such an angry exchange during the meeting that they did not speak to each other for many months. After a deliberation that extended into the early morning of January 7, a majority of the board voted to reelect Hutchins president, but only after he had agreed to several conditions that provided the board with more control over the Fund's operations. Hutchins was saved from his board crit-ics, but he was soon under attack from another powerful source—the House Un-American Activities Committee.[6]

Confrontation with HUAC

On June 11, Francis E. "Tad" Walter, an influential Democratic congressman from Pennsylvania and chairman of the House Committee on Un-American Activities (HUAC) announced that his committee would hold hearings on the Fund for the Republic on June 27. Walter charged that the Fund, "with its vast reservoir" of money, was financing activities that had been criticized by "members of Congress, prominent patriotic organizations, and individuals." Walter wanted to determine if the Fund was a "friend or foe in our national death struggle against the Communist conspiracy."

Walter's announcement came as no surprise to Hutchins or to Parten and his fellow directors. A few months before Walter's announcement, HUAC had demanded and received access to the Fund's administrative records, which Hutchins had assumed was in preparation for a formal investigation. Hutchins also knew that the HUAC staff had monitored the Fund for the Republic since its creation by the Ford Foundation. During its existence, the Fund had not endeared itself to HUAC members or to other conservative members of Congress. One of the Fund's first acts had been to provide money to the American Bar Association for a study of congressional investigating committees, with HUAC its obvious tar-get. The Fund had also distributed several thousand copies of published criticisms of HUAC by Erwin Griswold, Telford Taylor, and Alan Barth. The Fund's support of civil rights organizations had also angered a large number of southern con-gressmen. Because many of Rayburn's southern colleagues frequently complained about the Fund, the Speaker occasionally asked Parten for information that he could use to placate them. Hutchins and his colleagues did not know, however, that FBI director J. Edgar Hoover had actively encouraged HUAC to attack the Fund. Despite Hoover's public statements to the contrary, the FBI regularly fed confidential information from its files to HUAC for its use in the attack on the Fund. For example, the FBI sent its files on Theodore Draper and Alan Westin, two recipients of Fund grants, to HUAC investigator Karl Baarslag, with instructions that the FBI's involvement in the hearings on the Fund be kept secret.[7]

HUAC itself could do little harm to the Fund, but the hearings could give the Internal Revenue Service reason to revoke the Fund's tax exemption. It was critical, therefore, for the Fund to be allowed to answer allegations made by its enemies at the hearings. Parten actually welcomed the news of the planned hearings. The Fund had been the unrelenting target of Fulton Lewis and other right-wing, red-scare radio commentators and newspaper columnists, without having an opportunity to defend itself adequately in the media. Parten felt that this gave the Fund "a real opportunity to tell the world about the merits of our program and the newspapers would have to print it for a change." Parten had learned during his PAW service that "if you didn't have anything to hide, public investigations could be very helpful. They were the best type of advertising you could get if you had a worthy program."

Hutchins had a different reaction. He wrote Parten that the HUAC chairman "is doing the Fund for the Republic irreparable damage. We may have made mistakes, but they are not of a kind that suggest that we are in any way or in the slightest degree disloyal, unpatriotic, or un-American." Parten tried to assure Hutchins that the Fund had nothing to fear. "Let's just make certain," he told Hutchins, "that Walter is forced to hear our side of the story." Having no other acceptable options, Hutchins, Hoffman, Parten, and the entire board of directors made plans to attend the hearings and give testimony. Parten was eager for the confrontation, especially between the committee and Hutchins, who he knew could be devastating in such a forum. In 1949, when the Illinois legislature held hearings on alleged Communist infiltration of the University of Chicago, a legislator told Hutchins that one of the university's distinguished cancer researchers, who had belonged to some left-wing organizations, might be guilty of indoctrination. "Indoctrination?" Hutchins asked. "Of mice?"[8]

When the Fund notified HUAC that an impressive group of prominent citizens would testify on its behalf at the hearings, Richard Arens, the committee's staff director told reporters that Walter had no intention of allowing Hutchins or anyone else associated with the Fund to testify, implying that only critics of the Fund would be allowed to testify. On June 19, Parten was in Regina, Saskatchewan, on Woodley business, when Hutchins called and told him about Arens's statement. Parten replied that he would do "some investigating" with his friends in the Congress. He contacted Rayburn's legislative assistant to find out if it was true that the Fund would not be allowed to defend itself at the hearings. He asked the aide not to involve Rayburn in the request, he just wanted to know what Walter was planning to do. A few hours later, the aide confirmed the rumor, but quickly added that he "couldn't keep the boss out of this." Rayburn had told the aide to tell Parten that "there wasn't going to be any HUAC hearing on June 27." Rayburn wanted Parten to come to Washington as soon as possible, however, to meet personally with Congressman Walter to see if he could not be placated in some way.[9]

Rayburn was in an extremely uncomfortable political position. He and Francis Walter had been close friends and political allies for many years. Walter had become a power in the Congress as a result of his alliance with the Speaker, his position as head of the Democratic Patronage Committee, and his chairmanship of the much feared HUAC. The Pennsylvania congressman had even been mentioned as one of Rayburn's potential successors. More important, Walter was popular with the powerful bloc of conservative southern congressmen upon whom Rayburn depended for much of his support as Speaker. Parten assured Rayburn that he understood his problem and that had been one reason he had not wanted to get him involved personally. Rayburn replied that he could at least arrange a meeting with Walter for Parten to explain that the Fund simply wanted to have the opportunity to discuss its program at a public hearing. "I'm not sure that you'll get along very well," Rayburn said, "because Henry Ford has been down here and talked to Walter, and Ford doesn't seem to care what happens to the Fund for the Republic."[10]

Parten met with Congressman Walter the next morning, but as Rayburn had feared, the meeting resolved nothing. "Walter wanted to do all the talking," Parten said. After a few minutes, Walter announced that he had to go to a committee meeting and started walking out of his office. Parten followed him to the door, declaring that "there is only one request we have to make, and that is to let us have the opportunity to explain what we've been doing and why." Walter replied that the request was fair, but he would not promise him anything. Parten returned to Rayburn's office and told him about his unsatisfactory meeting with Walter. Not surprised, Rayburn assured Parten that if HUAC did conduct hearings on the Fund, he would do whatever he could to see that the Fund had an opportunity to defend itself. Before Parten left the Speaker's office, he told Rayburn that he suspected someone was giving money to HUAC to prosecute the Fund for the Republic. "I don't know who it is," Parten said, "but I am going to spend some of my money to try to find out."[11]

On June 20, Congressman Walter announced that the hearings on the Fund for the Republic were postponed indefinitely. Parten never asked Rayburn if he had pressured Walter about the hearings. He was sensitive about his relationship with the Speaker in a way that seems curiously old-fashioned today, but he always claimed that he never asked Rayburn for a favor, and there is no evidence to contradict that claim. Parten felt that even asking Rayburn if he had intervened in the HUAC affair was tantamount to making a request that he do so. Nevertheless, it seems reasonable to assume that Rayburn's obvious personal interest in the Fund may have had a chilling effect on Walter's plans to have a one-sided hearing. Whether or not Walter was getting pressure from Rayburn, he was definitely getting advice from J. Edgar Hoover, who warned Walter to postpone the hearings until HUAC could assemble more information on the Fund to "present better hearings than were originally scheduled."[12]

The Report on Blacklisting

The reprieve was short-lived. On June 24, the Fund published John Cogley's two-volume, six-hundred-page *Report on Blacklisting*, which provided detailed information about the practice of blacklisting in the television and movie industries. The Cogley report documented how HUAC had worked with the American Legion and smaller organizations such as AWARE, Inc., and with Hearst newspaper columnists George Sokolsky and Victor Riesel, among others, to deny employment in the movies and on television to anyone accused of being a Communist, of having Communist "sympathies," of associating with Communists, or of advocating controversial or nonconformist ideas. In addition, anyone who had invoked the Fifth Amendment when testifying at a HUAC hearing was placed on the blacklist. Only after the accused had applied for a "clearance," paid a fee, and publicly "recanted" whatever they had been accused of doing, did they have any chance to be reemployed in the industry. The victims, who numbered in the hundreds, included actors John Garfield, John Randolph, Jack Gilford, Gale Sondergaard, and Zero Mostel; writers Dalton Trumbo and Ring Lardner Jr.; and directors Carl Foreman and Martin Ritt. The report was a devastating indictment of HUAC, the American Legion, AWARE, Inc., and the broadcasting and movie-industry executives who had allowed the blacklisters to control their employment practices and trample the First Amendment rights of the blacklist victims.[13]

The Fund almost failed to publish the Cogley report. As board liaison for the study, Parten had received a copy of the completed manuscript for review. "When I read the galley proofs of Cogley's work," Parten said, "I was shocked and surprised by what I saw there. I knew that it was going to create a good deal of static as a result." Parten was impressed with Cogley's work, but had agreed with Elmo Roper and Ping Ferry when they suggested that it be sent out for evaluation by Earl Newsom, the public relations consultant for the Ford Motor Company and the Ford Foundation. Newsom returned the report a week later with the recommendation that it not be published. Although "thorough" and "objective," Newsom explained, the Cogley report would "revive widespread public controversy and confusion about a complex problem to which no solution has yet been found."[14]

At the meeting of the Fund's board of directors on March 22, Hutchins had requested permission to release the Cogley report to the public despite Newsom's recommendation. A spirited debate ensued in which some of the directors expressed concern about the storm of controversy the report was certain to create, which was likely to generate pressure on the IRS to remove the Fund's tax-exempt status. Parten joined with Ferry and Hutchins in favor of publication. If the Fund backed away from the work now, he stressed, it would be a major victory for the blacklisters. Cogley warned the board of directors that if they refused to publish the study, he would have someone else publish it. After a protracted and "heated"

John Henry Faulk (left) meets with his attorney, Louis Nizer in New York City. *CN 05709. Courtesy John Henry Faulk Photograph Collection, CAH.*

discussion, the board (by a split vote with Parten in favor) finally appropriated twenty thousand dollars to print ten thousand copies of the study on blacklisting.[15]

When it was released to the public on June 24, news about the blacklisting report was splashed across the front page of most of the major newspapers in the East, sending shock waves through HUAC and its allied organizations. The shock increased two days later when CBS radio personality John Henry Faulk filed a 1.5-million-dollar libel suit in the New York State Supreme Court against AWARE, Inc., and others. Faulk charged that AWARE and its allies had defamed him as part of a conspiracy to have him blacklisted. The timing of Faulk's suit and the publication of the Cogley report were coincidental, but both sent a message to HUAC and its cohorts that they now had a fight on their hands.[16]

HUAC and the blacklisters quickly went on the offensive. The Hearst newspaper chain denounced the report and called the Fund "anti-anti-Communist." HUAC announced that it would conduct hearings on the "Investigation of So-Called 'Blacklisting in the Entertainment Industry'." The committee also issued a subpoena for Cogley to appear at a hearing on July 10. Hutchins immediately sent a letter to Walter denouncing the hearings as an attack on the freedom of the press and demanding that the Fund be given an opportunity to present its own case and to cross examine witnesses. His demand was ignored. Hutchins also notified Parten about this latest HUAC assault on the Fund. Parten thought he had done all he could with Rayburn, knowing Rayburn's hands were tied because of his political relationship with Tad Walter. He did, however, contact Minnesota senator

Hubert Humphrey and Cong. Eugene McCarthy, with whom he had become friendly as a result of Great Northern's activity in the Twin Cities area. As it turned out, McCarthy was an old friend of Cogley's. Both men pledged their help. Humphrey subsequently placed into the Congressional Record strong statements of support for the Fund from various labor union leaders.[17]

HUAC opened its hearings on July 10. When Cogley entered the hearing room, he was accompanied by Congressman McCarthy, who, in a conspicuous gesture of support, walked in with his arm around Cogley. Richard Arens, HUAC staff director, began the hearings by accusing Cogley of relying on information supplied to him by persons of "suspect background" and of failing to list the alleged Communist affiliations of the individuals claimed to have been blacklisted. The latter accusation, of course, was a tacit admission that there *was* a blacklisting operation; which HUAC had declared did not exist. After Cogley's appearance, "an honor guard of the country's preeminent blacklisters," including leaders of the American Legion and AWARE, Inc., paraded before the committee to denounce Cogley and the Fund. The committee also examined the Fund's grant to the Plymouth Monthly Meeting in support of its hiring of Mary Knowles, more evidence that the hearings were aimed at the Fund as much as at Cogley. Walter pointed out that the five thousand dollars the Fund had given to the Quakers for hiring a "Communist" was tax-exempt money and that federal law prohibited foundations from spending money for politically partisan or propagandistic purposes. He charged that the Fund was a "multi-million dollar propaganda machine which enjoys tax exemption." This was a direct challenge to the Fund's tax-exempt status, one that the IRS would not ignore.[18]

Cogley was able to defend himself, but the Fund was denied an opportunity to provide witnesses on its behalf, despite repeated requests from Hutchins, Parten, and other directors. As one HUAC critic later observed, rather than conduct a fair hearing, HUAC "chose instead the tactic of hit-and-run assault and verdict by press release." At the conclusion of the hearings, Walter declared that the investigation had revealed that the "Fund for the Republic report is a partisan, biased attack on all persons and organizations who are . . . concerned in ridding the movie industry and radio and television of Communists and Communist sympathizers."[19]

While HUAC held its hearings on the Cogley report, Parten conducted his own investigation of the committee. Parten discovered that the HUAC staff member who had been giving them the most trouble, Karl Baarslag, a former staff member of Joseph McCarthy's subcommittee, had worked for H. L. Hunt's *Facts Forum* magazine. Hunt's magazine was published in Dallas, so Parten contacted Dallas merchant Stanley Marcus, for whom his wife Patsy had once worked as a fashion model, and asked him for a set of *Facts Forum* so that he could read Baarslag's articles. Marcus sent him copies of Hunt's magazine along with some copies of "Dan Smoot Speaks," another extreme-right-wing journal published in Dallas. Marcus told Parten that the articles documented "Baarslag's ideas thoroughly." As Parten leafed through the magazines, he became enraged by Baarslag's frequent references to the Democratic Party as "the party of treason." When Parten sent the magazines on to Frank Kelly, the recently hired public relations officer for the Fund, he wrote that he was amazed to learn "how much money seems to be available for such fascist material."[20]

Parten also sent copies of Baarslag's articles to Rayburn with a letter complaining about HUAC's employment of a man who had recently accused the Democratic Party of treason. Enraged by what he had read in *Facts Forum*, and somewhat frustrated by Rayburn's apparent inability to do anything about Walter and his HUAC colleagues, Parten's letter was unusually critical in tone, suggesting that Rayburn shared responsibility for Baarslag's and HUAC's activities. Baarslag's employment as a member of the staff of a House committee, Parten declared, did not "reflect credit upon the Democratic majority in the Congress. I feel it my duty to call it to your attention because I consider you the foremost Democrat of our party." Hutchins also challenged Rayburn. "As the chief officer of the House," he wrote, "we venture to hope that you . . . will find it possible to check the excesses of the Chairman of the House Un-American Activities Committee and its staff." Rayburn later admitted to Parten that he had been deeply distressed by the contents of the magazines and equally frustrated by Walter's behavior. A few weeks later, Baarslag quietly left the HUAC staff. The two men never discussed the issue again, but shortly after Rayburn's death in 1961, Parten learned that Rayburn had forced Walter to dismiss Baarslag from the HUAC payroll.[21]

Unable to do much about HUAC, Rayburn tried to help in other ways. Frank Kelly organized a black-tie dinner in Washington's Shoreham Hotel in February 1957 to show off the Fund's important backers and to send a message to HUAC. The large audience was filled with notables, including sixteen members of Congress. Among these was Rep. Morgan M. Moulder of Missouri, the second-ranking HUAC member, who announced after the dinner that he did not share Walter's suspicions about the Fund. And, as one observer later described it, "Speaker Sam Rayburn's bald head gleamed conspicuously at J. R. Parten's table." Rayburn's presence was pointed out to the audience by Elmo Roper, the master of ceremonies, and his attendance was emphasized by the Washington press corps.[22]

None of this kept Walter from continuing his almost obsessive pursuit of the Fund for the Republic. In his committee's annual report for the year 1956, Walter charged that the Fund had given "great aid and comfort to the Communist apparatus, particularly in the vital area of mass communications and entertainment." He continued to harass Cogley, threatening him twice in the first six months of 1957 with subpoenas, but backing down when Cogley sent word that he would not answer any questions about the report on blacklisting. Cogley even burned his notes and other research papers when he heard that HUAC might subpoena them. In June 1957, Walter declared that because he and his committee colleagues had to investigate subversive activities in San Francisco, and that the attempts to drag Cogley before the committee would be postponed until his return to Washington.[23]

While in San Francisco, however, Walter made a tactical mistake. He allowed HUAC hearings to be broadcast over a local television station, which violated

Rayburn's ban on televised coverage of any House proceedings. Rayburn learned about the violation when he read the news that a prospective witness had chosen to kill himself rather than be interrogated in front of a television camera—and immediately sent word to the committee that they were to cease the broadcasts. In a subsequent press conference in San Francisco, Walter declared that Rayburn's prohibition against television pertained "only to hearings in Washington and are no longer applied anyway. There is no such rule." Walter's remark enraged Rayburn, who told Cong. Wilbur Mills that "Tad Walter's investigative methods have gone too far." Walter's defiance was a challenge to his leadership as Speaker. Rayburn ordered Walter back to Washington. After a meeting with the HUAC chairman, Rayburn announced to the press that "Tad Walter is not going to tele-vise any meetings any more." One of Rayburn's staff later remarked that when the congressman left Rayburn's office he was "white and shaken. The old man obvi-ously pulled no punches." Cogley's long-delayed reappearance before HUAC was cancelled, and HUAC held no more hearings on the Fund.[24]

Early in 1958, however, Walter took one more shot at the Fund by leaking a report to the press claiming that IRS agents had determined in 1956 that the Fund for the Republic was distributing political "propaganda" rather than educational material, and thus the Fund no longer legally qualified for a federal tax exemption. Fulton Lewis broadcast the report and demanded that the IRS withdraw the Fund's tax exemption. Loss of its exemption, Lewis declared, "would mean—oh happy day—that the Fund for the Republic is out of business. . . ." Parten com-plained to Rayburn that the HUAC chairman had "declared publicly and assured me privately that . . . the Fund . . . would be given a hearing. . . . We have been given no day in court. It grieves me sorely to see a committee of a Democratic Congress embrace, nurture and practice the principles of 'McCarthyism'. . . ."[25]

Presumably as a result of Walter's actions, the IRS subsequently sent notice to the Fund to "show cause" why its tax exemption should not be revoked. Walter had made another mistake, however. When Hutchins received the IRS notice in March 1958, he again turned to Parten, whom he knew to be a friend of Robert B. Anderson, the secretary of the treasury. Parten had first met Anderson when the latter was a young assistant of Governor Allred's. The two men had also served together as directors of the Dallas branch of the Federal Reserve. Accompanied by Paul Hoffman, Parten met with Anderson in Washington. The secretary explained that he well understood that the Fund was not guilty of the charges Walter had made against it . He apologized to Parten for the inconvenience and assured him that the Fund's tax exemption would be preserved. In the presence of Parten and Hoffman, Anderson telephoned Rayburn, who was another old friend, and told him that the Fund's tax status remained secure. Anderson asked the Speaker, how-ever, to get Walter and HUAC "off of my back." Anderson's word was good, the Fund's tax exemption was saved and never threatened again. Hutchins's insistence when the Fund was being organized that its board of directors consist of individu-als with conservative and unassailable reputations had proven to be wise, as had been his selection of J. R. Parten.[26]

His experience with Tad Walter, HUAC, the blacklisting controversy, and McCarthyites such as Baarslag made a searing impression on Parten, giving him a renewed understanding of the important role the Fund could play in the civic health of the nation. He told Frank Kelly in August 1956 that he was outraged that HUAC could exist and engage in "McCarthyism," even though the Democratic Party had a majority in the House of Representatives. Parten declared that as "a life-long Democrat . . . the conduct of [HUAC] stirs me a lot more deeply than it might others." That same month, when Parten sent Frank Dobie some literature about the activities of the Fund for the Republic, he enclosed a letter admitting that his recent experience with HUAC had taught him and his fellow Fund directors that "Freedom and Justice are terms which are not as well understood as we first assumed." Parten later said that he believed that "one of the greatest things that the Fund for the Republic did was the investigation and the publication of the Cogley report. Cogley ran down and identified all of these culprits that were involved in blacklisting." Although the Cogley report did not end blacklisting in the entertainment industry, it contributed to its ultimate demise. Perhaps its most important contribution was to provide critical information which attorney Louis Nizer was able to use with devastating effect in the John Henry Faulk suit against AWARE, Inc. Faulk later confirmed that Nizer's legal team "made good use of [Cogley's] book in assembling the evidence for our case. And in no instance did we find him inaccurate."[27]

CHAPTER 28

"Ripe for Plucking"

The Political Civil War in Texas Continues, 1956–1957

While J. R. Parten worked to defend the Fund for the Republic from HUAC and its allies, he continued to be involved in the political maneuvering back in Texas as the 1956 elections approached. On March 7, Sam Rayburn issued a public statement calling on Lyndon Johnson to lead the Texas delegation to the national convention and to serve as the state's favorite-son candidate for the presidential nomination. It was obvious to Rayburn that Allan Shivers once again intended to control the Texas delegation to the national Democratic convention, which would give him an opportunity to repeat his performance of 1952 and work for an Eisenhower reelection. Rayburn had no intention of conceding party control to Shivers. He loathed the governor and wanted to destroy him politically. Parten assured Rayburn that the liberal faction would not fight Johnson's bid for control. Pledging his personal support, Parten stressed that Shivers had been tarnished by the scandals in his administration and was "ripe for plucking." Rayburn agreed. "Shivers is an angry, confused, frustrated man and can feel his ship going down," Rayburn told Parten. "If we all work like we should we will give Mr. Shivers a good beating in the May Convention." Rayburn's strategy dismayed many of the Texas liberals, but they were forced to cooperate in order to prevent Shivers from controlling the delegation.[1]

Shivers refused to relinquish control to Rayburn and Johnson. In the weeks prior to the party's precinct conventions, where delegates would be elected to the state convention, he travelled throughout Texas denouncing Johnson and Rayburn as "ultra liberals" who were captives of "radical" special-interest groups such as the NAACP, the CIO, and the Americans for Democratic Action. He compared Rayburn to Mexican military dictator Santa Anna, one of the arch villains of Texas history. Rayburn responded in kind, calling Shivers an expert in "rat alley politics." The Johnson-Rayburn forces, boosted by critical support from the liberal faction, were able to out-organize the Shivercrats at the grassroots level. Parten worked with his friend and fellow oil man Jim Abercrombie as cochairman of the campaign that succeeded in winning the Harris County precincts for Johnson in early May.[2]

The grassroots victory did not result in harmony within the anti-Shivers coalition, however. By supporting Johnson against Shivers, the liberals had assumed that they would receive a share of the party's offices, including one of the national committee positions. In addition, they did not want to pledge support beyond the first ballot for Johnson's favorite-son bid for president at the national convention. Johnson insisted that the Texas delegation pledge to vote for his candidacy on every ballot. He also had no intention of letting the liberals strengthen their faction by taking party offices.[3]

When Parten and Marlin Sandlin travelled to Dallas on May 20 as delegates from Harris County, they were shocked to learn that Johnson's convention manager, John B. Connally, would nominate Beryl "B. A." Bentsen, the wife of Lloyd Bentsen Jr., to serve in one of the national-committee posts. Parten knew that Bentsen, whose husband was a member of the Rayburn-Johnson group, was unacceptable to the liberals who were expecting to elect Frankie Randolph to the national committee. Parten was not committed to the idea of having one of the liberals appointed to the national committee, but, because of the land scandals in the Rio Grande valley in which her father-in-law had been deeply involved, he had strong reservations about a possible Bentsen nomination. Now that the Shivercrats had been vanquished, Parten did not want the loyalists to have any connection with the land scandals. He knew that B. A. Bentsen and her husband had not been involved with the land deal, but feared the liberals would raise the issue when they fought her nomination. He also felt that the national-committee post should go to a woman who had been active in Democratic Party affairs, which B. A. Bentsen had not been. Parten worried that a bitter fight at the convention over the nomination could split the party so badly that it could seriously damage Yarborough's next campaign for governor and destroy any chance the Democrats might have to win Texas in the presidential election in November.

Parten voiced these concerns to John Connally, whom he had known from Connally's days as a student organizer at the University of Texas during the Thompson campaign for governor in 1938. Parten had played a role in bringing the twenty-two-year-old Connally to Lyndon Johnson's attention in the spring of 1939, when Johnson had asked Parten for the names of some talented young men for his congressional staff. "John had impressed me as a gifted young man with a lot of potential," Parten recalled. "I thought he might be just what Lyndon needed." He also helped Connally secure a commission in the Naval Reserve in 1940. Although he and Connally had travelled in different circles in recent years and had not been close, they were still friends. Connally confirmed that Johnson wanted Bentsen on the national committee. "Mrs. Bentsen is undoubtedly one of the finest ladies in Texas," Parten replied, "but there is going to be some complaint against her because of those Rio Grande valley land fraud cases." Connally assured Parten that Bentsen's nomination "was taken care of," there would be no fight over it.[4]

When he attended some of the county caucuses the next night, however, Parten discovered that the liberals were planning a serious challenge to Bentsen's nomination. He decided to head off the confrontation. Rayburn was unable to help because he was in Bonham to be with his dying sister, Lucinda. Parten tried to call Johnson, but he was unable to get through to him. So he went back to Connally and warned him that there was going to be a fight over the nomination and that Bentsen might not win. He argued that if Connally dropped Bentsen, he did not have to replace her with Frankie Randolph or one of the other liberals. He could nominate the most conservative woman in the party, so long as it was someone who had been active in party affairs and was not a "card carrying" Shivercrat. "Well, it's too late now," Connally responded, "and besides, I've got the votes to do the job."[5]

At the convention on May 22, the coalition of Johnson-Rayburn forces and liberal factions outnumbered the Shivercrats by a three-to-one margin and took control of the party. As Parten had feared, however, the liberals fought Bentsen's nomination. They attracted enough votes (Parten's among them) to force Bentsen's withdrawal and to elect Frankie Randolph. Although Johnson won control of the Texas delegation to the national convention, Bentsen's defeat angered and embarrassed him. He later complained that he had been "double crossed" and "out maneuvered" by the liberals, whom he characterized as "the extremists." Johnson never forgave the liberals for the defeat, nor did they forgive or forget his attempt to shut them out after using them to take the party away from Shivers. Johnson's strategy, which Parten blamed partly on Connally's "arrogance," alienated the liberals and greatly exacerbated the factional problems within the state party, problems that grew worse at the next state convention in September.[6]

"Just a good middle of the road candidate"

Ralph Yarborough remained aloof from the party's factional squabble. Loyally and zealously supported by the liberal faction, Yarborough needed help from the Rayburn-Johnson moderates if he was going to prevail in his third attempt to be governor. Making his own move toward the moderates, Parten encouraged Yarborough not to do anything to alienate them. He advised Yarborough to step away from his "labor-liberal" reputation. "I would suggest that, whenever possible," Parten said, "you re-emphasize that you are *just a good middle of the road candidate.*"[7]

The 1956 gubernatorial race acquired an unanticipated dimension when Shivers announced that he would not run for reelection. A scandal in the Texas Veterans Land Program involving the bribery of land commissioner Bascom Giles and other Land Office employees had damaged Shivers's reputation, though he was never directly connected to the affair. Yarborough's main opponent was now U.S. senator Price Daniel, who was certain to be backed by the Shivers organization.

Complicating the race was the unexpected entry of former governor and senator W. Lee O'Daniel and right-wing conservative J. Evetts Haley. O'Daniel remained popular in the rural areas of Texas, while Haley was sure to draw votes from the conservative bastions in the Panhandle and High Plains of West Texas.[8]

Parten did not participate as actively in this campaign as he had in the previous two. Throughout the early summer of 1956, he focused on his business and his embroilment in the Fund for the Republic's fight with HUAC. Nevertheless, at several critical junctures in the campaign, Parten provided badly needed cash. He sent Yarborough a thousand dollar check, for example, to prevent the telephones in Yarborough's headquarters in Austin from being cut off. Heeding Parten's advice, Yarborough took to the middle of the road, campaigning in favor of increased funding for schools and public health, soil and water conservation, and an anti-lobby law, and avoiding the sensitive issue of racial integration. Nevertheless, Price Daniel easily won a plurality in the election on July 28, beating the second-place Yarborough by approximately 160,000 votes. Daniel failed to win a majority of the votes cast, however, and a runoff election was required.[9]

To Parten's surprise, Pappy O'Daniel threw his support to Yarborough in the runoff election, allowing him to attract a significant number of O'Daniel's rural supporters, especially in East Texas. As a result, Yarborough went slightly ahead of Price Daniel in the polls. His money problems continued, however. In the final week of the campaign, Parten had to rush two thousand dollars to Yarborough to keep the campaign afloat. Yarborough threw a fright into the Texas Democratic establishment, but he lost the runoff by a narrow margin. In an election marred by allegations of widespread voter fraud, Yarborough lost by less than four thousand votes out of nearly 1.4 million cast.[10]

The 1956 National Democratic Convention

During the first week of the gubernatorial runoff campaign in Texas, Parten's attention switched to Chicago and the Democratic national convention. Parten and Marlin Sandlin went to Chicago as members of the Texas delegation pledged to support Lyndon Johnson's presidential candidacy. Johnson's chances depended on the unlikely event of a deadlocked convention. Outwardly, Parten was a fully involved activist for Lyndon Johnson, working with his convention team to lobby other delegations in favor of a Johnson nomination. Despite his efforts on the floor of the convention on behalf of Johnson (and on behalf of a united loyalist effort in Texas in the presidential campaign), Parten knew that the senator from Texas would not be able to beat Adlai Stevenson, who was actually Parten's preferred candidate. "Stevenson was a real Democrat," Parten later observed. "He made a fine Governor of Illinois. He was just a civilized man and well educated man who used his talents admirably. Lyndon was not in the same league." Rayburn knew how Parten really felt, but he did not scold him because Rayburn was also strong for Stevenson. The Speaker never believed Johnson had a chance to get the nomination in 1956, but had pushed him to be the favorite-son candidate as part of the strategy to gain control of the party organization in Texas. Before leaving for

Left to right, Lloyd Bentsen, Sam Rayburn, and John Connally at the 1956 National Democratic Convention in Chicago. *CN 07780. Courtesy Rayburn Photograph Collection, CAH.*

Chicago, Parten had written a letter to Stevenson to assure him that "while we in Texas are pledged to support the candidacy of . . . Senator Johnson . . . I predict that you will receive the nomination upon an early ballot with the support of Texas." Parten confirmed this view in several chats with Stevenson during the convention and served as one of Stevenson's confidential informants from inside the Texas delegation.[11]

Stevenson won the nomination on the first ballot, with Lyndon Johnson placing a poor third behind New York governor Averell Harriman. When Stevenson instructed the convention to select its own candidate for vice president, Parten followed Johnson's and Rayburn's lead and voted with his fellow Texans for Sen. John F. Kennedy, who eventually lost the nomination to Tennessee senator Estes Kefauver. At a campaign finance meeting after the nominees had been selected, Stevenson asked Parten to serve as finance chairman of his campaign in Texas. Parten promised to give it serious consideration, but after he returned to Texas, he told Rayburn that someone else should take the job. "I am 'tarred with the brushes' of being 'too soft' on labor and of being a liberal," he explained to Rayburn. "I know that the large potential givers in Texas will do more for a Chairman of Finance who has not been so prominently identified with the liberal wing of the Party." Pledging to "work in the ranks" and a personal contribution of ten thousand dollars, Parten advised Rayburn to find "a prominent conservative Democrat

471

who would be more effective" in raising money. He did, however, accept an appointment as a member of the national finance committee and allowed his name to be used in the national campaign as a member of "Business Men for Stevenson and Kefauver ."[12]

"I have never heard anyone talk as strongly to Lyndon Johnson"

In September, Parten and Sandlin went to Fort Worth as delegates to the state Democratic convention. The liberals intended to use their majority to unseat the Shivercrats who had held on to their positions on the State Democratic Executive Committee. Although Parten had moved away from the liberals, he supported their request for seats on the state committee as fair and deserving. Lyndon Johnson, however, had other ideas. Stung by his defeat in the battle over the B. A. Bentsen appointment in May and desperate to keep the liberals from controlling the state's party machinery, Johnson decided to steal the convention. He packed the credentials committee with his allies, who subsequently seated conservative county delegations in place of the legally elected liberals. Connally confessed many years later that he and Johnson had "pulled one of the lowest stunts that had ever been pulled . . . it was a brutal display of raw power."[13]

Among those delegations denied credentials was the one led by Frankie Randolph from Harris County, which included Marlin Sandlin. Parten, who was a member of the unchallenged Madison County delegation, sneaked Sandlin into the convention as an alternate from Madison County. When Sandlin went to the area where Frankie Randolph and the other members of the Harris County delegation were supposed to be seated, he found it full of Texas Regulars and Shivercrats. Randolph, the newly elected national committeewoman, had been locked out of the convention. Outraged, Parten complained to Rayburn that Johnson's vendetta would destroy the party's efforts to form a united front in Texas. "Lyndon's backstage," Rayburn replied, "go talk to him. Tell him what you think." Parten found Johnson sitting on a table, "dangling his feet and enjoying himself." Parten confronted the senator. "Mister, you're making the biggest mistake of your life here," Parten warned, "allowing Frankie Randolph to stand out there in the foyer and refusing to let her delegation be seated. Lyndon, it is the legal delegation, unqualifiedly." Johnson smiled and said, "I've got Connally in charge of this thing, and I'm just going to let him run it. Frankie Randolph and her gang of 'red hots' should have stayed in line last May." Parten shook his finger in Johnson's face and declared, "you're going to pay for it. You just brace yourself." A witness to this backstage scene remembered it vividly many years later: "I have never heard anyone talk as strongly to Lyndon Johnson. Parten just chewed him out." Parten admitted to Rayburn that he had gotten "nowhere" with Johnson. "He just brushed me off, and said that he's paying Frankie Randolph off. Johnson's making wounds that will take many years to heal." Rayburn, no fan of the liberals and clearly comfortable with Johnson's strategy, said nothing.[14]

Johnson routed the liberals and elected a conservative state committee, but, as Parten had warned, it cost him dearly. The liberal faction in Texas never again trusted Johnson. They would hound and harass him until the end of his political career. Parten always believed that John F. Kennedy's near defeat in Texas in 1960 was the result of the hatred Texas liberals had for his running mate, Lyndon Johnson. As for Parten, Johnson's betrayal of the liberals and his treatment of Frankie Randolph pushed him away from Johnson and back toward the liberal camp.

Peace or Extinction?

Months before the nation's voters actually cast their ballots, the presidential election of 1956 was over. Facing an enormously popular incumbent president and hampered by a lackluster effort by his own party, Adlai Stevenson never had a chance. In Texas, there was no doubt about who would carry the state. Stevenson did not even bother to visit Texas during the campaign. Generally ignoring Stevenson, Lyndon Johnson and most of the congressional Democrats worked on behalf of Democratic candidates for Congress. Democratic control of the Senate and Johnson's position as majority leader were in danger because of the narrow Democratic majority.

Parten genuinely believed that Stevenson would make a better president than Eisenhower. He especially admired Stevenson's courageous stance against the testing of nuclear weapons. Since the dropping of the atomic bombs on Japan, Parten had been concerned about the threat of nuclear war. Stevenson's pledge to stop nuclear testing and to cease the effort to build ever-larger thermonuclear bombs resulted in widespread public discussion of the issue, educating Parten and many others on the dangers such testing posed to public health as well as on the insanity of creating weapons that, if ever used, would extinguish life on earth. It was a concern of Parten's that deepened as the nuclear-arms race escalated in the coming years. Because of Parten's admiration for Stevenson, he did what he could for his campaign, donating money and helping with fund-raising. Parten gave Marlin Sandlin the difficult assignment of raising money from Houston's oil men, the vast majority of whom disliked Stevenson as much as they admired Dwight Eisenhower, and Sandlin's efforts produced a grand total of $3,750, of which $2,000 was a donation from Parten.[15]

Stevenson lost to Eisenhower in a landslide. Eisenhower carried Texas by a larger margin than he had in 1952. The liberal faction blamed Stevenson's poor showing in Texas on Johnson and his dictatorial methods at the state convention the previous September, but Stevenson's campaign was doomed in Texas no matter what had happened at the convention. Despite Stevenson's overwhelming defeat, the Democrats maintained their majorities in both houses of Congress. Rayburn admitted to Parten that the election "proved that the people wanted Eisenhower, and it also proved that they do not want the Republicans." Parten wrote Stevenson to congratulate him for the "good fight" he had waged in the face of insurmountable odds. "You cannot beat a myth with a man," Parten stressed, adding that the nation was "heavily indebted" to him for his stand against nuclear testing. Parten assured the defeated candidate, that his "advocacy . . . for an international agreement to cease hydrogen bomb testing was nothing short of bold and courageous statesmanship for which future generations will remember and reward you." Stevenson's discussion of the nuclear issue had brought to light the fact that the military had hidden from the American public important information about the harmful effects of nuclear fallout. "It is simply unthinkable that . . . the military in this Democracy . . . should have kept the people so totally ignorant of the shocking implications of our continued building and testing of bigger and bigger hydrogen bombs," Parten told Stevenson.

Parten urged Rayburn to continue Stevenson's fight on the nuclear-testing issue. Rayburn, who had played a key role in winning congressional support for the appropriations necessary to develop the atom bomb during World War II, agreed with Parten, at least in private. "I do not see why President Eisenhower does not try to get these people together to stop the testing, and get an agreement not to use the hydrogen bomb in a future war," Rayburn told Parten, adding that "we must have peace or probably extinction."[16]

"Major . . . you have had the courage to stand against the tide"

Sen. Price Daniel's narrow defeat of Ralph Yarborough in the August 1956 Texas primary meant that a special election would have to be held in April 1957 to select someone to serve out the remaining two years of Daniel's term in the Senate. The special election presented an exceptional opportunity for Yarborough and his liberal backers. Unlike in the party primary, the winner would be whoever attracted the most votes, no matter how small the percentage of the total. If Yarborough could preserve his core of loyal supporters and if more than one major conservative candidate ran against him, Yarborough could win with only a minority of the vote. That was exactly what happened. Conservative Democratic congressman Martin Dies Jr. and Republican activist Thad Hutcheson also entered the race (along with twenty-one other minor Democratic candidates) and split the conservative vote. When an effort by conservative Democrats failed to get Dies to withdraw in favor of Lt. Gov. Ben Ramsey, an attempt was made to repeal the state law governing special elections and replace it with one requiring a runoff election in the event that no candidate won a majority of the votes. Johnson and Rayburn, fearful that a runoff might result in Hutcheson's election and thereby give the Republicans control of the Senate, did not support the effort to repeal the election law. It was subsequently defeated by a close vote in the legislature.[17]

Parten was among those who urged Yarborough to enter the special election campaign. Excited by the possibility of Yarborough going to the Senate, Parten devoted most of March 1957 raising funds for the campaign. He also purchased several hundred copies of the official Yarborough biographical campaign book and an equal number of the *Texas Observer* issue (February 19, 1957) endorsing Yarborough's election. He distributed both in several East Texas counties. Parten's help was not needed in Harris County because of the organizing work of Frankie Randolph and her liberal activists, who were able to mount an effective campaign for Yarborough in Houston. The newly formed "Democrats of Texas," which had been created by the liberal faction in reaction to Johnson's "theft" of the party machinery at the convention in September 1956, teamed with labor to give Yarborough a more highly organized campaign than he had enjoyed in previous election efforts.[18]

Yarborough won the election with 38 percent of the vote to Dies's 28 percent and Hutcheson's 23 percent. Parten was elated. "Your election has made ten's of thousands of your friends very happy," Parten told him, noting that he was "going into high office with as little obligation to pressure groups as any person who was ever elected in Texas." As for himself, Parten emphasized to the senator-elect that he had only one favor to ask. "For the little I have done for you, I will be amply repaid if you . . . make a good senator for all the people." Yarborough's victory was celebrated by liberal Democrats throughout the country. "Good news from Texas this morning," Ping Ferry proclaimed from his office at the Fund for the Republic in New York. "I mark it down as a straight 100% Parten triumph." Rayburn told Parten that "it was surely a fine showing you folks made for Yarborough . . . I think Ralph will make a good Senator." Parten knew that Rayburn would be supportive of Yarborough, but he was less confident about Johnson. He wrote Johnson the day after the election, stressing that Yarborough would need "a lot of help and I am sure you will cheerfully help him." Johnson replied that he had "talked to Ralph Yarborough on the phone and assured him that it will be my pleasure to cooperate with him all I can."[19]

Yarborough had finally tasted victory and he knew who was at the top of the list of people to thank. In a letter written a few weeks after the election, Yarborough stated: "Major, in 1952 you pledged two-thirds of all the money we had pledged over the State. . . . In the 1954 campaign, you . . . made it possible for me to announce . . . . You have had the courage to stand against the tide of the overwhelming majority of businessmen. Through one hard campaign after another you threw your continuing support on the side of good government in Texas and by your dedication . . . you have . . . played a major role in the victory we have won."[20]

CHAPTER 29

Victory at Last and the End of Woodley

1957–1961

T he last half of the 1950s was probably the happiest time in the Parten marriage. Patsy was actively involved in community affairs and had a wide circle of friends within Houston's River Oaks society. Patsy and J. R. belonged to an informal social group called the "Tuesday Club." During the evening on that day each week, the Partens joined Bill and Louise Moran and several prominent Houston physicians and their wives for dinner, drinks, and conversation at the home of one of the club's members. Patsy was artistically inclined and a painter. Dr. Lee Clark, the executive director of the University of Texas M. D. Anderson Cancer Hospital, lived next door to the Partens in River Oaks. When Patsy complained that the children's ward was "a dreary old place that no child would want to stay in," Clark invited Patsy's help, and she subsequently spent numerous hours painting nursery rhymes and figures on the walls in the children's wards at the hospital. She also spent much time as a volunteer designing and decorating the stage sets for plays at St. John's, the Episcopalian school where her daughter "Pepe" went to school.[1]

For the only time in his life, J. R. Parten was living the life of a millionaire oil man. He and Patsy bought the most expensive and fashionable clothes; they ate gourmet food and flew in private airplanes and each had a Cadillac. In 1955, they leased the huge three-story Heitman mansion in an exclusive neighborhood near Rice University called Shady Side. Randy Parten later remembered it as a "castle" of a house with a fish pond and a garden in the back, a three-car garage, and servants' quarters. The Partens employed two maids and a chauffeur, as well as a full-time governess for Randy. At the old family house in Madisonville where they spent weekends, they employed a full-time groundskeeper, handyman, and cook named Luther Johnson, who had been released from the state prison to work for the Partens.[2]

Parten's wealthy lifestyle reflected great success in his three principal business ventures: the Woodley Oil Company, the Great Northern Company, and—the biggest surprise of all—the Pan American Sulphur Company.

"There comes a time when you have to separate the men from the boys"

The Pan American Sulphur Company had entered the world sulphur market with a strength that stunned the established sulphur companies. Sitting on top of a mountain of easily extractable brimstone and led by the irrepressible and shrewd Harry Webb and his talented management team, Pan American was no longer an investment lark put together almost as an afterthought by the Little Mothers at the Dallas Athletic Club. It was now a major corporation playing an influential role in the international sulphur market, with shipments of its powdered yellow stone floating in the holds of ships scattered from Australia to Europe. As Harry Webb told the *Wall Street Journal,* the company had gone "beyond anything we dreamed about." Much of the company's success had been the result of fortunate geology, a world hunger for more and more sulphur, an arrogant competition, and a fair amount of hard work, tenaciousness, and sheer gall.[3]

By the mid-1950s, Pan American's Jaltipan plant was producing sulphur in significant amounts, thanks largely to Pan American's chemist, Dr. Frederick Gormley, who had developed a new filtration process to improve the quality of the company's product. The company now was providing all the sulphur the Mexican domestic market could absorb. That was a relatively small portion of Pan American's output, however, and the company was piling up a large amount of sulphur on the ground. It was obvious to Parten that the company had to attract customers from outside Mexico. He understood that Pan American would not be able to break the competition's hold on the U.S. market quickly enough to make much of a dent in their growing stockpile of brimstone. Instead, he turned his attention to markets in Europe and Australia. Bypassing the United States still left Pan American with a difficult task. The Texas Gulf Sulphur Company and the Freeport Sulphur Company also had a solid lock on most of the western European and British Commonwealth markets. "We knew that unseating those . . . companies, even to a partial extent, was going to be damn difficult," Leonard Townsend recalled.[4]

In the summer of 1954, Pan American devised a strategy for breaking into the European market . The dominant sulphur companies had kept the export price of sulphur at a steady thirty-one dollars per ton and European sulphur consumers were eager to find a cheaper alternative source. Parten calculated that Pan American's lower production costs would allow it to export its sulphur profitably at about twenty-nine dollars per ton. Offering lower prices and backed by a stockpile of two hundred thousand tons of sulphur, Parten launched an audacious but successful campaign to win supply contracts away from Texas Gulf and Freeport

Harry Webb and Parten inspecting Pan American Sulphur plant. *CN 09620. Courtesy Parten Photograph Collection, CAH.*

Sulphur. Within eighteen months, Pan American was selling sulphur in twenty-seven countries on six continents, most of it going to Europe.[5]

The company's success caught the complacent competition by surprise. *Fortune* magazine noted that Pan American had sneaked up on the "slumbering giants of the sulphur industry" and created "panic and havoc." Freeport and Texas Gulf quickly struck back. In February 1956, they lowered their export price to twenty-eight dollars per ton in an attempt to drive the upstart Pan American out of the market. Parten was not that easily cowed. Pan American not only cut its price to match its competition, it also entered the U.S. East Coast market where Texas Gulf had previously enjoyed no competition. Pan American staked its campaign on the advantage it had over Texas Gulf in transportation costs. U.S. maritime law required domestic companies to use U.S. flagships to transport to domestic markets. Pan American's Mexican subsidiary, however, could ship sulphur to the United States on foreign flag vessels, taking advantage of much cheaper transportation prices. Lower shipping expenses allowed Pan American to undercut Texas Gulf by about $1.50 per ton. The strategy was a stunning success, and Pan American's total shipments more than doubled by the end of 1956.[6]

Faced with a substantial drop in earnings resulting from Pan American's intrusion into its formerly tightly controlled market, Texas Gulf's president, Fred Nelson, decided to go after his unwelcome competitors with a vengeance. In

September 1957, Nelson cut Texas Gulf's domestic price by three dollars per ton, explaining to his associates that "there comes a time when you have to separate the men from the boys." Freeport and Jefferson Lake cut their export price by the same amount. Pan American immediately matched its competitors' reductions, initiating a major international price-war. When considering their attack on Pan American, Texas Gulf and Freeport had failed to understand two crucial factors. First was the generally bad image they had with their customers because of decades of monopolistic practices. Pan American not only retained the customers it had, it continued to attract new ones. The second factor was J. R. Parten. As one of Pan American's executives later noted, Parten was the "guiding genius of the company." He made certain that Pan American was extremely cost-efficient in its operations, making it possible for the company to hold its own in a cutthroat price war against an "infamous monopoly."[7]

In February 1958, the *Wall Street Journal* reported that in the last two years Pan American had tripled its share of the U.S. market and had "bitten a sizeable chunk out of U.S. sulphur companies' sales." Money flowed to its happy shareholders as the company's earnings soared from twenty cents per share in 1955 to $1.50 by the end of 1958. Texas Gulf's net income dropped from twenty-eight million dollars in 1957 to eighteen million in 1958, while Pan American's net income had risen sharply during the same period. Fred Nelson not only lost the price-cutting war, he also lost his job. Pan American was going to survive and its competitors were forced to live with that fact. Aided greatly by the company's innovative development of a method to ship sulphur while it was still in the molten state, Pan American had garnered approximately 14 percent of the world market and was entrenched in third place among the world's sulphur companies by the end of the 1950s.[8]

"Uncle Billy" Moran and the Fight for Control of Woodley

At the beginning of 1958, Parten's first love, the Woodley Petroleum Company, was also prospering. The company had just completed the best year in its thirty-six-year history. Net income was up nearly 50 percent over the previous year and daily production was increasing, mainly in Woodley's prolific Weyburn field in Saskatchewan, which was supplying ten thousand barrels of crude oil a day to the Great Northern refinery in Saint Paul. The company's Canadian operations were highly profitable, aided by the low cost of production and the ability to pipe its production into the United States without having to pay import taxes. Because of Woodley's favorable cash flow and some promising new fields in West Texas, Parten decided in early 1958 to significantly expand the company's exploration. He told the *Wall Street Journal* that it was "a good time to look for oil."[9]

Despite this happy situation, storm clouds loomed on the horizon. There were fewer possibilities for discovering major fields in the United States and many companies were being forced into offshore and foreign exploration, requiring enormous financial resources not only to finance such ventures but to survive the dry holes. The major oil companies were also importing much more oil from the Middle East and buying less crude from small producers like Woodley. The company had a reliable market for some of its production because of its Great Northern Refining operation in Saint Paul, but it was difficult to find additional markets. As a result of these factors and some wildcat failures in West Texas, the company had a steep decline in earnings for the first quarter of 1958.[10]

These problems plus the need for capital to expand his personal ventures in the natural gas business, convinced Woodley director Bill Moran that it was time to sell the company. A wave of mergers was sweeping the oil industry and Moran wanted Woodley to take advantage of a seller's market. As one of the three largest stockholders, Moran stood to make an enormous profit on his Woodley holdings. Moran was also frustrated by Parten's reinvestment of most of Woodley's profits back into the company's operations. Although it was one reason for the company's sound financial condition, the policy gave much smaller dividends to Woodley's shareholders. With his huge block of Woodley stock, Moran felt that he was being denied a substantial income. He understood, however, that Woodley would never be sold as long as J. R. Parten was in command. The company was Parten's pride and joy, his sense of self was largely defined by its existence. His feelings for Woodley, which he viewed as his personal creation (certainly the company as it existed in 1958 was of his making) were deeply, almost soulfully, entrenched.[11]

The two men had been friends for decades. Moran was the godfather of J. R.'s only son, Randy. He and Moran—"Uncle Billy" to Randy—had been especially close when Randy was a child. "He was a very loveable man," Randy recalled, "he didn't pass a kid on the street that he didn't talk to." Despite his relationship with Randy, Moran had never really been a member of Parten's inner circle. The two were opposites in personality. Moran was an extrovert and a major risk-taker. "He was Irish and had a little bit of the gambler in him," recalled Dallas Sherman. "J. R. was very quiet about what he did, Moran was a little more show-offish, a little bit more glamorous . . . much more of a backslapper." Parten had other close friends who had similar traits, but they had something Moran did not—Parten's trust. His personal secretary warned Parten one day in the office, "I don't know how you feel, but I wouldn't trust Mr. Moran as far as I could throw him." Parten nodded as he replied, "I know. I watch him pretty close."[12]

Early in 1958, Moran decided to launch a secret campaign to take control away from Parten. It was a gamble, but Moran knew that if he could enlist the help of one particular individual his goal could be accomplished. J. R. Parten was no longer the largest individual owner of Woodley stock—Bill Moran was. Parten had given half his Woodley stock to Opal at the time of their breakup in 1947. According to the divorce settlement, J. R. had control over Opal's votes at stockholder meetings for a period of ten years. That arrangement ended in 1958 and Opal took control of the stock and became a board member. Moran, who had maintained a close friendship with Opal and Dallas Sherman since the divorce, went to Opal with his plan. He tried to persuade Opal that selling Woodley would richly benefit everyone, including J. R. Parten. He pleaded with her to join forces with him to seize control of the company from J. R. so that Woodley could be placed on the market. Opal rejected Moran's invitation. "Opal never urged anybody to do anything that she thought was contrary to what J. R. wanted," Sherman says, "she was very true to J. R. in that way." One of Parten's longtime employees agreed: "Opal gave her solemn word that she would never vote against J. R. Her loyalty to him was indestructible."[13]

Naively, Moran apparently believed that Opal would not tell Parten about his plan. Opal's revelation, however, did not come as a complete surprise to Parten. He had been approached recently by several brokers and oil men asking him to consider selling Woodley, so he knew someone on the inside was stirring up the offers. Parten realized that he could not ignore Moran's efforts because he did not have absolute control of the majority of Woodley's stock. Moran's block was large enough to cause real trouble, especially if he could ally himself with other board members. "He . . . thought he was losing control of the company," his former secretary said. "He knew that he had better do something."[14]

Parten decided that if Woodley was going to be sold or merged, he would be the one to decide when, how, and to whom. He was also determined to arrange the sale or merger himself, without the services of brokers, whom he considered to be parasites. He simply could not abide the thought of paying huge commissions to brokers for doing a job he was quite capable of doing himself. He suspected that Moran, in contacting prospective buyers on his own, was hoping to collect special finders' fees. For most of the last months of 1958 and without Moran's knowledge, Parten quietly went to work to find his own deal.[15]

Another Yarborough Victory

While Parten sought a buyer for Woodley, he also gave some attention to an important political matter in 1958, the reelection of Ralph Yarborough to a full six-year term in the U.S. Senate. As usual, Parten's major contribution to Yarborough's campaign was as a financial backer, fund-raiser, and advisor. Unlike in his previous campaigns, however, Yarborough was an incumbent, so his reelection effort had more media attention and a better organization. His main opponent was William "Dollar Bill" Blakely, a multimillionaire conservative who had served a caretaker appointment to the Senate in 1957 during the months between Price Daniel's resignation and the special election.[16]

Parten joined with Fagan Dickson and Walter Hall to help form a statewide finance committee for Yarborough. At the committee's first meeting on May 17 in Austin, Parten helped formulate a general fund-raising program and a campaign strategy. As he had with previous races, he again urged Yarborough to campaign as a "middle-of-the-road" Texan who cared about basic bread-and-butter issues important to the average citizen and who was "sound" on issues of importance to the oil and gas industry. This strategy was adopted. Parten also wrote statements for Yarborough's use that praised the oil depletion allowance and called for the removal of controls on the price of natural gas at the wellhead. Yarborough told Parten that his "sage advice" was invaluable and that he had received "a great deal of benefit from . . . the wisdom and the warnings of old heads like you and Walter Hall. . . ."[17]

Parten worked hard to keep money flowing to Austin to pay Yarborough's campaign bills. In mid-June, after Parten sent Dickson a personal check for two thousand dollars attached to a note promising more later, Dickson replied that money was "coming in slower than I had anticipated; people are pleading hard times." Parten quickly responded with an additional five hundred dollars. Later, when Dickson reported that the campaign had bills totalling nine thousand dollars but no money with which to pay them, Parten went to work. He coaxed a thousand dollar contribution from his Pan American partner Roland Bond, who was an active Republican. He also solicited Houston millionaire and Democratic Party loyalist Will Clayton, who was upset by Yarborough's support for import tariffs, especially on oil. His involvement in Canadian oil had converted Parten into a free-trade man, even on oil, which was a complete turnaround from his position in the 1930s. "I know Yarborough is not fully in accord with us on free international trade," Parten stated, "but I think . . . he will come ultimately to our side." Clayton proved to be a hard sell at first. "You and I have nearly always thought alike on politics and many other things, and I have always been proud of that fact," Clayton told Parten. "I regret, however, that . . . I can't contribute. . . . I haven't been too pleased with his performance since he got in the Senate. . . ."[18]

Bill Blakely proved to be Yarborough's best campaign asset. His campaign stressed, almost to the exclusion of anything else, his right-wing views on racial integration, federal aid to education, and labor unions. Politically, the nation (and Texas with it) was moving into one of its more liberal phases and right-wing rhetoric such as Blakely was spouting had lost some appeal. His attack on federal aid to education, for example, was especially ill conceived in light of the general concern about the Soviet Union's successful launch of the Sputnik satellite. The situation had caused widespread public demand for increased funding for educational programs in science and mathematics. After one of Blakely's ill-informed statements on foreign policy appeared in the Houston newspapers, Clayton sent a check for a thousand dollars to Parten. Clayton told Parten that Yarborough's "position generally on foreign policy is so much more enlightened than that of [Blakely] that I have reluctantly made up my mind to help him.[19]

Parten also urged Sam Rayburn to endorse Yarborough, but the Speaker was reluctant to openly favor a candidate in a Democratic Party primary. A few days later, Rayburn received a donation of ten thousand dollars from Blakely for his library in Bonham. Attached to the check was a note pleading that no publicity be released about the donation. Rayburn believed that the donation was Blakely's attempt to buy his support. "Mr. Rayburn was offended by the timing of the donation," Parten recalled. "He told me that an announcement of his support for Yarborough would be released to the press, and it was." Rayburn's involvement in the campaign went beyond a simple endorsement. He and Parten frequently consulted on Yarborough's strategy, and Rayburn occasionally sent specific advice directly to the campaign. A Yarborough worker in Temple wrote Parten near the end of the campaign to thank him for his "valuable counsel. Ralph listened to it, knowing it came from you, and the same advice was relayed to him from Mr.

Rayburn. In fact, the similarity was so marked that I suspect you had a few words with the Speaker."[20]

Not only did Yarborough have Rayburn's public endorsement, he had a benign Lyndon Johnson. As part of Johnson's strategy to improve his chances for the presidential nomination in 1960, he was working hard to improve his standing with the liberal Democrats in the Senate. Accordingly, the Yarborough campaign kept up its momentum. "The campaign is moving along smoother than any Yarborough race ever has," Dickson reported to Parten in mid-June. "Mr. Blakely is conducting a very strange type of campaign. In fact it is so quiet that it makes us uneasy lest something ominous is brewing." Parten urged Yarborough to continue "to take the high road as an incumbent U.S. Senator and not get involved in pettiness or anything that might get 'Dollar Bill's' name on the front page." Yarborough won reelection with relative ease.[21]

Pure Enters the Picture

With Ralph Yarborough safely back in the Senate, Parten turned his full attention to one of the most personally significant business transactions in which he would ever be involved—selling Woodley. In early 1959, Parten quietly and informally met with those members of the board he could trust (enough to constitute a majority) and received permission to explore the possibility of selling or merging the company. Neither Moran nor any of the employees were told about this approval, but rumors spread through the company, forcing Parten to issue a denial that the company was for sale. Parten's secretary assured her colleagues that Parten "would just as soon sell [his son] Randy as to give up Woodley."[22]

Despite Parten's denial, J. Porter Langfitt, an executive vice president with Pure Oil Company in Chicago, knew something was going on. He was aware that Moran had talked to brokers in New York, and there were strong rumors that the Atlantic Oil Company had held meetings with Parten. Langfitt had met Parten during the PAW days and thought well of his skills as an oil executive. He viewed Woodley as one of the best-managed independent companies in the country. Woodley's net assets, which included 379 oil wells producing more than 10,000 barrels per day, totalled an estimated $75 million. Woodley also owned exploration rights to 600,000 acres of land and a one-third interest in the Great Northern refinery and 530 miles of pipelines stretching from Saskatchewan to Minnesota. It was Woodley's reserves, estimated to be approximately 75 million barrels of crude oil and 70 billion cubic feet of gas, that Langfitt especially coveted. Pure, an integrated oil company producing more than 60,000 barrels of oil a day, was a much larger company than Woodley, but its exploration program had not gone well. Pure desperately needed new oil reserves to keep its extensive refining and aggressive marketing program going.[23]

In July 1959, Langfitt approached Parten about a possible merger with Pure. Parten reacted favorably. He respected Langfitt and two of Langfitt's colleagues at Pure, chief geologist Ira Cram, a man Parten and many others in the industry considered to be one of the best oil-finders in the business, and Harris Van Zandt,

Pure's vice president for production. Parten was aware of Pure's need for oil, which Woodley could supply, and he liked Pure's extensive retail-marketing network, an enterprise in which Woodley had never engaged. Parten told Langfitt to submit a formal proposal, but to keep their discussion confidential. Once he had made the decision to initiate negotiations with Pure, Parten informed only Sandlin and the technical advisors who would evaluate the Pure proposal. The negotiations with Pure, which would have been complex and tedious under the best of circumstances, were made much more difficult when Langfitt suffered a serious stroke a few weeks after the talks began. His recovery proved to be slow and incomplete, so Pure president Robert L. Milligan took over the secret negotiations with Parten early in the fall of 1959.[24]

Woodley Merges with Pure

Parten's negotiations with Milligan, which for the sake of secrecy were conducted in a hotel room in Dallas and in a tiny storeroom in Parten's office building in Houston, continued throughout the fall of 1959. By early November, they had agreed on the basic structure of the deal. Pure would acquire all of Woodley's assets except for its 50 percent share of 7-J Stock Farm. The stock in 7-J would be distributed among Woodley's shareholders. Pure would acquire Woodley by exchanging Pure stock for Woodley stock, which would allow the two companies to combine without Woodley's stockholders having to pay taxes on the increased value of their holdings. How much Pure stock would be exchanged for Woodley stock, however, remained the only major unresolved issue. Parten was prepared to accept 1.1 shares of Pure for 1 share of Woodley stock, but he was hoping to do better. Parten met with Milligan in Dallas and offered 1 share of Woodley for 1.6 shares of Pure. Milligan immediately countered with an offer of 1.2 shares of Pure for 1 of Woodley. After a lengthy discussion, Parten lowered his request to 1.5 shares of Pure and Milligan countered with 1.3. "Finally," Parten said, "Milligan complained that he had to be back in Chicago that evening for a dinner engagement with his wife, so he made a quick proposition with me to split my 1.5 with his 1.3 and take 1.4, and that's the way the deal was made. He left a lot on the table . . . under the pressure of having to take his wife to dinner." Although Parten was pleased with the deal, he wondered how well Pure was being managed.[25]

Before the merger could be made final, Parten asked for a seat on Pure's board of directors to represent Woodley's stockholders. He also insisted that Pure agree to retain most of Woodley's seventy employees in jobs equal to or better than their current ones. On New Year's Eve, 1959, Milligan agreed to both requests and the deal was made. Parten flew to Las Vegas on New Year's Day to tell a surprised Bill Moran about the merger. Upon his return to Houston, Parten called a special directors' meeting on January 4 to consider the agreement. Moran did not attend. Opal, who made a special trip to Houston for the meeting, made the motion to approve the merger. The news of the fifty-million-dollar Woodley-Pure merger surprised investment analysts. The Houston *Post* called the deal "one of the industry's best-kept secrets of the past six months." Although Parten felt Milligan had left too much on the table when making the deal for Pure, *Business Week* disagreed, noting that Pure Oil "not only gains additional reserves and an increase in its import quota but also . . . has worked out a favorable exchange of shares."[26]

Parten was deeply ambivalent about giving up Woodley. He felt that he had negotiated a good deal and that prevailing business conditions argued in favor of making such a move. He believed that it was going to be difficult for Woodley to survive without getting involved in high-risk foreign exploration and production. Such an expansion would require enormous resources beyond Woodley's means. He admitted that it would be best if Woodley's shareholders could move into a company that had its own refining facilities and marketing outlets. "The oil industry today finds itself in a desperate struggle for markets," Parten told a Woodley stockholder, "and what Woodley has done, in effect, is to buy into a good market situation. Pure is short on crude and long on markets. Woodley on the other hand has crude but no markets."[27]

Nevertheless, Parten hated to give up a company that he had built over a period of four decades. Unlike Premier, which was as much or more the creature of Sylvester Dayson, or Pan American, which was a Little Mothers project from the beginning, the Woodley Company was J. R. Parten. Never motivated by the desire to acquire great personal wealth, Parten's goal had always been to make Woodley a model independent oil company, one that played by the rules, was efficient and profitable, and was respected by its competition. Parten's very self-identification had been deeply rooted in the soil of the Woodley Company and now that was gone. "It was against my better judgment to sell," Parten later claimed, "but my partners had decided that this was the time to sell, and hell, I had to." Twenty years later, he complained to the New York *Times* that the loss of Woodley was, in a sense, the price he paid for his divorce from Opal.[28]

Although he hated to give Woodley up, he at least did it on his terms, not on Moran's. No one made a brokerage fee out of the deal and Parten became a director of Pure Oil, making it possible for him to retain some influence over the company's direction. Parten had retained his beloved 7-J Stock Farm, of which he and his family now owned over 70 percent, but he lost control over Great Northern Refining and its associated pipeline companies. At the time, Woodley owned 40 percent of the pipeline and 38 percent of the refinery. Pure had little interest in Great Northern, so Parten considered spinning off its stock to Woodley's investors, the same way he had handled 7-J Stock Farm. His lawyers warned him, however, that such a move might upset the tax-free feature of the deal, so Pure swallowed its share of Great Northern in the merger. Parten always regretted not doing more to keep control of the refinery.[29]

Despite the bad feelings created by Moran's dealing behind Parten's back, the two men were able to maintain a semblance of friendship for many years to come. They remained partners in the 7-J oil and gas lease and Moran was now one of the largest individual stockholders in Pure. "They had oil up there on that field," Parten's secretary noted, "and there just wasn't any way they could get away from each other." Randy Parten believed that his father and Moran "kind of swept it under the rug." Nevertheless, the relationship chilled. Moran was heavily involved in the production of natural gas. "I remember J. R. being very distrustful of gas men after that," Randy Parten later stated. "As we would be riding around on horse back in a pasture, he would say to me—he must have said this to me a hundred times—'don't ever crawl up in a gas man's lap and go to sleep—and that includes your Uncle Billy'."[30]

Woodley and Pure merged officially on April 1, 1960. Parten, whose personal holdings totalled nearly 130,000 shares, now joined with Opal and Billy Moran to own about 5 percent of the Pure Oil Company. They were new investors in a fifty-year-old company built largely by Beaman and Henry Dawes. Originally chartered in Ohio, Pure moved its corporate headquarters to Chicago in 1926. Beaman and Henry Dawes ran the company until 1947, when they turned it over to a reorganized management structure, headed by Rawleigh Warner, who became the new chairman of the board of directors. Because of its highly visible marketing activities, Pure appeared from the outside to be a dynamic company. It was the nation's fifteenth-largest oil company, ranking 104 on the Fortune 500 list. The company had oil and gas wells in the United States, Canada, Algeria, Venezuela, and Italy; four refineries; and a distribution system spanning twenty-five states in the Southeast and Midwest supplying thirteen thousand service stations. Pure's management directed these operations from an impressive new headquarters in a sprawling complex of buildings in Palatine, thirty miles from Chicago. Parten eagerly assumed his position on Pure's board of directors and looked forward to playing an active and influential role in helping shape the policies of a major oil company.[31]

Part Five

1961–1992

CHAPTER 30

A Last Tour of Duty in Washington and the Death of Mr. Sam

1961

J R. Parten and Sam Rayburn were friends for most of three decades, their friendship deepening in the twilight of Rayburn's life. For several years, Rayburn had depended on Parten as a source of advice on the oil industry, but as the two men drew closer, Rayburn used Parten as a sounding board on a variety of issues ranging from Texas politics to international affairs. For example, during the 1961 election campaign in Texas to fill Lyndon Johnson's Senate seat, Rayburn shared with Parten his concern about Democratic candidate William "Dollar Bill" Blakely's chances to defeat Republican John Tower. Blakely, attempting to run to the ideological right of the conservative Tower (whom Rayburn called a "little squirt"), had thoroughly alienated liberal and middle-of-the-road Texas Democrats and was racing toward defeat. "It seems to me that Bill has done about everything he could do in order to defeat himself," Rayburn complained. "I told him . . . that he could not be more conservative than Tower." After the Bay of Pigs fiasco in April 1961 Parten complained to Rayburn that prominent Democrats in Texas were calling on the Kennedy administration to launch a full-scale invasion of Cuba, which Parten described as totally irresponsible. Rayburn agreed. "There is more nonsense going on about Cuba than anything I know," he admitted to Parten. "I try to tell everybody. . . . that even though they have a fool for the head of government that is no reason to invade the island and start a big war."[1]

JFK and LBJ

A few weeks prior to the 1960 Democratic national convention, Rayburn drew Parten into the fight over the Democratic presidential nomination. Parten's attention had been so distracted by his business and ranch work that he had been little involved in the state's political activities and was not a delegate to the convention. The leading candidate was John F. Kennedy. Although Lyndon Johnson had not entered the campaign, Rayburn told Parten in June that Johnson would challenge Kennedy. Rayburn and Johnson did not believe Kennedy could win on the first ballot, and thought the convention would turn to Johnson as a compromise candidate. Rayburn told Parten "that he would need my help if Johnson's candidacy somehow caught fire at the convention," Parten recalled. Although Parten disliked the way Johnson had treated the liberal faction of the Texas Democratic Party in 1956, he had no problem supporting him for the nomination. Parten was eager to do Rayburn a favor, and he was disturbed by a rumor (spread by John Connally) that Kennedy wanted to end the sacred 27.5 percent oil depletion tax allowance. A strong Johnson effort to get the nomination might force Kennedy to preserve the oil depletion allowance. Parten told Rayburn he would go to Los Angeles and do whatever he could to help Johnson.[2]

The Partens arrived in Los Angeles on July 9. By this time, Parten realized that Johnson was not going to win the nomination. Nevertheless, for three days Parten met with dozens of old friends talking up Lyndon Johnson's candidacy. He spent most of his free time in Rayburn's hotel suite. It was from that location on the night of July 13 that Parten watched Kennedy's first-ballot nomination. He shed no tears over Johnson's defeat. Despite his concerns about Kennedy's views on oil, he liked Kennedy's positions on most of the other issues. Equally important, he believed Kennedy could beat Nixon. Even Kennedy's religion attracted Parten. "I felt like I did during the Al Smith campaign," he recalled. "I thought it would be a healthy thing to have a Catholic as President."[3]

When Parten returned to Texas, he sent a check for six thousand dollars to the Kennedy-Johnson campaign in Texas, which was chaired by his old friend, former Texas attorney general Gerald C. Mann. He also promised Mann that he would help raise money for the campaign, but first he had to complete a project on one of his ranches. Two years earlier Parten had purchased Rattlesnake Ranch, a three-thousand-acre spread on the east bank of the Trinity River in Houston County, adjacent to 7-J Stock Farm. Parten now owned three ranches, including the thirty-five-hundred-acre Greenbrier, located six miles north of Madisonville in Madison County. Hoping to devote most of his time to his ranches, Parten had relinquished the chairmanship of Pan American Sulphur to Marlin Sandlin. With the company enjoying record profits, he readily gave up this post, though he remained one of the company's largest individual stockholders and thus retained much influence in its affairs.[4]

Parten's plan to help Mann was brought to an abrupt end in August when he was nearly killed on Rattlesnake Ranch as a work crew cut down trees. A large oak

Parten inspecting Greenbrier Ranch, late 1950s. *Courtesy Parten Photograph Collection, CAH.*

tree caught Parten as it fell after being cut, knocking him to the ground. The tree snapped the bones in his right leg and knocked him unconscious. Buried beneath limbs and leaves, Parten was eventually pulled free. The fracture was severe and the physicians feared that he might not regain full use of the leg. After an extended hospital stay, Parten was on crutches for several weeks.[5]

His leg injury ended Parten's active participation in the 1960 presidential campaign. He told one friend that though his broken leg had forced him to stay "pretty close" to home, "I am doing everything within my power for the Kennedy-Johnson ticket." On election day, J. R. and Patsy voted in Madisonville and then drove to Austin to Johnson's campaign headquarters. The vote margin between Kennedy and Nixon remained too close to call until the next morning. As Johnson, Connally, and their staff sweated out the returns, Parten remembered their treatment of Frankie Randolph and her associates in the liberal wing of the Texas Democratic Party in 1956. Many liberal Democrats in Texas had refused to help Johnson's campaign and some had called for liberals to "take a walk" on election day. Although Kennedy squeezed a tight victory in Texas, Parten believed that the political warfare in Texas four years earlier had nearly cost the Democrats the White House.[6]

After the victory, Sam Rayburn sent the Partens two tickets for VIP seats at the inauguration. Rayburn's friendship with Parten had grown stronger than ever.

"Words fail me," Rayburn told Parten, "when I try to express my gratitude to a friend like you for your unfailing helpfulness to me in everything that I undertake. You know I will never forget." The Partens went to Washington in mid-January 1961, and watched in the snow of a bitterly cold January day as Kennedy was sworn in.[7]

"If he was good enough for Harold Ickes, he's good enough for me"

While the Partens were in Washington, Rayburn informed J. R. that he and Oscar Chapman, with Lyndon Johnson's additional endorsement, had urged Stewart Udall, the new secretary of the interior, to make Parten his assistant secretary in charge of the Interior Department's Oil and Gas Division. Rayburn had been trying for years to get Parten to take an administrative post in the federal government and hoped that the Texas oil man would be available now that he no longer had an oil company to manage. Parten told Rayburn that he would consider an appointment, but only as Udall's nonpaid consultant for oil and gas matters.[8]

After Parten returned to Texas, Secretary Udall called and offered Parten the job as his oil and gas consultant. Udall, a former congressman from Arizona, admitted that he knew little about the oil industry and needed someone to help him "sort out his thinking" about oil and gas policy. When Udall subsequently announced the appointment at a press conference, he referred to Parten's experience with the PAW. "If he was good enough for Harold Ickes," Udall declared, "he's good enough for me." Parten's appointment was well received in Texas, where there were fears that the Kennedy administration might not be as protective of the state's oil interests as Eisenhower's had been.[9]

When Parten began his work at the Department of the Interior on February 10, 1961, the nation's energy picture was far different from the one he had confronted in his earlier tours of duty. The United States had increased its crude-oil imports from approximately 5 percent of the total U.S. demand in 1946 to more than 19 percent by the end of the 1950s. American independent producers, few of whom operated overseas, saw this dramatic increase in oil imports, which kept domestic retail prices low, as a serious threat to the future well-being of their segment of the industry. Because foreign oil was often cheaper to find and usually much cheaper to produce than domestic crude, the independents feared being slowly squeezed out of the industry. As a result, they demanded that the federal government impose oil-import restrictions. The Truman and Eisenhower administrations had resisted the demand for import controls as being too restrictive on trade with developing countries. In 1955 Congress finally responded to political pressures from the independents and granted the president authority to impose controls where needed for purposes of "national security." Eisenhower initiated a system of voluntary controls, but the level of imports increased and the program fell apart by late 1958. On March 10, 1959, Eisenhower imposed a mandatory oil-import quota system, to be administered by the Interior Department, that restricted imports to 9 percent of total domestic consumption. The independents were delighted. Domestic exploration and production increased significantly.[10]

As an independent, Parten had favored import quotas and tariffs as tools to encourage domestic exploration and production. As a producer of Canadian oil and Mexican sulphur, however, as well as a major shareholder in an integrated oil company involved in foreign exploration, he well understood the economic arguments against limiting imports. Nevertheless, his experience with the oil transportation crisis in World War II and his fear that another war could easily cut off those foreign sources, convinced him of the need for some level of federal control to prevent the country from becoming so dependent on foreign oil that national security was threatened.[11]

As Parten had anticipated, import control was the first issue about which Udall needed advice. Eisenhower's 1959 executive order had included import controls on residual fuel-oils, which had driven up the price on home-heating oil. Congressional representatives from New England asked Udall to remove controls on fuel-oil imports. Relations between the Soviet Union and the United States had worsened dramatically in the first days of the Kennedy administration, and Parten was concerned that in the event of a war the tankers that served as the main means of transportation of fuel oil to the East Coast would not be able to operate. Parten's PAW experience with the New England fuel-oil crisis also convinced him that the removal of import quotas would encourage East Coast industries and utilities to abandon coal as a fuel. He advised Udall to maintain import controls on fuel oil "certainly for the foreseeable future." For reasons of national defense, he argued, "it would seem wise policy for all industrial fuel consumers . . . to maintain at least one and possibly two alternative fuels." Udall accepted this advice and the policy remained.[12]

The Brownsville "Rinky-Dink"

Parten's good relationship with Udall proved to be short-lived. The culprit was the administrative complexity inherent in the Mandatory Oil Import Control Program, as it was formally titled. The oil-import program limited the total amount of oil that could be imported into the United States, but there was an important exception. Eisenhower's executive order had exempted oil imported into the United States by "overland" transportation such as by truck, rail, or pipeline. In 1960 the Eisenhower administration had granted PEMEX, Mexico's national oil company, a waiver for one year to move fifteen thousand barrels per day of residual fuel-oil through Brownsville, Texas. The exemption was granted because the import was refined oil rather than crude oil and because there was an alleged short-term local need. Parten learned that PEMEX was transporting fuel oil by tanker ships from Tampico, Mexico, to Brownsville, and then placing it in bonded storage controlled by U.S. Customs in Brownsville. After a few days, PEMEX removed the fuel oil from storage and, rather than sell it for local consumption as the exemption allowed, trucked it across the Rio Grande to

Matamoros, Mexico. There it was sold to an American company, which brought it back across the Rio Grande as a legal import covered by the overland transportation exemption. The fuel oil was shipped by tanker to the Northeast. This procedure violated the terms of PEMEX's exemption, allowing some American companies to circumvent the import quota. The operation also disturbed Parten because the main rationale for controls was based on the national security need to lessen U.S. dependence on oil transported via ocean routes.[13]

Although these operations were too small to affect the total pattern of U.S. imports, to Parten they were obvious circumventions of the law. His rigid code of honor prevented his overlooking them. The people involved were not playing by the rules and they were destroying respect for law. He was determined to end these activities for national security reasons, respect for law, and the sake of those who played by the rules. An equally important reason for Parten's hostile reaction to these circumventions of the rules was his desire to preserve his reputation for fairness and honesty. He could not abide the thought of being in his official position, knowing about these violations (which he called "rinky-dinks"), and being perceived as approving them.[14]

Parten went to Udall on March 1 and told him about the operations in Brownsville and in Puerto Rico. In the latter case, it was discovered that the Eisenhower administration had granted the two refineries in question special exemptions to increase their quotas. Parten believed that the exemptions had been granted for political purposes rather than for sound policy reasons, so he asked Udall to remove them. In the Mexican case, Parten discovered that the State Department had persuaded the Interior and Treasury Departments to allow the original PEMEX exception in 1960. Sympathetic to Parten's complaints, Udall passed them on to Sec. of State Dean Rusk. The State Department responded that it would ask for a report from the U.S. embassy in Mexico City about PEMEX's activities and plans. Meanwhile, Parten received confidential information from Morgan Davis, president of Humble Oil, that the Brownsville situation was worse than he had at first thought. PEMEX was actually shipping crude oil rather than fuel oil, shipments were double the amount allowed by the exemption, and PEMEX was considering increasing the amount it was shipping. Parten reported these charges to Udall.[15]

Parten believed that the Interior Department either had to enforce the law or change it through amendment. On March 14, he urged the Oil Import administrator, to secure a formal exemption to make legal the Brownsville operation to prevent "some developments which will prove . . . embarrassing." By this time, word had spread within the oil industry that Parten was trying to stop the Brownsville operation, which was known as the "Brownsville U-Turn" and "El Loophole." Ed Pauley, who had extensive business interests in Mexico, strong connections with PEMEX, and, as it turned out, involvement in "El Loophole," rushed to Washington to persuade his old friend Parten to ease up. Pauley's mission, which was doomed from the start, only served as further evidence for Parten that Pauley was an unethical deal-maker. If Pauley thought the rules and regulations that everyone else had to obey were unfair, he should get them repealed rather than violate them. "Ed decided that he wasn't going to do anything with me," Parten said, "so he gave up pretty quickly."[16]

Armed with the new information about PEMEX's blatant violation of the waiver agreement, Parten persuaded Udall to tell Rusk that Interior would no longer sanction the Brownsville situation and that the department would so inform U.S. Customs. He warned Udall that unless action was taken quickly, "this troublesome problem will become worse from week to week. . . ." He predicted State would stonewall the problem and not act. Udall should bypass State and request a legal opinion from the Justice Department to declare the current Brownsville operation a violation of the executive order. Udall could then send this legal opinion to Treasury and ask Customs to stop the importation of all but the original fifteen thousand barrels per day of fuel oil. This action was necessary to avoid "irreparable damage to the Oil Import Program."[17]

The State Department objected to Parten's plan because it could "arouse serious political antagonism on the part of the Mexicans." The State Department was eager to keep the Mexican government happy so that it would assist the U.S. effort to isolate Fidel Castro's Cuba and prevent the spread of "Castroism." Bowles added that Ed Pauley had informed the department of his plans to finance a pipeline from Mexico to the U.S. and that a pipeline was "a possible answer to the problem. . . ." Parten, who found Bowles's response unpersuasive, talked Udall into notifying the Bureau of Customs in Brownsville that it should enforce the original agreement allowing PEMEX to bring in only fifteen thousand barrels of residual fuel-oil per day. Crude-oil deliveries and shipments of residual fuel-oil in excess of the daily allowable were to be stopped.[18]

Satisfied that the problem had been resolved, Parten flew to Texas on March 31. When he returned to Washington in late April, he found that Udall had retreated from his earlier position in the face of continuing protest from the State Department and the White House. Parten saw Pauley's hand in the White House's intervention. A few days later, he read newspaper reports alleging that Udall had been involved in an ethically dubious campaign to solicit financial donations from the oil industry. Jack Evans, a Shell executive who was also a friend of Udall's, sent letters to fifty-six oil and gas industry executives and lobbyists asking them to buy $100-a-plate tickets to the Democratic Party's Jefferson-Jackson Day fund-raising dinner to be held in Washington on May 27. When some of the oil men complained about the letter, Udall called a press conference in which he said that he had merely asked Evans to help him sell "a few tickets."[19]

Parten was offended by Udall's solicitations, which gave the impression that the financial contributions might result in special treatment for the donor in dealing with Interior Department matters. Eager to disassociate himself from the Kennedy administration's handling of the oil-import program, Parten resigned. "I just could not have done anything else but what I did and face my good friends in the oil business and claim a conduct of decency," Parten later explained. He wrote Udall that he "may have overstayed the 'few weeks' mentioned at the outset" of his service. He asked Udall to make the announcement in order to avoid the appearance of a "resignation in protest." To Parten's chagrin, however, Udall failed to announce his resignation. After Parten returned home to Texas, oil industry people called him about Interior Department matters. "I called up Udall and told him that I was embarrassed," Parten complained, "because he hadn't announced my resignation. Udall said, 'Gonna do that right away,' but he didn't do it."[20]

On June 2, Parten went to Washington and demanded that Udall announce his resignation. Udall replied that the reason he had not released the news was because he was afraid that it would look like Parten had resigned as a result of the oil-industry fund-raising incident. Udall also explained that the State Department had succeeded in getting PEMEX to agree to limit their imports to thirty thousand barrels per day through Brownsville. He told Parten that he finally accepted this because it would keep PEMEX and Ed Pauley from building a crude-oil pipeline from Tampico to the United States and drowning the U.S. in Mexican oil. Parten disagreed, saying that with pipelines crisscrossing the Canadian border it would be extremely difficult politically as well as unfair to discriminate against the Mexicans whenever they wished to build such a pipeline.[21]

Faced with Udall's reluctance to act, Parten leaked the information that he had resigned from the Interior Department six weeks earlier. The news soon appeared in the *Oil Daily*. When the Houston *Post* called Parten to confirm the story, he emphasized only that he had "no connection with the department or any decision made by it . . . since May 2." Three days later, Udall finally confirmed publicly that Parten had resigned, expressing his "profound thanks . . . for [Parten's] fine work."[22]

The Mandatory Oil Import Control Program continued for another twelve years, its management, in the words of one historian, becoming "more and more Byzantine" as it lasted, developing into an "administrative nightmare" by the end of the Johnson administration. And the "Mexican Merry-Go-Round" in Brownsville not only continued, it expanded. Parten supported the oil-import program, which was highly successful in achieving its goal of protecting the domestic oil industry from cheap foreign oil, but he could not abide an administrative system that sanctioned cheating. He believed that it eroded respect for law and contributed to public cynicism about government. Parten's view may have been hopelessly naive and out of step with his times, but it was sincerely held. Although his protest was in vain and had no effect on the program, his behavior in the episode reflected the way he expected others in public office to behave, which is one reason he so deeply respected Sam Rayburn. To Parten, the Speaker was the model of the ideal public servant—a man with great potential power who was incorruptible, fair, and dedicated to the larger good.[23]

In fact, what bothered Parten the most about his experience with Udall was that Rayburn might think he had advised the secretary to initiate the ill-conceived fund-raising scheme. The day after he resigned, Parten sent Rayburn a note to assure him that Udall had not consulted him about the oil-company solicitation. "You don't have to tell me you were not consulted," Rayburn replied, "because if anybody had consulted you and taken your advice they would not have done such a foolish thing. . . ."[24]

The Death of Mr. Sam

When Parten resigned as a consultant to the Interior Department in May 1961, Rayburn scolded Udall for what the Speaker perceived as the secretary's mishandling of the situation. Arguing that Udall should have paid more attention to Parten's advice, Rayburn stressed that "my good friend, Major J. R. Parten . . . is a man of outstanding character and ability. He is honest, he is intelligent. . . ."

When Rayburn entered the hospital in October 1961, Parten donated sixty-five hundred dollars to the Rayburn Foundation. A contribution in support of the Rayburn Library in Bonham would mean far more to the Speaker than anything else that Parten could do. Parten admitted to a friend that Rayburn's terminal "illness has had a very depressing effect on many of his friends. It certainly has on me. I only hope that his doctors have chosen the right treatment. Frankly, I deplore the defeatist attitude which they announced at the outset." Rayburn died on November 16, 1961. J. R. and Patsy were among the crowd of mourners, including President Kennedy and former presidents Truman and Eisenhower, that overflowed Bonham's First Baptist Church for Rayburn's funeral.[25]

Rayburn's passing created a void in Parten's life. Years later, he listened intently to an argument among friends who had gathered in his living room. Someone declared that the country's political culture had "gone to Hell in a hand basket" after Kennedy's assassination, while another blamed Richard Nixon and his actions in the Watergate affair. Parten, who had remained silent throughout the discussion, finally said: "To me, Mr. Sam's death changed everything. Hell, it's almost as though he took political integrity to his grave. Congressional government has not been the same since he left us."[26]

CHAPTER 31

Parten versus Pure Oil

1962–1965

Although Parten's disagreement with Secretary Udall was the primary reason for his resignation as oil advisor in May 1961, management problems at Pure Oil Company also played a role. Parten's enthusiasm for the Pure Oil Company had waned considerably. The more he learned about the company that had swallowed up Woodley, the more he realized that it was not the dynamic operation he had thought it was. Despite the outward signs of success, Pure Oil was on the verge of serious trouble when Parten took his place on the board of directors in the spring of 1960. Parten discovered, for example, that Pure's refineries were obsolete, much of its production equipment worn out, and its most important retail markets threatened by gasoline price-wars. Pure's crude reserves were located mostly in states that severely restricted production, so the company could not depend on those reserves to meet its needs. Pure was withdrawing about twenty-five-million barrels of crude oil annually from its reserves without doing much to replace it. Because of its lack of crude, Pure had been forced for several years to buy high-priced oil from its competition to keep its refineries running. This meant that the company had to pay three dollars a barrel for oil that would have cost only one dollar a barrel if the company had produced it. These problems were exacting a high toll on Pure's individual shareholders. In pre-tax earnings per share of stock, Pure ranked thirteen out of fourteen comparable companies and ranked last in crude production per share. Pure's management had obviously seen the acquisition of Woodley's large reserves as a quick fix.[1]

Parten understood that a few of Pure's problems were beyond the company's control. He was convinced, however, that the main problem was an ossified, overpaid, and seemingly distracted management. The directors and officers owned a relatively small amount of Pure's stock, which meant to Parten that their main interest was in their salaries rather than in the company's stock value. Parten felt that Pure's management had become lazy and stagnant. For example, the board's executive committee met only every two months, while most of the oil companies with which Parten was familiar had executive committee meetings three times a week to respond to developments emerging from rapid changes in the industry. [2]

Parten was critical of Pure's top management, especially Bob Milligan and Rawleigh Warner, whose business experience had been strictly on the financial side. He felt that neither man knew anything about the oil business. He simply did not respect anyone trying to pass himself off as an oil man if he had not, as Parten liked to say, "done the work." He was also concerned by the significant influence his fellow Houstonian "Judge" James A. Elkins Sr., a director and Pure's general legal counsel, exerted over company affairs. The octogenarian Elkins, a powerful Texas political broker, banker, and senior partner of Houston's largest law firm, was a major holder of Pure stock and had dominated the affairs of Pure Oil for half a century. For years Parten had watched Elkins operate in Austin as a lobbyist working to kill progressive legislation in the areas of human welfare, taxation, labor relations, and education. "The Judge was drawing pay from utilities, telephone companies, oil companies, and sulphur companies," Parten later claimed, "and when the Legislature was in session, they all had some ax to grind, and he was grinding those axes for them." To Parten, Elkins was the antithesis of what a responsible businessman and citizen should be, and the two men were polar opposites in political outlook. "I knew the Judge pretty well," Parten once said. "He was strictly looking out after the Judge, not Pure Oil or its stockholders."[3]

At board meetings, therefore, Parten voiced his concerns openly about the manner in which Pure was being operated. These criticisms created tension between him and Milligan, who had been with the company since 1929. Although Pure had serious problems—exacerbated by bad management decisions—Parten may have been quick to criticize because of the personal problem he was having adjusting to his new business circumstances. He had gone from being in control of his own company to being just one among a group of directors, with little control over management. Dallas Sherman remembers how restless Parten was after the merger. "I always thought that J. R. was disappointed because he wasn't offered a job of some importance with Pure," Sherman observed. "For awhile there he seemed a little lost, because . . . all of a sudden he wasn't anything in the oil business."[4]

Two separate incidents related to company personnel heightened Parten's concerns about the quality of Pure's management. The first was Parten's discovery that Ira Cram, Pure's respected chief geologist, had left Pure to work for Conoco. Cram had been one of the main reasons Parten had been attracted to Pure during his quest for a merger partner. Cram left Pure because the company had been farming out his oil prospects to other companies. Afraid to take risks and wildcat their own leases, Pure had subleased many of what had turned out to be Cram's biggest discoveries to independents like Sid Richardson and Howard Keck. The second incident occurred in February 1962, when Warner and Milligan forced Porter Langfitt into early retirement. When Parten protested Langfitt's forced departure, Warner and Milligan explained that Langfitt had not carried his fair share of the work load as a result of a stroke he had suffered in October 1959.

Parten disagreed strongly and warned that Langfitt's removal would "prove very injurious to the Company." To placate Parten, Milligan appointed Harris Van Zandt to replace Langfitt as head of Pure's production and exploration program. Although Parten respected Van Zandt and supported his move into higher management, he objected to Langfitt's dismissal.[5]

Langfitt refused to retire, so at a board meeting on May 8, 1962, Pure's board of directors removed him as vice president. Parten voted against the removal and heatedly denounced Milligan for the action. In addition, Langfitt was not replaced on the board's executive committee, leaving it with only four members, none of whom were, in Parten's opinion, real oil men. To Parten, Pure was now an oil company run by accountants, bankers, and lawyers rather than by oil men. "Feeling as I do that the ablest oil man in the history of Pure . . . has been treated this way has been a violent shock to me," Parten admitted in a letter to Opal. "I will admit I have had some difficulty calming my emotions and feelings about the matter." Parten declared that he was "seriously disturbed about the management of The Pure Oil Company." He was now convinced that Milligan, Warner, Elkins, and their associates on the board of directors, were plundering the company to pay their own inflated salaries and fees and that their eventual goal was to sell the company and enrich themselves with commissions.[6]

"He didn't know what his own damn stocks were worth"

Because its earnings had been stagnant for four years, the price of Pure stock had declined steadily. Pure's assets, many of which it had acquired from Woodley, were much more valuable than indicated by the price of the company's stock. The low price of Pure stock relative to the higher value of its assets, coupled with the financial community's awareness of dissension on Pure's board of directors, made the company an attractive candidate for a corporate raid. During the spring of 1962, Parten discovered that one of Wall Street's most prestigious firms, the investment banking house of Loeb, Rhoades, and Company, had acquired four hundred thousand shares of Pure's common stock. One of Loeb, Rhoades, and Company's senior partners was his Parten's old friend, former secretary of the treasury Robert B. Anderson. Another partner, Mark J. Millard, a specialist in oil investments, had been a director of Pan American Sulphur for several years and had been a frequent visitor to Parten's Houston offices during that time. Loeb, Rhoades, and Company often forced itself into the management of companies in whose stock it had invested. When Parten informed Milligan of the stock purchases, Milligan admitted that he had never heard of Loeb, Rhoades and could not imagine why they would be buying Pure stock. "Bill was president of the company and didn't know what his own damn stocks were worth," Parten later complained. Milligan refused to be concerned about the stock purchases.[7]

Parten's curiosity was stronger than Milligan's however, so he travelled to New York to question his old friends at Loeb, Rhoades. "We think that company would go places if it had some management," Mark Millard said. His firm planned to buy more Pure stock. At some point in the future, Millard admitted, they would ask for representation on Pure's board of directors and demand a reorganization of the company's management. Parten told Millard that he looked forward to their intervention.[8]

In the fall of 1962, Harris Van Zandt resigned as a vice president of Pure because of fundamental disagreements with Milligan's management decisions. "I no longer have a feeling of loyalty or respect for [Milligan]," Van Zandt told Rawleigh Warner. Convinced by Van Zandt's abrupt departure that Milligan and his colleagues were destroying the company, Parten urged Millard to make his move. Loeb, Rhoades was now the largest single owner of Pure Oil stock and it was determined to protect that investment. In January 1963, Robert B. Anderson and Mark Millard informed Milligan and Warner that Loeb, Rhoades owned about 10 percent of Pure Oil and that the firm wanted representation on the company's board. Replying that they would have to study the request, Milligan and Warner immediately initiated a search for another oil company with which Pure could merge on terms beneficial to Pure's management. In the meantime, Judge Elkins notified Parten that he and Rawleigh Warner had a purchaser for the Loeb, Rhoades stock if it could be had for a reasonable price. Elkins warned Parten that if the Wall Street firm failed to sell its Pure stock and continued to insist on board representation, Pure would merge with a major oil company of its choosing. Parten told Milligan that he would oppose any attempt to merge Pure with another oil company. "It seems clear that there is entirely too much talk emanating from the Judge's office," Parten complained. "It appears that he has made up his mind to make war on Mark Millard which I consider contrary to the best interest of the Pure Oil Company."[9]

In the summer of 1963, after several months had passed without any official response from Pure, Mark Millard demanded a seat for himself and one for Marlin Sandlin on the board of directors. This was a message to Milligan that the Millard group was allied with his chief critic, J. R. Parten. "That just scared Milligan and Warner to death," Parten claimed. Milligan told Millard that he could join the Pure board but Sandlin was "unacceptable." Millard rejected the offer and Loeb, Rhoades purchased additional Pure stock, eventually acquiring eight hundred thousand shares. Frustrated by Pure's delaying tactics, Millard decided that his firm's only recourse was to purchase the company. In early 1964, Loeb, Rhoades, and Company assembled a syndicate consisting of Allied Chemical Corporation and Consolidation Coal Company which offered to buy Pure for seven hundred million dollars, which included paying Pure's long-term debt of ninety million. The remainder of the money would be distributed among Pure's stockholders, who would receive approximately sixty dollars per share (about six dollars per share more than the current stock price). The syndicate planned to create an entirely new operating company with Pure's assets. To entice Pure's stockholders and to put pressure on Milligan and Warner, Millard announced the offer with a press release to the *Wall Street Journal,* which emphasized Pure's poor earnings record.[10]

Millard's press release angered Pure's management. They were having enough problems with some of their stockholders because of the plunge in the price of the company's stock. Milligan, Elkins, and Warner also knew that Millard had no intention of bringing them into the new company he planned to create. It was obvious, however, that J. R. Parten was slated to assume a major role in the new company. Milligan was faced with a serious challenge, but he was far from help-less. Just as Parten had done when his control of Woodley was threatened, Milligan, Warner, and Elkins decided to negotiate a merger of their own choosing, one involving a tax-free exchange of stock and other benefits, including participa-tion in the management of the combined companies.

To buy time, Milligan informed his stockholders on July 6, 1964, that Pure would not reply to any merger offers until the company completed a detailed study of their crude reserves and other company assets. He also declared that any merger or buy-out would have to preserve "current Pure Oil management." At a subsequent board meeting that same month, when Parten demanded to know why Millard's bid had not been accepted, Milligan complained that the company was worth more than Loeb, Rhoades was offering. Parten disagreed and urged his fellow directors to overrule their president and accept Millard's cash offer. Elkins, however, asked his colleagues to disregard Parten's urgings and declared that he would "round up a better offer." The board voted to wait on the appraisals. Elkins dispatched a partner in his law firm to California to bring Union Oil (Unocal) into the merger picture.[11]

During the next four months, while Pure appraised its properties, Milligan fended off several new bidders by declaring that Pure would consider merger pro-posals only. As Pure's self-appraisal dragged on, the Loeb, Rhoades consortium withdrew its bid. Other bids and "feelers" poured into Milligan's office, including those from Houston and New Orleans independent John Mecom, Tenneco, Ashland Oil, the Armour Company of Chicago, Texas Eastern, and R. J. Reynolds Tobacco Company. Milligan kept most of these offers secret from Parten and the other directors. While Milligan turned away bidders during the fall of 1964, he negotiated with Fred Hartley, president of Union Oil. These discussions resulted in Union's tentative offer on January 11, 1965, to merge with Pure through an exchange of stock. Hartley also promised to place Milligan on Union's board of directors.[12]

At the meeting of Pure Oil's board of directors on January 25, Atlantic Refining submitted an offer to merge with Pure through an exchange of stock. Parten, unaware of Milligan's unofficial agreement with Union Oil, urged his fel-low directors to take a serious look at Atlantic's bid. Milligan, however, persuaded the board to reject the bid as too low. He also claimed that the Justice Department's Antitrust Division would never allow the merger because the two companies were in direct competition in several areas of the country. Parten once again dissented, arguing that an arrangement could be made that would satisfy the Justice Department. Milligan prevailed and the Atlantic offer was rejected without serious consideration. At the end of the meeting, the board granted Milligan per-mission to pursue merger discussions with Union Oil. Parten (like most of his fellow directors) not knowing that Milligan had already made a deal with Union, voted to give him permission to "initiate" talks.[13]

On January 29, 1965, Loeb, Rhoades, and Company, Allied Chemical Corporation, and the new partners, investment bankers Lazard Freres and Lehman Brothers, submitted a revised offer to purchase Pure. This new bid was for eight hundred million dollars (one hundred million more than their previous proposal), which would pay each stockholder $62.50 per share. This was followed by a much better offer from Atlantic Refining on February 10. The week before, however, Milligan had met secretly with Union's Fred Hartley in California and they had initialed an agreement to merge. Union offered an exchange of 1.3 shares of its stock for each share of Pure, which amounted to a value of sixty-seven dollars per share. Milligan and one other Pure representative joined Union's board of directors. When Union also promised to retain Judge Elkins as their Texas counsel, the deal was set.[14]

Without revealing his purpose, Milligan called a Pure board meeting for February 15 to get approval for the Union merger. At the meeting, Milligan placed the Union, the Atlantic, and the Loeb, Rhoades offers on the table. Parten, who had not known about Atlantic's offer, argued that all three bidders could be talked into raising their bids. Milligan told the board that the Loeb, Rhoades offer was unacceptable because it would cost Pure's shareholders too much in taxes. He argued once again that Atlantic's offer raised antitrust problems. Milligan also emphasized that Atlantic had insisted that their offer was final, so it was pointless to go back to them. On Milligan's motion, Pure's directors voted twelve to one to accept Union's offer in principle. Milligan was given permission to work out the final details. Parten, the largest individual owner of Pure stock, cast the only negative vote. He accused Milligan of "engineering" the merger of a billion-dollar company "without the directors' knowledge . . ."[15]

After the board meeting, Robert O. Anderson, chairman of Atlantic Refining, called Parten and complained that Milligan had lied about Atlantic's proposal. They had never refused to make another offer and had expected to have an opportunity to improve the one they had made. Anderson was the son of Hugo Anderson, a banker with the First National Bank in Chicago who had arranged oil loans for independents in Texas and Oklahoma during the 1930s when few banks were making such loans. Parten had been one of the independents to whom Hugo Anderson had loaned money and he had known the younger Anderson for several years. Parten respected Anderson and he was greatly attracted to the idea of him taking over Pure.[16]

With Parten's strong encouragement, Atlantic submitted a new bid that topped Union's by about one hundred million dollars and which would pay Pure's stockholders about ten dollars more per share than they would receive from Union. Milligan was able to kill it by getting a vote by mail from the directors. Parten was not given an opportunity to vote. He demanded a board meeting to discuss Atlantic's new offer but Milligan refused. Parten now began "to feel more strongly" that the merger had been "railroaded . . . on Union's . . . terms."[17]

Parten organizes the dissidents

Parten organized a group of dissident stockholders in an attempt to scuttle the merger. During the first week of March 1965, Parten met in Houston with other dissatisfied stockholders, including Mark Millard, Marlin Sandlin, Jack Blalock, and Bill Moran. The dissidents controlled a total of more than two million shares of Pure Oil stock, including the 120,000 shares Parten owned and another twelve thousand he controlled through trusts. Initially, Parten proposed that they file a suit in Ohio, where Pure was incorporated, demanding cash for their stock. Ohio law allowed dissenting shareholders in a corporate merger to demand fair market cash value for their stock. If the merging companies refuse to pay the price demanded by the shareholder, a state court was empowered to determine the fair market value. If the Ohio court ruled in their favor, Union would have to pay between $150 million and $200 million in cash, which would kill the merger. Although they all agreed that such a suit should be kept as an option, they decided to try another strategy first. The dissidents agreed to back Parten in a proxy fight at the annual stockholders' meeting in April to get Marlin Sandlin appointed to Pure's board of directors. A proxy fight would allow the dissidents to air their grievances publicly and attract other stockholders to their side. They also hoped a proxy fight would scare Union's board of directors into delaying the merger out of fear of a costly legal battle. Parten assured the group that one way or another, they would stop the merger or they would get a fair price for their stock. After the dissidents' meeting ended, Bill Moran told the *Wall Street Journal* that Parten was preparing for a "dog fight" with Pure's management.[18]

On March 30, Parten issued a statement to the press announcing the proxy fight. Charging that Union Oil, with Milligan's connivance, had based its offer on Pure's weak earnings, rather than on its highly valuable assets, Parten demanded that Union increase its offer by at least 10 percent. The Houston *Chronicle* characterized Parten's action as an attack on Judge Elkins because the Judge had provided "much of the initiative for the merger. . . ." To avoid the proxy fight at the annual meeting on April 10, Milligan agreed to appoint Marlin Sandlin to Pure's board of directors. This move did not, however, prevent a contentious stockholders' meeting. Milligan later claimed that the attacks by Parten and the other dissenting stockholders at the meeting made him feel "like the clown at the sideshow who has to stick his head through the canvas while people throw balls at him." The criticisms aired at the stockholders' meeting failed to stop the merger. At their meeting on April 29, Pure's board of directors voted to accept Union's original offer. Only Parten and Sandlin voted against the merger. An eager Robert Milligan signed the official agreement that same night on his dining-room table. Parten and Sandlin made a halfhearted effort to defeat the merger at the time of the stockholders' vote, but Pure's shareholders overwhelmingly approved the deal on July 2, 1965. The Justice Department subsequently ruled that the arrangement between Pure and Union did not violate antitrust laws, paving the way for the largest merger in the history of the U.S. oil industry up to that time.[19]

Pure Oil president Robert Milligan (left) and Union Oil president Fred Hartley sign the merger agreement, 1965. *CN 09715. Courtesy Parten Photograph Collection, CAH.*

To Parten, the Union offer had been "hastily presented to the Board of Directors of the Pure Oil Company with shockingly little . . . information, hastily approved by the board . . . and thereafter consummated with no effort whatsoever to improve its terms. . . ." As one of the largest owners of Pure stock, Parten believed he was a big loser. Although he correctly argued that Union had acquired Pure "on the cheap" and that a loss in potential value was a loss nonetheless, he still doubled the listed value of his holdings and wound up as a major stockholder in what was now the ninth-largest oil company in the U.S. The loss that Parten felt most acutely, however, was the loss of control. As the result of the Pure-Union merger, Parten was no longer a director of an oil company. Because of his highly visible opposition to Union's offer and his open dislike of Milligan, there was no chance of his playing any role in the management of Union. That was why Mark Millard's effort to buy Pure was so attractive to Parten. He undoubtedly would have played a major role in a new company controlled by Millard and his investment partners, none of whom were oil men.[20]

Parten was defeated, but he was not finished with Pure. He demanded payment for what he considered to be the fair market cash value for a portion of his stock holdings. He argued that the stock was worth one hundred dollars per share, based on a professional appraisal and the bid by Atlantic Refining. Pure offered him fifty per share and Parten countered with ninety. When Pure said he could take it or leave it, Parten sued. He hired Houston attorney Leon Jaworski, who later gained fame as the special prosecutor in the Watergate investigation. Jaworski filed suit in Columbus, Ohio. Because Parten had too much stock to ask for the market price for it all (the tax bill would have been high), the suit demanded cash for only one-fifth of his holdings. Jaworski and his Ohio lawyers convinced the state court that Pure's offer of fifty dollars per share was much too low. The court ordered Pure to pay eighty per share. Union offered not to appeal the decision if Parten would accept a settlement of seventy-five dollars per share. Parten accepted the offer. He retained nearly one hundred thousand shares of Union stock, but his vigorous opposition to the Pure-Union merger and the lawsuit that resulted meant that he would never be allowed to play a role in the management of the company.[21]

Parten's oil career was far from over, but much of his personal time from now on would be spent on Pan American Sulphur and on public affairs, not just because he had an interest in the latter, but because the times demanded it. The great civil and military shocks of the 1960s and 1970s shaped and influenced J. R. Parten in significant ways. Although deep into his seventh decade, Parten was still growing intellectually, and his capacity for outrage was deepening. During these years he had ample opportunity for outrage.

"A Breed So Rare"

1963–1965

B y the beginning of the 1960s, J. R. Parten had gained a reputation in
Texas as a political maverick. "He is . . . a millionaire Democrat and a
great liberal," Walter Prescott Webb said in 1961, "a breed so rare that
one should be preserved in brine." Parten's reputation as a liberal had its
foundations in Homer Rainey's campaign for governor in 1946. He earned his reputation, however, more from his consistent loyalty to the national Democratic
Party than from strict ideological affinity. For example, his strong opposition to
federal regulation of the domestic oil industry and his fervent support for the oil
depletion allowance clashed with the views of northern liberals such as Sen.
Hubert Humphrey. Parten was never actively involved in the civil rights or labor
movements in the 1950s, the defining issues for national liberals, though he was
sympathetic to both. As a director of the Fund for the Republic, Parten had proposed a grant program in 1957 to recognize southern whites who were making
courageous high-profile public stands against racial segregation and bigotry. He
also called for a program to support efforts to vote out of office "those local public
officials who thrive on agitating racial hatred. . . . It seems to me that the decent
people of this country must . . . make it unprofitable for politicians to promote
racial hatred."[1]

When considered in the context of national politics in the 1950s and early
1960s, Parten was a "Truman-Rayburn" middle-of-the-road Democrat. His "liberalism" was apparent only in the context of southern and Texas politics, where his
Democratic colleagues not only often failed to support the national party's candidates, but also vigorously opposed the northern liberals, especially on civil rights
for African Americans. Parten's support for the national Democratic Party
stemmed from family tradition, his loyalty to the charismatic Roosevelt legacy,
and, most important, his belief in the party's pro–civil liberties/anti-monopoly
(Jeffersonian-Jacksonian) heritage.

In the 1960s and 1970s, Parten's political world view broadened to include new concerns. Although he retained his conservative Jacksonian view of the proper relationship between government and private enterprise (especially with respect to oil), on issues of foreign policy and civil liberties Parten identified increasingly with the left wing of the Democratic Party. It was during this period—the last three decades of his life—that Parten earned his reputation as a maverick, especially among Texas businessmen. His move to the left on foreign-policy matters and on civil liberties was part of an evolutionary process. His opposition to the Cold War can be traced to his experiences in Moscow and at Potsdam, and his support for civil liberties was rooted in his experience as chairman of the University of Texas board of regents. But Parten's negative reaction to the rise of the extreme right wing in the Republican Party in the early 1960s, the U.S. military intervention in the civil war in Vietnam, and the escalation of the nuclear-arms race pushed him away from conventional establishment positions.

Although Parten's move to the left on foreign policy and other matters was fundamentally the result of his personal interpretation of and reaction to the tumultuous events of the time, there were two individuals who helped shape his political views in the 1960s and 1970s. One was his old friend at the Fund for the Republic, Robert Hutchins; the other was a new friend, humorist and civil libertarian, John Henry Faulk.

Parten and Faulk began their friendship in 1963. An up-and-coming radio and television personality on CBS, Faulk had been fired in 1956 and blacklisted for nearly seven years as a result of false allegations that he held subversive beliefs. Faulk had fought back by filing a lawsuit against his accusers. His attorney, Louis Nizer, conducted a brilliant courtroom campaign based on information about the practice of blacklisting compiled by the Fund for the Republic's John Cogley. Faulk won his case in the summer of 1962. Because Parten had monitored Cogley's work for the Fund, he had followed the Faulk case closely. That Faulk was also a Texan, a graduate of the University of Texas, and a protégé of J. Frank Dobie and Walter Prescott Webb heightened Parten's interest in his case.[2]

Parten eventually met Faulk on February 16, 1963, in San Antonio at the annual meeting of the Texas Institute of Letters, where Faulk had given a speech about his blacklist travail. Parten was delighted to hear Faulk acknowledge the importance of the Fund for the Republic's report on blacklisting in winning his case. "Johnny declared that Cogley had done their investigative work for them," Parten said. "Because of the report, they knew all the culprits and where the bodies were buried." After the meeting, Parten gave Faulk and J. Frank Dobie and his wife, Bertha, a ride back to Austin, where Parten's son Randy was attending prep school. "On the way back to Austin, we had one hell of a mighty enlightened discussion about the problems of the world," Faulk recalled. "It became apparent to me right then and there that Mr. J. R. Parten was my kind of people."[3]

Faulk and Parten became close friends. When *Fear on Trial,* Faulk's book on his blacklisting ordeal, was published in 1964, Parten purchased several dozen copies and distributed them to friends and relatives. He told Faulk his book was one that "every American should read, because this blacklisting racket is undoubt-edly one of the most un-American and vicious practices today." Parten admired the courage Faulk had shown in his battle against the red scare and he shared Faulk's opposition to the Cold War. Because Faulk's views on most political sub-jects were radical compared to Parten's, the latter found his conversations with the former to be challenging and thought provoking. Faulk's arguments forced Parten to seriously confront issues such as social and racial justice for the first time. On other issues, such as the nuclear-arms race and the threat of right-wing political extremism to civil liberties and democracy, the two men reinforced their shared beliefs. Faulk's influence on Parten's thinking increased dramatically after his per-manent return to Texas in 1968.[4]

A Failed Family Life

By the early 1960s, J. R.'s workaholic lifestyle and his inability to maintain emotional contact with his loved ones—the problems that had separated him from Opal—were beginning to have a destructive effect on his marriage with Patsy and on his relationship with Randy and Pepe. As a longtime associate observed, Parten "always found it difficult to let anyone get close to him. It has been a hand-icap in his personal relations. And it's such a pity because he just adored the ground Randy walks on. But he couldn't tell him that and that's sad." Those who knew J. R. well, realized that he cared and loved in his own silent way. And he occasionally let his guard down. "No widow ever weeped more than J. R. Parten over the loss of a family member," one friend noted. "He can show grief so easily and not be embarrased about it but he can't express his emotions otherwise. Its an interesting paradox. He's terrible at funerals."[5]

J. R.'s personal life began to unravel in 1961 when he moved his family from the spacious mansion in Shady Side to the Beaconsfield Apartments in downtown Houston, where they occupied the entire seventh floor. Pepe had married and Randy was the only child at home. Downtown Houston was not the best environ-ment for an adolescent. "There were no other kids around and nothing to do," Randy recalled. "It wasn't a place for a kid to live." J. R. realized that Randy need-ed to live in a more suitable area. He also wanted to get Randy out of the exclusive St. John's School. "J. R. hated St. John's," Randy recalled. "He felt it was a little rich kids school that taught the wrong values and he was right." J. R. also had no inten-tion of letting Randy get involved in what he perceived as the social life of the idle rich in Houston. He believed that St. John's students were spoiled rotten, and lazy. So J. R. enrolled Randy in St. Stephens, an Episcopalian boarding school located a few miles west of Austin.[6]

With no children at home, J. R. and Patsy soon grew tired of life at the Beaconsfield. J. R. no longer wanted to live in Houston, and yearned to make Madisonville his permanent residence. Patsy, however, did not want to live exclu-sively in Madisonville, nor did she desire to live in an apartment or another rent-ed mansion, no matter how luxurious. She wanted a house of her own in Houston, but J. R. was not interested. Instead, in early 1963 he and Patsy moved to the old Parten family home on Collard Street in Madisonville, a development that ultimately proved to be an unhappy one for Patsy. "I had ranches around Madisonville," J. R. explained, "and I had gotten pretty well involved in oil leases nearby. And I like the air up in Madison County better than the air on the Gulf Coast. I just enjoy the rural life." After the move to Madisonville, J. R.'s routine was to drive to his office in Houston at noon on Monday and stay until noon on Friday. During the work week, he lived in a room at the Lamar Hotel, usually leaving Patsy to languish in Madisonville.[7]

J. R. made his decision to move to Madisonville without much input from Patsy, as he frequently made important family decisions without first consulting with or even informing his wife. When Patsy realized that the move to Madisonville was permanent, she asked J. R. to build a new house, one that she could design and decorate for herself, preferably on a hill overlooking the beautiful pastures of Greenbrier Ranch. J. R. ignored Patsy's plea. Instead, he had the old family home remodelled and refurbished. "Mother desperately wanted to build her own house but J. R. found it inconvenient," Pepe said. "He was quite comfortable where he was." She added, somewhat bitterly, that "everyone made J. R. quite comfortable. I think he was spoiled by women when he was growing up and that's what he expected." J. R. later explained that he did not want to build a new house for himself and Patsy because he had "a perfectly adequate one" that had once been the home of his parents. He saw no reason to waste money on unnecessary personal expenses.[8]

Randy noted that the move to Madisonville was "a total defeat for my mother. To go from the palatial mansion in Shadyside to a funky old Madisonville house was a total cut back." One of Patsy's friends noted that "she had to live in this old house that J. R. would not let her do anything to and it was bad." Patsy was not even the boss in her own kitchen, frequently losing cooking disputes with Luther, the headstrong African American prison parolee brought in by J. R. as the family cook and handyman. Pepe also noted her mother's growing unhappiness. "She was not happy about moving to Madisonville and she was not happy with J. R.'s family, which included not only his sisters and brother, but their children. Many of them lived nearby and they were a plague to her. They were constantly asking J. R. for advice and money." J. R. was especially close to his sister Malcolm ("Aunt Mally"), who also lived in Madisonville. "To my Mother's great dismay," Randy said, "J. R. went out to Aunt Mally's house every afternoon and had a Scotch with her. My mother really resented that. She and Mally despised each other."[9]

Unlike Opal, Patsy refused to lead a separate life. She made an attempt to be active and productive, but within J. R.'s environment. Pepe recalled that her mother decided that "if she was going to have to live in Madisonville for the rest of her life, she was going to make it pretty." She tried to get the merchants on the courthouse square to redo their storefronts to make them more attractive, but few of them had any interest in the idea. Complaining that no one in Madisonville had any "taste or flair," she soon abandoned the project. Patsy also did volunteer work at the Madisonville hospital. In 1963, she persuaded J. R. to donate the money needed to build a new wing on the hospital, which was later dedicated to the memory of J. R.'s mother.[10]

Eventually, however, the sterility and banality of small-town life, combined with loneliness caused by an often absentee husband, took a toll on Patsy. One of her friends later observed, "Patsy was a very unhappy person. She was a suave and urbane woman who liked to entertain and be around people who were interested in art and fashion and it was not available in Madisonville. She wanted to go on vacations and she wanted J. R. to do things with her." The quintessential workaholic, J. R. disliked travel for any reason he considered frivolous, and that included anything not related to work or health—especially sight-seeing. "He never had an interest in going anywhere simply just to look and to observe and to just enjoy," Pepe claimed. "All the time I worked for him," his former secretary recalled, "Mr. Parten never took but one vacation that I know of, and that was when Mrs. Parten finally persuaded him to go on a Carribbean cruise on the *Stella Polaris*. Other than that, every time he went any place it was work-related." Pepe remembered that the cruise was a hard-earned victory for her mother. "Mother had a real bite," Pepe recalled. "J. R. agreed to go just to shut her up." After they returned, Patsy told friends that J. R. was bored and restless the entire voyage, eager to get back to Texas to work on his ranches. The family never went anywhere that was not related to J. R.'s business activities or to his health. They spent their annual family vacations, for example, in Rochester, Minnesota, where J. R. received his annual physical checkup at the Mayo Clinic. Randy remembered spending one summer vacation in the back seat of a car when he was a child, riding with his father through the endless prairie land of Saskatchewan, looking at oil leases.[11]

As the years passed, Patsy sought solace in alcohol. "Mama would sit on the couch and watch the television with J. R. when he was home," Randy said. "When he wasn't there, which was often, she would kill three bottles of gin a night." John Henry Faulk noted that "J. R. was certainly embarrassed by Patsy's drinking, but he didn't want to confront the real reasons for it. He believed that alcoholism was a moral failure; a failure of will and discipline. Patsy drank out of weakness, as far as he was concerned, and only she could do anything about it." Patsy did attempt to control her drinking. "Mama went to Alcoholics Anonymous meetings and made a pledge to reform and tried," Randy said, "but she was an incredibly frustrated and unfulfilled woman. She never really quit." During the last several years of their marriage, while J. R. continued his fast-paced political and business activities and stayed away from home more than ever, Patsy continued to drink. The last years of their marriage were sad and unhappy ones, especially for Patsy.[12]

"Kennedy will get his reward in hell!"

Parten had never been the victim of political extremism, but he had seen enough of it in his lifetime to make him its bitter foe. An incident in Dallas in the fall of 1963, however, was his first direct exposure to a mob driven by political hate.

Despite its relatively mild outcome, the incident made a deep impression on Parten, convincing him that the extreme right wing represented a real danger to the nation's constitutional freedoms, and motivating him to fight it whenever he could.

On October 24, 1963, J. R. and Patsy attended the Eleanor Roosevelt Foundation's reception and dinner in Dallas honoring Adlai Stevenson, who was serving the Kennedy administration as the U.S. ambassador to the United Nations. He had come to Dallas to deliver a public speech in observance of U.N. Day. The Partens were there at the invitation of department-store entrepreneur Stanley Marcus, an old friend, who had made the arrangements for the ambassador's visit. After the dinner, Parten went with Stevenson and Marcus to Memorial Auditorium in downtown Dallas to hear Stevenson's speech. When they arrived outside the auditorium, they were met by a large contingent of people carrying anti–United Nations signs. When Stevenson began his speech inside the auditorium, many in the crowd screamed, waved signs, and blew whistles and other noisemakers in an attempt to silence Stevenson and break up the meeting. One man in the audience screamed repeatedly: "Kennedy will get his reward in hell! And Stevenson is going to die! And he will burn, burn, burn!" Fistfights broke out in the audience and the police had to remove some of the more demonstrative protestors. As one man was being removed, Stevenson declared that he believed "in the forgiveness of sin and the redemption of ignorance."[13]

The demonstration was carefully orchestrated by retired U.S. Army general Edwin A. Walker and the local chapter of the John Birch Society.[14] Walker, who had been forced out of his command in Germany by President Kennedy because of his attempt to indoctrinate troops with the John Birch Society's political views, moved to Dallas, where he became a leader of right-wing extremists allied with the Birch Society and other anti-Communist zealots. Walker and his fanatical associates had been given a political legitimacy of sorts by the anti-Kennedy hate rhetoric spewed out by some of Dallas's conservative political and civic leaders, including Republican congressman Bruce Alger and the editorial management of the Dallas Morning News.[15]

Although many in the audience were unable to hear him over the howls of the right-wing mob, Stevenson persisted and gave his speech. Afterward, the Dallas police escorted Parten, Ambassador Stevenson, and Stanley Marcus off the stage and out a side door. Parten held Stevenson's right arm and Marcus held his left arm. "We walked out through this big crowd," Parten recalled, "and a young man . . . walked up and put out his arm as if to shake hands with the ambassador, but instead, he spat in his face." As the angry crowd moved around Stevenson and his companions, a woman hit the ambassador on the head with a sign that read "IF YOU SEEK PEACE, ASK JESUS." Before they could get into the car, Stevenson told one of the policemen arresting the woman who had struck him that he did not want to send her to jail, "I want to send her to school." As the stunned and horrified group drove away from the screaming crowd, Stevenson took his handkerchief out of his pocket and, as he wiped the spit off his face, asked his companions, "are these human beings or are these animals?" Little else was said as the group drove in shocked silence to a private reception.[16]

In Parten's mind, the anti-Stevenson protestors had violated every rule of civility and decency. Not even in the worst days of the Rainey campaign had Parten seen such virulent hatred directed at a public figure. This was his first direct exposure to the fanaticism of the hate-mongers on the extreme right-wing fringe (the so-called "radical right"), and the experience frightened and worried him profoundly. From that point on, Parten viewed the entire political right wing and the John Birch Society (the "Birchers," he called them) as one and the same. The memory of the violent protest against Stevenson was an important influence on Parten's political activities in the coming years. His fear and dislike of the political right wing not only strengthened his identification with the liberal wing of the Democratic Party, it resulted in his becoming increasingly supportive of and involved in organizations such as the Fund for the Republic, which he viewed as counterforces to the radical right.[17]

Reelecting Ralph Yarborough

In the early weeks of 1964, Parten's concerns intensified as extreme-right-wing groups made open preparations for the forthcoming presidential election. Arizona senator Barry Goldwater's campaign for the Republican Party's presidential nomination deepened Parten's anxieties. Goldwater was widely hailed as the darling of the political right, and his refusal to denounce the Birch Society or to reject its support convinced Parten that he had to do whatever he could to help Lyndon Johnson's presidential campaign. As it became obvious that Johnson would win the election easily, however, Parten focused most of his personal attention on Ralph Yarborough's efforts for reelection. Yarborough faced a tough reelection campaign in the Democratic primary against Dallas radio-station mogul Gordon B. McLendon, who charged that Yarborough had received financial support from the convicted swindler, Billie Sol Estes. McLendon's charges were false, but they created enough controversy to put Yarborough's reelection in doubt.

Once again, Parten was Yarborough's chief financial backer and fund-raiser. He also served as Yarborough's campaign advisor for issues related to the oil industry, providing a stream of information to the senator's staff about oil policy and related topics. The last week of the primary campaign, Parten wrote a letter that the Yarborough campaign reprinted and circulated among the leaders of the Texas oil industry. "Ralph's record shows that he is a responsible friend who understands our problems," Parten declared. "On every oil and gas issue before our nation, he has been a consistent and effective fighter for solutions which fairly treat his State's leading industry." He cited Yarborough's support for the depletion allowance, oil-import controls, and his opposition to Federal regulation of natural-gas prices at the wellhead as evidence of the senator's work on behalf of the industry.[18]

Yarborough won the Democratic primary, helped considerably by Lyndon Johnson's actions to keep more formidable Democratic opponents, such as South

Texas congressman Joe Kilgore, from running against him. Johnson wanted to prevent the disruptive factional political warfare that normally marked the state primary so that he would have a united party to help him carry Texas in the presidential election in November. Yarborough, however, now faced a potentially serious challenge from the Republican candidate, a wealthy young transplant from Connecticut named George Bush. An oil man who had recently made his home in Houston, Bush was an energetic and personable candidate with considerable financial backing.

Parten was prepared to work full time to help his friend win reelection. This campaign, however, was much different from other Yarborough campaigns. For Lyndon Johnson's sake, the state Democratic Party machinery worked hard for the entire ticket. Yarborough had more money for advertising, staff, and other needs than in any of his previous campaigns. Parten served on Yarborough's finance committee and contributed money to the campaign. He also arranged and financed a campaign program aimed specifically at voters in East Texas. Parten believed that radio commercials emphasizing Bush's "Yankee" origins, Yale education, and inherited wealth would be an effective campaign tool for Yarborough in East Texas, primarily a rural area with deep roots in the Old South. Parten persuaded John Henry Faulk to tape-record political commercials making fun of Bush's "sissified and spoiled" background in the voice of one of Faulk's "country bumpkin" characters. Yarborough liked the commercials, so with Parten paying the bills, Faulk's messages were broadcast with regularity throughout East Texas. In addition, Parten appeared with Yarborough on a live statewide television broadcast on the evening of October 22 and made a brief statement in support of the senator.[19]

The coattail effects of Lyndon Johnson's landslide victory over Barry Goldwater doomed George Bush's campaign. With LBJ's victory, Parten's status as an influential member of the nation's Democratic political establishment seemed secure for years to come. Always an active and loyal national Democrat, Parten had been banished from the inner circle of the dominant wing of the party in Texas ever since the Rainey affair. But the ascension of another loyal Texas Democrat to the White House, one with whom Parten had been associated for nearly thirty years, gave promise that Parten would continue to have influential access to the Democratic leadership at the national level, including the president and his closest advisors, many of whom were Texans who knew Parten well. There was much to celebrate, so J. R. and Patsy attended Johnson's inauguration in Washington and enjoyed themselves in the festivities held the evening before.[20]

Several weeks after the inauguration, Johnson asked Parten to serve as ambassador to Pakistan. Parten was tempted to accept the offer, but he was deeply involved in the power struggle at the Pure Oil Company and felt that he could not afford to be that far away from his business interests. He was also nearing his seventieth birthday. Pakistan was a critical diplomatic post, and with war between Pakistan and India a constant threat, the embassy in Islamabad would not be a tension-free place. Parten reluctantly declined the offer. "I took the position that a younger man ought to do that," Parten explained.[21]

The offer of the ambassadorship proved to be the last time the Johnson administration looked with favor on Parten. As the president and the military-industrial establishment began to push the United States ever deeper into the quagmire of Vietnam, Parten's support of Johnson soon came to an end.

CHAPTER 33

Pacem in Terris

1965–1970

I n late February 1965, one month after Lyndon Johnson's inauguration, J. R. Parten attended a convocation on international peace at the United Nations in New York . Sponsored by the Fund for the Republic, the convocation had been named for and inspired by Pope John XXIII's papal encyclical *Pacem in Terris*, which had called for peaceful coexistence between the United States and the Soviet Union and their respective allies. The three-day meeting brought together two thousand delegates from twenty nations, including the Soviet Union and Poland, to discuss ways to bring about worldwide peace. This major event attracted widespread and favorable attention during a time of increasing international tension stemming from U.S. military involvement in Indochina. The conference was the result of the work of an extraordinary institution with the unwieldy name of the Center for the Study of Democratic Institutions, which had been spawned six years earlier by Robert Hutchins, J. R. Parten, and their colleagues at the Fund for the Republic.[1]

During the year following the Fund for the Republic's nearly disastrous confrontation in 1958 with the Internal Revenue Service over its tax-free status, Robert Hutchins proposed to transform the Fund from a philanthropic agency to an institute of independent resident-scholars who would collectively identify, discuss, and clarify the concepts that are basic to freedom and justice in a democratic society. "I may be wrong," Hutchins told his directors, "but it seems to me that there is one set of underlying issues, and then many issues dependent upon it. The underlying issue is that of the meaning today of . . . freedom and justice, an issue that can be framed . . . by asking how much diversity a pluralistic society can stand and how much unity it requires." Hutchins believed that "men of the highest distinction," removed from mundane distractions and protected from some of the pressures of everyday life, could contemplate and discuss these underlying issues and eventually produce a coherent view of the requirements of a free society. As Hutchins later explained, the purpose of the institute was "to try to discover what a free society is and how it may be obtained." Hutchins explained that the institute "would be something like a university, except that it would be limited to the study of freedom, it would do no classroom teaching, it would not confer degrees, and it would not require them of its members." Hutchins later stated that his institute's "prejudice is democracy; its operating procedure, the dialogue."[2]

Some of the Fund's directors, including Howard Marshall and Erwin Griswold, thought Hutchins's institute was utopian. Others, including Parten, feared that the institute would divert the Fund from direct involvement in the struggle to protect civil liberties. Hutchins proposed to terminate the Fund for the Republic's grants program and channel its money exclusively to a program of its own. The majority of the board's members, however, were excited and strongly supportive of Hutchins's idea. The charismatic Hutchins eventually persuaded Parten and Marshall to accept his plan, while opponents such as Griswold resigned from the board. When Hutchins telephoned Parten in the spring of 1959 to tell him that he would present a fully developed proposal to create his institute (now called a "center") at the next board meeting, Parten encouraged him to proceed.[3]

At a meeting of the board of directors of the Fund for the Republic on May 20, 1959, Hutchins submitted his formal proposal for a basic-issues program to be operated as the Center for the Study of Democratic Institutions. Hutchins proposed that the Center should be located in Santa Barbara, California, where he had purchased land for his own home. Hutchins emphasized that he was impressed with the University of California's plan to expand and upgrade its Santa Barbara campus, which would provide library and other educational resources nearby. He had also located an ideal tract of land high above the town on which to site the Center, available at the reasonable price of $250,000. Known as Eucalyptus Hill, the property was forty-two acres in size and included a large house that could be easily converted into offices and conference rooms. Hutchins believed that the property would appreciate in value rapidly, creating a significant financial asset for the Fund for the Republic. Hutchins's recommendation was made even more attractive by a gift of one hundred thousand dollars from California donors. Parten and his fellow directors unanimously approved Hutchins's recommendations. In a public announcement, Hutchins declared that the Center had no intention of telling people what they should think. "If we succeed," he said, "we may tell them what they should be thinking about."[4]

By September 1, 1959, Hutchins and his staff, including vice presidents Frank Kelly and Ping Ferry, were settled into their new quarters in Santa Barbara. When Parten visited the site, he agreed that it was an ideal spot. Because of the charge that Hutchins was trying to establish a Platonic academy in an area dominated by Spanish Mediterranean architecture, Hutchins soon dubbed the main building "El Parthenon." From its wide terrace, situated adjacent to the conference room, one could see the majestic Pacific far below. "El Parthenon" was soon alive with activity, though not everyone took its mission as seriously as did Hutchins and his colleagues. A writer for the New York *Times* irreverently described the Center as housing "a jamboree of full-time scholars, sometime authors, one-time journalists, occasional iconoclasts, and perennial academics. Their mission is to think deeply and speak loudly, scorning no human problem as too difficult, evading no issue as too divisive."[5]

After the Center's resident fellows had been appointed, the chimes of a Benedictine bell called them forth three mornings a week to assemble in the marble-floored conference room to sit in comfortable chairs behind a large table and engage in a ninety-minute "dialogue." These dialogues were often edited and published, either in pamphlet form or in the *Center Magazine*. Even Hutchins's closest colleagues later admitted that the elegant building and surroundings gave support to his critics, who charged that the Center had created an "ivory tower far removed from the real world." Parten, however, believed in the Center's mission and supported it enthusiastically.[6]

The Center for the Study of Democratic Institutions was dominated by the strong personality of Robert Hutchins, who has been described as a man of "enormous presence and staggering charisma . . . arrogant in all things petty, he was immoderately tolerant of dissent." A former board member has said that when Hutchins "started talking, you knew you were in the company of a rare individual. There was no question he was a genius." Parten was among those in awe of Hutchins as an intellectual and he was content to let him manage the new Center as he wished. Nevertheless, Parten was not a passive director, he attended most board meetings and engaged actively in its deliberations, chaired board committees, participated in many of the programs, and worked hard to keep the Center financially solvent. His financial contributions during the Center's first five years totalled one hundred thousand dollars. Hutchins, in turn, considered Parten to be one of his most dependable board members. "I believe that the Center . . . will be a monument to you," Hutchins wrote Parten in May 1963. "I know there are a lot of others, including a large part of the University of Texas. From the first board meeting to the last you have always been the most stalwart member of our group."[7]

By the mid-1960s, Hutchins and the participants in the elite Center for the Study of Democratic Institutions excercised the most profound influence on Parten's increasingly progressive world view. In the sense of intellectual growth and expanded cultural horizons, Parten gained much from his involvement with Hutchins and the Center. As a member of the board of directors, Parten made friends with a number of prominent individuals whose political views significantly affected his own thinking about public affairs, especially within the realm of international relations. J. William Fulbright, the former chairman of the Senate Committee on Foreign Relations and an outspoken critic of the Vietnam war, for example, initially met Parten because of his involvement with the Center. Other important relationships that Parten made or that deepened through his work with the Center included those with Supreme Court justice William O. Douglas, who served as the chairman of the Fund's board of directors for several years; Harry Ashmore, a two-time winner of the Pulitzer Prize for journalism, and Hutchins's right-hand man at the Center; Eugene Burdick and Harvey Wheeler, coauthors of the best-selling novel *Fail-Safe*, which raised popular concern about the danger of accidental nuclear war; actor and director Paul Newman; nuclear physicist Isidor Rabi, a winner of the Nobel Prize; former New Deal brain-trusters Adolf A. Berle and Rexford G. Tugwell; diplomat and author George F. Kennan; Civil War writer Bruce Catton; Adm. Hyman Rickover; and former Episcopal bishop James A. Pike.[8]

Through the Center's public programs, Parten was also exposed to a wide variety of world views expressed by distinguished scholars and provocative opinion leaders. Parten long remembered his experience at a special board meeting held in May 1964 at "Wingspread," a local foundation's conference house in Racine, Wisconsin. Parten and his colleagues met with twenty-two invited guests to plan the Center's *Pacem in Terris* convocation. Among the guests were Senators George McGovern and Gaylord Nelson; Joseph Johnson, president of the Carnegie Endowment for International Peace; and representatives from the United Nations, the French National Assembly, the International Court of Justice, the Soviet Embassy to the United States, the National Council of Churches, the Vatican, and the Nigerian mission to the U.N. Such people were very different from those with whom Parten normally mixed, and he enjoyed the meeting immensely. As the participants planned the *Pacem in Terris* convocation, he was among those who urged that it include an in-depth discussion on the need for nuclear disarmament, a subject of long-standing importance to him.[9]

The *Pacem in Terris* convocation of February 1965 proved to be an enriching experience for many people, J. R. Parten among them. Questions raised and discussed included how to bring about peaceful coexistence between nations with radically different ideological systems; how to negotiate peaceful resolution of conflict; how to bring about nuclear disarmament; and how to eliminate racism in all countries. Speakers included U.N. general secretary U Thant , Vice President Humphrey, Chief Justice Earl Warren, British historian Arnold Toynbee, publisher Henry R. Luce, George F. Kennan, Soviet academician Yevgenyi Zhukov, and theologian Paul Tillich. The convocation was held at an auspicious time. Three days before it opened, President Johnson launched "Operation Rolling Thunder," a plan for the continuous bombing of North Vietnam. Although this ominous development did not dominate the convocation, Nobel laureate Linus Pauling denounced the president's bombing campaign, declaring that it could lead to "the catastrophe of a civilization-destroying nuclear war." In other sessions, speakers denounced Johnson's policy as "unjust" international vigilantism. Parten was deeply concerned by what he heard and, as a result, he began to look more closely and critically at that increasingly horrific affair in Southeast Asia. Pauling's statements about the increased threat of nuclear war, one of Parten's deepest fears, especially troubled him. His enthusiasm for Lyndon Johnson remained strong, but he believed that the president's military advisors were leading him astray.[10]

On the last evening of the convocation, the Center held a fund-raising dinner in honor of Hutchins. Parten joined Henry Luce, Israeli ambassador Abba Eban, Sen. Eugene McCarthy, and philosopher Mortimer Adler in giving testimonial speeches praising Hutchins. The convocation attracted 1.4 million dollars in much needed donations to the Fund for the Republic. Parten left New York more enthusiastic than ever about Hutchins and his program at Santa Barbara, an enthusiasm that led to his donation of a major block of Pure Oil stock to the Fund to help support the Center.[11]

"You're going to be responsible for getting Dick Nixon elected President of the United States"

Greatly influenced by what he had heard at the *Pacem in Terris* convocation, Parten became an early critic of the war in Vietnam. He was appalled when U.S. combat troops poured into South Vietnam during the summer of 1965. "I was diametrically opposed to it," Parten recalled. "I didn't see any sense in it whatsoever." A Center pamphlet, "How the United States Got Involved in Vietnam," written by journalist Robert Scheer and published in August 1965, was a strong influence on Parten's thinking. Scheer charged that the federal government and the mass media had misled and deceived the American public at every stage of the nation's involvement in Vietnam. Parten also discussed the war with John Henry Faulk during his visits to New York in 1965 and found himself agreeing with Faulk's heated denunciations of Johnson's policy in Southeast Asia.[12]

Parten's intellectual and moral concerns about the war were reinforced by a strongly personal one. His son, Randy, was nearing draft age. "I always felt that his main opposition to the war was to keep me from going," Randy has said. "He was kind of obsessed about that." Randy eventually received a medical deferment that he believed his father engineered with the help of a friend who was an orthopedic surgeon. Parten had the surgeon examine a knee Randy had injured several months earlier. After the examination, the surgeon wrote a letter to the Selective Service stating that Randy's knee was bad enough to disqualify him from military service, despite Randy's having had little difficulty with it. When asked if he and the physician had conspired to protect Randy from the draft, Parten would only say that he did not condemn anyone who had evaded the draft to avoid the Vietnam war. Parten recalled that he was "gung ho for the front lines in 1917, but I was young and stupid. That's why these old men start wars, they know its the young that must fight them."[13]

Deeply opposed to the war by early fall, 1965, Parten generally kept his views to himself. His friends and business colleagues in Houston were solidly behind Johnson's policies. Not only did Houston's business establishment subscribe to the "domino theory" of Communist aggression, some of its most influential members were making huge profits from the affair. Brown and Root, for example, served as one of the main contractors for some of the most lucrative military construction projects in South Vietnam. Parten also believed that he might be able to persuade Johnson to alter his military policy in Vietnam if he could make an appeal to the president in private. He feared that if Johnson knew how he felt about the war, he would have no opportunity to present his views to him. "Lyndon's greatest weakness was that he wouldn't talk to anybody on the other side," Parten said. "If people didn't agree with him, he had no time to spend with them and no respect for them."[14]

As the war escalated, Parten worried about the effect the war was having on American institutions and civil liberties. He feared a resurgence of McCarthyism and the onset of a police state. Johnson's inability to swiftly win the war was also resurrecting a political ghost from the past, one whom Parten especially despised. In June 1966, Parten complained to Senator Yarborough that Johnson had "to find some way to get out of this Viet Nam mess or else it might lead to something really horrible, namely, the election of Dick Nixon to the Presidency." Still refusing to break openly with Johnson, however, Parten tended to blame the military and Johnson's advisors, and he hoped that somehow an opportunity might arise for him to speak privately with Johnson in the White House.[15]

In July, J. R. and Patsy took Randy east to tour college campuses. While on the trip, J. R. decided to stay over in Washington, D.C., and Johnson invited the Partens to a private dinner at the White House. The dinner was scheduled to be served late because President Johnson and the First Lady were spending the early part of the evening on board a ship on the Potomac River visiting wounded Vietnam veterans.

When the Partens arrived at the White House, they were greeted warmly by the Johnsons. "Mama and Lady Bird were buddies from way back in school days," Randy recalled, "so they went off and did their chit-chat stuff. I wasn't about to sit and listen to that, so I tried to follow J. R. and the President around." It was a beautiful night, so Parten and Johnson walked out on the curved balcony extending from the private quarters, on the south side of the White House. Randy followed them. "All of a sudden," Randy says, "J. R. was on him like a bull dog." Johnson had made a joke about the "nervous Nellies" who were criticizing the war effort. Not laughing, Parten replied that he was one of those "nervous Nellies." Johnson was trying to laugh it off, telling him not to make such a big deal about it, but J. R. would not stop. Parten declared that the war made "no sense" and that the American people were not going to stand behind him much longer if the war did not end soon. Johnson growled, "Well, how would you do it?" Parten replied, "Mr. President, you've got to first make up your mind that you want to do it. And after that step is taken, the various steps by which to do it will come in a very orderly way." Randy, who was standing by silently while his father lashed out at the president, was horrified. "I was embarrassed and upset. Here was my father trying to tell the president of the United States how to run his business and being pushier than I had ever seen him before. They were standing there talking and J. R. just would not let go of him. I couldn't believe it." Parten warned Johnson that if he did not stop the war, he was "going to perpetrate a great injury on this whole country. You're going to be responsible for getting Dick Nixon elected President of the United States." Randy recalls that when his father warned Johnson about Nixon, "Lyndon gave him one of these condescending, 'you dumb son-of-bitch' looks. I have to say, I thought it was the stupidest thing I had ever heard. Nobody could imagine Richard Nixon coming back." Johnson finally laughed and said, "Well, that's just fine, because there's nobody I'd rather run against than 'Tricky Dick'." J. R.'s harangue about the war ended when Patsy and Lady Bird rejoined them and they went inside for dinner. Parten later admitted that Johnson did not take his complaint very seriously. "I don't think Lyndon wanted to stop that damn war," he said.[16]

A Capacity for Outrage

During the last half of the 1960s and the early 1970s, as the war in Vietnam continued unabated and as the nation's cities and college campuses became battle-fields of protest, Parten, now well into his seventies, sympathized more and more with the antiwar movement and other aspects of the counterculture's political protest. Convinced that "we cannot stand . . . another World War," he increased his involvement in and his financial donations to the Center for the Study of Democratic Institutions, encouraging Hutchins and his consultants to distribute more widely their views against the war and their warnings about the increasing threat to civil liberties caused by establishment reaction to the antiwar movement.[17]

Parten also contributed money to antiwar political candidates and to a variety of antiwar organizations. Chief among the latter was an antiwar group called Business Executives Move For Vietnam Peace (BEM), which was a nationwide organization of American entrepreneurs and business officers who worked to end the Vietnam war. Parten provided special financial support for BEM's newsletter *Washington Watch*, edited by Tristan Coffin, a journalist he greatly admired.[18] In 1968, when Sen. Eugene McCarthy of Minnesota declared his candidacy for president as a peace candidate and alternative to Lyndon Johnson, Parten announced his support and donated money. "I fear that the stopping of this crazy Vietnam War cannot be achieved by negotiation unless you win," Parten wrote McCarthy, "and for this I pray."[19] Parten also lobbied his contacts in the government, especially Senators Yarborough, McGovern, and Fulbright, to do all that they could to stop the war and to halt domestic political repression. "It seems that the cliche of 'anti-communism,' could easily bring this nation ultimately to the tragedy of Germany," Parten told Yarborough. "Our Military Industrial Complex, about which Eisenhower warned, really has me troubled. We must be reminded that Hitler, too, was fighting Communism with the aid of heavy industry. It seems to me that we must abandon this policy of policing the world to force our form of government upon all people." When Daniel Ellsberg was tried in federal court for his role in leaking to the press the so-called Pentagon Papers, Parten, seeing the case as an attack on the First Amendment, helped raise money for his defense fund. Ronnie Dugger noted that although Parten always worked quietly "behind the scenes," his criticism of the war "was a powerful influence."[20]

Because of their long and close relationship, Parten leaned particularly hard on Ralph Yarborough to fight in the Senate against the war. He was frustrated, however, by Yarborough's reluctance to speak out on the subject because of his fear of alienating the labor unions (which generally supported the war) and other important supporters, such as Dickinson banker Walter Hall, a liberal who was a "hawk" on Vietnam. "J. R. gave me fits about Vietnam," Yarborough recalled. In August 1967, Yarborough denounced what he perceived as preparations for a U.S. invasion of North Vietnam, declaring that anyone advocating such an action "should be prepared to justify to Congress a formal declaration of war. . . ." Delighted, Parten sent a message to Yarborough: "Hurrah! I do warmly congratulate you for the position taken in these statements. It is unthinkable to me that so many of our conservative Senators do not realize the impropriety of waging war . . . without a formal declaration by Congress." When Hall scolded Yarborough about his speech, Parten came to the senator's defense. "I think Ralph was wholly justified in making the statement he did in the Senate," Parten told Hall, adding that it "seems to be common knowledge that Secretary Rusk has been bent on escalating this war continuously."[21]

Parten was equally strong on other issues championed by the antiwar liberals, such as draft reform and gun control. He called for gun registration and the prohibition of mail-order shipment of guns. Nothing enraged Parten more, however, than the revelation that federal, state, and city law-enforcement agencies, as well as the military, were spying on citizens because of their political activities. Writing to several members of Congress, Parten stated that the news that the military had an organized spy system working on civilians was "both shocking and disturbing," and that the country was headed toward a police state. Parten complained to Ralph Yarborough that he had "come to shudder" whenever he thought about how much "we have already violated so many of the principles which were embodied in our original Declaration of Independence."[22]

The depth and sincerity of Parten's support for the antiwar movement and its associated causes in the late 1960s was surprising to many, even to those who were aware of his past activities. Larry Goodwyn, a former editor of the *Texas Observer* recalled that he was conversing with Parten in Houston on some matter when Parten asked him if he had ever heard of a record album Parten had recently purchased. Goodwyn confessed that he had never heard of it. "About ten days later," Goodwyn remembered "this record album arrived in the mail with a little note from J. R. asking me to pay special attention to a particular track called 'Are You Running With Me Jesus?' It was a virulent attack on the Southern Protestant clergy for their hypocrisy on issues of race and war and peace. I mean it was a radical, radical song. I was astonished that J. R. was pushing it. It's very rare to find somebody with extraordinary wealth who had the populist impulses that J. R. Parten had." Joseph Califano, a former White House aid to Lyndon Johnson, represented Parten on a legal matter in 1970. Califano had not met Parten previously. When he walked into Parten's office in Houston, the first thing he saw on the wall was a large anti–Vietnam war poster. "I was stunned," Califano said, "it wasn't exactly what I had expected to see in the office of a Texas oil man. I quickly learned that he was no ordinary Texan—or ordinary oil man for that matter."[23]

In 1968, Parten provided four thousand dollars as seed money to start a Pacifica radio station in Houston. Pacifica, a commercial-free, "alternative" radio concept created and sponsored by the Pacifica Foundation, had stations in San Francisco, Los Angeles, and New York City. Pacifica provided a forum for a wide range of political viewpoints, especially those of the antiwar and student movements. Parten's money sustained the station's organizers for more than a year while they conducted a successful campaign to raise the $120,000 required by the Federal Communications Commission for a broadcast license. Parten helped with the fund-raising. On May 12, 1970, not long after Pacifica went on the air, someone blew up its transmitter with dynamite. It was the first radio station in U.S. history to be silenced by a violent act. The station returned to the airwaves a month later, only to be bombed again on October 6, 1970. No longer insured because of the first attack, Pacifica faced an extended if not permanent period of silence. Recalling how Homer Rainey's opponents had sought to deny him access to the airwaves when he was running for governor in 1946, Parten gave Pacifica twenty-five thousand dollars to pay for a new transmitter. The station was soon back on the air.[24]

Bentsen defeats Yarborough

Although he donated money and supported Ralph Yarborough's return to the Senate, Parten was not actively involved in the Democratic primary reelection campaign in the spring of 1970. He devoted nearly all his attention that spring to a bitter corporate fight involving Pan American Sulphur. Yarborough's primary opponent, former congressman Lloyd M. Bentsen Jr., was also an old friend of Parten's. The two had met at one of Sam Rayburn's "Board of Education" meetings in the late 1940s. In the early 1960s, Parten had served with Bentsen on the board of directors of the Rayburn Foundation. "I knew Lloyd and I respected him. I did not agree with Lloyd's support of our Vietnam policy, so I continued to support Ralph. I really thought he would beat Bentsen, but I knew that if he didn't the world would not come to an end because Lloyd was reasonable . . . he would listen to both sides of an argument." Parten had planned to devote more attention to Yarborough's campaign against George Bush, who had won the Republican nomination and was preparing for his second race against Yarborough. Those plans were altered when Bentsen won an upset victory against Yarborough in the primary.[25]

Bentsen's victory was aided greatly by a demagogic television advertising campaign that smeared Yarborough as an antiwar radical who supported flag-burners and draft-evaders. In turn, Yarborough smeared Bentsen with accusations that his father, Lloyd Bentsen Sr., was a land swindler and exploiter of "wet back" labor from Mexico. "I was unhappy with both campaigns," Parten later said. "Obviously, Ralph was no traitor, but I was opposed to Ralph's attempt to blame the sins of the father on the son." After his victory, Bentsen was determined to avoid the Democratic factional split that had allowed Republican John Tower to win LBJ's former Senate seat in 1961. He decided to patch up his relations with some of Yarborough's key supporters, including Parten. In July 1970, Bentsen paid a surprise visit to Parten at his home in Madisonville. He convinced Parten that he would not ignore the legislative concerns of the liberals and that he would be fiercely protective of the oil industry, especially its independent component.

Bentsen's shrewd personal diplomacy paid off. Parten endorsed his candidacy against Bush and donated money to the cause. Bentsen, who went on to defeat Bush in the November general election, developed even closer ties with Parten as he became one of the Democratic leaders in the U.S. Senate.[26]

At the beginning of the 1970s, Parten was entering the middle of his seventh decade, well beyond the age of retirement for most people. He was "hip deep" in antiwar politics and the programs of the Center for the Study of Democratic Institutions, and he had become one of the few reliable sources for funds for the peace movement. Parten's business activities also continued without pause. Not only was he busy with his ranches near Madisonville, he remained involved in the immensely successful Pan American Sulphur Company.

CHAPTER 34

The End of Pan American

I n early 1967 the Mexican government passed a law requiring every mining and chemical company operating in Mexico to be majority-owned by Mexican citizens. This law forced Pan American to sell two-thirds of its Azufrera Mexicana stock to a consortium composed of individual Mexican investors and the Mexican government for seventy-six million dollars. Although forced to sell, Pan American received a fair price and favorable terms. For the down payment, Pan American was paid twenty million dollars in cash taken from Azufrera's treasury. Two notes for twenty-five million each were payable within two years after completion of the deal, with the remaining six million to be held in an open-ended interest-bearing note. Mexican president Diaz Ordaz, eager to demonstrate that foreign investments were safe in Mexico despite the new law, sent an official message to Parten giving his personal guarantee that the Mexican government would back the notes. Impressed by the president's personal interest and assured by his promise, Parten went through with the sale, which was completed on July 1, 1967. The new owners signed a five-year contract with Harry Webb, Leonard Townsend, and other Azufrera executives to operate the company during the transition to Mexican management.[1]

After the Mexican buyers delivered their second cash-payment in the summer of 1968, Pan American had nearly sixty million dollars sitting in a bank uninvested. It remained there for months as Parten and his fellow Pan American directors tried to decide what to do with it. Eager to return to the ranks of the major independents, Parten wanted to buy an oil company with the money. He moved with caution, however, taking the time to find some "good and solid" company to acquire with the cash. Stock analysts were critical of the long delay in investing the money. One characterized Pan American's management as being far too conservative and burdened by a "hesitant style." In the summer of 1968, Pan American finally joined with Phillips Petroleum in an effort to drill for hydrogen sulfide "sour" gas in Mississippi, but it was not a major investment and nothing came of it. Little else was done. A longtime Pan American employee later claimed that "the remnants of the Little Mothers Club were all tired old men and not creative any more. They could never find a deal to spend this money on. The money was sitting in the bank in simple certificates of deposit. We were just sitting ducks." Parten admitted that he should have been more concerned about corporate raiders. "We had all that money lying around, and we didn't get it invested quick enough."[2]

The Korholz Raid

The raid eventually came in October 1968, when Parten noticed brisk trading of Pan American stock, causing a rapid increase in value. The *Wall Street Journal* reported rumors that a takeover of the "cash heavy" Pan American was in the making, naming the Susquehanna Corporation of Alexandria, Virginia, as one of the possible raiders. Susquehanna had spotted Pan American's stockpile of uninvested cash and had decided to make a play for it. Susquehanna was controlled by Herbert Korholz, a fifty-five-year-old native of Holland, who had immigrated to the United States in 1936 after receiving his education in Paris and at Cambridge University in England. Upon becoming Susquehanna's chairman in 1965, Korholz had embarked on an aggressive acquisitions binge, taking over several small companies in a variety of industries, including uranium mines, digital electronic systems, building materials, and aerospace engineering and manufacturing. In 1967 Susquehanna had gone deeply into debt to merge with the Atlantic Research Corporation and Korholz needed Pan American's cash to keep the banking wolves away from the front door.[3]

In early October, Korholz notified Parten that Susquehanna wanted to buy as much as two million of Pan American's 4.7 million shares of outstanding stock for forty dollars a share, five dollars more than its current listed market price. Stressing that Susquehanna's intentions were friendly, Korholz hoped Pan American would not attempt to stop the purchase. Parten had never heard of Korholz, so he called his stepdaughter's husband, William Anderson, who was a member of a Wall Street brokerage firm, for information on Korholz. "He has less than a sterling reputation," Anderson warned, "I wouldn't have anything to do with him." That was enough for Parten, who convinced his fellow board members to reject Korholz's offer. Parten and his colleagues made a critical tactical error at this point. They did not understand how serious Korholz was in his effort to gain control of Pan American. In early November, the Susquehanna chairman made a surprise appearance at a Pan American board meeting and declared that he had arranged financing to buy 38 percent of Pan American's common stock (1.8 million shares) for seventy-one million dollars. He promised Pan American's directors that if the sale went through, Susquehanna would not use Pan American's assets to pay off Susquehanna's debts or to merge the company with another. He also pledged that the current management would be retained and the organization left basically as it was. Pan American would simply become the "natural resources arm" of Susquehanna.[4]

After the sale of Pan American's sulphur subsidiary to Mexican investors, the Securities and Exchange Commission had ruled that Pan American was an investment company subject to strict SEC regulation. The Securities and Exchange Act of 1934 required that a person or group acquiring more than 10 percent of the stock of a company it seeks to control must inform the SEC of any plans to merge or change the structure of the acquired company. This law required Korholz to file a petition with the SEC stating his plans for the company. It also compelled Parten and his fellow directors to inform their stockholders of the offer, which would facilitate Korholz's purchase of the stock. Faced with a situation over which they now had little control and comforted by Korholz's promises, which he had documented formally in his SEC petition, Pan American agreed not to fight Susquehanna's purchase.[5]

Within days, however, Korholz revealed his true intentions when he admitted to the *Wall Street Journal,* even before the sale was closed, that he would use Pan American's cash to help him acquire American Smelting and Refining Company (ASARCO). This news stunned Parten. It was now clear, as one of Pan American's executives later said, that Susquehanna simply "wanted to get its hands on all those millions that we had in the till. It was a pure raid. They were just crooks." Parten convinced a majority of his fellow directors that Korholz's purchase of Pan American stock had to be blocked. Pan American subsequently filed suit in federal district court in Boston to block Susquehanna's takeover bid. Pan American charged that Susquehanna had violated the Securities and Exchange Act and had committed fraud by failing to make a full and complete disclosure of its intentions to grab Pan American's cash assets to pay Susquehanna's corporate debts. The court dismissed the suit as being without merit, clearing the way for Susquehanna to purchase more than one-third of Pan American.[6]

Two months after Susquehanna had completed its purchase of more than one-third of Pan American's stock, the banks pressured Korholz to take control of Pan American and use its money to pay some of Susquehanna's seventy-one-million-dollar debt. A payment of fifteen million was due in July. Parten and his group, however, were determined not to let Korholz get their money. They had been actively seeking another company to serve as a "white knight" to buy a controlling interest in Pan American and rescue them from Korholz, but these efforts had failed because potential investors feared that buying into Pan American might ultimately result in becoming part of Susquehanna. The Parten group's determination to fight grew stronger when Korholz admitted to the *Wall Street Journal* that Pan American's large cash reserve made it "an ideal vehicle with which to make a major acquisition." Complaining that an acquisition could not be made as long as the Parten group remained in control of the board of directors, Korholz announced that Susquehanna would move immediately to take over the board. To help in that effort, Susquehanna had quietly bought stock on the open market to increase its share of Pan American to 40 percent. Parten immediately swung into action. Pan American filed suit in federal court in San Antonio seeking to force Susquehanna to divest its ownership of the company's stock on the grounds that it had committed fraud by lying to Pan American's stockholders about its intentions when it purchased the stock.[7]

A nasty court battle ensued. Korholz filed court papers accusing Webb and Sandlin of mismanaging and wasting Pan American's funds. He revealed that Webb and Sandlin had given themselves secret and "excessive" pay raises after the Mexican purchase of Azufrera. He also charged that both men had used a company plane and company apartments in Mexico and the Bahamas for personal pleasure and had run up outrageously high travel and entertainment expenses in the past year. Sandlin, for example, was accused of spending twenty thousand dollars of the stockholders' money for personal entertainment in 1968. These accusations, unfortunately, were not without foundation. Parten had criticized Sandlin and Webb frequently over the years for what he felt was their fondness for spending too much of the company's money on travel and entertainment. Sandlin had moved his residence to Mexico City in 1967 to manage Azufrera Mexicana for its new investors and Parten had been shocked by the luxurious lifestyle in which Sandlin had indulged since his move. He had thought that Sandlin's conspicuous consumption had been made possible by his exclusive Mexican import license for Polish vodka, but Korholz's charges convinced Parten that Sandlin's lavish lifestyle had also been subsidized by Pan American's stockholders. Parten was furious and, as a result, his longtime relationship with Sandlin deteriorated.[8]

On May 29, 1969, the San Antonio court issued an injunction against Susquehanna prohibiting it from taking any action to alter Pan American's board of directors until the suit could be tried. Two weeks later, however, Susquehanna's attorneys persuaded the Fifth Circuit Court of Appeals in New Orleans to rescind the injunction. The legal battle continued for another nine months, finally ending in Susquehanna's favor on March 17, 1970, when the Federal Court of Appeals in New Orleans ordered dismissal of Pan American's suit, despite the findings of an SEC examiner in August 1969 that Susquehanna had violated federal securities law. The examiner reported that Susquehanna had made "false and misleading statements" in its original petition to the SEC. Nevertheless, Supreme Court justice Hugo Black's denial of Pan American's application for a stay of the Appeals Court's decision brought the battle to a close on April 27, 1970.[9]

With the legal struggle over, Susquehanna was now free to merge with Pan American and to revamp its board of directors. Although he had won this particular battle, Korholz told the press that the victory was "a hollow one." The fight the Parten group had waged had kept Korholz away from Pan American's cash for nearly eighteen months, the legal fees had been costly, and Susquehanna's creditors were demanding payment. Korholz also knew that his war with Parten was far from over. Because the SEC still classified Pan American as an investment trust, Korholz would not be able to get Pan American's cash without SEC approval. As long as Parten was opposing him, Korholz knew that he would have trouble getting the SEC to let Susquehanna have Pan American's money. In May 1970, Korholz tried to persuade his nemesis to remain on the board of directors as a minority stockholders' representative and to participate in Korholz's various diversification schemes. Rejecting the offer, Parten resigned from the board, leaving him without an official position with Pan American for the first time since its founding in 1947. Parten later explained that he just "didn't want to be in business with Korholz. I figured that it was going to be a continual fight to preserve the rights of the minority stockholders and that I could do more good from the outside than from the inside."[10]

Korholz reorganized Pan American's management, becoming president and chairman of the board in the fall of 1970. He also took control of the board by appointing a majority of directors from Susquehanna. As he tightened his grip on the company, Korholz held off the banks that had financed his raid on Pan American, but by the end of 1970 knowing he was running out of time with his creditors, he quietly persuaded the newly constituted Pan American board to loan Susquehanna thirty-six million dollars to pay some of its corporate debt. Korholz had one major problem, however. The loan had to be approved by the SEC. To prevent Parten from interfering, Korholz planned to file the application and get it approved quickly without Parten's knowledge. Parten, however, learned about Korholz's scheme. After recruiting a small group of stockholders to join with him to form the PASCO Stockholders Protective Committee, Parten hired as counsel Joseph A. Califano Jr., who had been Lyndon Johnson's domestic policy chief and was now with a powerful Washington law firm headed by Edward Bennett Williams.[11]

Califano agreed to monitor the SEC to watch for Susquehanna's petition, and as soon as it was filed Califano would submit a petition asking the SEC to block the loan. Califano soon learned that the SEC had scheduled a hearing on the Pan American loan for the second week in January, and prepared a petition asking the commission to intervene and stop the loan. "Califano filed the petition back in Washington just thirty minutes before five o'clock on Friday afternoon," Parten later recalled. "Korholz's attorneys weren't tending to their business very closely, because they didn't learn about it until they read it in the *Wall Street Journal* on Monday morning. That frightened them." Parten told the *Journal* that because Susquehanna dominated the Pan American board of directors, it would not protect the rights of the eleven thousand minority stockholders. He accused Susquehanna of trying to "siphon" thirty-six million in cash from Pan American to repay loans it had received to buy Pan American. "Should Susquehanna default in repayment of the loan," Parten was quoted as saying, "Pan American would be left holding shares of its own stock as its primary security for the loan, but the value of the stock would be drastically impaired by the drainage of $36 million from the company's $77.1 million in assets."[12]

When he learned about Parten's request to the SEC to block the loan, Korholz announced that he would withdraw the loan request. Parten told the press that he did not believe that Susquehanna had given up on the loan and charged that the withdrawal was simply a "subterfuge to hide its intentions." He planned to monitor the situation to make certain that Korholz did not make another attempt to sneak the loan. Parten was concerned that Korholz would petition the SEC to exempt Pan American from being regulated by the Investment Companies Act. If the SEC agreed, Korholz could grab the money without having to ask government approval. Califano would file a counterpetition with the SEC if Korholz tried anything. Korholz now found himself in a difficult situation. Pressed hard by the banks, he either had to find a way to get Pan American's cash or he had to sell the company.[13]

Korholz Sells Out

Korholz finally made an attempt to buy off Parten. "Korholz asked me how much it would take financially to satisfy me," Parten claimed. "I told him it was very simple, 'just keep your cotton-picking hands off of the stockholders' money'." One of Parten's longtime employees later noted that Parten "had not been able to prevent Korholz from taking over Pan American, but he was certainly able to hold everything up long enough for the company to be traded. Korholz was not able to use the money like he had intended to." Out of options, the banks on his back, and profits down from his other enterprises, Korholz had no alternative but to get out. In June 1971, he sold Pan American to the Studebaker-Worthington company, an industrial conglomerate involved in a diverse range of enterprises and products, including STP motor-oil additive and a chain of gasoline stations.[14]

Parten was relieved to be rid of Korholz, but was angered by the terms of the sale, which allowed Studebaker-Worthington to get control of Pan American for a down payment of twenty-five million dollars. An additional payment, not to exceed $10.5 million would be due later, but the final amount to be paid would be determined by a thorough evaluation of Pan American's assets. In late June, Parten directed Califano to file another petition with the SEC, this time to stop Pan American's sale to Studebaker-Worthington on the grounds that the purchase price was "ridiculously low."[15]

Studebaker-Worthington's chairman and chief executive officer was Derald H. Ruttenberg, a fifty-five-year-old Yale- and Harvard-educated lawyer. Ruttenberg, who was as much a corporate raider as Korholz, described his company to *Forbes* magazine as one that looked for "good economic ventures on which we can make a reasonable return and which are not high-priced. Since the 1960's, our major acquisitions have been opportunistic." When the Parten group challenged his bid with the SEC, Ruttenberg met with Parten and Califano in New York in an attempt to resolve their problems. "Ruttenberg asked me to come back on the Board and help him invest our money," Parten later said. "He assured me that he was going to run this company . . . for the benefit of all the stockholders. That went a long way towards convincing me that they were sincere and earnest about it." Parten agreed to withdraw his challenge and to rejoin the Pan American board of directors after Ruttenberg agreed to let Parten find an attractive oil and gas prospect for the company to purchase with its cash. Ruttenberg also added to the board of directors Jack W. Boothe, one of Parten's longtime employees who had once served as treasurer for Pan American.[16]

Although Marlin Sandlin also remained on the Pan American board, Parten, unhappy about Sandlin's extravagant personal use of the company's money and bitter about his support of the loan to Korholz, no longer saw him as an ally. In fact, the thirty-year friendship between the two former business associates was at an end. Their estrangement deepened in 1972 when Sandlin became a member of John Connally's Democrats for Richard Nixon, an unforgivable sin to the strongly partisan Parten. Parten never again spoke to Sandlin, who died at the age of sixty-four at his beach home in Galveston in May 1974.[17]

Studebaker-Worthington assumed controlling interest in Pan American in July 1971. Two months later, Ruttenberg accomplished what Korholz had been unable to do: he changed Pan American's legal status from an investment company to an operational one that could make corporate acquisitions. The difference was that Parten agreed to the change. At the end of 1971, Pan American left the sulphur business entirely by selling its remaining share of stock in Azufrera to Mexican investors for four million dollars in cash. In May 1972, Ruttenberg became Pan American's CEO and chairman.[18]

"What happens if the ground breaks and all of that oil leaks away?"

In the meantime, Parten had initiated a search for an oil property for Pan American to acquire. With the help of Bill Anderson, a specialist in oil and gas for a Wall Street brokerage house, Parten identified Husky Oil as a sound company with strong oil reserves in Wyoming and undervalued stock. Parten sent Anderson to make a presentation to Ruttenberg. After Anderson emphasized the importance of Husky's underground oil reserves, Ruttenberg asked a question that shocked Parten when he heard about it. "What happens," Ruttenberg asked, "if the ground breaks and all of that oil leaks away? Do we lose our investment?" It was all Anderson could do to keep from laughing, but Parten did not see anything funny about the comment. It told him all he needed to know about Ruttenberg. There were few things he disapproved of more than someone who knew nothing about the oil business trying to run an oil company. The incident, humorous as it was, distorted Parten's view of Ruttenberg from then on. Ruttenberg agreed to make an offer to Husky, but his bid was much lower than Anderson had advised and it was rejected. Another company soon acquired Husky for the same price Anderson had recommended to Ruttenberg.[19]

Undaunted, Parten searched for other prospects. In August 1972, he contacted his old friend Robert O. Anderson, chairman of the Atlantic Richfield Company (ARCO), about the extensive oil properties in the western United States acquired by ARCO in its merger with Sinclair in 1969. Parten knew that the Justice Department was forcing Anderson to sell the property on antitrust grounds. When Anderson agreed to a tentative offer of $157 million, Ruttenberg approved the deal, which was closed on September 22. Pan American acquired seven oil fields in the Midwest and Wyoming, including an old but modernized Sinclair refinery in Rawlins, Wyoming, eighteen hundred Sinclair gas stations in a fourteen-state area extending from Louisiana to Wyoming, and partial interests in two pipeline systems. On December 29, Pan American officially changed its name to PASCO. In early January, Parten persuaded Ruttenberg to hire Art W. Winter, the former president of Great Northern, to manage PASCO, which was now an integrated oil company refining twenty thousand barrels of crude per day.[20]

A Dispute Over Stock Options

For the first two years of their corporate marriage, relations between the Parten group and Studebaker-Worthington were relatively good. Ruttenberg had followed Parten's recommendation to buy the former Sinclair property and had employed one of Parten's associates to run PASCO's oil operations. The relationship soured, however, in the fall of 1973. When Parten returned to his former position on Pan American's board of directors in 1971, he agreed to serve with Ruttenberg on the company's stock option committee. The bylaws of the committee prohibited its members from giving themselves stock options. In September 1973, Ruttenberg resigned from the committee while Parten was in the Mayo Clinic in Minnesota for his annual checkup. Ruttenberg was replaced by one of his associates. The new committee promptly granted valuable stock options to Ruttenberg and to Leslie Welsh, president of Studebaker-Worthington. Perfectly legal, it had become a common practice for corporate executives to take stock options in such circumstances. They had not informed Parten about their plan, however, aware that he would object. As a result, Parten felt that Ruttenberg had been dishonest and deceptive. Particularly galling to Parten was that one of the reasons given for granting the options to Ruttenberg was his "active" role in the ARCO deal. To Parten, this amounted to a finders' fee being paid to a man who had done very little to deserve it. "I had told many people that this was one large purchase that was bought without paying a commission," Parten said. Then for them to catch me in the hospital and claim that stock option didn't square with me very well."[21]

PASCO was making healthy profits, mainly because of skyrocketing oil prices resulting from the oil boycott imposed by the Arabs in October 1973, but tensions were building between Parten and Ruttenberg. The former, soon to be seventy-eight years old, was a cautious entrepreneur of the old school who wanted to make money, but who was equally intent on building a sound and responsible business that protected its stockholders and its customers. The latter, twenty-five-years younger than Parten, was an American corporate leader of the modern era, more interested in making quick and large profits than in building a business or protecting consumers. Ruttenberg, for example, wanted to merge Studebaker-Worthington's STP motor-oil-additive operation with PASCO, but Parten protested. He thought oil additives were a sham and he did not want to be associated with a business that he believed to be less than honest. In addition, he scorned Ruttenberg's lack of experience in and knowledge about the business, especially refining, and he deeply resented Ruttenberg's intrusions into PASCO's operations.[22]

The End of PASCO

The growing hostility between Parten and Ruttenberg did not bode well for PASCO's future, but external rather than internal developments eventually proved more damaging to the company. The great energy crisis of 1973–1974 inspired a bizarre and complex system of price controls, entitlements, and allocations that made the mandatory oil-import program of the 1960s seem simple. Under the Federal Energy Act of May 1973, the federal government established a program to subsidize refineries that processed foreign oil. These refineries, many of them small independents, were forced to buy oil at substantially higher prices than refineries that ran on domestic oil. Federal policy-makers determined that the country needed these refineries to prevent a massive products shortage, so a plan was devised to make the domestic-crude refiners make payments called entitlements to the foreign-crude refiners for every barrel of domestic crude they refined. This would make up the cost differential, subsidize the foreign-crude refiners, and maintain product prices evenly, allowing the foreign-crude refiners to compete with the domestic refiners. The general idea was to help independents remain competitive with majors, but the program had the opposite result. In many cases, the domestic refiner was an independent, while the refiner of foreign oil was a major. [23]

As an independent with a refinery in Wyoming running on its own domestic supply, PASCO was compelled by law to pay entitlements to major oil companies that were refining foreign oil. "We found ourselves paying eight dollars a barrel on the crude oil that we ran from our own production through our own refinery," Parten complained, "and one of the companies that was eligible for the sale of these rights was ARCO from whom we had bought this property." The entitlement program was costing PASCO dearly. Working with Califano, Parten won some relief from Congress, which granted small refiners an exemption from entitlement payments for the first fifty thousand barrels per day of domestic crude refined. Even with that exemption, PASCO's internal problems continued. "We could see nothing but trouble from Ruttenberg's lack of knowledge and lack of willingness to be patient and learn anything about refining and production of crude oil and marketing," Parten said. "That finally caused us to sell the property and liquidate PASCO."

In December 1975, PASCO sold their oil and gas fields in Wyoming to AMOCO for $225 million, but retained the refineries, pipelines, and gas stations. On December 30, 1975, soon after the AMOCO sale was closed, PASCO announced plans to liquidate. It distributed to its shareholders the cash it earned from the AMOCO deal and sold its remaining assets (gas stations, pipelines, and the refinery) to the new Sinclair Company in June 1976. When PASCO finally closed its offices in December 1976, it distributed to its stockholders a company liquidation profit of more than one hundred million dollars. Parten was bitter about having to sell the old Sinclair properties and liquidating PASCO. Refraining from saying anything about his problems with Ruttenberg, he instead publicly blamed federal regulation for PASCO's demise. He complained to the *Texas Observer* that the entitlements program was destroying "the fabric" of the industry and destroying competition.[24]

Thus ended the last of J. R. Parten's major business enterprises. What had begun thirty years before as an interesting little gamble for Parten and his friends in the Little Mothers Club, and which subsequently had taken on the world's major sulphur companies and succeeded beyond any of their dreams, was no more.

CHAPTER 35

"My Graduate Education in the Liberal Arts"

Robert Hutchins and the Malcolm Moos Affair, 1972–1975

B y the early 1970s, J. R. Parten, whose annual donations had averaged one hundred thousand dollars for a number of years, had become the largest financial contributor to the Center for the Study of Democratic Institutions. As one of the two original directors of the Fund for the Republic still on the board, Parten took deep pride in the Center's growth and accomplishments. Since 1969, when Hutchins reorganized the Center around nine resident senior fellows, the Center had attracted much attention nationally with highly publicized convocations and research projects. It had a membership in excess of one hundred thousand and it published an official journal, the *Center Magazine*, and a series of book-length *Occasional Papers*.[1]

Parten found the Center's work important and stimulating, but he was less than enthusiastic about its financial behavior. Hutchins spent money as quickly as he raised it, constantly pushing the budget into the red. The Center had received thirty million dollars since its creation but Hutchins had resisted advice to set any of it aside for an endowment to support operations. He had a special ability to bring in money whenever there was a financial crisis, so he saw no reason not to spend whatever money was at hand. Although bothered by Hutchins's blase attitude about the budget, Parten had always stepped forward with cash whenever necessary to ward off insolvency.[2]

Robert Hutchins could also depend on Parten's moral support. Hutchins often complained to his staff about how difficult it was to persuade his board members to support controversial policies and how easily criticism from their business associates swayed them. Parten was an exception, however. "J. R. is the best man on the board and one of the best men I've ever met," Hutchins told Frank Kelly, the Center's publicist. "He's a man with that inner strength who doesn't depend on the opinions of other people for his own self-esteem. He can . . . go through these battles and not waver."[3]

Parten and Hutchins had forged a strong professional alliance, but not a close personal friendship. "I didn't have the sense that they were intimate personal friends," one staff member observed. "They were very different people in terms of background and personal taste." Nevertheless, Hutchins's respect for Parten was both practical and sincere. "What would we do without you," he asked Parten in 1971. "You have got to live forever."[4]

In late 1971, Robert Hutchins decided to honor J. R. Parten for his financial and moral support with a special convocation and fund-raising dinner in Houston. Making arrangements for the event, Hutchins's second in command, Harry Ashmore, told one of the Center's board members that "God knows [Parten] deserves the tribute." By having the dinner in Houston, Hutchins could also bring recognition to three of Parten's associates from Texas who were serving on the board: J. Howard Marshall, who had served since the 1950s; Fagan Dickson, who had been appointed in 1970; and Bernard Rapoport, an insurance company entrepreneur from Waco who joined the board in 1971. Parten had recruited all three. An event in Houston in honor of Parten would publicize the Center's Texas connections, which Hutchins hoped might also attract new financial contributers for the Center.

In April 1972, however, Parten asked Rapoport to postpone the event. His active role in the current election campaigns, as well as his vocal opposition to the Vietnam war, had angered the business establishment in Houston to the point that fund-raising would be difficult. "J. R . . . is getting a lot of flack in Houston," Rapoport reported to Hutchins. Agreeing to the postponement, Hutchins could not resist the temptation to tease Parten the next time he talked to him on the telephone: "This is the Kremlin calling 'Comrade' Parten," Hutchins declared gleefully when J. R. answered the call.[5]

Sissy and Barney

Parten was "getting flack" for his highly visible support of Frances "Sissy" Farenthold's bid for the Democratic nomination for governor of Texas and of Sen. George McGovern's campaign for the Democratic presidential nomination in the spring of 1972, candidates who were considered by Parten's conservative business associates to be much farther to the left of the political spectrum than anyone Parten had supported previously. The "radicalism" of both candidates, however, stemmed more from their fervent call for social justice and their strong antiwar and anti–arms race views than from their positions on economic issues. An advocate of women's rights and a civil libertarian, Farenthold had attracted popular attention as a reformer in the Texas legislature during the Sharpstown banking scandal. Her gubernatorial campaign was an open challenge to the conservative "good old boy" state political establishment and its candidate Lt. Gov. Ben Barnes. Senator

Sissy Farenthold, 1972. *CN 09619. Courtesy Farenthold Papers, CAH.*

McGovern's presidential campaign, on the other hand, was more of a one-issue affair. He parted company with many liberals and nearly all conservatives by pledging, if elected president, to withdraw U.S. military forces from Vietnam unilaterally and immediately and to end the nuclear-arms race with the Soviet Union. These controversial positions, however, attracted Parten to McGovern. Ignoring the Texas business establishment's strong disapproval of his candidates, something to which he had long ago become accustomed, Parten joined with Bernard "Barney" Rapoport and the wealthy iconoclastic Houston art patron Jean de Menil to raise most of the campaign funds for the Farenthold and McGovern campaigns in Texas.[6]

Although Parten's consistent support for liberal Democrats placed him far to the left in Texas political circles in the late 1960s and early 1970s, he was usually joined there by two other businessmen: Dickinson banker Walter Hall, and, most consistently, Barney Rapoport, his friend and colleague on the board of the Center for the Study of Democratic Institutions. These liberal businessmen did not agree on every issue—Hall was a hawk on Vietnam, for example—but they generally supported the same candidates (especially Ralph Yarborough) and they were unanimously in support of the political journal the *Texas Observer* as a much needed voice of the liberal cause.[7]

Of the group, Parten was closest to Rapoport, whom he first met in 1967. Parten was a regent when Rapoport was a student at the University of Texas and he had won Rapoport's respect and admiration for his support of Homer Rainey. When John Henry Faulk introduced Rapoport to Parten in 1967, Rapoport was in awe of the liberal oil man. "At that time," Rapoport recalled, "J. R. was reputed to be one of the richest guys in Texas. Coming from my kind of background, I'd never met anyone with that kind of money." Rapoport was also in awe of Parten because of his relationship with Bob Hutchins, who was one of Rapoport's idols. Nearly opposites in personality, Parten and Rapoport nonetheless shared important concerns. To Ronnie Dugger, who worked closely with both men for many years, Parten was "reserved, distant, and dignified. He seemed very 'Old World' to me, like an English gentleman." Rapoport, however, he described as "openly passionate and driven by these deep ethical emotions about the human race. Their common characteristic was political and moral passion. It was interesting to see how differently it was manifested in each." Parten and Rapoport rapidly became good friends as well as close political allies.[8]

The 1972 Texas Democratic primary was one of the political campaigns in which Parten and Rapoport played an active and significant role as a team. Both were early and enthusiastic supporters of Sissy Farenthold for governor and their joint financial support and fund-raising efforts helped make Farenthold's campaign possible. John Henry Faulk, who had moved to Austin four years before, initially got Parten and Rapoport interested in Farenthold. Parten had never met Farenthold, but she was the granddaughter of Judge Tarlton, his real property professor in law school, and the daughter of Dudley Tarlton, a lawyer in Corpus Christi whom he had known well. When he met her and had an opportunity to discuss issues with her, Parten was even more pleased. "I was impressed . . . that Sissy Farenthold was a real Democrat," Parten recalled. "She had a good . . . understanding of the need to defend and protect our constitutional liberties." After that first meeting, Farenthold came to count Parten as one of her most important sources for political advice. "I have always learned from being around Major Parten," she said. "I always feel he is going to be on the side of the angels politically. As a consequence, whenever I hear that the Major thinks that and says this, I'm going to pay a lot of attention to it."[9]

Parten joined with Rapoport, de Menil, and Houston banker Robert Lanier to loan sixty thousand dollars to the Farenthold campaign, and at a particularly critical juncture a few weeks before the election he contributed six thousand dollars to keep her state campaign office open. Farenthold ran her campaign without a professional public relations person, without billboards (she opposed them), and with only a little radio and television time. In addition to her opposition to the Vietnam war and her support of George McGovern's presidential candidacy, Farenthold demanded that the Texas Rangers be disarmed because of their record for suppressing Mexican American and labor union protest, called for strict gun-control legislation, and argued for the enactment of a corporate-profits tax.[10]

Helped by a staff described as a "zealous, if disorganized, band of newly enfranchised students and old Yarborough hands," Farenthold surprised nearly everyone by receiving 28 percent of the vote to wind up in a runoff with rancher and former legislator Dolph Briscoe Jr. of Uvalde. Briscoe had spent over $900,000 to her $212,000. Heavily favored Ben Barnes (a protégé of John Connally), as well as incumbent governor Preston Smith, both of whom had been tainted by the Sharpstown banking scandal, failed to make the runoff. Delighted by the outcome, Parten told Farenthold that she had run an "intelligent and effective campaign. It is our earnest hope that you may gain the democratic nomination . . . in order that we might surely see a total elimination of corruption in our state government." Parten also helped finance Farenthold's runoff campaign, but Briscoe was able to attract most of the Barnes and Smith votes to win the nomination. "I was disappointed that Sissy lost," Parten said. "Looking back, I guess she was too liberal for most Texans. But I was pleased that Smith and Barnes had been tossed out of office."[11]

The McGovern Campaign

Two major objectives drove Parten's activities during the 1972 presidential campaign. One was his deep desire to stop the war in Southeast Asia. The other was to rid the country of Richard Nixon. "Surely it has come time to get this crazy and undeclared war in Vietnam over," Parten told Houston congressman Bob Eckhardt. Parten added that U.S. war policy "seems nothing short of criminal under the Nuremberg principles under which we hung many Germans after WWII. The blood is on all of our hands. As a citizen, I feel deeply that it is my duty to protest." Parten supported George McGovern, despite his dislike of McGovern's domestic-economy proposals, which Parten felt would place too many restrictions on private enterprise. Because of McGovern's views on economic policy, Parten had supported Maine senator Edmund Muskie in the early primaries. But once Muskie had withdrawn and McGovern became the leading candidate, Parten shifted his support to the antiwar senator from South Dakota, whom he had known personally for several years through the Center for the Study of Democratic Institutions.[12]

Although Parten endorsed McGovern's candidacy in April 1972, his formal entry into the McGovern camp occurred on May 1, when he attended a campaign fund-raising party in New York City. Parten joined forty prominent people, including entertainers Shirley McLaine, Warren Beatty, and Barbara Streisand, and General Motors heir Stewart Mott, who attended the party to demonstrate their support for McGovern and to raise one million dollars for his campaign. Parten agreed to team with Rapoport to raise money for McGovern's Texas campaign.[13]

Parten was delighted by McGovern's successful bid for the Democratic presidential nomination and he approved McGovern's selection of Missouri senator Thomas Eagleton to serve as his vice presidential running mate. Parten had identified Eagleton earlier as a promising young Democrat who could contribute much to the party. He was outraged, however, when a controversy arose a few days after the Democratic convention about Eagleton's medical history and pressure built on McGovern to dump him from the ticket. Parten wired McGovern: "We must remember your opposition in this race is the military industrial complex first and Richard Nixon second. Tom Eagleton they have cause to dread and therefore will go to any length to force you to drop him. I still like the team of McGovern and Eagleton against the War Hawks." Only a few days after pledging his complete support for Eagleton, McGovern removed him from the ticket and replaced him with former Peace Corps director Sargent Shriver. "The worst thing McGovern did was when he fired Eagleton just because the Pentagon didn't want him," Parten declared. "I always thought Sargent Shriver was a lightweight."[14]

540

McGovern's action soured Parten on his candidacy. Nevertheless, Parten's intense dislike of Nixon and the war kept him involved as a fund-raiser for the campaign. "I don't know how many hundreds of thousands of dollars J. R. and I raised together for McGovern," Rapoport recalled. "We had luncheons and gatherings for him in Houston. I was the pitchman. J. R. always sat quietly in a corner and people came to him. We had about 30 or 40 people in Houston that were good for a $1000 to $10,000. Jean de Menil was probably the most important member of that group. J. R. and I would just call these luncheons. Then I'd make the pitch and the money would come in." The most successful fund-raising event Parten and Rapoport held in Houston was a luncheon for Shriver at the Sheraton-Lincoln Hotel on September 13. Though only twenty-five people attended, Rapoport and Parten succeeded in raising nearly one hundred thousand dollars. "That was a lot of money in 1972," Rapoport noted, "and it was desperately needed by the campaign." Parten's donation of twenty-five thousand was matched by de Menil and Bob Lanier. After the luncheon, Shriver told reporters that he had just come from "a very enthusiastic luncheon of men of means."[15]

Parten personally contributed a total of forty-five thousand dollars to McGovern's ultimately unsuccessful campaign, contributions which were closely watched by Nixon's vindictive reelection campaign organization. A few months after Nixon's reelection, auditors from the Internal Revenue Service arrived at Parten's office and demanded access to his financial records. "Well, I always expect that," Parten later admitted. "I learned a long time ago that there's nothing you can do about income tax, except be honest, pay it, and expect your accountants to protect you and see that you don't overpay." The auditing team worked for several weeks going through Parten's records. The IRS eventually presented Parten with a bill for $350,000 in back taxes, which included a claim that Parten owed gift taxes on his contributions to the McGovern campaign because they had not been routed through a legally approved political committee. Parten protested the tax claim, but he eventually paid fifteen thousand dollars in gift taxes because McGovern's finance people had failed to run the contributions through the proper committee. "After I paid the bill, it occurred to me that there's some wickedness in this thing," Parten said. "Ol' Nixon did that to me. And later, I found out he had done it to a lot of people that had opposed him."[16]

Parten's suspicions about his tax audit were confirmed later during the Watergate hearings when it was revealed that Nixon's domestic policy chief John Ehrlichman had compiled a list of 490 individuals considered to be enemies of Nixon. Ehrlichman had given the list to White House special legal counsel John Dean, who was told to submit it to the IRS commissioner with the instructions that those listed should undergo special tax audits. This so-called "Nixon enemies list" included J. R. Parten, Bernard Rapoport, and Frances Farenthold as well as such nationally prominent McGovern supporters as Shirley McLaine, Gary Hart, and Pierre Salinger. The use of the IRS to harass and embarass Nixon's political opponents constituted one of the articles of impeachment drawn up by the House Judiciary Committee. When a reporter asked Parten for his reaction to being on the list, he replied that he was "deeply honored," adding that the list was proof that Nixon was "a rare combination of a crook and a fool."[17]

Parten was disappointed by Nixon's landslide victory over McGovern, but he and many other McGovern supporters enjoyed some vindication when the Watergate scandal drove Nixon from the presidency in August 1974. Throughout the Watergate hearings, Parten had sent a stream of telegrams to Sen. Sam Ervin, chair of the Senate Watergate Committee, urging him to press forward with the investigation. "The revelations . . . are forcing the American people to understand what our government has been doing to endanger the Republic," Parten declared.[18]

The Search for Hutchins's Successor

On March 3, 1973, the Center for the Study of Democratic Institutions finally held its long-delayed event in honor of J. R. Parten. Feeling that partisan political tensions had eased sufficiently for it to be a success, Bob Hutchins and his staff joined local and state civic and educational leaders at Houston's Sheraton-Lincoln Hotel to participate in a day-long special convocation on current issues. That evening, the Center paid homage to Parten at a fund-raising dinner in his honor. A keynote address by former attorney general Ramsey Clark was followed by speeches in tribute to the dinner's honoree. Among the speakers was Bernard Rapoport, who praised Parten for his lonely stand "against anachronistic and evil men on the [University of Texas] Board who fired a great university president." The last speech was reserved for Hutchins, who declared that there would never have been a Fund for the Republic or a Center for the Study of Democratic Institutions without Parten. Hutchins emphasized Parten's role in persuading Henry Ford to provide fifteen million dollars to allow the Fund to become independent as well as the decisive part Parten had played in the effort to preserve the Fund's tax-exempt status.[19]

After the dinner, Hutchins met privately with Parten to scold him gently about a matter of importance to the Center's future. "J. R., you are letting me down," he complained. "You are not trying to find my successor." Hutchins had been diagnosed with bladder cancer in 1971 and Parten had arranged for him to be evaluated at Houston's famed M. D. Anderson Cancer Hospital. While in Houston undergoing treatment, Hutchins's health problems and advancing age forced him to consider retirement. He had asked Parten to find his replacement as head of the Center, but Parten had ignored his request. "I just figured that Bob wasn't ready to retire," Parten later explained. "I just couldn't visualize the Center going on without him as its head. I dragged my feet for months." Now, two years later, Hutchins was telling Parten as firmly as he could that he was serious about retiring and that he was depending on him to find an appropriate successor. Reluctantly, Parten agreed to initiate the search.[20]

Some of Parten's reluctance might have been due to the fact that the high-profile searches in which he had participated as a regent of the University of Texas had resulted in much contention and controversy. Given the effects the Rainey and

Spies affairs had on the university, it is understandable that Parten did not want to plunge into a similar effort that had the potential to adversely affect the Center.

In the summer of 1973, the search for Hutchins's successor was initiated by Parten as chair of the Fund's committee on organization, which included board members Harold Willens, Arnold Grant, and James Douglas. Parten wanted Hutchins's replacement to be a substantial figure in the academic world from outside the Center. He was aware that senior fellow and member of the board Harry Ashmore coveted the job. Hutchins had delegated much authority for the Center's daily operations to Ashmore and to Dr. Norton Ginsburg, a geographer on leave from the University of Chicago who was the Center's dean of senior fellows. But Parten and his colleagues on the search committee felt that Ashmore lacked the necessary scholarly credentials and reputation. Parten also thought Ashmore had little regard for budgetary constraints and that he lacked a sense of urgency in his work. Spending was something that Parten was determined to bring under strict control. "I believed in a balanced budget," he said. "That removed from consideration Ashmore and several others around him who were spending money very freely." With the Center once again facing a financial crisis, Parten wanted someone who would eliminate its $850,000 deficit.[21]

Parten's committee considered fifteen candidates recommended by Hutchins. "We didn't interview a man Hutchins didn't nominate," Parten claimed. "I saw that anybody that came in had to have Hutchins' protection to get along with Ashmore and the Senior Fellows." The committee eventually picked three finalists: Malcolm Moos, president of the University of Minnesota; Harlan Cleveland, president of the University of Hawaii; and Russell Peterson, former governor of Delaware. Moos, who had been on Hutchins's personal list of potential candidates, soon became the front-runner. Parten was especially impressed when he learned that Moos had drafted most of President Eisenhower's farewell address, which had included the famous warning about the increasing power of the military-industrial complex. Parten had often quoted the warning in his own letters to Congress.[22]

A slender man with bushy eyebrows and a sharply angled face, Moos was fifty-eight years old. A native of Minnesota, with a doctorate from the University of California at Berkeley, Moos had been on Hutchins's original list of candidates. He had taught political science at Johns Hopkins for twenty-one years and had authored or coauthored eleven books. Moos worked in the White House during Eisenhower's second term and he later served as an adviser on public affairs to the Rockefeller brothers. Appointed president of the University of Minnesota in 1967, Moos had announced that he would retire in July 1974. As president of the University of Minnesota, he had his share of enemies and critics. Some of his regents felt that he had been too soft in his handling of students who had protested on campus against the war in Vietnam, while faculty members who were attempting to unionize saw him as too much of a regents' man. Moos had referred to Watergate as an attempted "coup d'etat" by Richard Nixon, thereby alienating Republican members of the state legislature. He had also angered Minnesota's medical establishment by merging the university's medical branch with the Mayo

Clinic. Recalling Homer Rainey's experience, Parten was not troubled by Moos's campus critics. Instead, he was impressed by the fact that Moos had raised Minnesota's endowment from a rank in the lower quarter to one in the upper quarter of the nation's state universities.[23]

Convinced that Moos would be an effective fund-raiser and impressed with his academic credentials and experience, Parten submitted his name to Hutchins, who approved the choice. When Parten warned Hutchins about the criticism of Moos, Hutchins replied that such criticism of a university president could just as easily be interpreted to mean that he was doing a good job. Disagreement later arose as to whether Hutchins had endorsed Moos, but Parten was sure he had. "If I had thought that Hutchins didn't want Moos, that would have been enough for me," he stressed.[24]

At a Center board meeting in Washington on October 8, 1973, held prior to the opening of the Center's covocation *Pacem in Terris III*, he announced that Moos was his committee's choice for chairman of the Center. To smooth the way financially, Parten informed the board that he would make a personal gift to Moos of twenty-five thousand dollars to serve as a down payment on a new house and that Rapoport's insurance company had agreed to finance the mortgage. Moos, however, would not be able to assume his new duties until July 1, 1974. After a discussion, the board voted to make Moos an offer, and his appointment as chairman was announced during the *Pacem in Terris III* convocation—but not before Parten and Rapoport settled some last-minute demands. When Rappoport called to offer him the job, Moos asked for guaranteed tenure, the outright purchase of a house for him in Santa Barbara, and the designation of Harvey Wheeler as the head of the Center's academic program. Moos's unexpected attempt to change the agreement governing his appointment irritated Parten, but he still believed Moos was the best person for the job. At Parten's request, Rapoport persuaded Moos to withdraw his new conditions.[25]

Dissension in Santa Barbara

Moos's last-minute demands, particularly the proposal to make Wheeler the new dean, warned of problems ahead. Moos and Wheeler had been colleagues at Johns Hopkins and they were good friends, but Ashmore and some of the other senior fellows disliked Wheeler intensely. Moos's attempt to give Wheeler administrative authority was a particularly alarming development to Ashmore, who hoped to preserve his own power base at the Center. Parten and some of the Center's staff members believed that Ashmore expected Moos to raise funds to pay for the continuation of Ashmore's pet (and expensive) programs, such as the *Pacem in Terris* convocations, while Ashmore ran the Center.[26]

Parten had other ideas, however. He and J. Howard Marshall persuaded Moos that the Center's money was being wasted. Faced with a projected deficit of nearly one million dollars for the coming fiscal year, firm action was required to bring the budget under control. Parten urged Moos to reduce the size of the staff and implement a long-range plan with a realistic budget tied to a new fund-raising effort. Parten also told Moos that he had to work much more closely with the board of directors than had Hutchins, and that to establish his own management authority Ashmore's power had to be reduced.[27]

Agreeing with Parten's recommendations, Moos said that he planned to revitalize the Center with new programs to attract money from potential donors who had refused to give money to the organization when Hutchins led it. He promised to present a long-range plan to the board during its February 1974 meeting. Armed with Parten's strong backing, Moos informed Ashmore in late November that he did not want the staff to commit the Center to any new programs before he assumed the chairmanship. Further, he told Ashmore that the Center's financial situation was not good and needed a retrenchment program "as we catch our breath and move ahead with new intellectual direction and a muscular, long-range funding program." He emphasized that this meant that there would be no *Pacem in Terris IV*, one of Ashmore's favored projects.[28]

Moos's declarations sparked a fight over control of the Center, one pitting Ashmore and his allies against Parten, Moos, and their supporters. Already bitter about not being selected to be Hutchins's successor and aware of Parten's personal lack of respect for him, Ashmore launched a counterattack against Parten and Moos. Ashmore's attack was greatly aided by Moos's decision to stay in Minnesota until July 1974, which gave Ashmore eight months to bring Hutchins over to his side and to undermine Moos's relationship with the board. Ashmore gathered information about Moos's problems at Minnesota and circulated it among the staff and board members. He also spread the rumor that Parten had unilaterally selected Moos.[29]

Another problem was Harvey Wheeler, who acted as though he were in charge and alienated many people during Moos's last months in Minnesota. Irritated by Wheeler's heavy-handed and unauthorized actions, Parten complained to Moos, who assured him that Wheeler was not in control and that the resignations were not wanted. Ashmore, however, used the incident to breed suspicions among both the staff and the board that Moos planned to turn the Center over to the unpopular Wheeler.[30]

Ashmore's campaign convinced some of the board members that Moos's appointment should be cancelled. When these views reached Parten in late January 1974, he called the dissident board members and urged them to give Moos an opportunity to do his job. He then warned Moos about "considerable confusion at the Center" which he blamed on Wheeler, who "has shown monumental deficiency in . . . working with people." Moos should work directly with the fellows rather than using Wheeler as an intermediary and go slow with staff changes at the Center.[31]

At the next board meeting on February 15, Moos expressed his desire to raise funds to endow the salaries of the senior fellows, whose annual pay currently depended on year-to-year fund-raising. His longer-range plan, however, was to convert the Center into something he called a "communiversity," which would bring in students to interact with the fellows. Students would add an essential

545

ingredient to the intellectual process, forcing the fellows to confront new ideas and perspectives. Moos's model was Rockefeller University. He and others, including Parten and Marshall, realized that the Center could not operate as it had without Hutchins. "The concept of a few brilliant people sitting on a hill looking at the world and discussing great thoughts and solving the world's problems without *engaging* in the world just wasn't working," observed one former staff member. "One of the things we have learned is if you want to contribute to change you have to be actively involved in making the change. Just having a good idea is not likely to be good enough."[32]

Moos's statements alarmed Ashmore and the old guard, who believed that Moos was determined to destroy Hutchins's Center. Board member Blair Clark charged that the proposal "represented a radical change" in the Center's mission. Other directors criticized his handling of personnel matters and opposed his giving Wheeler administrative authority. Moos insisted that Wheeler would not have such authority and that he would meet with staff to resolve any problems in that area. With these assurances, the board agreed to Moos's request that his title of chairman of the board be transferred to J. R. Parten. Moos assumed the new title of board president and chief executive officer. The board also approved Moos's recommendation that Ashmore be named executive vice president. Privately, Moos was reluctant to give Ashmore such authority, but he wanted to placate Ashmore's allies on the board.[33]

"I don't care much for my successor—nobody ever does, I suppose"

Hutchins had been conspicuously silent during the February board meeting. "Bob was the key to this deal," Parten recalled. "If Hutchins turned against Moos, I knew it would create a very difficult problem." In the weeks after the board meeting, Parten sought to smooth over any possible problems between Hutchins and Moos. Ashmore and his colleagues told Hutchins that Moos's plan would ruin the Center, and they pleaded with him not to retire. "I don't care much for my successor—nobody ever does, I suppose," Hutchins admitted to his friend Thornton Wilder. "But this one seems to have done an unusual job of getting off on the wrong foot. . . ."[34]

In April, Moos told Parten that he wanted to add three new members to the board who were sympathetic to his ideas. Moos's nominees were Bernard Ridder Jr., publisher of the St. Paul *Pioneer Press*; Arthur A. Burck of Palm Beach, Florida, a management consultant; and Dr. L. Emmerson Ward, chairman of the board of the Mayo Foundation in Rochester, Minnesota. Because of his years of involvement in the refinery business in Minnesota, Parten knew Ridder and Ward and he endorsed their nominations, as did Hutchins. Ashmore, on the other hand, organized a group of directors to oppose Moos's nominations. Anticipating a battle at the next board meeting, Parten notified his allies and collected the proxies of Moos supporters Paul Newman, Howard Marshall, and Harold Willens.[35]

On the evening of May 15, 1974, a fire, apparently caused by his wife's smoking, destroyed Parten's old family home in Madisonville. Parten was in Houston preparing for the Center's board meeting on May 17. At home alone, Patsy Parten narrowly escaped death by jumping into the swimming pool at the rear of the house. She avoided burns but the shock put her in the hospital. The loss of his family home and much of his personal library was a terrible blow to Parten. Typically, however, he put his professional life ahead of his personal life, refusing to forego the board meeting in Saint Paul. He had promised Moos that he would get his nominees elected to the board. Parten left Madisonville with his wife in the hospital and the ruins of his home still smoking. He did not tell the board until after the meeting about his loss. He had made a commitment and he stood by it, but his behavior revealed how insensitive he could be toward his family.[36]

As Parten had feared, Ashmore's allies on the board opposed Moos's nominees. For the first time in the history of the Fund for the Republic, individuals nominated by the board's committee were challenged by other board members. With the help of Rapoport and Joseph Antonow, however, Parten defeated the challenge and elected Moos's nominees to the board. Nevertheless, Blair Clark persuaded the board to pass a resolution instructing Moos not to make any organizational or programmatic changes at the Center without the prior approval of the board.[37]

Parten now took Moos's enemies seriously. He saw the situation as similar to one in which he had been involved years before. "There's no doubt that J. R. saw the attacks on Moos as something like the Homer Rainey affair," John Henry Faulk later observed. "He felt personally responsible for bringing Moos into this place, just as he had with Rainey, and he sure as hell didn't want the same results." Despite the attack on Moos, Parten remained confident that the new president would do well. Those feelings were bolstered after the contentious board meeting in Minnesota when Hutchins told Parten that "Moos and the Center will make it." Hutchins added that it would "not be the first time this organization has owed its survival to you."[38]

Financial Crisis

In June, as Moos prepared to take over the Center, Parten led an effort to raise ten million dollars to create an endowment that would guarantee the Center's future existence. Parten announced that he would give or raise one hundred thousand a year for the next three years and challenged each director to match his pledge. He was disappointed, however, when he realized that the dissension on the board had become so deep that his colleagues would not respond to his challenge. The endowment drive died before it could get started.[39]

By the end of the summer, with no money pledged other than his own, Parten called an emergency meeting in Houston, attended by Moos and members of two board committees. Parten explained that the absence of donations had forced him to concentrate on the problem of basic short-term survival. He stressed that the Center was spending more money from its investment fund than it was receiving in income and at the current rate of expenditure the reserve fund would be depleted in only a few months. In response, the committee members endorsed Parten's proposal to mortgage the Center's Santa Barbara estate and close the Washington office. Moos also agreed to explore a number of other options to reduce expenditures, including placing the fellows and the staff on a half-time, half-pay status.[40]

The Center's future was now much in doubt. Parten had made a personal commitment to Hutchins to do whatever he could to maintain the founder's original vision, but he knew change was needed. It was obvious to him that the board would never be able to attract large donations of money with the only purpose being to pay for a group of elitist intellectuals to sit on top of a hill in Santa Barbara to discuss the ongoing problems of democracy. Making matters worse, of course, was the continuing factional dissension on the board and the petty rancor among the board members, the fellows, and the support staff.

No matter which direction the Center might take eventually, the failure to attract financial support meant that it would soon be out of money unless drastic measures were taken. At its next meeting, on November 4, 1974, the board approved Moos's plan to slash the budget. Moos subsequently terminated most of the clerical and secretarial staff and closed the Washington and Los Angeles offices, thereby reducing his operational expenses by half. The board also created a committee, with Hutchins as chair, to investigate a move to Chicago or some other site. Meanwhile, the internal attacks on Moos continued.[41]

While Parten worked to end the bickering among members of the board, his problems with Ashmore worsened. In December, Ashmore allegedly told officials of the Fund for Peace that Moos had lost the support of the Center's board and was on his way out. This allegation soon got back to Parten, who saw it as definitive proof of Ashmore's insubordination. When Ashmore denied the story, Parten conducted a private investigation of the matter. The result convinced him that the allegation against Ashmore was true. Parten had had enough of Ashmore and his allies on the board, especially Frances McAllister. The latter's term as a director was soon to expire and Parten believed that he had enough votes to prevent her reelection at the next board meeting. He also decided to confront Ashmore at the meeting about his disloyal activities.[42]

Parten's effort to dump McAllister failed when two of the board members he had counted on voted to reelect her. His effort to get rid of McAllister soundly defeated, he dropped his plan to accuse Ashmore of insubordination. After Parten announced that he was willing "to let the matter rest," the board passed a resolution clearing Ashmore of the allegations of misconduct. In an obvious slap at Parten, the board also approved Stewart Mott's motion prohibiting the investigation of officers of the Fund for the Republic by board members without the entire board's approval. Parten was bitter about the outcome. He feared that Moos's enemies would now feel free to escalate their efforts against him.[43]

The board finally concluded its meeting with a lengthy discussion about how to prevent the Center's fast-approaching bankruptcy. Unless the Center received a quick infusion of cash it would be out of money within five months. Parten asked how many directors would join him in giving or raising one hundred thousand dollars to sustain the Center for the remainder of the year. Rapoport accepted Parten's challenge, but the others remained silent. Further action was delayed. Moos recommended that the Center reorganize and either remain in Santa Barbara with only four resident fellows or accept an offer from the University of California at San Diego to relocate to their campus. Moos's opponents rejected those options and called instead for the dissolution of the organization as it now existed and the creation of another Center with a new staff in Chicago. It was evident that Moos would not be part of the proposed reorganization. The board agreed to postpone its decision until April 19 to give Moos more time to raise the money needed to avoid bankruptcy.[44]

Other than Parten's and Rapoport's pledges, Moos failed to raise enough money to take care of immediate needs. Parten refused to give up, however. In an attempt to give Moos's fund drive some momentum, Parten's foundation pledged one hundred thousand dollars if an additional two hundred thousand could be raised from other sources. This pledge also went unmatched. Parten then urged his fellow directors to sell the Center's Eucalyptus Hill property and move to rented office space in Santa Barbara. He believed the Center could make a profit of at least one million dollars from the sale of the property.[45]

The Death of Patsy Parten

On April 16, Parten spent the night in Houston rather than Madisonville because he had to fly to California early the next morning to meet with Moos to prepare for the April 19 board meeting. He dreaded the meeting because neither he nor Moos had raised the money they needed to prevent the Center's dissolution and removal to Chicago. The next morning, he received a telephone call and learned that his wife, Patsy, had died in her sleep during the night, apparently of a heart attack. When Parten told Moos of Patsy's death, Moos cancelled the board meeting and flew with Frank Kelly to Texas to attend the funeral.[46]

Patsy's funeral was held on April 19 in Madisonville. Her daughter and son-in-law, Pepe and Bill Anderson, who were now residing in Connecticut, flew to Texas for the services. Randy Parten, who was working for his father and living at 7-J Stock Farm, was already in Madisonville. The funeral attracted a large contingent of the Partens' friends and relatives from around the country, but Hutchins and Ashmore remained in Santa Barbara, where they held an informal meeting with some of the anti-Moos board members. Hutchins's failure to come to Patsy's funeral was a bitter disappointment to J. R.[47]

Moos Leaves the Center

Immediately following Patsy Parten's funeral, Frank Kelly called Hutchins from Madisonville and learned that Hutchins had decided to recommend to the board that the Center be moved to Chicago and that Moos be dismissed. Kelly later recalled that he could see "the pain in Parten's face" when he told him about Hutchins's intentions. Parten had refused to believe that Hutchins would openly endorse Moos's removal. "Why didn't Hutchins call me and tell me that?" Parten asked. He told Kelly that "it was all over" if Hutchins was demanding Moos's dismissal. This was an especially bitter defeat for Parten. He felt he had done what Hutchins had wanted: he had found a successor—one that Hutchins had endorsed—and he had persuaded that successor to come to California with a promise of solid support from the Fund for the Republic's board of directors. Feeling a strong personal obligation to Moos, Parten resolved to secure him the best severance-pay arrangement possible.[48]

On May 10, 1975, the directors dissolved the Center as it then existed, and terminated the contracts of Moos, the fellows, and the support staff. At Parten's insistence, the board agreed to give Moos a severance payment totalling seventy-five thousand dollars, but only after Moos agreed not to criticize the Center in public. Reluctantly, Parten advised Moos to accept the restriction on his free speech to avoid getting the severance matter into a lengthy legal battle. A Center press release depicted Moos's departure as part of the overall reorganization that also included the termination of more than twenty other employees.[49]

The board also agreed to create a new Center with offices in Chicago and Santa Barbara, with Hutchins administering a drastically reduced academic program in the latter city. The Chicago office would conduct its program with part-time fellows drawn from the University of Chicago and other institutions of higher education in the city. Board members from Chicago personally guaranteed financial support for the new program. The Fund was now obligated to pay not only Moos's severance but also that of the other terminated employees, a financial obligation totaling $560,000, to be paid at a rate of $16,000 a month. These severance payments were to be secured by the Center's real estate. Accordingly, the board voted to place the Eucalyptus Hill property in a trust and authorized its sale or mortgage if future developments so required.[50]

Before the board meeting, Morris Levinson and several other directors had asked Parten to remain as chairman. Although Parten was angry with Moos's enemies on the board and had little hope that the Center could survive its current crisis, he agreed to serve as chairman only if Hutchins resumed his duties as president. Hutchins agreed and the board unanimously approved the appointments. "Hell, I wasn't going to be in the position of being Chairman and let him run the damn thing without being President," Parten declared later. "I wanted him to have official responsibility." Parten retained the chairmanship to make certain that the board fulfilled its severance-pay obligations to Moos and the other employees who were losing their jobs. Parten also wanted Hutchins to clean up the mess that he believed Hutchins had created by undermining Moos.

Moos departed gracefully. "He was splendid about it," Parten later recalled. "Moos came in after the massacre and thanked the Board and Hutchins and told them that he would continue to support the Center." Parten was the only director to voice his formal appreciation to Moos for the work he had done as president. Frank Kelly later remembered the episode as "sad and depressing." After the meeting had adjourned, Ashmore walked over to Hutchins and said: "Well, Bob, you're back in the saddle."[51]

The Moos affair left a sour taste in Parten's mouth. Hutchins had misled him about wanting to retire and several of his colleagues on the board had behaved abominably. These directors, especially Blair Clark, felt the same about Parten. However, one of Parten's best friends on the board, Bernard Rapoport, also concluded that Moos had been "a terrible mistake." Reflecting on the affair several years later, Rapoport charged that Moos had shown no leadership qualities as head of the Center.[52]

Rapoport may have been correct in his criticism of Moos, but Moos never had a real opportunity to prove himself. Ironically, the reorganization eventually implemented by the board resembled Moos's plan to reduce the number of resident fellows and rely on academicians affiliated with cooperating universities to conduct the Center's intellectual dialogue. Moos's most serious problem was Hutchins, who, despite ill health and professions of his desire for retirement, ultimately could not let go of the Center. As a result, he fed and encouraged the rebellion that led to Moos's removal. Criticism of Parten ignores the fact that he nominated Moos only after Hutchins himself had approved Moos. "J. R. was only doing what he thought Hutchins wanted him to do," Rapoport noted. "As a result, he really felt a personal obligation to Moos."[53]

Despite his anger and disappointment about the battle over Moos and his termination, Parten retained his belief that the Center had an important role to play as an independent island of intellectual thought and discussion, confronting and seeking imaginative solutions to problems related to civil liberties, social justice, the environment, and international peace. Just a few days after Moos's departure, Parten wrote a check for twelve thousand dollars to help pay the Center's overdue bills.[54]

After Hutchins reassumed his position as president, board member Seniel Ostrow contributed one hundred thousand dollars to take care of immediate needs and to give Hutchins time to plan. The recent shake-up had generated some unfavorable press, leading Hutchins to decide that a major convocation, specifically a fourth *Pacem in Terris,* could demonstrate the Center's continuing existence and vitality. He secured Henry Kissinger's commitment to participate, and believed he had a good chance to get Pres. Gerald Ford to deliver the keynote address. Parten, however, argued that a convocation would cost more than the Center could afford and that it would distract the board from the important task of raising an endowment to insure the Center's future existence. Hutchins nevertheless prevailed over Parten's strong objection. At a board meeting on June 28, 1975, Parten was the only director to vote against *Pacem in Terris IV.* Ignoring the continuing financial problem, Hutchins proceeded with plans for a full program of meetings and conferences in Santa Barbara for the summer of 1975.[55]

As Hutchins expanded his program and planned for *Pacem in Terris IV,* Parten worried that the Fund for the Republic would go broke. Parten felt that

Hutchins was ignoring the board's instructions to establish a trust and was reluctant to trade his majestic surroundings at Eucalyptus Hill for a less impressive office suite in downtown Santa Barbara. His anxiety turned to alarm when Hutchins told him that the Center had an opportunity to get a loan equal to 60 percent of the appraised value of Eucalyptus Hill. Parten objected to this plan, warning Hutchins that it would be a "big mistake" to mortgage the property with interest rates high. He urged Hutchins to sell Eucalyptus Hill while real estate prices were high, invest the profit, and use the earnings to help pay the severance obligations.[56]

By the end of the summer, Hutchins had taken no action. When Parten asked him for a progress report, he replied that the executive committee would discuss what should be done. This was surprising news to Parten because the board had voted in May to place the property in trust. He suspected that Hutchins was planning to mortgage Eucalyptus Hill to get money to support the Center before the property could be placed in trust as security for the severance payments. The rift between himself and Hutchins had now grown too wide for him to continue as chairman or a board member. Hutchins was no longer consulting with him on important Center matters and Parten refused to be a figurehead chairman. He also had no intention of being legally responsible for the ex-employees' severance pay. Parten blamed Hutchins's behavior on his cancer and felt the real culprit was Harry Ashmore.[57]

Parten concluded that it was time to end his twenty-five years of service with the Fund for the Republic. He was the last of the original board members. On September 25, he wrote Hutchins that his plan to mortgage the property without securing it for the severance payments was "a breach of trust." Under the circumstances, therefore, Parten felt that he had to resign as an officer and trustee of the Fund. "I will continue to wish you well," Parten said. Although Hutchins was wounded by Parten's accusation that he had committed a breach of trust, he did not want his longtime associate to leave the board. Believing he could work through mutual friends to lure Parten back into the fold, he asked Howard Marshall to talk Parten out of his decision, but Marshall refused. He told Hutchins that he not only agreed with Parten's opinion of the situation at the Center, he felt "more strongly about what is proposed" than Parten. Marshall told Hutchins that perhaps it was "the old Quaker" in him that made him believe that "we ought to take care of our obligations first, and only spend on other things when our obligations are covered in full." Marshall's resignation from the board of directors soon followed Parten's. Fagan Dickson also resigned as soon as he heard that Parten had quit the board. Bernard Rapoport, however, remained on the board and he maintained his friendship with Hutchins and Harry Ashmore. Rapoport was the only one of Parten's close associates on the board who felt that he had misunderstood and over-reacted to the trust situation, though he did not express that opinion to Parten. "The whole . . . controversy is . . . a tragedy," Rapoport lamented to a board colleague, "more because of the personal animosities that resulted among lifetime friends than for any other reason."[58]

Hutchins appealed directly to Parten, telling him that he had served the Fund for the Republic for "so long and with such distinction that I hate to have you resign on the basis of actions that I think you have misinterpreted. . . ." He assured Parten that the mortgage money was not for operating expenses. It would be placed in a trust for the severance payments. This explanation failed to placate Parten. He was "astonished" that Hutchins seemed not to understand the danger of using Eucalyptus Hill as collateral for the trust fund. Parten believed that Hutchins's failure to follow the board's instructions was "an injustice. . . to the dismissed employees to whom we had made a commitment." Parten's resignation would stand. "Bob, you and I have been friends since we worked on that famous joint venture . . . in 1935 that resulted in the McDonald Observatory," he noted. "It is my earnest hope that . . . this disagreement . . . should not adversely affect this longstanding relationship." Despite this declaration, Parten and Hutchins never spoke or saw each other again. In March 1976, Eucalyptus Hill was placed in trust, just as Hutchins had promised. Parten's resignation focused so much attention on the issue that Hutchins had been forced to do it. Parten may simply have misinterpreted Hutchins's intentions but the trust dispute served merely as the catalyst for Parten's resignation and rift with Hutchins. The Moos affair was the real cause. Parten was equally unhappy with most of the remaining directors of the Fund for the Republic and his departure from the board was an inevitable result.[59]

The break with Hutchins and the Center was a traumatic experience for the seventy-nine-year-old Parten. When Supreme Court justice William O. Douglas, who had once served with Parten on the Fund for the Republic board of directors, announced his retirement from the Court one month after Parten's resignation from the Center, Parten wrote with sadness to Douglas "that this year, 1975, has been an uncommonly bad year for me. First, I suffered the loss of my dear wife in the month of April. . . . Second, I had to give up my . . . work with The Fund for the Republic, Inc., on account of a disagreement over financial and administrative policies . . . and now . . . I have lost my favorite member of the Supreme Court. . . ."[60]

Hutchins remained as president of the new version of the Center until his death on May 14, 1977. The Center limped along until June 1979, when its directors voted to dissolve the Fund for the Republic and turn its remaining assets over to the University of California at Santa Barbara. The university established the Robert M. Hutchins Center for the Study of Democratic Institutions, which became a standard academic think tank. It was closed in 1987.[61]

The Fund for the Republic and its most ambitious program, the Center for the Study of Democratic Institutions, made a number of contributions to the civic good, including John Cogley's *Report on Blacklisting*, Michael Harrington's *The Other America* (which inspired LBJ's War on Poverty), and the series of international convocations inspired by Pope John XXIII's encyclical *Pacem in Terris*. More important, it enriched and raised the level of public discourse.[62]

Despite his final, bitter estrangement from Hutchins and the Fund for the Republic, J. R. Parten took pride in his lengthy association with both. He was especially proud of its investigation of the blacklist and its opposition to the red scare.

In addition, Parten believed that the Center's dialogues, conferences, and convocations brought meaningful public attention to the issues of racism, poverty, civil liberties, public education, militarism, and the threat of nuclear war. Parten also understood the influential role Hutchins and the Fund had played in broadening his own world view. In a letter to Hutchins in the summer of 1974, Parten stressed that their friendship of forty years had "indeed meant a great deal to me. It has contributed in no small way to my education which prior to that time was woefully incomplete." Parten held that view until the end of his life. "The Fund for the Republic was my graduate education in the liberal arts," Parten admitted, "and Bob Hutchins was the director of my dissertation."[63]

CHAPTER 36

"His Name Is Not Exactly a Household Word in Texas— but it Ought to Be"

The Final Years, 1976–1992

P arten's resignation from the Fund for the Republic and the liquidation of PASCO gave him an opportunity to withdraw from the world of public affairs and business to enjoy the winter of his life in comfortable retirement. Retirement, however, was not a word in his vocabulary. When Parten celebrated his eightieth birthday in February 1976, he declared that being an octogenarian meant that you did things "a little bit slower, it sure as hell doesn't mean you're dead." Blessed with remarkably good health and stamina for his age, Parten devoted much of his time in the late 1970s and early 1980s to Parten Oil, a small independent company he founded after his break with Pure. In 1965, Parten Oil discovered a deep pocket of natural gas on property adjacent to the southeast section of his 7-J ranch. This significant find covered about fifteen thousand acres. In 1970, Parten discovered another field, but this one was on his own land, the west eight thousand acres of 7-J ranch.[1]

By the early 1980s, Parten had drilled ten successful oil wells and two gas wells in the Madisonville area. Parten Oil branched out to West Texas, where it participated in several new wells in the Permian Basin. Parten was deeply satisfied by his continuing success as an oil man, especially at his age. With much pride, he told the Dallas *Morning News* in an interview in July 1981 that he was producing oil and gas "close to home" in Houston County and Madison County. "It's not big oil production or big gas production, but it's good and solid."[2]

Parten was directly involved in every one of his business enterprises almost until the day of his death. He drove himself down Interstate 45 to Houston (nearly one hundred miles from Madisonville) nearly every Monday, checked into a hotel, and worked in his office until Thursday, when he drove back to Madisonville. Not until he was in his late eighties did he grudgingly give in to the exhortations of his family and allow someone to drive him back and forth to Houston. During his three-day weekends in Madisonville, Parten divided his time between his ranches and his oil-well sites. Among his major enterprises in his last years was a cattle-breeding business. Parten loved to drive his Cadillac around Greenbrier and the 7-J to inspect the fences and check out his herd.[3]

At lunch or in the evenings, Parten usually visited with friends who travelled to Madisonville from California, New York, Washington, D.C., Austin, and elsewhere to pay their respects and talk about current events, or to discuss a project they hoped Parten might fund. Parten established a small foundation to support scholarships, civil liberties programs, and public policy projects. If he had no guests, which was rare, Parten sat by his fireplace in the living room and read. And he read voraciously, concentrating on current affairs and history, especially the history of World War II. Sometimes if a book really impressed him, he sent copies to dozens of his friends with a cover letter urging them to read the book as soon as possible.

A Yellow Dog Democrat

In his last decade Parten maintained his deep interest in politics and current affairs. He no longer participated in election campaigns, but he contributed financially to his favored candidates, contributing thirty thousand dollars to Lloyd Bentsen's reelection campaign in 1982, for example. Other Parten favorites to whom he made generous contributions included Texas gubernatorial candidates John Hill, Mark White, and Ann Richards; Congressmen Bob Eckhardt, Jim Mattox, and Jim Wright; Senators Alan Cranston and Frank Church; and presidential candidates Jimmy Carter, Walter Mondale, and Michael Dukakis.[4]

In most cases, Parten supported whoever eventually won the Democratic nomination for any office. He was a "yellow dog" Democrat, always pulling the straight Democratic lever. Any nominee who was openly critical of the oil industry risked Parten's wrath, however. For example, Parten supported Jimmy Carter's election in 1976, but the Carter administration's lengthy delay in removing price controls on natural gas outraged him. The Carter administration also established a confusing set of pricing categories. To Parten, Carter's program was yet another example of governmental interference in an economic activity for which it was ill suited. Parten complained that "there is an enormous push today by people thinking that the government should get into the business of producing oil. My opinion is that though it is essential that government be run by politicians, it is impossible for politicians to run a business. . . ."[5] Although Parten had voted for and given money to every Democratic presidential candidate since 1920, he waited until late in the campaign to help Carter in 1980. After Cong. Bob Eckhardt cast several votes in support of Carter's energy policies, Parten refused to help raise funds for Eckhardt's reelection campaign in 1980. "It was a difficult question but I thought

Left to right, John Henry Faulk, Parten, unidentified woman, and Patsy Parten attend a symposium at the LBJ Library in the early 1970s. *CN 09618. Courtesy Faulk Photograph Collection, CAH.*

we needed controls to keep the price down and avoid a deep recession in the late 1970s," Eckhardt recalled. "J. R., however, had a very strong free-market view and felt that we had to keep oil down to a rate that was within reason." Parten had been one of Eckhardt's most important financial backers ever since his election to Congress in 1966. Eckhardt lost to his Republican opponent, Jack Fields.[6]

John Henry and Liz

One particular source of joy for Parten in the late years of his life was his close relationship with John Henry and Elizabeth Faulk. With Parten's urging, the Faulks had made Madisonville their home in April 1974. "We'll have a Center for the Study of Democratic Institutions—East," Parten had joked. John Henry and J. R. grew especially close in the late 1970s. Until the Faulks moved back to Austin in the summer of 1981, they saw J. R. almost daily. Parten and Faulk rode horses on Greenbrier Ranch nearly every Sunday morning and John Henry was a primary influence on J. R.'s political thinking. "J. R. and I straighten out the world over breakfast," Faulk told the Houston *Post* in 1980. "John Henry had striking, populistic views and whatever he thought about anything you heard about it," former *Texas Observer* editor Lawrence Goodwyn noted. "So I knew that J. R. had been exposed to the totality of John Henry's world view on everything. What was interesting to me was that J. R. agreed with them."[7]

Parten and John Henry Faulk at 7-J Stock Farm, about 1976. *CN 09605. Courtesy Parten Photograph Collection, CAH.*

Throughout the late 1970s and 1980s, Faulk sent a steady stream of information on current events to Parten laced with his own strong opinions. For example, in the mid-1980s when Texas congressman Charles Wilson made a highly publicized trip to Afghanistan during the Soviet Union's military involvement in that country, Faulk sent Parten a news clipping with the comment that "our East Texas congressman . . . seems to have replaced General Curtis LeMay as one who not [only] wants to kill Russians, but wants to kill Russia!" When Boston University president John Silber, a former University of Texas faculty member and dean, was quoted in the press as supporting a massive increase in the U.S. military budget, Faulk sent the news clipping to Parten with the annotation that Silber "seems to have gone over to Reagan completely." A George Will column attacking a public figure's criticism of Israeli foreign policy was sent to Parten with Faulk's comment that Will was "savaging any who dare ask for understanding and open dialogue on the Middle East." These and scores of similar comments from Faulk filled Parten's mailbox. Parten repeated Faulk's comments in his own letters to other friends— usually without mentioning their source.[8]

This is not to say that Parten did not have strong opinions of his own. He simply could not articulate those opinions as well or in as colorful a style as Faulk. "John Henry could say things that J. R. felt but could not verbalize," noted Pepe Anderson. Although Parten and Faulk agreed on most subjects, especially international relations and civil liberties, they differed over government regulation of business. Faulk was a democratic socialist who had a low opinion of the free market and laissez-faire capitalism. Keenly aware of Parten's opinions on the subject as well as his knowledge of the business world, Faulk knew better than to challenge his friend in that area.

In the realm of ideas, the Faulk-Parten relationship was not one-sided. Parten's views on the Bill of Rights and the meaning of the Declaration of Independence helped shape Faulk's thoughts in a variety of ways. When Faulk wrote his one-man play "Deep in the Heart," Parten served as the inspiration for Tom Willis, one of the play's characters. The Parten-inspired character is an elderly man whose nephew is circulating a petition urging censorship of pornography. Willis lectures his nephew on the meaning of the First Amendment and the importance of safeguarding free-speech rights—even for those with whom you strongly disagree. In the late 1970s, John Henry landed a job as the folk philosopher on the popular television program "Hee Haw." Faulk managed to weave his personal interpretation of the First Amendment and the Declaration of Independence into his skits. As he prepared for his "Hee Haw" appearances, he often discussed them with Parten while they rode on horseback on Greenbrier Ranch. As a result, Parten's views on the Constitution and civil liberties were frequently integrated into Faulk's discussions on "Hee Haw." Although "Hee Haw" was a low-brow attempt at "Hillbilly" humor, it was watched by millions of people. Parten greatly relished the idea that his and Faulk's progressive ideas on civil liberties might somehow be absorbed by some portion of this audience.[9]

Faulk also served as Parten's connection to individuals and liberal organizations in need of financial support. In the fall of 1979, for example, Faulk brought to Parten's attention historian Athan Theoharis's work on the House Committee on Un-American Activities. Parten subsequently paid some of Theoharis's research expense. Faulk also persuaded Parten to join with Bernard Rapoport to match grants for some project of interest to all three. In 1979, for example, Parten and Rapoport funded John Henry's lawsuit against the Federal Bureau of Investigation. Faulk was seeking an uncensored version of his own FBI file. "J. R. and I didn't consider giving John Henry money a good deed," Rapoport said. "We thought that was just an investment in a better world. John Henry would ask for money for those things he knew we were as passionate about as he was."[10]

Despite Parten's impressive accomplishments and his devoted work on behalf of the public good, he remained generally unknown to the public at large. And as death inevitably narrowed his circle of old friends over the years, his record and work became less known even among the political and business elite, especially those from younger generations. Having never sought public acclaim, Parten was undisturbed by his relative anonymity. Faulk, however, believed that Parten deserved recognition. In an article Faulk wrote for the *Texas Observer* in December 1974, he tried to bring more attention to his friend. "[Parten's] name is not exactly a household word in Texas, but it ought to be," Faulk wrote. He added that:

> Mr. Parten is the kind of citizen that people should know about.
> J. R. Parten's approach to civil liberties is direct and uncomplicated. He
> understands with great clarity that the intent of the Constitution is to

protect, not only those ideas we cherish, but those we despise. He believes quite devoutly that basic to all our liberties is the freedom of each citizen to speak, to write, and to establish his thoughts not merely without restraint, but without the possibility of restraint. Mr. Parten not only holds these opinions, he acts on them.[11]

In the summer of 1976, largely as a result of the *Observer* piece and Faulk's quiet lobbying, *Texas Monthly* magazine selected Parten as the "best rich man in Texas." Parten's image, shaped by his liberal views on civil liberties, his opposition to the Vietnam war, his criticism of American policy toward the Soviet Union, his respect for learning and higher education, and his identification with the liberal wing of the Democratic Party, was in stark contrast to the popular stereotype of the wealthy Texas oil man. Accordingly, Faulk was eventually able to attract the interest of some important news journals. He persuaded New York *Times* editor and columnist Abe Rosenthal to have lunch with Parten at his home in Madisonville. That visit led in 1980 to a major personality profile on Parten in the *Times*. In 1981, Faulk persuaded the Dallas *Morning News* to publish a lengthy article on Parten. The following year, *Parade Magazine* brought national attention to Parten by publishing a cover story entitled "The 'Real' J. R. Speaks His Mind."[12]

"You'll burn this whole earth up. Kill everything on it"

The issue that caused J. R. Parten more concern than any other in the last years of his life was the nuclear-arms race. His interest dated from December 1945, when he attended a program on the issue at the Waterman Park Hotel in Washington. Parten's opposition to the arms race was one of the reasons for his involvement with the Center for the Study of Democratic Institutions. When the Reagan administration launched a massive build-up of U.S. nuclear forces, Parten feared that nuclear war was an increasingly real possibility. He spoke out against the arms race at every opportunity and provided whatever financial support he could to individuals and organizations who were working to stop it. His concern was his grandchildren and their world. Randy had married and was now the father of two boys who were the apples of J. R.'s eyes.[13]

Parten complained to the Dallas *Morning News* that the Reagan administration was building "an awesome war machine that is frightening." The reason the Reagan administration was escalating the arms race was to put money "into the pockets of defense contractors who have a self-serving interest in global unrest." He denounced Reagan's "Star Wars" proposal as both an "idiot's dream" and a huge hoax on the American people. Reagan had surrounded himself with advisors who believed that the United States could win a "limited" nuclear confrontation with the Soviet Union. "There's no such thing as a limited nuclear war," Parten declared. "How could it be limited? I'm convinced that the time is past on this planet when you can win a war." In another interview, Parten declared that "this talk of limited nuclear war . . . is for the birds. Who's going to limit the war? You'll burn this whole earth up. Kill everything on it. It would . . . turn this old earth into cinder." Reagan's

Parten inspecting his ranch in the 1980s. *CN 09591. Courtesy Parten Photograph Collection, CAH.*

representatives during his second term successfully negotiated a reduction in the number of nuclear weapons in the U.S. and Soviet arsenals, but by then Parten's health had become a serious problem and he was not as mentally engaged in these issues. That was even more the case during George Bush's presidency.[14]

In his fight against the nuclear-arms race, Parten also provided financial support to two national nonpartisan organizations that he identified as being among the most effective and responsible of the groups involved in the nuclear-armaments debate: the American Committee on East-West Accord and the Center for Defense Information (CDI). Parten became involved in the Committee on East-West Accord after a visit to Madisonville by Adm. Noel Gayler, who was a member of the committee's board of directors. The committee's purpose was to reduce tensions between the U.S. and the U.S.S.R. by strengthening public understanding of strategic-arms agreements and by fostering mutually beneficial programs in science, culture, and trade. The Center for Defense Information, headed by retired Rear Adm. Gene R. LaRocque, gathered and disseminated information about U.S. military programs and strategies to provide Congress and the public with an alternate source of technical and fiscal information with which to evaluate Defense Department policy. Parten served as a member of the CDI advisory board and became good friends with Admiral LaRocque, who was a frequent visitor to Madisonville.[15]

Parten also criticized the Reagan administration's economic policies, its cozy relationship with Wall Street, and its lack of interest in the antitrust laws. He watched in frustration as conservative Southern Democrats joined with the

Republicans to pass Reagan's legislation. He was especially galled by the fact that he was a constituent of Cong. Phil Gramm, one of the leaders of these so-called pro-Reagan "Boll Weevils." Parten had a visceral loathing for the former economics professor from Texas A&M. "That man offends every bone in my body," Parten blurted out after seeing Gramm on a television program. When Gramm resigned from the Democratic Party in January 1983 and returned to Texas to run as a Republican for reelection to Congress, Parten resolved to do whatever he could to defeat him.[16]

When it appeared that no Democrat would oppose Gramm, Parten persuaded John Henry Faulk to enter the race. Not only did Parten want Gramm defeated, he also relished the idea of "Congressman" John Henry Faulk stirring up the House of Representatives. "I feel your going to Congress," Parten told Faulk, "would help to keep us out of war and avoid an atomic energy plant in every county in Texas." Assured of financial support from Parten, Bernard Rapoport, and the Menil family in Houston and New York, Faulk declared his candidacy. Faulk and Parten had counted on the support of the Democratic Party establishment, but the party backed state representative Dan Kubiak, who made a last-minute decision to oppose Gramm. Bitterly disappointed by the refusal of politicians for whom he had worked so hard in the past to campaign for him, Faulk nevertheless threw all his energy into the fight. As Faulk later described it, however, "it was an uphill battle with a short stick." With a truncated campaign period of only three weeks, neither Faulk nor Kubiak had enough time to counter the overwhelming advantages of an incumbent candidate. Gramm easily won reelection. In hindsight, the effort was hopelessly quixotic. Parten, however, refused to second-guess the decision to go after Gramm. "Whether he ever knows it or not," Parten said, "Gramm will be a better man by having had some opposition."[17]

The campaign against Phil Gramm proved to be Parten's last active foray into the political arena. He made financial contributions until the last year of his life— he gave one hundred thousand dollars to the Democratic National Committee during the 1988 Dukakis presidential campaign—but, increasingly hampered by the physical decline of a person in his nineties, Parten participated in no more political campaigns.[18]

Reconciliation with the University

One of the most satisfying personal developments in Parten's life in his last years was his reconciliation with the University of Texas at Austin. His bitter experience in the Rainey affair alienated him from the people who controlled the university. Although he served as a member of its development board in the late 1940s and early 1950s, Parten basically kept his distance from the university for a period of nearly two decades. The main reason was that Allan Shivers and his appointees to the board of regents dominated University of Texas affairs during most of those years. The feud between Parten and Shivers lasted until the latter's death in 1985.[19]

Parten had a reconciliation with the university in the late 1960s, but it was temporary. University president and later chancellor Harry Ransom, a longtime admirer of Parten, worked quietly to lure him back into the university fold. In 1966, appreciative of Ransom's attention and impressed with his plans to make the University of Texas a world-class educational institution, Parten became a charter member of Ransom's Chancellor's Council. He was delighted to be a member once again of the university's extended family. Making up for lost time, he became involved in a number of projects of personal interest to him. In 1966, he recruited John Henry Faulk, author Lon Tinkle, and architect O'Neil Ford, to join him on a committee to raise seventy-six thousand dollars for the university to purchase the late J. Frank Dobie's Paisano Ranch. Parten contributed five thousand dollars toward the purchase and played the leading role in raising the remainder of the funds. Houston businessman Ralph A. Johnston had saved the ranch from being subdivided after Dobie's death in 1964. Parten's committee raised the money to reimburse Johnston, who donated the ranch to the university to serve as a writer's retreat. "It was most gratifying to have you give my Dobie Paisano project the support you did," Johnston told Parten. "You were really the best supporter I had . . ."[20]

Other substantive contributions Parten made to the university during the late 1960s included a fund to support a book series at the University of Texas Press, gifts in support of scholarly conferences, and numerous grants in support of graduate research in the College of Arts and Sciences. His contributions to the College of Arts and Sciences resulted from his friendship with John Silber, an iconoclastic philosophy professor who served as dean of the college. In 1968, when Silber organized an Arts and Sciences Foundation as a means to raise excellence funds and scholarship support, Parten became an active member.[21]

Parten's reconciliation with the university ended abruptly, however, in the summer of 1970, his break the result of a series of actions taken by the university's chairman of the board of regents, Frank Erwin. A political crony of Lyndon Johnson and John Connally, Erwin had won notoriety during his service on the board as a result of his frequent and highly public clashes with students and faculty in disputes ranging from his attempts to fire teachers to his efforts to stifle campus protests against the war in Vietnam. Erwin was intolerant of any opposition to his policies from the university's administration and that included powerful deans such as Page Keeton of the School of Law and John Silber of the College of Arts and Sciences.

After forcing Chancellor Harry Ransom and President Norman Hackerman out of their administrative positions, Erwin engineered the appointment of Fine Arts dean Bryce Jordan as acting president without faculty consultation. Parten was upset by Erwin's selection of medical doctor Charles "Mickey" LeMaistre to replace Ransom as chancellor. LeMaistre had angered Parten by his public declaration after a student rally against the Vietnam war that "protest is one of the silliest ways I know to express yourself." The fiercely independent John Silber, himself no stranger to controversy, was next on Erwin's list. To reduce Silber's power at the university, Erwin decided to split up the College of Arts and Sciences, which was the largest college on campus. Silber publicly opposed Erwin, but he eventually lost the battle and was removed as dean on July 24, 1970. Parten considered Silber's dismissal to be yet another example of the continuing tradition of regental politi-cal interference in the administration of the university.[22]

Parten sent a telegram to Chancellor LeMaistre denouncing Erwin and declaring that he was severing all ties with the University of Texas. Parten also issued a press release accusing Erwin of being among those who wished "to put our schools under a police state." Charging that the regents had interfered improperly in the internal administration of the university, Parten also criticized the manner in which Jordan and LeMaistre had been selected. He told the Houston *Chronicle* that he could "never again face my respected friends on the faculty . . . without protesting loudly the irrational actions of the administration and the board of regents."[23]

Parten's break with the university seemed permanent. A vocal critic of the institution's board of regents throughout the 1970s, his alienation only deepened when Allan Shivers became a regent in January 1973. Gradually, however, Parten was again lured back into the university's circle. He had maintained friendships with a number of faculty and these contacts had kept him informed of and inter-ested in various programs, especially those in the liberal arts. After Peter Flawn became president in 1979, Parten accepted his invitation to serve on the universi-ty's Centennial Committee. He attended some of the committee's meetings in Austin, where he renewed his friendships with a number of his old acquaintances from among the university's prominent ex-students. [24]

After William H. Cunningham became president in 1986, Parten's return as an honored member of the university's community of ex-students and former regents was completed. Cunningham made several trips to Madisonville to have lunch with Parten and tour his ranches. In October 1987, Parten received the uni-versity's Distinguished Alumnus Award. Presented by the Ex-Students Association, the award was long-overdue recognition from the university for the valuable contributions he had made to the institution as a regent and former stu-dent over a period of more than six decades. The award ceremony and the atten-dant programs were among the most personally fulfilling events of Parten's long life. Although ninety-one years old and too frail to stand without help (Randy Parten stood at his side throughout the two days of events), Parten summoned enough of his remaining energy to stand almost as tall and erect as the handsome young army major that he had been many years before.[25]

The Last Years

Beginning in 1988, Parten's physical condition weakened greatly. His ailments were mainly those associated with advanced age. Nevertheless, his mind was sharp and alert and his interests in public affairs and in his university were as keen as ever. He entertained visitors to his home in Madisonville, including old friends such as John Henry and Liz Faulk, Ronnie Dugger, Molly Ivins, and Sissy Farenthold; his former colleagues at the Fund for the Republic, Frank Kelly and Leonard Townsend; and his many friends from the University of Texas.

His thoughts drifting more and more to things of the past, Parten's interest in history intensified and he piled his reading table with the latest books on the history of the United States and Europe in the twentieth century. His love of history and his understanding of the need to preserve materials that make the writing of history possible led him to establish in December 1988, a $500,000 endowment at the University of Texas's Barker Texas History Center (now the Center for American History). President Cunningham secured approval from the board of regents to add $250,000 from the Available Fund to Parten's gift to establish a $750,000 J. R. Parten Chair in the Archives of American History. Parten's last major gift to the University of Texas was in response to the loss of one of the closest friends he had ever had: John Henry Faulk. After a long battle with inoperable cancer, Faulk died at his home in Austin on April 9, 1990. On April 24, Parten donated $100,000 to the university's Center for American History to establish the John Henry Faulk Fund for the First Amendment, an endowment to support research and programs on issues related to freedom of expression.[26]

Parten's last two years were difficult—in and out of the hospital, no longer ambulatory, his eyesight fading to the point that he could not read. Randy arranged to have nurses stay with him around the clock. In late September 1992, Parten's physician told Randy that there was nothing anyone could do for the Major. The end finally came in the early morning of November 9, 1992. J. R. Parten died in his bed at home in Madisonville, four months shy of his ninety-seventh birthday.

The news of Parten's death was little noted by the nation's news media. Not even the New York *Times*, whose obituary page is filled daily with notices of the deaths of obscure lawyers, real estate developers, and investment bankers, printed the news of Parten's passing. He had lived his life too quietly and too long and he had died in too small a town to get the attention he deserved in the end. Nationally syndicated columnist Molly Ivins, however, took note. "J. R. Parten of Madisonville died yesterday," Ivins announced in her column. The "immensely civilized" Parten, Ivins wrote, had left Texas "shy of both the vision and integrity that have enriched our state for many years." After listing a few of Parten's contributions to his state and nation, Ivins declared that she had never known anyone "quite as good as J. R. Parten at simply Doing the Right Thing without ever counting the cost, simply because it never occurred to him to do anything else. Rest in peace, Major Parten."[27]

On November 11, following an early morning Episcopalian service in Madisonville's First Methodist Church attended by an overflow of mourners, Major Parten was buried near Patsy and his mother and father in the soil of "the county named for the greatest of all Americans." Before Parten was laid to rest, his family and friends who filled the church heard Frank Kelly eulogize his old friend and former associate. "Men and women with a noble concern for humanity, with compassion for the whole human race, have been rare in the history of this world," Kelly declared. "Mr. Parten was such a person."

It is appropriate that such a man was born in a town named for James Madison. . . . I see Mr. Parten standing now with Madison, Jefferson, Washington, and all the other noble citizens who created this nation and who worked to keep it . . . free through all the ages. Thomas Merton once said that it is "a glorious destiny to be a member of the human race." When I think of J. R. Parten, I know that is certainly true.[28]

Conclusion

J R. Parten was an entrepreneur, a man who was never happier or more energized and satisfied than when he was building one of his companies. Creating jobs, building business facilities, organizing entrepreneurial projects, and making decisions upon which future profits and growth depended were the activities that mattered most to him. Ranked first on Parten's personal list of lifetime accomplishments was his founding of the Woodley Petroleum Company and its development as a successful enterprise, admired widely throughout the industry as a well-managed and responsible corporation. Parten also took great pride in his Premier Refining, Great Northern, and Pan American Sulphur Companies. The success of Pan American Sulphur, which dared to challenge the established companies that dominated the sulphur industry, especially pleased him. And though he suffered disappointments large and small in all his business activities—his feud with the management of Pure Oil Company, for example—Parten's overall business record is indisputably one of solid achievement.

For all his business success, however, Parten's historical importance stems from his lifelong involvement in public affairs. One of his most consequential roles was the one he played in helping shape the nation's energy policy. No one spent more personal time, money, or energy to fight federal control of the oil industry during the 1930s than J. R. Parten. For a period of six critical years, from the early days of martial law in East Texas to the fight in Washington to defeat the last Ickes bill, Parten or one of his representatives was at the center of nearly every important oil battle. He continued to play a role in the shaping of the nation's energy policy for another fifty years after this federal regulation fight in the 1930s. As head of the Transportation Division of the PAW during World War II, Parten implemented a complete revolution in the petroleum transportation system of the United States and he was among those most responsible for ensuring that Allied forces in Europe had sufficient fuel to wage the war. His work in organizing the Petroleum Administration for Defense helped end the nation's aviation-gasoline crisis and provided the military with the fuel it needed to defend South Korea. The

PAD earned a reputation as one of the most efficient emergency agencies in the federal government. Parten's return to federal oil service in 1961 ended unhappily, but his protest against the so-called "Brownsville Rinky-Dink" and related issues is an example of his refusal to participate in any activity that violated his moral sense.

Parten's accomplishments as a regent of the University of Texas were the ones that gave him the most satisfaction, as well as an experience he considered his "second university education." Convinced that Texas's prosperity and civic health required a great state university, Parten worked hard to make his alma mater a "university of the first class." Knowing that little could be done without sufficient financial resources, he was especially proud of his successful effort to significantly increase the revenues the university earned from its oil lands and the appropriations it received from the legislature. The leader in the process to select Homer Rainey as university president, Parten later teamed with Rainey to plan and implement an ambitious university program to help create a progressive "New Texas." Although Rainey and Parten were unable to see that hope realized, the legacy of their vision remained to inspire future university leaders such as Harry Ransom and Peter Flawn to continue the quest for excellence. Parten's tenure as a regent exposed him to new ideas and reshaped his politics. By the time of his departure from the board, Parten had developed a deep appreciation for and an understanding of freedom of expression and inquiry, and he continued to the end of his life to staunchly defend both.

Parten's Jeffersonian passion for education gave him an open mind and a hunger for knowledge that allowed him to grow and to develop intellectually throughout his life. Until his mid-forties, Parten's views about American foreign policy and civil liberties were conventional and conservative. He was a strict constructionist in his interpretation of the federal constitution and a firm believer in states' rights. He was little concerned with public-policy issues not directly affecting his own narrow oil-business interests. Beginning in the mid-1930s, however, a series of events and experiences drove Parten to look at the world in new ways. His experience in the Petroleum Administration for War and his work with Harold Ickes made him identify more closely with FDR and the national Democratic Party. Parten became a strong adherent of the brand of liberalism symbolized by Roosevelt, a man whose memory Parten came to revere. The most profound influence on Parten's political views, however, came as a result of Homer Rainey's dismissal as University of Texas president and his subsequent defeat in the 1946 Democratic Party primary election. The Rainey affair strengthened Parten's identification with the national Democratic Party and activated his latent civil libertarianism. The affair also alienated him from the conservative Texas political and business establishment, pushing him into the Loyal Democratic faction of the state party. The Rainey affair also marked Parten as the "liberal oil man" who could be counted upon for financial support for progressive causes.

During this same period, Parten's experiences in the Soviet Union as a result of his participation in the reparations negotiations made him critical of the Cold War and an opponent of the nuclear-arms race. Parten's opinions about the nature of the Soviet government changed as the evils of Stalinism became more evident, but he never retreated from his basic belief in the need to maintain good relations with the Soviet Union. He never believed that the Soviet Union was solely responsible for the Cold War. Based on his own experiences, he knew that the United States deserved its share of the blame. Even in the darkest days of the Cold War, Parten's memories of the devastated Stalingrad continued to bolster his belief in the need to maintain the peace. His fear of nuclear war convinced him that everything possible had to be done to maintain the peace between the two superpowers having the capability to destroy the world. As the arms race escalated, the cause of peace became one of his burning passions.

Parten's experience in the Rainey affair as well as his opposition to the Cold War also deepened his antipathy to superpatriotic political demagoguery, the first real taste of which he had experienced as a regent in his dealings with Cong. Martin Dies. Parten later said that he had "learned from seeing how Mr. Dies operated that you have to challenge a demagogue or there's no end to it." Parten's confrontation with Dies, his clash with Rainey's accusers, and his Jeffersonian ideology made him a vocal critic of the post–World War II red scare and the activities of Sen. Joseph McCarthy. Few things outraged Parten more than the practitioners of McCarthyism. "What makes Parten great," Bernard Rapoport once said, "is that he knows when to be outraged. And when he gets outraged, you know it."

It was Parten's capacity for outrage and his profound concern for civil liberties that led him into the Fund for the Republic, which brought him into contact with a wide variety of diverse ideas and causes espoused by intellectuals, journalists, educators, artists, and political and social activists of whom he would never have otherwise known. One of the Fund's most influential directors, Parten inspired its "fear in education" project, which resulted in Paul Lazerfield's *The Academic Mind: Social Scientists in a Time of Crisis* (1955). Lazerfield's study provided compelling evidence that the red scare was severely and adversely affecting the nation's colleges and universities. Parten also backed the Fund's exposé of the blacklisting system in the entertainment industry, which later provided critical information in support of John Henry Faulk's lawsuit against AWARE, Inc. In addition, Parten's support of the Center for the Study of Democratic Institutions enabled it to sponsor conferences and convocations that brought meaningful public attention to the issues of racism, poverty, civil liberties, public education, militarism, and the threat of nuclear war. In the summer of 1974, when Parten looked back on his many years of association with the Fund, he admitted that it had contributed "in no small way to my education which prior to that time was woefully incomplete."

While Parten's world view broadened, his basic philosophical beliefs remained the same throughout his life. Equally suspicious of Big Government and Big Business, Parten never abandoned his Jacksonian economic conservatism. In an interview with the New York *Times* in 1980, Parten insisted that the "chief thing the government should do for industry is to see that fair competition is preserved." In addition, Jeffersonian democratic principles, with their emphasis on personal liberty, toleration, and the critical need for an educated citizenry, dominated Parten's political and social world view until the day he died. A reverence for Jeffersonian democracy and a belief in the sanctity of individual liberty nurtured his sense of social justice and fairness, providing him with the value system that guided his behavior and shaped his world view. In the early 1980s when Reaganism was sweeping the country and it became politically faddish to attack Social Security, Medicare, and other components of the welfare state such as food stamps, Parten voiced his strong support for these programs, arguing that the inequalities inherent in the free-enterprise system made them necessary. The Jeffersonian Parten saw no conflict between his economic conservatism and his passion for civil liberties, equal rights and opportunities, and basic constitutional guarantees.

Despite encouragement and numerous invitations to run for elected office, J. R. Parten never accepted that challenge, preferring to remain behind the scenes as counselor and promoter rather than as public leader. "J. R. Parten," John Henry Faulk noted, "is a very low profile gentleman." Parten's sense of personal dignity and his consistent adherence to larger principles never permitted him to seriously consider running for public office. Although he understood and accepted the realities of the American political system, he found distasteful the thought of having to make promises that he might not be able to keep and of having to wheel and deal in a political culture he considered characterized by overblown and false rhetoric. "I always want to stay behind the political scenes," Parten once said. "If you get into office . . . you are crippled from the beginning because you have all of these people you have to placate, you can't say what you think, you have to play this one off against that other one and I don't want to have to do that." Parten, however, was more than capable of playing one interest off against another in his behind-the-scenes political involvements as well as in the business arena.[1]

Despite Parten's preference for a location backstage rather than in the spotlight, Bernard Rapoport believed that J. R. Parten was "as influential as any person that ever lived in this state. He was not well-known at all and yet, among that inner circle of people that understand what has made things move in the state of Texas and this nation [he was well known]." Parten's connections with political figures such as Huey Long, Sam Rayburn, Harold Ickes, Jesse H. Jones, Harry Truman, Oscar Chapman, Arthur Vandenburg, Edwin Pauley, Lyndon Johnson, Leon Jaworski, and Joseph Califano extended his influence well beyond the borders of the Lone Star State. Noting "a certain Victorian reserve, almost an asceticism" about J. R. Parten, the New York *Times* asked in a profile published in 1980, "How, then, has Parten made his influence felt? Through half a century of associations with powerful people and institutions—and through the money he has given them." Parten's friendships and connections were not simply the result of his self-made wealth, however. His managerial and entrepreneurial skills, his abilities as a clear and focused thinker, his capacity for hard work, and his solid reputation for honesty and integrity, made J. R. Parten more than just another rich man. Because of those personal qualities, Parten was a man to whom others in positions of authority frequently turned for help as well as money and as a result, he enjoyed a position in a wide range of situations of importance to his university, state, country, political party, and industry.[2]

J. R. Parten was more than an influential businessman and public servant; his life of accomplishment and influence is also a study in apparent contradictions. He led his life against the grain, behaving in ways that transcended the expected. He was a wealthy Texas businessman with conservative economic views who remained to the end of his life a vocal advocate for liberal social principles; an activist who played an important role in Democratic Party politics for more than half a century yet remained relatively unknown to the public; an independent oil man and cattle rancher whose quiet, formal, and reserved manner did not fit the flamboyant stereotype; a former army major who nearly chose the military as his career yet who opposed the Vietnam war and denounced the nuclear-arms race; a Texan with deep rural roots who traveled away from North America only once but was a fervent internationalist who supported the United Nations, called for a harmonious relationship with the Soviet Union, and worked for world peace. "What you've got is a patrician humanist and an intellectual and that's remarkable to come out of the Establishment," Ronnie Dugger noted. "People like J. R. Parten are critical to the possibility that democracy is going to achieve its latent ideal of self government. By Marx's standards Parten should be a part of the oppressive and exploitive class. And yet without people like him, how could you even have a democracy? Look how much it costs to run for office now. These people are critical. It's a paradox, but its people like him who make social change possible. J. R. Parten gave strength to the people."[3]

Walter Prescott Webb once described J. R. Parten as "a breed so rare." He was a remarkable man who lived during remarkable times, and for almost a century he was actively involved in the events and ideas of those times. He was a patriot who during World War I, World War II, and the Korean War served his country in the ways he was best able to at the time, yet his patriotism also encompassed a belief in civil liberties and the right to free speech, the right to tell the President of the United States that the Vietnam war was wrong. He was a passionate believer in the value of education and he remained willing to grow and change intellectually throughout his life. He loved the University of Texas and the state of Texas, and he believed that all the causes he supported could help his university and state be the best that they could be. His passing left many people and causes without a champion. This state, country, and world would be better places if there were more men like J. R. Parten.

Author's Note

I first heard of "Major" J. R. Parten in the late 1960s when I was researching my master's thesis on McCarthyism in the Houston, Texas, public schools during the 1950s. His reputation intrigued me greatly: a wealthy Texas oil man from a small East Texas town who had fought McCarthyism and who opposed the ongoing war in Vietnam. Here was someone who did not fit the rigid stereotype of the typical Texas oil man, much less the typical Texan with a military title. He was not flamboyant like the famous wildcatter Glenn McCarthy; he was educated and well read, unlike oil man Hugh Roy Cullen; and his politics were not reactionary like H. L. Hunt and so many other Texas oil men. I did not know what to make of this man. I went on to other things, but I kept Parten in the back of my mind.

In the fall of 1972, J. R. Parten's name again came to my attention while I was working in the quixotic crusade to elect Sen. George McGovern president of the United States. I was in the Houston campaign headquarters to receive a newly arrived supply of McGovern bumper stickers. Knowing that the Nixon campaign was swimming in money while we had little, I asked one of the staff how we could afford to buy anything. The answer got my attention: "If it wasn't for Major Parten and [Waco insurance executive] Barney Rapoport, we would be out of business." My curiosity about Parten deepened.

I would not meet Parten, however, for another ten years. That first meeting was arranged by our mutual friend John Henry Faulk, the humorist and civil liberties activist who was raising money to make it possible for me to finish my book *Red Scare!* John Henry knew that Parten would be interested in my work on McCarthyism, a subject about which they both had an intense personal interest. We first met in January 1982. Parten, who then was eighty-five years old, told me about his confrontation with Cong. Martin Dies in the early 1940s and his subsequent involvement with the anti–red scare organization, the Fund for the Republic. I left Parten's office eager to know more about his life, but with no real plan to do anything about it. Parten's small foundation subsequently granted me the funds that I needed to complete my book.

In the spring of 1983, Faulk and J. R. Parten's son, Randy, asked me to conduct an oral history project to record J. R. Parten's oral autobiography. This was a wish come true. I spent most of the summer of 1983 with J. R. at his house in Madisonville taping his life story. J. R. helped the project significantly by allowing me unrestricted access to his voluminous personal papers and business records, which were stored in his company office in Houston. Filling dozens of cabinet drawers, the Parten papers preserved an almost complete documentary picture of his career since 1919. The availability of those papers made it possible for me to question J. R. about matters of importance to his life about which he had long forgotten and about which I would not have otherwise known. The papers also allowed me to correct the factual errors that inevitably occur when one attempts to recall events that happened, in J. R.'s case, sixty to seventy years earlier. On the whole, however, I was amazed at the quality of J. R.'s memory. Our interviews produced a lengthy transcript full of detail and rich in perception.

After completing the Parten oral history project, I realized that the memoir and the availability of his papers made it possible for me to write a full-scale biography. I embarked on this biographical project with J. R.'s blessing and encouragement, but it is not an "official" work. J. R. never sought to control any portion of it. He never even asked to see the rough drafts of the earliest chapters. J. R.'s cooperation extended beyond allowing me unrestricted access to his papers. He spent hours answering questions that I had failed to ask during the oral history project, and he persuaded his friends and associates to let me interview them. A list of these individual interviews is in the bibliography.

In "Reflections of a Biographer," an essay about his research on Texas empressario Stephen F. Austin, Eugene C. Barker wrote that "in a present so filled with unavoidable annoyances, why resurrect from the past a man one doesn't like and write about him? I, for one, will not." [1] I readily identify with Barker's implied admission that his biography of Austin was not free of personal bias. I do not claim that this biography is free of bias, and I do not offer it to the reader as an example of objectivity. Because so much of this book is built upon J. R. Parten's oral-history life memoir, it reflects in large measure his interpretation of the events that intersected his life. The book is, therefore, something of a hybrid—a mixture of autobiography and biography. As a professionally trained historian, however, I have been careful to search the relevant documentary evidence widely and in depth, so that the facts of J. R. Parten's life could be presented as accurately as possible. My interpretation of events generally match Parten's, but I have not hesitated to express a different opinion or be critical of Parten's behavior or actions when I felt it necessary .

Every historian depends on the work of those who preceded him or her, and although a selected bibliography is included at the end of the narrative, I want to acknowledge those whose prior research proved especially valuable to my work.

---

1 Eugene C. Barker, "Reflections of a Biographer," ms., n.d., box 2B108, Eugene C. Barker Papers (CAH).

Doctoral dissertations by Barbara Sue Thompson Day and Alice Carol Cox, the former on the oil and gas industry and Texas politics and the latter on the Homer Rainey affair, are essential starting places for anyone interested in those subjects. James A. Clark's unpublished history of the Pan American Sulphur Company, "Miracle at Jaltipan," provided crucial information about the formation and early development of that business enterprise. I also relied heavily on the published work of Bruce K. Brown, Ronnie Dugger, John W. Frey and H. Chandler Ide, George Norris Green, William Haynes, Arthur M. Johnson, Frank K. Kelly, Gerald D. Nash, Norman E. Nordhauser, David F. Prindle, Thomas C. Reeves, Robert Sheehan, and Daniel Yergin.

My greatest debt, of course, is to J. R. Parten and John Henry Faulk. Without their cooperation, support, and encouragement I could not have written this book. John Henry and I spent many pleasant hours together driving to and from Austin and Madisonville. His memories and observations informed me in more ways than I can catalog here. Johnny was a wonderful friend and comrade in arms. I miss him very much. Many others helped along the way. They include John R. "Randy" Parten, Bill and Pepe Anderson, Myrna Bernier, L. Tuffly Ellis, Ron Tyler, William H. Cunningham, Louise O'Connor, John Crain, Tom Kreneck, Barbara Griffith, H. G. Dulaney, and Suzette Dayson Shelmire. Chester Burns helped me sort out the complex Spies affair at the University of Texas Medical School. Two University of Texas graduate students, Sheree Scarborough and Mark Young, tracked down some elusive sources. Katherine J. Adams, my friend and associate at the Center for American History, read most of the manuscript in draft form. Her sharp pencil and perceptive editorial eye greatly improved the narrative. Another colleague and friend at the Center, Alison Beck, gave me the encouragement to keep working on this project when I doubted that I would ever have the time to finish it. Lewis Gould, who also read several chapters in draft, provided invaluable critiques that reshaped significant portions of the manuscript. My former boss, Harold W. Billings, director of The University of Texas at Austin General Libraries, gave me a critical period of time off to write the first draft of this book. My debt to him is great indeed.

Several librarians and archivists—the essential partners of any research project—provided helpful reference support. They include Ralph Elder, The University of Texas Center for American History; Ben Primer and Nanci Young, Princeton University Mudd Library; Dawn Letson, Southern Methodist University DeGolyer Library; Robert Colasacco, the Ford Foundation; Chris Laplante, Texas State Archives; Nancy Boothe, Rice University Woodson Research Center; Patricia Meador, Louisiana State University at Shreveport Library; Robert Martin, Louisiana State University at Baton Rouge Library; Beth Schnieder, the Haley Library; and Linda Hanson and Claudia Anderson, Lyndon B. Johnson Library.

Because I am the full-time director of The University of Texas Center for American History, most of this book was researched and written at night and during weekends, vacation, and other "time-off" periods. My wife Suzanne and our children, Ian and Aunna, therefore, have made their own significant contribution to this work by enduring my long absences while I hid in my study and clicked away at a computer keyboard. Because my children have heard about "J. R." ever since they were born, he is like an ancestor to whom references are made but who remains a distant, unknown figure. Hopefully, this book will now give identity to the mysterious "J. R." about whom they have heard so much.

Selected Bibliography

I. Archival and Manuscript Collections

American Heritage Center, University of Wyoming, Laramie, Wyo.
  Ralph K. Davies Papers
M. D. Anderson Library, University of Houston
  James V. Allred Papers
Bancroft Library, University of California at Berkeley
  Ernest O. Lawrence Papers
  Robert Gordon Sproul Papers
Center for American History, University of Texas at Austin
  Clarence E. Ayres Papers
  Eugene C. Barker Papers
  Roy Bedicheck Papers
  John H. Bickett Papers
  George C. Butte Papers
  Lillian Collier Papers
  Sylvester Dayson Papers
  Frederick Duncalf Papers
  Robert C. Eckhardt Papers
  Frances "Sissy" Farenthold Papers
  John Henry Faulk Papers
  Ralph Frede Papers
  John C. Granbery Papers
  J. Evetts Haley Papers
  John A. Lomax Papers
  J. Howard Marshall Papers
  Maury Maverick Sr. Papers
  Dan Moody Papers
  Jubal R. Parten Papers
  Bernard Rapoport Papers
  Ernest O. Thompson Papers
  Sam Rayburn Papers
  Homer Price Rainey File, Richard T. Fleming Collection
  University of Texas, Minutes of the Board of Regents, 1936–1941
  University of Texas, Records of the Office of the President
  Walter P. Webb Papers
  Dudley K. Woodward Papers
  Works Projects Administration, Texas Division Records
  Ralph W. Yarborough Papers
DeGolyer Library, Southern Methodist University, Dallas, Tex.
  Everette Lee DeGolyer Sr. Papers

Haley Library, Midland, Tex.
  J. Evetts Haley Papers
Lyndon Baines Johnson Library and Museum, Austin, Tex.
  Lyndon Baines Johnson Papers
  D. B. Hardeman Papers
  Drew Pearson Papers
The Library, Louisiana State University, Baton Rouge, La.
  Huey Long Papers
The Library, University of California at Santa Barbara
  Center for the Study of Democratic Institutions Archives (CSDI)
The Library, University of Texas at Arlington
  James Sewell Papers
Library of Congress, Washington, D.C.
  Harold L. Ickes Papers
Mudd Library, Princeton University, Princeton, N.J.
  Fund for the Republic Archives (FFR)
National Archives, Washington, D.C.
  Petroleum Administration for War, Record Group 253 (PAW Records)
Harry Ransom Humanities Research Center, University of Texas at Austin (HRC)
  J. Frank Dobie Papers
Franklin D. Roosevelt Library, Hyde Park, N.Y.
  Franklin D. Roosevelt Papers
Southern Historical Collection, University of North Carolina, Chapel Hill, N.C.
  Frank Porter Graham Papers
Texas State Library, Archives Division, Austin, Tex.
  W. Lee O'Daniel Papers
  Coke Stevenson Papers
Harry S. Truman Library, Independence, Mo.
  Oscar L. Chapman Papers
  Will Clayton Papers
  Ralph K. Davies Papers
  Stephen Mitchell Papers
  Harry S. Truman Papers
Woodson Research Center, Rice University, Houston, Tex.
  Fagan Dickson Papers
  Walter Hall Papers
  Frankie Carter Randolph Papers

Selected Bibliography

II. Oral History Transcripts
Texas Collection, Baylor University, Waco, Tex.
    Bernard Rapoport
Butler Library, Columbia University, New York City
    Paul Benedum
    D. B. Hardeman
    Maury Maverick Jr.
    Henry A. Wallace
    Palmer Webber
Center for American History, University of Texas at Austin
    John B. Connally
Ford Foundation, New York City
    Robert M. Hutchins
    W. H. Ferry
Lyndon Baines Johnson Library and Museum, Austin, Tex. (LBJ)
    Paul Bolton
    Oscar Chapman
    Walter Hall
    D. B. Hardeman
    John E. Lyle
    J. R. Parten
    Edwin Pauley
    Allan Shivers
    Claude C. Wild Sr.
The Library, Louisiana State University at Shreveport (LSU)
    Don Ewing
    Carl Jones
    Cecil Morgan
    Scott Wilkinson
Harry S. Truman Library, Independence, Mo.
    Josiah E. Dubois
    Isador Lubin
The Library, University of North Texas, Denton (UNT)
    Jo Betsy Allred
    Earle Cabell
    Alla Clary
    Price Daniel
    Wick Fowler
    Homer Rainey
    Allan Shivers
    Coke Stevenson

III. Interviews
(conducted by the author, unless otherwise noted; recordings, notes, and transcripts in author's possession)

Pepe Anderson, Mar. 21, 1992, Houston, Tex.
William A. Anderson, Mar. 21, 1992 and Mar. 5, 1993, Houston, Tex.
James Calloway, June 7, 1988, Houston, Tex.
Lloyd M. Bentsen Jr., Aug. 26, 1993, San Diego, Calif.
Jack Blanton, May 22, 1992, Austin, Tex.
Jack and Marguerite Boothe, Oct. 23, 1987, Houston, Tex.
Gary Cadenhead, Apr. 14, 1992
Joseph Califano Jr., Feb. 26, 1992, by telephone
Edward Clark, July 26, 1990, Austin, Tex.
Lanier Cox, May 10, 1989, Austin, Tex.
Ronnie Dugger, Nov. 29, 1989, Austin, Tex.
H. G. Dulaney, May 18, 1988, Bonham, Tex.
Robert C. Eckhardt, Dec. 1, 1989, Austin, Tex.
Frances "Sissy" Farenthold, June 7,1989, Houston, Tex.
Creekmore Fath, Nov. 2, 1990, Austin, Tex.
John Henry Faulk, Mar. 14 and Aug. 18, 1987; Oct. 23 and Nov. 14, 1988 Austin, Tex.
Liz Faulk, Aug. 18, 1987, Austin, Tex.
Jenkins Garrett, Oct. 26, 1989, Fort Worth, Tex.
Miles Glaser, Jan. 30, 1994, Houston, Tex.
Lawrence Goodwyn, Aug. 16, 1990, Austin, Tex (with Barbara Griffith)
Charlotte Gray, Oct. 22, 1987, Houston, Tex.
J. Evetts Haley, Apr. 14, 1989, Midland, Tex.
Walter Hall, June 8, 1989, Dickinson, Tex..
Mozelle Ilfrey, Oct. 22, 1987, Houston, Tex.
Frank Kelly, Apr. 13, 1988, Madisonville, Tex.
Eugene McCarthy, Mar. 12, 1997, Washington, D.C.
George McGovern, Mar. 12, 1997, Washington, D.C.
Gerald C. Mann, Apr. 24, 1989, Dallas, Tex.
Stanley Marcus, Apr. 15, 1994, Dallas, Tex.
Morton "Pat" Marr, Mar. 18, 1993, Dallas, Texas
J. Howard Marshall, Feb. 12, 1986, Houston, Tex.
Fred Mayer, June 26, 1989, Dallas, Tex.
Eugenia Miller, Sept. 12, 1990, Houston, Tex.
Fred Moore, May 24, 1985, Austin, Tex.
John Randolph "Randy" Parten, Jan. 17, 1992, Houston, Tex.

J. R. Parten, Jan. 19, 1980, Madisonville, Tex.
(with Anthony Champagne)
Bernard Rapoport, Mar. 7, 1992, Waco, Tex.
Audre Rapoport, Mar. 7, 1992, Waco, Tex.
Suzette Shelmire, Feb. 8, 1989, Dallas, Tex. and
Apr. 23, 1989, Tyler, Tex.
Dallas Sherman, Feb. 27, 1988, New York City
Leonard J. Townsend, June 17, 1988,
Madisonville, Tex.
Logan Wilson, Nov. 4, 1988, Austin, Tex.
Justin R. Wolf, Mar. 1, 1988, Washington, D.C.
Ralph W. Yarborough, Apr. 10, 1987, Austin,
Tex.

IV. Official and Semi-Official Publications
Board of Regents of the University of Texas
System. *Permanent University Fund
Investments for the Fiscal Year Ended
August 31, 1990* . Austin, Tex., 1990.
Congressional Record, 78th Cong., 1st Sess.,
Senate, volume 89, part 3. Washington,
D.C.: GPO, 1943.
U.S. Tenth Census (1880), Madison County,
Tex. Population Schedules.
U.S. Twelfth Census (1900), Madison County,
Tex. Population Schedules.
U.S. Congress. House of Representatives. H.R.
6999. *Hearings*, House Committee on
Rivers and Harbors. 77th Cong., 2nd sess.
Washington, D.C.: GPO, 1942. Short cita-
tion: House *Hearings* on Rivers and
Harbors.
U.S. Congress. House of Representatives.
Hearings, House Subcommittee of the
Committee on Naval Affairs. 78th Cong.,
1st sess. Vol. 3. Washington, D.C.: GPO,
1942. Short citation: House *Hearings* on
Naval Affairs.
U.S. Congress. House of Representatives.
*Petroleum Investigation: Hearings on House
Resolution 441.* House Subcommittee of
the Committee on Interstate and Foreign
Commerce. 73rd Cong., Recess. 4 vols.;
Washington, D.C.: GPO, 1934. Short cita-
tion: House *Petroleum Investigation.*
U.S. Congress. House of Representatives.
Committee on Un-American Activities.
Annual Report for the Year 1956 .
Washington, D.C.: GPO, 1957.
U.S. Congress. Senate. *Hearings Pursuant to S.
Res. 241: A Resolution to Investigate
Whether the Use of Inland Waterways for
the Transportation of Petroleum Products*

and other Commodities May be Increased,
Senate Subcommittee of the Committee
on Commerce. 77th Cong., 2nd Sess.
Washington, D.C.: GPO, 1942. Short cita-
tion: Senate *Hearings Pursuant to S. Res.
241.*
U.S. Department of State. *Foreign Relations of
the United States, Diplomatic Papers. The
Conference of Berlin (The Potsdam
Conference), 1945.* Vols. I and II.
Washington, D.C.: GPO, 1960. Short cita-
tion: State Department, *The Conference of
Berlin.*

V. Unpublished Books, Papers, Theses, and Dissertations
Atkinson, William Eugene, "James V. Allred:
A Political Biography, 1899–1935," Ph.D.
diss., Texas Christian University, Fort
Worth, 1978.
Brown, David L., "Homer Price Rainey and
the Campaign of 1946," Senior Honors
thesis, University of Texas at Austin, 1989.
Burlage, Robb K., "James V. Allred: Texas'
Liberal Governor," unpublished paper,
1959, copy in JRP Papers (CAH).
Clark, James A., "Miracle at Jaltipan," unpub-
lished book-length manuscript, n.d., per-
sonal collection of Jack W. Boothe,
Houston, Tex.
Cox, Alice Carol, "The Rainey Affair: A
History of the Academic Freedom
Controversy at the University of Texas,
1938–1946," Ph.D. diss., University of
Denver, 1970.
Day, Barbara Sue Thompson, "The Oil and
Gas Industry and Texas Politics,
1930–1935," Ph.D. diss., Rice University,
Houston, 1973.
Eakens, Robert Henry Seale, "The
Development of Proration in the East
Texas Oil Field," Master's thesis,
University of Texas, Austin, 1937.
Koppes, Clayton R., "Oscar L. Chapman: A
Liberal at the Interior Department,
1933–1953," Ph.D. diss., University of
Kansas, Lawrence, 1974.
Martindale, Robert, "James V. Allred,"
Master's thesis, University of Texas at
Austin, 1958.
Parker, Donald, "The Texas Gubernatorial
Campaign of 1954," Master's thesis, Texas
Christian University, Fort Worth, 1975.

Perkins, William Coy, "A History of Wheeler County, Texas," Master's thesis, University of Texas, Austin, 1938.

Reeves, Thomas Charles, "The Fund for the Republic, 1951–1957: An Unusual Chapter in the History of American Philanthropy," Ph.D. diss., University of California at Santa Barbara, 1966.

Wolfe, Thomas Herndon, "Dimensions of a Prominent American Graduate School, The Graduate School of the University of Texas in Austin, 1883–1969," Master's thesis, University of Texas, Austin, 1970.

VI. Newspapers and Periodicals

Alcalde (University of Texas at Austin)
Business Week
Daily Texan (University of Texas at Austin)
Dallas *Morning News*
Dallas *Times Herald*
Forbes Magazine
Fort Worth *Star-Telegram*
Houston *Chronicle*
Houston *Post*
Houston *Press*
Huntsville (Tex.) *Item*
Life
Madisonville (Tex.) *Meteor*
New York *Times*
St. Paul (Minn.) *Dispatch-Pioneer Press*
San Antonio *Express-News*
Saturday Evening Post
Shreveport *Journal*
Shreveport *Times*
Texas Independent
Texas Oil Journal
Tyler (Tex.) *Courier-Times Telegraph*
Wall Street Journal
Washington *Post*

VII. Books

Alperovitz, Gar. *Atomic Diplomacy: Hiroshima and Potsdam: The Use of the Atomic Bomb and the American Confrontation with Soviet Power.* New York: Simon and Schuster, 1985.

Ambrose, Stephen E. *Eisenhower: The President.* New York: Simon and Schuster, 1984.

Ashmore, Harry S. *Unseasonable Truths: The Life of Robert Maynard Hutchins.* Boston: Little, Brown, 1989.

Ball, Max W., Douglas Ball, and Daniel S.

Turner. *This Fascinating Oil Business.* Indianapolis: Bobbs- Merrill, 1965.

Beaton, Kendall. *Enterprise in Oil: A History of Shell in the United States.* New York: Appleton-Century-Crofts, 1957.

Bedichek, Roy. *Letters of Roy Bedichek.* Austin: University of Texas Press, 1985.

Bennett, David Harry. *The Party of Fear : From Nativist Movements to the New Right in American History.* Chapel Hill: University of North Carolina Press, 1988.

Berry, Margaret C. *The University of Texas: A Pictorial Account of Its First Century.* Austin: University of Texas Press, 1980.

Board of Governors of the Federal Reserve System. *The Federal Reserve System: Purposes and Functions.* Washington, D.C.: Government Printing Office, 1954.

Bohlen, Charles E. *Witness To History: 1929–1969.* New York: Norton, 1973.

Brown, Bruce K. *Oil Men in Washington: An Informal Account of the Organization and Activities of the Petroleum Administration for Defense During the Korean War, 1950–1952.* Evanil Press, 1965.

Brown, Norman. *Hood, Bonnet, and Little Brown Jug: Texas Politics, 1921–1928.* College Station: Texas A&M University Press, 1984.

Brureggerhoff (publisher), *Shreveport City Directory,* 1918; 1919; 1921; 1922; 1932; 1935.

Bullock, Alan. *Hitler and Stalin: Parallel Lives.* New York: Knopf; distributed by Random House, 1992.

Burns, James MacGregor. *Roosevelt : The Lion and the Fox.* New York: Harcourt, Brace & World, 1956.

Byrnes, James F. *Speaking Frankly.* New York: Harper, 1947.

Cactus. Texas Student Publications, University of Texas. 1913–1918, 1935–1941, 1944.

Calvert, Robert W. *Here Comes the Judge: From State Home to State House.* Waco: Texian Press, 1977.

Carleton, Don E. *Red Scare !: Right-Wing Hysteria, Fifties Fanaticism, and Their Legacy in Texas.* Austin: Texas Monthly Press, 1985.

———. *Who Shot the Bear? J. Evetts Haley and the Eugene C. Barker Texas History Center.* Austin: Wind River Press, 1984.

Caro, Robert A. *The Years of Lyndon Johnson: The Path to Power.* New York: Knopf, 1982.

————. *The Years of Lyndon Johnson: Means of Ascent.* New York: Knopf, 1990.

Castaneda, Christopher J. and Joseph A. Pratt. *From Texas to the East: A Strategic History of Texas Eastern Corporation.* College Station: Texas A&M Press, 1993.

Caute, David. *The Great Fear: The anti-Communist purge under Truman and Eisenhower.* New York: Simon and Schuster, 1978.

Ceplair, Larry and Steven Englund. *The Inquisition in Hollywood: Politics in the Film Community.* New York: Anchor Press/Doubleday, 1980.

Champagne, Anthony. *Congressman Sam Rayburn.* New Brunswick, N.J.: Rutgers University Press, 1984.

Chapman, Margaret and Carl Marcy, eds. *Common Sense in U.S.-Soviet Trade.* Washington, D. C.: American Committee on East-West Accord, 1983.

Clark, James A. *Three Stars for the Colonel.* New York: Random House, 1954.

Clark, James A. and Michel T. Halbouty. *The Last Boom.* Bryan, Tex.: Shearer Publishing, 1984.

Cochran, Bert. *Harry Truman and the Crisis Presidency.* New York: Funk & Wagnalls, 1973.

Cogley, John. *Report on Blacklisting.* 2 vols. New York: Fund for the Republic, 1956.

Connally, John B. *In History's Shadow: An American Odyssey.* New York: Hyperion, 1992.

Cotner, Robert. *James Stephen Hogg: A Biography.* Austin: University of Texas Press, 1959.

Cumley, R. W. and Joan McCay, comps. and eds. *The First Twenty Years of The University of Texas, M. D. Anderson Hospital and Tumor Institute* (Houston: Dept. of Publications, M. D. Anderson Hospital, 1964).

Dallek, Robert. *Lone Star Rising: Lyndon Johnson and His Times, 1908–1960.* New York: Oxford University Press, 1991.

Daniels, Jonathan. *The Man of Independence.* Philadelphia: Lippincott, 1950.

Davidson, Chandler. *Race and Class in Texas Politics.* Princeton: Princeton University Press, 1990.

Davidson, T. Whitfield. *The Memoirs of T. Whitfield Davidson.* Waco: 1972.

Deutscher, Isaac. *Stalin: A Political Biography.* New York: Oxford University Press, 1966.

Dilling, Elizabeth. *The Red Network; A "Who's Who" and Handbook of Radicalism for Patriots.* Kenilworth, Ill.: The author, 1935.

Dobie, J. Frank. *Some Part of Myself.* Boston: Little, Brown, 1967.

Donovan, Robert J. *Conflict and Crisis: The Presidency of Harry S. Truman, 1945–1948.* New York: Norton, 1977.

Dugger, Ronnie. *Our Invaded Universities: Form, Reform, and New Starts.* New York: Norton, 1974.

————. *The Politician: The Drive for Power, From the Frontier to Master of the Senate.* New York: Norton, 1982.

Dunagan, J. Conrad. *Eugene Holman, A Texan of Distinction.* [Monahans, Tex.] Historical Association of Ward County, 1989.

Egerton, John. *Speak Now Against the Day: The Generation Before the Civil Rights Movement in the South .* New York: Knopf, 1994.

Engler, Robert. *The Politics of Oil: A Study of Private Power and Democratic Directions.* New York: Macmillan, 1961.

Evans, David S. and J. Derral Mulholland. *Big and Bright: A History of McDonald Observatory.* Austin: University of Texas Press, 1986.

Faulk, John Henry. *Fear on Trial.* Austin: University of Texas Press, 1983.

Franks, Kenny A. and Paul F. Lambert. *Early Louisiana and Arkansas Oil: A Photographic History, 1901–1946.* College Station: Texas A&M University Press, 1982.

Frantz, Joe B. *The Forty-Acre Follies: An Opinionated History of the University of Texas.* Austin: Texas Monthly Press, 1983.

Freidel, Frank. *Franklin D. Roosevelt: Launching the New Deal.* Boston: Little, Brown, 1973.

Frey, John W. and H. Chandler Ide. *A History of the Petroleum Administration for War, 1941–1945.* Washington, D.C.: Government Printing Office, 1946.

Fried, Richard M. *Men Against McCarthy.* New York : Columbia University Press, 1976.

————. *Nightmare in Red: The McCarthy Era in Perspective.* New York: Oxford University Press, 1990.

Gaddis, John Lewis. *The United States and the*

Origins of the Cold War, 1941–1947. New York: Columbia University Press, 1972.

Galbraith, John Kenneth. *A Life in Our Times: Memoirs*. New York: Houghton Mifflin, 1981.

Ganrud, Pauline Jones, comp. *Marriage Records of Marengo County, Alabama, 1818–1860*. Memphis: 1970.

Giebelhaus, August W. *Business and Government in the Oil Industry: A Case Study of Sun Oil, 1876–1945*. Greenwich, Conn.: JAI Press, 1980.

Goodman, Walter. *The Committee: The Extraordinary Career of the House Committee on Un-American Activities*. New York: Farrar, Straus, and Giroux, 1968.

Goodwyn, Lawrence. *Texas Oil, American Dreams: A Study of the Texas Independent Producers and Royalty Owners Association*. Austin. Texas State Historical Association, 1996.

Gulick, Luther H. *Administrative Reflections from World War II*. Birmingham, Ala.: Univ. of Alabama Press, 1948.

———. *Papers on the Science of Administration*. New York: Institute of Public Administration, Columbia University, 1937.

Grant, Lyman and William A. Owens, eds. *Letters of Roy Bedichek*. Austin: University of Texas Press, 1985.

Green, George Norris. *The Establishment in Texas Politics: The Primitive Years, 1938–1957*. Westport, Conn.: Greenwood Press, 1979.

Haigh, Berte. R. *Land, Oil, and Education*. El Paso: Texas Western Press, 1986.

Hair, William Ivy. *The Kingfish and His Realm: The Life and Times of Huey P. Long*. Baton Rouge: Louisiana State University Press, 1991.

Haley, J. Evetts. *The University of Texas and the Issue*. Clarendon, Tex.: Clarendon Press, 1945.

Hardeman, D. B., and Donald C. Bacon. *Rayburn: A Biography*. Austin: Texas Monthly Press, 1987.

Hardin, J. Fair. *Northwestern Louisiana: A History of the Watershed of the Red River, 1714–1937*, Vol. 2. 2 vols. [Shreveport]: 1938.

Hawley, Ellis W. *The New Deal and the Problem of Monopoly: A Study in Economic Ambivalence*. Princeton: Princeton University Press, 1966.

Haynes, Williams. *Brimstone: The Stone that Burns; The Story of the Frasch Sulphur Industry*. Princeton: Princeton University Press, 1959.

Henderson, Richard B. *Maury Maverick: A Political Biography*. Austin: University of Texas Press, 1970.

Herken, Gregg. *The Winning Weapon: The Atomic Bomb in the Cold War, 1945–1950*. New York: Knopf; distributed by Random House, 1980.

Hofstadter, Richard. *Social Darwinism in American Thought, 1860–1915*. Philadephia: University of Pennsylvania Press, 1944.

House, Boyce. *Oil Boom: The Story of Spindletop, Burkburnett, Mexia, Smackover, Desdemonia, and Ranger*. Caldwell, Idaho: Caxton Printers, 1941.

Hurt, Harry. *Texas Rich: The Hunt Dynasty from the Early Oil Days through the Silver Crash*. New York: Norton, 1981.

Hyman, Sidney. *Marriner S. Eccles: Private Entrepreneur and Public Servant*. Stanford, Calif.: Graduate School of Business, Stanford University, 1976.

Ickes, Harold L. *Fightin' Oil*. New York: Knopf, 1943.

———. *The Secret Diary of Harold L. Ickes*: Volume I: *The First Thousand Days, 1933–1936*. New York: Simon and Schuster, 1953.

———. *The Secret Diary of Harold L. Ickes*: Volume III: *The Lowering Clouds, 1939–1941*. New York: Simon and Schuster, 1954.

Ivins, Molly. *Nothin' but Good Times Ahead*. New York: Random House, 1993.

Johnson, Arthur M. *Petroleum Pipelines and Public Policy, 1906–1959*. Cambridge, Mass.: Harvard University Press, 1967.

Jones, J. Edward. *'And So—They Indicted Me!"*: *A Story of New Deal Persecution*. New York: J. E. Jones Publishing, 1939.

Jones, Jesse H. *Fifty Billion Dollars: My Thirteen Years with the RFC (1932–1945)*. New York: Da Capo Press, 1951.

Kanfer, Stefan. *A Journal of the Plague Years*. New York: Atheneum, 1973.

Kelly, Frank K. *Court of Reason: Robert Hutchins and the Fund for the Republic*. New York: Free Press, 1981.

Kennan, George F. *Memoirs, 1925–1950.* Boston: Little, Brown, 1967.

King, John O. *Joseph Stephen Cullinan: A Study of Leadership in the Texas Petroleum Industry, 1897–1937.* Nashville: Vanderbilt University Press, 1970.

Kuklick, Bruce. *American Policy and the Division of Germany: The Clash with Russia over Reparations.* Ithaca, N.Y.: Cornell University Press, 1972.

LaFeber, Walter. *America, Russia, and the Cold War, 1945–1975.* 3rd edition. New York: Wiley, 1976.

Larson, Henrietta M. and Kenneth W. Porter. *History of Humble Oil and Refining Company: A Study in Industrial Growth.* New York: Harper, 1959.

Leslie, Warren. *Dallas: Public and Private.* New York: Avon, 1964.

Lipartito, Kenneth J. and Joseph A. Pratt. *Baker & Botts in the Development of Modern Houston.* Austin: University of Texas Press, 1991.

Louisiana Publishers Association. *Louisiana: Its Builders and Its Industries: A Newspaper Reference Work.* [New Orleans?]: Louisiana Publishers Assoc., 1924.

McClure, Lilla and J. Ed Howe. *History of Shreveport and Shreveport Builders.* Shreveport: Journal Printing, 1937.

McComb, David G. *Houston, A History.* Austin: University of Texas Press, 1981.

McCullough, David. *Truman.* New York: Simon and Schuster, 1992.

McDanial, Ruel. *Some Ran Hot.* Dallas: Regional Press, 1939.

McKay, Seth Shepard. *Texas and the Fair Deal, 1945–1952.* San Antonio: Naylor Co., 1954.

———. *Texas Politics, 1906–1944.* Lubbock: Texas Tech Press, 1952.

———. *W. Lee O'Daniel and Texas Politics, 1938–1942.* Lubbock: Texas Technological College Research Funds, 1944.

McKeever, Porter. *Adlai Stevenson: His Life and Legacy.* New York: Morrow, 1989.

Madison County Historical Commission. *A History of Madison County, Texas.* Madisonville, Tex.: The Commission, 1984.

Madisonville Chamber of Commerce. *Industrial Inventory of Madisonville, Texas.* Madisonville, Tex.: Madisonville Chamber of Commerce, 1955.

Marshall, J. Howard. *Done in Oil: An Autobiography.* College Station: Texas A&M University Press, 1994.

Martin, John Bartlow. *Adlai Stevenson and the World: The Life of Adlai E. Stevenson.* New York: Doubleday, 1977.

Mathews, John Joseph. *The Life and Death of an Oilman: The Career of E. W. Marland.* Norman: University of Oklahoma Press, 1951.

Maverick Delegation. *The Texas Story: Democrats-Vs-Dixiecrats, 1952 National Democratic Convention.* Austin: 1952.

Mee, Charles L., Jr. *Meeting At Potsdam.* New York: M. Evans, 1975.

Messer, Robert L. *The End of an Alliance: James F. Byrnes, Roosevelt, Truman, and the Origins of the Cold War.* Chapel Hill: University of North Carolina Press, 1982.

Montague, George William. *History and Genealogy of Peter Montague.* Amherst, Mass.: 1894.

Montgomery, Robert H. *The Brimstone Game: Monopoly in Action.* New York: Vanguard Press, 1940.

Muller, H. J. *Out of the Night: A Biologist's View of the Future.* New York: Vanguard Press, 1935.

Nash, Gerald D. *United States Oil Policy: 1890–1964.* Pittsburg: University of Pittsburg Press, 1968.

———. *World War II and the West: Reshaping the Economy.* Lincoln: University of Nebraska Press, 1990.

Nicholson, Patrick J. *Mr. Jim: The Biography of James Smither Abercrombie.* Houston: Gulf Publishing Co., 1983.

Nordhauser, Norman E. *The Quest for Stability: Domestic Oil Regulation, 1917–1935.* New York: Garland Publishing, 1979.

Olien, Roger and Diana Davids Olien. *Wildcatters: Texas Independent Oilmen.* Austin: Texas Monthly Press, 1984.

O'Pry, Maude Hearn. *Chronicles of Shreveport.* Shreveport: Journal Printing, 1928.

Patenaude, Lionel V. *Texans, Politics, and the New Deal.* New York: Garland, 1983.

Payne, Robert. *The Rise and Fall of Stalin.* New York: Simon and Schuster, 1965.

Pettengill, Samuel B. *Hot Oil: The Problem of Petroleum.* New York: Economic Forum Co., 1936.

Phillips, William G. *Yarborough of Texas.* Washington, D.C : Acropolis Books, 1969.

Polenberg, Richard. *War and Society: The United States, 1941–1945.* Philadelphia: Lippincott, 1972.

Pool, William C. *Eugene C. Barker: Historian.* Austin: Texas State Historical Association, 1971.

Porter, Millie Jones. *Memory Cups of Panhandle Pioneers: A Belated Attempt at Panhandle History. . . .* Clarendon, Tex.: Clarendon Press, 1945.

Presley, James. *A Saga of Wealth: The Rise of the Texas Oilmen.* New York: Putnam, 1978.

———. *Never in Doubt: A History of Delta Drilling Company.* Houston: Gulf Publishing Co., 1981.

Prindle, David F. *Petroleum Politics and the Texas Railroad Commission.* Austin: Univeristy of Texas Press, 1981.

Rainey, Homer P. *The Tower and the Dome: A Free University Versus Political Control.* Boulder, Colo.: Pruett Publishing, 1971.

Reeves, Thomas C. *Freedom and the Foundation: The Fund for the Republic in the Era of McCarthyism.* New York: Knopf, 1969.

———. *The Life and Times of Joe McCarthy : A Biography.* New York : Stein and Day, 1982.

Reston, James, Jr. *The Lone Star: The Life of John Connally .* New York: Harper and Row, 1989.

Rhodes, Richard. *The Making of the Atomic Bomb.* New York: Simon and Schuster, 1986.

Rister, Carl Coke. *Oil! Titan of the Southwest.* Norman: University of Oklahoma Press, 1949.

Rostow, Walt W. *The Division of Europe after World War II: 1946.* Austin: University of Texas Press, 1981.

Schlesinger, Arthur M., Jr. *The Crisis of the Old Order, 1919–1933 .* 3 vols. Boston: Houghton Mifflin, 1957.

Sherwin, Martin J. *A World Destroyed: The Atomic Bomb and the Grand Alliance.* New York: Knopf, 1975.

Smith, Gaddis. *American Diplomacy during the Second World War, 1941–1945.* New York: Wiley, 1965.

Smith, Henry Nash. *The Controversy at the University of Texas, 1939–1945: A Documented History.* Austin: University of Texas, Students' Association, 1945(?).

Steger, Charles, comp. *William and Jane Law and Some of Their Descendants.* Decorah, Iowa: Anundsen Publishing Co., 1985.

Stoff, Michael, B. *Oil, War, and American Security: The Search for a National Policy on Foreign Oil, 1941–1947.* New Haven: Yale University Press, 1980.

Sweet, George Elliott. *Gentleman in Oil.* Los Angeles: Science Press, 1966.

Theoharis, Athan G. and John Stuart Cox. *The Boss: J. Edgar Hoover and the Great American Inquisition.* Philadelphia: Temple University Press, 1988.

Thomson, Bailey and Patricia L. Meador. *Shreveport: A Photographic Remembrance, 1873–1949.* Baton Rouge: Louisiana State University Press, 1987.

Tindall, George Brown. *The Emergence of the New South, 1913–1945.* Baton Rouge: Louisiana State University Press, 1967.

Tinkle, Lon. *An American Original: The Life of J. Frank Dobie.* Boston: Little, Brown, 1978.

Traylor, Melvin A. *The Human Element in Crises: An Address before the International Chamber of Commerce.* Washington, D.C.: Melvin A. Traylor, 1931.

Ulam, Adam B. *The Rivals: America & Russia Since World War II.* New York: Viking Press, 1971.

University of Texas Faculty and Staff. *The University of Texas Medical Branch at Galveston: A Seventy-Five Year History.* Austin: University of Texas Press, 1967.

Volkogonov, Dimitri. *Stalin: Triumph and Tragedy,* ed. and trans. Harold Shukman. New York: Grove Weidenfeld, 1996.

Watkins, T. H. *Righteous Pilgrim: The Life and Times of Harold L. Ickes, 1874–1952.* New York: H. Holt, 1990.

Weaver, Jacqueline Lang. *Unitization of Oil and Gas Fields in Texas: A Study of Legislative, Administrative, and Judicial Policies.* Washington, D.C.: Resources for the Future, 1986.

Webb, Walter Prescott. *Divided We Stand: The Crisis of a Frontierless Democracy..* New York: Farrar and Rinehart, 1937.

Webb, Walter Prescott, H. Bailey Carroll, and Eldon Stephen Branda, eds. *Handbook of Texas.* 3 vols. Austin: Texas State Historical

Association, 1952, 1976.

Welty, Earl M. and Frank J. Taylor. *The 76 Bonanza: The Fabulous Life and Times of the Union Oil Company of California.* Menlo Park, Calif.: Lane Magazine and Book Co., 1966.

Werth, Alexander. *Russia at War, 1941–1945.* New York: Dutton, 1964.

White, Graham J. *Harold Ickes of the New Deal: His Private Life and Public Career.* Cambridge, Mass.: Harvard University Press, 1985.

Williams, T. Harry. *Huey Long.* New York: Knopf, 1969.

Williamson, Harold; Ralph L. Andreano; Arnold R. Daum; Gilbert C. Klose. *The American Petroleum Industry: Volume II, The Age of Energy, 1899–1959.* 2 vols. Evanston, Ill.: Northwestern University Press, 1963.

Wolfe, Jane. *The Murchisons: The Rise and Fall of a Texas Dynasty.* New York: St. Martin's Press, 1989.

Woodward, Dudley K. *Reasons of Dudley K. Woodward, Jr., Chairman of the Board of Regents of the University of Texas, for Voting Against the Election of Dr. Homer P. Rainey as President of the University of Texas.* Austin, Jan. 26, 1945. N.p.

Wright, Lawrence. *In the New World: Growing Up with America, 1960–1984.* New York: Knopf, 1988.

Yergin, Daniel. *The Prize: The Epic Quest for Oil, Money and Power.* New York: Simon and Schuster, 1990.

VIII. Articles

Ayres, Clarence E., "Academic Freedom in Texas," *New Republic,* 111 (Dec. 4, 1944), 740–742.

Banta, Brady M., "The Pine Island Situation: Petroleum, Politics, and Research Opportunities in Southern History," *Journal of Southern History,* 52 (Nov., 1986), 589–610.

Bernstein, Barton J., "The Atomic Bomb and American Foreign Policy, 1941–1945: An Historiographical Controversy," *Peace & Change* (Spring, 1974).

Broder, David S., "The Freedom that Education Built," Washington *Post,* May 18, 1977.

Buckalew, A. R. and R. B., "The Discovery of Oil in South Arkansas, 1920–1924," *Arkansas Historical Quarterly,* 33 (Autumn, 1974), 195–238.

Buenger, Walter L., "Between Community and Corporation: The Southern Roots of Jesse H. Jones and the Reconstruction Finance Corporation," *Journal of Southern History,* 56 (Aug., 1990), 481–510.

Carleton, Don E. and Katherine J. Adams, "'A Work Peculiarly Our Own': Origins of the Barker Texas History Center, 1883–1950," *Southwestern Historical Quarterly,* 86 (Oct., 1982), 197–230.

Childs, William R., "Origins of the Texas Railroad Commission's Power to Control Production of Petroleum: Regulatory Strategies in the 1920s," *Journal of Policy History,* 2 (1990), 353–387.

———, "The Transformation of the Railroad Commission of Texas, 1917–1940: Business-Government Relations and the Importance of Personality, Agency, Culture, and Regional Differences," *Business History Review,* 65 (Summer, 1991), 285–344.

Cogley, John, "Return Engagement," *Commonweal* (June 7, 1957), 251–254.

Dugger, Ronnie, "Double the Stakes," *Texas Observer* (Mar. 30, 1973), 20.

Dugger, Ronnie, and Kaye Northcott, "Pacifica Silenced by Bomb," *Texas Observer* (May 29, 1970), 7, 8.

Engler, Robert, "Just So They Vote Right," *New Republic* (Sept. 5, 1955), 11–15.

Faulk, John Henry, "Tributes for Two Good Men," *Texas Observer* (Dec. 27, 1974), 8.

Forbes, Gerald, "A History of Caddo Oil and Gas Field," *Louisiana Historical Quarterly,* 29 (Jan., 1946), 59–72.

Gardner, Don, "Notes on a Native Son," *Texas Observer* (June 15, 1990), 23.

Goodwyn, Lawrence, "Dugger's Observer," *Texas Observer* (Dec. 27, 1974), 5.

Gould, Lewis L., "The University Becomes Politicized: The War with Jim Ferguson, 1915–1918," *Southwestern Historical Quarterly,* 86 (Oct., 1982), 255–276.

Hall, Sam, "Inside Texas," *Texas Spectator* (Jan. 25, 1946), 5.

Hardwicke, Robert E., "Legal History of Proration of Oil Production in Texas," *Texas Law Review,* 56 (Oct., 1937), 99–128.

Hart, James P., "Oil, the Courts, and the

Railroad Commission," *Southwestern Historical Quarterly*, 44 (Jan., 1941), 303–320.

Huttlinger, Joseph B., "PAD Makes Good Start," *World Petroleum* (Nov., 1950), 51.

Ickes, Harold I., "The Battle of Oil," *Nation*, 155 (Aug. 1, 1942), 86–87.

Ivins, Molly, "How Not to Regulate the Oil Business," *Texas Observer*, 68 (Feb. 27, 1976), 6, 7.

———, "The Soves' Revenge," *Texas Observer*, 67 (Oct. 17, 1975), 17–20.

Lamp, Irwin, "When Oil's Fleets 'Put Out to Sea'," *Pure Oil News*, 26 (June, 1943), 4–8.

Lear, Linda J., "Harold L. Ickes and the Oil Crisis of the First Hundred Days," *Mid-America: An Historical Review*, 63 (Jan., 1981), 3–17.

Malavis, Nick, "To Protect and Serve: Houston's 'Judge' James A. Elkins Defends the Pure Oil Company, 1931," *Houston Review*, 14 (1992), 153–174.

Miller, Elton, "The Yarborough Story," *Texas Observer* (Oct. 16, 1964), 3.

Murphy, Charles J. V. "Texas Business and McCarthy," *Fortune*, 49 (May, 1954), 100, 101, 208, 211, 212, 214, 216.

Navasky, Victor, et al., "Robert Hutchins's Platonic Grove," *Nation* (Jan. 30, 1988), 119–124.

Nelson, Tom, "The 'Real' J. R. Speaks His Mind," *Parade Magazine* (Apr. 25, 1982), n.p., clipping in J. R. Parten vertical file (CAH).

Northcott, Kaye, "Without Billboards . . .," *Texas Observer* (May 26, 1972), 3, 4.

Parten, J. R., "'Big Inch' Stands as Monument to Nation's Oil Men," *Oil and Gas Journal* (Jan. 7, 1943), 49–50.

Pohl, James W., "The Bible Decade and the Origin of National Athletic Prominence," *Southwestern Historical Quarterly*, 86 (Oct., 1982), 299–320.

Pratt, Joseph A., "The Petroleum Industry in Transition: Antitrust and the Decline of Monopoly Control in Oil," *Journal of Economic History* 40 (Dec., 1980), 815–837.

Prindle, David F., "Oil and the Permanent University Fund: The Early Years," *Southwestern Historical Quarterly*, 86 (Oct., 1982), 277–298.

Rundell, Walter, "A Historian and Federal Policy: W. P. Webb as a Case Study," *Prologue*, 15 (Winter, 1983), 215–228.

Sheehan, Robert, "The 'Little Mothers' and Pan American Sulphur," *Fortune* (July, 1960), 96–103, 199, 200, 203, 204, 206, 209.

Stocking, George Ward, "Stabilization of the Oil Industry: Its Economic and Legal Aspects," *American Economic Review*, 23 (Mar., 1933, supplement), 55–70.

———, "Chaos in the Oil Industry," *Nation*, 136 (June, 1933), 634–636.

Turner, Earl, "J. R. Parten: An Independent Oilman Who Has Made a Difference," *Tipro Reporter* (Fall, 1983), 24–28.

Wise, T. A., "The Curious Pursuit of Pure Oil," *Fortune* (July, 1965), 112–115, 226, 228, 230, 232.

Yarborough, Ralph, "Tiger Jim," *Texas Observer* (Jan. 28, 1977), 21–23.

Notes

Chapter One

1. The name "Jubal" came from Jubal O. Eddings, a member of Ella May Parten's extended family. JRP interview; "Madisonville, Texas," *Handbook of Texas*, ed. Walter Prescott Webb, H. Bailey Carroll, and Eldon Stephen Branda (3 vols.; Austin: Texas State Historical Association, 1952, 1976), II, 128; "Madison Co. History," WPA records, box 4H255 (Center for American History, University of Texas at Austin; cited hereafter as CAH).

2. Wayne Lafayette Parten was born on August 19, 1858, and Ella May Brooks was born on February 25, 1865. Ella May's father was John Caperton Brooks. Sometime around 1835, at the age of ten, Brooks immigrated to Texas from Tennessee. After serving in the military during the Mexican War, the State of Texas granted him land in Madison County. He also served in the Confederate Army. Brooks died on May 30, 1870. Asa Parten joined Company A of the Ninth Battalion of the Georgia Infantry as a private on March 4, 1862; Nancy Parten died on October 14, 1861. JRP interview; Madison County Historical Commission, *A History of Madison County* (Madisonville, Tex.: The Commission, 1984) 412–416; "A. J. Partin," service record, photocopy from the National Archives, J. R. Parten Papers (CAH; cited hereafter as JRP Papers); JRP to the Georgia Department of Archives and History, Mar. 17, 1984, ibid.; Asa J. Parten probate record, Mar. 27, 1866, Marengo County, Alabama, ibid.; Lizzie Parten Leonard, "Sarah Eunice Law's Move to Texas with Her Family and Relatives in 1866," typescript, 1954, ibid.; and news clipping, Madisonville *Meteor*, Nov. 21, 1940, ibid.

3. Emily Brooks (April 9, 1830–May 18, 1895) was born in rural Fayette County, Tennessee. She married John Brooks on August 10, 1848. George William Montague, *History and Genealogy of Peter Montague* (Amherst, Mass.: 1894), 203; JRP interview; *A History of Madison County*, 416; United States Tenth Census (1880), Madison County, Texas, Population Schedules, 20; Willie Caperton Brooks to JRP, undated, JRP Papers; Mrs. George Anthony Rather to Ella Parten, Nov. 27, 1940, ibid.; W. L. Parten scrapbook, ibid.

4. Wayne and Ella Parten had four daughters by the time they moved to Madisonville: Agnes (b. 1884), Lizzie (b. 1886), Lucy (b. 1888), and Malcolm (b. 1892). Seven more children were born in Madisonville: Elizabeth (b. 1894), Jubal (b. 1896), Grace (b. 1899), George (b. 1900), Cleo Alice (b. 1903), Sam (b. 1905), and Ella Susan (b. 1911). *A History of Madison County*, 416; letterhead, Parten & Parten, Feb. 15, 1930, JRP Papers; Rodney Chambliss, "Ella Brooks Parten," Oct. 10, 1963, typescript, ibid.; JRP interview.

5. JRP interview.

6. Sherman interview; JRP interview.

7. JRP interview.

8. JRP interview; New York *Times*, Aug. 17, 1980.

9. For more about James S. Hogg and the Railroad Commission, see Robert Cotner, *James Stephen Hogg: A Biography* (Austin: University of Texas Press, 1951).

10. JRP interview.

11. Ibid.

12. Ibid.

13. Ibid.; O. A. Parten to W. L. Parten, Dec. 2, 1900, JRP Papers; Webb, Carroll, and Branda (eds.), *Handbook of Texas*, II, 415; Huntsville *Item*, July 24, 1933; Norman Brown, *Hood, Bonnet, and Little Brown Jug: Texas Politics, 1921–1928* (College Station: Texas A&M University Press, 1984), 5; clipping in Madison County Scrapbook (CAH).

14. JRP interview; JRP to Jo Christian Sproul, Mar. 15, 1977, JRP Papers.

15. JRP interview.

16. Ibid.; Leonard, "Sarah Eunice Law's Move to Texas."

17. JRP interview.

18. Ibid.

19. JRP interview; *Daily Texan* (UT-Austin), Nov. 1, 1916.

20. The son of Oscar Parten, Ben lived near Jube when they were children and they had been good friends growing up together in Madisonville. JRP interview; JRP to E. O. Thompson, Sept. 12, 1936, JRP Papers.

21. Parten earned three C's and two B's in his freshman year. "Jube Richard Parten," Official Transcript, The University of Texas at Austin, certified copy in JRP Papers; JRP interview.

22. JRP interview; *Cactus* (Austin: Texas Student Publications, UT-Austin, 1915), 233; "Walter Elmer Pope," Biographical Vertical Files (CAH).

23. JRP interview; "Jube Richard Parten," Official Transcript, The University of Texas at Austin, JRP Papers.

24. Parten kept a copy of Marsden's book on his office bookshelf until his death. Author's personal observation; JRP interview.

25. Another professor who made a major contribution to Jube's intellectual growth and development was

Judge Benjamin Dudley Tarlton, his real property and criminal law professor. In his senior year, Jube served as president of the law society sponsored by Judge Tarlton. JRP interview; "George C. Butte," *Handbook of Texas*, ed. Webb, Carroll, and Branda, I, 258; Brown, *Hood, Bonnet, and Little Brown Jug*, 246.

26. JRP interview; Butte, untitled lecture ms., 1915, box 2B171, George C. Butte Papers (CAH).

27. Class roll, 1915, box 2B171, Butte Papers; JRP interview.

28. Fifty-eight years later when Parten saw a story in the New York *Times* about recently opened secret documents in the State Department confirming that the *Lusitania* had been carrying munitions to Great Britain, he told his friend Robert Hutchins about his debate. Hutchins replied that he had "always suspected that *Lusitania* business. Now it appears that you were right all along. You should have been President." JRP to Robert M. Hutchins, May 9, 1973 and Hutchins to JRP, May 15, 1973, both in JRP Papers; JRP interview.

29. JRP interview; "Jube Richard Parten," Official Transcript, The University of Texas at Austin, JRP Papers.

30. JRP interview; *Cactus* (1916), 356 and unnumbered page following 230.

31. JRP interview; *Cactus* (1916), 139, 188.

32. For more on George and the single tax, see Richard Hofstadter, *Social Darwinism in American Thought, 1860–1915* (Philadephia: University of Pennsylvania Press, 1944); JRP interview; *Daily Texan* (UT-Austin), Oct. 1, 1916; "Jube Richard Parten," Official Transcript, The University of Texas at Austin, JRP Papers.

33. *Cactus* (1917), 256, 258; "Texas-Colorado Debate," broadside, Apr. 6, 1917 (CAH); JRP interview.

34. The military science requirement soon resulted in the removal of more than four hundred students from the school rolls. Most of the expelled students eventually were allowed to re-enroll, *Daily Texan* (UT-Austin), Apr. 6, 9, 1917; J. Frank Dobie, *Some Part of Myself* (Boston: Little, Brown, 1967), 216, 224; JRP interview.

35. *Daily Texan* (UT-Austin), Apr. 24, 27, 1917; JRP interview.

36. JRP interview.

37. For more on the Ferguson episode, see Lewis L. Gould, "The University Becomes Politicized: The War with Jim Ferguson, 1915–1918," *Southwestern Historical Quarterly*, 86 (Oct., 1982), 255–276.

38. JRP to Mrs. E. L. Leonard, July 1, 1932, JRP Papers; JRP interview.

39. Parten's law school grades ranged from a low of 85 for Mortgages to a high of 98 for Real Property, "Jube Richard Parten," Official Transcript, The University of Texas at Austin, JRP Papers; JRP interview.

40. JRP interview; JRP, "Application for Insurance," Bureau of War Risk Insurance, Feb. 1, 1918, JRP Papers.

41. JRP interview; Special Orders, No. 158, C. D. Garrison to JRP, Nov. 27, 1917, JRP Papers.

42. JRP interview; Madisonville *Meteor*, n.d., clipping in JRP Papers.

43. JRP interview; JRP to Lucy Myers, Dec. 23, 1939, JRP Papers.

44. JRP interview.

45. JRP interview; JRP to Phillip Booker, Feb. 18, 1930, JRP Papers.

46. There was speculation later that Parten may have been the youngest man of that rank in all of the army, but that remains unverified. Statement of Gen. Robert Danford, chief of field artillery, U.S. Army, quoted in undated Shreveport *Journal* clipping, JRP Papers; Official Orders, Sept. 21, 1918, ibid.; JRP interview.

47. JRP interview.

Chapter Two

1. A native of Gadsden, Alabama, Woodley grew up near the town of Brownwood, Texas. There he married Minnie Roberts and eventually they had four children. In the early 1900s, the Woodleys moved to the Texas Panhandle village of Shamrock, where E. L. became the local agent for the Santa Fe Railroad. Woodley eventually became Shamrock's first mayor and named two of Shamrock's new residential streets after his daughters Opal and Mary Lynn. Millie Jones Porter, *Memory Cups of Panhandle Pioneers: A Belated Attempt at Panhandle History* . . . (Clarendon, Tex.: Clarendon Press, 1945), 373; William Coy Perkins, "A History of Wheeler County, Texas" (M.A. thesis, University of Texas, Austin, 1938), 92; JRP interview; Sherman interview; Brureggerhoff (publisher), *Shreveport City Directory* (1918), 473; Biographical Questionnaire, "Who's Who In Oil," Aug. 15, 1922, JRP Papers.

2. Gerald Forbes, "A History of Caddo Oil and Gas Field," *Louisiana Historical Quarterly*, 29 (Jan., 1946), 59–72; Bailey Thomson and Patricia L. Meador, *Shreveport: A Photographic Remembrance, 1873–1949* (Baton Rouge: Louisiana State University Press, 1987), 171; Kenny A. Franks and Paul F. Lambert, *Early Louisiana and Arkansas Oil: A Photographic History, 1901–1946* (College Station: Texas A&M University Press, 1982), 43; Brady M. Banta, "The Pine Island Situation: Petroleum, Politics, and Research Opportunities in Southern History," *Journal of Southern History*, 52 (Nov., 1986), 591; JRP interview.

3. JRP interview; Sherman interview.

4. New York *Times*, 1980; JRP interview.

5. Brureggerhoff (publisher), *Shreveport City Directory* (1920); JRP interview.

6. Gerald D. Nash, *United States Oil Policy: 1890–1964: Business and Government in Twentieth Century America* (Pittsburg: University of Pittsburg, 1968), 43, 45, 73 82; Banta, "The Pine Island Situation," 591, 592; Henrietta M. Larson and Kenneth W. Porter, *History of Humble Oil and Refining Company: A Sudy in Industrial*

Growth (New York: Harper, 1959), 104–105.

7. Thomson and Meador, *Shreveport*, 171; Franks and Lambert, *Early Louisiana and Arkansas Oil*, 43.

8. Sam Mims, *Oil is Where You Find It* (Boston: Marshall Jones Co., 1940), 85; *Shreveport Louisiana: Center of the Greatest Lumber, Oil, Gas and Agricultural Field in the South* (Shreveport: 1919), n.p.

9. Brureggerhoff (publisher), *Shreveport City Directory* (1920); JRP interview.

10. Harry Hurt, *Texas Rich: The Hunt Dynasty from the Early Oil Days through the Silver Crash* (New York: Norton, 1981), 71, 72; JRP interview.

11. JRP interview.

12. Larson and Porter, *History of Humble Oil*, 120–122; Jones interview, oral history transcript (Louisiana State University-Shreveport; cited hereafter as LSU); JRP interview.

13. Franks and Lambert, *Early Louisiana and Arkansas Oil* , 107; JRP interview.

14. Franks and Lambert, *Early Louisiana and Arkansas Oil*, 107; Carl Coke Rister, *Oil! Titan of the Southwest* (Norman: University of Oklahoma Press, 1949), 210; JRP interview.

15. Franks and Lambert, *Early Louisiana and Arkansas Oil*, 108, 110; JRP interview.

16. Rister, *Oil!*, 212; JRP interview; Max W. Ball, et al., *This Fascinating Oil Business* (Indianapolis: Bobbs-Merrill, 1965), 249.

17. A. R. and R. B. Buckalew, "The Discovery of Oil in South Arkansas, 1920–1924," *Arkansas Historical Quarterly*, 33 (Autumn, 1974), 206–208; Hurt, *Texas Rich*, 50–51.

18. Hurt, *Texas Rich*, 51, 53; JRP interview.

19. JRP interview; Franks and Lambert, *Early Louisiana and Arkansas Oil*, 109.

20. A resident of Shreveport since 1886, Andrew Querbes started in business as the owner of a wholesale grocery, which he built into a successful firm. A progressive southern businessman typical of the era, his work on behalf of civic improvement won him a reputation as the "father of good roads" in Shreveport. He served as mayor of Shreveport from 1902 until 1904. After selling his grocery business, Querbes became an officer of Shreveport's First National Bank, rising to the bank presidency in 1908. Lilla McLure and J. Ed Howe, *History of Shreveport and Shreveport Builders* (Shreveport: Journal Printing, 1937), 451; J. Fair Hardin, *Northwestern Louisiana: A History of the Watershed of the Red River, 1714–1937* (2 vols.; Shreveport: 1938), II, 423–424; Louisiana Publishers Association, *Louisiana : Its Builders and Its Industries: A Newspaper Reference Work* ([New Orleans]: Louisiana Publishers Association, 1924), 113, 174; Wilkinson interview, oral history transcript (LSU); JRP interview; JRP to Querbes, Feb. 3, 1933, JRP Papers.

21. Long allegedly hated Standard of Louisiana because of losses he incurred in his own oil investment in Pine Island resulting from Standard's refusal to buy Pine Island's low-quality crude after the end of the war. T. Harry Williams, *Huey Long* (New York: Knopf, 1969), 96–97; JRP interview; Misc. documents, folder 1072, box 26, Huey Long Papers (Louisiana State University-Baton Rouge); Banta, "The Pine Island Situation," 594; Morgan interview, oral history transcript (LSU).

22. Long's work for Woodley included a breach-of-contract suit and a legal problem related to the theft of some of Woodley's drilling equipment. He also recruited attorneys in Arkansas to represent the Woodley Company in legal matters in that state. Woodley Files, box 20, folder 773; box 24, folders 959–963; and box 28, folders 1122, a and b, Long Papers. Also, Morgan interview, oral history transcript; Williams, *Huey Long*, 92, 96, 97; JRP interview.

23. JRP interview; Morgan interview, oral history transcript (LSU). For more about Morgan's role in Long's career, see Williams, *Huey Long*.

24. Woodley was incorporated in Delaware, with permits for operation in Arkansas and Louisiana. Long's papers include a folder on his work incorporating Woodley, including instructions on how to do it. box 20, folder 773, Long Papers; JRP interview.

25. Woodley's assets included crude production at El Dorado of approximately five hundred barrels per day; 228 leased acres in the Caddo field with a production of about three hundred barrels per day; small acreage in "Bull" Bayou in DeSoto Parish with negligible production; and some wildcat acreage scattered throughout northern Louisiana and southern Arkansas. In addition, Woodley owned six complete drilling outfits and had field and office organizations. Monthly earnings in the late spring of 1922 averaged about $35,000. Woodley financial information is in Huey Long to Howe, Snow, Corrigan & Bertles, July 12, 1922, box 20, folder 773, Long Papers.

26. Ibid.; Williams, *Huey Long*, 117–118; JRP interview.

27. Franks and Lambert, *Early Louisiana and Arkansas Oil*, 124; JRP interview.

28. JRP interview; Buckalew and Buckalew, "The Discovery of Oil in South Arkansas," 220, 221, 228.

29. JRP interview; Buckalew and Buckalew, "The Discovery of Oil in South Arkansas," 221.

30. Ball, *This Fascinating Oil Business*, 76–77; JRP interview.

31. JRP interview.

32. Ibid.; Woodley Petroleum, board minutes, July 1923, JRP Papers; Buckalew and Buckalew, "The Discovery of Oil in South Arkansas," 236; Rister, *Oil!*, 214.

33. JRP interview; Buckalew and Buckalew, "The Discovery of Oil in South Arkansas," 236; Rister, *Oil!*, 214; Marr interview.

34. Drilling resumed in January 1924. Woodley Petroleum, board minutes, July 1923, JRP Papers; Nash, *United States Oil Policy*, 82.

35. The Partens purchased the Jordan Street house after renting for several months a local architectural landmark at 1746 Irving Place known as the "Levy House." Brueggerhoff (publisher), *Shreveport City Directory* (1921); Shreveport *Journal*, June 25, 1965; Wilkinson interview, oral history transcript (LSU); Thomson and Meador, *Shreveport*, 72, 110; *Cactus* (1917), 289; JRP interview.

36. Sherman interview; JRP interview; Woodley Petroleum, board minutes, Dec. 13, 1924, JRP Papers.

37. Woodley Petroleum, board minutes, Feb. 15, 1926, JRP Papers; J. Fair Hardin, *Northwestern Louisiana*, 400–401; JRP interview.

38. JRP interview; J. Conrad Dunagan, *Eugene Holman, A Texan of Distinction* ([Monahans, Tex.]: Historical Association of Ward County, 1989), 22; Sherman interview; Maude Hearn O'Pry, Chronicles of Shreveport (Shreveport: 1928), 291; JRP to Carl Estes, Jan. 24, 1935, JRP Papers; Holman to JRP, Nov. 5, 1926, ibid. For more on the Humble Company's early history, see Larson and Porter, *History of Humble Oil*.

39. Holman to JRP, Aug. 4, 1926, JRP Papers; JRP to Holman, Aug. 6, 1926, ibid.; Woodley Petroleum, board minutes, ibid.; JRP to Lamar Hart, June 10, 1927, ibid.; JRP interview.

40. JRP interview.

41. Woodley eventually acquired the total assets of the Moutray Oil Company in May 1930. Woodley Petroleum, annual reports, 1928, 1931, JRP Papers; JRP to Querbes, Dec. 1, 1928, ibid.; JRP interview.

42. Don Ewing, oral history transcript (LSU), 16; JRP interview.

43. William Ivy Hair, *The Kingfish and His Realm: The Life and Times of Huey P. Long* (Baton Rouge: Louisiana State University Press, 1991), 164; Williams, *Huey Long*, 308, 309.

44. JRP interview; JRP to Warren J. Dale, May 31, 1928, JRP Papers.

45. JRP interview; Hair, *The Kingfish and His Realm*, 168.

46. JRP interview; Williams, *Huey Long*, 345, Hair, *The Kingfish and His Realm*, 177.

47. JRP interview. For a discussion of Long and LSU, see Williams, *Huey Long*, 492–521; for Long's impeachment and its connection to the oil-tax issue, see ibid., 347–383, 445.

48. In 1930 Parten purchased six airplanes for a new flying service called Wings, Inc., managed by Currie Sanders and some pilot friends in Shreveport. Wings, Inc., offered chartered passenger service and crop-dusting for the extensive cotton fields surrounding the Shreveport area. The business lasted only two years because of stiff competition from a company flying out of Monroe, Louisiana, the "Delta Dusters," which eventually became Delta Airlines. Thomson and Meador, *Shreveport*, 128; Shreveport *Times*, Nov. 15, 1970; Howard F. Noble to JRP, Sept. 24, 1929, JRP Papers; bill of sale, Howard F. Noble to JRP, Oct. 28, 1929, ibid.; JRP Engine Log Book, n.d., ibid.; entry, "Pilot's Log Book," ibid.; *Shreveport City Directory* (1931); JRP interview.

Chapter Three

1. JRP interview.

2. JRP interview; Larson and Porter, *History of Humble Oil*, 448.

3. JRP interview; Larson and Porter, *History of Humble Oil*, 448; Kendall Beaton, *Enterprise in Oil: A History of Shell in the United States* (New York: Appleton-Century-Crofts, 1957), 383; Lawrence Goodwyn, *Texas Oil, American Dreams: A Study of the Texas Independent Producers and Royalty Owners Association* (Austin: Texas State Historical Association, 1996), 12.

4. Larson and Porter, *History of Humble Oil*, 119, 266–267; JRP interview.

5. JRP interview; Woodley Petroleum, annual report, 1931, JRP Papers.

6. "Myron Geer Blalock," *Handbook of Texas*, ed. Webb, Carroll, and Branda, I, 171; JRP interview; T. Whitfield Davidson, *The Memoirs of T. Whitfield Davidson* (Waco: 1972), 62–63; Yarborough interview; Shelmire interview; Dallas *News*, Dec. 29, 1950; JRP interview (with A. Champagne).

7. Until his marriage, Dayson had a reputation for fast-living. He was a frequent visitor to Pistol Hill and Hamburger Row and regularly gambled at H. L. Hunt's casino. When he made Dayson a director of Lion Oil in 1928, the company president counseled him: "Now Dayson, I hope that you grow to a point where you are capable and worthy of this confidence. . . . it should mean more dignity and less parties." Winters to Dayson, Sept. 17, 1928, and Dan E. Lydick to Allen E. Richardson, Jan. 16, 1953, Sylvester Dayson Papers (CAH); JRP, affidavit, Jan. 17, 1941, "Dayson" file, JRP Papers; JRP interview; Shelmire interview; James Presley, *Never in Doubt: A History of Delta Drilling Company* (Houston: Gulf Publishing Co., 1981), 67, 401–402.

8. Barton to Dayson, Oct. 29, 1930, Dayson Papers; JRP interview; Presley, *Never in Doubt*, 125.

9. JRP to Querbes, Jan. 22, 1931, JRP Papers; JRP to K. A. Hackler, Feb. 11, 1931, ibid.; JRP interview.

10. The bank required Parten to build an eighty-thousand-barrel steel holding tank on a Woodley lease near Kilgore to store the oil as security for the loan. Parten was also required to spend an additional $30,000 to build

storage tanks and railroad loading racks on Woodley's Moutray field. The Woodley lease Querbes used to secure the loan was on the J. M. Peterson farm south of Kilgore, where the company had a successful well with strong production. Woodley Petroleum, annual report, 1930, JRP Papers; Querbes to JRP, Dec. 12, 1930, ibid.; JRP to Myron Blalock, Mar. 30, 1931, ibid.; JRP to Andrew Querbes, Aug. 19, 1931, ibid.; JRP to R. J. O'Brien, Jan. 11, 1931, ibid.; news clipping, n.d., no title, ibid.; clipping, Shreveport *Times*, June 3, 1931, ibid.; JRP interview.

11. Dayson and Parten secured additional financing for Centex from Continental Supply Company of St. Louis. Mayer interview; Shreveport *Times*, June 3, 1931; Woodley Petroleum, annual report, 1931, JRP Papers; JRP to Dayson, May 30, 1931, ibid.; Moran to JRP, Oct. 7, 1931, ibid.; JRP to Moran, Oct. 8, 1931, ibid.; Parten to E. L. Eppenauer, Jan. 13, 1932, ibid.; JRP to Holman, Apr., 2, 1932, ibid.; Woodley to JRP, Mar. 12, 1931, ibid.; JRP interview; Sherman interview.

12. Shelmire interview; Dayson to JRP, May 22, 1931, JRP Papers; JRP to Dayson, May 30, 1931, ibid.; JRP to R. J. O'Brien, Jan. 11, 1932, ibid.; Mayer interview; Presley, *Never in Doubt*, 402, 403.

13. Larson and Porter, *History of Humble Oil*, 266–267; David F. Prindle, *Petroleum Politics and the Texas Railroad Commission* (Austin: University of Texas Press, 1981), 26; Beaton, *Enterprise in Oil*, 383.

14. The term "hot oil" originated from the fact that when a well produces at a high or "flush" rate, the oil comes out much warmer than normal because the temperature of oil increases with depth. If the oil is being produced rapidly, it will come up from a deeper level and at a higher temperature. As one former federal investigator later recalled, "if you are looking for someone who's been illegally producing oil, and it's winter, and everything's supposed to be shut in, but you put your hand on a pipe and it's very warm, he's producing oil he shouldn't. . . ." Marshall interview; JRP, "The Texas Oil Case," (pamphlet; Independent Petroleum Association of Texas, 1933; copy in JRP Papers), 3; Ball, et al., *This Fascinating Oil Business*, 146, 151; Larson and Porter, *History of Humble Oil*, 316.

15. Larson and Porter, *History of Humble Oil*, 49–50; Jacqueline Lang Weaver, *Unitization of Oil and Gas Fields in Texas: A Study of Legislative, Administrative, and Judicial Policies* (Washington, D.C.: Resources for the Future, 1986), 49–50.

16. Goodwyn, *Texas Oil, American Dreams*, 13 (quotation). For more on prorationing and the East Texas field, see Prindle, *Petroleum Politics*, 21–40.

17. Carl Estes, an East Texas newspaper publisher and early critic of prorationing, voiced an opinion shared by many small independents when he declared that "the monopolistic companies are advocating proration as a means of holding up the price of oil. . . . They are open and loud about it." Ruel McDanial, *Some Ran Hot* (Dallas: Regional Press, 1939), 78.

18. Larson and Porter, *History of Humble Oil*, 324, 325.

19. JRP interview; Woodley Petroleum, annual report, 1930, JRP Papers.

20. "I always frowned upon the idea of compulsory unitization by law," Parten declared in 1983, "I still am opposed to it. The state doesn't need to unitize all oil fields. I was making a frontal attack on that idea." JRP interview; J. R. Parten, "Why 'Market Demand' Oil Proration?," *Texas Independent*, 1 (Aug., 1932), 3–4; J. R. Parten, "Oil and Economics," *Texas Independent*, 1 (Sept., 1932), 5, 6, 9, 10, 16, 20.

21. Prindle, *Petroleum Politics*, 31; JRP interview.

22. JRP to Huey Long, May 5, 1931, JRP Papers; JRP interview.

23. The plan is usually referred to as the Cranfill plan, but it was also called the Tyler plan and the East Texas plan. Production was to be held to three hundred barrels per day for each twenty-acre tract, but wells completed before June 10 were allowed to produce up to three hundred barrels per day no matter what size the field in which they were located. Robert Henry Seale Eakens, "The Development of Proration in the East Texas Oil Field" (M.A. thesis, University of Texas, Austin, 1937), 49–51; JRP interview.

24. JRP to Joe Danciger, July 2, 1931, JRP Papers; Minutes, East Texas Oil Arbitration Committee, June 18, 1933, ibid.; JRP to Stephen L. Pinckney, June 20, 1931, ibid.; J. F. Lucey and J. R. Parten to the Texas Railroad Commission, June 18, 1931, ibid.; McDanial, *Some Ran Hot*, 101–103.

25. JRP to Estes, June 20, 1931, JRP Papers; Barbara Sue Thompson Day, "The Oil and Gas Industry and Texas Politics, 1930–1935" (Ph.D. diss., Rice University, 1973), 99, 100.

26. Dallas *Morning News*, June 23, 1931; Shreveport *Times*, June 27, 1931; Eakens, "The Development of Proration in the East Texas Oil Field," 56; JRP interview.

27. Day, "The Oil and Gas Industry and Texas Politics," 103, 104; Norman E. Nordhauser, *The Quest for Stability: Domestic Oil Regulation, 1917–1935* (New York: Garland Publishing, 1979), 80; Weaver, *Unitization of Oil and Gas Fields*, 43; Mcdanial, *Some Ran Hot*, 119 (Sterling quote); Eakens, "The Development of Proration in the East Texas Oil Field," 54.

28. *Alfred MacMillan et al. v. Railroad Commission et al.*, 51 F (2nd) (W.D. Tex., 1931), 400, 408; Day, "The Oil and Gas Industry and Texas Politics," 103–105; Nordhauser, *The Quest for Stability*, 82, 83; Weaver, *Unitization of Oil and Gas Fields*, 43; Goodwyn, *Texas Oil, American Dreams*, 13; JRP to Andrew Knight, Nov. 9, 1931, JRP Papers; Eakens, "The Development of Proration in the East Texas Oil Field," 60; Larson and Porter, *History of Humble Oil*, 458.

29. Larson and Porter, *History of Humble Oil*, 458; Daniel Yergin, *The Prize: The Epic Quest for Oil, Money, and Power* (New York: Simon and Schuster, 1991), 250.

30. James Clark and Michael T. Halbouty, *The Last Boom* (Bryan, Tex.: Shearer Publishing, 1984), 168–173; Yergin, *The Prize*, 250.

31. JRP interview; JRP to Andrew Knight, Nov. 9, 1931, JRP Papers.

32. Eakens, "The Development of Proration in the East Texas Oil Field," 69–71; Rister, *Oil!*, 321; Woodley Petroleum, annual report, 1931, JRP Papers.

33. Eakens, "The Development of Proration in the East Texas Oil Field," 65; Day, "The Oil and Gas Industry and Texas Politics," 110; Woodley Petroleum, annual report, 1931, JRP Papers; JRP to Querbes, Nov. 3, 1931, ibid.

34. News clipping, Dallas *Morning News*, Nov. 4, 1931, JRP Papers; McDanial, *Some Ran Hot*, 145; August W. Giebelhaus, *Business and Government in the Oil Industry: A Case Study of Sun Oil, 1876–1945* (Greenwich, Conn.: JAI Press, 1980), 202–204 (Pew quotation); JRP interview.

35. Wild to JRP, July 9, 1931, JRP Papers.

36. Larson and Porter, *History of Humble Oil*, 469.

37. Dallas *Morning News*, Dec. 14, 1931; Independent Petroleum Association of Texas (IPAT), minutes of directors meeting, Dec.15, 1931, JRP Papers; JRP, "Unitization," printed version of speech, Dec. 15, 1931, ibid.; Wild to Parten, Dec. 17, 1931, ibid.; JRP interview.

Chapter Four

1. News clipping, unidentified newspaper, Jan. 16, 1932, JRP Papers; JRP to W. T. Saye, July 27, 1932, ibid.; Shreveport *Times*, Feb. 13, 1932.

2. Claude C. Wild Sr. biographical file (CAH); Wild interview, oral history transcript (Lyndon Baines Johnson Library and Museum, Austin; cited hereafter as LBJ); JRP interview.

3. IPAT, minutes of directors meeting, Feb. 24, 1932, JRP Papers; JRP to Claude Wild, Dec. 23, 1931, ibid.; Wild to JRP, Dec. 23, 1931, Mar. 31, 1932, ibid.

4. JRP to Harry Reynolds, Mar. 22, 1932, JRP Papers; Claude Wild to JRP, Mar. 31, Dec. 13, 1932, ibid.

5. *Constantin v. Smith*, 57 F. (2d), 231. The U.S. Supreme Court later upheld the Constantin ruling on December 12, 1932. Some troops remained in the field to assist the commission in enforcing its proration order. Robert E. Hardwicke, "Legal History of Proration of Oil Production in Texas," *Texas Law Review*, 56 (Oct., 1937), 111; Rister, *Oil!*, 321; Nordhauser, *The Quest for Stability*, 90–91; JRP to Carl Everett, Feb. 2, 1932, JRP Papers; JRP interview.

6. In the early 1930s, oil imports did account for 9 to 12 percent of U.S. domestic demand. As Daniel Yergin points out in *The Prize*, however, "tariff proponents rarely noted that the United States remained a net oil exporter . . . American oil exports were as much as two times the volume of imports." (p. 258); JRP to Wirt Franklin, Jan. 4, 1932, JRP Papers; JRP to Claude Wild, Jan. 14, 1932, ibid.; JRP to Ike Felsenthal, Mar. 11, 1932, ibid.; JRP to J. M. Lee, Mar. 10, 1932, ibid.

7. News clipping, unidentified newspaper, JRP Papers; Dallas *Morning News*, Mar. 11, 1932; Shreveport *Times*, Mar. 22, 1932; JRP to Huey Long, May 9, 1932, JRP Papers; JRP to Wirt Franklin, May 11, 1932, ibid.; Franklin to JRP, May 20, 1932, ibid.; George Elliott Sweet, *Gentleman in Oil* (Los Angeles: Science Press, 1966), 154; Larson and Porter, *History of Humble Oil*, 731n.47; JRP interview.

8. Nash, *United States Oil Policy*, 126, 127; JRP interview; Claude Wild, "Swattin' Hokum," *Texas Independent*, I (July, 1932), 11.

9. The founder of the Texas Company, Joseph S. Cullinan, had urged federal control of the nation's oil industry as early as 1916. John O. King, *Joseph Stephen Cullinan: A Study of Leadership in the Texas Petroleum Industry, 1897–1937* (Nashville: Vanderbilt University Press, 1970), 210, 211; JRP interview; JRP to Wirt Franklin, June 27, 1932, JRP Papers.

10. For more information on Roeser's views, see his testimony, House Subcommittee of the Committee on Interstate and Foreign Commerce, 73rd Cong., Recess, *Petroleum Investigation: Hearings on House Resolution 441* (4 vols.; Washington, D.C.: Government Printing Office, 1934; cited hereafter as House *Petroleum Investigation*), IV, 2315–2350; J. R. Parten, "Meeting an Organized Age," typescript of a statement released in Fort Worth, Feb. 23, 1932, JRP Papers; Larson and Porter, *History of Humble Oil*, 464, 465; Day, "The Oil and Gas Industry and Texas Politics," 137; JRP interview.

11. Claude Wild to JRP, May 7, 1932, JRP Papers; J. R. Parten, "Forward from the President," *Texas Independent*, I, (July, 1932), 1; JRP interview.

12. For Farish's views see Yergin, *The Prize*, 224; Wild, "Swattin' Hokum," *Texas Independent*, 1 (July, 1932), 7, and ibid. (Dec., 1932), 21; JRP interview.

13. "Will Farish didn't have any choice," Parten later claimed, "Standard of New Jersey did it for him." JRP interview; JRP to Claude Wild, July 18, 1932, JRP Papers; JRP to Hines Baker, July 27, 1932, ibid.; Baker to JRP, July 28, 1932, ibid.

14. KWKH's broadcasts, which crowded out local stations across the U.S. that had the misfortune of being on

the same frequency, played a role in the creation of the Federal Radio Commission. George B. Tindall, *The Emergence of the New South, 1913–1945* (Baton Rouge: Louisiana State University Press, 1967), 595; Thomson and Meador, *Shreveport*, 117; JRP interview.

15. JRP interview; Larson and Porter, *History of Humble Oil*, 338, 337; William Eugene Atkinson, "James V. Allred: A Political Biography, 1899–1935" (Ph.D. diss., Texas Christian University, Fort Worth, 1978), 200–208; "James V. Allred," *Handbook of Texas*, ed. Webb, Carroll, and Branda, III, 21–22; JRP to Fred Upchurch, Nov. 18, 1931, JRP Papers; Allred interview, oral history transcript (University of North Texas, Denton; cited hereafter as UNT).

16. JRP interview; Houston *Chronicle*, Mar. 11, 1935; Yarborough interview.

17. JRP to Mrs. E. L. Leonard, July 1, 1932, JRP Papers; Claude Wild to IPAT directors, July 18, 1932, ibid.; Claude Wild to Myron Blalock, July 25, 1932, ibid.; JRP to Fred Upchurch, June 18, 1932, ibid.; JRP interview; Atkinson, "James V. Allred," 271.

18. Claude Wild to Myron Blalock, July 25, 1932, JRP Papers; Ernest Alexander to JRP, July 7, 1932, ibid.; JRP to Mrs. E. L. Leonard, July 1, 1932, ibid.

19. JRP to C. V. Terrell, June 24, 1932, JRP Papers; JRP to Mrs. E. L. Leonard, July 1, 1932, ibid.; Gene B. Lasseter to JRP, Oct. 28, 1932, ibid.; "Charles Vernon Terrell," *Handbook of Texas*, ed. Webb, Carroll, and Branda, III, 964; JRP interview.

20. JRP to J. O. Fox, Mar. 1, 1932, JRP Papers; *Cactus* (1917), 72, 266; Prindle, *Petroleum Politics*, 35; JRP interview; James A. Clark, *Three Stars for the Colonel* (New York: Random House, 1954), 54–64.

21. JRP interview; E. O. Thompson to JRP, Oct. 7, 1932, JRP Papers.

22. Clark, *Three Stars for the Colonel*, 77; Atkinson, "James V. Allred," 272; JRP interview; JRP to E. O. Thompson, Aug. 26, 1932, JRP Papers.

23. JRP interview; JRP to Carl B. Calloway, Oct. 5, 1932, JRP Papers.

24. JRP interview. Parten's political views in 1932 are derived from his letters to friends and political associates at the time, for example see JRP to Myron Blalock, Apr. 5, 1932, JRP Papers.

25. JRP to Huey Long, June 18, 1932, JRP Papers; JRP to Myron Blalock, Apr. 15, 1932, ibid.

26. David H. Bennett, *The Party of Fear: From Nativist Movements to the New Right in American History* (Chapel Hill: University of North Carolina Press, 1988), 254, 256; JRP to Father Coughlin, Apr. 4, 1932, JRP Papers; Coughlin to JRP, June 8, 1932, ibid.; JRP to W. T. Saye, July 27, 1932, ibid.; JRP interview.

27. Jerome Beatty, "It's Time to Throw a Monkey Wrench," *American Magazine* (Nov., 1931), reprint in "Politics-1932" folder, Dan Moody Papers (CAH); Arthur M. Schlesinger Jr., *The Crisis of the Old Order, 1919–1933* (3 vols.: Boston: Houghton Mifflin, 1957–1960), I, 284; JRP to Raymond O'Brien, Jan. 11, 1932, JRP Papers; M. R.Walton to JRP, Mar. 11,1932, ibid.; JRP to Myron Blalock, Apr. 15, 1932, ibid.

28. At one point, Roosevelt's advisors feared that Traylor might actually win control of the Illinois, Kentucky, and Texas delegations to the national convention because of his claim on all three states as his "home." Jouett Shouse to John Costello, Sept. 26,1931, President's Personal Files, 220, Franklin D. Roosevelt Papers (Franklin D. Roosevelt Library, Hyde Park, N.Y.; cited hereafter as FDR Papers); Fort Worth *Star-Telegarm*, Aug. 10, 1931; Houston *Chronicle*, Aug. 16, 1931; JRP to Willard Drown, July 8, 1932, JRP Papers.

29. *People's Petroleum Producers, Inc., et al. v. Lon Smith, et al.*, 60 F. (2nd), 1041, 1 F. Supp., 361; Eakens, "The Development of Proration in the East Texas Oil Field," 93; Prindle, *Petroleum Politics*, 31; Nordhauser, *The Quest for Stability*, 91; JRP interview; JRP to Carl Estes, Oct. 24, 1932, JRP Papers; Claude Wild to JRP, Oct. 25, 1932, ibid.; JRP to Wild, Sept. 19, 1932, ibid.; JRP to George Sawtelle, Sept. 19, 1932, ibid.; JRP to Carl Estes, Sept. 26, 1932, ibid.

30. JRP interview; Weaver, *Unitization of Oil and Gas Fields*, 61–64; Eakens, "The Development of Proration in the East Texas Oil Field," 93, 94.

31. For a detailed statement of Thompson's views at this time, see Ernest O. Thompson, "Federal Control of Oil Production," *Texas Independent*, I (Dec., 1932), 10–13; JRP interview; Atkinson, "James V. Allred," 250.

32. For a case study of James Elkins's activity as a lobbyist in the prorationing battles of the early 1930s, see Nick Malavis, "To Protect and Serve: Houston's 'Judge' James A. Elkins Defends the Pure Oil Company, 1931," *Houston Review*, 14 (1992), 153–174; JRP to Carl Estes, Jan. 31, 1933, JRP Papers; JRP interview.

33. Weaver, *Unitization of Oil and Gas Fields*, 61, 63; 74–75, 315; JRP interview; Eakens, "The Development of Proration in the East Texas Oil Field," 95; Larson and Porter, *History of Humble Oil*, 471; Day, "The Oil and Gas Industry and Texas Politics," 154–157.

34. Weaver, *Unitization of Oil and Gas Fields*, 61–63; Marshall interview (quotation); JRP to E. O. Thompson, Nov. 9, 1932, JRP Papers.

35. JRP to Russell B. Brown, Nov. 7, 1932, JRP Papers; J. R. Parten, "Expediency vs. Principle," *Texas Independent*, I (Dec., 1932), 32; JRP interview.

36. News clipping, Tyler *Courier-Times Telegraph*, Nov. 27, 1932, JRP Papers; JRP to Claude Wild, Nov. 29, 1932, ibid.

37. Eakens, "The Development of Proration in the East Texas Oil Field," 98; Larson and Porter, *History of Humble Oil*, 474; JRP to E. O. Thompson, Dec. 2, 1932, JRP Papers; Thompson to JRP, Dec. 7, 1932, ibid.

38. Eakens, "The Development of Proration in the East Texas Oil Field," 101, 102; Weaver, *Unitization of Oil and Gas Fields*, 64.

39. Eakens, "The Development of Proration in the East Texas Oil Field," 102–104; Larson and Porter, *History of Humble Oil*, 475; JRP to E. O. Thompson, Dec. 17, 1932, JRP Papers; JRP to Tom Cranfill, Jan. 18, 1933, ibid.

40. JRP to Eugene Holman, Apr. 2, 1932, JRP Papers; JRP to Andrew Querbes, June 17, 1932, ibid.; Myron Blalock to Amon G. Carter, July 6, 1934, ibid.; Woodley Petroleum, annual report, 1932, ibid.; JRP interview.

41. Parten, "Expediency vs. Principle," 6–9, 19, 20, 31, 32.

42. Claude Wild to JRP, Aug. 2, Oct. 17, 1932, Jan. 26, 1933, JRP Papers; JRP to George Hill, Oct. 5, 1932, ibid.; JRP to Claude Wild, Jan. 7, Feb. 1, 1933, ibid.; R. F. Schoolfield to JRP, Feb. 18, 1933, ibid.; JRP to Rollin V. Hill, Mar. 22, 1933, ibid.

43. Wild to JRP, Feb. 22, 23, 1935, Jan. 3, 1938, JRP Papers; JRP to Wild, Mar. 11, 30, 1938, ibid.

44. The oil in East Texas was under high pressure at a relatively shallow depth and could be drilled without difficulty. Because of the Depression, labor costs were negligible, so the overhead for a small-time operator was much lower than was typical elsewhere. JRP interview; Eakens, "The Development of Proration in the East Texas Oil Field," 110, 114 (commission quote re Texaco); Larson and Porter, *History of Humble Oil*, 475; JRP to Carl Estes, Jan. 31, 1933, JRP Papers; Nordhauser, *The Quest for Stability*, 92.

45. Eakens, "The Development of Proration in the East Texas Oil Field," 108–109 (Dudley quote); Marshall interview; JRP interview.

Chapter Five

1. James MacGregor Burns, *Roosevelt: The Lion and the Fox* (New York: Harcourt, Brace, and World, 1956), 163; Nash, *United States Oil Policy*, 129.

2. W. Forbes Morgan to M. H. McIntyre, Mar. 10, 1933, with enclosed proposals from the API for federally mandated prorationing, Harold L. Ickes Papers (Library of Congress, Washington, D.C.); Nordhauser, *The Quest for Stability*, 96–97; Nash, *United States Oil Policy*, 129, 130.

3. Roosevelt included Kansas, a state with a relatively small amount of production, because its governor, Alfred Landon, was a Republican whose presence would give the conference more of a bipartisan flavor. Frank Freidel, *Franklin D. Roosevelt: Launching the New Deal* (Boston: Little, Brown, 1973), 426; Nash, *United States Oil Policy*, 130, 133; T. H. Watkins, *Righteous Pilgrim: The Life and Times of Harold L. Ickes, 1874–1952* (New York: H. Holt, 1990), 341–342; Nordhauser, *The Quest for Stability*, 99; Linda J. Lear, "Harold L. Ickes and the Oil Crisis of the First Hundred Days," *Mid-America: An Historical Review*, 63 (Jan., 1981), 6.

4. Ickes had spent most of his adult years as a social reformer involved in a wide range of liberal causes that included labor reform, antitrust work, and civil rights activism. A fervent supporter of Theodore Roosevelt during "Teddy's" progressive-reform phase, Ickes was appointed interior secretary after playing a leading role in bringing progressive Republicans over to Franklin Roosevelt's side in the 1932 election campaign. For more on Ickes see Watkins, *Righteous Pilgrim*, and Graham White and John Maze, *Harold Ickes of the New Deal: His Private Life and Public Career* (Cambridge, Mass.: Harvard University Press, 1985).

5. Although one scholar has argued that Ickes was more interested in raising the price of oil than he was in conserving a natural resource, others have argued to the contrary. The most important point is that he felt both goals were important and that they both required federal action, Nordhauser, *The Quest for Stability*, 109–110; Lear, "Harold L. Ickes and the Oil Crisis of the First Hundred Days," 15; Harold L. Ickes Diary, p. 6795, Ickes Papers; Michael B. Stoff, *Oil, War, and American Security: The Search for a National Policy on Foreign Oil, 1941–1947* (New Haven: Yale University Press, 1980), 10, 12, 13, 15.

6. Lear, "Harold L. Ickes and the Oil Crisis of the First Hundred Days," 6; Watkins, *Righteous Pilgrim*, 342; J. Edward Jones, *"And So—They Indicted Me!": A Story of New Deal Persecution* (New York: J. E. Jones Publishing, 1939), 24; JRP interview; JRP to Ickes, Mar. 17, 1933, JRP Papers.

7. Wirt Franklin to JRP, Mar. 21, 1933, JRP Papers; JRP interview.

8. JRP interview; Jones, *"And So—They Indicted Me!"*, 30, 31.

9. Wallace Pratt of Jersey Standard later said of Wirt Franklin that he "stood with us on proration as few independents did. We relied on him and he merited our trust." The Pratt quote is from an advertising circular for George Sweet's *Gentleman in Oil*, private collection of author; JRP interview.

10. JRP interview; Wirt Franklin to JRP, Nov. 25, 1932, Apr. 4, 1933, JRP Papers.

11. JRP interview; Jones, *"And So—They Indicted Me!"*, 33.

12. JRP interview; Watkins, *Righteous Pilgrim*, 342; *New York Times*, Mar. 27, 1933; *Washington Post*, Mar. 27, 1933; "Committee of 15 to Harold Ickes," Mar. 29, 1933, Ickes Papers; Day, "The Oil and Gas Industry and Texas Politics," 218, 219; Nordhauser, *The Quest for Stability*, 101, 102.

13. Jones, *"And So—They Indicted Me!"*, 39, 40; JRP interview.

14. Memorandum, E. S. Rochester to Ickes, Mar. 27, 1933, Ickes Papers; Freidel, *Franklin D. Roosevelt*, 428.

15. JRP interview; Harold L. Ickes, *The Secret Diary of Harold L. Ickes* (3 vols.; New York: Simon and Schuster, 1953–1954), Volume I, *The First Thousand Days, 1933–1936*, p. 10; Jones, *"And So—They Indicted Me!"*, 45–54.

16. JRP interview; House *Petroleum Investigation*), IV, 2404 (Blalock quote); Nordhauser, *The Quest for Stability*, 101–103; New York *Times*, Mar. 29, 1933.

17. Nash, *United States Oil Policy*, 131; Ickes, *The Secret Diary*, Volume I, 10–11; Association letter to Ickes, Mar. 29, 1933, FDR Papers; Jones, *"And So—They Indicted Me!"*, 57, 58; Nordhauser, *The Quest for Stability*, 101–102, 104–105; JRP to C. Dwight Dorough, Apr. 6, 1961, JRP Papers.

18. JRP, "Brief History of the Oil Conference, Washington, DC, 1933," JRP Papers; Independent Petroleum Association Opposed to Monopoly to Ickes, Mar. 29, 1933, Ickes Papers; Jones, *"And So—They Indicted Me!"*, 58–61; Nash, *United States Oil Policy*, 131; JRP interview.

19. Freidel, *Franklin D. Roosevelt*, 427; FDR to Ickes, Apr. 5, 1933, Ickes Papers; JRP, "Brief History of the Oil Conference," JRP Papers.

20. For an example of the protest against pipeline divorcement, see R. C. Holmes to FDR, Apr. 17, 1933, FDR Papers; Nordhauser, *The Quest for Stability*, 105–106; Day, "The Oil and Gas Industry and Texas Politics," 221–222, 223; Ickes to Albert Brunker, Apr. 11, 1933, Ickes Papers; Ickes to Hiram Johnson, Apr. 11, 1933, ibid.

21. Day "The Oil and Gas Industry and Texas Politics," 222; Franklin to JRP, Apr. 4, 1933, JRP Papers; JRP interview.

22. Day, "The Oil and Gas Industry and Texas Politics," 198, 199; JRP interview.

23. JRP interview; Day, "The Oil and Gas Industry and Texas Politics," 200.

24. Nordhauser, *The Quest for Stability*, 92–93; Larson and Porter, *History of Humble Oil*, 475; JRP interview.

25. Yergin, *The Prize*, 252; JRP to John Elliot, Apr. 22, 1933, JRP Papers; Nordhauser, *The Quest for Stability*, 93, 94; Fort Worth *Star-Telegram*, Apr. 25, 1933.

26. JRP interview; Fort Worth *Star-Telegram*, Apr. 25, 1933; Day, "The Oil and Gas Industry and Texas Politics," 203–204.

27. Burns refused to press charges against Roeser and his friends and no one was ever prosecuted; Day, "The Oil and Gas Industry and Texas Politics," 203–204; JRP interview.

28. JRP, *The Texas Oil Case* (pamphlet; IPAT; copy in JRP Papers). The IPAT published Parten's testimony in a pamphlet with this title and distributed more than ten thousand copies nationally. Parten had the pamphlet reprinted in 1978.

29. Ibid., n.p.; JRP interview; JRP to Bailey Hardy, May 13, 1933, JRP Papers; JRP to Lawson Taylor, May 14, 1933, ibid.; JRP to Elliot, May 10, 1933, ibid.; George S. Heyer to JRP, Aug. 23, 1933, ibid.; JRP to Bryce Claggett, May 3, 1933, ibid.; JRP to Elliot, May 10, 1933, ibid.; James Presley, *A Saga of Wealth: The Rise of the Texas Oilmen* (New York: Putnam, 1978), 155–157; Day, "The Oil and Gas Industry and Texas Politics," 206.

30. Eakens, "The Development of Proration in the East Texas Oil Field," 116; Day, "The Oil and Gas Industry and Texas Politics," 209, 210.

31. For more on the hot-oil wars, see Presley, *Saga of Wealth*, 137–180; Day, "The Oil and Gas Industry and Texas Politics," 211; Wolf interview; Murray quote from transcript of documentary film, *The Hot Oil Wars*, in author's possession.

32. JRP to Elliot, May 10, 1933, JRP Papers; JRP to C. D. Neff, May 10, 1933, ibid.

Chapter Six

1. Day, "The Oil and Gas Industry and Texas Politics," 224; Nash, *United States Oil Policy*, 132; Nordhauser, *The Quest for Stability*, 106–108.

2. Ickes to FDR, May 1, 1933, FDR Papers; Ickes to Hiram Johnson, May 8, 1933, Ickes Papers.

3. Nordhauser, *The Quest for Stability*, 99; Nash, *United States Oil Policy*, 132; Lear, "Harold L. Ickes and the Oil Crisis of the First Hundred Days,"10; Ferguson to Ickes, May 5, 1933, Ickes Papers; Morgan Sanders to FDR, May 13, 1933, FDR Papers.

4. John B. Elliot to JRP, May 23, 1933, JRP Papers; Richard Blalock to Jack Blalock, May 31, 1933, ibid.; JRP to Jack Blalock, July 1, 1933, ibid.; JRP interview; Patrick J. Nicholson, *Mr. Jim: The Biography of James Smither Abercrombie* (Houston: Gulf Publishing Co., 1983), 275.

5. JRP interview; for Murchison's hot-oil activities, see Jane Wolfe, *The Murchisons: The Rise and Fall of a Texas Dynasty* (New York: St. Martin's Press, 1989), 82–88.

6. Myron Blalock to Bailey Hardy, May 30, 1933, JRP Papers; JRP interview; Nordhauser, *The Quest for Stability*, 108, 109.

7. Jack Blalock to JRP, telegram, n.d., JRP Papers; JRP interview.

8. Nordhauser, *The Quest for Stability*, 112; Jack Blalock to Bailey Hardy, June 8, 1933, JRP Papers; John B. Elliot to JRP, June 9, 1933, ibid.

9. For more on the NIRA, see Ellis W. Hawley, *The New Deal and the Problem of Monopoly: A Study in*

Economic Ambivalence (Princeton: Princeton University Press, 1966); Nash, *United States Oil Policy*, 134; Nordhauser, *The Quest for Stability*, 111–112; John B. Elliot to JRP, June 9, 1933, JRP Papers.

10. Stoff, *Oil, War, and American Security*, 10; Bailey Hardy to A. L. Guiberson, June 15, 1933, copy in JRP Papers; JRP interview.

11. Nash, *United States Oil Policy*, 135–137; John B. Elliot to JRP, June 18, July 5, 14, 1933, JRP Papers; JRP to Elliott, July 8, 14, 1933, ibid.; JRP interview.

12. Ickes to FDR, July 10, 1933, Ickes Papers; Louis Howe to Ickes, July 12, 1933, ibid.; Nash, *United States Oil Policy*, 136; Nordhauser, *The Quest for Stability*, 113–115.

13. JRP to Jack Blalock, July 1, 1933, JRP Papers; Jack Danciger to JRP, June 29, 1933, ibid.; JRP to Harry Pennington, July 1, 1933, ibid.; JRP to John B. Elliott, July 5, 1933, ibid.; JRP, "To Texas Oil Producers," circular letter, n.d., ibid.; JRP interview.

14. For a detailed discussion of Marshall's views on federal regulation of the oil industry during the early 1930s, see his autobiography *Done in Oil: An Autobiography* (College Station: Texas A&M Press, 1994), as well as his testimony before Subcommittee of the Committee on Interstate and Foreign Commerce in House *Petroleum Investigation*, IV, 2599–2666; Marshall interview; Norman L. Meyers and J. Howard Marshall, "Memorandum to the Secretary," July 26, 1933, Oil file, Ickes Papers.

15. Marshall interview; JRP interview; Marshall, *Done in Oil*, xviii; Meyers and Marshall, "Memorandum to the Secretary," July 26, 1933, Oil file, Ickes Papers.

16. JRP, "Statement to General Hugh S. Johnson, Administrator, Industrial Recovery Administration," Memeographed document, July 1933, JRP Papers; Elliott to JRP, July 8, 1933, ibid.; Blalock to JRP, July 12, 1933, ibid; Nash, *United States Oil Policy*, 138, 139.

17. Elliott to JRP, July 5, 1933, JRP Papers; JRP to Elliott, July 13, 1933, ibid.; James V. Allred, "1st meeting with Ickes," typescript of a partial memoir, ibid.; Atkinson, "James V. Allred," 327–328.

18. Day, "The Oil and Gas Industry and Texas Politics," 229; Nash, *United States Oil Policy*, 138; JRP, "Washington Petroleum Code Conference," Aug. 28, 1933, JRP Papers; JRP to J. G. Puterbaugh, Aug. 24, 1933, ibid.; Parten to Bailey Hardy, n.d., ibid.; JRP interview.

19. JRP to W. G. Williams, Aug. 30, 1933, JRP Papers; Day, "The Oil and Gas Industry and Texas Politics," 229; Nash, *United States Oil Policy*, 137, 138.

20. Nash, *United States Oil Policy*, 138–140; Watkins, *Righteous Pilgrim*, 350–351; Stoff, *Oil, War, and American Security*, 11; Nordhauser, *The Quest for Stability*, 125–130; Marshall interview; Elliott to Jack Blalock, Aug. 31, 1933, JRP Papers; Day, "The Oil and Gas Industry and Texas Politics," 230.

21. Joe Danciger to JRP, Sept. 2, 1933, JRP Papers; JRP to Joe Danciger, Sept. 5, 1933, ibid.; JRP to Elliott, Sept. 5, 1933, ibid.; Elliott to JRP, Sept. 8, 1933, ibid.; and "Comment," n.d., IPAT file, ibid.; JRP to H. B. Fell, Nov. 21, 1933, ibid.

22. Nordhauser, *The Quest for Stability*, 134, 135, 141; Beaton, *Enterprise in Oil*, 386; Nash, *United States Oil Policy*, 141, 142; JRP to Querbes, May 13, Aug. 25, 1933; Woodley Petroleum, Annual Report, 1933, ibid.

23. Wild to Hardy, June 9, 13, Nov. 6, 1933, JRP Papers; Hardy to Mel Davis, June 16, 1933, ibid.; JRP to Harry Pennington, June 22, 1933, ibid.; Wild to Parten, Oct. 22, 1932, ibid.

24. JRP, "An Address to the Membership of the IPAT—Annual Meeting, Dec. 18, 1933, JRP Papers.

25. Robert Engler, *The Politics of Oil: A Study of Private Power and Democratic Directions* (New York: Macmillan, 1961), 273–274.

Chapter Seven

1. Opal had returned to the University of Texas in 1921 to complete her bachelor's degree. JRP interview; Sherman interview; JRP to Opal, telegram, Sept. 16, 1927, JRP Papers.

2. JRP to Littlefield, Oct. 7, 1931, JRP Papers; JRP to W. J. Disch, Dec. 30, 1929, ibid.; JRP to Thompson, May 21, 1935, ibid.; JRP interview.

3. JRP to Disch, Sept.17, 1931, JRP Papers; Clyde Littlefield to JRP, May 7, Aug.19, Dec. 10 (quote), 1932, Feb. 6, 1933, ibid.

4. Although Shreveport's bid nearly fell victim to a feud between the city's business elite and Gov. Huey Long, they eventually won the intense competition for the base in 1931, beating out more than eighty other towns across the country. The city of Shreveport purchased a choice site in Bossier Parish and then donated it to the U.S. Army, which named the new five-million-dollar air base after an early army aviator named Eugene Barksdale. Thomson and Meador, *Shreveport*, 11, 118; for the Shreveport–Huey Long feud, see Williams, *Huey Long*, 329.

5. Sherman interview; San Antonio *Express*, Feb. 2, 3, 1933; Williams, *Huey Long*, 699; JRP interview.

6. JRP to Stephen L. Pinckney, Jan. 15, 1932, JRP Papers; JRP interview; Sherman interview.

7. Sherman interview; JRP interview.

8. Sherman interview.

9. Ibid.; Miller interview.

10. Nordhauser, *The Quest for Stability*, 141, 142; David C. McCaleb and J. R. Lewis, "Conditions attending the investigation in Texas of the Legal Status of Petroleum or the Products thereof which move into Interstate Commerce," Oct. 1934, Ickes Papers; Carl Estes to JRP, Mar. 26, 1934, JRP Papers; Nash, *United States Oil Policy*, 144; E. O. Thompson to Connally, Mar. 2, 1934, box 4Ze136, Thompson Papers; Thompson to E. N. Stanley, Mar. 22, 1934, ibid.

11. House *Petroleum Investigation*, IV, 2777; Ickes quote from his *Secret Diary*, I, 158–159; Marshall quote from his statement in House *Petroleum Investigation*, IV, 2619, 2620; Bailey Hardy to the Directors of the Independent Petroleum Association of Texas, Apr. 30, 1934, JRP Papers.

12. Day, "The Oil and Gas Industry and Texas Politics," 254–257; Nash, *United States Oil Policy*, 144; JRP interview; Nordhhauser, *The Quest for Stability*, 157.

13. Houston *Chronicle*, May 7, 1934; JRP interview; JRP, press release, May 15, 1934, JRP Papers; Blalock to JRP, May 9, 1934, ibid.; John Elliot to JRP, May 9, 1934, ibid.; John Elliot to FDR, May 31, 1934, box 56A, FDR Papers.

14. For the Garner-Rayburn relationship, see D. B. Hardeman and Don Bacon, *Rayburn: A Biography* (Austin: Texas Monthly Press, 1987), 136, 137; FDR to Ickes, Aug. 19, 1933, Oil folder # 9, box 218, Ickes Papers; Ickes to Charles Fahy, ibid.; Day, "The Oil and Gas Industry and Texas Politics," 264; Blalock to Strake, May 16, 1934, JRP Papers; Blalock to JRP, May 16, 1934, ibid.; JRP interview.

15. Marshall's statement in House *Petroleum Investigation*, IV, 2638–2639; Jack Blalock to JRP, May 17, 1934, JRP Papers; JRP interview (with A. Champagne); Thompson to Blalock, May 17, 1934, box 4Ze136, Thompson Papers.

16. Amon Carter to FDR, June 9, 1934, box 56A, FDR Papers; Miriam Ferguson to FDR, June 4, 1934, ibid.

17. Hardeman and Bacon, *Rayburn*, 53; Robert A. Caro, *The Years of Lyndon Johnson: The Path to Power* (New York: Knopf, 1982), 306–333; JRP interview.

18. JRP interview (Champagne); Nicholson, *Mr. Jim*, 277; JRP interview; Dulaney interview; Fath interview; Dugger interview.

19. JRP interview; JRP to Long, May 26, 1934, JRP Papers.

20. Williams, *Huey Long*, 678, 679; JRP interview.

21. Williams, *Huey Long*, 865; JRP interview.

22. Dallas *Morning News*, May 18, 1934.

23. JRP, transcript, "Testimony before the Interstate and Foreign Commerce Committee," June 5, 1934, JRP Papers.

24. Meyers to Ickes, undated note, Ickes Papers; Ickes to Roosevelt, June 9, 1934, box 56A, FDR Papers; Ickes, *The Secret Diary*, I, 169; JRP interview.

25. JRP to Joe Danciger, June 11, 1934, JRP Papers; Marshall's statement in House *Petroleum Investigation*, IV, 2665; Dallas *News*, June 15, 1934; Jack Blalock to Ernest Thompson, June 14, 1934, Thompson Papers; Ernest Thompson to Jack Blalock, June 14, 1934, ibid.; Ernest Thompson to Sam Rayburn, June 14, 1934, ibid.

Chapter Eight

1. Allred made a speech to the Young Democrats of Texas in May 1935 that was so critical of the New Deal that the governor of New Mexico wrote Roosevelt to complain about it. See Clyde Tingley to FDR, June 13, 1935, PPF 236, FDR Papers. For an example of Parten's advice to Attorney General Allred, see JRP to Allred, Oct. 6, 1933, Allred Papers (M. D. Anderson Library, University of Houston); see also boxes 185 and 190, in ibid. Allred to JRP, Mar. 8, 1934, JRP Papers; Atkinson, "James V. Allred," 300, 316; JRP interview.

2. JRP interview; JRP to Claude Wild, Mar. 7, 1934, JRP Papers; Allred to JRP, May 20, 1934, ibid.

3. Rapoport interview; Clark interview; Yarborough interview; JRP interview.

4. Seth Shepard McKay, *Texas Politics, 1906–1944* (Lubbock: Texas Tech Press, 1952), 257–262.

5. JRP interview.

6. Ibid.; Robert W. Calvert, *Here Comes the Judge: From State Home to State House: Memoirs* (Waco: Texian Press, 1977), 97; JRP to Allred, July, 3, 1934, JRP Papers.

7. JRP to Paul Wakefield, July 12, 1934, JRP Papers; also see Lee Armer to JRP, July 25, 26,1934, ibid.

8. McKay, *Texas Politics*, 269; Atkinson, "James V. Allred," 345; Lee Armer to JRP, July 25, 1934, JRP Papers; JRP to Elliott, July 24, 1934, ibid.

9. McKay, *Texas Politics*, 274–275; Atkinson, "James V. Allred," 353; JRP to Allred, Aug. 6, 1934, box 81, Allred Papers.

10. Atkinson, "James V. Allred," 357, 358; JRP to Allred, Aug. 20, 1934, JRP Papers; JRP interview.

11. *Ferguson Forum*, Aug. 23, 1934; JRP interview.

12. McKay, *Texas Politics*, 276; JRP, typescript, n.d., Allred file, JRP Papers.

13. JRP interview; McKay, *Texas Politics*, 278–279; Atkinson, "James V. Allred," 363.

14. JRP interview; Atkinson, "James V. Allred," 361; copies of Hunter's letter to Allred can be found in the Allred file, JRP Papers, and in the Allred Papers.

15. JRP interview; Calvert, *Here Comes the Judge,* 98; McKay, *Texas Politics,* 278; Atkinson, "James V. Allred," 361.

16. For the vote tabulation, see the *Texas Almanac* (Dallas: Dallas Morning News, 1936), 477; for demagoguery in Texas gubernatorial campaigns, see George N. Green, *The Establishment in Texas Politics: The Primitive Years, 1938–1957* (Westport, Conn.: Greenwood Press, 1979); JRP to Allred, Aug. 25, 1934, box 81, Allred Papers; JRP interview.

17. JRP interview; for a very different view of Stevenson, see Robert A. Caro, *The Years of Lyndon Johnson: Means of Ascent* (New York: Knopf, 1990).

18. Allred later appointed Sarah Hughes to serve as the first woman district judge in Texas, and Calvert was elected Speaker in 1937. Hughes was the federal judge who administered the oath of office to Lyndon Johnson in Dallas the day of the Kennedy assassination. JRP to Allred, Dec. 24, 1934, JRP Papers; Robert Martindale, "James V. Allred" (Master's thesis, University of Texas, 1958), 52, 56, 86; Dallas *Morning News,* Jan. 9, 1935; JRP interview; Calvert, *Here Comes the Judge,* 86, 88; Stevenson interview, oral history transcript (UNT); Caro, *Means of Ascent,* 163, 164.

19. JRP interview.

Chapter Nine

1. The Tender Board was J. Howard Marshall's idea. See his *Done in Oil,* 60. E. O. Thompson to Homer Cummings, Aug. 22, 1934, box 4Ze136, Thompson Papers; JRP interview; Marshall interview; Nash, *United States Oil Policy,* 145; Nordhauser, *The Quest for Stability,* 149, 150; Charles Fahy to Harold Ickes, Oct. 26, 27, 1934, Ickes Papers; Homer Cummings to FDR, Dec. 20, 1934, FDR Papers.

2. Hawley, *The New Deal and the Problem of Monopoly,* 215; Beaton, *Enterprise in Oil,* 387; Nash, *United States Oil Policy,* 148; speech by Ickes, Nov. 14, 1934, mimeographed document, Ickes Papers.

3. Nash, *United States Oil Policy,* 149; John Joseph Mathews, *Life and Death of an Oilman: The Career of E. W. Marland* (Norman: University of Oklahoma Press, 1951), 247–249; JRP interview; Hawley, *The New Deal and the Problem of Monopoly,* 215, 216; Robb K. Burlage, "James V. Allred: Texas' Liberal Governor" (May, 1959) unpublished typescript of paper for Tutorial Course 359, UT-Austin, pp. 31, 32, copy in JRP Papers.

4. JRP interview; McDanial, *Some Ran Hot,* 107, 108.

5. The Parten-Zeppa relationship is an example of Parten's ability to create business relationships and even maintain friendships with individuals with whom he differed drastically in political viewpoint. Zeppa's ultra-conservative political views were anathema to both Parten and Dayson and he rejected just as fiercely their political and social liberalism. See Presley, *Never in Doubt,* 67, 125, 126; JRP interview; Shelmire interview.

6. Shelmire interview; JRP interview.

7. McDanial, *Some Ran Hot,* 109; JRP interview; Mayer interview.

8. By 1933, Parten had supervised the drilling and operation of more than four hundred oil and gas wells and had produced more than seven million barrels of crude oil. JRP, "Affidavit, in re: Hunt Production Company v. Lon A. Smith, et al.," May 28, 1933, JRP Ppaers; JRP to John R. Palmer, Sept. 15, 1934, ibid.; Woodley Petroleum, Annual Report, 1934, ibid.

9. JRP interview; JRP to E. O. Thompson, Mar. 1, 1935, JRP Papers; JRP to Andrew Querbes, Feb. 23, 1935, ibid.

10. J. Hugh Watson, the chairman of Shreveport's First National Bank, thanked Parten for his offer, but told him that regulations required the bank to pay the going rate of 8 percent. Watson to JRP, Nov. 11, 1985, JRP Papers; Justin R. Querbes Jr. to JRP, Nov. 18, 1985, ibid.; Andrew Querbes to JRP, Mar. 1, 1935, ibid.; JRP to Querbes, Mar. 23, 1935, ibid.; JRP to Querbes, Sept. 25, 1935, ibid.; and JRP to J. Hugh Watson, Nov. 7, 1985, ibid.

11. Houston *Chronicle,* Nov. 3, 1968; JRP interview.

12. Beaton, *Enterprise in Oil,* 387; Nordhauser, *The Quest for Stability,* 153, 154; Nash, *United States Oil Policy,* 145; Hawley, *The New Deal and the Problem of Monopoly,* 216; JRP to Thompson, Jan. 7, 1935, box 4Ze136, Thompson Papers; JRP interview.

13. Marshall interview; Marshall, *Done in Oil,* 60, 61; Beaton, *Enterprise in Oil,* 386, 387; Stoff, *Oil, War, and American Security,* 15; Nordhauser, *The Quest for Stability,* 154, 155; Meyers to Ickes, Jan. 8, 1935, Ickes Papers.

14. Clark, *Three Stars for the Colonel,* 115, 116; JRP interview; Nordhauser, *The Quest for Stability,* 154.

15. Thompson to Blalock, Jan. 23, 1935, box 4Ze136, Thompson Papers; Blalock to Thompson, Jan. 31, 1935, ibid.; Thompson to Rayburn, Feb. 5, 1935, ibid.; JRP to Blalock, Feb. 2, 1935, JRP Papers; JRP interview; Beaton, *Enterprise in Oil,* 386–389; Nordhauser, *The Quest for Stability,* 155.

16. Ickes, *The Secret Diary,* I, 417–418; Carl Estes to JRP, Mar. 28, 1935, JRP Papers; JRP to Blalock, Apr. 13, 1935, ibid.; James A. Farley to JRP, June 12, 1935, box 218, folder 9, Ickes Papers; Ickes to FDR, Aug. 10, 1935, ibid.; Marshall interview; JRP interview.

17. JRP interview; Burlage, "James V. Allred," p. 38, JRP Papers; Rayburn to Allred, Mar. 1, 1935, box 236, Allred Papers.

18. JRP interview.

19. McIntyre to FDR, Apr. 15, 1935, FDR Papers; Burlage, "James V. Allred," p. 38, JRP Papers; JRP interview.

20. JRP interview; Houston *Post*, undated clipping of a James Clark newspaper column, JRP Papers.

21. FDR to Charles West, May 10, 1935, file 56, FDR Papers; Ickes to FDR, May 21, 1935, ibid.; FDR to Rayburn, May 23, 1935, ibid.; JRP interview.

22. Hawley, *The New Deal and the Problem of Monopoly*, 216, 217; Nash, *United States Oil Policy*, 151, 152.

23. Clark, *Three Stars for the Colonel*, 134; JRP interview; Hawley, *The New Deal and the Problem of Monopoly*, 217–219; Stoff, *Oil, War, and American Security*, 12, 16; Nordhauser, *The Quest for Security*, 165.

24. Nash, *United States Oil Policy*, 155, 156; JRP to George Morgan, Oct. 28, 1935, copy in box 4Ze136, Thompson Papers.

25. JRP interview.

Chapter Ten

1. JRP interview; *Daily Texan* (UT-Austin), Jan. 15, Mar. 12, 1935; Frederick Duncalf to JRP, Nov. 15, 22, Dec. 6, 18, 1934, JRP Papers; JRP to Duncalf, Nov. 19, 1934, ibid.; R. L. Batts to JRP, Nov. 22, 1934, ibid.; JRP to H. Y. Benedict, Dec. 8, 1934, ibid.; Benedict to JRP, Dec. 10, 1934, ibid.

2. JRP to Jester, Dec. 23, 1931, JRP Papers; Allred announced his support for lump-sum appropriations on February 4, 1935. See *Daily Texan* (UT-Austin), Feb. 5, 1935; JRP interview; Clark interview.

3. The University of Texas still awaits an objective scholarly history, nonetheless much information about the history of the board of regents and the relationship between the board and its various constituencies can be found in Ronnie Dugger, *Our Invaded Universities: Form, Reform, and New Starts* (New York: Norton, 1974); Joe B. Frantz, *The Forty-Acre Follies: An Opinionated History of the University of Texas* (Austin: Texas Monthly Press, 1983); Gould, "The University Becomes Politicized," 255–276; Green, *The Establishment in Texas Politics*; Homer P. Rainey, *The Tower and the Dome: A Free University Versus Political Control* (Boulder, Colo.: Pruett Publishing Co., 1971); and Brown, *Hood, Bonnet, and Little Brown Jug*.

4. *Daily Texan* (UT-Austin), Feb. 22, Mar. 12, 1935; Houston *Chronicle*, Mar. 12, 1935; Longview *Daily News*, Mar. 20, 1935; Batts to JRP, Mar. 15, 1935, JRP Papers; Woodley to Allred, Mar. 31, 1935, box 106, Allred Papers; Allred to Woodley, Apr. 6, 1935, ibid.

5. *Daily Texan* (UT-Austin), Mar. 20, 1935; JRP interview; Fath interview; Clark interview; Yarborough interview; JRP, "The University of Texas Controversy," 5, JRP Papers; Jo Betsy Allred's diary entries for Jan. 10, Feb. 28, June 21, July 4, Oct. 15, 1937, Allred Papers; Allred to JRP, July 24, Aug. 3, Nov. 18, 1935, JRP Papers; Yarborough to JRP, Jan. 8, 1935, ibid.; JRP to Allred, July 26, 30, 1935, ibid.

6. JRP interview.

7. Information about Parten's regental colleagues comes from their individual biographical files (CAH); *Daily Texan* (UT-Austin), Mar. 31, 1935; University of Texas, Minutes of the Board of Regents, 1936–1941 (CAH; cited hereafter as Board of Regents Minutes), Mar. 30, 1935, p. 331; JRP interview; Bert R. Haigh, *Land, Oil, and Education* (El Paso: Texas Western Press, 1986), 255; Brown, *Hood, Bonnet, and Little Brown Jug*, 146.

8. Individual biographical files (CAH); JRP interview; *Daily Texan* (UT-Austin), Dec. 5, 1936.

9. "Harry Yandell Benedict," Webb, Carroll, and Branda (eds.), *Handbook of Texas*, I, 146; Brown, *Hood, Bonnet, and Little Brown Jug*, 354; JRP interview.

10. JRP interview; Dugger, *Our Invaded Universities*, 23.

11. *Daily Texan* (UT-Austin), Mar. 31, 1935; JRP interview.

12. For more about Bedichek, see Frantz, *The Forty-Acre Follies*, 161–166; JRP interview.

13. Dobie, *Some Part of Myself*, 218; Roger Griffin, "To Establish a University of the First Class," *Southwestern Historical Quarterly*, 86 (Oct., 1982), 135; David Prindle, "Oil and the Permanent University Fund: The Early Years," ibid., 278; JRP interview.

14. Mather to JRP, Apr. 24, 1935, JRP Papers; JRP interview.

15. JRP to regents, May 13, 1935, JRP Papers; Regents Legislative Committee to regents, June 1, 1935, ibid.; JRP to Frank Andrews, May 23, 1935, ibid.; JRP to Allred, May 15, 1935, ibid.

16. David G. McComb, *Houston: A History* (Austin: University of Texas Press, 1981), 115, 116; JRP interview; Sherman interview.

17. Dallas Sherman to JRP, Aug. 15, 1935, JRP Papers; JRP interview; Sherman interview.

18. JRP to Fred Adams, Aug. 31, 1935, JRP Papers; JRP to Aynesworth and Morgan, Nov. 18, 1935, ibid.; JRP to Lester Charles Uren, Aug. 23, 1935, ibid.; JRP to Hines Baker, Aug. 29, 1935, ibid.; *Daily Texan* (UT-Austin), Aug. 8, 1935.

19. JRP to George Morgan, July 3, 13, 15, 1935, JRP Papers; JRP to Aynesworth and Fairchild, Sept. 27, 1935, ibid.; JRP interview.

20. JRP interview; Prindle,"Oil and the Permanent University Fund," 296, 297.

21. JRP interview; Dallas *News*, Mar. 25, 1936.

22. Haigh, *Land, Oil, and Education*, 256, 266; JRP interview; Prindle, "Oil and the Permanent University Fund," 297; Lohman to JRP, Oct. 17, 1935, JRP Papers; JRP to Aynesworth, Sept. 26, 1935, ibid.; Leslie Waggener

to JRP, Mar. 9, 1936, ibid.; Aynesworth to JRP, June 16, 1936, ibid.; Hines Baker to JRP, Mar. 20, 1936, ibid.; JRP interview.

23. *Daily Texan* (UT-Austin), July 18, 1937; Merton Harris, assistant attorney general, to JRP, Oct. 24, 1935, JRP Papers; Harris to Aynesworth, May 16, 1936, ibid.; JRP to Aynesworth, Apr. 23, May 25, 1936, ibid.; Lohman to JRP, Oct. 17, 1935, ibid.; Haigh, *Land, Oil, and Education*, 267–268, 270.

24. The university had earned an average of $19.78 an acre for leases during the previous five years. The first open auction, however, generated $37.36 an acre; Prindle, "Oil and the Permanent University Fund," 295; Austin *American*, July 21, 1936; JRP to Gordon Burns, July 31, 1939, JRP Papers; JRP to George Morgan, July 24, 1936, ibid.; Board of Regents of The University of Texas System, "Permanent University Fund Investments for the Fiscal Year Ended August 31, 1990," Appendix A, 82 (report distributed by UT System; copies at UT System offices).

25. JRP interview.

26. JRP to Lohman, Sept. 2, 18, 1936, JRP Papers; JRP to Morgan, Sept. 18, 1936, ibid.

27. Wild to JRP, Feb. 24, 1937, JRP Papers; JRP interview; Prindle, "Oil and the Permanent University Fund," 298.

28. Fort Worth *Star-Telegram*, Feb. 12, 1961; Haigh, *Land, Oil, and Education*, 269, 270; Clark interview; Garrett interview; Blanton interview; Rapoport interview; JRP to author, Dec. 3, 1986, letter in author's possession.

Chapter Eleven

1. Stocking's speech was reprinted as "Stabilization of the Oil Industry: Its Economic and Legal Aspects," *American Economic Review*, 23 (Mar., 1933), 70; a condensed and revised version was printed as "Chaos in the Oil Industry," *Nation* (June, 1936), 634–636; JRP to Allred, Jan. 17, 1933, Allred Papers; JRP interview.

2. John Kenneth Galbraith, *A Life in Our Times: Memoirs* (New York: Houghton Mifflin, 1981), 24.

3. Fath interview; Dugger interview; Eckhardt interview; Dugger, *Our Invaded Universities*, 39–41.

4. Don E. Carleton, *Red Scare!: Right-Wing Hysteria, Fifties Fanaticism, and Their Legacy in Texas* (Austin: Texas Monthly Press, 1985), 22; Dugger, *Our Invaded Universities*, 39–41; Clarence R. Wharton to Haley, Dec. 2, 1935, box 2D264, J. Evetts Haley Papers (CAH).

5. Fort Worth *Star-Telegram*, July 2, 1935; Frazier Moss to JRP, July 2, 1935, JRP Papers; JRP to Moss, July 3, 1935, ibid.; JRP to Scott, July 3, 1935, ibid.; Scott to JRP, July 5, 1935, ibid.

6. Benedict's interpretation of academic freedom did not apply to Communists or to those strongly suspected of having Communist sympathies. Official university policy prohibited the employment of members of the Communist Party. JRP interview.

7. Parten later secured an appointment for Montgomery as an economic consultant to a branch of the Federal Reserve; *Daily Texan* (UT-Austin), July 5, 1935; JRP interview.

8. *Daily Texan* (UT-Austin), Nov. 17, 1935; JRP to Benedict, Nov. 21, 1935, JRP Papers.

9. Frances Perkins, Roosevelt's secretary of labor, appointed Stocking to serve as a mediator in a longshoremen's strike in Galveston in December. Stocking to JRP, Jan. 20, May 23, JRP Papers; JRP to Stocking, Jan. 25, May 29, 1936, ibid.; for Parten's problems with the *Daily Texan*, see next chapter.

10. Adams to Morgan, Dec. 17, 1935, copy in JRP Papers; JRP to Adams, Dec. 20, 1935, ibid.; *Daily Texan* (UT-Austin), Nov. 27, 1935.

11. JRP to J. O. Guleke, Dec. 19, 1935, JRP Papers; Guleke, to JRP, Dec. 30, 1935, ibid.; Haley to W. C. Murphy Jr., Nov. 25, 1935, box 2D264, Haley Papers (CAH); JRP to Dean William Masterson, Feb. 17, 1936, ibid.; Don E. Carleton, *Who Shot the Bear? J. Evetts Haley and the Eugene C. Barker Texas History Center* (Austin: Wind River Press, 1984); JRP interview.

12. Elizabeth Dilling, *The Red Network: A "Who's Who" and Handbook of Radicalism for Patriots*, 5; JRP to Allred, Dec. 20, 1935, JRP Papers.

13. JRP interview.

14. *Daily Texan* (UT-Austin), Jan. 30, Apr. 28, 1936; Muller, *Out of the Night: A Biologist's View of the Future* (New York: Vanguard Press, 1935), vii, 74; JRP interview.

15. *Daily Texan* (UT-Austin), Jan. 30, Apr. 28, 1936; Herman J. Muller to Benedict, Mar. 30, 1932, "Investigations" file, University of Texas, Records of the Office of the President (CAH; cited hereafter as Records of Office of the President); Benedict to Muller, Apr. 11, 1932, ibid.; R. L. Batts to Edward Crane, July 13, 1932, ibid.; Dugger, *Our Invaded Universities*, 32.

16. The June 1932 number is the only known issue of the *Spark* , a rare copy is in the Texas Newspaper Collection (CAH); Austin *American*, June 28, 1932; Dallas *News*, June 29, 1932; Batts to Benedict, June 23, 1932, "Investigations" file, Records of Office of the President; Edward Crane to Batts, July 12, 1932, ibid.; Batts to Crane, July 13, 1932, ibid.

17. Maco Stewart to Edward Randall, Sept. 30, 1932, "Investigations" file, Records of Office of the President; Randall to Benedict, Oct. 6, 1932, ibid.; Muller to Benedict, Feb. 22, 1933, ibid.

18. *Daily Texan* (UT-Austin), Jan. 10, 30, Apr. 28, 1936; Benedict to Muller, Jan. 18, Apr. 27, 1936, Muller folder, "Investigations" file, Records of Office of the President; Muller to Benedict, Feb. 23, Apr. 3, 1936, ibid.

19. *Daily Texan* (UT-Austin), Jan. 10, 30, Apr. 28, 1936; Benedict to Muller, Jan. 18, Apr. 27, 1936, Muller folder, "Investigations" file, Records of Office of the President; Muller to Benedict, Feb. 23, Apr. 3, 1936, ibid.; JRP interview.

20. Muller (1890–1967) fled to Scotland in 1939 as a result of Stalin's purges and eventually denounced the Soviet Communist Party. He was awarded the Nobel Prize in 1946 and retired as a professor at the University of Indiana in the 1960s. The real reason for his resignation from the University of Texas faculty remained confidential until the publication of Ronnie Dugger's *Our Invaded Universities* in 1974. See Dugger, 26–32; also the *Daily Texan* (UT-Austin), Mar. 24, 1967; JRP interview.

21. Martindale, "James V. Allred," 79; JRP interview.

22. JRP interview; JRP to Thompson, June 24, 27, 1936, JRP Papers.

23. Clark, *Three Stars for the Colonel*, 140, 141.

24. JRP interview; JRP to Ben L. Parten, Aug. 6, 1936, JRP Papers; photograph of a letter, Lon Smith to Price Campbell, n.d. (ca. June 1936), ibid.; typed transcript of a pamphlet by Lon A. Smith, n.d., ibid.

25. JRP to Knight, July 3, 1936, JRP Papers; JRP to N. U. Caldwell, July 3, 1936, ibid.; Webb to JRP, July 4, 1936, ibid.

26. Clark, *Three Stars for the Colonel*, 144, 145; McKay, *Texas Politics*, 301; JRP to C. H. Siadous, Aug. 5, 1936, JRP Papers; JRP interview.

27. JRP to Grover Hill, Aug. 1, 1936, JRP Papers; JRP to Siadous, Aug. 5, 1936, ibid.; JRP to Dayson, Aug. 6, 1936, ibid.; I. P. Bradley to JRP, Aug. 10, 1936, ibid.; Jack Danciger to JRP, Aug. 14, 1936, ibid.

28. JRP to Thompson, Aug. 4, 1936, box 4Ze136, Thompson Papers; JRP interview; Clark, *Three Stars for the Colonel*,145, 146; Ernest Thompson, memeographed copy of speech, Aug. 17, 1936, JRP Papers; JRP to Joe E.Webb, Aug. 18, 1936, ibid.; JRP to Thompson, Aug. 17, 1934, box 4Ze136, Thompson Papers.

29. Thompson to JRP, Aug. 21, 1936, JRP Papers; Pete Biggers to JRP, Aug. 26, 1936, ibid.

30. *Daily Texan* (UT-Austin), July 9, Sept. 18, 1936; Richard B. Henderson, *Maury Maverick: A Political Biography* (Austin: University of Texas Press, 1970), 125; for more on Wirtz, see Caro, *Path to Power*, 373–379; JRP interview.

31. JRP interview; William McGill to JRP, Nov. 8, 1935, JRP Papers; Garrett interview.

32. JRP interview; *Daily Texan* (UT-Austin), July 23, 1936; JRP to Waggener, Sept. 8, 1936, JRP Papers.

33. JRP interview; *Daily Texan* (UT-Austin), Aug. 6, 1936.

34. Waggener to JRP, Sept. 4, 1936, JRP Papers; *Daily Texan* (UT-Austin), Aug. 6, 9, 1936; Henderson, *Maury Maverick*, 124; JRP interview.

35. Austin *American Statesman*, July 30, 1936; *Daily Texan* (UT-Austin), Aug. 6, 1936; San Antonio *Light*, Aug. 2, 1936; Henderson, *Maury Maverick*, 126; Longview *Daily News*, Aug. 5, 1936; *Daily Texan* (UT-Austin), Aug. 30, 1936.

36. *Daily Texan* (UT-Austin), Aug. 11, 1936; Houston *Press*, n.d., clipping in JRP Papers.

37. JRP to Waggener, Sept. 8, 1936, JRP Papers; JRP interview; *Daily Texan* (UT-Austin), Aug. 9, 1936.

38. Tom Dailey Jr. to Blalock, Sept. 3, 1936, JRP Papers; Myron Blalock biographical file (CAH); Houston *Chronicle*, Sept. 16, 1936.

39. Press release, UT Free News Service, Sept. 16, 1936, JRP Papers; Benedict to JRP, Sept. 18, 1936, ibid; *Daily Texan* (UT-Austin), Sept. 17, 1936.

40. JRP to George F. Howard, Dec. 2, 1936, JRP Papers.

41. See chapter 13 for the *Daily Texan* censorship controversy.

42. Carleton, *Who Shot the Bear?*, 7; Don E. Carleton and Katherine J. Adams, "'A Work Peculiarly Our Own': Origins of the Barker Texas History Center, 1883–1950," *Southwestern Historical Quarterly*, 86 (Oct., 1982), 197–230.

43. University Library Regents Committee on Complaints and Grievances, Report, Apr. 27, 1936, Board of Regents Minutes, Apr. 27, 1936, p. 347; Board of Regents Minutes, July 27, 1936, p. 10.

44. Haley was a founding member of the Jeffersonian Democrats, Haley to Orville Bullington, May 16, 1936, box 2D263, Haley Papers (CAH); Green, *The Establishment in Texas Politics*, 25; Lionel V. Patenaude, *Texans, Politics, and the New Deal* (New York: Garland Publishing, 1983), 112–117; Board of Regents Minutes, Aug. 24, 1936, p. 7; President's Docket, Aug. 24, 1936, p. 5, Board of Regents Minutes (CAH).

45. Haley to Benedict, Aug. 24, 1936, box 2D263, Haley Papers (CAH); *Daily Texan* (UT-Austin), Sept. 18, 1936; Carleton, *Who Shot the Bear?*, 9, 11; JRP interview.

46. Haley to Ruby Mixon, Sept. 10, 1935, box 2D264, Haley Papers (CAH); Haley to Dobie, Dec. 4, 1936, J. Frank Dobie Papers (Harry Ransom Humanities Research Center, University of Texas at Austin; cited hereafter as HRC); Carleton, *Who Shot the Bear?*, 11–13; Haley interview; Dallas *News*, Sept.13, 1936.

47. JRP interview; Waggener to JRP, Sept. 17, 21, 1936, JRP Papers; JRP to Waggener, Sept.18, 1936, ibid.; *Daily Texan* (UT-Austin), Sept. 18, 1936.

48. Randall to Haley, Dec. 3, 1935, box 2D263, Haley Papers (CAH); Aynesworth to Haley, Oct. 24, 1935, ibid.
49. JRP interview.
50. Roy Miller (1884–1946), mayor of Corpus Christi (1913–1917) and publisher of the Corpus Christi *Caller*, was also lobbyist for the Port of Corpus Christi. He played a key role in getting the Texas portion of the Intracoastal Canal completed. "Roy Miller," biographical file (CAH); Lyle interview, oral history transcript (LBJ); for Miller's expenses, see *Daily Texan* (UT-Austin), Feb., 4, 1937; Fath interview.
51. JRP interview; *House Journal*, 44th Leg., special session 3 (1936), 28, 43, 50–54, 78; *Daily Texan* (UT-Austin), Sept. 30, Oct. 2, 7, 1936.
52. Montgomery's retort about the profit system was incorrectly cited in the author's book *Red Scare!* as having occurred during another legislative investigation of Montgomery conducted in 1948. The author is pleased to have an opportunity to correct that error here; Caldwell got into trouble when it was revealed by Herman Wright that a letter the committee chairman had read at the hearing had been stolen from his files as secretary of the Progressive Democrats. Caldwell was later forced to hire an attorney to fend off a criminal investigation by the District Attorney's Office of the alleged theft; Benedict quote is from Fath interview; *Daily Texan* (UT-Austin), Oct. 14, 1936; Houston *Post*, Oct. 13, 14, 1936; Cuero *Record*, Oct.14, 1936; Houston *Press*, Oct. 14, 1936.
53. *House Journal*, 44th Leg., special session 3 (1936), 491–493; Green, *The Establishment in Texas Politics*, 72; *Daily Texan* (UT-Austin), Oct. 28, 29, 1936; Fath interview.
54. *Daily Texan* (UT-Austin), Dec. 8, 1936, Feb. 6, Mar. 7, June 1, 1937; JRP to Marguerite Fairchild, Mar. 5, 1937, copy in Texas Student Publications files, VF-5, Records of Office of the President; Henderson, *Maury Maverick*, 126.

Chapter Twelve

1. Parten sometimes arranged to have financial payments made directly to the athletes. For example, he persuaded Lutcher Stark in August 1936 to subsidize the living expenses of J. W. ("Beefus") Bryant, a running back, during the upcoming school year. Parten reminded Stark that "you told me to find you an outstanding junior college prospect who . . . had outstanding athletic ability. . . . Well, I have now found that man. He is . . . speedy, kicks, passes, and runs . . . I told him you would help him with fifty dollars a month . . ." JRP to Stark, Aug. 19, 1936, JRP Papers; JRP to Jack Chevigny, Jan. 14, 1934, ibid.; JRP interview; Frantz, *The Forty-Acre Follies*, 66.
2. A few weeks before joining the board of regents, Parten arranged for and cosigned a sixteen-hundred-dollar note with W. L. Moody and Company to allow Chevigny to cover his gambling debts. A year later, Parten bailed Chevigny out of a $7,552 gambling debt. JRP interview; George S. Heyer to JRP, Mar. 15, 1935, JRP Papers; JRP to Heyer, Mar. 21, 1935, ibid.; John A. Gracy to JRP, July 20, 1936, ibid.; JRP to Gracy, July 24, 1936, ibid.; JRP to Stark, Aug. 1, 1936, ibid.
3. Jane Weinert, the regent's daughter and herself a future university regent, was dating Chevigny and the Weinerts were very fond of the young coach. Weinert had also played the leading role in bringing Chevigny to the university. Weinert to JRP, Nov. 17, 1936, JRP Papers; JRP to Weinert, Nov. 18, 1936, ibid.; JRP to Oliver W. Fannin, Oct. 28, 1936, ibid.; Frantz, *The Forty-Acre Follies*, 68, 69; JRP interview.
4. JRP interview; *Daily Texan* (UT-Austin), Nov. 11, 1936.
5. JRP interview; JRP to Benedict, Nov. 20, 1936, JRP Papers; JRP to Oliver W. Fannin, Nov. 17, 1936, ibid.; JRP to C. B. Smith, Oct. 4, 1978, ibid.; Scott to JRP, Nov. 25, 1936, ibid.
6. JRP interview; *Daily Texan* (UT-Austin), Nov.15, 1936.
7 After Chevigny left the university, Parten got him a job as an attorney with the state tax board, but he soon moved to Illinois to work for Hilmer Weinert in a newly developing oil field. Commissioned as a U.S. Marine lieutenant after the outbreak of World War II, he was killed in battle at Iwo Jima in 1945. JRP interview; JRP to Dolley, Dec. 2, 14, 1936, JRP Papers; Hogg to Dolley, Dec. 1, 1936, ibid.; Dolley to JRP, Dec. 3, 1936, ibid.; JRP to Waggener and Aynesworth, Dec.12, 1936, ibid.; *Daily Texan* (UT-Austin), Dec. 9, 1936; James W. Pohl, "The Bible Decade and the Origin of National Athletic Prominence," *Southwestern Historical Quarterly*, 86 (Oct., 1982), 301–302; Frantz, *The Forty-Acre Follies*, 70.
8. Joe Frantz has noted that Bible was "probably the only coach in the world named for a Greek historian." Frantz, *The Forty-Acre Follies*, 187; JRP interview; *Daily Texan* (UT-Austin), Jan. 17, 1937.
9. JRP interview; Pohl, "The Bible Decade," 302.
10. JRP interview.
11. Ibid.; Jo Betsy Allred diary, Jan. 10, 1937, Allred Papers; Waggener to JRP, Jan. 19, 1937, JRP Papers; JRP to Waggener, Jan. 22, 1937, ibid.; JRP to Weinert, Jan. 13, 1937, ibid.; Weinert to JRP, Jan. 13, 1937, ibid.; *Daily Texan* (UT-Austin), Jan. 17, 1937.
12. New York *Times*, Jan. 16, 1937; *Daily Texan* (UT-Austin), Jan. 16, 1937; clipping, unknown paper, Jan. 18, 1937, JRP Papers.
13. Pohl, "The Bible Decade," 303; JRP interview.
14. JRP interview; Pohl, "The Bible Decade," 303.
15. JRP interview; JRP to Waggener, Jan. 22, 1937, JRP Papers.

16. Houston *Chronicle*, Jan. 22, 1937; *Daily Texan* (UT-Austin), Jan. 23, Mar. 25, 1937; JRP to Bible, Jan. 23, 1937, JRP Papers.

17. JRP interview.

18. For more about Bible and his subsequent career at the University of Texas, see Pohl, "The Bible Decade," 299–320; JRP interview.

19. "Board of Regents to Allred, et al.," Jan. 9, 1937, printed circular, Records of Office of the President; *Daily Texan* (UT-Austin), Dec.14, 1936, Jan. 28, Apr. 23, 1937; JRP interview.

20. Aynesworth to JRP, Feb. 5, 1936, JRP Papers; Waggener to JRP, Feb. 4, Nov. 21, 1936, ibid.; Fairchild to JRP, Dec. 16, 1936, ibid.; Robert L. Holliday to JRP, Mar. 3, 1937, ibid.; Randall to Allred, Dec. 1, 1936, box 348, Allred Papers; JRP interview; *Daily Texan* (UT-Austin), Feb. 28, 1937.

21. JRP interview; Jo Betsy Allred, diary, Feb. 28, 1937, box 1, Allred Papers; JRP, "Some of the University's Problems," typescript, Mar. 2, 1937, JRP Papers; Houston *Chronicle*, Mar. 5, 1937.

22. "George C. Butte," *Handbook of Texas*, ed. Webb, Carroll, and Branda, I, 258; Butte to JRP, May 28, 1937, JRP Papers.

23. Houston *Chronicle*, Mar. 5, 1937; *Daily Texan* (UT-Austin), Apr. 9, 1937.

24. JRP interview.

25. *Daily Texan* (UT-Austin), Mar. 31, 1937; JRP to Rex Harlow, May 25, 1937, JRP Papers; JRP to Waggener, May 8, 1937, ibid.; JRP interview.

26. *Daily Texan* (UT-Austin), May 11, 12, 1937; William A. Owens and Lyman Grant (eds.), *Letters of Roy Bedichek* (Austin: University of Texas Press, 1985), 159; JRP interview; JRP to Harry Cross, May 18, 1937, JRP Papers.

27. The distinguished professorship paid $6,500 a year, $1000 more than the highest paid full professors. Funding was provided for fourteen distinguished professors, ten at Austin and four at Galveston. JRP to A. C. Krey, May 26, 1937, JRP Papers; JRP to Rex Harlow, May 25, 1937, ibid.; Report of Legislative Committee on University Appropriation, May 31, 1937, ibid.; Wild to JRP, May 26, 1937, ibid.; Randall to JRP, May 20, 1937, ibid.; *Daily Texan* (UT-Austin), May 23, June 9, 1937.

28. JRP interview; Houston *Post*, Jan. 23, 1938.

29. Dallas *Morning News*, undated clipping, JRP Papers; George Howard to JRP, May 31, 1937, ibid.; JRP to E. L. Woodley, June 9, 1937, ibid.; JRP to Wythe, July 14, 1937, ibid.; JRP interview.

30. *Daily Texan* (UT-Austin), June 1, 1937; JRP interview.

31. The faculty search committee also included Eugene C. Barker, Alton Burdine, Charles Ramsdell, and B. F. Pittenger. Robert L. Holliday to JRP, Aug. 31, 1937, JRP Papers; JRP interview.

32. JRP interview; JRP to Holliday, Aug. 9, 1937, JRP Papers; JRP to Aynesworth, June 16, 1937, ibid.

33. JRP to Randall, July 3, 1937, JRP Papers; JRP to C. B. Smith, Oct. 4, 1978, ibid.; JRP to Harry Cross, May 18, 1937, ibid.; Alice Carol Cox, "The Rainey Affair: A History of the Academic Freedom Controversy at the University of Texas, 1938–1946" (Ph.D. diss., University of Denver, 1970), 13; JRP interview.

34. JRP interview; *Daily Texan* (UT-Austin), Sept. 26, 28, Oct. 15, 20, 1937.

35. JRP interview; JRP, "The University of Texas Controversy," p. 5, JRP Papers.

36. Cox, "The Rainey Affair," 14; "Homer P. Rainey," biographical files (CAH); Rainey interview, oral history transcript (UNT).

37. Parten's colleagues were not familiar with Webb's book, so Leo Haynes, board of regents secretary who was traveling with the search committee, purchased each member of the committee a copy of *Divided We Stand* after they arrived in New York. JRP interview. For more on the general influence of Webb's book, see Walter Rundell, "A Historian and Federal Policy: W. P. Webb as a Case Study," *Prologue*, 15 (Winter, 1983), 215–228; Walter P. Webb, *Divided We Stand* (New York: Farrar and Rinehart, 1937); Tindall, *The Emergence of the New South*, 596, 597.

38. JRP interview; Luther H. Gulick, *Papers on the Science of Administration* (New York: Institute of Public Administration, Columbia University, 1937).

39. More on Hutchins's life and educational philosophy can be found in Harry S. Ashmore, *Unseasonable Truths: The Life of Robert Maynard Hutchins* (Boston: Little, Brown, 1989).

40. JRP to Herman James, Mar. 11, 1938, JRP Papers; JRP interview.

41. Hutchins to Randall, May 20, 1937; Randall to JRP, Mar. 21, 1938, JRP Papers; Ashmore, *Unseasonable Truths*, 108, 165; Norman Cousins, "A Giant in the Land," *Saturday Review* (June 11, 1977), 4; Hutchins interview, oral history transcript (Ford Foundation, New York City); Kelly interview; JRP interview.

42. Randall to JRP, Mar. 11, 1938, JRP Papers; JRP to Randall, Mar. 12, 1938, ibid.

43. Gulick to Randall, Mar. 17, 1938, JRP Papers; Rainey to Randall, Mar. 30, 1938, ibid.

44. JRP, "Our Changing University," typescript of Apr. 27, 1938, speech, JRP Papers ; JRP to John A. McCurdy, May 2, 1938, ibid.

45. JRP interview; JRP to Calhoun, Aug. 19, 1938, Records of Office of the President.

46. Randall to JRP, Apr. 6, 1938, JRP Papers; JRP to Randall, Apr. 8, 1938, ibid.

47. T. Whitfield Davidson to JRP, June 30, 1937, JRP Papers; JRP interview; Houston *Post*, Apr. 10, 1938.

48. Aynesworth to JRP, Apr. 18, 1938, JRP Papers; JRP to Aynesworth, Apr. 20, 1938, ibid.; Parlin to Randall, Apr. 29, 1938, ibid.

49. JRP interview; JRP to Lucy Myers, Dec. 23, 1939, JRP Papers; JRP to McNutt, May 2, 1938, ibid.; McNutt to JRP, July 23, 1938, ibid.; Waggener to JRP, Aug. 5, 1938, ibid.

50. JRP to Weinert, May 25, 1938, JRP Papers; JRP to Randall, Apr. 20, 1938, ibid.; JRP interview (with A. Champagne).

51. Coffman to JRP, May 2, 1938, JRP Papers; JRP to Fairchild, May 10, 1938, ibid.; JRP to Randall, May 24, 1938, ibid.

52. Pauley interview, oral history transcript (LBJ); JRP to John Calhoun, June 3, 1938, JRP Papers; Randall to JRP, June 4, 1938, ibid.; Waggener to JRP, June 8, 11, 1938, ibid.

Chapter Thirteen

1. Allred was sixteen thousand dollars in debt when he left the governor's office. Allred interview, oral history transcript (UNT); JRP interview; Martindale, "James V. Allred," 95.

2. JRP interview; Seth S. McKay, *W. Lee O'Daniel and Texas Politics, 1938–1942* (Lubbock: Texas Technological College Research Funds, 1944), 24; JRP to Ed Bullard, July 10, 1938, JRP Papers.

3. JRP interview; Yergin, *The Prize*, 259.

4. Dan Moody to Pink L. Parrish, June 15, 1938, "Politics, 1938" folder, Moody Papers.

5. JRP interview; Allred, "On O'Daniel in 1938," typescript statement, n.d., JRP Papers; McKay, *W. Lee O'Daniel*, 32; Green, *The Establishment in Texas Politics*, 23.

6. Dan Moody to Pink L. Parrish, June 15, 1938, "Politics, 1938" folder, Moody Papers; McKay, *W. Lee O'Daniel*, 38; McKay, *The Establishment in Texas Politics*, 312, 313; JRP interview.

7. JRP interview; John B. Connally, *In History's Shadow: An American Odyssey* (New York: Hyperion, 1992) 55, 56.

8. JRP interview.

9. Ibid.

10. JRP interview; Clark, *Three Stars for the Colonel*, 153.

11. JRP interview; Clark, *Three Stars for the Colonel*, 153, 155; anti-McCraw poster in JRP Papers.

12. JRP interview; Sam Fore to Thompson, July 10, 1938, box 4Ze136, Thompson Papers; Arthur J. Drossaerts to R. J. Boyle, July 14, 1938, ibid.

13. Thompson to JRP, July 23, 1938, JRP Papers; JRP interview.

14. For an excellent description of O'Daniel's campaign, see Caro, *The Path to Power*, 695–703; McKay, *W. Lee O'Daniel*, 315, 316.

15. Eastus to Farley, June 29, 1938, file 300, Texas, FDR Papers; Dan Moody to Pink L. Parrish, July 8, 1938, "Politics, 1938" folder, Moody Papers; Dan Moody to Robert L. Holliday, July 13, 1938, ibid.; Allred, "On O'Daniel in 1938," JRP Papers.

16. JRP interview.

17. Ibid.; Allred, "On O'Daniel in 1938," JRP Papers; Robb K. Burlage, "James V. Allred," unpublished typescript, p. 141, JRP Papers.

18. Green, *The Establishment in Texas Politics*, 25; McKay, *W. Lee O'Daniel*, 46; JRP to Edgar Wakefield, July 29, 1938, JRP Papers; Randall to Calhoun, July 26, 1938, VF-4, Records of Office of the President; JRP to Calhoun, July 30, 1938, ibid.

19. Gulick to JRP, July 21, 1938, JRP Papers; Aynesworth to JRP, July 28, 1938, ibid.; Randall to JRP, Aug. 1, 1938, ibid.; JRP to Holman, July 26, 1938, ibid.; Randall to Waggener, Aug. 8, 1938, ibid.; JRP to Gulick, Aug. 13, 1938, ibid.

20. JRP interview.

21. Ibid.; Mart H. Royston to Mrs. I. D. Fairchild, July 14, 1939, JRP Papers.

22. JRP interview; Aynesworth to JRP, Jan. 11, Mar. 5, 7, 9, 1938, JRP Papers; JRP to Randall, Mar. 9, 1938, ibid.

23. JRP interview; JRP to Randall, June 2, 1938, JRP Papers; Spies to Randall, July 21, 1938, ibid.; Randall to JRP, July 27, 1938, ibid.; Aynesworth to Randall, July 27, 1938, ibid.; New York *Times*, Feb. 28, 1960.

24. Tom Spies to Randall, Aug. 4, 1938, JRP Papers.

25. "John W. Spies," biographical files (CAH); Tom Spies to JRP, Sept. 1, 1938, JRP Papers; Randall to JRP, Aug. 17, 18, 30, 1938, ibid.

26. JRP interview; JRP to Randall, Oct. 31, 1938, JRP Papers.

27. JRP interview.

28. Ibid.; JRP to Randall, Oct. 31, 1938, JRP Papers; Aynesworth to JRP, Nov. 1, 1938, ibid.; Calhoun to JRP, Nov. 8, 1938, ibid.

29. JRP interview; JRP to Holman, Nov. 17, 1938, JRP Papers.

30. *Daily Texan* (UT-Austin), Nov. 11, 1938; JRP to Randall, Nov. 11, 1938, JRP Papers; JRP to Weinert, Nov. 15,

1938, ibid.; JRP to Aynesworth, Nov. 16, 1938, ibid.; Gulick to Randall, Dec. 2, 1938, ibid.; JRP to Gulick, Dec. 15, 1938, ibid.; JRP interview.

31. Cox, "The Rainey Affair," 13, 14; JRP interview; Randall to JRP, May 2, 1939, JRP Papers; JRP to George Reynolds, Jan. 5, 1939, ibid.

31. JRP interview.

Chapter Fourteen

1. Aynesworth to JRP, Dec. 21, 1938, JRP Papers; Waggener to JRP, Dec. 24, 1938, ibid.

2. Cox, "The Rainey Affair," 14; Rainey interview, oral history transcript (UNT); Rainey to JRP, Jan. 2, 1939, JRP Papers; Randall to JRP, Mar. 31, 1939, ibid.; *Daily Texan* (UT-Austin), Feb. 5, 1939; Houston *Chronicle*, Feb. 8, 1939; Rainey, *The Tower and the Dome*, 19; JRP interview.

3. For Graham's record at the University of North Carolina, see John Egerton, *Speak Now Against the Day: The Generation Before the Civil Rights Movement in the South* (New York: Knopf, 1994), 130–134; Rainey interview, oral history transcript (UNT); JRP interview.

4. *Daily Texan* (UT-Austin), Feb. 8, 1939. Disappointed by the lack of enthusiasm in the legislature for the Latin American Studies program, the board of regents eventually voted in April 1939 to proceed with its creation whether or not legislative funding was available. *Daily Texan* (UT-Austin), Apr. 23, 1939; JRP interview.

5. Rainey interview, oral history transcript (UNT); JRP interview; George Morgan to JRP, May 18, 1939, JRP Papers.

6. Houston *Chronicle*, Jan. 2, 1939; JRP to Rainey, Jan. 11, 1939, JRP Papers; Dallas *News*, n.d., clipping in JRP Papers; *Daily Texan* (UT-Austin), Feb. 7, 1939.

7. JRP to Edward Randall, Jan. 30, 1939, JRP Papers; JRP to E. H. Thornton and Morris Roberts, May 13, 1939, ibid.; Waggener to JRP, May 17, 1939, ibid.; JRP interview; Houston *Chronicle*, Feb. 8, 1939; *Daily Texan* (UT-Austin), Feb. 8, 1939.

8. Wild to JRP, Feb. 14, 1939, JRP Papers; JRP to J. M. Heflin, May 24, 1939, ibid.; *Daily Texan* (UT-Austin), Feb. 22, 1939; JRP interview.

9. JRP interview; Dallas *Morning News*, Mar. 3, 1939; *Daily Texan* (UT-Austin), Mar. 3, 1939.

10. JRP interview; *Daily Texan* (UT-Austin), May 31, 1939.

11. For more about the origins of the McDonald Observatory, see David S. Evans and J. Derral Mulholland, *Big and Bright: A History of McDonald Observatory* (Austin: University of Texas Press, 1986); JRP interview.

12. *Daily Texan* (UT-Austin), May 4, 1939; JRP interview.

13. JRP interview; Richard Rhodes, *The Making of the Atomic Bomb* (New York: Simon and Schuster, 1986), 363, 364; Evans and Mulholland, *Big and Bright*, 80, 83.

14. JRP to Robert Lee Bobbitt, May 8, 1939, JRP Papers; JRP interview.

15. JRP interview; Rainey to JRP, Mar. 17, 1939, JRP Papers.

16. JRP interview; JRP to Rainey, May 9, 1939, JRP Papers.

17. *Daily Texan* (UT-Austin), Feb. 23, June 22, 1939; JRP to J. M. Heflin, May 24, 1939, JRP Papers; JRP interview; Wolfe, *The Murchisons*, 148, 149.

18. JRP interview; Dallas *Morning News*, June 3, 1939.

19. A. O. Singleton (1882–1947) was a nationally known surgeon who pioneered a number of widely used surgical techniques. *The University of Texas Medical Branch at Galveston: A Seventy-Five Year History by the Faculty and Staff* (Austin: University of Texas Press, 1967), 147, 148, 163; JRP interview; Aynesworth to JRP, Apr. 1, 1940, JRP Papers; Spies to Singleton, Jan. 19, 1940, ibid.; *Daily Texan* (UT-Austin), July 20, 1941; Galveston *News*, Feb. 21, 1942.

20. Randall to JRP, June 2, 1939, JRP Papers; JRP interview.

21. Randall to JRP, June 2, 1939, JRP Papers; JRP to Randall, June 3, 1939, ibid.; Randall to JRP, June 21, 1939, ibid.; Aynesworth to Randall, July 18, 1939, ibid.; Spies, typescript, "Memorandum Regarding the Meeting of the Executive Committee, Medical Branch," July 21, 1939, ibid.; JRP interview.

22. JRP interview; Spies, "Memorandum Regarding the . . . Medical Branch," July 21, 1939, JRP Papers; Galveston *Daily News*, Feb. 23, 1942.

23. JRP interview; Rhodes, *The Making of the Atomic Bomb*, 143, 144.

24. Rainey to Lawrence, Sept. 15, 1939, carton 17, Lawrence Papers (Bancroft Library, University of California at Berkeley); Lawrence to Robert G. Sproul, Sept.18, 1939, ibid.; JRP interview.

25. Joel H. Hildebrand to Sproul, Sept. 16, 1939, carton 17, Lawrence Papers; Lawrence to Rainey, Sept. 19, 1939, ibid.; Lawrence to Sproul, Sept. 18, 1939, ibid.; Sproul to Lawrence, Sept. 21, 1939, ibid.

26. Rainey to JRP, Oct. 6, 1939, JRP Papers; JRP to Rainey, Oct. 10, 1939, ibid.; JRP to Waggener, Oct.13, 1939, ibid.; Lawrence to Thelma Lockwood, Oct. 13, 1939, carton 17, Lawrence Papers; *Daily Texan* (UT-Austin), Nov. 26, 1939; JRP interview.

27. Moody to Holliday, Jan. 18, 1937, "Politics, 1937" folder, Moody Papers; Lawrence to Rainey, Oct. 29, 1939, carton 17, Lawrence Papers; Rainey, *The Tower and the Dome*, 26; JRP interview.

28. JRP interview; Los Angeles *Times*, Nov. 24, 1939.

29. Rainey to Hines Baker, Jan. 2, 1940, VF B-1, Records of the Office of President; JRP interview.

30. Rhodes, *The Making of the Atomic Bomb*, 360; Rainey to Lawrence, Apr. 8, 1940, carton 17, Lawrence Papers; Rainey, *The Tower and the Dome*, 26; JRP interview.

31. Rhodes, *The Making of the Atomic Bomb*, 270; JRP interview.

32. JRP interview; JRP to Aynesworth, Aug. 1, 1939, JRP Papers.

33. JRP to Rainey, Aug. 1, 1939, JRP Papers; JRP to Randall, Aug. 3, 1939, ibid.; JRP interview.

34. Spies was accused of causing the suicides of Dr. W. T. Dawson and Dr. Harry. O. Knight. Dawson, widely understood to have suffered from depression for many years, died in his laboratory after ingesting a large amount of nicotine. Knight ended his life when he concluded that he had developed Parkinson's disease. *The University of Texas Medical Branch at Galveston*, 119, 154. JRP to Fairchild, Oct. 12, 1939, JRP Papers; typescript, "Galveston Meeting, Summary of Testimony," Oct. 7–9, 1939, ibid.; *Daily Texan* (UT-Austin), July 20, 1941.

35. Aynesworth to JRP, Oct. 13, 1939, JRP Papers; Waggener to JRP, Oct. 16, 1939, ibid.; JRP to Fairchild, Oct. 12, 1939, ibid.; JRP to Spies, Oct. 24, 1939, ibid.

36. JRP interview; JRP to Fairchild, Oct. 23, 1939, JRP Papers.

37. Aynesworth to JRP, Oct. 28, 1939, JRP Papers; JRP to Singleton, Nov. 28, 1939, ibid.; Aynesworth to JRP, Nov. 29, 1939, ibid.; Singleton to JRP, Dec. 1, 1939, Feb. 5, 1940, ibid.; JRP to Stark, Nov. 23, 1939, ibid.; JRP interview.

38. JRP, typescript of speech, Dec. 9, 1939, JRP Papers; Rainey to JRP, Mar.17, 1939, ibid.; Austin *Statesman*, Dec. 9, 1939; Dallas *Morning News*, Dec. 10, 1939.

39. Rainey to JRP, Mar. 17, 1939, JRP Papers; Dallas *Morning News*, Dec. 8, 1939; *Daily Texan* (UT-Austin), Dec. 8, 1939; JRP interview.

40. Rainey's inaugural address was subsequently published by the University of Texas under the title *The State and Public Education*. Rainey interview, oral history transcript (UNT); Austin *American-Statesman*, Dec. 12, 1971; Dallas *Morning News*, Dec. 10, 1939.

41. Dallas *Morning News*, Dec. 10, 1939; JRP to Rainey, Dec. 11, 1939, drawer 4/E, Records of Office of the President; Rainey, *The Tower and the Dome*, 21; Dugger, *Our Invaded Universities*, 37.

Chapter Fifteen

1. For a detailed analysis and discussion of the Texas corporate-political establishment during the late 1930s and 1940s, see Green, *The Establishment in Texas Politics*.

2. JRP to Aynesworth, Jan. 2, 3, 1940; UT Board of Regents Meeting No. 393, Jan. 13, 1940, Board of Regents Minutes; Cox, "The Rainey Affair," 20; JRP interview.

3. Houston *Chronicle*, Jan. 29, 1940; Randall to JRP, Feb. 3, 1940, JRP Papers.

4. "Edward Randall," biographical files (CAH); Randall to D. B. Hardeman, Apr. 9, 1935, Hardeman Papers (LBJ); Thornton to JRP, Jan. 6, 1940, clipping from the Clifton *Record*, Dec. 22, 1939, JRP Papers; JRP to Thornton, Jan. 9, 1940, ibid.; JRP interview.

5. R. A. Weinert to Rainey, Oct. 5, 1939, JRP Papers; Hilmer Weinert to JRP, n.d., ibid.; JRP to R. A. Weinert, Oct. 12, 1939, ibid.; Rainey, *The Tower and the Dome*, 41; JRP interview.

6. Green, *The Establishment in Texas Politics*, 83; Spies to JRP, Feb. 5, 1940, JRP Papers; *Daily Texan* (UT-Austin), Feb. 1, 1940; Weinert to O'Daniel, Jan. 25, 1940, box 230, W. Lee O'Daniel Papers (Texas State Library, Archives Division, Austin); JRP interview.

7. Randall to JRP, Feb. 3, 12, 1940, JRP Papers; JRP to Stark, Mar. 2, 1940, ibid.; JRP interview.

8. JRP to Stark, Mar. 2, 1940, JRP Papers; Aynesworth to JRP, Mar. 6, 1940, ibid.

9. Rainey to Randall, Mar. 7, 1940, JRP Papers; Randall to Rainey, Mar. 8, 1940, ibid.; JRP interview.

10. Aynesworth to JRP, Mar. 12, 1940, JRP Papers; JRP interview.

11. JRP interview; JRP to Aynesworth, Mar. 15, 1940, JRP Papers; Aynesworth to Spies, Mar. 23, 1940, ibid.

12. Carney to Board of Regents, May 27, 1940, Records of Office of the President; Cox, "The Rainey Affair," 24 (Rainey quote); JRP interview; Randall to JRP, Mar. 29, 1940, JRP Papers; JRP to Randall, Apr. 2, 1940, ibid.

13. JRP to Mart Royston, Apr. 1, 1940, JRP Papers; Spies to JRP, Apr. 16, 1940, ibid; Aynesworth to JRP, May 16, 1940, ibid.; JRP to Aynesworth, May 17, 1940, ibid.; JRP interview.

14. Moore to O'Daniel, Jan. 29, 1940, box 220, O'Daniel Papers; JRP interview.

15. JRP interview.

16. Ibid.; Rainey, *The Tower and the Dome*, 42.

17. UT Board of Regents Meeting No. 401, May 31, 1940, Board of Regents Minutes; JRP, "The University Controversy," p. 6, JRP Papers; Rainey, *The Tower and the Dome*, 42.

18. *Daily Texan* (UT-Austin), June 16, 1940.

19. Other than vote for the president and make a modest financial contribution, Parten played no role whatsoever in the 1940 Roosevelt campaign in Texas. His personal involvement in politics, which had been minimal

that year for the reasons discussed, continued to be restricted to state contests. JRP interview; Thompson to JRP, July 1, 1940, JRP Papers.

20. Carl L. Phinney to Homer Rainey, June 21, 1940, "Texan-Goodman" folder, VF5D, Records of Office of the President; Green, *The Establishment in Texas Politics*, 73; John Henry Faulk interview; for the CPSU in Texas during this period, see Carleton, *Red Scare!*, 26–63.

21. Houston *Press*, June 20, 1940; Goodman to Rainey, June 19, 1940; Mrs. Cummings to Rainey, June 21, 1940; "Texan-Goodman" folder, VF5D, Records of Office of the President.

22. JRP to Thompson, July 9, 1940, JRP Papers; JRP to Phinney, June 21, 1940, ibid.; *Daily Texan* (UT-Austin), June 23, 1940; Rainey to Goodman, June 21, 1940, "Texan-Goodman" folder, VF5D, Records of Office of the President.

23. Boyd Sinclair served with distinction in the Twelfth Air Service Group in the China-Burma Theater. He also served as the director of selective service for Texas in the postwar period. He died in 1990. Austin *American-Statesman*, Apr. 9, 1990; Thompson to JRP, July 1, 1940, JRP Papers; JRP to Thompson, July 8, 9, 1940, ibid.; Green, *The Establishment in Texas Politics*, 29; "Ernest Othmer Thompson," *Handbook of Texas*, ed. Webb, Carroll, and Branda, III, 1004.

24. Parten had asked Karl B. Calloway, an attorney in Dallas who had connections with the Federal Bureau of Investigation, to make a confidential request to the FBI "to determine whether there is a . . . group . . . at the University of Texas acting in an un-American manner subversive to the best interests of the United States." Calloway relayed this information to his partner Rollo E. Kidwell who happened to be in Washington on business. Kidwell went to the FBI, where he was interviewed by agent K. R. McIntire on June 20. Kidwell asked the FBI not to do anything more until he had had a chance to discuss the matter with Parten. Although the FBI assured Kidwell that they would do nothing else, Dallas congressman Hatton Sumners, under pressure from local American Legion leaders and officers of the Texas National Guard, subsequently contacted FBI director J. Edgar Hoover to demand an FBI investigation of the situation at the University of Texas. The congressman's request was followed by a highly publicized demand by Texas state representative J. H. Goodman for an FBI investigation. It is not known if Hoover followed through with an investigation, but the Bureau certainly knew that there was a tiny band of students at the university who were members of the Texas Communist Party. The party had a public office in Houston and operated openly in the state throughout the 1930s and 1940s, holding conventions and running candidates for office, as it had every legal right to do. Subsequent events indicate that the FBI, motivated by Parten's inquiry and under pressure from Sumners, Goodman, and others, may have leaked information about students at the University to Texas to the Dies Committee. K. R. McIntire to H. H. Clegg, June 21, 1940, "J. R. Parten FBI file," JRP Papers; JRP interview; Athan Theoharis and John Stuart Cox, *The Boss: J. Edgar Hoover and the Great American Inquisition* (Philadelphia: Temple University Press, 1988), 155, 156.

25. The committee investigator was Robert Stripling. JRP interview; Houston *Post*, July 31, 1940; Dallas *News*, Aug. 3, 1940; JRP to Dies, July 31, 1940, JRP Papers.

26. JRP interview; Dallas *Morning News*, Aug. 14, 1940; Houston *Post*, Aug. 14, 1940; Dies to JRP, Aug. 13, Dec. 13, 1940, JRP Papers; JRP to Dies, Oct. 2, Dec. 3, 1940, ibid.; Fowler to JRP, Oct. 7, 1940, ibid.; JRP to Fowler, Oct. 28, 1940, ibid.; Green, *The Establishment in Texas Politics*, 72, 73.

27. Winfree repeated these charges a few days later at a Jackson Day dinner in Houston. Some members of the legislature were appalled by Winfree's grandstanding. For example, G. C. Morris of Greenville openly dissented, arguing that Sinclair had a right to write or say anything he pleased. Houston *Chronicle*, Mar. 27, 1941; Dallas *News*, Mar. 28, 1941; Houston *Post*, Mar. 28, 1941; Ed Syers to Lyndon B. Johnson, Mar. 31, 1941, LBJA, LBJ Papers (LBJ).

28. JRP interview; Ed Syers to Lyndon B. Johnson, Mar. 31, 1941, LBJA, LBJ Papers; *Daily Texan* (UT-Austin), Apr. 3, 1941.

29. Houston *Press*, Apr. 8, 1941; Green, *The Establishment in Texas Politics*, 73; JRP to Waggener, Apr. 10, 1941, JRP Papers; Waggener to JRP, Apr. 15, 1941, ibid.

30. This account of Thornton's visit to Parten is from the latter's testimony at a state Senate committee hearing in 1944, which was later published as "The University of Texas Controversy." Much additional information was provided by Parten during several conversations with the author. See also Green, *The Establishment in Texas Politics*, 83, 84. Thornton later denied that he visited Parten or that he had any knowledge of the alleged meeting between O'Daniel and his supporters in Houston. Thornton to JRP, Nov. 20, 1944, JRP Papers. For more on this incident, see chapter 20.

31. For Weinert's relations with O'Daniel, see footnote 14; JRP, "The University of Texas Controversy," p. 6, JRP Papers; JRP interview; Green, *The Establishment in Texas Politics*, 84.

32. Of the ten surviving children, only Lucy, living half the world away in the Philippines, was unable to be present. Lucy had made the Philippines her permanent home after she retired as a U.S. Army nurse and married J. L. Myers, a retired U.S. Army officer. When J. R. sent a letter to Lucy in July to report on their father's condition, he expressed his deep concern about her safety if war broke out in the Pacific. "With this world situation

what it is," J. R. wrote, "I hope that you both are thinking in terms of getting back to the States to live before long." JRP to Lucy Myers, July 12, 1940, JRP Papers; Madisonville *Meteor*, Nov. 21, 1940; JRP interview.

33. At Parten's suggestion, the board of regents asked for an opinion from Texas attorney general Gerald Mann on whether the university could cancel its contract with the City of Galveston and assume sole control of the hospital. Mann subsequently ruled on January 5, 1941, that the university could indeed cancel its contract with the city. *The University of Texas Medical Branch at Galveston*, 163; Galveston *News*, Jan. 6, 1941; JRP to Tom Spies, Sept. 30, 1940, JRP Papers.

34. "The people whom [O'Daniel] listened to while governor," former Texas governor Price Daniel declared in an oral history interview, "were the big corporation presidents and leaders in industry of the state. . . . All of his close advisors were . . . from big business in some way or another. And so he got the votes by appealing to the people and criticizing the big interests, but after having gotten elected, the big interests were the ones that he listened to." Daniel interview, oral history transcript (UNT); Green, *The Establishment in Texas Politics*, 83, 84; Carleton, *Who Shot the Bear?*, 12, 13, 20; Haley interview; JRP interview.

35. Haley was rejected for strictly partisan reasons, McKay, *W. Lee O'Daniel*, 359, 360, 370; JRP interview.

36. "I got Harrison and Bullington some votes," Parten recalled, "but I didn't have any luck with old Clay Cotton. He looked at me and said, 'now, look here, J. R., I'd do most anything for you. But I just can't stoop to vote for those renegades.' And he didn't." JRP interview; JRP, "The University of Texas Controversy," p. 6, JRP Papers; JRP to Branson, Jan. 29, 1941, ibid.; Sam Hall, "Inside Texas," *Texas Spectator* (Jan. 25, 1946), 5; McKay, *W. Lee O'Daniel*, 361.

37. Houston *Chronicle*, Jan. 15, 1941; *Daily Texan* (UT-Austin), Jan. 21, 1941.

38. For an example of a typical letter praising Parten's performance as a regent, see Hines Baker to JRP, Jan. 20, 1941, JRP Papers; Holman to JRP, Jan. 31, 1941, ibid.; Calhoun to JRP, Feb. 8, 1941, ibid.; Singleton to JRP, Jan. 24, 1941, ibid.

39. Many years after Parten's service on the board had been completed, Walter Hall wrote Parten that Ed Clark, the powerful lobbyist and ex-University of Texas regent had declared at a dinner party that in his judgement J. R. Parten had done more for the university than had any other chairman of the board of regents since Jimmy Allred's term as governor. Hall, a banker and liberal political activist agreed, telling Parten that "the contributions you made to the University will certainly stand high on the list of things in which you can take pride." Hall to JRP, Aug. 2, 1985, JRP Papers; JRP interview.

40. John Henry Faulk, "Tributes for Two Good Men," *Texas Observer* (Dec. 27, 1974), 8.

41. JRP interview; Woodley Petroleum Company, Nineteenth Annual Report (1941), no pagination, copy in JRP Papers.

42. The formal agreement between the university and the foundation was eventually reached in August, 1942. JRP interview; Rainey to W. B. Bates, Aug. 15, 1942, VF9/D, Records of the Office of President; R. W. Cumley and Joan McCay (comps. and eds.), *The First Twenty Years of the University of Texas, M. D. Anderson Hospital and Tumor Institute* (Houston: Dept. of Publications, M. D. Anderson Hospital, 1964), 16, 17, 19.

43. JRP interview.

44. Dr. Pat I. Nixon, an ultra-conservative physician in San Antonio urged Bullington to fire Spies. "There are many people in Texas who are very sympathetic with you in the Spies case," Nixon argued, "as to Dr. Spies . . . he is a trouble maker of the first order and . . . he will continue to be as long as he remains in Galveston." Pat I. Nixon to Bullington, July 25, 1941, Haley Papers (Haley Library, Midland); Bullington to J. I. Kilpatrick, Mar. 26, 1942, ibid.; Aynesworth to Bullington, July 14, 19, 1941, ibid.; Harrison to Bullington, July, 1941, ibid.

45. Houston *Post*, July 23, 1941; Dallas *News*, July 23, 1941; Houston *Chronicle*, July 17, 1941; Rainey, *The Tower and the Dome*, 51; *The University of Texas Medical Branch at Galveston*, 164; JRP to Aynesworth, Aug. 1, Oct. 15, 1941, JRP Papers.

46. JRP interview; Jack Love to JRP, Feb. 21, 1942, JRP Papers; *Daily Texan* (UT-Austin), Feb. 22, 1942; Galveston *News*, Feb. 22, 1942; George Hermann to Orville Bullington, Feb. 23, 1942, Haley Papers (Haley Library, Midland).

47. Rainey believed that Spies would not have been removed if Parten had been reappointed to the board of regents. "Parten had made a careful study of the unhappy Medical School situation in Galveston," Rainey declared in his memoirs, "and we were well on the way to a sound solution of that problem when he was not reappointed to the Board." Rainey, *The Tower and the Dome*, 86, 87; *Daily Texan* (UT-Austin), Feb. 27, May 11, June 7, 1942; *The University of Texas Medical Branch at Galveston*, 167, 168.

48. Spies was eventually appointed head of the Cancer Control Division of the State of Delaware. He retired as a physician in the 1960s and died in Austin in July 1971. Austin *American-Statesman*, Feb. 9, 1949, July 26, 1971; JRP interview.

Chapter Sixteen

1. Stoff, *Oil, War, and American Security*, 17; Harold Williamson, Ralph Andreano, et al., *The American Petroleum Industry*: Volume 2, *The Age of Energy, 1899–1959* (2 vols.; Evanston, Ill.: Northwestern University

Press, 1963), 753; Nash, *United States Oil Policy*, 158, 159–160; Yergin, *The Prize*, 372; Harold L. Ickes, *Fightin' Oil* (New York: Knopf, l943); JRP interview; "Conference with Representatives of the Oil Industry," June 19, 1941, transcript of Ickes speech, Ralph K. Davies Papers (Harry S. Truman Library, Independence, Missouri; cited hereafter as Truman Library).

2. Ickes, *Fightin' Oil*, 71, 74; "Conference with Representatives of the Petroleum Industry," June 19, 1941; Davies Papers; Watkins, *Righteous Pilgrim*, 704; JRP interview.

3. Bert Cochran, *Harry Truman and the Crisis Presidency* (New York: Funk & Wagnalls, 1973), 8, 9, 11, 12; John W. Frey and H. Chandler Ide, *A History of the Petroleum Administration for War, 1941–1945* (Washington, D.C.: Government Printing Office, 1946), 65; Engler, *The Politics of Oil*, 281.

4. Marshall, *Done in Oil*, 113–116; Stoff, *Oil, War, and American Security*, 17; Engler, *The Politics of Oil*, 277, 285–287; Nash, *United States Oil Policy*, 160; Beaton, *Enterprise in Oil*, 556, 557; JRP interview.

5. Engler, *The Politics of Oil*, 280; Stoff, *Oil, War, and American Security*, 22; Watkins, *Righteous Pilgrim*, 704; Beaton, *Enterprise in Oil*, 558; Marshall, *Done in Oil*, 120; Ickes to JRP, July 12, 1941, JRP Papers; JRP to Ickes, July 14, 1941, ibid.

6. Yergin, *The Prize*, 754; JRP interview; Marshall interview.

7. Frey and Ide, *A History of the Petroleum Administration for War*, 19, 20, 380–382; Yergin, *The Prize*, 373; JRP interview; JRP to Aynesworth, Oct. 15, 1941, JRP Papers.

8. Stoff, *Oil, War, and American Security*, 20–21; JRP interview; Marshall interview.

9. Parten's sister Lucy and her husband remained in the Phillipines despite the increasing threat of war. Before the Japanese conquest of the Phillipines, the Myers had evacuated women and children from Hong Kong on their large sailboat and had received a medal from the British government for heroism. When the Japanese invaded the Phillipines two weeks later, J. R. was cut off from any news of his sister's fate for nearly three years. In June 1944, he received a Red Cross telegram from Lucy's husband informing him of Lucy's death at the age of 56 from cancer while a prisoner of the Japanese. J. R. then learned for the first time that the Japanese had imprisoned his sister and brother-in-law with other Americans in Camp Santo Tomas near Manila. JRP interview; J. L. Myers to JRP, June 27, 1944, JRP Papers.

10. JRP interview, oral history transcript (LBJ); Dugger, *The Politician: The Life and Times of Lyndon Johnson; The Drive for Power, from the Frontier to Master of the Senate* (New York: Norton, 1982), 193; Hardeman and Bacon, *Rayburn*, 273, 274.

11. JRP interview; Yergin, *The Prize*, 375.

12. JRP interview; for the British viewpoint on convoys to Murmansk and the Soviet reaction, see Alexander Werth, *Russia at War, 1941–1945* (New York: Dutton, 1964), 475–477.

13. The importance of oil and the role it played in World War II has been the subject of numerous studies. The best overview, however, is Daniel Yergin's extensive treatment of the topic in *The Prize*; see also New York *Times*, June 1, 1943.

14. Nash, *United States Oil Policy*, 157, 158; Beaton, *Enterprise in Oil*, 555.

15. Ickes diary, pp. 6359, 6360, Ickes Papers.

16. Marshall interview.

17. JRP to Yarborough, Jan. 20, 1945, JRP Papers; JRP interview; Marshall interview.

18. Marshall interview; Clark and Halbouty, *The Last Boom*, 268; JRP interview; Stoff, *Oil, War, and American Security*, 19.

19. Parten and Dayson had built a Premier refinery near the Cotton Valley field that produced intermediate naphtha from gas distillate. In the spring of 1942, he and Dayson were negotiating a nine-million-dollar federal loan from the Defense Plant Corporation and the Defense Supplies Corporation to expand the Cotton Valley refinery to produce hundred-octane aviation gasoline and to make butadiene for synthetic rubber for the military. JRP to C. H. Siedous, Mar. 18, 1942, JRP Papers; JRP to Davies, Mar. 31, 1942, ibid. JRP interview; Sherman interview.

20. JRP interview; JRP to Rainey, Mar. 31, 1942, JRP Papers; Wolf interview.

21. Petroleum Administration for War press release, Apr. 24, 1942, RG 253, PAW Records (National Archives, Washington, D.C.; cited hereafter as PAW Records); JRP interview; Frey and Ide, *A History of the Petroleum Administration for War*, 311; JRP to John D. Ewing, Jan. 14, 1943, JRP Papers.

22. SOCAL is now known as Chevron. Stoff, *Oil, War, and American Security*, 18; San Francisco *Chronicle*, June 10, 1941, scrapbook, box 15, Davies Papers; Wolf interview.

23. JRP interview; Wolf interview.

24. Marshall interview; Ickes diary, p. 6976, Ickes Papers; Wolf interview; Stoff, *Oil, War, and American Security*, 19; Frey and Ide, *A History of the Petroleum Administration for War*, 305; JRP interview.

25. J. H. Marshall to James R. Schlesinger, Mar. 22, 1979, JRP Papers.

26. Engler, *The Politics of Oil*, 288; Luther H. Gulick, *Administrative Reflections from World War II* (Birmingham, Ala.: Univ. of Alabama Press, 1948), 113, 114; Marshall to James R. Schlesinger, Mar. 22, 1979, JRP Papers; Ickes diary, p. 6704, Ickes Papers.

27. Ickes diary, p. 6995, Ickes Papers; JRP interview.

28. Ickes diary, pp. 6442–6443, 6475, Ickes Papers; *Business Week* (Apr. 17, 1943), 57; JRP interview; Frey and Ide, *A History of the Petroleum Administration for War*, 87, 88; JRP to Dayson, Apr. 10, 1942, JRP Papers.

29. Frey and Ide, *A History of the Petroleum Administration for War*, 88, 89; Irwin Lamp, "When Oil's Fleets 'Put Out to Sea'," *Pure Oil News*, 26 (June, 1943), 5; JRP interview; Opal Parten to Lohman, May 8, 1942, JRP Papers; JRP to Pope, June 30, 1942, ibid.

30. JRP interview; Ickes diary, pp. 6514, 6563, Ickes Papers; Marshall interview.

31. Wiess, "Presentation of Distinquished Service Award to J. R. Parten," JRP Papers; Ickes diary, p. 6577, Ickes Papers; JRP interview; JRP testimony, May 22, 1942, in *Hearings Pursuant to S. Res. 241: A Resolution to Investigate Whether the Use of Inland Waterways for the Transportation of Petroleum Products and other Commodities May be Increased,* Senate Subcommittee of the Committee on Commerce, 77th Cong., 2nd Sess. (Washington, D.C.: Government Printing Office, 1942; cited hereafter as Senate *Hearings Pursuant to S. Res. 241*), 92, 93.

32. Frey and Ide, *A History of the Petroleum Administration for War*, 101, 102; Nash, *United States Oil Policy*, 163, 164; Watkins, *Righteous Pilgrim*, 738, 739; Richard Polenberg, *War and Society: The United States, 1941–1945* (Philadelphia: Lippincott, 1972), 8, 11.

33. Hull to JRP, Mar. 19, 1942, JRP Papers; JRP to Hull, Mar. 30, 1942, ibid.; JRP to Davies, Nov. 24, 1943, PAW Records.

34. Arthur M. Johnson, *Petroleum Pipelines and Public Policy, 1906–1959* (Cambridge: Harvard University Press, 1967), 315–318.

35. Polenberg, *War and Society*, 8, 11.

36. Lamp, "When Oil's Fleets 'Put Out to Sea'," 6; Opal Parten to Lohman, May 8, 1942, JRP Papers; JRP interview.

37. Ickes diary, pp. 6577, 6578, Ickes Papers.

38. Johnson, *Petroleum Pipelines and Public Policy*, 342; JRP interview.

39. JRP interview; Williamson, Andreano, et al., *The American Petroleum Industry*, 549, 550, 554, 584.

40. New York *Times*, May 23, 1942; JRP testimony, in House *Petroleum Investigation*, 32–72; JRP testimony, May 22, 1942, in Senate *Hearings Pursuant to S. Res. 241*, 67–101.

41. Marshall interview; Wolf interview; JRP testimony, May 22, 1942, in Senate *Hearings Pursuant to S. Res. 241*, 101; Ickes diary, p. 6893, Ickes Papers; Memorandum, Davies to Ickes, July 11, 1942, PAW Records.

42. New York *Times*, Apr. 2, 1942; JRP testimony, May 21, 1942, in H.R. 6999, *Hearings* of House Committee on Rivers and Harbors (Washington, D.C.: Government Printing Office, 1942; cited hereafter as House *Hearings* on Rivers and Harbors), 215–250; JRP "Statements," box 4189, PAW Records; JRP interview; JRP "Daily Record," Apr. 22, 1942, JRP Papers; Dallas *News*, Mar. 12, 1943; Ickes diary, p. 7546, Ickes Papers.

43. JRP interview; JRP "Daily Record," Apr. 22, 27, June 1, 1942, JRP Papers; Wolfe, *The Murchisons*, 116.

44. Ickes diary, pp. 6642–6644, Ickes Papers; New York *Times*, May 23, June 1, 1942; JRP, "Daily Record," JRP Papers; JRP interview; Frey and Ide, *A History of the Petroleum Administration for War*, 105; Ickes diary, pp. 6695, 6696, 6709, Ickes Papers.

45. The eleven oil companies represented at the meeting were Atlantic Refining, Cities Service, Consolidated, Gulf, Pan American, Shell, Standard of New York (Mobil), Standard of New Jersey (Exxon), Sun, Texas (Texaco), and Tidewater. Frey and Ide, *A History of the Petroleum Administration for War*, 108; JRP interview.

46. JRP to Cullen, June 21, 1942, JRP Papers; Johnson, *Petroleum Pipelines and Public Policy*, 322, 323; JRP interview.

47. The Big Inch gave Bert Hull the status of a living legend among pipeline professionals, but he did not stop with that project. After the war, he became president of Trans-Arabian Pipeline Company. Before his retirement in 1951, Hull built most of the important pipelines in the Middle East, including the 1,040-mile, 31-inch-diameter pipeline (called Tapline) from the Persian Gulf to the Mediterranean coast of Lebanon. Unidentified newspaper clipping, n.d., JRP Papers; Rister, *Oil!*, 358; Yergin, *The Prize*, 426, 427; New York *Times*, Nov. 9, 1958.

48. JRP interview; Ickes diary, p. 6720, Ickes Papers; JRP, Daily Record, June 15, 1942, JRP Papers; Johnson, *Petroleum Pipelines and Public Policy*, 323; OPC press release, July 25, 1942, PAW Records ; Polenberg, *War and Society*, 19; Watkins, *Righteous Pilgrim*, 739; Jesse H. Jones, *Fifty Billion Dollars: My Thirteen Years with the RFC, 1932–1945* (New York: Da Capo Press, 1951), 343, 344.

49. JRP interview; JRP statement to House Appropriations Committee, June 28, 1943, PAW Records.

50. Polenberg, *War and Society*, 19; JRP interview.

51. Johnson, *Petroleum Pipelines and Public Policy*, 318, 320, 322; JRP, "Pipelines and War Demands," 1942, Speech, box 4186, PAW Records.

52. JRP to Davies, Nov. 23, 1943, PAW Records; Frey and Ide, *A History of the Petroleum Administration for War*, 99; JRP testimony, May 20, 1942, in House *Petroleum Investigation*, 32–72; JRP testimony, May 21, 1942, in House *Hearings* on Rivers and Harbors, 215–250; JRP testimony, May 22, 1942, in Senate *Hearings Pursuant to S. Res. 241*, 74.

53. JRP to Dan Rogers, June 21, 1942, JRP Papers; JRP interview.

54. *Hearings*, House Subcommittee of the Committee on Naval Affairs, 78th Cong., 1st Sess. (Washington, D.C.: Government Printing Office, 1942; cited hereafter as House *Hearings* on Naval Affairs), III, 1330, 1331; June 29, 1942, Senate *Hearings Pursuant to S. Res. 241*, 2, 6, 158–162; Hurt, *Texas Rich*, 121, 135; JRP interview.

55. JRP interview; JRP Daily Record, June 30, 1942, JRP Papers; June 29, 1942, Senate *Hearings Pursuant to S. Res. 241*, 208–210.

56. June 29, 1942, Senate *Hearings Pursuant to S. Res. 241*, 69–105, 114, 115; Hurt, *Texas Rich*, 135.

57. New York *Times*, July 9, 1942; House *Hearings* on Naval Affairs, III, 1546, 1547.

58. JRP to Ralph K. Davies, Mar. 31, 1942, JRP Papers; A. Rosen to E. A. Tamm, Oct. 27, 1947, "J. R. Parten," FBI file, ibid.; Belmont to Ladd, Mar. 25, 1953, ibid.; JRP interview.

59. Parten and Dayson struck back at H. L. Hunt in October 1945, when they persuaded Attorney General Tom Clark to file an antitrust suit against Hunt, Magnolia Oil Company, and the other members of the Cotton Valley operators committee (CVOC). Parten and Dayson accused the CVOC of conspiring to cut off the crude-oil supply to Premier's refinery so that the CVOC could take it over. The case was eventually terminated in 1950 when the U.S. Supreme Court refused to reverse a lower court's decision to dismiss the suit because of the Justice Department's refusal to turn over FBI files on the case. A. Rosen to E. A. Tamm, Oct. 27, 1947, in "J. R. Parten," FBI file, JRP Papers; Belmont to Ladd, Mar. 25, 1953, ibid.; JRP to Davies, Sept. 3, 1942, ibid.; JRP interview; Marshall interview; Wolf interview.

60. JRP, "Pipelines and War Demands," box 4186, PAW Records; Frey and Ide, *A History of the Petroleum Administration for War*, 106, 107.

61. Frey and Ide, *A History of the Petroleum Administration for War*, 108; JRP interview.

62. Hull to JRP, Oct. 27, 1942, JRP Papers; New York *Times*, Sept. 21, 1942; JRP interview.

63. JRP interview; Ickes diary, pp. 7029, 7055, 7142, 7143, Ickes Papers.

64. Johnson, *Petroleum Pipelines and Public Policy*, 323; Ickes, *Fightin' Oil*, 32.

65. *Business Week* (Apr. 17, 1943), 57.

Chapter Seventeen

1. JRP interview; Frey and Ide, *A History of the Petroleum Administration for War*, 116, 117.

2. Ickes's speech transcript, May 27, 1942, box 4189, PAW Records; Ickes diary, p. 6760, Ickes Papers; JRP interview; Frey and Ide, *A History of the Petroleum Administration for War*, 123; Ickes, *Fightin' Oil*, 59, 60.

3. JRP to L. R. Cowles, Sept. 28, 1942, box 4187, PAW Records; Boyd Wilson to JRP, Sept. 30, 1942, ibid.; JRP to Davies, Oct. 6, 1942, ibid.; Davies to Brown, Oct. 9, 1942, box 4182, ibid.

4. Ickes diary, pp. 7192–7193, Ickes Papers.

5. JRP interview; Ickes diary, p. 7333, Ickes Papers.

6. In his autobiography, J. Howard Marshall gives Parten credit for the steel-drum innovation, but it was Ickes's idea. Marshall, *Done in Oil*, 124; JRP, "Daily Record," Dec. 30, 1942, JRP Papers; JRP interview.

7. JRP interview; James F. Byrnes, *Speaking Frankly* (New York: Harper, 1947), 17, 18; Polenberg, *War and Society*, 35; Ickes diary, Jan. 2, 1943, Ickes Papers.

8. Ickes diary, Jan. 3, 1943, Ickes Papers; JRP, "Daily Record," Dec. 31, 1942, JRP Papers; JRP interview.

9. Roosevelt issued an executive order on December 2, 1942, establishing the Petroleum Administration for War (PAW) as a formal administrative agency. Ickes's title was changed to Petroleum Administrator for War and he became a member of the WPB. Watkins, *Righteous Pilgrim*, 737, 738; Frey and Ide, *A History of the Petroleum Administration for War*, 375–377; Marshall to Yorty, May, 1943, J. Howard Marshall Papers (CAH); JRP, "Daily Record," Jan. 2, 1943, JRP Papers; Ickes diary, Jan. 2, 1943, Ickes Papers; JRP interview.

10. Frey and Ide, *A History of the Petroleum Administration for War*, 96; JRP interview; PAW press releases, Jan. 13, 14, 1943, box 4184, PAW Records; JRP to John W. McCormack, June 11, 1943, box 4182, ibid.

11. JRP interview; J. H. Thacher Jr. to JRP, Sept. 2, 1943, box 4186, PAW Records; JRP to Bruce K. Brown, Sept. 3, 4, 1943, box 4185, ibid.

12. Ickes diary, pp. 6685–6686, Ickes Papers; Maloney to JRP, Jan. 22, 1943, box 4182, PAW Records; Calvin D. Johnson to JRP, Jan. 23, 1943, ibid.; Walter Lynch to JRP, Feb. 9, 1943, ibid.; JRP to W. Lee O'Daniel, Jan. 5, 7, 1943, ibid.; JRP to Davies, Jan. 9, 1943, ibid.; Legislative Reference Service, War Service Bulletins, Series G: Summaries of Committee Hearings, Senate Special Committee on Oil, Hearing of January 4, 1943 (Library of Congress), copy in Senatorial file, Truman Papers (Truman Library); *Business Week* (Apr. 17, 1943), 57; JRP interview.

13. Frey and Ide, *A History of the Petroleum Administration for War*, 105, 434; JRP to Bruce K. Brown, memo, Jan. 14, 1943, PAW Records; Ickes diary, p. 7425, Ickes Papers.

14. JRP interview.

15. Ibid.

16. Verbatim Record of Proceedings of Senate Committee Investigating National Defense Program, Feb. 17, 1943, pp. 654–655, Senatorial file, Truman Papers; Legislative Reference Service, War Service Bulletins, Series G: Summaries of Committee Hearings, Senate Special Committee on Oil, Hearing of Jan. 4, 1943, ibid.; JRP to

Truman, Feb. 18, 1943, box 4182, PAW Records; Ickes diary, p. 7466, Ickes Papers; Marshall, *Done in Oil*, 131.

17. Ickes diary, p. 7513, Ickes Papers; Verbatim Record of Proceedings of Senate Committee Investigating National Defense Program, Mar. 3, 1943, pp. 663–684, Senatorial file, Truman Papers; JRP interview; C. R. Musgrave to JRP, Mar. 29, 1943, PAW Records; JRP to Musgrave, Apr. 16, 1943, ibid.; H. C. Weiss to Ickes, Feb. 11, 1943, Ickes Papers.

18. Hendricks specifically named the PAW, but Parten was by far the most visible opponent within the PAW. New York *Times*, Mar. 6, May 6, 7, July 6, 1943; JRP to Colegrove, Feb., 24, 1943, box 4182, PAW Records; JRP to Vandenberg, Mar. 1, Apr. 16, 1943, ibid.; JRP to Rep. Lex Green, Apr. 19, 1943, ibid.; JRP to George J. Bates, Mar. 26, 1943, ibid.; JRP "Daily Record," Apr. 15, 1943, JRP Papers; Ickes diary, p. 7546, Ickes Papers; JRP interview.

19. Frey and Ide, *A History of the Petroleum Administration for War*, 122; *Congressional Record*, 78th Cong., 1st Sess., Sen., vol. 89, part 3, pp. 3269, 3270.

20. JRP to McCormack, May 1, 1943, box 4182, PAW Records; JRP to Lodge, July 3, 1943, ibid.; JRP to Curley, June 14, 1943, ibid.; Washington *Post*, June 11, 1943; New York *Times*, June 8, 1943; JRP, "Daily Record," June 7–10, 1943, JRP Papers; JRP interview.

21. JRP, "Daily Record," July 7, 1943, JRP Papers; JRP interview.

22. JRP interview; Marshall interview; Fort Worth *Star-Telegram*, June 8, 1943.

23. JRP to Davies, July 16, 1943, box 4185, PAW Records.

24. JRP interview; JRP to Cumming, Aug. 10, 1943, box 4186, PAW Records.

25. JRP interview; Frey and Ide, *A History of the Petroleum Administrtion for War*, 425, 426.

26. JRP interview.

27. Ibid.

28. Ibid.; JRP to Davies, Aug. 12, 1943, PAW Records; Frey and Ide, *A History of the Petroleum Adminsitration for War*, 108.

29. JRP interview; JRP "Daily Record," Aug. 26, 1943, JRP Papers; JRP to Davies, Sept. 18, 1943, box 4185, PAW Records.

30. At this point in Woodley's development, Parten owned approximately 30 percent of the capital stock of Woodley and 15 percent of the stock of Premier. His financial statement as of January 1, 1940, indicated $386,128 in assets; his actual debt was $42,435. JRP, affidavit submitted to FCC, Oct. 21, 1940, copy in JRP Papers; JRP to Davenport, Feb. 14, 24, 1942, ibid.; JRP to J. R. Pope, Apr. 5, 1942, ibid.; Davenport to JRP, Feb. 5, 1943, ibid.; JRP interview.

31. JRP interview; Funkhouser to JRP, July 14, 1943, JRP Papers; Pope to JRP, Aug. 23, 1943, ibid.

32. JRP interview; JRP to Pope, Aug. 31, Sept. 17, 1943, JRP Papers; Pope to JRP, Sept. 2, 10, 1943, ibid.; van der Sluys to JRP, Sept. 14, 1943, ibid.; Davenport to JRP, Sept. 11, 1943, ibid.; JRP, "Daily Record," Sept. 18, 1943, ibid.; JRP to Cook, Sept. 27, 1943, ibid.; JRP to Moran, Oct. 19, 1944, ibid.

33. JRP interview.

34. Bert Hull was recognized as the outstanding representative of the major companies for 1943. Wiess, "Presentation of Distinguished Service Award to J. R. Parten," Oct. 14, 1943, JRP Papers; Harry Weiss to JRP, Nov. 23, 1943, ibid.; John Suman to J. Edgar Pew, Aug. 30, 1943, Everett Lee DeGolyer Sr. Papers (DeGolyer Library, Southern Methodist University, Dallas); George C. Gibbons to the Distinguished Service Awards Committee, Aug. 24, 1943, ibid.

35. Wilson succeeded Parten as director of transportation on November 26, 1943. JRP interview; JRP to Davies, Oct. 21, 1943, JRP Papers; Davies, "Statement made to the Lea Committee," Oct. 21, 1943, PAW Records.

36. JRP interview; JRP to Davies, Oct. 11, 1943, box 4185, PAW Records; JRP to Davies, Nov. 23, 1943, ibid.

37. JRP to Ickes, Mar. 16, 1944, Ickes Papers; Watkins, *Righteous Pilgrim*, 747–752; JRP interview; Ickes diary, pp. 8755, 8390, Ickes Papers; New York *Times*, Nov. 23, 1943; PAW press releases, Nov. 22, 26, 1943, PAW Records; Fort Worth *Star-Telegram*, Nov. 23, 1943.

38. Pyron to Ickes, Nov. 25, 1943, Ickes Papers; Ickes to Pyron, Nov. 29, 1943, ibid.; Pipkin to JRP, Nov. 23, 1943, JRP Papers; Hamon to JRP, Nov. 23, 1943, ibid.; Houston *Chronicle*, Nov. 23, 1943.

39. Thomas to JRP, Nov. 30, 1943, JRP Papers; Statement from Subcommittee on Naval Affairs, cited in Payton Ford to O. Chapman, Feb. 16, 1951, copy in Ickes Papers.

40. The Big and Little Inch lines were sold by the government in February 1947 to a syndicate headed by Parten's former debate coach, Charles I. Francis, and George and Herman Brown. The purchase price was 143 million dollars, only three million less than it had cost the government to build the lines. The Brown brothers invited Parten to join the original investment group, but he turned them down. "I just didn't want to get into it," Parten said later. "I'd helped create the thing, and I didn't want anybody to feel that I had laid the ground-work for utilizing it after the war was over." Sen. W. Lee O'Daniel had questioned Parten in committee hearings about the use of the Big Inch pipeline after the war. "He kept asking me what I was going to do with the big pipelines," Parten later remembered. "I told him that I was only interested in winning this war. If they could be used for gas or oil or wine or whatever was of no real concern to me personally because I would have nothing to do with the pipelines once they were built." Parten's ethics proved costly. Texas Eastern, the company organized

by the syndicate, developed into an enterprise worth hundreds of millions of dollars. For the definitive history of Texas Eastern see Christopher J. Castaneda and Joseph A. Pratt, *From Texas to the East: A Strategic History of Texas Eastern Corporation* (College Station: Texas A&M University Press, 1993); see also Engler, *The Politics of Oil!*, 170; *Time* (Nov. 24, 1947); Frey and Ide, *A History of the Petroleum Administration for War*, 90–91; Supply and Transportation Division, "History: Petroleum Pipeline Transportation During War Period" (Oct., 1945), box 4184, PAW Records; Johnson, *Petroleum Pipelines and Public Policy*, 325–327; Jones, *Fifty Billion Dollars*, 343; Nash, *United States Oil Policy*, 164, 165.

    41. Johnson, *Petroleum Pipelines and Public Policy*, 326; Stalin is quoted in Yergin, *The Prize*, 382.

    42. JRP interview; Lamp, "When Oil's Fleets 'Put Out to Sea'," 8.

Chapter Eighteen

    1. The hard work paid off by late summer. "There is an old-time boom in the oil business with the enormous war demand for petroleum," Parten happily reported to a friend. "You may be interested to know that Mississippi has about four good oil fields." JRP to Woody Weir, Jan. 7, Aug. 22, 1944, JRP Papers; DeGolyer and MacNaughton,"Preliminary Report of Woodley Petroleum Company as of Dec. 31, 1945," Apr., 1946, ibid.; Tom Dailey to JRP, Dec. 19, 1943, ibid.; "Marlin Sandlin," biographical files (CAH); JRP interview.

    2. JRP interview; Dallas *News*, June 15, 1942; *Daily Texan* (UT-Austin), June 20, 1942.

    3. Austin *American-Statesman*, Dec. 12, 1971; JRP interview.

    4. Rainey, *The Tower and the Dome*, 7, 8; Green, *The Establishment in Texas Politics*, 84, 86; Cox, "The Rainey Affair," 41–52; Davidson to Bullington, Mar. 25, 1942, Haley Papers (Haley Library); Bullington to Davidson, Mar. 26, 1942, ibid.

    5. L. H. Cullum to Bullington, July 11, 1942, Haley Papers (Haley Library); Cox, "The Rainey Affair," 59–60.

    6. Bullington to John A. Lomax, Dec. 28, 1942, July 5, 21, 1943, Mar. 17, 1944, Haley Papers (Haley Library); Rainey, *The Tower and the Dome*, 68; Cox, "The Rainey Affair," 89.

    7. For a detailed account of the incidents in the controversy between Homer Rainey and the board of regents, see Cox, "The Rainey Affair"; Rainey, *The Tower and the Dome*, 43, 92.

    8. JRP, "The University of Texas Controversy," p. 6, JRP Papers; JRP interview; Cox, "The Rainey Affair," 62–67.

    9. Dobie to Lomax, Apr. 14, 1943, "Rainey Controversy" file, box 2E387, John A. Lomax Papers (CAH); JRP to Dobie, Aug. 31, 1943, "Recipient File," Dobie Papers; Dobie to JRP, Sept. 4, 1943, ibid.; JPR interview.

    10. Rainey to JRP, Oct. 16, 1943, JRP Papers; clipping, Dallas *Morning News*, Oct. 15, 1943, ibid.; JRP to Mann, Nov. 15, 1943, ibid.; Mann to JRP, Nov. 26, 1943, ibid.; Mann interview.

    11. Bickett replaced Leslie Waggener as a regent. Roy Bedichek, *Letters of Roy Bedichek* (Austin: University of Texas Press, 1985), 248.

    12. Bullington to Lomax, July 5, 21, 1943, Lomax Papers; Cox, "The Rainey Affair," 81–84; Rainey, *The Tower and the Dome*, 100–110.

    13. "University Problems," *Alcalde* (Nov., 1944), 30, 33; Cox, "The Rainey Affair," 90; JRP interview; *Daily Texan* (UT-Austin), Oct. 14, 1944.

    14. JRP to Rainey, Oct. 20, 1944, JRP Papers; JRP interview; JRP, "The University of Texas Controversy," p. 7, JRP Papers.

    15. Rainey to JRP, Oct. 21, 1944, JRP Papers; JRP to Gordon Fulcher, Oct. 20, 1944, ibid.

    16. Bullington to Lomax, Oct. 17, 1944, Lomax Papers; Eugene Hollon to Walter P. Webb, Oct. 25, 1944, Rainey files, Walter P. Webb Papers (CAH).

    17. "University Problems," *Alcalde* (Nov., 1944), 29; Cox, "The Rainey Affair," 92–94; JRP interview.

    18. JRP interview; Cox, "The Rainey Affair," 94, 95.

    19. Fairchild to JRP, Feb. 1, 1945, JRP Papers.

    20. Bullington, Schreiner, and Strickland issued a statement that they intended to resign "very soon," but they did not. The terms of Stark and Fairchild were due to expire in less than two months. Weinert to Coke Stevenson, Nov. 21, 1944, box 4, Stevenson Papers; JRP interview; JRP, "The University of Texas Controversy," p. 7, JRP Papers; Cox, "The Rainey Affair," 96–100, 104, 106.

    21. Painter to Dudley K. Woodward, June 30, 1950, Box 3R110, Dudley K. Woodward Papers (CAH); JRP interview.

    22. JRP to Coke Stevenson, Nov. 2, 1944, JRP Papers; JRP interview; *PM* (Dec. 21, 1944), clipping in Rainey File, Richard Fleming Collection (CAH); Cox, "The Rainey Affair," 103.

    23. Cox, "The Rainey Affair," 100, 105; JRP to Bobbitt, Nov. 8, 1944, JRP Papers; Kern Tips to JRP, telegram, Nov. 7, 1944, ibid.; Sandlin to Tips, Nov. 11, 1944, ibid.; JRP to W. H. Francis, Nov. 7, 1944, ibid.; JRP to John McCurdy, Nov. 7, 23, 1944, ibid.

    24. JRP interview; Graham to Battle, Nov. 2, 1942, Frank Porter Graham Papers (University of North Carolina); JRP to Graham, Jan. 24, 1945, ibid.; Graham to JRP, Feb. 1, 1944, JRP Papers.

    25. Barker to Haley, Nov. 16, 1944, Haley Papers (Haley Library).

26. Houston Harte to Dan Moody, Dec. 5, 1933, Politics file, Moody Papers; Green, *The Establishment in Texas Politics*, 91, 92; Morgan to JRP, Nov. 15, 1944, JRP Papers; Cox, "The Rainey Affair," 111, 112; JRP interview.

27. Cox, "The Rainey Affair," 106, 112; Austin *American*, Nov. 10, 1944; JRP interview, Faulk interview; JRP to Dobie, Feb. 22, 1947, Dobie Papers; Hollon to Webb, Nov. 21, 1944, Rainey files, Webb Papers.

28. Bullington testimony, Senate Proceedings, I, 450, 465; Cox, "The Rainey Affair," 114, 115, 119; Ralph E. Himstead to Penrose Metcalfe, Nov. 20, 1944, copy in Graham Papers; *State Observer*, Nov. 20, 1944; Bullington to Lomax, Dec. 22, 1944, Lomax Papers.

29. Strickland testimony, Senate Proceedings, II, 687; Austin *American*, Nov. 19, 1944; Cox, "The Rainey Affair," 115.

30. Strickland and Bullington made no secret of their racism and their rigid opposition to racial integration at the university. Bullington, for example, in a letter to John Lomax the previous January, declared that "there is not the slightest danger of any negro attending the University of Texas as long as the present board are on the throne . . . regardless of what Franklin D.[Roosevelt], Eleanor [Roosevelt], or the Supreme Court says. . . ." Bullington to Lomax, Jan. 7, 1944, box 2E387, Lomax Papers; Cox, "The Rainey Affair," 116.

31. JRP interview; George Morgan to JRP, Nov. 15, 1944, JRP Papers; Rainey testimony, Senate Proceedings, I, 61, 63; Burdine Testimony, Senate Proceedings, II, 903; San Antonio *Light*, Nov. 21, 1944.

32. Taylor died a few days after his appointment. Stevenson left his position open until January. Cox, "The Rainey Affair," 122, 123; William C. Pool, *Eugene C. Barker: Historian* (Austin: Texas State Historical Association, 1971), 200, 201; Dobie to JRP, Feb. 22, 1945, Dobie Papers; JRP interview.

33. JRP interview.

34. JRP, "The University of Texas Controversy," JRP Papers.

35. JRP interview; JRP, "The University of Texas Controversy," JRP Papers; JRP to Thornton, Nov. 6, 1944, ibid.; Thornton to JRP, Nov. 20, 1944, ibid.; JRP to Thornton, Feb. 4, 1945, ibid.

36. Austin *American*, Nov. 28, 1945; Andrews to JRP, Dec. 9, 1944, JRP Papers; Lillian Collier to JRP, Dec. 18, 1944, ibid.; LBJ to JRP, Dec. 16, 1944, ibid.; Harte to JRP, Dec. 2, 1944, ibid.; JRP to Houston Harte, Dec. 7, 1944, ibid.; Harold Ickes to JRP, Dec. 23, 1944, box 239, Ickes Papers.

37. For discussions of the Houston "Gag" Conference, see Green, *The Establishment in Texas Politics*, 84; Rainey, *The Tower and the Dome*, 6, 7; and Cox, "The Rainey Affair," 15–17; also, Charles I. Francis to JRP, Dec. 14, 1944, JRP Papers; Lomax to Barker, July 11, 1945, "Rainey Controversy" file, Box 2E387, Lomax Papers. Unless some heretofore unknown written document is eventually uncovered, there will never be any way to know for certain if the Houston "Gag" Conference ever occurred or, if so, if it had any connection with the Rainey affair. This writer, however, believes Parten's story that Thornton and Branson told him about the conspiracy. To have lied about this incident at all, much less in a legislative hearing, would have been completely out of character for J. R. Parten. Whether or not Thornton and Branson were telling Parten the truth, however, is another matter. Nevertheless, that these two men gave Parten this information independently and for reasons intended to be of benefit to him, is a strong indication that they had credible knowledge. Other circumstantial evidence, essentially based on the chain of events and letters to O'Daniel written by Orville Bullington, Hilmer Weinert, Jim West, and others discovered by historian George Green in O'Daniel's papers in the Texas State Archives give further credence to the allegation. Green, *The Establishment in Texas Politics*, 83, 84.

38. Mewhinney to Webb, undated and Hollon to Webb, Jan. 18, 1945, "Rainey Files," Webb Papers; Haley interview.

39. Haley to Lomax, Dec. 23, 1944, Jan. 5, 1945, "Rainey Controversy" file, box 2E387, Lomax Papers; Barker to Haley, Dec. 30, 1944, Jan. 2, 1945, Haley Papers (Haley Library); Haley interview.

40. J. Evetts Haley, *The University of Texas and the Issue* (Clarendon, Tex.: Clarendon Press, 1945), 14; San Antonio *Express*, Jan. 15–20, 1945; Hollon to Webb, Jan. 18, 1945, Rainey files, Webb Papers.

41. JRP to E. B. Stroud, Dec. 11, 1944, JRP Papers; Clements to Bickett, May 21, 1945, John H. Bickett Papers (CAH); JRP interview.

42. JRP, "Statement Made to The Ex-Students of the University of Texas . . .," Dec. 15, 1944, memeographed speech transcript, JRP Papers; JRP interview.

43. JRP interview; undated clippings, Houston *Post*, 1944, Bickett Papers; Pinckney to Haley, Dec. 29, 1944, Haley Papers (Haley Library); JRP to W. H. Francis, Dec. 16, 1944, JRP Papers; JRP to Fairchild, Dec. 20, 1944, ibid.

44. Bedichek, *Letters*, 249; Yarborough to JRP, Jan. 8, 12, 1945, JRP Papers; JRP to Yarborough, Jan. 20, 1945, ibid.

45. Joe Sheldon to JRP, Jan. 18, 1945, JRP Papers; JRP to Joe Sheldon, Feb. 17, 1945, ibid.; Dobie to JRP, Feb. 22, 1945, ibid.

46. Fath interview; Minnie Fisher Cunningham to Frank Graham, Oct. 20, 1945, May 7, 1946, Graham Papers; Green, *The Establishment in Texas Politics*, 88; JRP to Fairchild, Feb. 10, 1945, JRP Papers.

47. Marguerite Fairchild and Lutcher Stark were not renominated to the board. The new nominees were Dudley K. Woodward, David Warren, Edward B. Tucker, E. E. Kirkpatrick, Dr. C. O. Terrell, and Dr. Walter

Scherer (who was replacing the recently deceased Judson Taylor). The day after the regents voted not to reinstate Rainey, Alton Burdine resigned as vice president and returned to his tenured position as a professor of government. Cox, "The Rainey Affair," 123–125; Dudley K. Woodward, "Reasons . . ." (Austin: n.p., Jan. 26, 1945); JRP to R. B. Anderson, May 4, 1950, JRP Papers; Bullington to Lomax, Jan. 31, 1945, Lomax Papers; Henry Nash Smith, *The Controversy at the University of Texas, 1939—1945: A Documented History* (Austin: University of Texas, Students' Association, 1945?), 17–19.

48. Because Sandlin shared Parten's liberal political views for most of the years of their relationship, he often served as Parten's political emissary. Ralph Yarborough recalled that when he was in the U.S. Senate, if Parten wanted him to vote in favor of a bill he knew that Yarborough did not like, he would send Marlin Sandlin to Washington to ask him to do it. "Most of the time Sandlin came to see me, it was for something I didn't want to do and didn't do," Yarborough said. "I preferred it that way. It allowed me to say no to Sandlin rather than to Parten, which kept my relationship with Parten at a higher level." Yarborough interview; JRP interview.

49. Rainey said in an interview in 1967 that Strickland's remark about preferring a Japanese invasion was "more right" than he knew, because "you can stop an invasion of tanks, guns, and ships with other tanks, guns, and ships, but I didn't know any way to stop the spread of good ideas. So in that sense, I was a dangerous man," Rainey interview, oral history transcript (UNT); Austin *American*, Feb. 1, 2, 9, 1945; JRP interview.

50. Cox, "The Rainey Affair," 126; Dobie to JRP, Feb. 22, 1945, Dobie Papers.

51. As a result of the Rainey affair, the Southern Association for Colleges and Secondary Schools placed the University of Texas on probation in July 1945, and the AAUP placed it on its censured list for nine years beginning in 1946. JRP interview; Duncalf to JRP, Feb. 25, 1945, JRP Papers.

52. Rapoport interview; Faulk interview.

Chapter Nineteen

1. Edwin Pauley founded the Petrol Corporation in California in 1929. JRP interview.

2. John Lewis Gaddis, *The United States and the Origins of the Cold War, 1941–1947* (New York: Columbia University Press, 1972), 215; Gaddis Smith, *American Diplomacy during the Second World War, 1941–1945* (New York: Wiley, 1965), 135; Adam B. Ulam, *The Rivals: America and Russia Since World War II* (New York: Viking Press, 1971), 74 (quotation).

3. Truman's first choice to serve as head of the reparations delegation was Postmaster General Frank C. Walker, but Walker did not want the job. He and Democratic Party chairman Robert Hannegan persuaded Truman to appoint Pauley instead. Francis S. Wyman to author, Oct. 8, 1995; Gaddis, *The United States and the Origins of the Cold War*, 216, 217, 220, 221; Lubin interview, oral history transcript (Truman Library); Robert J. Donovan, *Conflict and Crisis: The Presidency of Harry S. Truman, 1945–1948* (New York: Norton, 1977), 78; U.S. Department of State, *Foreign Relations of the United States, Diplomatic Papers: The Conference of Berlin (The Potsdam Conference), 1945.* (Washington, D.C.: Government Printing Office, 1960; cited hereafter as State Department, *The Conference of Berlin*), III, 1290, 1291.

4. Marshall, *Done in Oil*, 168; Bruce Kuklick, *American Policy and the Division of Germany: The Clash with Russia over Reparations* (Ithaca: Cornell University Press, 1972), 129; Charles L. Mee Jr., *Meeting at Potsdam* (New York: M. Evans, 1975), 148; Marshall interview; Justin Wolf to Everett DeGolyer, Apr. 30, 1945, box 15, DeGolyer Papers. For Pauley's activities at the 1944 Democratic Convention see Cochran, *Harry Truman*, 320; and McCullough, *Truman*, 306, 307, 312, 314, 316.

5. Gaddis, *The United States and the Origins of the Cold War*, 220; Marshall interview; Wolf interview; JRP interview.

6. Gaddis, *The United States and the Origins of the Cold War*, 220–221; Pauley to Harry S. Truman, May 10, 1945 (letter annotated by Truman "approved"), box 424, Official File 85-C, Truman Papers.

7. Other appointees included Ernest Mahler of Wisconsin for plant and equipment appraisal; Richard B. Scandrett, for international law; George Johnson of Wisconsin, for machine tools and metals; and Lawrence Richardson of Massachusetts, for rolling stock. Henry L. Stimson to Truman, May 10, 1945, box 424, Official File 85-C; Paul Blazer to Truman, May 9, 1945, ibid.; Houston *Press*, May 15, 1945; Marshall interview; JRP interview.

8. JRP interview; Gaddis, *The United States and the Origins of the Cold War*, 230.

9. Marshall, *Done in Oil*, 167, 168; JRP interview; "Memo re Watches," undated, "Ed Pauley" folder, box G240, Drew Pearson Papers (LBJ).

10. Gaddis, *The United States and the Origins of the Cold War*, 221; Wolf interview; JRP interview.

11. JRP interview; Parten to Duncalf, May 17, 1945, JRP Papers.

12. Maj. Charles Kindelberger agreed to be Pauley's representative at the State Department. Pauley to Edward McKim, May 20, 1945, box 424, Official File 85-C, Truman Papers; Wolf interview; JRP interview; Wolf to DeGolyer, June 8, 1945, box 15, DeGolyer Papers; Pauley to Matt Connelly, Oct. 24, 1945, box 424, Official File 85-C, Truman Papers.

13. Sherman interview.

14. JRP interview; George F. Kennan, *Memoirs, 1925–1950* (Boston: Little, Brown, 1967), 259, 260; Gaddis, *The United States and the Origins of the Cold War*, 221–222 (Harriman quote).

15. Pauley's wife accompanied him, an action for which Pauley would later be severely criticized by newspaper columnist Drew Pearson. Pearson accused Pauley of taking his wife on a junket at taxpayer expense and charged that the Soviets had paid for her expenses in Russia. Pauley denied the charges; a denial supported by Lubin. Pauley to Eugene Meyer, Sept. 5, 1945, copy in General File, Truman Papers; see also Isador Lubin to Drew Pearson, Sept. 4, 1945, "Ed Pauley" folder, box G240, Pearson Papers; JRP interview; Opal Parten to Ella Parten, May 23, 1945, JRP Papers; Opal Parten to Claire Dayson, May 23, 1945, Dayson Papers.

16. JRP, "Memorandum for the Files," Sept. 28, 1945, JRP Papers; JRP to Opal Parten, May 23, 1945, ibid.; JRP interview.

17. Pauley to Truman, May 28, 1945, box 2, Confidential File, "Allied Reparations Commission," Truman Papers; JRP interview; "Inspection Itinerary," May, 1945, box 54, folder 1, Robert Gordon Sproul Papers (Bancroft Library); Houston *Post*, Sept. 21, 1945, JRP Papers; JRP to Opal Parten, June 12, 1945, ibid.

18. Pauley to Truman, June 12, 1945, box 424, Official Files, Truman Papers; JRP interview.

19. JRP interview; JRP to Dayson, Aug. 2, 1945, Dayson Papers; Shelmire interview.

20. The Pauleys and Lubin were given quarters in the U.S. ambassador's residence, Spaso House. JRP interview; mission itinerary, JRP Papers.

21. JRP interview; JRP to Opal, June 12, 1945, JRP Papers.

22. JRP interview.

23. JRP interview; Gaddis, *The United States and the Origins of the Cold War*, 220–221.

24. JRP interview.

25. JRP to Fogelson, Mar. 11, 1986, JRP Papers; JRP Interview.

26. Houston *Post*, Sept. 21, 1945; JRP to Opal, July 1, 1945, JRP Papers; JRP to Ella Parten, Aug. 2, 1945, ibid.

27. JRP interview.

28. Inexplicably, Howard Marshall's autobiography fails to even mention Parten's name in the section about his service on the U.S. delegation to Moscow. Marshall, *Done in Oil*, 165–170; Marshall interview; JRP interview.

29. JRP interview; Will Clayton to Roger Makins, June 6, 1945, box 1,"June, 1945" folder, Will Clayton Papers (Truman Library); Isaac Deutscher, *Stalin: A Political Biography* (New York: Oxford University Press, 1966), 549; Robert Payne, *The Rise and Fall of Stalin* (New York: Simon and Schuster, 1965), 687.

30. JRP interview; JRP to Opal, June 24, 1945, JRP Papers; Payne, *The Rise and Fall of Stalin*, 687, 688; Werth, *Russia at War*, 1002; Deutscher, *Stalin*, 549.

31. Pauley to Secretary of State, June 19, 1945, enclosed in memorandum, Samuel I. Rosenman to Truman, June 23, 1945, box 2, Confidential Files, Truman Papers.

32. JRP interview; information from Parten notebook, JRP Papers.

33. JRP interview; Gaddis, *The United States and the Origins of the Cold War*, 239, 240; State Department, *The Conference of Berlin*, I, 550; F. Byrnes, *Speaking Frankly*, 82, 83.

34. July 4, 11 entries, JRP notebook, JRP Papers; Byrnes, *Speaking Frankly*, 75–76.

35. In the 1950s, Marshall told the FBI his suspicions about Lubin. One can only speculate about how much damage Marshall's unsubstantiated charges did to Lubin's career during the red scare. In an interview with the author, Marshall failed to provide any evidence of Lubin's alleged subversive activities. Marshall interview; Marshall, *Done in Oil*, 168; June 25 entry, JRP notebook, JRP Papers; JRP interview; Houston *Post*, Sept. 21, 1945; Kuklick, *American Policy and the Division of Germany*, 132, 133, 142.

36. Anonymous ms., ca. June, 1945, JRP Papers.

37. JRP interview; JRP to Opal, July 1, 1945, JRP Papers.

38. Jonathan Daniels, *The Man of Independence* (Philadelphia: Lippincott, 1950), 305; Lubin interview, oral history transcript (Truman Library); JRP interview; Gar Alperovitz, *Atomic Diplomacy: Hiroshima and Potsdam; The Use of the Atomic Bomb and the American Confrontation with Soviet Power* (New York: Simon and Schuster, 1985), 212; Kuklick, *American Policy and the Division of Germany*, 132, 133.

39. July 3, 11 entries, JRP notebook, JRP Papers; JRP interview; Alperovitz, *Atomic Diplomacy*, 134, 211.

40. JRP interview; State Department, *The Conference of Berlin*, II, 872–876.

41. Charles E. Bohlen, *Witness to History, 1929–1969* (New York: Norton, 1973), 232, 233.

42. Gaddis, *The United States and the Origins of the Cold War*, 239, 242, 243; Kennan, *Memoirs*, 259, 260; State Department, *The Conference of Berlin*, III, 1200, 1203–1205; JRP interview; Lubin interview, oral history transcript (Truman Library).

43. July 14, 15 entries, JRP notebook, JRP Papers; JRP to Opal, July 18, 1945, ibid.; JRP interview. For more on the details of the Potsdam Conference, see Mee, *Meeting at Potsdam*, and the numerous published memoirs of key participants such as James F. Byrnes and Admiral William D. Leahy.

44. Clayton, an assistant secretary of state, was a businessman from Houston whom Parten had known for several years. JRP interview; JRP to Dayson, Aug. 6, 1945, Dayson Papers; State Department, *The Conference of Berlin*, II, 942.

45. JRP interview; JRP notebook, JRP Papers; JRP to Opal, July 18, 20 1945, ibid.; JRP to Dayson, July 18, 1945, Dayson Papers.

46. JRP to Opal Parten, July 18, 1945, JRP Papers; JRP interview; Sherman interview; JRP to Dayson, July 18, 1945, Dayson Papers.

47. JRP interview; July 23 entry, JRP notebook, JRP Papers; Byrnes, *Speaking Frankly*, 83.

48. Alperovitz, *Atomic Diplomacy*; Robert L. Messer, *The End of an Alliance: James F. Byrnes, Roosevelt, Truman, and the Origins of the Cold War* (Chapel Hill: University of North Carolina Press, 1982), esp. chapters 6 and 7; Martin J. Sherwin, *A World Destroyed: The Atomic Bomb and the Grand Alliance* (New York: Knopf, 1975); Gregg Herken, *The Winning Weapon: The Atomic Bomb in the Cold War, 1945–1950* (New York: Knopf; distributed by Random House, 1980).

49. The news about the atomic bomb was not a complete surprise to Parten. While working in the White House preparing for the trip to Moscow, he had heard rumors about some type of new weapon under development. Because of his experiences as a university regent, he was also well aware of the nuclear research going on at the University of Chicago and at the University of California in Berkeley. He had learned of Ernest Lawrence's work when he and Rainey had tried to bring him to the University of Texas. JRP interview; Alperovitz, *Atomic Diplomacy*, 54; Josiah E. DuBois interview, oral history transcript (Truman Library).

50. Donovan, *Conflict and Crisis*, 84; Bohlen, *Witness to History*, 228; JRP interview; JRP notebook, JRP Papers.

51. Byrnes, *Speaking Frankly*, 83; Gaddis, *The United States and the Origins of the Cold War*, 240.

52. July 25 entry, JRP notebook, JRP Papers; JRP interview.

53. July 27, 28 entries, JRP notebook, JRP Papers; State Department, *The Conference of Berlin*, II, 888, 889.

54. July 28 entry, JRP notebook, JRP Papers; Alperovitz, *Atomic Diplomacy*, 216, 217; Byrnes, *Speaking Frankly*, 84; Bohlen, *Witness to History*, 232.

55. July 30 entry, JRP notebook, JRP Papers; Ulam, *The Rivals*, 75; Byrnes, *Speaking Frankly*, 85, 86; Gaddis, *The United States and the Origins of the Cold War*, 240, 241; Alperovitz, *Atomic Diplomacy*, 216–218.

56. JRP to Dayson, Aug. 2, 1945, JRP Papers; Dayson to JRP, Aug. 10, 1945, ibid.

57. Aug. 3, 4 entries, JRP notebook, JRP Papers; Pauley to Lt. Gen. Lucius D. Clay, Aug. 4, 1945, box 424, Official Files, Truman Papers; JRP to Opal Parten, Aug. 11, 1945, JRP Papers.

58. Parten returned, briefly, to the Southwest sooner than he had planned, however, when he received word that his oldest sister, Agnes Emma Brown, was mortally ill. He flew to Agnes's home in Clovis, New Mexico, on August 27. She died on September 6 and Parten returned to Washington a few days after her funeral. Charles Steger (comp.), *William and Jane Law and Some of Their Descendants* (Decorah, Iowa: 1985), 100l; JRP interview; Aug. 20–22, 27 entries, JRP notebook, JRP Papers; JRP to Ella Parten, Aug. 20, 1945, ibid.

59. Houston *Chronicle* and Houston *Post*, Sept. 21, 1945; Shreveport *Times*, Sept. 3, 1945.

60. Parten's views on the potential for business with the Soviet Union were later echoed in the 1980s and 1990s by the U.S. corporate establishment with respect to the People's Republic of China. "Major J. R. Parten Sees Big Opportunity For U.S. Understanding With Russia," *Texas Oil Journal* (Oct., 1945), 13.

61. JRP to Henry Fox, Oct. 24, 1945, JRP Papers.

62. Since the break-up of the Soviet Union, Stalin's crimes have been cataloged in detail. Among others see for example Dimitri Volkogonov, *Stalin: Triumph and Tragedy*, ed. and trans. Harold Shukman (New York: Grove Weidenfeld, 1991); JRP interview.

63. Pauley to JRP, Dec. 8, 1945, JRP Papers; JRP interview.

64. JRP interview.

65. JRP interview; clipping from the Houston *Chronicle*, Feb. 13, 1950, JRP Papers.

66. JRP interview; JRP to Pauley, Dec. 29, 1945, JRP Papers; Watkins, *Righteous Pilgrim*, 830–832; McCullough, *Truman*, 483, 484.

67. Nash, *World War II and the West: Reshaping the Economy* (Lincoln: University of Nebraska Press, 1990), 183; Pearson column, n.d., clipping in JRP Papers.

68. JRP to Sen. David I. Walsh, Feb. 26, 1946, JRP Papers; Watkins, *Righteous Pilgrim*, 836.

69. Donovan, *Conflict and Crisis*, 350; JRP interview.

70. Alan Bullock, *Hitler and Stalin: Parallel Lives* (New York: Knopf; distributed by Random House, 1992), 902, 903.

Chapter Twenty

1. Rainey to Granbery, Apr. 17, July 12, 17, 1945, box 2P423, John C. Granbery Papers (CAH); David L. Brown,"Homer Price Rainey and the Campaign of 1946" (Senior Honors thesis, University of Texas at Austin, 1989), 55; JRP to Wallace, Apr. 20, 1946, JRP Papers; Rainey to Dobie, Aug. 11, 1945, Dobie Papers; JRP interview; Rainey interview, oral history transcript (UNT).

2. When Rainey was asked years later who he relied on most strongly when he was making the decision to run, he replied that "by all odds Major J. R. Parten. He . . . had been active in the political life of the state and

knew it very well, indeed." Rainey interview, oral history transcript (UNT); Rainey to JRP, Oct. 15, 1945, JRP Papers; Cox,"The Rainey Affair," 127.

3. Robert Dalleck, *Lone Star Rising: Lyndon Johnson and His Times, 1908–1960* (New York: Oxford University Press, 1991), 278; Rainey interview, oral history transcript (UNT); JRP interview; Brown,"Homer Price Rainey," 63; Rainey to JRP, Dec. 15, 1945, JRP Papers.

4. JRP interview; Hardeman interview, oral history transcript (LBJ); JRP to Rainey, Feb. 1, 1946, JRP Papers; Bond to JRP, June 7 1946, ibid.; JRP to Hardeman, Feb. 6, Mar. 4, 1946, ibid.; Bobbitt to Rainey, Mar. 26, 1946, ibid.; JRP to Lubin, Apr. 23, 1946, box 76, Lubin Papers.

5. Brown, "Homer Price Rainey," 68; JRP interview; Green, *The Establishment in Texas Politics*, 90–94; JRP to Henry Fox, May 29, 1946, JRP Papers.

6. Rainey, mimeograph copy of speech, May 23,1946, JRP Papers; Green, *The Establishment in Texas Politics*, 94; JRP interview; JRP to Lubin, May 31, 1946, box 76, Lubin Papers.

7. Rainey interview, oral history transcript (UNT); JRP interview; Cox,"The Rainey Affair," 129; Rainey, mimeograph copy of speech, May 23, 1946, JRP Papers; Washington *Post*, May 26, 1946.

8. Rainey interview, oral history transcript (UNT); Washington *Post*, May 26, 1946.

9. JRP to Chambliss, Aug. 6, 1946, JRP Papers; JRP to Julien Elfenbein, July 9, 1946, ibid.; JRP to T. J. Caldwell, July 25, 1946, ibid.

10. JRP to Davies, July 27, 1946, JRP Papers; JRP, typescript of speech text, n.d., ibid.; JRP interview.

11. Seth S. McKay, *Texas and the Fair Deal, 1945–1952* (San Antonio: Naylor Co., 1954), 106; JRP interview; Bobbitt to Rainey, Mar. 26, 1946, JRP Papers.

12. JRP interview; JRP to Connally, June 18, 1946, JRP Papers.

13. Rayburn had played a key role in getting much of Roosevelt's New Deal legislation passed and the Texas Regulars wanted him out. They persuaded state senator Grover Cleveland Morris to oppose Rayburn in the Democratic primary on July 22. Parten donated money and raised funds from some friends to help Rayburn, who defeated Morris by six thousand votes. Ickes diary, Aug. 15, 1944, Ickes Papers; JRP interview; Hardeman and Bacon, *Rayburn*, 297–300; Rayburn to JRP, Oct. 16, 1944, JRP Papers; Green, *The Establishment in Texas Politics*, 48.

14. JRP interview; Dulaney interview; Lyle interview, oral history transcript (LBJ); Lloyd M. Bentsen Jr. interview (CAH).

15. JRP interview; Hardeman and Bacon, *Rayburn*, 303–307; U.S. Statutes at Large, 1946, Vol. LX, Part I, 23–26; JRP interview (with A. Champagne).

16. JRP interview; Truman appointment calendar," June 21, 1946," Truman Papers; JRP to Truman, June 24, 1946, JRP Papers; New York *Times*, June 24, 1946; Houston *Chronicle*, June 21, 1946.

17. Undated clipping, Houston *Chronicle*, JRP Papers; Houston *Chronicle*, June 27, 1946; JRP interview.

18. An example of Parten's research activities was his gathering of information on public health from Eliot Janeway and Frieda Hancock through the Committee for the Nation's Health in New York. See JRP to Lois Jacoby, July 17, 1946, JRP Papers; JRP interview; Bernard Rapoport interview, oral history transcript (Baylor University, Waco); Wolf interview; "Houston Supporters of Dr. Homer P. Rainey," typescript list, n.d., JRP Papers; Ralph Frede to D. B. Hardeman, July 18, 1946, Ralph Frede Papers (CAH); Rainey interview, oral history transcript (UNT).

19. Financial records, Rainey Campaign, 1946, box 19, Hardeman Papers; Rainey interview, oral history transcript (UNT); JRP to Lubin, May 31, 1946, box 76, Lubin Papers.

20. Bernard Rapoport to John C. Granbery, box 2P423, Granbery Papers; Rapoport interview, oral history transcript (Baylor); for financial contributions to Rainey's opponents, see Green, *The Establishment in Texas Politics*, 96.

21. Opal to JRP, June 12, 1946, JRP Papers; JRP to Jack Lewis, July 8, 1946, ibid.; JRP to Burdine, July 3, 1946, ibid.; JRP to Henry Fox, May 29, 1946, ibid.

22. JRP to Hardeman, July 10, 1946, JRP Papers; JRP to Cora Mae Sloan, July 15, 1946, ibid.

23. JRP interview; JRP to Hardeman, Apr. 25, 1946, JRP Papers; Rainey campaign press release, May 31, 1946, ibid.; JRP to Hardeman, May 31, 1946, ibid.

24. "I . . . could not buy commercial time at twice the . . . political rates," Rainey later explained. "They wouldn't give me that opportunity to pay for it!" The four stations of the TQN were KPRC in Houston, WFAA in Dallas, WOAI in San Antonio, and WBAP in Fort Worth. Rainey interview, oral history transcript (UNT).

25. JRP interview; Rainey interview, oral history transcript (UNT); Rainey to FCC, June 7, 1946, JRP Papers; T. J. Slowie to Rainey, June 11, 1946, ibid.; Hardeman to Marks, June 19, 1946, ibid.; memeographed Rainey Campaign press release, July 1, 1946, ibid.; JRP to Bobbitt, July 9, 1946, ibid.; Charlotte Carr to Boyd Sinclair, July 10, 1946, ibid.; McKay, *Texas and the Fair Deal*, 102–104.

26. Green, *The Establishment in Texas Politics*, 95; McKay, *Texas and the Fair Deal*, 79, 105, 111; Rainey interview, oral history transcript (UNT).

27. McKay, *Texas and the Fair Deal*, 104, 115; *PM* (Dec. 20, 1944), clipping in Rainey File, Fleming Collection; Green, *The Establishment in Texas Politics*, 92.

28. McKay, *Texas and the Fair Deal*, 99, 107, 112; Green, *The Establishment in Texas Politics*, 92; Haley interview.

29. McKay, *Texas and the Fair Deal*, 117; JRP to Lou Harris, July 31, 1946, JRP Papers.

30. JRP interview;"Daily Record of Phone Calls," in Ralph Frede to D. B. Hardeman, July 19, 20, 1946, Frede Papers; Rainey, memeographed speech, July 5, 1946, JRP Papers.

31. JRP interview; Lewis, mimeograph copy of speech, July 12, 1946, JRP Papers; Hobby's review was in the Sept. 27, 1936 issue of the Houston *Post*, clipping in "Rainey" file, JRP Papers.

32. JRP interview; Fairchild, memeograph copy of speech, n.d., JRP Papers; Frede to Hardeman, July 19, 1946, Frede Papers.

33. JRP to Rogers, July 5, 1946, JRP Papers; Rogers to JRP, July 17, 1946, ibid.; JRP to Hardeman, July 6, 1946, ibid.

34. Lizzie Parten Leonard to JRP, July 1946, JRP Papers.

35. JRP interview; Sandlin to Hardeman, July 20, 1946, Rainey file, box 19, Hardeman Papers; Hardeman quote from his notes in ibid.; Rainey, mimeographed copy of speech, Olney, Texas, July 20, 1946, JRP Papers.

36. The University remained on the AAUP censure list until 1953. JRP to Lou Harris, July 31, 1946, JRP Papers; JRP interview; McKay, *Texas and the Fair Deal*, 84; Rainey interview, oral history transcript (UNT).

37. First quote from Dugger, *Our Invaded Universities*, 51. Hardeman would later not recall having made the circumcision remark, but he did admit that it was an accurate reflection of his feelings, ms. of a letter written by Hardeman "intended for but never sent" to Ronnie Dugger, Aug. 1971, box 19, Hardeman Papers; McKay, *Texas and the Fair Deal*, 109, 114.

38. Jester received nearly 444,000 votes and carried 212 counties, while Rainey attracted 291,000 votes and won only 8 counties. McKay, *Texas and the Fair Deal*, 117, 118.

39. Eckhardt interview; JRP interview; Carr to JRP, Aug. 9, 1946, JRP Papers; Rainey, "To the Women of Texas," mimeographed copy of speech, Aug. 13, 1946, ibid.

40. JRP interview; McKay, *Texas and the Fair Deal*, 119.

41. Mimeographed copy of speech text, n.d., JRP Papers; ms. of a letter written by Hardeman intended for but never sent to Ronnie Dugger, Aug. 1971, box 19, Hardeman Papers.

42. Eckhardt interview; JRP interview; Green, *The Establishment in Texas Politics*, 96; JRP and Allred to Hardeman and Wild, "Suggestions for This Week," carbon copy of typescript, n.d., JRP Papers; Rainey, mimeograph copy of speech texts, Aug. 3 and 5, 1946, ibid.

43. JRP and Allred to Hardeman and Wild, "Suggestions for This Week," carbon copy of typescript, n.d., JRP Papers; and Rainey, mimeographed copies of speech texts, Aug. 6 and 8, 1946, ibid.

44. JRP to Harris, July 31, 1946, JRP Papers; JRP interview; Henry Wallace interview, oral history, Reel 2, 4920–23 (Butler Library, Columbia University, New York; cited hereafter as Butler Library).

45. JRP interview; Allred, mimeographed copy of speech text, Aug. 14, 1946, JRP Papers; JRP to Marcus, Aug. 14, 1946, ibid.; JRP to Marks, Aug. 9, 1946, ibid.; Dallas *Morning News*, Aug. 22, 1946.

46. JRP, typescript of speech text, n.d., JRP Papers; JRP to Pauley, Aug. 23, 1946, ibid.

47. For a thorough analysis of the Rainey-Jester election results, see Green, *The Establishment in Texas Politics*, 96–100 and Chandler Davidson, *Race and Class in Texas Politics* (Princeton: Princeton University Press, 1990); McKay, *Texas and the Fair Deal*, 129, 130; JRP to Ed Winton, Aug. 26, 1946, JRP Papers; Wolf to JRP, Sept. 4, 1946, ibid.

48. JRP interview; JRP to Robert Elliott, Sept. 16, 1946, JRP Papers; JRP to George M. Reynolds, Sept. 4, 1946, ibid.; Jim Lindsey to JRP, Aug. 27, 1946, ibid.; Rainey to JRP, Sept. 1, 1946, ibid.; JRP to Rainey, Sept. 5, 1946, ibid.; Rainey to Field, Sept. 12, 1946, ibid.; JRP to Harris, Sept. 15, 1946, Oct. 7, 1946, ibid.

49. Rainey served as president at Stephens College until June 1952, when he resigned in a dispute with the trustees. He eventually joined the faculty at the University of Colorado, where he retired as a professor of education in 1964. He died in Boulder, Colorado, in 1990. Austin *American-Statesman*, June 22, 1952, May 1, 1956; Field to Rainey, Sept. 18, 1946, JRP Papers; JRP to Marks, Dec. 11, 1946, ibid.; JRP interview.

50. Marks to JRP, Jan. 21, 1946, JRP Papers; Rainey to Marks, Jan. 29, 1946, ibid.; Rainey to JRP, Jan. 29, 1946 (quotation), ibid.; Rainey interview, oral history transcript (UNT).

51. Hardeman interview, oral history transcript (UNT); Dobie to JRP, Nov. 6, 1946, Dobie Papers; JRP to Mac Hill, July 28, 1947, JRP Papers.

52. Holman became chairman of Standard in 1946, see "Cowboy of Fifth Avenue" in *Saturday Evening Post* (Aug. 22, 1959); Dunagan, *Eugene Holman*, 24; "Eugene Holman," biographical files (CAH).

53. Dobie eventually paid for his support of Rainey and his involvement in the liberal cause. Late in 1945, Bullington had complained to John Lomax that Dobie "may . . . have a political bee in his bonnet, because he seems to be cultivating negroes and the labor unions, and apparently has been tarred with the Rainey brush, so I do not have much hope for his regeneration, and think he has gone 'where the woodvine twineth and the whangdoodle mourneth'." In 1947, the University of Texas board of regents removed him from the faculty.

Bullington to Lomax, Sept. 2, 1945, "Rainey Controversy" file, box 2E387, Lomax Papers; Hall, "Inside Texas," *Texas Spectator* (Jan. 25, 1946), 5; Ed Clark interview; JRP to Davies, July 27, 1946, JRP Papers; Holman to DeGolyer, July 23, 1940, box 6-757, DeGolyer Papers.

54. In 1946, when LBJ defeated Coke Stevenson in a controversial election to the U.S. Senate, Parten wrote to Rainey, then president of Stephens College in Missouri: "Lyndon Johnson summarily defeated your friend Coke Stevenson. . . . It is my opinion that the school teachers of the state should celebrate, for I firmly believe that Stevenson is the most formidable enemy of education that Texas has ever had." JRP to Rainey, Nov. 10, 1948, JRP Papers; Rainey to JRP, Nov. 3, 1964, ibid.; Rainey interview, oral history transcript (UNT).

55. Harry Ransom to JRP, Apr. 28, 1969, Dobie-Paisano file, JRP Papers; Clark interview.

Chapter Twenty-One

1. Tom Dailey to JRP, Dec. 19, 1943, JRP Papers; JRP to Frederic Duncalf, Sept. 9, 1944, ibid.; JRP to Opal, June 7, 1944, ibid.; JRP interview; Fath interview; Miller interview; Ilfrey interview; Shelmire interview; Sherman interview; Opal Parten to Claire Dayson, Feb. 12, 1947, Dayson Papers; New York *Times*, Aug. 17, 1980.

2. The divorce became final on March 8, 1947. Opal and J. R. traded their River Oaks home for some vacant lots in the same subdivision and J. R. moved into the Lamar Hotel in downtown Houston. Opal kept the lots in River Oaks and J. R. got Greenbrier, the ranch in Madison County. Sherman, "Remembrances," JRP Papers; Sherman interview; Opal Parten to Claire Dayson, Feb. 12, 1947, Dayson Papers; Ilfrey interview; Miller interview.

3. Board of Governors of the Federal Reserve System, *The Federal Reserve System: Purposes and Functions* (Washington, D.C.: Government Printing Office, 1954). For information on Marriner Eccles, see Sidney Hyman, *Marriner S. Eccles: Private Entrepreneur and Public Servant* (Stanford, Calif.: Graduate School of Business, Stanford University, 1976); JRP interview.

4. Chester Morrill to JRP, Dec. 31, 1943, JRP Papers; JRP to Evans, Jan. 6, 1944, ibid.; Board of Governors, *The Federal Reserve System*; Houston *Chronicle*, Jan. 3, 1947.

5. JRP interview; Townsend interview; Stanley Marcus interview.

6. For more information on Frasch and the sulphur industry, see Williams Haynes, *Brimstone: The Stone That Burns; The Story of the Frasch Sulphur Industry* (Princeton, N.J.: Van Nostrand, 1959); Yergin, *The Prize*, 229–232.

7. James Clark, "Miracle at Jaltipan," unpublished ms. history of Pan American Sulphur Company, no pagination, privately held by Jack Boothe, Houston, Texas; Robert Sheehan, "The 'Little Mothers'and Pan American Sulphur," *Fortune Magazine* (July, 1960), 99.

8. Clark, "Miracle at Jaltipan"; Sheehan, "The 'Little Mothers'," 101.

9. JRP interview; JRP memorandum to the Woodley files, Nov. 27, 1958, JRP Papers; Hubert Herring, *A History of Latin America from the Beginnings to the Present* (2nd ed.; New York: Knopf, 1961), 387–389.

10. JRP interview; Sherman interview.

11. JRP to Andrade, Mar. 18, Apr. 17, 1947, JRP Papers; Clark, "Miracle at Jaltipan."

12. JRP interview; Haynes, *Brimstone*, 191; Clark, "Miracle at Jaltipan."

13. In total, the Little Mothers paid $300,000 (at 43.5 cents per share) and issued one million common shares. They gave nearly 290,000 shares to the Bradys for their Jaltipan rights and $82,500 in cash to cover expenses they had incurred in drilling the exploratory well that discovered the sulphur. They also agreed to pay the Bradys a royalty of one dollar per ton for any sulphur that might be produced in the future. Haynes, *Brimstone*, 190; JRP interview; JRP to Andrade, Apr. 17, 22, 1947, JRP Papers; Clark, "Miracle at Jaltipan"; Sheehan, "The 'Little Mothers'," 101, 102, 203; Miller interview; Ilfrey interview.

14. JRP interview.

15. JRP interview; Robert H. Montgomery, *The Brimstone Game: Monopoly in Action* (New York: Vanguard Press, 1940); JRP to Roland S. Bond, Apr. 29, 1947, JRP Papers.

16. JRP interview; JRP to Pauley, June 30, July 22, 1947, JRP Papers; JRP to William Brady, May 12, 1947, ibid.; JRP to Roland Bond, Sept. 15, 1947, ibid.; Clark, "Miracle at Jaltipan."

17. Judson to DeGolyer, Aug. 6, 1947, folder 884, DeGolyer Papers; JRP interview.

18. JRP to Lawrence Brady, July 21, 1947, JRP Papers.

19. Clark, "Miracle at Jaltipan"; Haynes, *Brimstone*, 12; Perry Allen to JRP, Aug. 25, 1947, JRP Papers; JRP to William Baker, Sept. 16, 1947, ibid.

20. Patsy Puterbaugh, born on October 28, 1910, was the daughter of Clara and Walker G. Edwards, a lawyer who lived at 3609 Gillon Street in Highland Park. Clipping in Dayson Papers, Longview *Sunday Journal*, Nov. 2, 1947; JRP interview; Randy Parten interview; Pepe Anderson interview; Shelmire interview.

21. Ilfrey interview; Shelmire interview; Pepe Anderson interview; JRP interview.

22. Steger (comp.), *William and Jane Law*, 100; JRP interview.

23. JRP interview; Pepe Anderson interview.

24. JRP interview; Madison County Historical Commission, *A History of Madison County*, 191.

25. JRP interview; Presley, *Never in Doubt*, 126; Mayer interview.
26. JRP interview.
27. During the negotiations for the refineries, Parten realized that the co-ops had no interest in Premier's share of the 7-J Stock Farm, so he and Dayson persuaded the co-op's directors to let them buy those shares for the same price Premier had paid for them several months before. Parten and Dayson had formed different companies to operate their refineries. Premier, for example, owned the Longveiw plant; the Baird Refining Company owned the plant in Baird, Texas; and the Octane Oil Refining Company owned the plant in Fort Worth. At the time of the sale, Woodley Petroleum Company owned stock in the latter two companies but not in Premier. All of the refining companies were liquidated. JRP, "Woodley Petroleum Company Twenty-Sixth Annual Report: 1948," p. 2, JRP Papers; Presley, *Never in Doubt*, 127–128; Dayson testimony, Woodley v. Dayson, 211–214, ibid.; JRP to Earl Petty, Aug. 20, 1948, ibid.; JRP interview.
28. Opal Sherman to JRP, Aug. 27, 1948, JRP Papers; JRP to Opal Woodley, Sept. 17, 1948, ibid.
29. JRP to Roland Bond, Feb. 19, 1949, JRP Papers; Carl Basland to JRP, Apr., 12, July 8, 1949, ibid.; JRP to Herbert Lord, June 22, 1949, ibid.; JRP to John D. Manley, Nov. 15, 1949, ibid.; JRP to R. Lee Kempner, Aug. 17, 1950, ibid.; Sandlin to Jerome Sale Hess, June 29, 1950, ibid.; JRP to R. B. Anderson, Mar. 22, 1951, ibid.; JRP to James Boyd, Dec. 12, 1950, ibid.; JRP interview.
30. JRP interview; Clark, "Miracle at Jaltipan."
31. JRP interview; Clark, "Miracle at Jaltipan."
32. JRP interview; Clark, "Miracle at Jaltipan."
33. JRP interview; Clark, "Miracle at Jaltipan."
34. JRP interview.
35. JRP interview; Clark, "Miracle at Jaltipan."
36. JRP, memorandum, "To the Stockholders," Apr. 16, 1951, JRP Papers; JRP to I. H. Kempner, Nov. 15, 1951, ibid.; Clark, "Miracle at Jaltipan"; JRP interview.
37. Haynes, *Brimstone*, 13; Sheehan, "The 'Little Mothers'," 103; *Wall Street Journal*, Aug. 9, 1954; JRP to R. B. Anderson, Mar. 22, 1951, JRP Papers; JRP to I. H. Kempner, Mar. 6, 1951, ibid.

Chapter Twenty-Two

1. JRP interview; Nash, *United States Oil Policy*, 195.
2. Bruce K. Brown, *Oil Men in Washington: An Informal Account of the Organization and Activities of the Petroleum Administration for Defense during the Korean War, 1950–1952* (Evanil Press, 1965), 22.
3. For more on Chapman, see Clayton R. Koppes, "Oscar L. Chapman: A Liberal at the Interior Dept., 1933–1953" (Ph.D. diss., University of Kansas, Lawrence, 1974); Watkins, *Righteous Pilgrim*, 328; JRP interview; Oscar Chapman interview, oral history transcript (LBJ).
4. Wolf later became assistant deputy administrator and general counsel to the Petroleum Administration for Defense. PAD press release, Feb. 15, 1951, box 15, folder 2022, DeGolyer Papers; McCullough, *Truman*, 791; JRP interview; Houston *Post*, Sept. 26, 27, 1950; JRP interview; Marshall interview.
5. JRP interview; Brown, *Oil Men in Washington*, 13, 15, 16.
6. JRP interview; Brown, *Oil Men in Washington*, 16; Engler, *The Politics of Oil*, 293; JRP interview; Marshall interview.
7. JRP interview; Brown, *Oil Men in Washington*, 1; Houston *Chronicle*, n.d., clipping in JRP Papers.
8. Koppes, "Oscar L. Chapman," 171, 172; JRP interview; Marshall interview; Chapman interview, oral history transcript (LBJ).
9. Brown, *Oil Men in Washington*, 17, 19, 23 (quotation); JRP interview; Chapman interview, oral history transcript (LBJ).
10. *Wall Street Journal*, Sept. 29, 1950; Brown, *Oil Men in Washington*, 21–23.
11. New York *Times*, Sept. 29, 1950.
12. "Parten Named Consultant for National Oil and Gas Agency," Department of the Interior press release, Sept. 27, 1950, Oscar L. Chapman Papers (Truman Library); Spencer to JRP, Oct. 2, 1950, JRP Papers; *National Petroleum News*, n.d., clipping in PAD files, JRP Papers; E. O. Thompson, "Industry is Given the Ball in Oil Defense Setup," *TIPRO Magazine*, n.d., clipping in ibid.; "Oil Industry in Good Hands," *Texas Oil Journal* (Oct., 1950), 6.
13. Truman's Executive Order was number 10161; Nash, *United States Oil Policy*, 195; Chapman, "Order No. 2591, Petroleum Administration for Defense," Oct. 3, 1950, transcript in Chapman Papers.
14. Cochran, *Harry Truman*, 340; JRP interview; Marshall interview; Wolf interview; Koppes, "Oscar L. Chapman," 438, 439; Engler, *The Politics of Oil*, 294.
15. JRP interview; Marshall interview; Joseph B. Huttlinger, "PAD Makes Good Start," *World Petroleum* (Nov., 1950), 51.
16. JRP interview, Marshall interview; Wolf interview; Brown, *Oil Men in Washington*, 25, 30; Koppes, "Oscar L. Chapman," 447, 448; Brown to JRP, undated note, PAD file, JRP Papers.

17. JRP interview; Marshall interview; Wolf interview; Brown, *Oil Men in Washington*, 25, 26.

18. JRP interview; Marshall interview; Wolf interview.

19. JRP interview; Brown, *Oil Men in Washington*, 122, 130–134.

20. JRP to Chapman, Oct. 30, 1950, JRP Papers; JRP to Charles S. Jones, Nov. 18, 1950, ibid.

21. JRP to Chapman, Nov. 17, 1950, JRP Papers; Brown, *Oil Men in Washington*, 31; Koppes, "Oscar L. Chapman," 448; JRP interview.

22. Brown, *Oil Men in Washington*, 31; JRP interview.

23. A copy of Truman's executive order is in the PAD file, JRP Papers; JRP to Brown, Feb. 23, 1956, ibid.; JRP to Symington, Nov. 15, 1950, ibid.; official press release, Department of the Interior, Nov. 22, 1950, ibid.; Jones to JRP, Nov. 30, 1950, ibid.; Brown, *Oil Men in Washington*, 32, 33; JRP interview.

24. JRP interview.

25. Ibid.; Brown, *Oil Men in Washington*, 123, 126.

26. JRP interview; Brown, *Oil Men in Washington*, 124.

27. JRP interview; Brown, *Oil Men in Washington*, 127, 128.

28. One reason for Symonds's strong feelings against Texas Eastern was that it had out-bid Symonds for the Big Inch lines when the government put the lines up for sale. See Castaneda and Pratt, *From Texas to the East*, 33–53; Kenneth J. Lipartito and Joseph A. Pratt, *Baker and Botts in the Development of Modern Houston* (Austin: University of Texas Press, 1991), 164, 165; McCullough, *Truman*, 864.

29. Brown, *Oil Men in Washington*, 128; JRP interview.

30. Brown, *Oil Men in Washington*, 128; JRP interview.

31. Chapman to Ford, Jan. 29, 1951, JRP Papers.

32. Ford to Chapman, Feb. 16, 1951, copy in Ickes Papers. For details on the Naval Affairs subcommittee and the PAW, see chapter 19.

33. Marshall interview; JRP interview; memorandum, Joseph V. Machugh to JRP and Marshall, Mar. 28, 1951, JRP Papers; telegram, Bruce K. Brown to JRP, Apr. 3, 1951, ibid.; Chapman to Ford, Apr. 13, 1951, copy in Ickes Papers.

34. JRP to Rayburn, May 17, 1951, JRP Papers; JRP interview.

35. JRP to Chapman, May 3, 1951, JRP Papers; JRP interview.

36. JRP interview; JRP to Chapman, Jan. 14, 1953, JRP Papers; Nash, *United States Oil Policy*, 197.

37. Koppes, "Oscar L. Chapman," 450, 456; Engler, *The Politics of Oil*, 295.

38. JRP interview; Brown to Chapman, Jan. 11, 1952, Chapman Papers.

39. Engler, *The Politics of Oil*, 295; McCullough, *Truman*, 896–901; Brown, *Oil Men in Washington*, 292.

Chapter Twenty-three

1. JRP to Lillian Collier, Apr. 11, 1951, JRP Papers; Carleton, *Red Scare!*, 97, 98; Frantz, *Forty-Acre Follies*, 85, 86; JRP interview.

2. JRP interview.

3. The literature on the post–World War II red scare and "McCarthyism" is vast. For useful overviews see Richard M. Fried, *Nightmare in Red: The McCarthy Era in Perspective* (New York: Oxford University Press, 1990), and David Caute, *The Great Fear: The Anti-Communist Purge under Truman and Eisenhower* (New York: Simon and Schuster, 1978).

4. Hart's tenure as chancellor was soon ended. Pressure from the conservatives in control of the board of regents eventually led to his resignation. For more on the attack on Ayres and Hart, see Carleton, *Red Scare!*, 98.

5. JRP interview.

6. Walter Hall interview, oral history transcript (LBJ); JRP interview.

7. Davidson, *Race and Class in Texas Politics*, 161; Green, *The Establishment in Texas Politics*, 110, 111, 141, 143; JRP interview.

8. JRP interview; Collier to JRP, July 23, 1951, JRP Papers; and Cunningham to JRP, Aug. 8, 1951, ibid.; Green, *The Establishment in Texas Politics*, 143.

9. Margaret Reading to JRP, Aug. 10, 1951, JRP Papers; JRP to Harry Seay, Sept. 26, 1951, ibid.; JRP interview; Fath interview; Green, *The Establishment in Texas Politics*, 147; Austin *Statesman*, Feb. 22, 1948.

10. JRP interview; JRP to Tristram Coffin, Nov. 13, 1979, JRP Papers.

11. Margaret Reading to JRP, June 13 1952, JRP Papers; JRP interview; Fath interview; Hall interview.

12. JRP interview; Fath interview.

13. JRP interview; Hall interview; Fath interview; Dugger interview. For more on Jim Sewell, see Ralph Yarborough, "Tiger Jim," *Texas Observer* (Jan. 28, 1977), 21–23.

14. JRP interview; Dallek, *Lone Star Rising*, 417; Hardeman and Bacon, *Rayburn*, 361.

15. For an excellent summary of Yarborough's career, see Michael L. Collins, "Ralph Yarborough," in Kenneth F. Hendrickson Jr. and Michael L. Collins (eds.), *Profiles in Power: Twentieth Century Texans in Washington*

(Arlington Heights, Ill.: Harlan Davidson, Inc., 1993), 149–173; Yarborough interview; JRP interview.

16. Michael Deutch to JRP, Feb. 3, 1952, JRP Papers; Connelly to JRP, Feb. 8, 1952, Truman Papers; JRP to Connelly, Feb. 9, 1952, ibid.

17. Truman Daily Calendar, Feb. 14, 1952, Truman Papers; JRP interview.

18. JRP interview; Fagan Dickson to Maury Maverick Sr., Apr. 7, 1952, Maury Maverick Sr. Papers (CAH); Green, *The Establishment in Texas Politics*, 143–145; Hall, Sandlin, JRP, and Underwood to McKinney, Mar. 21, 1952, JRP Papers; Hall to Rayburn, Apr. 15, 1952, ibid.

19. "Memo of conversation between Sen Johnson & Weldon Hart," Apr. 22, 1952, box 1, Notes and Transcripts of Conversations, LBJ Papers.

20. JRP interview.

21. Ibid.; "Memo from the Files,"Apr. 24, 1952, box 1, LBJ Papers.

22. JRP interview; Yarborough interview; Green, *The Establishment in Texas Politics*, 142; Davidson, *Race and Class in Texas Politics*, 32.

23. Yarborough later wrote Parten that he "alone made it possible for me to run in 1952. . . ." JRP interview; Yarborough interview; Yarborough to Creekmore Fath, Sept. 15, 1967, copy in JRP Papers; Elton Miller, "The Yarborough Story," *Texas Observer* (Oct. 16, 1964), 3; Yarborough, typescript of a radio speech, May 19, 1952, box 2R559, Ralph W. Yarborough Papers (CAH); Yarborough to JRP, Apr. 16, 1952, ibid.; Yarborough to JRP, Feb. 13, 1955, JRP Papers; William G. Phillips, *Yarborough of Texas* (Washington, D.C : Acropolis Books, 1969), 34; Allan Shivers interview, oral history transcript (UNT).

24. Maverick to Lawrence Westbrook, May 6, 1952, Maverick Papers; Maverick to Truman, May 7, 1952, ibid.; Dallas *Morning News*, May 22, 1953.

25. Austin *Statesman*, May 7, 1952; Fagan Dickson to William Neal Roach, May 9, 1952, box 13, Walter Hall Papers, (Woodson Research Center, Rice University, Houston); JRP interview.

26. Houston *Chronicle*, May 28, 1952; JRP interview; Hall interview; Fath interview; Green, *The Establishment in Texas Politics*, 145; Houston *Post*, May 28, 1952; Dickson to JRP, June 24, 1952, folder 5, Fagan Dickson Papers (Woodson Research Center, Rice University); Collier to JRP, June 3, 1952, Maverick Papers; Collier to Maverick, June 3, 1952, ibid.

27. Dickson to JRP, May 30, June 23, July 9, 1952, folder 5, Dickson Papers; JRP to Dickson, July 10, 1952, ibid.; Creekmore Fath to Drew Pearson, June 4, 1952, "Creekmore Fath" folder, box G231q3, Drew Pearson Papers; JRP to Rayburn, June 2, 1952, JRP Papers; Hardeman and Bacon, *Rayburn*, 361; JRP interview.

28. Working behind the scenes on Shivers's behalf, Johnson called party chairman Frank McKinney to urge his support for seating the Shivers delegates, telling McKinney that Shivers had "a better record than the other people." "Telephone Conversation between Senator Johnson and Governor Shivers, June 11, 1952 at 10:25 AM," box 1 , LBJ Papers; Dallek, *Lone Star Rising*, 417; Hardeman and Bacon, *Rayburn*, 361.

29. Houston *Press*, July 16, 1952.

30. JRP interview; Houston *Press*, July 16, 1952; JRP to Shivers, July 16, 1952, JRP Papers; JRP to Truman, July 16, 1952, ibid.; JRP to Yarborough, July 16, 1952, ibid.

31. JRP interview.

32. Allan Shivers interview, oral history transcript (LBJ); JRP interview.

33. Years later, Shivers recalled that "Lyndon [Johnson] and I never had any real conflict over the 1952 convention or my support of Eisenhower." Shivers interview, oral history transcript (LBJ); JRP interview; Fath interview; Dallek, *Lone Star Rising*, 417.

34. Green, *The Establishment in Texas Politics*, 145; Shivers interview, oral history transcript (LBJ); JRP interview; Fath interview; Hall interview; Yarborough interview.

35. Green, *The Establishment in Texas Politics*, 142; McKay, *Texas and the Fair Deal*, 407, 408; JRP to Yarborough, Apr. 2, 1953, JRP Papers.

36. Porter McKeever, *Adlai Stevenson: His Life and Legacy*, 212, 213; Dallek, *Lone Star Rising*, 419; Green, *The Establishment in Texas Politics*, 145; Shivers interview, oral history transcript (LBJ); JRP interview; JRP to Rayburn, Aug. 27, 1952, JRP Papers; Rayburn to JRP, Sept. 1, 1952, ibid.

37. JRP interview; Haynes, *Brimstone*, 13.

38. Freeport offered to buy 50 percent of Pan American so that the two companies could work Jaltipan together and split the risks. As a writer for *Fortune Magazine* later noted however, "Parten wanted a buyer, not a partner." Sheehan, "The 'Little Mothers'," 200; JRP interview.

39. JRP interview; Sheehan, "The 'Little Mothers'," 200; JRP interview; *Wall Street Journal*, Aug. 9, 1954.

40. JRP, "Memorandum for the files of the Pan American Sulphur Company," Aug. 14, 1952, JRP Papers; JRP interview; Sheehan, "The 'Little Mothers'," 200.

41. JRP interview.

42. JRP interview; Leonard J. Townsend interview.

43. JRP interview; Hardeman and Bacon, *Rayburn*, 370, 371.

44. McKay, *Texas and the Fair Deal*, 413, 414; Houston *Post*, Oct. 18, 19, 1952; JRP to McKinney, Oct. 8, 1952,

JRP Papers; Sandlin to W. N. Roach, Oct. 10, 1952, ibid.; JRP to DNC, Oct. 7, 1952, ibid.; Rayburn to JRP, Oct. 20, 1952, ibid.; Conn to JRP, Oct. 24, 1952, ibid.; JRP interview.

45. Townsend interview; Houston *Press*, Oct. 30, 1952; Houston *Post*, Oct. 31, 1952.

46. JRP interview; Houston *Press*, Oct. 30, 1952; JRP to Rayburn, Nov. 8, 1952, 1952 file, drawer 3, "General Misc.," Rayburn Papers; Rayburn to JRP, Nov. 15, 1952, ibid.

47. JRP interview; JRP to Stevenson, Nov. 8, 1952, JRP Papers.

Chapter Twenty-four

1. Thomas C. Reeves, *Freedom and the Foundation: The Fund for the Republic in the Era of McCarthyism* (New York: Knopf, 1969), 22–24; JRP interview.

2. JRP interview.

3. JRP interview; Hoffman to JRP, Aug. 29, 1952, JRP Papers; JRP to Hoffman, Sept. 4, 1952, ibid.; Kelly interview; Frank K. Kelly, *Court of Reason: Robert Hutchins and the Fund for the Republic* (New York: Free Press, 1981), 17.

4. JRP interview; Kelly interview; JRP interview (with A. Champagne).

5. Reeves, *Freedom and the Foundation*, 32–33 (quotation).

6. Ibid., 33, 34; Hutchins interview, oral history transcript (Ford Foundation); quote about Parten is from Kelly, *Court of Reason*, 17; W. H. Ferry interview, oral history transcript (Ford Foundation); Ashmore, *Unseasonable Truths*, 331, 332.

7. Joining Parten from the South had been Malcolm Bryan, the president of the Federal Reserve Bank in Atlanta, Georgia. Bryan had resigned after the first board meeting because of the Fund's interest in supporting the civil rights movement. Attorney John Lord O'Brian soon replaced Bryan. JRP interview; Reeves, *Freedom and the Foundation*, 34, 35, 38; Kelly, *Court of Reason*, 19, 20; JRP to David F. Freeman, Dec. 17, 1952, box 3, Fund for the Republic Archive ; cited hereafter as FFR (Mudd Library, Princeton University, Princeton).

8. Kelly, *Court of Reason*, 19; Reeves, *Freedom and the Foundation*, 36, 38, 42, 43, 49; Ashmore, *Unseasonable Truths*, 333; JRP interview.

9. For more on Cullen's political activities and public statements, see Carleton, *Red Scare!*, 89–93; JRP interview; JRP to Rayburn, Jan. 16, 1953, JRP Papers; Rayburn to JRP, Jan. 24, 1953, ibid.

10. JRP interview.

11. Kelly, *Court of Reason*, 17; Reeves, *Freedom and the Foundation*, 45, 47; JRP interview.

12. Griswold to JRP, Dec. 7, 1956, JRP Papers; Hoffman to JRP, Feb. 25, 1953, ibid.; Reeves, *Freedom and the Foundation*, 47, 48; Ashmore, *Unseasonable Truths*, 335; Kelly, *Court of Reason*, 13–18; JRP interview.

13. Reeves, *Freedom and the Foundation*, 49; Edward C. Solomon to JRP, Mar. 4, 1953, ibid.; Alfred A. Knopf to JRP, Mar. 10, 1953, ibid.; Frieda B. Hennock to JRP, Mar. 27, 1953, ibid.; and JRP to Hennock, Apr. 2, 1953, ibid.

14. Reeves, *Freedom and the Foundation*, 51, 52; Joseph R. McCarthy to Paul Hoffman, May 1, 1953, box 10, FFR; J. R. Parten FBI File, Mar. 25, 1953, JRP Papers.

15. Reeves, *Freedom and the Foundation*, 53, 54; Hutchins interview, oral history transcript (Ford Foundation); JRP interview.

16. JRP interview; Ferry interview, oral history transcript (Ford Foundation).

17. For the Ebey affair and the Houston situation, see Carleton, *Red Scare!*

18. Dallas *News*, Sept. 18, 1953; JRP interview; Stephen Mitchell to Aubrey Gasque, July 8, 1954, "State File-Texas," box 40, Stephen Mitchell Papers (Truman Library); the Browns made their contribution in cash, see Charles I. Francis to JRP, Nov. 11, 1953, JRP Papers; JRP to Rayburn, July 25, 1953, ibid.; JRP to Rayburn, Nov. 4, 1953, ibid.; and Rayburn to JRP, Nov. 11, 1953, ibid.

19. Rayburn to JRP, Feb. 27, 1954, JRP Papers.

20. JRP to Freeman, Oct. 21, 1953, JRP Papers; JRP to Hutchins, Oct. 27, 1953, ibid.; Reeves, *Freedom and the Foundation*, 58, 59; JRP interview.

21. JRP to Clifford Case, Dec. 15, 1953, box 3, FFR; "Minutes," board meeting, Nov.18, 1953, box 21, ibid.; Reeves, *Freedom and the Foundation*, 59, 60; Carleton, *Red Scare!*, 239, 240; JRP interview.

22. Reeves, *Freedom and the Foundation*, 74, 75; David S. Broder, "The Freedom That Education Built," Washington *Post*, May 18, 1977; JRP interview.

23. Hoffman to JRP, July 9, 1954, JRP Papers; JRP interview.

24. Hoffman to JRP, July 17, 1954, JRP Papers; JRP to William Frye, July 21, 1954, ibid.; Thomas C. Reeves, *The Life and Times of Joe McCarthy: A Biography* (New York : Stein and Day, 1982), 641; Richard M. Fried, *Men Against McCarthy* (New York : Columbia University Press, 1976), 295; JRP interview; Carleton, *Red Scare!*, 273.

25. Baltimore *Sun*, July 23, 1954; New York *Times*, July 23, 24, 1954.

26. Alfred Kohlberg to JRP, July 27, 1954, JRP Papers; Howard Gilhouser, to JRP, July 23, 1954, ibid.; Robert Engler, "Just So They Vote Right," *New Republic* (Sept. 5, 1955), 13.

27. Reeves, *Freedom and the Foundation*, 76, 77, 84, 88; Kelly, Court of Reason, 39; JRP interview; Carleton, *Red Scare!*, 239, 240

28. Reeves, *Freedom and the Foundation*, 83–86; JRP interview
29. Reeves, *Freedom and the Foundation*, 86; JRP interview.

Chapter Twenty-five

1. Woodley Petroleum, Annual Report (1948), p. 3, JRP Papers; ibid. (1949), p. 8, ibid.; JRP interview.
2. Carbon copy to JRP of Marshall to board of directors, Ashland Oil, JRP Papers; JRP to Marshall, Mar. 31, 1952, ibid.; Rainey to JRP, Feb. 16, 1952, ibid.; JRP to Jules G. Kranich, Feb. 19, 1954, ibid.; Marshall, *Done in Oil*, 197; JRP testimony, *Woodley v. Dayson*, p. 128, Dayson Papers.
3. JRP interview; Miller interview; Brown, *Oil Men in Washington*, 47, 48; Dayson testimony, *Woodley v. Dayson*, p. 218, Dayson Papers.
4. Each Great Northern investor purchased 3600 shares of stock at $1 per share. The company was incorporated on February 7, 1951. J. H. Marshall and JRP testimonies, *Woodley v. Dayson*, Dayson Papers; Sandlin to Charles N. Caldwell, Jan. 29, 1951, JRP Papers; Dayson to J. R. White, Feb. 5, 1951, ibid.
5. JRP interview; Marshall, *Done in Oil*, 204; *Woodley v. Dayson*, p. 230, Dayson Papers.
6. Sheehan, "The 'Little Mothers'," 200; JRP interview; Clark, "Miracle at Jaltipan."
7. In his autobiography, Marshall indicated that his opinions about Dayson had not changed in more than forty years. Marshall, who misspelled Dayson's name ("Dasone"), grudgingly described Parten's old friend as a "fairly good refiner in a technical sense." He characterized Dayson, however, as a "too greedy" liar and con artist. *Done in Oil*, 206, 207; Miller interview; Shelmire interview; JRP to Marshall, Dec. 15, 1952, JRP Papers.
8. Miller interview; Anderson interview; Ilfrey interview; Moore interview; JRP interview.
9. Shelmire interview; Presley, *Never in Doubt*, 402, 403.
10. JRP interview; JRP testimony, *Woodley v. Dayson*, p. 130, Dayson Papers; Marshall to Allen E. Richardson, Nov. 26, Dec. 23, 1952, JRP Papers; Marshall to J. B. Cook, July 23, 1953, ibid.; Dayson to JRP, Aug. 28, 1952, ibid.
11. Townsend interview; JRP interview.
12. Sylvester Dayson was appointed vice president and Roland Bond became secretary-treasurer. Although Dick Andrade remained as a major stockholder, he did not take a position on the board of directors because of his investments in other sulphur companies. Townsend interview; Haynes, *Brimstone*, 192; Clark, "Miracle at Jaltipan"; Sheehan, "The 'Little Mothers'," 203.
13. By the beginning of 1957, Pan American was putting 7.5 million in U.S. dollars into the Mexican economy. Haynes, *Brimstone*, 194, 195; Clark, "Miracle at Jaltipan."
14. Haynes, *Brimstone*, 193, 194; Townsend interview; Clark, "Miracle at Jaltipan."
15. J. Howard Marshall later claimed that Mobil's management stalled while it made plans to build its own refinery in Minnesota. *Done in Oil*, 205; JRP to Jules G. Kranich, Feb. 19, 1954, JRP Papers; JRP interview.
16. JRP interview.
17. JRP, "Outline of statement to be made at the St. Paul Dinner on March 9, 1954," Marshall to JRP, July 20, 1953, JRP Papers; JRP to Harold H. Liebman, Feb. 8, 1954, ibid.; Sandlin testimony, *Woodley v. Dayson*, p. 60, Dayson Papers; St. Paul *Dispatch-Pioneer Press*, Mar. 10, 1954; Marshall, *Done in Oil*, 204.
18. Woodley and Southern Production provided six million dollars in equity for the refinery. A banking consortium led by the First National Bank of Chicago and the First National Bank of Saint Paul financed the remaining nineteen million dollars at 5 percent interest. Chase Bank of New York also participated in Great Northern's financing. Marshall, *Done in Oil*, 205, 206; JRP to J. B. Cook, June 22, 1953, JRP Papers; St. Paul *Dispatch-Pioneer Press*, Mar. 10, 1954; JRP interview; Marshall interview.
19. Mayer interview; JRP interview; Shelmire interview.
20. In his autobiography, Marshall gives a different version of Dayson's demands. He claims that Dayson refused to invest his own money in the refinery deal and demanded that Parten, Marshall, and the other investors pay his share of the stock price and carry the interest. Marshall, *Done in Oil*, 206; JRP interview; JRP testimony, *Woodley v. Dayson*, p. 167, Dayson Papers; Joe Levin to JRP, Nov. 15, 1953, JRP Papers; clipping, Minneapolis *Morning Tribune*, Nov. 13, 1953, ibid.
21. JRP interview; Marshall interview.
22. *Wall Street Journal*, Dec. 23, 1953; JRP, "Outline of a speech to be made at the St. Paul Dinner on Mar. 9, 1954," JRP Papers; JRP to Allan J. Haggerty, July 26, 1956, ibid.; Marshall, *Done in Oil*, 207.
23. Dayson died on April 6, 1978. Shelmire interview; JRP testimony, *Woodley v. Dayson*, p. 167–171, Dayson Papers; Allen E. Richardson to JRP, Apr. 15, 1954, JRP Papers; Suzette Shelmire to JRP, Dec. 4, 1967, ibid.; JRP interview.

Chapter Twenty-six

1. Yarborough interview; JRP interview; Yarborough to JRP, July 27, Aug. 17, Nov. 5, 1953, JRP Papers; JRP to Yarborough, Nov. 4, 1953, ibid.
2. Mitchell to JRP, Feb. 1, 1954, JRP Papers; JRP interview.
3. Creekmore Fath in particular had alienated the Speaker by his confrontational activities during the fight

over the Maverick delegation in 1952 and by his subsequent public criticisms of national Democratic Party chairman Stephen Mitchell, whom Fath had accused of being weak and incompetent. Fath was not happy with Rayburn either. He felt that Rayburn's support for seating the Shivers delegation to the national convention in Chicago had been a betrayal of the loyalist cause. Fath complained to muckraking journalist Drew Pearson that Stephen Mitchell "has the imagination of a guppy . . . [he] is a squarehead who thinks he's an egghead." Fath to Pearson, Jan. 20, 1954, "Creekmore Fath" folder, box G231q3, Pearson Papers; JRP interview; Fath interview; JRP to Mitchell, Feb. 18, 1954, JRP Papers; Hardeman to JRP, Mar. 5, 1954, ibid.

4. JRP interview; Yarborough interview; Yarborough to JRP, Feb. 6, 1954, JRP Papers; Sandlin, manuscript notation to JRP, Apr. 9, 1954, on carbon copy of Mozelle Chapman to Yarborough, Mar. 25, 1954, ibid.; JRP to Rayburn, Apr. 30, 1954, ibid.; JRP to Mitchell, Apr. 30, 1954, ibid.; Rayburn to JRP, May 21, 1954, ibid.; Fath interview; Fath to Pearson, Jan. 20, 1954, "Creekmore Fath" folder, box G231q3, Pearson Papers.

5. For more on the insurance scandal and the political environment surrounding the 1954 gubernatorial campaign, see Green, *The Establishment in Texas Politics*, 152; JRP interview.

6. JRP interview; Deposition of Allan Shivers, *Charles Landergott vs. Lloyd M. Bentsen, Sr.*, Sept. 29, 1952, photocopy in JRP Papers.

7. The water permit allowed the taking of water during dry season only when the river was flowing at a certain rate as measured at a gauge at Rio Grande City. Shivers deposition, *Landergott vs. Bentsen*, Sept. 29, 1952, JRP Papers; Green, *The Establishment in Texas Politics*, 153; JRP interview.

8. JRP interview; Yarborough interview; Austin *American*, May 18, 1954; JRP to Rayburn, May 19, 1954, JRP Papers.

9. JRP interview; Austin *American*, June 26, 1954; Fath interview.

10. Austin *American*, June 26, 1954.

11. Ibid., June 3, 1954; D. B. Hardeman to JRP, June 7, 1954, JRP Papers; Yarborough to JRP, June 28, 1954, ibid.; Yarborough interview.

12. For more on Shivers and the red scare, see Carleton, *Red Scare!*, 255–276; Austin *American*, July 14, 1954; Dallas *News*, July 19, 1954.

13. Rayburn to JRP, May 21, 1954, JRP Papers; JRP to Yarborough, June 1, 1954, ibid.; JRP interview, Yarborough interview; Carleton, *Red Scare!*, 276.

14. Transcript, "Yarborough Meets the People," July 22, 1954, 1954 campaign file, Yarborough Papers; Fath interview; JRP interview; Yarborough interview.

15. Yarborough won 119 of the state's 254 counties, trailing the governor by only 24,000 votes out of the more than 1.3 million votes cast. Green, *The Establishment in Texas Politics*, 157.

16. Green, *The Establishment in Texas Politics*, 151–165.

17. Ibid., 156.

18. JRP to Sawtelle, Aug. 18, 1954, Yarborough-Shivers folder, JRP Papers; JRP to Marlin Sandlin, manuscript note, n.d., Yarborough-Shivers folder, ibid.; [Boyce] House to JRP, n.d., ibid.; JRP interview.

19. JRP, ms. draft, undated and untitled, Yarborough-Shivers folder, JRP Papers; Dallas *Morning News*, Aug. 26, 1954; Green, *The Establishment in Texas Politics*, 162, 163; JRP to W. H. Bryant, Oct. 1, 1954.

20. Opal to JRP, Sept. 15, 1954, JRP Papers; JRP to Opal, Sept. 17, 1954, ibid.

21. Yarborough to JRP, Oct. 20, 21, 1954, JRP Papers.

22. JRP interview; Goodwyn, "Dugger's Observer," *Texas Observer* (Dec. 27, 1974), 5.

23. Dugger interview; Walter Hall interview; JRP interview; Helen Ainsworth to Mozelle Chapman, Nov. 6, 1953, JRP Papers.

24. JRP interview; Dugger interview; Goodwyn, "Dugger's Observer," 5.

25. Mozelle Chapman to Ferry, Apr. 15, 1955, JRP Papers; Ferry to JRP, Apr. 1, 1955, ibid.

26. James McEnteer, *Fighting Words: Independent Journalists in Texas* (Austin: University of Texas Press, 1992), 187, 188; Dugger interview; JRP interview.

27. Dugger interview; Lawrence Goodwyn interview; Dallas *Morning News*, July 19, 1981.

28. Rapoport interview; Dugger interview; JRP interview; Goodwyn interview.

29. Parten had too many personal and business distractions to be involved in LBJ's campaign for the Senate against Coke Stevenson in 1948. He was eager to see Stevenson defeated, but he did little on Johnson's behalf except to make a financial contribution and to urge his former colleagues in the Rainey campaign to vote for him. LBJ's campaign organization welcomed Parten's money and his moral support, but his strong identification with Rainey's liberal cause eliminated the possibility of any visible role in the campaign for the Houston oil man. As LBJ political operative Ed Clark later recalled, "we didn't tell the Major to stay home because we didn't have to, but he was too connected to Rainey to help us much, so that's the way things just worked out." Clark interview; JRP interview; Dallek, *Lone Star Rising*, 498, 499.

30. JRP to Will Clayton, Oct. 13, 1954, JRP Papers; Sewell to JRP, Sept. 28, 1954, ibid.; JRP to Sewell, Oct. 15, 1954, ibid.; JRP interview.

31. JRP interview; Houston *Post*, Aug. 5, 1955; JRP to W. B.Crossley, Sept. 8, 1955, JRP Papers; Green, *The*

Establishment in Texas Politics, 168.
32. Collier to JRP, Sept. 20, 1955, JRP Papers; JRP to Collier, Sept. 27, 1955, ibid.
33. Stevenson to JRP, Nov. 3, 22, 1955, JRP Papers; JRP to Stevenson, Nov. 11, 1955, ibid.
34. JRP interview; Dugger interview.

Chapter Twenty-seven

1. Kelly, *Court of Reason,* 50–54.
2. Reeves, *Freedom and the Foundation,* 117–123, 185.
3. Philip E. Beach to JRP, Aug. 14, 1955, JRP Papers; Jackson P. Dick to JRP, Apr. 12, 1956, ibid.; JRP to Thompson, July 8, 1955, ibid.; JRP to Jackson P. Dick, May 14, 1956, ibid.
4. Ferry interview, oral histroy transcript (Ford Foundation); Ferry to JRP, Dec. 20, 1955, box 3, FFR.
5. Reeves, *Freedom and the Foundation,* 177; Griswold to Hoffman, Dec. 19, 1955, copy in JRP Papers.
6. Griswold to JRP, Dec. 7, 1956, JRP Papers; JRP to Griswold, Jan. 24, 1957, ibid.; Reeves, *Freedom and the Foundation,* 184, 189; Kelly interview.
7. Walter Goodman, *The Committee: The Extraordinary Career of the House Committee on Un-American Activities* (New York: Farrar, Straus, and Giroux, 1968), 399, 400; Reeves, *Freedom and the Foundation,* 56; JRP interview; Theoharis and Cox, *The Boss,* 319.
8. Hutchins to JRP, n.d., JRP Papers; JRP interview; Broder, Washington *Post,* May 18, 1977.
9. Reeves, *Freedom and the Foundation,* 206, 207; Ashmore, *Unseasonable Truths,* 370; JRP interview (with A. Champagne); Mozelle Chapman to Paul Hoffman, June 19, 1956, box 21, FFR.
10. Hardeman and Bacon, *Rayburn,* 424; Alla Clardy interview, oral history transcript (UNT); JRP interview.
11. JRP interview; Reeves, *Freedom and the Foundation,* 339.
12. Theoharis and Cox, *Rayburn,* 319; JRP interview (with A. Champagne); JRP interview; Kelly, *Court of Reason,* 92–93; Ashmore, *Unseasonable Truths,* 370.
13. John Cogley, *Report on Blacklisting* (2 vols.; New York: Fund for the Republic, 1956). For a detailed discussion of the blacklist and how it worked against one victim, see John Henry Faulk, *Fear on Trial* (Austin: University of Texas Press, 1983); for the blacklist in general, see Victor S. Navasky, *Naming Names* (New York: Viking Press, 1980); Stefan Kanfer, *A Journal of the Plague Years* (New York: Atheneum, 1973); David Caute, *The Great Fear: The anti-Communist Purge under Truman and Eisenhower* (New York: Simon and Schuster, 1978), 621–650; and Larry Ceplair and Steven Englund, *The Inquisition in Hollywood: Politics in the Film Community* (New York: Anchor Press/Doubleday, 1980), 478–504; Reeves, *Freedom and the Foundation,* 211.
14. Reeves, *Freedom and the Foundation,* 193, 210; JRP interview.
15. Reeves, *Freedom and the Foundation,* 70, 192; Kelly, *Court of Reason,* 73, 74; JRP interview.
16. Faulk, *Fear on Trial,* 28; Faulk interview.
17. Reeves, *Freedom and the Foundation,* 211, 212, 231, 232; Eugene McCarthy interview; JRP interview.
18. Reeves, *Freedom and the Foundation,* 215–230, 236, 237.
19. Goodman, *The Committee,* 402–406; Kelly, *Court of Reason,* 107.
20. Kelly interview; Reeves, *Freedom and the Foundation,* 191, 196; JRP interview; Marcus interview; Marcus to JRP, July 3, 20, 1956, JRP Papers; JRP to Marcus, July 6, 1956, ibid.; Kelly, *Court of Reason,* 106; JRP to Kelly, Aug. 8, 1956, box 3, FFR.
21. JRP to Rayburn, Aug. 9, 1956, JRP Papers; Hutchins to Rayburn, Aug. 7, 1956, Rayburn Papers; Kelly, *Court of Reason,* 106; JRP interview.
22. Kelly, *Court of Reason,* 108; Ashmore, *Unseasonable Truths,* 372.
23. HUAC annual report (1956), viii, 24; Kelly, *Court of Reason,* 108–110.
24. Hardeman and Bacon, *Rayburn,* 424, 425.
25. JRP to Rayburn, Mar. 27, 1958, JRP Papers.
26. Ashmore, *Unseasonable Truths,* 373; Kelly, *Court of Reason,* 110, 111; Reeves, *Freedom and the Foundation,* 269; Houston *Chronicle,* Jan. 3, 1947, Jan. 5, 1948; Hardeman interview; JRP interview.
27. JRP to Kelly, Aug. 9, 1956, JRP Papers; JRP to J. Frank Dobie, Aug. 26, 1957, Dobie Papers; JRP interview; Faulk interview; Faulk, *Fear on Trial,* 31.

Chapter Twenty-eight

1. Green, *The Establishment in Texas Politics,* 172; Dallek, *Lone Star Rising,* 500; Hardeman and Bacon, *Rayburn,* 398; JRP interview; JRP to Rayburn, Mar. 9, 1956, JRP Papers; Rayburn to JRP, Mar. 30, 1956, ibid.; Anthony Champagne, *Congressman Sam Rayburn* (New Brunswick, N.J.: Rutgers University Press, 1984), 147.
2. Dallek, *Lone Star Rising,* 500; Green, *The Establishment in Texas Politics,* 173; Hardeman and Bacon, *Rayburn,* 400; JRP interview; Fath interview.
3. Connally interview; Fath interview; Green, *The Establishment in Texas Politics,* 173.
4. See Dallek, *Lone Star Rising,* 186, for a slightly different version of how Connally and LBJ got together. JRP

interview; James Reston Jr., *The Lone Star: The Life of John Connally* (New York: Harper and Row, 1989), 30, 31, 56; JRP to Frank Knox, Sept. 16, 1940, "John Connally," box 15, LBJ Papers.

5. JRP interview; Hardeman and Bacon, *Rayburn*, 412.

6. JRP interview; Green, *The Establishment in Texas Politics*, 174; Dallek, *Lone Star Rising*, 501.

7. Green, *The Establishment in Texas Politics*, 167, 168, 174; Yarborough interview; JRP interview; JRP to Yarborough, July 3, 1956, JRP Papers.

8. Green, *The Establishment in Texas Politics*, 174, 175; JRP interview.

9. Haley's campaign stressed the issue of racial integration, calling it "a communist plot to destroy the white race." At one point, Haley promised to use Texas Rangers to stop at the Red River any federal authorities who tried to enter Texas to enforce racial integration. O'Daniel's appeal had been equally racist, labelling the Supreme Court's decision in the Brown case "communist inspired." In the election, O'Daniel placed third and Haley fourth. Green, *The Establishment in Texas Politics*, 174, 175; JRP to Yarborough, May 31, 1956, JRP Papers; Yarborough to JRP, June 9, 1956, ibid.; JRP interview; Yarborough interview.

10. Joe Cook to Yarborough, Aug. 20, 1956, JRP Papers; Yarborough to JRP, May 18, 1957, ibid.; Yarborough interview; Green, *The Establishment in Texas Politics*, 176.

11. JRP to Butler, May 18, 1956, JRP Papers; LBJ to JRP, July 30, Aug. 7, 1956, ibid.; JRP to Stevenson, Aug. 9, 1956, ibid.; Hardeman and Bacon, *Rayburn*, 401, 402; JRP interview; photograph of JRP, Sandlin, and Joe Kilgore wearing "Love that Johnson" buttons at the caucus at the Palmer House, Houston *Chronicle*, Aug. 14, 1956.

12. Dallek, *Lone Star Rising*, 503; JRP interview; Roger L. Stevens to JRP, Aug. 17, 1956, JRP Papers; JRP to Stevens, Oct. 15, 1956, ibid.; JRP to Matthew H. McCloskey, Oct. 2, 1956, ibid.; Rayburn to JRP, Sept. 19, 1956, ibid.; Lou Poller to JRP, Sept. 24, 1956, ibid.; JRP to Rayburn, Sept. 14, 1956, Rayburn Papers.

13. Connally claimed that Johnson had been forced to kick the liberals out of the convention because they were planning to seize control of the party offices to deny the certification of Price Daniel as the party's nominee for governor. There is no substantive evidence, however, to support Connally's claim. Connally interview (with A. Champagne); Yarborough interview; JRP interview; Fath interview; Green, *The Establishment in Texas Politics*, 177, 178; Dallek, *Lone Star Rising*, 505.

14. JRP interview.

15. C. T. McLaughlin to JRP, Oct. 4, 1956, JRP Papers; JRP to McLaughlin, Oct. 23, 1956, ibid.

16. JRP to Stevenson, Nov. 8, 1956, JRP Papers; Rayburn to JRP, Nov. 12, 1956, ibid.

17. Green, *The Establishment in Texas Politics*, 182; Dallek, *Lone Star Rising*, 510.

18. JRP to Yarborough, Mar. 12, 1957, JRP Papers; Marshall to Yarborough, Mar. 14, 1957, ibid.; Mozelle Chapman to Joe Webb, Mar. 25, 1957, ibid.

19. JRP to Yarborough, Apr. 3, May 9, 1957, JRP Papers; Ferry to JRP, Apr. 4, 1957, ibid.; JRP to LBJ, Apr. 3, 1957, ibid.

20. Yarborough to JRP, May 18, 1957, JRP Papers.

Chapter Twenty-nine

1. Pepe Anderson interview; Randy Parten interview.

2. Randy Parten interview.

3. Sheehan, "The 'Little Mothers'," 96; *Wall Street Journal*, Aug. 9, 1954.

4. Sheehan, "The 'Little Mothers'," 96; JRP interview; Townsend interview.

5. Pan American Sulphur Company, "Annual Report to the Stockholders," Dec. 1954, JRP Papers; Townsend interview; JRP interview; *Forbes* (Sept. 1, 1960), 23; Sheehan, "The 'Little Mothers'," 203.

6. Clark, "Miracle at Jaltipan"; Sheehan, "The 'Little Mothers'," 96; Townsend interview; JRP interview.

7. *Wall Street Journal*, Dec. 9, 1957, Feb. 11, 1958; Sheehan, "The 'Little Mothers'," 203, 204; Jack and Marguerite Boothe interview; Townsend interview; Miller interview.

8. Sheehan, "The 'Little Mothers'," 97; *Forbes* (Sept. 1, 1960), 23; JRP interview; Townsend interview; *Wall Street Journal*, Feb. 11, 1958; Haynes, *Brimstone*, 189; Pan American Sulphur Company, "Annual Report to the Stockholders," Dec. 1954, JRP Papers.

9. *Wall Street Journal*, Feb. 17, 19, May 8, 1958.

10. Miller interview; JRP to Else E. Hensie, Apr. 29, 1958, JRP Papers.

11. Miller interview; *Forbes* (Mar. 15, 1960), 16; JRP interview.

12. Miller interview; Marr interview; Sherman interview; Ilfrey interview.

13. New York *Times*, Aug. 17, 1980; Sherman interview; Ilfrey interview; Miller interview.

14. JRP interview; Ilfrey interview.

15. JRP interview; Miller interview.

16. JRP interview.

17. JRP interview; Green, *The Establishment in Texas Politics*, 202; JRP to Fagan Dickson, May 12 , 15, 20, 1958, JRP Papers; Yarborough to JRP, May 19, 1958, ibid.; JRP to Yarborough, July 2, 1958, ibid.

18. JRP to Billy Goldberg, July 21, 1958, JRP Papers; JRP to Yarborough, Aug. 5, 1958, ibid.; JRP to Dickson, June 16, 27, Aug. 15, 1958, ibid.; Sandlin to Dickson, Aug. 22, 1958, ibid.; Dickson to JRP, June 20, 30, 1958, ibid.; JRP to Bond, July 17, 1958, ibid.; JRP to Clayton, July 3, 1958, ibid.; Clayton to JRP, July 7, 1958, ibid.

19. Green, *The Establishment in Texas Politics*, 202; "Yarborough's Opponent," *New Republic*, 138 (April 21, 1958), 4–5; Clayton to JRP, July 23, 1958, JRP Papers.

20. Rayburn accepted Blakely's donation, but he had his library fund-raiser acknowledge it. Hardeman and Bacon, *Rayburn*, 348; JRP interview; Harry Blanding to JRP, July 20, 1958, JRP Papers.

21. JRP interview; Green, *The Establishment in Texas Politics*, 202; Dickson to JRP, June 20, 30, 1958, JRP Papers; JRP to Dickson, June 27, 1958, ibid.; Yarborough to JRP, Dec. 19, 1958, ibid.

22. JRP interview; Woodley Petroleum, board minutes, Jan. 4, 1960, JRP Papers; *Wall Street Journal*, Jan. 8, 1959; Ilfrey interview.

23. Notes in Pure Oil file, JRP Papers; *Wall Street Journal*, Aug. 5, 1959, Jan. 5, 1960; Houston *Chronicle*, Jan. 5, 1960; JRP interview.

24. Parten's negotiations were interrupted on September 27 by the death of Jimmy Allred. Parten attended Allred's funeral in Wichita Falls. JRP interview; JRP to Opal Sherman, Feb. 7, 1962.

25. Miller interview; *Wall Street Journal*, Mar. 8, 1960; JRP interview.

26. Woodley Petroleum, board minutes, Jan. 4, 1960, JRP Papers; Houston *Chronicle*, Jan. 5, 1960; Houston *Post*, Jan. 5, 1960; *Wall Street Journal*, Jan. 5, 1960; "Pure Offers to Buy Out Woodley Petroleum," *Oil and Gas Journal*, 58 (Jan. 11, 1960), 59; Ilfrey interview; JRP interview; Houston *Post*, Jan. 5, 1960; *Business Week*, Jan. 9, 1960, n.p., clipping in Pure Oil file, JRP Papers.

27. JRP interview; JRP to J. E. Keyser, Jan. 20, 1960, JRP Papers.

28. JRP interview; New York *Times*, Aug. 17, 1980.

29. After Pure later merged with Union Oil Company of California, Union sold its share of the refining company to Koch Industries of Wichita, Kansas, which for many years continued to operate the highly profitable refinery. Koch itself eventually became a "cash cow," making J. Howard Marshall, who kept his outside shares in Great Northern, a very wealthy man. JRP interview; Marshall interview; Marshall, *Done in Oil*, 253, 254.

30. Ilfrey interview; Randy Parten interview.

31. Beaman and Henry Dawes' brother, Charles, was Calvin Coolidge's vice president. Earl Welty, *The 76 Bonanza: The Fabulous Life and Times of the Union Oil Company of California* (Menlo Park, Calif: Lane Magazine and Book Co., 1966), 285, 286, 310, 311, 314; Houston *Post*, Mar. 24, 1960; *Wall Street Journal*, Mar. 25, 1960; T. A. Wise, "The Curious Pursuit of Pure Oil," *Fortune* (July, 1965), 114.

Chapter Thirty

1. Dulaney interview; JRP interview; C. Dwight Dorough to JRP, Oct. 7, 1960, JRP Papers; Rayburn to Udall, May 19, 1961, Rayburn Papers; Rayburn to JRP, May 19, 1961, ibid.

2. JRP interview; Reston, *The Lone Star*, 188; JRP to Elmo Roper, June 24, 1960, JRP Papers.

3. Patrick J. O'Connor to JRP, Aug. 1, 1960, JRP Papers; Marshall interview; JRP interview.

4. *Wall Street Journal*, Apr. 25, Aug. 9, 1960; JRP interview; Miller interview.

5. JRP interview; JRP to Henry Jackson, Aug. 24, 1960, JRP Papers; JRP to Gerald C. Mann, Aug., 24, 1960, ibid.; Mann interview; JRP to Kelly, Aug. 31, Nov. 18, 1960, box 138, FFR.

6. Kennedy won Texas by slightly more than 46,000 votes. Dallek, *Lone Star Rising*, 588; JRP to Kelly, Aug. 31, 1960, box 138, FFR; JRP interview.

7. Rayburn to JRP, Dec. 13, 1960, JRP Papers.

8. JRP interview; Udall to JRP, May 12, 1961, JRP Papers; *Petty's Oil Letter*, Dec. 17, 1960, clipping in ibid.; Fort Worth *Star Telegram*, Feb. 12, 1961.

9. Houston attorney Leon Jaworski told Parten that his going to Washington meant that he no longer had to worry "about how well our Department of the Interior will function." Jaworski to JRP, Feb. 9, 1961, JRP Papers; "Notification of Personnel Action," U.S. Civil Service Commission, Feb. 5, 1961, ibid.; clipping, Dallas *Times Herald*, n.d., ibid.; Houston *Press*, Feb. 8, 1961; Max B. Skelton, "Veteran Texas Oilman to Serve Government," Dallas *Morning News*, Feb. 13, 1961.

10. Williamson, et al., *The American Petroleum Industry*, 815; Ambrose, *Eisenhower*, 446–447; Yergin, *The Prize*, 536–538.

11. JRP interview.

12. JRP to Udall, Mar. 2, 1961, JRP Papers; JRP interview.

13. Morgan Davis, president of Humble Oil, told Parten about a similar operation in Puerto Rico. Davis claimed that several companies were running crude oil from Venezuela through two independent refineries in Puerto Rico and then shipping the products to the U.S. Special exemptions had been granted to refineries in Puerto Rico and in the U.S. Virgin islands in an effort to boost local economic development, but the amount of oil imported into the island territory exceeded legal quotas. The companies were claiming that the oil was for Puerto Rican consumption, but Davis charged that it was double the amount needed to meet local demand.

Davis to JRP, Mar. 24, 1961, JRP Papers; clipping, "Why Don't We Solve Oil Imports?," editorial in *Our Sun* (Winter, 1961), ibid.; JRP interview.

14. Marshall interview; Wolf interview; JRP interview.

15. JRP interview; JRP to Udall, Mar. 3, 1961, JRP Papers.

16. JRP interview; JRP to O'Connor, Mar. 14, 1961, JRP Papers; JRP appointment calendar, entry for Mar. 23, ibid.; Yergin, *The Prize*, 539.

17. JRP to Udall, Mar. 23, 1961, JRP Papers; Udall to Rusk, Mar. 27, 1961, copy in ibid.

18. Bowles to Udall, Mar. 28, 1961, copy in JRP Papers; Udall to Office of Collector of Customs, Brownsville, Texas, Apr. 17, 1961, ibid.

19. JRP interview; Houston *Post*, May 3, 1961.

20. Houston *Press*, May 2, 1961; JRP to Udall, May 2, 1961, JRP Papers; JRP interview.

21. JRP interview.

22. JRP to Sandlin, June 8, 1961, JRP Papers; JRP to Neville G. Penrose, June 20, 1961, ibid.; Wolf to JRP, June 7, 1961, ibid.; *Oil Daily*, June 7, 1961, clipping in 1961 file, "General," Rayburn Papers;" Wolf interview; Houston *Post*, June 8, 1961; New York *Times*, June 12, 1961.

23. Yergin, *The Prize*, 538, 539.

24. JRP to Rayburn, May 3, 1961, 1961 file, "General," Rayburn Papers; Rayburn to JRP, May 10, 1961, ibid.

25. JRP to Buster Cole, Oct. 5, 1961, JRP Papers; JRP to Horace Busby, Oct. 19, 1961, ibid.; Hardeman and Bacon, *Rayburn*, 473.

26. Parten encouraged University of Houston professor C. Dwight Dorough to write Rayburn's biography, and subsequently raised money to fund Dorough's research. Parten joined Will Clayton, Oveta Culp Hobby, and Lloyd Bentsen on the board of the Rayburn Foundation in October 1962, and he continued to provide financial support for the Rayburn Library until his death, donating, for example, $100,000 to the Library in 1991. In April 1973, J. R. and Patsy donated to the National Portrait Gallery a bronze bust of Rayburn done by Jimilu Mason. Houston *Chronicle*, Oct. 4, 1962; JRP interview.

Chapter Thirty-one

1. Welty, *The 76 Bonanza*, 317; Wise, "The Curious Pursuit of Pure Oil," 115; *Business Week* (June 27, 1964), 130, (July 4, 1964), 20, and (Feb. 27, 1965), 122; JRP interview.

2. JRP interview.

3. For more about Elkins and his relationship with Pure Oil, see Malavis, "To Protect and Serve," 153–174; Wise, "The Curious Pursuit of Pure Oil," 114; Carleton, *Red Scare!*, 66–67; *Wall Street Journal* (Dec. 14, 1961); JRP interview.

4. Wise, "The Curious Pursuit of Pure Oil," 115; Sherman interview; Miller interview, Ilfrey interview.

5. JRP interview; JRP to Milligan, May 3, 1962, JRP Papers; Milligan to JRP, May 4, 1962, ibid.; JRP to Opal Sherman, May 17, 1962, ibid.

6. Welty, *The 76 Bonanza*, 318; JRP to L. S. Wescoat, May 24, 1962, JRP Papers; JRP to Opal Sherman, May 17, 1962, Mar. 13, 1963, ibid.; JRP interview.

7. Before its involvement with Pure, Loeb, Rhoades had forced its way into the management of Curtis Publishing Company and Twentieth Century Fox Film Corporation and had received much publicity due to its activities with the latter company. *Wall Street Journal*, Jan. 23, 1963, June 24, 1964; *Business Week* (June 27, 1964), 130, and (Feb. 27, 1965), 122, 124, 126, 128; JRP interview; Miller interview; Welty, *The 76 Bonanza*, 324.

8. *Business Week* (Feb. 27, 1965), 122; JRP interview.

9. Harris Van Zandt to Robert Milligan, Sept. 20, 1962, JRP Papers; JRP to Bill Milligan, May 9, 1963, ibid.; *Business Week* (July 4, 1964), 20, and (Feb. 27, 1965), 122; JRP interview.

10. Welty, *The 76 Bonanza*, 324; *Business Week* (Feb. 27, 1965), 122, 124; Wise, "The Curious Pursuit of Pure Oil," 226; JRP deposition, *Parten vs. Pure*, 1966, JRP Papers; JRP interview; *Time* (July 3, 1964); Welty, *The 76 Bonanza*, 325–326; *Wall Street Journal*, June 24, 1964.

11. *Business Week* (July 4, 1964), 20, and (Feb. 27, 1965), 124, 126; Welty, *The 76 Bonanza*, 327; *Wall Street Journal*, July 1, 1964, Feb. 15, 1965; JRP deposition, *Parten vs. Pure*, JRP Papers; Wise, "The Curious Pursuit of Pure Oil," 226; JRP interview.

12. *Business Week* (Feb. 27, 1965); *Wall Street Journal*, Jan. 29, 1965; JRP deposition, *Parten vs. Pure*, JRP Papers; JRP interview.

13. Welty, *The 76 Bonanza*, 329–330; *Business Week* (Feb. 27, 1965); Parten deposition, *Parten vs. Pure*, JRP Papers; Wise, "The Curious Pursuit of Pure Oil."

14. *Wall Street Journal*, Feb. 1, 15, 1965; *Business Week* (Feb. 27, 1965), 126.

15. *Wall Street Journal*, Feb. 16, 1965; *Business Week* (Feb. 27, 1965), 126; Welty, *The 76 Bonanza*, 332; JRP deposition, *Parten vs. Pure*, JRP Papers; Wise, "The Curious Pursuit of Pure Oil."

16. JRP interview; Yergin, *The Prize*, 570–571.

17. *Business Week* (Feb. 27, 1965), 128; *Time* (Feb. 26, 1965); JRP deposition, *Parten vs. Pure*, JRP Papers; JRP interview.

18. *Wall Street Journal*, Mar. 9, 1965; JRP interview.

19. *Wall Street Journal*, Feb. 18, 25, Mar. 9, 31, 1965; JRP and Sandlin depositions, *Parten vs. Pure*, JRP Papers; Wise, "The Curious Pursuit of Pure Oil," 232; Houston *Chronicle*, Mar. 31, 1965; *Business Week* (Apr. 17, 1965), 58–60; Welty, *The 76 Bonanza*, 330, 333; Hutchins to JRP, June 14, 1965, box 94, CSDI Archives (The Library, University of California at Santa Barbara); JRP interview.

20. JRP deposition, *Parten vs. Pure*, JRP Papers; JRP interview.

21. Parten requested payment for 26,375 shares out of his total holdings of 120,000 shares. "Statement to Appraisers on Behalf of Dissenting Shareholders Setting Forth Their Position Regarding Fair Cash Value," undated legal brief enclosed in David A. Johnston Jr. to Marlin E. Sandlin, Nov. 1, 1966, JRP Papers; JRP deposition, *Parten vs. Pure*, ibid.; Houston *Chronicle*, Sept. 30, 1965.

Chapter Thirty-two

1. As an example of the type of behavior Parten believed should be recognized and rewarded, he had cited the efforts of state legislators Henry B. Gonzales of San Antonio and Abraham Kazen Jr. of Laredo to defeat segregation bills in the Texas legislature in the spring of 1957. JRP to Herbert H. Lehman, May 22, 1957, box 3, FFR; Walter Webb to Terrell Maverick, Aug. 23, 1961, Webb Papers; for an example of Parten's fervor in support of the oil depletion allowance, see JRP to Yarborough, May 17, 1969, JRP file, Yarborough Papers.

2. For more on the Faulk case see his book, *Fear on Trial*; Dallas *News*, Feb. 24, 1963; JRP interview; J. H. Faulk interview.

3. JRP interview; J. H. Faulk interview.

4. J. H. Faulk interview; JRP to J. H. Faulk, Jan. 8, 1965, JRP Papers.

5. J. H. Faulk interview; Miller interview.

6. Pepe Anderson interview; JRP interview; Randy Parten interview.

7. JRP interview; Pepe Anderson interview; Randy Parten interview.

8. Pepe Anderson interview; Randy Parten interview; JRP interview.

9. Randy Parten interview; Pepe Anderson interview; Bill Anderson interview; Audre Rapoport interview .

10. Randy Parten interview; Pepe Anderson interview.

11. Pepe Anderson interview; Randy Parten interview; Ilfrey interview.

12. Audre Rapoport interview; Randy Parten interview; Bernard Rapoport interview; J. H. Faulk interview; Liz Faulk interview.

13. JRP interview; Marcus interview; McKeever, *Adlai Stevenson*, 539; Lawrence Wright, *In the New World: Growing up with America, 1960–1984* (New York: Knopf, 1988), 40.

14. Founded by Massachusetts businessman Robert Welch in 1958, the Birch Society espoused the belief that communism is a "front" for a secret and diabolical conspiracy to conquer the world planned by a mysterious group of men called the Illuminati, which had been formed in 1776 in Europe. Welch claimed that this evil (and mythical) group had been responsible not only for every war and revolution on earth since 1789, it had orchestrated every social and economic reform in American history. Carleton, *Red Scare!*, 298, 299.

15. Wright, *In the New World*, 29, 30, 38–40; Warren Leslie, *Dallas: Public and Private* (New York: Avon, 1964).

16. For a different version of the Stevenson incident see an interview with Earle Cabell, who was serving as Dallas mayor at the time. Cabell interview, oral history transcript (UNT); Leslie, *Dallas: Public and Private*, 188–198; John Bartlow Martin, *Adlai Stevenson and the World: The Life of Adlai E. Stevenson* (New York: Doubleday, 1977), 774, 775; for an outstanding description of the political and cultural environment in Dallas in the early 1960s, see Wright's *In the New World*, especially pp. 24–44; Marcus interview; JRP interview.

17. A month after the Stevenson incident, J. R. and Patsy were driving to Austin to attend a dinner in honor of President Kennedy when the news of the president's assassination was announced on the radio. Initially, Parten agreed with those who blamed Kennedy's death on the hate atmosphere in Dallas fostered by the extreme right wing and believed that the assassination served as further evidence that the political far right posed a serious threat to American democracy and world peace. Parten reminded Ralph Yarborough "that . . . Governor Allred said many times that the great danger to our form of government and our way of life was from the . . . fascists instead of from the leftists or communists." Although Parten's views about the direct role of the right wing in the Kennedy assasination changed as information about Lee Harvey Oswald's left-wing ideology became known, he continued to believe that the atmosphere of hate in Dallas somehow encouraged Oswald's action. JRP to Yarborough, Feb. 14, 1964, Yarborough Papers; JRP interview.

18. JRP to Yarborough, Mar. 26, 1964, Apr. 24, 1964, Yarborough files, JRP Papers.

19. Yarborough interview; J. H. Faulk interview; JRP interview; JRP to Fagan Dickson, Sept. 24, 1964, JRP Papers; Woodrow Seals to JRP, Oct. 28, 1964, ibid.

20. JRP to J. H. Faulk, Jan. 8, 1965, John Henry Faulk Papers (CAH).

21. JRP interview.

Chapter Thirty-three

1. For detailed discussions of the *Pacem in Terris* convocation, see Kelly, *Court of Reason*, 257–271, and Ashmore, *Unseasonable Truths*, 431–437.

2. Kelly, *Court of Reason*, 119, 126, 127; Victor Navasky, et al., "Robert Hutchins's Platonic Grove," *Nation* (Jan. 30, 1988), 119.

3. Griswold resigned in the fall of 1958 after a series of disputes with Hutchins. Griswold to Hutchins, Sept. 26, 1958, box 1, FFR; Kelly interview; Marshall interview; JRP interview.

4. JRP interview; Kelly, *Court of Reason*, 171, 172; Kelly, "Remembrances . . .", JRP Papers; Navasky, et al., "Robert Hutchins's Platonic Grove," 123, 124.

5. JRP interview; New York *Times*, June 5, 1974, clipping in JRP Papers.

6. "Demise of the Center," *Time* (May 26, 1975), 64; JRP interview.

7. David S. Broder, "The Freedom that Education Built," Washington *Post*, May 18, 1977; New York *Times*, June 5, 1974, clipping in JRP Papers; Financial statement, JRP file, box 94, CSDI; Hallock Hoffman to JRP, June 5, 1964, ibid.; Hutchins to JRP, May 21, 1963, ibid.; JRP interview; Rapoport interview.

8. Jimmy Allred, calling Parten his "very dear friend, a high class gentleman," introduced him to William O. Douglas in 1941. James V. Allred to William O. Douglas, Nov. 7, 1941, box 171, Allred Papers; Fulbright, "Remembrances . . . ", JRP Papers; JRP interview.

9. JRP interview; Hallock Hoffman to JRP, June 5, 1964, box 94, CSDI; Kelly, *Court of Reason*, 246–247; Ashmore, *Unseasonable Truths*, 432.

10. Ashmore, *Unseasonable Truths*, 436; Kelly, *Court of Reason*, 259, 262; JRP interview.

11. Kelly to JRP, Jan. 21, 1965, box 207, CSDI; Hutchins to JRP, June 14, 1965, box 94, ibid.; Ashmore, *Unseasonable Truths*, 431–437; Kelly, *Court of Reason*, 271; JRP interview.

12. JRP interview; J. H. Faulk interview; Kelly, *Court of Reason*, 272–274.

13. Randy Parten interview; JRP interview.

14. JRP interview.

15. JRP to Yarborough, June 23, 1966, JRP Papers; JRP interview.

16. JRP interview; "Daily Diary," The White House, July 18, 1966, LBJ Papers; Randy Parten interview.

17. One of his most important financial donations to the Center during this period was a large block of Union Oil stock, which was used to help finance the Center's world peace convocation in Geneva, Switzerland, in 1967. JRP to Hallock Hoffman, Mar. 30, 1967, box 94, CSDI; JRP to Opal, June 28, 1967, JRP Papers.

18. BEM leaders included investor Palmer Weber of Virginia, businessman Harry Niles of Maryland, businessman Bernard Rapoport and investor Harold Willens of California. Rapoport recalled that BEM members "lobbied other businessmen to tell them that the war was against their best interests. We also lobbied the Congress." BEM brochure, n.d., Coffin file, JRP Papers; Coffin to JRP, Mar. 28, 1972, ibid.; JRP to Coffin, May 6, 1971, ibid.; JRP interview; Rapoport interview.

19. Parten eventually supported Hubert Humphrey after his nomination in Chicago. He and Marlin Sandlin helped organize a mass rally for Humphrey at Houston's Astrodome the Sunday before election day. The event attracted an estimated fifty thousand people, the largest rally of the Humphrey campaign. Lyndon Johnson, who had not campaigned for Humphrey, made a "surprise" appearance. Parten and Ralph Yarborough were among those on the stage with Humphrey and Johnson. When Johnson came on the platform, Parten stood up to shake hands with him. To Parten's surprise, instead of shaking his hand, Johnson gave him a warm embrace, saying "I knew you would be here, J. R." JRP interview; McCarthy interview; JRP to Eugene McCarthy, June 6, 1968, JRP Papers; Houston *Post*, Nov. 4, 1968.

20. JRP to Yarborough, Feb. 28, 1968, JRP Papers; JRP to Bernard Rapoport, Feb. 15, 1973, Bernard Rapoport Papers (CAH); JRP interview; Marshall interview; Yarborough interview; Dugger interview.

21. JRP to Yarborough, Sept. 7, 1967, JRP Papers; Hall to Yarborough, Sept. 6, 1967, Yarborough Papers; JRP to Hall, Oct. 25, 1967, ibid.

22. JRP to Yarborough, Feb. 28, 1968, JRP Papers; JRP to Yarborough, Jan. 8, 1969, ibid.; JRP to Yarborough, June 20, 1968, ibid.; JRP to Yarborough; Dec. 18, 1970, ibid.; JRP to Robert Eckhardt, Dec. 18, 1970, ibid.

23. Goodwyn interview; Califano interview.

24. Don Gardner, "Notes on a Native Son," *Texas Observer* (June 15, 1990), 23; Ronnie Dugger and Kaye Northcott, "Pacifica Silenced by Bomb," *Texas Observer* (May 29, 1970), 7, 8; "Bombed Again," *Texas Observer* (Nov. 13, 1970), 11; Bernard Rapoport to JRP, Aug. 13, 1970, JRP Papers; Minute Book, Parten Foundation, Nov. 18, 1970, ibid.

25. Houston *Chronicle*, Oct. 4, 1962; JRP interview.

26. Parten became one of Bentsen's most dependable financial backers. In 1982, for example, he contributed $30,000 to Bentsen's "Circle" club. JRP to Bentsen, Feb. 23, 1982, JRP Papers; Bentsen to JRP, Mar. 23, 1979, ibid.; JRP interview; Rapoport interview; Bentsen to JRP, July 21, 1970, JRP Papers; Bentsen interview.

Chapter Thirty-four

1. Pan American also retained minority investments in a Mexican fertilizer plant and a small sulphur company. Townsend interview; JRP interview; *Wall Street Journal,* June 22, 1967.

2. *Wall Street Journal* reported on October 8, 1968, that "several analysts think [Pan American] has been excessively slow in diversifying." JRP interview; Miller interview; *Wall Street Journal,* Sept. 9, 1968, Mar. 24, 1969.

3. "Herbert Korholz," *Who's Who in America: 1968; Wall Street Journal,* Oct. 8, 1968, Mar. 24, 1969; JRP interview; Miller interview; Townsend interview; Boothe interview; Ilfrey interview.

4. JRP interview; Anderson interview; *Wall Street Journal,* Nov. 1, 7, Dec. 26, 1968, Mar. 24, 1969.

5. Anderson interview.

6. *Wall Street Journal,* Nov. 27, Dec. 2, 3, 9, 12, 1968; Townsend interview; JRP interview.

7. *Wall Street Journal,* Mar. 12, 17, 24, 26, 1969; JRP interview.

8. *Wall Street Journal,* Mar. 26, 1969; JRP interview; Anderson interview.

9. *Wall Street Journal,* June 2, 11, Aug. 21, 1969, Mar. 17, Apr. 27, 1970.

10. *Wall Street Journal,* Mar. 26, May 18, 1970; JRP interview; Anderson interview.

11. *Wall Street Journal,* Oct. 19, 1970; JRP interview; Anderson interview; Califano interview.

12. JRP interview; Califano interview; *Wall Street Journal,* Jan. 11, 1971.

13. *Wall Street Journal,* Jan. 15, 1971; JRP interview; Anderson interview.

14. JRP interview; *Wall Street Journal,* Mar. 26, 1971; Ilfrey interview; Anderson interview.

15. *Forbes* (Sept. 15, 1973), 54; *Wall Street Journal,* June 3, 30, 1971; JRP interview; *Wall Street Journal,* June 28, 1971; FBI File, JRP Papers.

16. Harry Webb, Roland Bond, and DeWitt Ray had resigned from the Pan American board in February 1971. *Wall Street Journal,* Feb. 17, 1971; *Forbes* (Sept. 15, 1973), 54; JRP interview; Boothe interview.

17. Miller interview; JRP interview; Anderson interview; Houston *Chronicle,* May 30, 1974.

18. *Wall Street Journal,* July 9, Sept. 24, Dec. 7, 1971, May 18, 1972.

19. JRP interview; Anderson interview.

20. Pan American paid $65 million of its own cash to ARCO and borrowed the remainder. JRP interview; Yergin, *The Prize,* 570–571; Anderson interview; New York *Times,* Sept. 1, 23, Dec. 30, 1972; *Wall Street Journal,* Jan. 2, 3, 1973; PASCO, Inc., "Proxy Statement," Apr. 19, 1973, pp. 7, 8, copy in Rapoport Papers.

21. PASCO, Inc., Stock Option Committee, "Minutes of Meeting Held," Sept. 27, 1973, copy attached to letter, John D. Hartigan to JRP, Oct. 31, 1973, Rapoport Papers; JRP to R. H. Guthrie, Nov. 15, 1973, JRP Papers; JRP interview; Anderson interview.

22. Anderson interview; JRP interview.

23. Yergin, *The Prize,* 659–660.

24. PASCO's shareholders received $50.50 per share upon liquidation. JRP interview; Califano interview; New York *Times,* May 22, Aug. 23, Sept. 30, Oct. 3, Dec. 31, 1975, May 18, 29, June 30, 1976; *Wall Street Journal,* Apr. 8, 1975, Dec. 30, 1976; Ivins, "How Not to Regulate the Oil Business," 6, 7.

Chapter Thirty-five

1. Ping Ferry, Bishop James A. Pike, and a few others were removed in the reorganization. Harry Ashmore, Frank Kelly, and John Cogley were among those who remained. Ferry sued the Fund for the Republic when his position was terminated. Kelly, *Court of Reason,* 347–370, 379.

2. One Center project that attracted much publicity was Rexford G. Tugwell's effort, initiated in 1966, to rewrite the U.S. Constitution. Tugwell eventually produced more than forty drafts. Tugwell's project, however, was one Center activity that Parten disliked. He believed that the orginal Constitution was as perfect a document as humans were capable of producing. Kelly, *Court of Reason,* 276; JRP interview.

3. Kelly interview; Gary Cadenhead interview; JRP to Hutchins, Dec. 2, 1970, JRP Papers.

4. Cadenhead interview; Hutchins to JRP, Nov. 12, 1971, JRP Papers.

5. Ashmore to Rapoport, Nov. 24, 1971, box 91, CSDI; Rapoport to Hutchins, Apr. 7, 1972, ibid.; JRP interview.

6. JRP interview; J. H. Faulk interview; Ed Clark interview; George McGovern interview.

7. Jean de Menil died in 1973. Rapoport interview, oral history transcript (Baylor University), 312, 313; Dugger interview.

8. Bernard Rapoport was born in 1917 in San Antonio, the son of Russian Jewish immigrants. His father had been a socialist revolutionary in Russia. Rapoport built a hugely successful company that specialized in providing insurance to labor union members. Rapoport interview, oral history transcript (Baylor University), 289, 366, 367, 370; Rapoport to JRP, Nov. 7, 1966, JRP Papers; JRP to Rapoport, Nov. 11, 1966, ibid.; JRP interview; J. H. Faulk interview; Dugger interview.

9. Rapoport claimed in an oral history interview in 1980 that he and Parten persuaded Farenthold to run for governor rather than attorney general because of their preference for John Hill in the latter race. Parten and

Farenthold denied this, claiming instead that Farenthold entered the gubernatorial race because of Ralph Yarborough's decision not to run for governor and that no one talked her out of running for attorney general. Rapoport interview, oral history transcript (Baylor University), 421, 422; JRP interview; Fath interview; Farenthold interview.

10. JRP interview; Fath to JRP, July 17, 1973, Jan. 16, 1974, JRP Papers; Kaye Northcott, "Without Billboards," *Texas Observer* (May 26, 1972), 3.

11. Farenthold attracted 888,000 votes to Briscoe's 1.1 million. Northcott, "Without Billboards," 3; Jean Childers to JRP, Apr. 10, 1972, JRP Papers; JRP to Farenthold, May 11, 1972, ibid.; Farenthold interview; J. H. Faulk interview; JRP interview.

12. JRP to Eckhardt , Jan. 5, 1973, JRP Papers; McGovern interview.

13. JRP interview; McGovern interview; New York *Times*, May 4, 1972.

14. JRP to McGovern, July 28, 1972, JRP Papers; JRP interview.

15. Lanier, who was a bank president in 1972, was later elected mayor of Houston. New York *Times*, Sept. 14, 1972; Houston *Post*, Sept. 14, 1972; JRP interview; Rapoport interview.

16. JRP to Bernard Rapoport, Sept. 21, 1972, July 22, 1976, Rapoport Papers; JRP interview.

17. Dallas *Morning News*, July 19, 1981; Washington *Post*, Dec. 21, 1973; Houston *Chronicle*, Dec. 21, 1973.

18. JRP to Coffin, Feb. 23, 1973, JRP Papers; JRP to Ervin, Aug. 17, 1973, ibid.

19. Ballew to Rapoport, Mar. 7, 1973, Rapoport Papers; Bernard Rapoport, manuscript copy of speech, "Introduction of J. R. Parten," Mar. 3, 1973, ibid.; Houston *Chronicle*, Mar. 4, 1973; Ronnie Dugger, "Double the Stakes," *Texas Observer* (Mar. 30, 1973), 20.

20. Ashmore, *Unseasonable Truths*, 480; JRP to Hutchins, June 1, 1971, JRP Papers; Deposition of Jubal R. Parten, *Comfort v. The Fund for the Republic*, Apr. 21, 1976, pp. 38, 39, JRP Papers, cited hereafter as JRP deposition, *Comfort v. Fund*; JRP interview; Rapoport interview.

21. Gary Cadenhead, the Center's financial officer, claimed that Ashmore was lavish with his expense accounts, favoring luxury hotels, fine restaurants, and first-class plane travel. "That irritated J. R. very much," Cadenhead declared. JRP interview; Kelly interview; Rapoport interview; Cadenhead interview.

22. Hutchins's list included Sen. Eugene McCarthy; former University of Texas dean John Silber; economist John Kenneth Galbraith, and retired army general James Gavin. JRP interview; JRP deposition, *Comfort v. Fund*, 39, 40, JRP Papers; Cadenhead interview; Board Docket and Minutes, Oct. 8, 1973, box 149, CSDI; Rapoport interview; Stephen Ambrose, *Eisenhower: The President* (New York: Simon and Schuster, 1984), 611.

23. Bernard Rapoport, who knew Minnesota governor Wendell Anderson, later claimed that because of widespread discontent against Moos, Anderson "wanted him out of there. He really did." Rapoport interview; Minneapolis *Star*, Jan. 29, 1982; Kelly, *Court of Reason*, 509; Cadenhead interview; JRP interview; Ashmore, *Unseasonable Truths*, 503.

24. Ashmore later claimed that Parten misunderstood Hutchins's "sardonic reaction" to be an endorsement of Moos. Ashmore, *Unseasonable Truths*, 504; Minneapolis *Star*, Jan. 29, 1982; Kelly, *Court of Reason*, 508, 512; Parten interview; Rapoport interview.

25. Ashmore, *Unseasonable Truths*, 499–501; Minutes, Annual Meeting of the Board of Directors of the Fund for the Republic, Oct. 8, 1973, box 114, CSDI; Parten interview; Rapoport interview; JRP to Hutchins, Oct. 17, 1973, JRP Papers.

26. Rapoport interview; JRP interview; Cadenhead interview; Marshall interview; Kelly interview.

27. Kelly, *Court of Reason*, 428, 516, 517; Ferry interview, oral history transcript (Ford Foundation); *Time* (May 26, 1975), 64; JRP interview; Rapoport interview.

28. Moos to Ashmore, Nov. 23, 1973, box 119, CSDI; Ashmore, *Unseasonable Truths*, 505; JRP interview; Rapoport interview; Kelly, *Court of Reason*, 516, 517, 522, 523.

29. JRP interview; Rapoport interview; Cadenhead interview; Kelly interview; Ashmore, *Unseasonable Truths*, 503.

30. Kelly, *Court of Reason*, 525, 529; Kelly to JRP, Mar. 3, 1975, JRP Papers; JRP deposition, *Comfort v. Fund*, 190, ibid.; Cadenhead interview; Kelly interview; JRP interview; Ashmore, *Unseasonable Truths*, 503.

31. Kelly, *Court of Reason*, 530–532; JRP interview.

32. Cadenhead interview.

33. Minutes, Annual Meeting of the Board of Directors of the Fund for the Republic, Feb. 15, 1974, box 114, CSDI; Kelly, *Court of Reason* 535, 536; JRP interview.

34. JRP interview; Marshall interview; Ashmore, *Unseasonable Truths*, 509, 514.

35. Kelly, *Court of Reason*, 540; JRP interview.

36. JRP interview; Randy Parten interview; Pepe Anderson interview.

37. Cadenhead interview; Kelly, *Court of Reason*, 541–542; Rapoport interview.

38. JRP interview; Rapoport interview; Randy Parten interview; J. H. Faulk interview; Hutchins to JRP, June 24, 1974, JRP Papers.

39. Paul Newman to JRP, Oct. 24, 1974, JRP Papers; JRP interview.

40. JRP to Blair Clark, June 13, 1974, box 119, CSDI; Minutes of the Joint Meeting of the Endowment Committee and the Executive Committee, Sept. 10, 1974, box 149, ibid.

41. Minutes, Executive Committee, Nov. 4, 1974, box 149, CSDI; Kelly, *Court of Reason*, 558, 561–564; JRP to McAllister, Dec. 11, 1974, JRP Papers.

42. Kelly, *Court of Reason*, 555, 568, 569, 580, 581, 584, 585; JRP interview; JRP deposition, *Comfort v. Fund*, 89, 221, 225, JRP Papers; Ashmore to JRP, Jan. 15, 1975, box 119, CSDI; JRP to the Board of Directors of The Fund for the Republic, Feb. 6, 1975, JRP Papers; JRP et al. to the Board of Directors of The Fund for the Republic, Feb. 6, 21, 1975, ibid.; Hutchins to JRP, Jan. 6, 1975, ibid.; JRP to Hutchins, Jan. 16, 1975, ibid.; Kelly to JRP, Feb. 20, 1975, ibid.; JRP to Blair Clark, Mar. 11, 1975, ibid.; Minutes, Executive Committee Meeting, Feb. 4, 1975, box 149, CSDI; JRP interview; Rapoport interview.

43. Rapoport interview; JRP to Moos, Mar. 13, 1975, JRP Papers; Minutes, Feb. 22, 1975, box 149, CSDI; Kelly, *Court of Reason*, 585–587.

44. Kelly, *Court of Reason*, 590, 591; Minutes, Annual Meeting of the Board of Directors of the Fund for the Republic, Feb. 22, 1975, box 149, CSDI.

45. Kelly, *Court of Reason*, 593; JRP to Monsignor Francis J. Lally, Mar. 12, 1975, JRP Papers; JRP to Morris Levinson, Mar. 10, 1975, ibid.

46. Six months prior to Patsy's death, Parten's first wife, Opal, died in Brownwood, Texas. Opal and Dallas Sherman had moved to Brownwood after his retirement from Pan American Airlines a few years before and had continued their friendship with J. R. until Opal's death on October 12, 1974. Several years later, when Parten was asked for his thoughts about Opal's passing, the only words that he could get out before being silenced by his own tears was that "she was a beautiful, wonderful girl." JRP interview; Dallas *Times Herald*, Oct. 13, 1974; Sherman interview.

47. Parten's estranged friend Sylvester Dayson attended the funeral. Shelmire interview; JRP interview; Houston *Post*, Apr. 18, 1975; Pepe Anderson interview; Randy Parten interview; Kelly interview; Kelly, *Court of Reason*, 593.

48. JRP to Moos, Mar. 13, 1975, JRP Papers; Kelly, *Court of Reason*, 594, 595; JRP interview.

49. JRP interview; Rapoport interview; Kelly, *Court of Reason*, 595, 601.

50. Minutes of the Special Board Meeting, Fund for the Republic, May 10, 1975, box 149, CSDI.

51. The board decided that it had to keep an office in Santa Barbara to avoid being sued by Alex Comfort, a Center fellow whose contract required his employment specifically in Santa Barbara. Moos and Parten remained good friends until Moos's death in January 1982. JRP interview; Minneapolis *Star*, Jan. 29, 1982; JRP deposition, *Comfort v. Fund*, 129, JRP Papers; Kelly, *Court of Reason*, 595–603; Rapoport interview; Ashmore, *Unseasonable Truths*, 514.

52. Animosities between board members deepened after Moos's resignation. Blair Clark charged that Parten's actions in the Moos affair had been "ourtrageous." He also wrote a hot-headed letter to Arthur Burck accusing him of ignorance and characterizing his performance on the board as "destructive and foolish." Parten told Burck that Clark was "a reckless and wicked man." Clark to Burck, May 13, 1975, copy in Rapoport Papers; JRP to Burck, May 23, 1975, JRP Papers; JRP interview; Clark to Kelly, Aug. 8, 1977, box 114, CSDI; Cadenhead interview; Rapoport interview.

53. Hutchins admitted to Thorton Wilder that Moos could not have been appointed without his approval. "I didn't select [Moos], but the Board would not have selected him if I had objected." Ashmore, *Unseasonable Truths*, 514; JRP interview; Kelly, *Court of Reason*, 606.

54. JRP to Peter Tagger, July 5, 1975, JRP Papers; Kelly, *Court of Reason*, 612.

55. Peter Tagger to Rapoport, Sept. 4, 1975, Rapoport Papers; Hutchins to JRP, June 11, 1975, JRP Papers; Kelly, *Court of Reason*, 610–611; JRP interview; Docket and Minutes, June 28, 1975, box 149, CSDI.

56. Hutchins to JRP, June 11, 1975, JRP Papers; JRP to Hutchins, July 9, 1975, ibid.; Kelly, *Court of Reason*, 614.

57. JRP interview; Kelly, *Court of Reason*, 612, 613; JRP to Hutchins, Sept. 5, 1975, JRP Papers; Hutchins to JRP, Sept. 8, 1975, ibid.; JRP to Dugger, Oct. 29, 1975, ibid.

58. Marshal later claimed that the Center "spent money like the Russians were coming up the river. You didn't have to do anything but look at the balance sheet . . . to make a good guess as to what was going to happen: insolvency." JRP to Hutchins, Sept. 25, 1975, JRP Papers; JRP deposition, *Comfort v. Fund*, 78, 109, ibid.; Marshall interview; Marshall to Hutchins, Oct. 1, 13, 1975, box 94, CSDI; Kelly, *Court of Reason*, 634; Rapoport to James Douglas, Oct. 18, 1975, Rapoport Papers.

59. For another view of Parten's final break with Hutchins, see Ashmore, *Unseasonable Truths*, 518. Hutchins to JRP, Sept. 29, 1975, JRP Papers; JRP to Hutchins, Oct. 8, 1975, ibid.; James Douglas to JRP, Apr. 16, 1976, copy in Rapoport Papers; Kelly, *Court of Reason*, 614–616; JRP interview.

60. JRP to Douglas, Nov. 13, 1975, JRP Papers.

61. Ashmore, *Unseasonable Truths*, 527, 537; Navasky, "Robert Hutchins's Platonic Grove," 119.

62. Kelly interview.

63. Hutchins to JRP, June 24, 1974, JRP Papers; JRP to Hutchins, July 17, 1974, ibid.

Chapter Thirty-six

1. His son Randy joined the company after graduating from the University of Texas School of Law in the mid-1970s. JRP interview; Randy Parten interview; Marshall interview; New York *Times*, Aug. 17, 1980.

2. JRP interview; Dallas *Morning News*, July 19, 1981.

3. This and the following discussion of Parten's activities in his final years is based largely on the author's personal observations and his interviews with Parten's employees and associates.

4. JRP to Bentsen, Feb. 23, 1982, JRP Papers; Bentsen to JRP, Mar. 1, 1982, ibid.; Bentsen to JRP, Nov. 24, 1982, ibid.; J. H. Faulk interview; JRP interview.

5. JRP to Coffin, Nov. 13, 1979, JRP Papers; Marshall interview; JRP interview.

6. Eckhardt interview; JRP interview.

7. J. H. Faulk interview; Pepe Anderson interview; Goodwyn interview.

8. The author heard several of Parten's Faulk-inspired discourses. Faulk's direct link to Parten's views was made clear by copies of Faulk's letters to Parten the author received *before* he heard Parten discuss the issue at hand. In addition, the author was present on several occasions when Faulk expressed to Parten his opinions on a variety of topics. During subsequent visits by the author, Parten repeated these opinions, almost verbatim, as his own. Faulk was very aware of his strong influence on Parten with respect to most foreign policy issues. J. H. Faulk interview; Faulk to JRP, May 28, July 8, Aug. 14, 1985, copies in the personal files of the author.

9. Parten was also a financial underwriter for Faulk's theatrical productions of "Deep in the Heart" and its earlier version, "Pear Orchard." J. H. Faulk interview; J. H. Faulk, "Tom Willis," *Deep in the Heart*, ms. in Faulk Papers; JRP interview.

10. J. H. Faulk interview; Rapoport interview; see also the discussion on Pacifica in Chapter 35. For one of dozens of other examples of Faulk's influence with Parten with respect to grants, see JRP to Phil Record, Jan. 23, 1986, JRP Papers, concerning a project on the First Amendment; JRP to Athan Theoharis, Dec. 12, 1979, JRP Papers; J. H. Faulk interview.

11. Faulk, "Tributes for Two Good Men," 8.

12. In May 1979, Parten's support of higher education was recognized by Haverford College in Philadelphia, which gave him an honorary degree. Marshall interview; J. H. Faulk interview; *Texas Monthly* (July, 1976); New York *Times*, 1980; Tom Nelson, "The 'Real' J. R. Speaks His Mind," *Parade Magazine* (Apr. 25, 1982).

13. JRP interview; J. H. Faulk interview; JRP to Walter Hall, Dec. 15, 1982, JRP Papers; Nelson, "The 'Real' J. R. Speaks His Mind."

14. Dallas *Morning News*, July 19, 1981; *Oil and Gas News* (May, 1982), clipping in JRP Papers; JRP interview.

15. As a result of his activities in support of the antinuclear-arms movement, the Nuclear Age Peace Foundation honored Parten on his ninetieth birthday with its first Citizen Peace Maker Award. "American Committee on East-West Accord," *Encyclopedia of Associations* (1985), 13196; Margaret Chapman and Carl Marcy (eds.), *Common Sense in U.S.-Soviet Trade* (Washington, D. C.: American Committee on East-West Accord, 1983); JRP to Rapoport, Oct. 27, 1977, Rapoport Papers; *Wall Street Journal*, Apr. 24, 1972; JRP interview.

16. JRP to Walter Hall, Jan. 13, 1982, JRP Papers.

17. Although Parten could only donate the legal maximum of $1,000 to Faulk's campaign, he arranged for several additional $1,000 contributions from various family members, employees, and friends. Randy Parten served as Faulk's campaign treasurer. JRP to Faulk, Feb. 2, 1983, Faulk Papers; JRP interview; J. H. Faulk interview; JRP to Dugger, Mar. 1, 1983, JRP Papers.

18. JRP interview; James Calloway interview.

19. JRP interview.

20. Ibid.; Ralph A. Johnston to JRP, May 19, 1966, Dobie-Paisano file, JRP Papers.

21. JRP interview; Goodwyn interview.

22. JRP to Ayres, Sept. 18, 1970, JRP Papers.

23. JRP to LeMaistre, Aug. 5, 1970, JRP Papers; San Angelo *Standard Times*, Aug. 6, 1970, clipping in "JRP" vertical file (CAH); San Antonio *Express*, Aug. 5, 1970, ibid.; Houston *Chronicle*, Aug. 5, 1970.

24. JRP interview.

25. Parten's award was largely the result of lobbying by regents chairman, Jack Blanton; Parten received the award at ceremonies on the University of Texas campus, Oct. 2, 1987. Clark interview.

26. In 1990, when the University of Texas assumed permanent responsibility for the Sam Rayburn Library and Museum in Bonham, Parten donated $100,000 to support the Library's special programs. Don Carleton, "Comment," *Discovery*, vol. 13, no. 3 (1993), 3, 4.

27. Molly Ivins, *Nothin' but Good Times Ahead* (New York: Random House, 1993), 169–171.

28. Frank Kelly, "Eulogy—J. R. Parten Funeral," audiotape cassette recording, in author's personal possession.

Conclusion

1. J. H. Faulk interview; Kelly interview.
2. William K. Stevens, "J. R. Parten: Reclusive oil baron steps in to limelight," New York *Times,* Aug. 16, 1980; J. H. Faulk interview; Kelly interview; Rapoport interview, oral history transcript (Baylor University), 363–365; Dugger interview.
3. Dugger interview.

Index

Photographs are indicated by boldfaced page numbers.

Brazos County: and 1936 Railroad
Commission race, 162
Breceda, Alfredo: sulphur concession, 377, 379,
389
Bridges, Styles: 289, 291
Bridwell, L. S.: 295
Brimstone Game: Monopoly in Action, The: 381
Briscoe, Dolph, Jr.: and 1972 governor's race,
539–540
Brooks, Emily Montague: 7–8
Brooks Airfield (San Antonio): 106
Brown, Bruce: and PAD, 398–403, 405, 406
Brown, George: and S. Rayburn, 430
Brown, Herman: and S. Rayburn, 430
Brown, John: and PAW, 285, 290
Brown County: Woodley Petroleum in, 45
Brown and Root: and Vietnam war, 520
Brownlee, Houghton: and Rainey controversy,
310
Brownsville, Texas: PEMEX illegal oil imports
through, 493–496, 568
Brown v. Board of Education: 448
Brownwood, Texas: Woodley Petroleum in, 45
Buchanan, James "Buck": *Daily Texan* and,
163
Buck, E. O.: 79
Bucknell University: H. Rainey and, 186, 188
Bull Bayou oil field: 32–33, 34, 35, 38
Bullington, Orville: 311; and 1946 governor's
race, 352; and faculty tenure rule, 302–303;
and J. Haley, 168; and Rainey controversy,
301–323, 362; and UT board of regents,
244–246; and UT medical school contro-
versy, 248–249
Burck, Arthur A.: 546
Burdick, Eugene: 518–519
Burdine, Alton: and 1946 governor's race, 359;
and Rainey controversy, 304, 310, 313
Burford, Freeman: 161
Burns, Gordon: 93, 94
Burris, Ward: 179
Bush, George: 1964 Senate race, 514; 1970
Senate race, 524–525; Parten and presidency
of, 561
Business Executives Move For Vietnam Peace
(BEM): 522
Business Week: and Woodley/Pure merger, 485
Butte, George C.: 20; Parten and, 19–22, 24,
183
Byers, Tom: 13
Byrnes, James F. "Jimmy": and Potsdam
Conference, 340, 342, 343–344; and WWII
oil transport, 284

C

Caddo Lake oil field: 29, 31
Caldwell, Joe: and UT, 169–171
Calhoun, John: and McDonald Observatory,
219; and medical school, 208, 209, 221; and
Parten, 246; as UT acting president, 186,
193, 205
Califano, Joseph A., Jr.: and Pan American
Sulphur, 530–531, 534; and Parten, 523, 570
California: and oil production control, 84, 86,
88; oil and tidelands of, 348. *See also*
University of California
Callahan County: and 1936 Railroad
Commission race, 162; and 1946 governor's
race, 358; Moutray Oil in, 45; Woodley
Petroleum in, 45, 53–54
Calloway, Carl: 74
Calvert, Robert: and 1934 governor's race, 118,
119; and D. Bible, 178–179; stands for Texas
Speaker, 122; and UT appropriations, 183
Camp Jackson (Columbia, S.C.): Parten at, 27
Camp Leon Springs. *See* Leon Springs Military
Reservation
Camp Mabry (Austin): W. O'Daniel speaks at,
237
Camp Stanley. *See* Leon Springs Military
Reservation
Camp Travis (Fort Sam Houston): Parten at,
25, 27
Canada: Woodley Petroleum Co. in, 434–437,
439–441, 479
Capper, Arthur. *See* Marland-Capper bill
Cardenas, Pancho: 388
Cardenas, Pres.: and Pan American Sulphur,
388–389
Carnegie Endowment for International Peace:
and *Pacem in Terris,* 519
Carroll, Hulen R.: 171
Carter, Amon: and Ickes oil legislation, 110
Carter, Jimmy: Parten and, 556
Carter, W. S.: 206
Carthaus, William J.: 441
Case, Clifford P.: and Fund for the Republic,
428–429, 431, 433
Castro, Americo: 230
Castro, Fidel: 495
Catton, Bruce: 519
Center for Defense Information (CDI): 561
Centex Refining Co.: and 1936 Railroad
Commission race, 162; created, 54–55; end
of, 386; and Woodley Petroleum finances,
80
Champlin, H. H.: 88

G

imports, 494; and Smackover field, 41–42

Humphrey, Hubert: and Fund for the Republic, 463; and oil industry, 507; and *Pacem in Terris*, 519

Hunt, Bruce: 34

Hunt, Harold C.: 431

Hunt, H. L.: and El Dorado field, 35; E. Texas oil, and fortune of, 51, 69; and Florida barge canal, 275; and McCarthyism, 426, 432, 463–464; and oil production control, 69, 134, 452–453

Hunt, H. L., Jr. "Hassie": and Florida barge canal, 275–277

Hunter, Tom: and 1934 governor's race, 116–123; and 1938 governor's race, 198; J. Ferguson and, 118–120; and general sales tax, 120–121

Husky Oil Co.: and Pan American Sulphur, 532

Hutcheson, Joseph C.: 306, 319

Hutcheson, Thad: 1956 Senate race of, 474–475

Hutchins, Robert Maynard: 191; death of, 553; and FFR's Center, 516–517, 520, 536–537, 542–544, 545, 546, 547, 548, 550–554; and Ford Foundation, 423, 430; and Fund for the Republic, 423–425, 430, 431–433, 456–459, 461–465; genius of, 518; illness of, 542; and McDonald Observatory, 190, 216, 219, 553; and Parten, 190–191, 508, 518, 537, 549, 553, 554; and *Texas Observer*, 452; and UT presidency, 179, 190–191, 192; and Vietnam war, 522

Hutchins Center for the Study of Democratic Institutions, Robert M.: established, 553

Huxley, Julian: 157

hydrogen bomb: 347–348, 473–474

I

Ickes, Harold L.: and Big Inch, 258–259, 263–267, 270–271, 274, 280; and Connally Hot Oil Act, 129–130; and Federal Tender Board, 124; and Florida barge canal, 270; and Little Inch, 280; and New Deal, 84; oil control legislation of, 105–114, 116, 129–130, 130–133, 134, 567, 568; and oil production control, 84–85, 87–90, 96–104, 124, 154; and OPC (PAW), 253–256, 261, 264, 283–285, 287–288, 289, 290, 291, 297, 298, 299, 396, 404; and PAD, 402–403; and E. Pauley naval appointment, 348, 349; Parten and, 354, 568, 570; and PIWC, 256; and Rainey controversy, 316; on J. Smith, 363; and

Tanker Control Board, 255; on U-boat danger, 258

Ideson, Julia: 318

Illinois: oil, and WWII, 258; university appropriations in, 215. *See also* Big Inch pipeline

Independent Petroleum Association of America (IPAA): and NRA code, 102; and oil import tax, 68; and oil production control, 63, 65, 85, 85–86, 89, 90–91

Independent Petroleum Association of California: 86

Independent Petroleum Association Opposed to Monopoly: Parten and, 88–90

Independent Petroleum Association of Texas (IPAT): and J. Allred, 72; controlled membership of, 69; and Ickes oil legislation, 109, 110; and NRA code, 99–103; and oil import tax, 68; and oil production control, 63, 65, 66–70, 77, 78, 79, 80, 94, 95, 99–103, 134; and C. Wilde suit, 103–104

Internal Revenue Service: and Fund for the Republic, 459, 461, 463, 465, 516; Nixon's use of, 541

International Court of Justice: and *Pacem in Terris*, 519

Interstate Commerce Commission: 273

Intracoastal Canal Assoc.: 270

Ivins, Molly: and Parten, 564, 565; and *Texas Observer*, 452

Ivy, John: 384–385

J

Jackson, Andrew: influence on Parten, 11, 12, 31, 74, 507, 508, 569

Jacques Power Tool Co. (Denison): 358

Jaltipan, Mexico. *See* Pan American Sulphur Co.

James, Herman: 230

Japan: Potsdam Conference and, 342, 343, 345. *See also* atomic bomb

Jaworski, Leon: Parten and, 506, 570

Jefferson, Thomas: influence on Parten, 11, 12, 31, 195, 457, 507, 568, 569–570

Jeffersonian Democrats: J. Haley and, 166–168, 244

Jefferson Lake Sulphur Co.: 381, 479

Jehovah's Witnesses: and Big Inch, 280

Jenner, William: 428, 429

Jennings, Brewster: 439

Jersey Standard Oil Co.: and oil production control, 59, 71

Jester, Beauford: and 1946 governor's race, 352,

Pew, J. Edgar: and oil production control, 62, 69, 134; and PAW, 295
Pew, John: and PAW, 295
Phillips Petroleum Co.: and Little Inch, 287; and Pan American Sulphur, 526
Phillips, Wade: 287
Phinney, Carl: 239
Pike, James A.: and FFR's Center, 519
Pinckney, Steve: and Rainey controversy, 319; and UT board of regents, 246
Pine Island oil field: 29, 31, 32, 33, 35, 38, 294
Pipkin, James H.: 297
Plantation pipeline: 274
Poland: and *Pacem in Terris,* 516; WWII, and war reparations commission, 326, 332, 343
Pope, Joe: 294
Pope, Walter "Uncle" Elmer: Parten and, 19; and UT legislative appropriations, 145, 156, 164
Pope John XXIII: *Pacem in Terris* of, 516, 553
Port Arthur, Texas: and 1954 governor's race, 448; and WWII oil transport, 274
Potsdam Conference (Berlin): atomic bomb and, 342, 344, 345; Parten and, 2, 324, 339, 340-345, 348-349, **341**
Pratt, Wallace: and Latin American studies program, 192–193; and OPC, 255; and UT presidential search, 193, 195, 210
Premier Oil and Refining Co.: **126**, 567; Cotton Valley refinery, 393; S. Dayson and, 125–128, 247, 277, 386, 485; end of, 386; established, 125–128; and hot oil, 277; and 1936 Railroad Commission race, 162; and Pan American Sulphur, 380; and 7-J farm, 385; and WWII, 256
Price, Granville: and censorship of *Daily Texan,* 164
Progress and Poverty: 23
Progressive Democrats of Texas: UT chapter, 170
prohibition: W. Dean and, 14
Proxmire, William: and 1952 Democratic Convention, 418
Public Works Administration (PWA): and UT, 163
Puerto Rico: and oil import controls, 494
Pure Oil Co.: and Fund for the Republic, 520; merger with Union Oil, 502–506; merger with Woodley Petroleum, 483–486; Parten and management of, 498–500, 567; and production control, 77
Pure Oil News: 266
Pushing to the Front: 19

Pyron, Walter: 275–276, 297

Q

Quakers: red scare and, 456–457, 463
"quantity" tax (Louisiana): H. Long and, 47–48
Querbes, Andrew: and H. Long, 46, 48; Parten and, 36–37, 43, 46, 54, 62, 80, 103, 128; and W. L. Woodley, 55

R

Rabi, Isidor: and FFR's Center, 519
race. *See* civil rights
radio: FCC and 1946 governor's race, 360–361
railroads: H. Long and, 37; symbol trains, 272, 273, 283; W. Parten's distrust of, 11, 12; and WWII oil transport, 265, 267, 272, 273, 283–286, 287, 288, 295, 297. *See also* Texas Railroad Commission
Rainey, Helen: 188
Rainey, Homer Price: **229**; and 1944 governor's race, 303–304, 305; and 1946 governor's race, 350–355, 357–374, 507, 568; background of, 188; and black enrollment at UT, 313, 363, 365, 366; as candidate for UT presidency, 186–189, 191–196, 205–206, 210–211; controversy over UT presidency, 300–323, **307, 308,** 309, 362, 374, 408, 425, 547, 562, 568, 569; demogoguery of, 369–370; and faculty radicalism, 232–233, 236–237, 238–239, 300, 304, 308, 318; and FCC, 360–361; and Houston Buffs, 216; and HUAC, 241–242; inauguration as UT president, 219, 228–230; and legislative appropriations, 213–216, 220–221; and McDonald Observatory, 219; and medical school controversy, 226–228, 232–236, 242–243, 244, 248–250, 304, 315; "New Texas" vision of, 231, 245, 353, 568; and Parten, 212, 247, 260; and H. Urey, 226
Ramsey, Ben: and 1956 Senate race, 474
Randall, Edward, Sr.: **141**; and 1938 governor's race, 205; and D. Bible, 179; and censorship of *Daily Texan,* 171; and J. Haley, 169; and McDonald Observatory, 219; and medical school controversy, 206–209, 221–222, 226–228, 232, 233–236, 238, 242–243, 244, 248–249; and Parten, 140, 182, 212; resigns as regent, 232–233; and H. Stark, 143–144; and UT presidential search, 186, 187, 191, 193–196, 205–206, 210
Randolph, Frankie Carter: and 1956 Democratic Convention, 468–469, 472–473,

COLOPHON

The typeface used for the text is Adobe Minion and Minion Expert, designed by Robert Slimbach. The display face is Compugraphic Cloister.

Two thousand copies printed at Edwards Bros., Inc., Ann Arbor, Michigan, on 50 lb. Glatfelter